Echoes of Empire

ECHOES OF EMPIRE

MEMORY, IDENTITY AND COLONIAL LEGACIES

Edited by Kalypso Nicolaïdis, Berny Sèbe and Gabrielle Maas

I.B. TAURIS

LONDON · NEW YORK

This book has been made possible by financial support from the Institut universitaire de France

Published in 2015 by I.B.Tauris & Co Ltd
www.ibtauris.com

Distributed worldwide by I.B.Tauris & Co Ltd
Registered office: 6 Salem Road, London W2 4BU

Cover images: Detail from a folding screen depicting Portuguese merchants in Japan. Japanese, *c.* early seventeenth century (Photo by Werner Forman/Universal Images Group/Getty Images);
Soldiers from British East Africa during World War I, 1916
(Photo by Culture Club/Getty Images);
'Colonel Mordaunt watching a cock fight at Lucknow', India, 1790 (Photo by Ann Ronan Pictures/Print Collector/Getty Images).
Cover design: www.paulsmithdesign.com

ISBN: 978 1 78453 050 1 (HB)
ISBN: 978 1 78453 051 8 (PB)
eISBN: 978 0 85773 896 7

A full CIP record for this book is available from the British Library
A full CIP record is available from the Library of Congress

Library of Congress Catalog Card Number: available

Designed and Typeset by Riverside Publishing Solutions, Salisbury SP4 6NQ

Contents

Contributors   ix

Acknowledgements   xi

Echoes of Empire: The Present of the Past   1
Kalypso Nicolaïdis, Berny Sèbe and Gabrielle Maas

Part I: Colonialism and Modernity: Views from the Receiving End

Imperial Parasitism: British Explorers and African Empires   19
Dane Kennedy

Colonial Modernities: A View from the Imperial Verandah, *c*.1880–1960   35
Jan-Georg Deutsch

Fading Echoes: Legacy of Empire and Democracy in India   47
Sarmila Bose

The Imperial Question in the History of Ibero-America:
The Importance of the Long View   63
Jean-Frédéric Schaub

Epilogue: The History, Identity, Crisis and Endemic Submission of the
American Continent   81
Juan José Rossi

Part II: Return to Sender? Imperial Visions, Imperial Legacies

The Echoes of Rome in British and American Hegemonic Ideology   105
Ali Parchami

Towards Cosmopolitan Perspectives on Empires and their Echoes?
The Case for a European Framework   123
  Berny Sèbe

Between Memory, History and Historiography: Contesting Ottoman
Legacies in Turkey, 1923–2012   141
  Nora Fisher Onar

The Russian Empire and the Soviet Union: Too Soon to Talk of Echoes?   155
  Alexander Morrison

State of Insecurity: Self-Defence and Self-Cultivation in the Genesis of
Japanese Imperialism   175
  Christopher Harding

Epilogue: Analysing 'Echoes of Empire' in Contemporary Context:
The Personal Odyssey of an Imperial Historian (1970s–present)   189
  John M. MacKenzie

Part III: From Imperial to Normative Power:
the EU Project in a Post-Colonial World

Building Eurafrica: Reviving Colonialism through European
Integration, 1920–60   209
  Peo Hansen and Stefan Jonsson

Echoes of Colonialism in Trade Negotiations between the
European Union and African, Caribbean and Pacific Countries   227
  Emily Jones and Clara Weinhardt

From the Soviet Bloc to the New Middle Age: East-Central Europe's
Three Imperial Moments   251
  Dimitar Bechev

The EU and its Eastern Neighbours: Why 'Othering' Matters   267
  Elena Korosteleva

Southern Barbarians? A Post-Colonial Critique of EUniversalism   283
  Kalypso Nicolaïdis

Epilogue: Chinese Empire Meets the West: A Centennial Conundrum
for China   305
  Zhu Liqun and Feng Jicheng

Part IV: Globalism: From the Colonial to the Post-Colonial Worlds

European Power and the Mapping of Global Order   323
  Karoline Postel-Vinay

Legal Child vs Step Child? The Impact of Colonial Legacies on Brazil's
and India's Global Trajectories   337
  Vinícius Rodrigues Vieira

Echoes of Imperialism in LGBT Activism   355
  Rahul Rao

From the Anti-Colonial Movements to the New Social Movements   373
  Robert J. C. Young

Colonization and Globalization   383
  Jacques Frémeaux and Gabrielle Maas

Epilogue: After-Images of Empire   393
  Bernard Porter

Afterword   407
  John Darwin

Index   411

Contributors

Dimitar Bechev is a senior policy fellow and Head of the Office of the European Council on Foreign Relations in Sofia.

Sarmila Bose is Senior Research Associate, Centre for International Studies, Department of Politics and International Relations, University of Oxford.

John Darwin is the Beit University Lecturer in the History of the British Commonwealth at the University of Oxford.

Jan-Georg Deutsch is University Lecturer in African History at the University of Oxford.

Jacques Frémeaux is Professor of Contemporary History at the University of Paris-Sorbonne (Paris IV) and member of the Institut universitaire de France.

Peo Hansen is Professor of Political Science at the Institute for Research on Migration, Ethnicity and Society (REMESO), Linköping University, Sweden.

Christopher Harding is Lecturer in Asian History at the University of Edinburgh.

Feng Jicheng is Associate Professor of International Studies at China Foreign Affairs University.

Emily Jones is Deputy Director of the Global Economic Governance Programme, University of Oxford.

Stefan Jonsson is Professor of Ethnic Studies at the Institute for Research on Migration, Ethnicity and Society (REMESO), Linköping University, Sweden.

Dane Kennedy is the Elmer Louis Kayser Professor of History and International Affairs at George Washington University.

Elena Korosteleva is Jean Monnet Chair and Professor of International Politics and Director of the Global Europe Centre in the School of Politics and International Relations, University of Kent.

Zhu Liqun is Professor of International Relations and Vice President at China Foreign Affairs University.

Gabrielle Maas is an independent scholar and former fellow of the Institute of Historical Research. She received her doctorate from the University of Oxford.

John M. MacKenzie is Honorary Professorial Fellow at the University of Edinburgh.

Alexander Morrison is Professor of History at Nazarbayev University, Astana, Kazakhstan.

Kalypso Nicolaïdis is Professor of International Relations and Director of the Centre for International Studies at the University of Oxford.

Nora Fisher Onar is a transatlantic fellow at the German Marshall Fund, and a research associate of the Centre for International Studies, University of Oxford.

Ali Parchami is a senior lecturer in the Department of Defence and International Affairs at RMA Sandhurst.

Bernard Porter is Emeritus Professor of Modern History at the University of Newcastle.

Karoline Postel-Vinay is Directrice de recherche at Sciences Po, Paris.

Rahul Rao is Senior Lecturer in Politics at SOAS, University of London.

Vinícius Rodrigues Vieira completed his doctorate in International Relations at Nuffield College, University of Oxford.

Juan José Rossi is a professor at the Universidad Autónoma de Entre Ríos (Concepción del Uruguay, Argentina), and director of the ethnographical and historical museum Ivy marä ey ('The Land Without Evil').

Jean-Frédéric Schaub is Professor of Early Modern History at the École des hautes études en sciences sociales (Paris).

Berny Sèbe is Lecturer in Colonial and Post-Colonial Studies at the University of Birmingham.

Clara Weinhardt is a research associate at the Global Public Policy Institute in Berlin and a member of associated academic staff at the Willy Brandt School of Public Policy at the University of Erfurt.

Robert J. C. Young is Julius Silver Professor of English and Comparative Literature, New York University.

Acknowledgements

The editors of this book had two aims: firstly, to develop new avenues of investigation by bringing together historians and international relations scholars at the University of Oxford; secondly, to expand this initial remit to scholars around the world, eventually including twenty-eight authors from four continents. We would like to thank our colleagues who have contributed to the development of this idea over the years, and encouraged our efforts to move between disciplines. *Echoes of Empire* draws on discussions initially held at the interdisciplinary workshop *Echoes of Imperialism: Rethinking European Colonialisms*, which brought together historians and international relations scholars at the University of Oxford, organized in Oxford in 2008 and funded jointly by Oxford University's Modern History Faculty, the Department of Politics and International Relations, the European Studies Centre and the Maison française d'Oxford, with additional support from OxPo. The book also benefitted from subsequent annual workshops of the programme RENEW (Rethinking Europe in a Non-European World) supported by the European Studies Centre (St Antony's College), the Centre for International Studies (DPIR) and OxPo. The co-editors would also like to thank the Beit Fund and the European Research Group for co-funding the workshop, as well as the co-convenors Jan-Georg Deutsch, Judith M. Brown, John Darwin and Rahul Rao, and Alexis Tadié, then director of the Maison française d'Oxford, for his active support of the initiative. Finally, we would like to thank Victoria Petitjean and Dorian Singh for their thorough organizational and editing work.

The chapters by Jean-Frédéric Schaub and Juan José Rossi were translated from the French and Spanish respectively by Brian Melican in Hamburg.

The editors would also like to thank the following institutions for their financial support to the publication of this book: RAMSES programme (St Antony's College,

University of Oxford and Maison méditerranéenne des sciences de l'homme, Aix-en-Provence), FP7 funding (European Union), the School of Languages and Cultures, Art History and Music at the University of Birmingham and the Institut universitaire de France.

Note: Unless otherwise stated, titles in English are published in London.

Echoes of Empire:
The Present of the Past

Kalypso Nicolaïdis, Berny Sèbe and Gabrielle Maas

[F]or the pattern is the action
And the suffering, that the wheel may turn and still
Be forever still.

T. S. Eliot, Murder in the Cathedral (1935)

EU diplomats in search of fresh air between negotiation rounds can stroll through a pleasant leafy park at the heart of Brussels' European District: the Parc du Cinquantenaire. They may be surprised to discover a monument inscribed with the words of King Leopold II: 'I undertook the conquest of the Congo in the interest of civilization and for the good of Belgium'. Another of the inscriptions on the Congo memorial – 'the heroism of the Belgian soldier crushes the Arab slave-trader' – has been erased and reinstated several times, further to requests from the Arab League and the Royal Circle of Former Officers of African Campaigns respectively.[1]

Europe's colonial past is still ubiquitous: in monuments and cityscapes, but also in memories, symbols and political battles. National attempts to digest it rarely pass without emotive reaction, either in former colonies or former metropoles. Through its eastwards enlargement, the European Union has brought former colonial and colonized states into the same nominal membership group; if EU rhetoric talks of a 'community of memory', the memory of World War II referred to in this collective narrative frequently eclipses another less convenient memory: that of overseas colonization and decolonization, and their vestiges in the national and international narratives of a globalized world. This is hardly surprising, given that despite initiatives such as the Union for the Mediterranean, the apparent convergence between former colonial and colonized states witnessed in Eastern

Europe has failed to materialize towards the south. Beyond this, can we even speak of a properly European 'colonial past', or only of a series of national colonial pasts with metropoles that happen to be European? How has the EU dealt with the colonial past in its external relations – by amnesia, rejection or atonement?

Global politics, on the other hand, is largely predicated on a myth that the world is now resolutely and universally past colonialism, claiming to organize a society of equal sovereign states abiding by the rule of international law. This vision posits a 'post-colonial' world that has seen off the scourge of empire and succeeded it with a 'clean slate' alternative system; but the term has another possible meaning: a world that is not yet past colonialism, but continues to hear and interpret its echoes well beyond the end of empire as hard political reality.

Memory of the colonial past and its meanings now lives on in other political guises. As well as a justification for continued dominance, the colonial past often serves as a totem for contemporary political rivals within a former metropolis. Debates over the rights and wrongs of colonialism in North Africa have repeatedly been the pretext for controversies on 'national identity' and immigration in France over the past decade, and in her chapter Nora Fisher Onar draws our attention to another case of politicized memory: that of 'Ottomanism' in contemporary Turkey. As she demonstrates, empires (whether overseas, as in the case of French expansion, or continental in the Ottoman case) and the transition out of them have in themselves become a *lieu de mémoire*, sites where 'memory, history and historiography overlap in charged ways'.

This project builds on an already impressive body of work on the present of Europe's pasts. There are still a number of shortcomings in mainstream scholarship, however. Comparisons between national imperial traditions in Europe, let alone between European and non-European imperialisms, are still comparatively rare;[2] old Eurocentric habits die hard, as does the tendency for historians and political scientists to remain behind disciplinary walls and fail to engage fully with the insights of complementary disciplines such as anthropology or critical theory; and finally, there is still a dearth of analysis linking colonial international relations with the post-colonial world, including their impact on EU politics and current patterns of globalization. This volume is a contribution to the ongoing process of addressing these challenges through interdisciplinary work.

The Meanings of Echoes

In John Darwin's formulation, 'imperialism may be defined as the sustained effort to assimilate a country or region to the political, economic or cultural system of another power'. Though this definition is originally based on the case of the British Empire, it remains valid for all the other case studies we examine. Within this broad definition, we can usefully distinguish between formal imperialism – which 'aimed to achieve this object by the explicit transfer of sovereignty and, usually, the imposition of direct administrative control' – and 'informal imperialism', which 'relied upon the links created by trade, investment or diplomacy, often supplemented by unequal treaties and periodic armed intervention, to draw new regions into the world-system of an imperial power'.[3] European colonialism cannot be reduced to the settlement of *coloni* (farmers, colonists) in overseas territories: it has come to refer more broadly to the power relations between a metropole and its colonies. Whilst we are aware of the etymological implications of each concept, we use the two terms interchangeably in this book.[4]

The hinge on which this book turns is the post-war process of decolonization, which saw the collapse of European empires against the backdrop of the Cold War, marked by the emergence of two superpowers whose rhetoric was resolutely set against the old colonial empires. From the late 1940s to the early 1960s, the world underwent a deep 're-ordering' – to borrow Kristin Ross' concept, which referred to the radical reconceptualization of French culture and practices in the wake of the loss of Indochina and Algeria.[5] With settlers repatriated, hierarchies shaken and new voices heard on the international arena, it seemed that an entire world order had crumbled: this was the advent of a 'post-colonial' world, which would infuse generations of scholars and thinkers as the voices of the 'subalterns' were heard at last, reclaiming an intellectual, political and symbolic space in which their presence had previously been made difficult or impossible.[6] At the same time, old colonial projects crumbled; a good example is the staggering speed at which the Eurafrica narrative retold in this volume was eclipsed and forgotten.

Though this 're-ordering' was clearly visible from the Franco-British humiliation of Suez until the fall of the Berlin Wall, the advent of what Francis Fukuyama labelled the 'end of history' in the late 1990s, which sealed the apparent triumph of the capitalist model, seemed to allow for the resurfacing of old habits. The EU project, which appeared to go from strength to strength in the late twentieth and early twenty-first centuries, gave member states a feeling of rejuvenation. Until the eurozone crisis, Europe seemed to be growing bolder, asserting itself as a major international player even at the risk of 'neo-colonial' undertones as perceived from Rio, Jakarta or Capetown.[7] And so we must ask: are we witnessing a return of the repressed, an attempt (conscious or otherwise) to override the legacy of colonialism and return to a more direct assertion of claims, values and interests in bilateral and multilateral relations?

Colonial Echoes Across Time and Space

In order to answer this question, we juxtapose and suggest routes between interpretations of empires and their echoes from different times, places and disciplines. Bringing together historians of empire and analysts of contemporary EU and global politics, the book establishes a dialogue between what are often watertight compartments in thinking about the legacy of colonial rule. Unsurprisingly, historians of empire are not necessarily concerned with the contemporary implications of their findings, and political scientists may overlook the weight of the past in their understanding of contemporary European affairs and international relations. Our contributors seek to create trading routes between past and present. This volume has another aim: to bring together scholars working in and on different geographical regions, often separated by institutional divisions of area studies and regional history. John MacKenzie, in his epilogue to Part II, offers an example of fruitful scholarly engagement with various interconnected fields. He argues that 'British historians, not least of the imperial variety, have been much too introverted for far too long. They have also too often had their noses firmly stuck in the official records and their eyes on the grand processes and meta-narratives of imperial history. Such history, in missing the local and the apparently micro, has missed the vital insights that can be secured from a greater range of documents and techniques, as well as a focus upon real people facing their own problems, dilemmas and sometimes opportunities in specific locations.' His intellectual trajectory exemplifies the type of cross-fertilization which the present volume seeks to foster.

We present interpretations of colonial 'echoes' both across past and present and as they are heard around the world. Some chapters focus on colonial echoes as abstract ideas; others illustrate how they find voice in the actual conduct of national, European and international politics. Our definition of the 'echoes of empire' therefore extends far beyond the allegations of neo-colonialism or dependency that often dominate analysis of North–South relations. We intend to challenge the assumption that we can understand imperialism merely by examining a past international society made up of half a dozen empires with their capital cities crowded together at the far end of the Eurasian continent. We seek instead to 'decentre' our understanding of imperialism, both geographically and conceptually as a form of power.

Some of our chapters are indeed about direct historical or power relationships between ex-metropoles and former colonies. Emily Jones and Clara Weinhardt thus analyse how the struggles of the European Partnership Agreement (EPA) negotiations with African, Caribbean and Pacific countries are influenced by the memories of colonial economic imbalances, while Vinícius Rodrigues Vieira traces the divergent 'inheritance routes' of Brazil and India from their former colonizers. Beyond these direct legacies, however, we examine several other types of echoes.

Between colonial or neo-colonial projects of different eras, firstly: Ali Parchami outlines how discourses of Roman imperial power as a benign, pacifying power have influenced British and more recently US imperial and neo-imperial practice. Echoes between colonial enterprises and modern nation state practices come next, with chapters from Nora Fisher Onar, Alexander Morrison and Sarmila Bose all touching in different ways on the continuities between imperial practice and the institutional life of the successor nation state, from Turkey to Russia to India.

Continuities also emerge between a shared colonized past and the contemporary reimagination of regional identities, be it Dimitar Bechev's exploration of the contemporary use and abuse of the Soviet *imperium*'s multicoloured legacies in the eastern parts of Europe or Jean-Frédéric Schaub's analysis of the way in which Spanish and Portuguese imperial traditions continue to shape the sociopolitical reality of Latin American countries. Kalypso Nicolaïdis, meanwhile, explores the different ways in which the European Union has 'internalized' the colonial pasts of its member states, attempting to steer a narrow course between forgetting and remembering, denial and atonement.

We listen too for echoes between European and non-European imperial projects, with chapters on Japanese, Chinese and Ottoman imperialisms each contributing to a decentred view of imperial power. Though our main focus is on the interplay between European and non-European experiences of empire, we present a number of chapters that draw an implicit contrast between different imperial powers within Europe. Berny Sèbe thus re-examines British and French imperial traditions with an eye to instances of competition and cross-fertilization; he argues further that apprehending these legacies as cosmopolitan processes can help us reassess the after-lives of 'Greater Britain' and *La plus grande France*, as each former metropole reformulates its global ambitions as part of an evolving European project.

Ideology, Discourse and Practice

Above all, we listen for ideological echoes of colonialism or anti-colonialism in more latent domains – places where colonial ideas live on less as practice than as pervasive mindsets or frameworks of power relations. Rahul Rao thus explores how both proponents and critics of Western LGBT activism have construed it as a quasi-imperialist civilizing mission. He highlights the dangers of this simplistic narrative, which fails to acknowledge how the colonial encounter itself may have planted the seeds of what LGBT activists now seek to challenge, and forgets to differentiate between radically divergent suggestions within LGBT activism about 'how to export [a common] ontology to the rest of the world'. Sarmila Bose, meanwhile, contests the wisdom of analysing contemporary Indian democracy as a colonial inheritance. She argues instead that the very notion of democracy is unsuited to a highly regionalized state, where localized or interest-based political movements seek to capture representation rather than democratic legitimacy *sensu stricto*. In each of these cases, moving from the historical to the normative, we find a colonial past constructed around a 'rescue narrative' and we are moved to ask: what, if anything, can we rescue from this rescue narrative?

The end of administrative colonization does not mean the end of imperialist mindsets, which may persist either vis-à-vis formerly colonized territories and new dependent or indeed subordinate groups within the new nation state. As Robert Young observes, the achievement of national sovereignty rarely meant full sovereignty, and with an incomplete transfer of power usually come latent forms of resistance and an increased sensitivity to threats 'from below'. This is fertile long-term ground for echoes – both of colonialism and anti-colonialism – to return cyclically in response to contemporary events. In his chapter, Alexander Morrison thus highlights the layered echoes of colonialism in today's Russia, ranging from racism towards migrants from former satellite states to imperial nostalgia for the heyday of Tsarist military glory to romanticized visions of the Caucasus and its insurgents as Russia's threatening yet alluring boundary.

As several of our contributors demonstrate, imperial ideologies and practices were never separate. In his chapter, Jan-Georg Deutsch reminds us that European discourses on progress and the modern condition are far from a mere 'backdrop' to colonial enterprises in Africa over the nineteenth and twentieth centuries. Changing notions of modernity and where it resides, he suggests, in fact determined broad shifts in the administrative practice of empire in Africa. What is more, these shifts occurred in response to changes not in the colonized territories but in the heart of Europe's own experience. Nineteenth-century *mission civilisatrice* discourses thus lost ground when Europeans confronted their own lack of 'civility' after World War I, giving way to ideals of 'protecting' Africa from the perils of modernity and then to a discourse of colonial development and welfare. As Peo Hansen and Stefan Jonsson remind us in their chapter, the latter became the basis for early post-war blueprints of European integration, which sought to translate imperial ideology into a new aggregative praxis of pooling sovereignty *in order* to pool colonies.

From a different angle, Dane Kennedy also alerts us to the dangers of assuming that Western empires were in some way uniquely 'modern'. He offers a powerful reading of expedition histories as evidence for the primacy of indigenous power structures in controlling the terms and findings of European colonial discovery. The colonialist narrative of explorers penetrating Africa's interior and its subsequent post-colonial interpretations here give way to a reverse narrative of gatekeepers and natural barriers over which Europeans had no control. We find the same partial reversal in Jones and Weinhardt's account of how African states have resisted Europe's attempts to renegotiate the terms of its economic penetration in the post-colonial period.

This relationship between discourse, practice and agency raises a further question that runs through the contributions to this volume: do all imperialisms ultimately tell us more about the metropolitan inside than the outside? As Kennedy shows, colonial territory has often acted as a metaphor for the unknowable. And as Christopher Harding illustrates in his chapter, imperial projects may therefore appear to be looking and expanding outwards while in fact predicated on inward-looking, defensive notions of cultural loss and national self-cultivation. In a different perspective, Hansen and Jonsson draw our attention to European notions of 'spiritual unity' behind the drive for a unified attempt to create a third geopolitical pole perched between US and Soviet ambitions: 'Eurafrica'.

These chapters suggest that in order to understand anything about colonialism and its legacies, there is only one place to start: from the domestic self-image of the nations that masked their insecurities behind a confident imperial swagger. As Bernard Porter remarks in his epilogue to Part IV, 'underneath the display and noise and strutting and silly dressing-up that Britain's political elite employed and encouraged in order to give the *impression* of power and glory, the British Empire was really a very vulnerable thing'.

The EU in a Post-Colonial World

Though the scope of this volume is global and its guiding thread that of decentring from a Eurocentric apprehension of colonialism, an outstanding question remains: that of the future of post-colonial Europe in an increasingly 'non-European' world. There is palpable tension, both in the national arenas of Europe's former metropoles and in region-wide debates about the EU as global actor, between the two definitions of 'post-colonial' outlined earlier: denying as opposed to dealing with Europe's colonial past. As Dimitar Bechev observes, today's EU can no longer take refuge as easily as it once could in romantic notions of a shared past. For many of its Eastern European members the memory of imperial satellite status is barely more than two decades old; and new 'echoes of colonialism' in contemporary Russia mean that many in Eastern Europe lean more towards Washington than Brussels as representative of the 'new values' of freedom and democracy.

The EU is increasingly caught between two conflicting demands on it. Messages emanating from the south, and especially from the BRICS powers, often encourage its leaders to acknowledge that Europe lies at the 'periphery' of a new world order; yet they also call for it to assume global responsibilities commensurate with its historical legacies and contemporary economic might. Can the EU be all things to all people, ambitious where required and humble where chastened, cognisant of the troubled relationship with its past that defined its very inception yet able to reform and look forward? As Kalypso Nicolaïdis observes, EU foreign policy actors have all too often dealt with this contradiction through selective amnesia, denying the EU's descendance from member states that had themselves so recently acted as imperial hegemons. What is more, as Dimitar Bechev demonstrates, this also requires forced suppression of the radical differences between dominant historical memories and legacies in the core and on the periphery of Europe.

This sleight of hand no longer passes unchallenged. The EU, as well as a community of ideas and memory, is a regional power fighting for influence in an increasingly competitive global arena; and its influence still depends in large part on its ability to wield normative power. Ian Manners introduced the concept of Normative Power Europe (NPE), or the 'ability to shape conceptions of "normal" in international relations', in order to move beyond the narrow contrast between military versus civilian power and consider the influence of the EU as constituted by what it is rather than what it does or says.[8] But as Elena Korosteleva observes, this very question – that of 'who we [Europeans] are' – calls up the past to legitimate the present. Notions of today's Europe as a 'credible force for good' thus become paradoxically yet inextricably linked to past visions of European universalism, often colonial in origin. To what extent, then, can we distinguish contemporary European normative power from 'hard' forms of economic neo-colonialism, or the kind of civilizing mission rationale which characterized the era of empires? And normatively, is it possible to imagine a truly post-colonial approach to global affairs in our second definition of the term – one that does not pretend that we live in a brand new world but instead acknowledges and reflects on the danger of perpetuating colonialism by other means? In order to address these questions in all their complexity, we devote a section of the book to the role of the EU in an international system whose terms Europe can no longer define.

Universalism and Globalization

We are concerned, then, with systems of both colonial and post-colonial knowledge and practice, and with the relationship between the two. In today's world, one word often suffices to elicit either unquestioning endorsement or vehement rejection of the post-colonial order: globalization, or more simply globalism. While some glorify globalism as the benign face of the communications and exchange routes instituted by colonial powers, others condemn the so-called global order as the continuation of empire by other means. Global, say its critics, is not a value term but merely one of scope: it does not guarantee inclusion for all, but merely designates the power sweep of the few actors who *do* wield truly 'earth-wide' influence.

Global forces are at the centre of the remaining broad theme that runs through the volume: that of universalism versus particularism. As Nicolaïdis observes, 'universalism [...] has historically served to name *particular* discursive traditions [...] originating in Europe and directed outside Europe'. Is this an inevitable feature of national or regional thinking? Does every claimant to power take refuge in a notion of itself as uniquely predisposed to export its ideas? And if so, how can we avoid seeing a mere succession of worlds in a succession of sand grains – is there any such thing as a global order at all, even now?

Karoline Postel-Vinay argues that the apparent unsustainability of universalism as a political project today derives from the conflation of the notion of universality with that of globality, a conflation which is intrinsically linked to the nature of European power in the late nineteenth century. The specificity of what economic historians have called the 'first globalization' is that it produced an international order that was determined by the geophysical finitude of the planet, where no political community – whether colonized or not – could escape from the 'civilizing' power of the European-defined international order. This obsession with globality informed Europe's vision of universalism and led to a problematic conflation that is clearly at play in the way non-Western powers are contesting international institutions and order today. Jacques Frémeaux and Gabrielle Maas, meanwhile, identify the inequalities engendered by today's globalism with colonial hierarchies of knowledge, arguing that 'modern global networks [...], like colonial routes, create power imbalances and rifts even as they connect places'. On the premise that 'the challenge of [colonial] conquest was also an epistemological challenge', their chapter investigates how expanding knowledge paradoxically leads to ossified categories and hierarchies.

How we go about decentring also depends on our personal experience, and its intimate connection with the writing of history. If 'echoes' find their way into political practice and discourse, they also shape the writings of historians and political scientists. This depends not merely on where in the world one is writing from, or what one's politics are; as John MacKenzie vividly describes in his epilogue to Part II, new lines of academic investigation are often sparked by chance echoes arising from the writer's own instinctive cultural sensibility, upbringing or intellectual context. MacKenzie's visceral disagreement with Said's interpretation of *Aida*, which led to the publication of *Orientalism: History, Theory and the Arts*, leads him to conclude that 'individual historians are formed out of their genes, out of their personal experiences, or put at its most basic, out of their gut reactions'.

A similar assumption lies behind this volume: we are listening not only for objective 'echoes', but also for the more emotive strains of memory and interpretation that determine what we choose to hear. We acknowledge the importance of this reflexive dimension to the volume through the inclusion of four epilogues, concluding each of the book's parts. The epilogues foil the chapters with a consciously subjective, sometimes emotive, commentary on the broad section theme. Juan José Rossi's contribution in Part I thus delivers an attack on European 'compulsive colonialism' driven, he argues, by the 'endemic illness' of a minuscule continent's pathological need to expand. Zhu and Feng's epilogue to Part III, meanwhile, gives a similarly incisive critique of Western influence and what they perceive as its destruction of Chinese 'traditional culture' since the early nineteenth century. Their chapter provides a powerful foil to a section offering readings of the EU's evolving role in global power relations and critiques of what Nicolaïdis in Part III terms an ongoing 'EUniversalism'.

Bernard Porter's epilogue to the final section on globalism concludes the journey by describing the 'after-images' of empire as a retinal impression: something which, though no longer real in a material sense, lives on in the mind, taking on new shapes and meanings. Here, we come full circle to the relationship between practice and discourse, past and present: in Porter's words, 'the [colonial] myth has sprouted wings. And also some rather sharp teeth.' The 'myth' – how we think about colonialism today – and its sometimes very real teeth, are in equal parts the subject of this book.

Disciplinary Strands and Critical Endeavours

As we glance over the wealth of approaches, primary materials and intellectual traditions needed to explore the manifold echoes of Europe's colonial past, how could we not start where the journey of post-colonial poets and novelists has taken us, along the theoretical paths opened by the likes of Edward Said, Homi Bhabha, Gayatri Chakravorty Spivak and several others.[9] Many of the symbolic and effective types of oppression which they unveiled and fought still exist; but the echoes are fainter, more confusing and less stark than in their immediately post-colonial times. Power is more diffuse and hybridity more pervasive. We need to update talk of the post-colonial condition for these new circumstances.

Several historical traditions are on offer here. With the post-war decline of Western universalisms, coterminous with decolonization, came a radical reappraisal of the practice and epistemological underpinnings of writing non-European history. In this regard, African history offers an illuminating case study. Growing academic interest in Africa (research often carried out in the US, with federal funding) has given birth to a new approach to the history of the continent. Sources hitherto neglected (oral testimonies, or archives in non-European languages) have been reinstated,[10] leading to a reconceptualization of African history as a field in its own right (contrary to the pessimistic predictions of Hugh Trevor-Roper and others).[11] More recently, 'global' or 'world history', with its emphasis on decentring traditional historical frameworks of interpretation, has provided useful templates for thinking about the sheer scope of the exchanges of ideas, practices, people and goods which have been and remain subject to power struggles and constant renegotiation.[12]

We must also take into account successful examples of methodological cross-fertilization, some of which have demonstrated the fluidity of post-colonial analytical frameworks and challenged the temporal and geographical boundaries of their original contexts.[13] Naturally, in our search for the modern 'echoes' of the colonial past, the precedent of World War II and the Holocaust illuminates questions of memory and forgetfulness, of 'a past that does not pass' in Henry Rousso's formula.[14] Our approach also takes into account a growing historiography focusing on issues of memory, commemoration and cultural exchanges, and on the interaction between former metropoles and former colonies.[15] This ranges from studies of contemporary echoes of the imperial mindset at home, exposing how the empire has 'struck back' in many more ways than previously imagined,[16] to the development of diasporic communities,[17] the commemoration of the empire in the metropoles, or the after-effects of decolonization struggles and the quest for new national narratives.[18] In this vein, historians as well as sociologists and political scientists have probed the meaning of (post-colonial) republicanism in France, and the contradiction between its avowed universal principles and the colonial project, while their peers in Britain have argued over the future of the Commonwealth, conceived as 'a surrogate for colonial rule', at a time when its initial role is radically out of step with twenty-first-century realities.[19]

To be sure, the patterns of power-through-knowledge that post-colonial theory interpreted as the heart of the colonial era[20] are alive and well in certain areas of political science and international relations. The oft-cited history of IR is itself constructed in Western terms: the omission of post-colonial perspectives in mainstream theory was due, perhaps ironically, to a first kind of decentring, namely the migration of the metropolitan (European) academy to the United States and the foundation of IR as an 'American social science'.[21] In response, European scholarship both contested a US-centrism that echoed its own and internalized analytical frameworks pioneered in the US.[22] Characteristically, the 'three traditions' (Hobbesian, Grotian and Kantian) proposed in the classical international society strand of IR scholarship emanate from the European canon, and reproduce the logic of unilinear diffusion of European practices from the European core to the periphery – a process Hedley Bull famously referred to as the *expansion of European society*.[23]

A critically minded new generation of international society scholars have revisited such frames, exploring the ways in which thinkers like Locke and Grotius were appropriated by the imperial enterprise. In *Provincializing Europe* (2000), Dipesh Chakrabarty charted the subaltern history of the Indian struggle for independence, and countered Eurocentric scholarship about non-Western peoples and cultures by proposing that Western Europe simply be considered as culturally equal to the other regions of the world – as 'one region among many' in human geography.[24] Keene (2006), meanwhile, traces how Grotian ideas were deployed to rationalize a legal and normative apparatus in which sovereign recognition was accorded to those deemed 'civilized/European' while capitulations were the fate of the 'semi-civilized' and colonization of the 'barbaric' or 'savage'.[25] In this vein, IR scholars have questioned the central tenet of formal sovereign equality under anarchy in the contemporary international system, exploring the enduring place of hierarchy and its implications for the reproduction of former patterns of exploitation.[26] Such ventures seem to run in parallel with critical international political economy, which however has perhaps the oldest disciplinary pedigree in contesting Eurocentric narratives through theories of dependency, world systems, post-development and post-Marxist scholarship.[27] A particularly fascinating question is that of how perceptions of the colonial era are changing amidst current global power shifts which cast radical doubt on the lasting value of what Samuel Huntington called the 'great divergence', and the economic supremacy of the West at the heart of 'modernity'.[28] Against the backdrop of contemporary geopolitical change, post-colonial international relations has only recently started to make headway in the mainstream study of international relations, a trend to which we hope to contribute.[29]

Book Structure

The book is structured in four parts. It starts with in the viewpoint of countries which were subject to European imperialisms from the Iberian age of imperialism onwards, before turning in Part II to the varied imperial traditions of European states. Part III goes on to examine the imperial roots of the normative ambitions which buttress the EU project and the reminiscent echoes of the universalist claims which sustained imperial projects. Lastly, Part IV moves beyond the EU, and takes a global perspective to consider the shift from a colonial to a post-colonial world. Each section ends with an epilogue: either a testimony relevant to the section considered, or a provocative statement on the 'echoes of empire' as they are perceived from outside Europe.

The first section (*Colonialism and Modernity: Views from the Receiving End*) introduces our topic with hindsight, examining how the connection between a colonial past and a globalized present plays out in different regions of the world. On the one hand, colonial rule often seemed to project indigenous societies directly from a pre-industrial stage to the post-colonial era and imperialism appeared as a powerful agent of modernity in most of these former colonies. On the other hand, an increasing body of evidence tends to indicate the existence of pre-colonial agents of modernity. How do we adjudicate between these two sides of the argument? This part of the book aims to analyse the extent to which European ideas, practices and concepts of modernity have survived, declined or prospered in former colonies.

The second section (*Return to Sender? Imperial Visions, Imperial Legacies*) turns this initial viewpoint around by going back to examine the imperial enterprise itself, emphasizing the diversity of imperial visions and therefore legacies. Beyond this diversity, the chapters highlight common threads and ask whether the 'echoes' from different colonial traditions produce a cacophony or a recognizable pattern. By moving around the globe rather than following the classic distinction between European and non-European empires, this section intends to 'decentre' the study of imperialism[30] and to evaluate the extent to which colonial projects and practices were dictated as much by factors internal to the conquering power as by the conditions that prevailed in conquered territories. Part II thus examines the pan-European idea of imperialism and questions not only the fundamental divide between land-based and sea-borne empires, but also the common distinction between early modern and late modern empires.

The third section (*From Imperial to Normative Power: the EU Project in a Post-Colonial World*) takes a contemporary and prescriptive turn, drawing on the preceding sections to detect and analyse the echoes of colonialisms in contemporary relationships of power and cooperation orchestrated by the EU. We start with the EU's policies and narratives today, and evaluate the varied contemporary imperial legacies in different member states, including those which were the object rather than the subject of imperial rule. The prospect for a truly post-colonial agenda for today's Europe depends on its ability to free the EU project from the 'colonial DNA' of some of its member states and to transcend these combined imperial legacies. To what extent and how is such an evolution possible? We believe that one precondition is for Europeans to reflect on how deeply rooted in colonial patterns was the original project of European integration, and why many chose to forget this. In the process, we also need to understand different meanings of the 'imperial past' between countries in East and Central Europe, Southern or Northern Europe. Ultimately, Europeans must grasp how former European former colonies see the EU through the lens of their own post-colonial status.

The last part of the book (*Globalism: From the Colonial to the Post-Colonial Worlds*) moves beyond the EU to explore the normative constitution of ideas and practices, both of imperialism and of resistance to it. Our chapters analyse the normative influence that imperialisms of the past still exert on the present, as well as the influence of earlier normative thinking about resistance to imperialism on contemporary struggles and movements. Are hierarchical relationships inevitable irrespective of a colonial past, or does this past actively influence them? The chapters also ask whether Western-inspired 'universal' values are bound to be imperialist, as Immanuel Wallerstein has argued,[31] or whether a future global arena is possible in which relationships between nations are (re)founded on cosmopolitan principles of mutuality, reciprocity and equal dignity.

Notes

1 'L'Héroïsme militaire belge anéantit l'Arabe esclavagiste'. More information on the memorial and the controversies it generated can be found at http://www.irismonument.be/fr.Bruxelles_Extension_Est.Parc_du_Cinquantenaire.A004.html (accessed 14 October 2012).

2 Though there are of course notable exceptions, including: K. Pomeranz, *The Great Divergence: China, Europe, and the Making of the Modern World Economy* (Princeton, NJ, 2000); J. Darwin, *After Tamerlane: The Rise and Fall of Global Empires, 1400–2000* (2007); J. Burbank and F. Cooper, *Empires in World History: Power and the Politics of Difference* (Princeton, NJ, 2010); and J. M. Headley, *The Europeanization of the World: On the Origins of Human Rights and Democracy* (Princeton, NJ, 2007). A positive appraisal of the legacy of empires can be found in N. Ferguson, *Empire: How Britain Made the Modern World* (2004) and J. Frémeaux, *Les Empires coloniaux dans le processus de mondialisation* (Paris, 2002) (second edition: *Les Empires coloniaux, une histoire-monde*, Réédition CNRS [Paris, 2012]). For a critical appraisal, see W. Rodney, *How Europe Under-Developed Africa* (Washington, 1973) or, more recently, K. Kwarteng, *Ghosts of Empire: Britain's Legacies in the Modern World* (2011).

3 J. Darwin, 'Imperialism and the Victorians: The Dynamics of Territorial Expansion', *English Historical Review*, 112, 447 (June 1997), pp. 614–42.

4 For a good discussion of the possible, and still controversial, differences between imperialism and colonialism, see the entry on Colonialism in the Stanford Encyclopedia of Philosophy: M. Kohn, 'Colonialism', *The Stanford Encyclopedia of Philosophy (Summer 2012 Edition)*, ed. Edward N. Zalta, http://plato.stanford.edu/archives/sum2012/entries/colonialism/ (accessed 15 December 2012). For a discussion of the shortcomings of the term 'post-colonialism', see A. McClintock, 'The Angel of Progress: Pitfalls of the Term "Post-Colonialism"', *Social Text*, 31/32, Third World and Post-Colonial Issues (1992), pp. 84–98.

5 K. Ross, *Fast Cars, Clean Bodies* (Cambridge, MA, 1996). See also T. Sheppard, *The Invention of Decolonization: The Algerian War and the Remaking of France* (Ithaca, NY, 2006).

6 G. Chakravorty Spivak, 'Can the Subaltern Speak?', in C. Nelson and L. Grossberg (eds), *Marxism and the Interpretation of Culture* (Urbana, IL, 1988), pp. 271–313. See also M. Fee, 'Why C. K. Stead Didn't Like Keri Hulme's *The Bone People*: Who Can Write as Other?', *Australian and New Zealand Studies in Canada*, 1 (1989), pp. 11–32.

7 On neo-colonialism, see for instance, on Africa: M. Beti, *Main basse sur le Cameroun* (Paris, 1972); M. Beti and O. Tobner, *La France contre l'Afrique: retour au Cameroun* (Paris, 1993); F.-X. Verschave, *La Françafrique, le plus long scandale de la République* (Paris, 1998); F.-X. Verschave, *De la Françafrique à la Mafiafrique* (Paris, 2005). For an analysis of Anglo-American imperial continuities, see W. R. Louis and R. Robinson, 'The Imperialism of Decolonization', *The Journal of Imperial and Commonwealth History*, 22, 3 (1994), pp. 462–511 as well as B. Porter, *Empire and Superempire* (New Haven, CT, 2006). On South–South exchanges in Africa, see M. Beuret and S. Michel, *La Chinafrique* (Paris, 2009). On the post-colonial recycling of 'Eurafrica' and the need to reconceptualize the relationship between Europe and Africa, see A. Adebajo and K. Whiteman (eds), *The EU and Africa: From Eurafrique to Afro-Europa* (New York, NY, 2012); P. Hilaire, *Le Multiculturalisme franco-africain à l'épreuve des puissances* (Paris, 2013).

8 I. Manners, 'Normative Power Europe: A Contradiction in Terms?', *Journal of Common Market Studies*, 40, 2 (June 2002), pp. 235–58.

9 E. Said, *Orientalism* (1978) and *Culture and Imperialism* (1993); G. Spivak, 'Can the Subaltern Speak?', in P. Williams and L. Chrisman (eds), *Colonial Discourse and Post-Colonial Theory* (New York, NY, 1992), pp. 66–111; H. Bhabha, *Nation and Narration* (1990) and *The Location of Culture* (1994). See also A. Memmi, *Portrait du colonisé, précédé par Portrait du colonisateur* (Paris, 1957); F. Fanon, *Les Damnés de la terre* (Paris, 1961); A. Césaire, *Discours sur le colonialisme* (Paris, 1955); K. Nkrumah, *Consciencism* (Paris, 1970); M. Beti, *Peuples noirs, peuples africains*, bimonthly review, 1978–91. On the origins of post-colonialism, see M. Majumdar, *Postcoloniality, The French Dimension* (Oxford, 2007).

10 See for instance T. O. Ranger, *Revolt in Southern Rhodesia, 1896–7* (1967); J. M. MacKenzie, 'Southern Rhodesia and Responsible Government', *Rhodesian History*, 9 (1978), pp. 23–40; or more recently J. M. MacKenzie, this volume; Ghislaine Lydon, 'Writing Trans-Saharan History: Methods, Sources and Interpretations across the African Divide', *The Journal of North African Studies*, 10, 3–4 (2005), pp. 293–324.

11 See for instance H. Trevor-Roper, *The Rise of Christian Europe* (New York, NY, 1974), p. 9: 'Then indeed we may neglect our own history and amuse ourselves with the unrewarding gyrations of barbarous tribes in picturesque but irrelevant corners of the globe.'

12 For recent examples of works in global history, see J. Darwin, *After Tamerlane* or Burbank and Cooper, *Empires in World History*.

13 L. Festa and D. Carey (eds), *The Postcolonial Enlightenment* (Oxford, 2009); M. Broers, *The Napoleonic Empire in Italy, 1796–1814: Cultural Imperialism in a European Context?* (Basingstoke, 2004).

14 H. Rousso, *Le Syndrome de Vichy* (Paris, 1987). On the parallels between the Holocaust and the colonial experience, see M. Silverman, 'Interconnected Histories: Holocaust and Empire in the Cultural Imaginary', *French Studies*, 62, 4 (2008), pp. 417–28.

15 On the importance of indigenous cooperation for the colonial project, see. R. Robinson and J. Gallagher, 'The Imperialism of Free Trade', *The Economic History Review*, 6, 1 (1953), pp. 1–15.

16 See books by J. M. MacKenzie, especially *Propaganda and Empire* (Manchester, 1984), as well as A. Thompson, *The Empire Strikes Back* (2005); Said, *Culture and Imperialism*; A. Appadurai, *After Colonialism: The Cultural Consequences of Globalization* (1996).

17 See for instance P. Gilroy, *There Ain't no Black in the Union Jack* (1987) and *The Black Atlantic* (1993); L. Back and A. Nayak (eds), *Invisible Europeans: Black People in the 'New Europe'* (Birmingham, 1993); S. Hall and P. du Gay (eds), *Questions of Cultural Identity* (New York, NY, 1996); H. Bhabha, *The Location of Culture* (1994).

18 See for instance O. Dard and D. Lefeuvre (eds), *L'Europe face à son passé colonial* (Paris, 2009); C. Baker and J. Jahn (eds), *Postcolonial Slavery: An Overview of Colonialism's Legacy* (Newcastle, 2009); S. Dulucq and C. Zytnicki (eds), *Décoloniser l'histoire? De l'histoire 'coloniale' aux histoires nationales en Afrique et en Amérique latine (19e–20e siècle)* (Paris, 2003).

19 See for instance N. Bancel and P. Blanchard, *De l'indigène à l'immigré* (Paris, 1998); N. Bancel, P. Blanchard and S. Lemaire (eds), *La Fracture coloniale. La société française au prisme de l'héritage colonial* (Paris, 2005); O. Lecour Grandmaison, *Une mauvaise décolonisation. La France: de l'Empire aux émeutes des quartiers populaires* (Paris, 2007); M. Rigouste, *L'Ennemi intérieur. La généalogie coloniale et militaire de l'ordre sécuritaire dans la France contemporaine* (Paris, 2009); Lillian Thuram et al., *Appel pour une République multiculturelle et postraciale* (Paris, 2010); K. Marsh, N. Frith (eds), *France's Lost Empires: Fragmentation, Nostalgia, and La Fracture Coloniale* (Lanham, MD, 2011). The expression 'surrogate for colonial rule' comes from K. Srinivasan, *The Rise, Decline and Future of the British Commonwealth* (Basingstoke, 2007), p. 1.

20 F. Cooper, *Colonialism in Question: Theory, Knowledge, History* (Berkeley, CA, 2005), pp. 18–19; Said, *Orientalism*.

21 S. Hoffmann, 'An American Social Science: International Relations', *Daedalus*, 106, 3 (1977), pp. 41–60.

22 For a discussion see N. Fisher Onar and K. Nicolaïdis, 'The Decentering Agenda: Rethinking European in a Non-European World', in K. Nicolaïdis and R. Whitman (eds), *Conflict and Cooperation*, Special Issue on Normative Power Revisited (June 2013). P. Darby, 'Pursuing the Political: A Post-Colonial Rethinking of Relations International', *Millennium*, 33, 1 (2004), pp. 1–32; J. Hobson, 'Is Critical Theory Always for the White West and for Western Imperialism? Beyond Westphalian towards a Post-Racist Critical IR', *Review of International Studies*, 33 (2007), pp. 91–116; A. Acharya, *Whose Interests Matter?* (Ithaca, NY, 2011).

23 H. Bull and A. Watson (eds), *The Expansion of International Society* (Oxford, 1985), Chapters 1, 8 and 14; S. Seth, 'Historical Sociology and Postcolonial Theory: Two Strategies for Challenging Eurocentrism', *International Political Sociology*, 3, 3 (2009); K. Alderson and A. Hurrell (eds), *Hedley*

Bull on International Society (Basingstoke, 2000), Chapters 3 and 8; A. Anghie, *Imperialism, Sovereignty and the Making of International Law* (Cambridge, 2005); T. Barkawi and M. Laffey, 'The Post-Colonial Moment in Security Studies', *Review of International Studies*, 32 (2006), pp. 329–52; B. Buzan, 'Culture and International Society', *International Affairs*, 86, 1 (2010), pp. 1–25. D. Chakrabarty, *Provincializing Europe: Postcolonial Thought and Historical Difference* (Princeton, NJ, 2000); R. Doty, *Imperial Encounters* (Minneapolis, MN, 1996).

24 Chakrabarty, *Provincializing Europe*.

25 E. Keene, *Beyond the Anarchical Society: Grotius, Colonialism and Order in World Politics* (Cambridge, 2002). See also T. McCarthy, *Race, Empire, and the Idea of Human Development* (Cambridge, 2009), especially Chapter 3; W. H. McNeill, *Arnold J. Toynbee: A Life* (Oxford, 1989); S. Suzuki, *Civilization and Empire: China and Japan's Encounter with European International Society* (2009); S. Vucetic, *The Anglosphere: A Genealogy of Racialized Identity in International Relations* (Stanford, CA, 2011).

26 J. Hobson and J. C. Sharman, 'The Enduring Place of Hierarchy in World Politics', *European Journal of International Relations*, 11, 1 (2005), pp. 63–98; R. Foot, J. L. Gaddis and A. Hurrell (eds), *Order and Justice in International Relations* (Oxford, 2003).

27 M. Cox, T. Dunne and K. Booth (eds), *Empires, Systems and States: Great Transformations in International Politics* (Cambridge, 2001); I. Wallerstein, *The Modern World-System* (1974).

28 C. Bayly, *The Birth of the Modern World, 1780–1914* (Oxford, 2004); D. Ludden, 'Modern Inequality and Early Modernity', *American Historical Review*, 107, 2 (April 2002), pp. 470–80; J. Hobson, *The Eastern Origins of Western Civilisation* (Cambridge, 2004).

29 See inter alia G. Chowdry and S. Nair (eds), *Power, Postcolonialism and International Relations: Reading Race, Gender and Class*, (2002); P. Darby, 'Pursuing the Political: A Postcolonial Rethinking of Relations International', *Millenium*, 33 (2004), pp. 1–32; A. Acharya, *Whose Interests Matter?* (2011); D. Harvey, *The New Imperialism* (Oxford, 2003).

30 We acknowledge that the term was already used by one of the contributors to the present volume: D. Kennedy and D. Ghosh (eds), *Decentering Empire: Britain, India, and the Transcolonial World* (Hyderabad, 2006).

31 I. Wallerstein, *L'Universalisme européen, de la colonisation au droit d'ingérence* (Paris, 2008).

Part I

Colonialism and Modernity:
Views from the Receiving End

Imperial Parasitism:
British Explorers and African Empires[1]

Dane Kennedy

The exploration of Africa in the nineteenth century is usually seen as setting the stage for European imperial expansion across the continent. British explorers in particular are presented as men who helped make empire, blazing the trails that would be followed by conquering armies and mapping the terrain that would be claimed as colonial territories. But whose empire did they advance? The answer to this question seems so self-evident that it is rarely asked. After all, most British explorers saw themselves as the agents of British interests. Moreover, the British Empire did in fact become the primary beneficiary of the 'scramble' for African territory by the end of the century. But a close examination of the contexts in which explorers undertook their expeditions shows that their contributions to British imperialism were not as direct and determinative as we have been led to believe.[2] The most effective means of accessing much of the African interior came by way of routes controlled by several gateway states, and these states only permitted explorers to access these routes when it furthered their own political and economic interests in the region. Although these gateway states' ambitions and achievements have since been submerged under the meta-narrative of the European Scramble for Africa, they made bids for empires in Africa that would be echoed by Britain and other European imperial powers. The benefits that British exploration brought to the British Empire need to be reconceived as a consequence of its parasitic dependence on the ambitions of these gateway states.

British explorers confronted a complex and highly contested political terrain in Africa. Indigenous and other non-Western polities did much to shape the terms under which expeditions were conducted, as well as to determine their outcomes. Most viable routes to the interior were controlled by Arab or black African states, whose cooperation was essential to any expedition that sought to set out from their shores. These states supplied much of the geographical expertise, political leverage, and logistical support that explorers relied on for their success and indeed their very survival. As they ventured into the African interior, explorers encountered a complex mosaic of polities whose allegiances and rivalries, shaped to varying degrees by ethnic, economic, and religious factors, made safe passage difficult. Their ability to move through this fractious and ever shifting political landscape had far less to do with their affiliations to Britain and its empire than with the assistance they received from the gateway states and their agents, who sought to exert their own imperial influence on the interior. To ask 'whose empire?', then, is to acknowledge that British exploration of Africa occurred against the backdrop of the intertwined ambitions of various empires, which both colluded and collided with one another.

The argument I will advance here diverges in an important respect from Ronald Robinson's well-known thesis about the role of indigenous collaborators in European imperial expansion.[3] That thesis, which characterized certain members of colonized communities as active agents and beneficiaries of colonial rule, was premised on the understanding that the European colonizers held the balance of power in the relationship with these indigenous collaborators, however tentative or fragile that power may have seemed at the time. What distinguishes the circumstances examined in this chapter is that the balance of power rested with the indigenous gateway states, not the explorers or the European governments they represented. Insofar as there was a collaborative relationship between the explorers and gateway states, the explorers were more often the collaborators, acting as agents of these indigenous states' interests.

The inspiration for this analysis derives in large part from a new wave of comparative studies of empires. This research is eroding the exceptionalist claims that have long been made on behalf of the British and other Western empires. At the heart of these claims is the conviction that such empires were uniquely modern.[4] Recent work has shown instead that they often built on the institutional foundations of the older empires they replaced, and that contemporaneous non-Western empires often adopted similar strategies of rule.[5] Ann Laura Stoler and Carole McGranahan, among others, have pointed to 'the portability of practices and ideas [...] across imperial systems'.[6] As a result of this comparative research on empires, it has become increasingly difficult to sustain the long-standing distinction between 'modern' Western empires and 'pre-modern' non-Western ones. Furthermore, modernity itself has been exposed as such an elusive and problematic term that its value as an analytic category is open to question.[7] Its significance for our understanding of Western empires may have less to do with any innovative practices they introduced than it does with the ideological poses they adopted.

What is required, then, is a reconsideration of the associations that historians have conventionally drawn between European expeditions into Africa, European empires, and their exceptionalist claims to modernity.

Most of the literature on African exploration, both in its popular and academic guises, has minimized the role that non-European actors, institutions, and interests may have played in the character and outcome of expeditions. Until recently, the few historians who did devote attention to the role of non-Europeans in the European exploration of Africa regarded them as subordinates to and agents of European-driven enterprises, a view consistent with the collaborative model advanced by Ronald Robinson.[8] To be sure, historians of Africa have been tracing for some time the trading interests and political influence that various African, Arab, and other non-European parties established across parts of the continent.[9] Surprisingly little notice, however, has been given to the ways they interacted with and imposed their own will on European efforts to explore these same regions.

British explorers became entangled in the agendas of non-European parties because these parties controlled most viable points of entry to the African interior and, hence, often set the terms of their admission. Suitable sites for launching expeditions were far fewer than might be supposed. The logistics of such operations necessitated a staging ground that could be counted on to provide a secure and reliable source of supplies, trading goods, modes of transportation, knowledgeable guides, and more. These requirements tended to be found at the coastal or riverine termini of established trade routes to the interior. Suitable sites were often controlled by non-European states and traders, who had their own interests to protect and promote.

Three states that proved particularly important to British exploration in Africa were Tripoli (now Libya), Egypt, and Zanzibar, each of which was ruled for a significant portion of the nineteenth century by new, dynamic, and expansionist Muslim regimes. Tripoli was transformed by Yusuf Karamanli, who seized the throne in 1795 and temporarily revived his state's naval presence in the Mediterranean, then projected its power across the Sahara. Muhammad Ali took control of Egypt in 1805, asserting its autonomy from Ottoman overlords, expanding its rule into Arabia and the Sudan, and establishing a dynasty that lasted until the Urabi revolution and British invasion of the early 1880s. The Omani ruler Seyyid Said moved his capital from Muscat to Zanzibar in the 1830s, founding a vigorous trading state that extended its sway into the East African interior and retained its independence until 1890. Taken together, these states served as the staging grounds for most of the major British expeditions into West, East, and Central Africa: only the continent's southern triangle was explored by parties that set out from mainly British-controlled territories. The implications that these non-British points of entry carry for our understanding of British exploration and empire will be examined here.

The first region to attract the systematic attention of British explorers was the interior of West Africa. British and other European merchants had established a profitable presence along the West African coast as a result of the slave trade, but indigenous states and a deadly disease environment limited their access to the interior. By the end of the eighteenth century, economic interests, scientific curiosity, and geopolitical rivalry with France had created stronger incentives for the British to explore the region. Their coastal settlements, however, were poor staging grounds for such endeavours. Mungo Park's miraculous journey from the mouth of the Gambia River along a slave caravan corridor to the banks of the upper Niger River in 1795–7 stirred hopes about that route's feasibility, but Parks and his entire party of 50 men died during a second attempt in 1805. The British sent an even larger expeditionary force on much the same route at the conclusion of the Napoleonic Wars, but the obstructionist tactics of a local ruler prevented it from penetrating more than a few hundred miles into the interior. Nor did the trade factories along the Guinea Coast provide viable points of entry. The African states and merchants that supplied slaves to European traders sought to safeguard their own political and economic interests by keeping Europeans sequestered on the coast, and their suspicions of the British were heightened when Parliament voted to end the slave trade in 1807. According to the would-be explorer Henry Nicholls, a leading African trader in Calabar warned him that 'if I came from Wilberforce [the Parliamentary leader of the British campaign to abolish the slave trade] they would kill me'.[10] Nicholls succumbed instead to fever. His fate was a common one. Malaria and yellow fever posed the other major barrier to expeditions setting out from the West African coast. Even large, well-equipped river-bound expeditions failed to overcome the problem of disease. The Royal Navy's expedition up the Congo River in 1816–17 disintegrated when most of the crew died of yellow fever, and disease defeated several attempts to journey up the Niger River, killing 40 of the 49 European participants in Macgregor Laird's privately financed expedition of 1832–3 and 55 of the 159 Europeans in the government-sponsored Niger Expedition of 1841–2.[11] Only a few especially hardy (and lucky) British explorers, such as the Lander brothers, succeeded in penetrating the interior of West Africa from its coast.

North Africa proved a far more stable launching pad for expeditions into the region. Disease presented less of a threat to outsiders and the Sahara desert, for all its challenges, had been traversed by transhumant tribes and trade caravans for centuries. One of the shortest routes to the savannah region where the kingdom of Bornu and the Hausa states held sway had its northern terminus in Tripoli on the Barbary Coast. This Muslim maritime state had been one of the main promoters and havens of the privateers that plagued the Christian west with coastal raids, the capture of vessels, and the ransom of hostages, but its predations were brought to an end by European and American navies in the early nineteenth century. As a result, Tripoli's ambitious pasha, Yusuf Karamanli, turned to commercial and political opportunities in the interior, asserting tributary claims to the crucial network of oases in Fezzan, exerting influence over the traders who controlled the routes across that part of the Sahara, and establishing Tripoli's presence as a political force to be reckoned with among the states further south.[12] It was therefore able to provide explorers with the escorts and assurance of safe passage that they so obviously lacked when setting out from the Gambia, the Gulf of Guinea, or elsewhere along the West African coast.

The earliest attempts by the British to launch expeditions into the African interior from Tripoli were no less star-crossed than the efforts they made from Gambia and the Guinea Coast, but their prospects improved as Tripoli began to project its own power into the Sahara. In 1788, the African Association recruited a long-time English resident of North Africa, Simon Lucas, to cross the Sahara from Tripoli, but reports of warfare along the caravan route convinced him that the undertaking was too risky. Friedrich Hornemann, another explorer sponsored by the African Association, retreated for a time to the safety of Tripoli when his efforts to reach West Africa from Cairo in 1798 stalled in Fezzan. He launched his second attempt from Tripoli in 1800, but died of dysentery during the journey. When the Napoleonic Wars came to an end, Tripoli became the point of departure for several Colonial Office-sponsored expeditions. The first ended prematurely with the death of one of the two explorers. The second, however, was a huge success. In 1822–5, Dixon Denham and Hugh Clapperton reached Bornu and the Hausa states. Travelling under the protection of Yusuf Karamanli, Denham claimed that the route from Tripoli to Bornu was no more dangerous than the one from London to Edinburgh.[13] Soon thereafter, Alexander Laing set off from Tripoli in search of Timbuktu, the holy grail of West African explorers, and became the first European to enter that fabled city in 1826. The loss of Fezzan to Arab and Berber rebels in 1831 and the civil war that followed Yusuf Karamanli's fall from power in 1832 closed the route from Tripoli for a time, but the Ottomans reopened it in 1835. One beneficiary was Heinrich Barth, a German scientist who joined a British-sponsored expedition that set out from Tripoli for the interior in 1850. While James Richardson, the original leader of the expedition, soon died, Barth survived and travelled across much of West Africa over the next five years, returning to Europe to publish the most detailed and informed account of the region ever written by an explorer.[14]

Why did Yusuf Karamanli permit the British to launch these expeditions from Tripoli's shores? He was able to advance his own imperial ambitions. He extracted a fee of £25,000 (equivalent to approximately £1,500,000 in today's currency) from the British government in exchange for allowing the Denham and Clapperton expedition to enter the interior. The British consul who negotiated the deal explained to his superiors that the money would be used to help Karamanli conquer the interior states of Bornu and Sudan, which would in turn 'enable Him to relinquish the Slave Trade'.[15] Karamanli did indeed have aims of conquest, but he had no intention of relinquishing the trade in slaves. He used the British funds to finance an army that accompanied Denham and Clapperton across the Sahara and to raid local communities, sending captives as slave labourers for the fields of Fezzan and to North African slave markets. Tripoli conducted this operation under the pretence of protecting the explorers from the very peoples who were its targets.[16] When Alexander Laing arrived in Tripoli in 1825 to launch his expedition in search of Timbuktu, Karamanli prevented him from setting out until the British consul-general paid 8,000 Spanish dollars, supplemented by a second 'Secret Present' of 1,000 dollars.[17] In return for these payments, Laing received a letter of credit and a promise of safe passage across the Sahara. This was useful so far as it went, but Karamanli's influence did not extend into the vicinity of Timbuktu, where Laing was eventually murdered.[18]

Tripoli's imperial ambitions were reasserted under the Ottomans, who regained control of Fezzan in 1842, stationed garrisons at other oases, and sent an expedition to conquer the territory of Tibesti in 1859. The aim was to protect the trans-Saharan caravan routes and pre-empt French expansionist ambitions – one among many examples of the enduring interactions between Western and non-Western imperialism.[19] This projection of power was advantageous to travellers, who often obtained a written promise of safe passage from authorities in Tripoli. The weight of that promise – known in Islamic discourse as *aman* – was generally respected by the Muslim states in the sub-Saharan savannah region.[20] The *aman* permitted Heinrich Barth to travel through the region with relative freedom and safety. At one point in his travels he was arrested in the emirate of Massina on suspicion of spying for the British, but Islamic legal authorities ruled that he had entered the *dar al-Islam* as a protected non-Muslim and could not be detained nor have his property confiscated.[21] He was freed and permitted to continue on his way. Thus, even in those regions where Tripoli did not wield direct political power, it did carry influence as an important partner in the economic and religious system that bound the region together. British and other European explorers were the beneficiaries of that system: indeed, their very survival often depended on it.

Egypt provided a second important entry point to the African interior for European explorers. The beys who ruled Egypt prior to its invasion by Napoleon in 1798 had granted letters of protection to several British travellers seeking entry to the West African interior, though the route from Tripoli proved shorter and safer.[22] A more attractive destination for expeditions originating in Cairo was up the Nile to Sudan and Ethiopia. In the aftermath of the French withdrawal from Egypt, Muhammad Ali came to power and launched a concerted campaign to modernize and westernize the country, giving an Islamic register to the transformative designs that Napoleon had initiated with his abortive occupation. Muhammad Ali's policies provided an opportunity for British explorers to probe the lands south and east of Egypt. The most famous and successful of these explorers was Jean Louis Burckhardt, whose travels from 1812 to 1816 under the sponsorship of the African Association took him up the Nile nearly as far as Khartoum, then overland to the Red Sea, followed by visits to Mecca and Medina and a voyage along the coast to Suez. Several Britons ventured up the Nile into unfamiliar territory during the following decade and a half, though few of them survived to tell the tale.

The determinative context for these and subsequent expeditions by British explorers was the systematic campaign of imperial expansion conducted by Muhammad Ali and his successors.[23] Egypt won control over the Red Sea's littoral zone, wrestled Mecca and Medina from the Wahhabis (who had previously driven out the Ottomans), and even invaded greater Syria, though it was pushed back when Britain and several other European states intervened on the Ottomans' behalf. Its most successful and lasting effort to establish an empire, however, occurred along the upper Nile. Muhammad Ali conquered much of northern Sudan in 1821 and Egyptian forces soon pushed further southward, establishing a base at Khartoum that became the political and economic capital of their Sudanese domain. Eve Troutt Powell has aptly characterized Egyptian claims to Sudan 'a different shade of colonialism.'[24] Egyptian forces conducted campaigns to enslave indigenous inhabitants (who were impressed into the Egyptian army and put to work on plantations and in other enterprises), expropriate their cattle, and obtain ivory, gold, and other natural resources. By the 1840s Egypt's reach extended as far south on the White Nile as Gondokoro, the front line for an increasingly profitable ivory and slave trade.[25] This imperial enterprise elicited a mixed reaction from the British. Although troubled by reports of slave raiding, the British became convinced that in other respects the Egyptians were bringing the benefits of civilization into a savage land.

Egyptian expansion southward proved useful to Europeans eager to trace the source of the White Nile and gain access to the Great Lakes region of Africa. When in 1863 John Hanning Speke and James Grant left the shores of Lake Victoria to follow the Nile north to Cairo, the route they took to Gondokoro had been pioneered at least in part by Egyptian traders. At Gondokoro, they encountered Samuel Baker and his Hungarian mistress Florence, who were using the station as a staging ground for their own push in the other direction. Baker carried a royal mandate or *firman* from the khedive that permitted him to call on assistance from Egyptian agents. From Gondokoro he and his party accompanied an Arab trade caravan much of the way south to Lake Albert. Although Baker often complained about the caravan's delays and detours, he relied on it for logistics and security. His party's survival became far more precarious once it set out on its own, becoming virtual prisoners of the king of Bunyoro for a time.[26]

The lesson Baker drew from his experience was that 'the only means of commencing the civilization of Central African races [...] [is] by *annexing* to Egypt the equatorial Nile Basin.'[27] Ismail Pasha, Egypt's ruler at the time, shared those sentiments, and in 1869 he appointed Baker as governor general of his newly proclaimed province of Equatoria. Accepting the post ostensibly in order to suppress the slave trade, Baker understood that his main task was to impose Egyptian imperial rule on the peoples of the upper Nile. He had been granted 'despotic powers', he stated, in order 'to subdue to our authority the countries situated to the south of Gondokoro [...] to open to navigation the great lakes of the equator [...] [and] to establish a chain of military stations and commercial depots [...] throughout Central Africa'.[28] He arrived with an armada of nearly 60 vessels, over 1,600 Egyptian and Sudanese soldiers, and two artillery batteries. He proceeded to conduct a brutal military campaign against the native population, justifying it as promoting progress and civilization. Although his efforts to impose Egyptian authority on the peoples of the region met with limited success, this famed British explorer was a willing agent of a non-European state's imperial ambitions.[29] The fact that Egypt's imperial designs on southern Sudan and the Lakes region preceded those of the European powers suggests that in this part of the continent at least, the 'Scramble for Africa' was neither an unprecedented rupture with the past nor an entirely European initiative.

While British explorers benefitted in many respects from Egyptian imperialism, they also found that it made their attempts to gain access to certain territories much more difficult. The Ethiopian explorer Mansfield Parkyns was blocked by African authorities from venturing into the Sahara west of Sudan because he was suspected of spying on behalf of the Egyptians.[30] Similar suspicions forced Richard Burton to abandon his disguise as an Arab trader during his expedition to the Ethiopian city-state of Harar, which feared Egyptian more than European expansion.[31] And the principal reason why the ruler of Bunyoro detained Baker and his party was that he suspected them of being agents of Egyptian imperial designs on his kingdom. As it happened, this is exactly what Baker became. Time and again, explorers seeking to move beyond Egypt's imperial frontiers found that their passage was obstructed by peoples fearful that they were acting as the outliers of Egyptian expansionist ambitions.

A third important gateway for British and other European explorers was Zanzibar, which proved to be a far more commonly travelled and convenient avenue of entry to the Lakes region than Egypt. Like Tripoli, Zanzibar was a Muslim maritime state that provided an entrepôt for the exchange of goods between overseas traders and inhabitants of the interior. Like Egypt, it was a modernizing state of surprisingly cosmopolitan character. And like both, it was aggressively expansionist in its ambitions. In the 1830s the Omani ruler Seyyid Said shifted his capital to the island of Zanzibar, making it the principal trading port along the East African coast. Ships from around the world unloaded cloth, beads, brass coil, and furniture for domestic markets and loaded ivory, copal, hides, cloves, and slaves for overseas markets.[32] Zanzibar's dominion soon stretched along the coast from Mogadishu in the north to Cape Delgado in the south. Its influence also extended hundreds of miles inland. Arab agents of Zanzibar established trading stations at Tabora, Ujiji, and elsewhere in the interior, where they sought not only to expand commercial opportunities but to exert political influence. The sultan, in turn, bolstered their interests against the Nyamwezi and other African competitors, even dispatching his army into the hinterland to defend the Arab traders on several occasions. One indication of how far his authority extended can be seen in his government's response to the murder of a German explorer on the northern shore of Lake Nyasaland in 1859. Zanzibari pressure forced the local chief to hand over the perpetrators, who were sent to the capital, tried, and executed.[33] Zanzibar, in brief, held sway over what its leading historian, Abdul Sheriff, has referred to as a 'commercial empire' that stretched from Uganda in the north-east to eastern Zaire in the west and northern Zambia in the south-west.[34] Although Zanzibar's seaborne capabilities would become increasingly circumscribed by Britain and other European powers, those powers' prospects for sending explorers into the interior were dependent on the approval and assistance of Zanzibar's government and its agents.

The first British explorers to use Zanzibar as the staging ground for their expedition were Richard Burton and John Hanning Speke, who famously returned from their arduous 1857–9 journey to report the existence of Lakes Tanganyika and Victoria. The sultan appointed their caravan leader and supplied them with eight of his soldiers to protect the expedition. He also granted the explorers letters of safe passage and access to credit from traders in the interior. The caravan flew the red flag of Zanzibar, not the British Union Jack.[35] As it marched into the interior, it followed what Burton referred to as the 'Arab line of traffic', the main caravan route that carried ivory and other goods from the interior to Zanzibar.[36] When Speke returned to East Africa in 1860, determined to prove that Lake Victoria was the source of the Nile, he turned once again to Zanzibar and its traders for logistical support. He and his companion, James Grant, followed the standard caravan route west to Tabora, then took another route pioneered by Arab traders to Lake Victoria. Several decades later, Henry Morton Stanley would sneer at the explorers who had preceded him in the region for following what he termed the 'Arab parcel post', but he did much the same on his 1871–2 expedition in search of Livingstone and again during the initial portion of his trans-African journey of 1874–7.[37] So too did Verney Lovett Cameron and various other explorers whose expeditions originated in Zanzibar.

What did Zanzibar hope to gain from permitting this steady stream of explorers to pass through its profitable trading hinterland? No one seems to have asked this question. It is simply assumed that Zanzibar acted at the behest of the British because it was pressured to do so. But this assumption both exaggerates the influence that Britain wielded over Zanzibar and underestimates the authority Zanzibar wielded over the interior, at least until the final decade or two of the nineteenth century. Zanzibar permitted British explorers to set out from its shores and provided them with assistance because it benefitted from the relationship. One of those benefits was the infusion of capital into the local economy as explorers hired porters and purchased supplies, trade goods, and other necessities. It cost Burton and Speke about £2,500 to outfit their expedition and hire a crew in 1857; by the early 1870s Cameron had to spend some £11,000, a sum that shocked his Royal Geographical Society backers. Beyond this, Zanzibar's rulers and merchants recognized that the British shared their interest in opening new regions of the interior to trade. This was a task that explorers were well trained to carry out, taking notes and collecting samples of plants and minerals that might be profitably exploited in the territories through which they passed. The sultan of Zanzibar actually hired the explorer Joseph Thomson in 1882 to prospect the Ruvuma and Lugenda rivers for coal or other valuable mineral deposits. (At about the same time Richard Burton was leading a gold-prospecting expedition into the Midian region of Arabia on behalf of the khedive of Egypt.)

Perhaps the most striking examples of the relationship that was forged between explorers and Zanzibar occurred during the trans-African expeditions of Cameron and Stanley. Once the two men reached the region west of Lake Tanganyika, they turned for assistance to Tippu Tip (Hamid ibn Muhammad), an ambitious Zanzibari trader who had begun to push the frontiers of Zanzibar's trading empire into this territory. Tip provided them with porters and protection, while they in turn provided him with information about routes and trading opportunities that lay further west. Stanley's discovery that the Lualaba River flowed into the Congo, for example, made it possible for Tip to move into the region. By the early 1880s Tippu Tip had established effective control over the upper reaches of the Congo, making it 'a vital component of the Zanzibar system'.[38] 'I am a subject of the Sultan Seyyid Barghash,' declared Tip, 'and the country [...] over which I rule, both it and I are under the authority of Seyyid.'[39] As an agent of the sultan's state, Tip extracted ivory, slaves, and other resources from the Congo basin and sent them back to markets in Zanzibar. Although the British government objected to the slave trade and pressured Zanzibar to stop it, the explorers who set out from this gateway state into the African interior were complicit in its expansion.

The only part of Africa where the British had an effective point of access to the interior was in the far south, where Cape Town and other settlements along the coast served as gateways northward. Yet the existence of a large and expanding British and Boer settler presence in the region paradoxically meant that there was less impetus for formal expeditions than elsewhere. Much of the exploration of the southern frontier was carried out by cattle herders, petty traders, prospectors, and big game hunters, each probing for new opportunities to make a profit. Even here, however, indigenous African polities played some role in determining the course and character of British exploration and expansion. The most famous explorer of Southern Africa was David Livingstone, drawn there by his work as a Christian missionary. His first great expedition across the continent was made possible because he won the support of Sekeletu, the chief of the Kololo people, who provided him with guides and porters. What accounted for this act of generosity is seldom explained, but it is worth taking seriously the claim made by one of Livingstone's most recent biographers: that Livingstone was actually 'leading an African expedition, as an African leader under the authority of Sekeletu.' As Livingstone himself acknowledged, Sekeletu hoped that the expedition would forge routes to new markets for the ivory he hoped to export, though he was less forthcoming about the guns Sekeletu also wanted to purchase with his profits.[40]

Viewed through a Eurocentric lens that anticipates the Scramble for Africa and interprets probes of the continent by explorers as portents of that upheaval, the aims and initiatives of Zanzibar, Egypt, and Tripoli might seem insignificant since they appear in that context as little more than the unwitting accomplices – and victims – of British imperial ambitions. This perspective, I have argued, seriously underestimates the enterprise of these states and misinterprets their stance towards British and other European explorers. These three gateway states shared several characteristics that often caused them to regard expeditions organized by outsiders as opportunities to advance their own interests. Each was a relatively autonomous and dynamic Muslim state, seeking opportunities for economic development, expansion of territorial boundaries, and influence over neighbouring peoples. Each promoted the production and export of agricultural goods (cotton, cloves, and so on) and the targeting of African hinterlands for slaves, ivory, cattle, and other commodities. And each embraced a strikingly cosmopolitan strategy to achieve those ends, drawing on the talents and resources of individuals of varied ethnic origins and cultural identities. The sultans of Zanzibar, for example, relied on an Indian firm to oversee its customs and finances and encouraged American and European governments and merchants to establish an active presence on their island capital. The khedives of Egypt were equally welcoming to foreign bankers and traders, and employed Italians, Frenchmen, and other Europeans in many capacities, including service as officers in Egyptian armies and leaders of Egyptian expeditions.[41] It was entirely within the character of these regimes to recruit individuals of any background whose talents were likely to advance their commercial and political interests. To assume that the British explorers of Africa acted as the inexorable agents of Britain's imperial designs is to lose sight of the influence these gateway states exerted over the character and outcome of their expeditions. It also ignores some explorers' susceptibility to the professional inducements offered by these states, which were able to persuade British subjects such as Samuel Baker and Joseph Thomson to serve more than one master.

The most distinctive characteristic of British explorers through most of the nineteenth century was their weakness and vulnerability to the depredations of local rulers and peoples. From Mungo Park onward, it became a common refrain for explorers to lament the various occasions when they were subjected to extortion, detention, assault, and more, all of which highlighted their powerlessness. There was little if anything that the British Empire could do to protect them or punish their persecutors. Often the only polities that possessed the political muscle to smooth their passage through the interior were the gateway states, and even their power had its limits. Once explorers passed beyond their spheres of influence, they either had to buy their way out of trouble or persuade those who controlled their fate that cooperation could bring benefits through privileged access to arms or other resources. Speke used this strategy to win the cooperation of Mutesa, the powerful and ambitious *kabaka* of Buganda, as did other explorers in negotiations with African rulers elsewhere across the continent. But it remained the case that local rulers, not explorers, usually held the upper hand in these negotiations. The balance of power only began to change in the late nineteenth century as Henry Morton Stanley and other explorers were able to organize much larger, more heavily armed expeditions that resorted more readily to violence to push their way through territories where indigenous peoples were resistant to their presence.[42] These expeditions marked the real transition from exploration to empire-building by Britain and other European states.

What significance does this analysis of the exploration of Africa hold for our broader understanding of empires? First, it demonstrates that British explorers in Africa should not be regarded simply as agents of British imperial interests. They were enmeshed, however unwittingly, in the expansionist designs of non-European gateway states as well. As a corollary, this analysis suggests that whatever imperial designs the British government may have had toward the African continent, it was unable to act upon its intentions at will. The struggle to project power into Africa was a more complex and collusive process than the standard historiography appreciates, a process that merged British interests with and in some instances subordinated them to the interests of non-European states and peoples. Tripoli, Egypt, and Zanzibar may have been different kinds of empires from those established by the British and their European rivals, but they were empires nonetheless. And the fact that they were active in Africa at the same time as Britain and other European powers raises larger questions about how we draw historical distinctions between 'modern' European empires and 'pre-modern' non-European empires. These cases suggest that such distinctions are underwritten by an unsustainable teleology. They need to be re-examined and replaced by a more nuanced understanding of the complex and often reciprocal relationships that arose between empires. Another way to put it is to say that we need to decentre our understanding of empire, replacing the notion of a closed bilateral circuit between a single imperial metropole and its colonial periphery with a much more open, multilateral system that entailed interactions across a number of imperial circuits.[43] This, in turn, requires us to rethink the exclusive relationship that has been asserted between the British Empire in particular (and Western empires more generally) and the rise of modernity.

Finally, and in keeping with the theme of this book, we might make better sense of post-colonial events in Africa by being more aware of the past interactions between these colluding and contending empires. Consider, for example, the merger of Tanganyika and Zanzibar in 1964, which reconstituted much of the sultan of Zanzibar's commercial empire and created what has been to date the remarkably stable country of Tanzania. Or consider the failure of the Arab Muslim-dominated Sudanese state to reconcile the alienated and oppressed populations of Darfur in the west and Bar al-Ghazal in the south to its rule, a failure that led directly to the creation in 2011 of Africa's newest state, South Sudan. Or, finally, consider the recent crisis posed by Islamist movements in Mali, Nigeria, and neighbouring states. While commentators might attribute its immediate causes to Islamic extremists' terrorist ambitions or decrepit African governments' failure to meet the basic needs of their citizens, the problem can be traced back further than that – to ethnic tensions and competition for resources that originated at least in part in Tripoli's prior ambitions in the region, which reverberate in the illicit arms and ex-militiamen from Libya that helped to precipitate the crisis. Although Britain, France, the United States, and other Western countries continue to exert considerable influence in these regions, they are in some respects mere bystanders to processes driven by other agents and agendas, much as they were in the nineteenth century.

Notes

1 This chapter is a modified version of a chapter from my book, *The Last Blank Spaces: Exploring Africa and Australia* (Cambridge, MA, 2013).

2 The titles of several important books on British exploration demonstrate this association between exploration and empire: R. A. Stafford, *Scientist of Empire: Sir Roderick Murchison, Scientific Exploration and Victorian Imperialism* (Cambridge, 1989); J. L. Newman, *Imperial Footprints: Henry Morton Stanley's African Journeys* (Washington, DC, 2004); F. Driver, *Geographic Militant: Cultures of Exploration and Empire* (Oxford, 2001).

3 R. Robinson, 'Non-European Foundations of European Imperialism: Sketch for a Theory of Collaboration', in R. Owen and B. Sutcliffe (eds), *Studies in the Theory of Imperialism* (1972), pp. 117–41.

4 One of the most important recent works to offer this line of interpretation is D. B. Abernethy, *The Dynamics of Global Dominance: European Overseas Empires 1415–1980* (New Haven, CT, 2000).

5 See, for example, M. Adas, 'Imperialism and Colonialism in Comparative Perspective', *International History Review*, 20, 2 (June 1998), pp. 371–88; C. Elkins and S. Pedersen (eds), *Settler Colonialism in the Twentieth Century* (New York, NY, 2005); C. S. Maier, *Among Empires: American Ascendancy and Its Predecessors* (Cambridge, MA, 2006); D. Khoury and D. Kennedy (guest eds), 'Comparing Empires', *Comparative Studies of South Asia, Africa and the Middle East*, 27, 2 (2007), pp. 233–344; A. L. Stoler, C. McGranahan and P. C. Perdue (eds), *Imperial Formations* (Santa Fe, NM, 2007); J. Darwin, *After Tamerlane: The Global History of Empire Since 1405* (2008); J. Burbank and F. Cooper, *Empires in World History: Power and the Politics of Difference* (Princeton, NJ, 2010).

6 Stoler and McGranahan, 'Introduction: Refiguring Imperial Terrains', in *Imperial Formations*, p. 6.

7 F. Cooper, *Colonialism in Question* (Berkeley, CA, 2005), Chapter 5.

8 Robinson, 'Non-European Foundations of European Imperialism'. D. Simpson, *Dark Companions: The African Contribution to the European Exploration of East Africa* (New York, NY, 1976) is characteristic of the work that presents Africans as agents of European ambitions.

9 An excellent example is S. J. Rockel, *Carriers of Culture: Labor on the Road in Nineteenth-Century East Africa* (Portsmouth, NH, 2006).

10 R. Hallett (ed.), *Records of the African Association 1788–1831* (1964), p. 194.

11 P. D. Curtin, *The Image of Africa: British Ideas and Actions, 1780–1850* (Madison, WI, 1964), pp. 165–6, 296, 303.

12 See K. Folayan, *Tripoli During the Reign of Yusuf Pasha Qaramanli* (Ile-Ife, Nigeria, 1979), Chapter 4.

13 Major D. Denham and Captain H. Clapperton, *Narrative of Travels and Discoveries in Northern and Central Africa: In the Years 1822, 1823 and 1824*, 2 vols (Boston, MA, 1826), p. x.

14 H. Barth, *Travels and Discoveries in North and Central Africa, Being a Journal of an Expedition Undertaken Under the Auspices of H.B.M.'s Government in the Years 1849–1855*, 3 vols (1965 [1857]).

15 E. W. Bovill, 'Introduction' in *Missions to the Niger*, vol. II: *The Bornu Mission 1822–25*, 1 (Cambridge, 1966), p. 10.

16 Bovill, 'Introduction', p. 9, fn. 3.

17 'The Letters of Major Alexander Gordon Laing, 1824–26', in *Missions to the Niger*, vol. I (Cambridge, 1964), p. 225. The Spanish dollar was the standard medium of exchange in Tripoli and much of the Mediterranean at this time.

18 Although Tripoli's British consul was convinced that a prominent government minister had conspired with the French consul to murder Laing, his son-in-law. Folayan, *Tripoli*, pp. 149–50.

19 L. Anderson, 'Nineteenth-Century Reform in Ottoman Libya', *International Journal of Middle East Studies*, 16, 3 (August 1984), pp. 328–35.

20 M. S. Umar, 'Islamic Discourses on European Visitors to Sokoto Caliphate in the Nineteenth Century', *Studia Islamica*, 95 (2002), pp. 135–59.

21 Letter by Ahmad al-Bakayi ibn Sayyid Muhammed to Amir Ahmad, item 19 in Library of Congress exhibit, 'Ancient Manuscripts from the Desert Libraries of Timbuktu', www.loc.gov/exhibits/mali/mali-exhibit.htm, accessed 21 April 2008.

22 Hallett, *Records*, p. 57.

23 See H. A. Ibrahim, 'The Egyptian Empire, 1805–1885', in M. W. Daly (ed.), *The Cambridge History of Egypt*, vol. II: *Modern Egypt, From 1517 to the End of the Twentieth Century* (Cambridge, 1998), pp. 198–216.

24 E. M. Troutt Powell, *A Different Shade of Colonialism: Egypt, Great Britain, and the Mastery of the Sudan* (Berkeley, CA, 2003).

25 See S. Sekwat Poggo, 'Zande Resistance to Foreign Penetration in the Southern Sudan, 1860–1890', in J. Spaulding and S. Beswick (eds), *White Nile, Black Blood: War, Leadership, Ethnicity From Khartoum to Kampala* (Lawrenceville, NJ, 2000), pp. 263–78.

26 See S. W. Baker, *The Albert Nyanza, the Great Basin of the Nile and Explorations of the Nile Sources* (1866).

27 Samuel Baker to Roderick Murchison, 8 March 1867, M6a, Russell E. Train Africana Collection, Joseph Cullman Library, National Museum of Natural History, Washington, DC.

28 Samuel W. Baker, *Ismailia: A Narrative of the Expedition to Central Africa for the Suppression of the Slave Trade*, 2 vols (1874), I, pp. 7–8.

29 The fullest account of Baker's campaign of conquest is provided by A. Moore-Harell, *Egypt's African Empire: Samuel Baker, Charles Gordon, and the Creation of Equatoria* (Brighton, 2010).

30 D. Cumming, *The Gentleman Savage: The Life of Mansfield Parkyns 1823–1894* (1987), p. 128.

31 D. Kennedy, *The Highly Civilized Man: Richard Burton and the Victorian World* (Cambridge, MA, 2005), pp. 87–8.

32 See J. Prestholdt, *Domesticating the World: African Consumerism and the Genealogies of Globalization* (Berkeley, CA, 2008), Chapters 3 and 4.

33 Simpson, *Dark Companions*, p. 24.

34 A. Sheriff, *Slaves, Spices and Ivory in Zanzibar* (Oxford, 1987), p. 172.

35 Simpson, *Dark Companions*, p. 14.

36 R. F. Burton, *Zanzibar: City, Island, and Coast*, 2 vols (1872), II, p. 292.

37 Quoted in T. Jeal, *Stanley: The Impossible Life of Africa's Greatest Explorer* (2007), p. 226.

38 N. R. Bennett, *Arab versus European: Diplomacy and War in Nineteenth-Century East Central Africa* (New York, NY, 1986), p. 116.

39 H. ibn Muhammad, *Maisha Ya Hamed bin Muhammed el Murjebi Yaani Tippu Tip* (Nairobi, 1966), p. 109. Tip also reports that he kept in constant communication with the sultan (p. 117).

40 A. C. Ross, *David Livingstone: Mission and Empire* (2002), p. 98; D. Livingstone, *Missionary Travels and Researches in South Africa*, new ed. (1899), pp. 253, 344.

41 Powell, *A Different Shade of Colonialism*, p. 43.

42 See Newman, *Imperial Footprints*, and F. Driver, 'Henry Morton Stanley and His Critics: Geography, Exploration and Empire', *Past & Present*, 133 (November 1991), pp. 134–66.

43 See D. Ghosh and D. Kennedy, 'Introduction', in D. Ghosh and D. Kennedy (eds), *Decentring Empire: Britain, India and the Transcolonial World* (Hyderabad, 2006), pp. 1–15.

Colonial Modernities: A View from the Imperial Verandah, c.1880–1960

Jan-Georg Deutsch

Colonialism is both a set of institutions, and also, emphatically, a set of discourses.

S. Kaviraj[1]

European perceptions of Africa as modernity's 'Other' have a long tradition. In 1830, for instance, Friedrich Hegel famously asserted that Africa lies 'on the threshold of the World's History', but is not part of it.[2] The following chapter explores how European ideas about Africa's supposed essential 'nature' in relationship to 'Western modernity' changed over time in the late nineteenth and early twentieth centuries.[3] This is not merely an inquiry into the history of thought or political argument. European perceptions of Africa guided administrative practice by colonial and indeed post-colonial governments, which arguably had significant and wide-ranging consequences. Even today, the lasting legacy of nineteenth-century and early twentieth-century stereotypes about Africa's supposed lack of modernity is all too noticeable in public discourse, both in Europe and – sadly so – in Africa itself.[4] Most of the examples in this chapter are drawn from the history of the British Empire in Africa.

There is little, if any, agreement in the sociological, historical or philosophical literature about what constitutes 'modernity'.[5] The answer to the question what 'it' is (or, indeed, what 'it' was, according to some post-modern thinkers), when 'it' all started, whether 'it' has local varieties and what 'it' actually means shows a bewildering variety of responses. Beyond a broad and abstract consensus that the emergence of European modernity involved fundamental changes in all spheres of society and that they were to a degree interrelated, there is deep disagreement about when they happened, how important they were in each of these spheres, how precisely they were related to each other and what these changes meant for the non-European part of the world. 'Modernity' originated either in the scientific revolutions of the sixteenth and seventeenth centuries, or in the political revolutions of the late eighteenth century, or in the Industrial Revolution of the early nineteenth century, or only finally came about as a result of the profound alterations that had occurred in the arts and with the move to abstraction in the early twentieth century, or indeed any combination thereof.

As Frederick Cooper and Ann Laura Stoler have pointed out, each of these movements is frequently associated with the idea of 'human progress'. However, they were accompanied by processes that did not fit into that particular idea at all.[6] Thus, for instance, the extension of democratic rights in Europe, as exemplified by the widening franchise granted to European (male) citizens in the nineteenth century, went together with an unprecedented extension of colonial empires and thus authoritarian rule in non-European parts of the world, particularly in Asia and Africa. Similarly, the emergence of industrial, largely wage-labour-based economies in the global 'North' in the early nineteenth century was tied in with, if not based upon, the rapid growth of agrarian, slave or indentured-labour-based economies in the global 'South'.[7] Moreover, 'modernity' in whatever form, disguise or definition is conceived not merely to have effected changes in economic and political structures or to be concerned with the emergence of particular institutions, for instance in the field of education, but has also involved transformation in modes of thought (e.g. spread of witchcraft) and sets of practices (e.g. forms of punishments, such as incarceration for lengthy periods of time).[8]

Given the variety of opinions and the complexity of defining what 'modernity' is or was, it is surprising to note that at least until the mid twentieth century there was widespread agreement that Africa was somehow not part of that 'Modern World'. The reason for taking such a perspective is deceptively simple. As many commentators have pointed out, perceiving Africa as Europe's barbarian 'Other' was predominantly self-congratulatory. It made Europeans feel good and arguably had often little to do with the continent itself.[9] Imagining Africa as the 'Heart of Darkness' would not have mattered that much to most people living in Africa, if Europeans had stayed away from the interior of the continent beyond maintaining precarious trade relations with coastal communities. As far as Europe was concerned, even the transatlantic slave trade, vast as it was, only rarely involved more than gaining a tiny territorial foothold on the continent. After all, up to the early 1870s, except for the French possessions in North and West Africa (Algeria and part of the Senegal) and British possessions in Southern Africa (mainly the Cape Colony), the European presence in the continent was barely experienced. In many parts of West Africa, for instance, Europeans were largely perceived to be merely annoying outsiders who occasionally knocked on the doors of African power holders to ask for favours; they were not seen as posing a serious threat to African sovereignty.

However, the period between c.1870 and 1960 saw the unprecedented projection of European power into Africa, notably by establishing colonial rule. Thus, the history of the set of ideas that legitimized the 'colonial project' (of which the alleged absence of modernity in Africa was an important aspect) arguably merits closer scrutiny, since colonial practices were closely linked to them. This chapter argues that the meaning of European modernity for Africa against the backdrop of its perceived absence in Africa itself underwent substantial change from the onset of the European Scramble for Africa in the 1870s until African independence in the 1960s. In short, while it is not at all clear what at any given point in time European 'modernity' actually was, it might be fruitful to explore what the colonial authorities thought about Africa's supposed deficiencies in this regard and what that peculiar designation meant for the areas concerned.[10]

'Modernities' à la carte

There appear to be three distinct periods which one might want to distinguish in the history of 'modernity' in Africa. Until World War I, proponents of colonial expansion strongly contrasted European 'modernity' and its dynamism with supposedly stagnant African barbarism, arguing that 'modernity' and 'civilization' had to be brought to Africa, if needed by forceful means. The idea of the 'civilizing mission' in one or the other variant dominated public discourse. After World War I, however, colonial enthusiasts no longer perceived European modernity to be unquestionably 'progressive' and 'civilized'. On the contrary, they believed that 'modernity' constituted such a 'threat' to Africa that it urgently needed to be contained and only highly selectively implemented. Finally, after World War II a third, far more radical set of colonial ideas and corresponding practices swept through the continent. Now it was believed that Africa needed to be rapidly modernized by more direct and forceful European intervention, a belief that perhaps was only abandoned in the mid 1970s. In the following each of these 'echoes of modernity' and their discrete histories will be briefly outlined.

Conquista Modernity

Until World War I, it was assumed that Africa was a continent that needed to be civilized by the spread of the Bible and the introduction of the plough. Even a cursory glance at well-informed nineteenth-century explorers such as David Livingstone, Verney Lovett Cameron or Richard Burton shows that they depicted the interior of East Africa as a place filled with wily witch doctors, hungry cannibals and devious Muslim slave raiders, who were deemed to be responsible for the perceived general lack of African 'economic and moral progress'. Whether or not these groups really existed or what kind of influence they actually exerted might be an interesting question to explore, but for the purpose of this chapter, it is sufficient to highlight that these writers thought that in order to civilize Africa, the activities of these groups had to be firmly suppressed, if necessary by violent means.[11] Thus, for instance, in the 1880s and 1890s conquest period, one of the foremost reasons given for the establishment of colonial rule was the assumed barbaric nature of Africa, particularly the alleged widespread practice of slavery and slave raiding. It was a 'dark continent' not because Africans happened to be black but because they were believed to be subjected to oppression and exploitation, which European colonial rule, the development of Africa's productive resources, and the 'civilizing mission' were promising to bring to an end – to 'enlighten', if one wants to extend the metaphor of the 'dark continent'.

In reality, however, colonial rule looked remarkably different from that vision. The importance of the fact that colonial rule was meant to cost little to European taxpayers cannot be overstated. Thus, the military and financial means available to colonial governments on the ground were strictly limited. Colonial governments at least until World War I were run by and large on a 'shoestring' budget. In the case of slavery little was done actually to suppress the 'evil institution' except to deny it official legal recognition by the colonial authorities, and even that was only enacted in parts of the British, French and Portuguese empires and not at all in the German colonies in Africa.[12] There was thus a curious gap between colonial aspirations – bringing 'civilization' and 'modernity' to Africa – and colonial practices that more or less openly condoned social conditions that were explicitly perceived to be modernity's negation. The 'moral high ground' that had justified colonial conquest – for instance, the suppression of slavery in Africa – was remarkably easily sacrificed to the expediency of colonial rule.

Moreover, already by the turn of the century, the belief that in some ways European 'modernity' was by itself good for Africa came increasingly under pressure from European public opinion itself. In economic terms, the colonies proved to be more of a burden than a source of wealth. Metropolitan governments had invested considerable economic and political resources into the colonies, but with a few notable exceptions such as South Africa the returns were frequently meagre at best. Moreover, the conduct of the South African War, King Leopold's Congo policies or German atrocities in South-West Africa, let alone the persistence of large-scale African resistance to repressive forms of colonial rule and instances of ferocious economic exploitation (that had to be put down at great human and material cost), severely undermined the claims of colonial enthusiasts that all was well with the colonial project in Africa. There was increasing doubt both at the periphery and in the centre about the purpose of colonial rule, what it had achieved in the 1890s and 1900s and where it was actually heading for in the future. While the enemies of empire often remained politically powerless and numerically small, they were vocal and their popular support was perceived to be rising after the turn of the century, especially in the early 1910s.

That not all was well in Africa was further reinforced when the disastrous effects of World War I on Africa became more widely known. The forced recruitment of African soldiers in French West Africa to fight and die in the trenches in Flanders, the incompetent and brutal conduct of war in East Africa that directly or indirectly cost up to a quarter of a million of East African civilians their lives, and the South African sub-imperialist land-grabbing in South-West Africa ran directly counter to the ideas associated with the European 'civilizing mission'. Moreover, World War I shook European beliefs in the 'natural' superiority of European culture, its economic rationality or political mastery. If large-scale and hitherto unimaginable violent conflict between civilized nation states was part of the 'modernity/civilizing mission' package, the more perceptive observers were forced to conclude, Africa could do without it.[13]

Against mounting criticism and doubt both at the local and metropolitan level a new rationale for colonial rule thus had to be found. 'Imperialism' as a distinctive set of ideas had to be reinvented in order to construct a new moral high ground that ideally would provide both ethical purpose and political legitimacy to the enterprise and unite the critics of empire and its proponents. That is not to say that the notion of a 'civilizing mission' was simply discarded, but that it took on a new and rather different meaning. Instead of transforming Africa wholesale according to some preconceived notions of supposedly universally accepted moral norms (that demanded the suppression of 'traditional' practices, deemed to be unacceptable to European sensibilities), protecting Africa from the 'strenuous conditions of the modern world'[14] came to be the leitmotif of the years following World War I.

Paternalist Modernity

In the interwar years 'modernity' and 'European civilization' came at least partially to be seen as a kind of contagious disease that seemed to threaten the moral well-being of African societies and traditions. The spectre of the 'de-tribalized' African was haunting the European imagination. In no other area can this be more clearly seen than in the political sphere. While still maintaining that Africa had to be developed economically – not least for government tax revenue purposes and for the benefit of European commercial companies – European administrations embarked all over Africa, but particularly in the British sphere, on a policy that aimed to preserve African political institutions, customs and traditions and even to restore them in those areas in which they were believed to have been destroyed by European rule. This approach is usually associated with the multi-purpose 'indirect rule' policy of the

British colonial administration in the interwar years and was most forcefully expressed in the widely cited, though perhaps not equally widely read, book *The Dual Mandate in British Tropical Africa* (1921) by Frederick (later Lord) Lugard, former governor general of Nigeria. In this book, Lugard emphatically insisted that the 'cardinal principle of British policy in dealing with native races' was to recognize that the political institutions and methods of 'native administration' had to be 'deep-rooted in their traditions'. These traditions had to be preserved rather than radically altered or abolished.[15] Consequently, African political institutions had to be incorporated in one form or the other into the structures of colonial rule and governance.

Lugard proposed that 'indirect rule' should not be seen as a predetermined administrative blueprint, but should be tailored to local circumstances. As a result, 'indirect rule' covered an almost infinitely broad variety of circumstances and practices. Later commentators were thus inclined to argue that the idea of 'indirect rule' resembled more an abstract 'philosophy' or vague 'sentiment' than a discrete set of discernible policy recommendations. They also claimed that 'indirect rule' was primarily an expedient measure to carry on running colonial administrations 'on the cheap' as the alternative – the replacement of African political power holders by local level European administrators – was not feasible, mainly for cost reasons.[16] What these commentators arguably underestimated is that the 'indirect rule' philosophy gave the administration a new moral purpose. Preserving Africa from the onslaught of 'modernity' was perceived to be a noble idea that seemingly bridged the gap between the critics and proponents of the colonial project, both at the local and metropolitan level. By giving colonial rule a new powerful moral purpose, it arguably acquired a new lease of life. Thus at least in the early interwar years, with a few notable exceptions, popular criticism of the imperial project significantly declined. In the metropole, critics found it difficult to raise objections against the avowed goal of protecting Africans from outright repression and exploitation, while in Africa itself local power holders enjoyed the manifold fruits of their official recognition and by and large had little appetite for promoting, let alone leading, popular resistance to colonial rule.

Yet the notion that administrative policy had to be rooted in local customs and traditions was invariably compromised when administrators found out that local political structures could not carry the weight of the colonial administration. The colonial state was meant to rest on hierarchically structured local institutions that in the interwar years were called 'Native Authorities'. Where centralized local political institutions had been present before the arrival of European administrators, the policy seems to have worked well: for instance, in Northern Nigeria or in Uganda. However, in other parts of West and East Africa, notably in Southern Nigeria, Kenya and Tanganyika, such hierarchical institutions frequently did not exist. In such areas, rather than deep-rooting the administration in customs and traditions, the administration constructed 'Native Authorities' that fitted into the 'steel frame' of the colonial administration. In the eyes of their local subjects, these 'Native Authorities' and their agents – African chiefs – became mouthpieces of the colonial administration and it is thus not surprising that many of them lacked any kind of local political legitimacy, 'traditional' or otherwise.[17]

The African power holders' peculiar lack of legitimacy would probably not have mattered to the colonial administration too much if the 'Native Authorities' had been proven useful in dealing with the fallout of the Great Depression. In the early 1930s plunging export prices and steeply declining tax revenues led to a fiscal crisis of the colonial state. Colonial governments all over Africa reacted to this crisis with retrenchment, severely cutting services such as health, education and agricultural extension that were deemed not to be of vital importance to the functioning of colonial rule. They also tried to ameliorate the situation by encouraging export production, the idea being that the fiscal loss stemming from falling prices would be mitigated by rising export volumes. However, this policy failed, as the institutions through which the government had hoped to achieve success – the 'Native Authorities' – proved to be spectacularly ineffective in this regard. By and large, the subjects of the 'Native Authorities' refused to take notice of the exhortation of their chiefs to increase production. Their ineffectiveness became even more apparent during World War II. With a few notable exceptions, such as Kenya and South Africa, the conflict in Europe shut off African colonial territories from their markets, leading to a severe decline in export prices and volumes and an acute shortage of imports. Again, colonial government tried to use the 'Native Authorities' to mitigate the ensuing crisis and again they failed miserably to achieve any significant success in this respect. Much more successful were the attempts to impose central government control over the import and export trade.

Moreover, the more pressure the colonial authorities put on African chiefs for administrative purposes, the more they undercut the power even of those chiefs who actually could command a degree of legitimacy and respect from their subjects.[18] It is perhaps no coincidence that in the later 1930s early nationalist movements in West Africa began to articulate popular discontent when the legitimacy of African chiefs was eroded by demands from the colonial administration. The economic and political alignment between the colonial administration and African power holders opened a political space for nationalist movements, a space that was to widen during World War II and in the immediate post-war years. After World War I colonial economic change had hastened the twin processes of migration and urbanization. At the same time, the small mission-educated African elite became more vocal. Neither the urban labour migrants nor the emerging elites fitted well into the colonial 'indirect rule' framework. For those groups, 'modernity' in whatever form was not a threat, but a condition for their very existence. Their numbers were small, amounting to perhaps less than three per cent of the population, but they were vocal, increasingly interested in politics, and started to get organized in various associations that turned out to be more often than not the predecessors of the political parties that came to dominate the political struggle for independence in the 1950s.

Thus, already by the late 1930s, the idea of 'indirect rule' was seen to be going nowhere.[19] In addition, political pressures arising from the mobilization of colonial resources for the war effort at the local level as well as opposition to the colonial project by the Allied Powers (both from the United States and the Soviet Union) made a continuation of the old 'indirect rule' policy after World War II untenable. The idea had lost its glamour as it seemingly no longer fitted the purpose for which it had been originally developed. Similar to what had happened after World War I, a new rationale for colonial rule had to be created that would take care of the mounting criticism and doubt expressed both at the local and metropolitan level. Ideally such a new policy would provide both moral purpose and political legitimacy to the enterprise and unite the critics of empire and its proponents at home, abroad and in the colonies. Again the new paradigm had to be multipurpose. In retrospect one can only marvel at how well the 1930s idea of 'colonial development and welfare' fitted that bill in the turbulent years following World War II.

Authoritarian Modernity

The history of the origins of the 'colonial development and welfare' policy and its expanding application after World War II has been told by many authors and does not need to be retold in this chapter in greater detail.[20] The main issue from the beginning was that 'colonial development and welfare', like 'indirect rule', comprised an almost infinitely broad variety of policies and practices, ranging from small and low-key primary-education projects to large-scale investment in mechanized agriculture. The supposed beneficiaries included African urban dwellers, rural producers, African colonial governments, the imperial exchequer as well as metropolitan consumers. It was perceived to be a 'noble idea', but the projects were implemented with little regard for the local population or indeed for the local administration. This is why some commentators characterize this period as a 'Second Colonial Occupation'.[21] The colonial state finally reached even the more remote rural areas and more broadly started to affect the livelihoods of increasing numbers of colonial peoples negatively. Moreover, the implementation of 'colonial development and welfare' policies threw into stark relief the deeply authoritarian nature of the colonial state.

Importantly, apart from supposedly nurturing economic growth, the idea of 'colonial development and welfare' served a variety of political purposes: meeting criticism from anti-colonial nationalist groups in various colonial territories, accusing Britain of having done too little for Africa in the interwar years, as well as counter balancing the moral disquiet about the purpose of colonial rule emerging in Britain, especially about policies grotesquely favouring white settlers in colonies such as Kenya or Southern Rhodesia. Finally, the new policy aimed at mitigating at least partially the critique of empire that had emerged in the US and the Soviet Union in the aftermath of World War II, in that 'colonial development and welfare' could be dressed up as a means to prepare colonies in Africa for their eventual independence. Respecting 'the right of nations to self-determination' as the Atlantic Charter of 1941 had stated could thus be postponed for another day.[22]

For the purpose of this chapter, it is perhaps sufficient to highlight that 'development and welfare' surprisingly smoothly replaced the notions of 'indirect rule'. Preserving traditions in Africa from the pernicious effects of 'modernity' was apparently no longer considered to be vital for the maintenance of colonial rule; rather, the very opposite dominated the agenda. Africa was now perceived to be in need of rapid modernization, both politically and economically. In the years following World War II the immediate impact on Africa of these policies was initially limited by the shortage of manpower and material resources, but later substantially deepened. Moreover, one of the most pressing concerns at the time was the need to put the European wartime command economies on a viable post-war footing. This meant that whatever few resources were available at the time for development in Africa, they would be invested predominantly in large projects that promised to provide immediate benefits to metropolitan rather than African economies, like the disastrous Groundnut Scheme in colonial Tanganyika. Indeed, until the early 1950s, African producers, peasants and workers alike were squeezed hard to provide resources for the development and welfare of their European overlords rather than vice versa. Again, the moral high ground that seemed to give the colonial project a new purpose was remarkably easily sacrificed to expediency.

In the 1940s and 1950s, the political tension arising from implementing 'development and welfare' policies brought about a great deal of political reform in colonial Africa, at least insofar as West Africa and parts of East Africa were concerned. In the British case, the local institutions of 'indirect rule' were surreptitiously reformed into local councils while a small number of Africans were invited to participate in the management of colonial government affairs at the central level by virtue of being first nominated, but then increasingly elected members of colonial legislative and executive councils. As far as the non-settler colonies in Africa were concerned, accelerating wider participation in government mapped out a remarkably fluid and peaceful path to independence.

Thus, during the war and in the immediate post-war years a pattern emerged that was to dominate European attitudes towards Africa for a considerable time to come. The 'development and welfare' paradigm reigned supreme well into the 1970s, long after the immediate conditions that had given rise to the idea of 'colonial development and welfare' had vanished. 'Development and welfare' was eagerly adopted by post-independence governments not only because it was perceived to be inherently of merit – a 'noble idea' – but also because it gave credence to an almost infinitely broad range of policies and practices. Importantly, post-colonial 'development and welfare' policies also took on board the authoritarian tradition of colonial administration.[23] Development was understood as a technical rather than political problem and if those who were meant to benefit from these policies were dissatisfied with its result, so be it. There are numerous examples of the authoritarian nature of development policies in the immediate post-independence years, ranging from the exploitation of export commodity producers in West Africa by statutory marketing boards to forced resettlement policies initiated under the banner of 'African Socialism' in East Africa.

Conclusion

This chapter has shown that discourses about the lack of modernity in Africa followed a clear sequence. Each of them built upon the central tenets of its predecessor, discarding some while retaining other elements of the previously dominant ideas. They were propelled forward when external factors and internal developments, both political and economic, coincided to create such a crisis of the 'colonial project' and its rationale to hold on to power that the refashioning of the previously dominant discourse was made unavoidable. Moreover, I have argued that the discourses about African modernity say more about the 'West' than about 'Africa': in their crudest form, they were merely a heuristic device for self-gratification and not even remotely concerned with Africa's past or present.

The last phase in the drama of 'modernity in Africa' opened with the disillusionment over the effects of the 'colonial development and welfare' policies in Africa in the 1970s, an attitude that further deepened during the 1980s and 1990s. 'Colonial development and welfare' policies seemed not to work as internal political turmoil, such as the replacement of various democratically elected governments by military leaders, and external economic shocks, like the oil crises of the mid 1970s, undercut the rationale and high expectations of even the better-designed post-colonial 'development and welfare' plans. However, there is no great hope that the long-standing and by and large self-serving 'modernity' discourse in Europe about Africa has finally run its course.

One conclusion one could easily draw from the discussion above is that 'modernity' – ill-defined as it is – is a useless category of historical analysis. Yet, as much as this might be true in academic terms, the concept itself has still-powerful resonances in everyday life in Africa. Research on what it means for Africans to be 'modern' is unfortunately scant,[24] but arguably would offer rich rewards to the researcher who is interested in the history of vernacular perceptions of 'modernity' that do not fit into the European model of constructing 'Others'.

Notes

1   S. Kaviraj, 'On the Contruction of Colonial Power: Structure, Discourse, Hegemony', in D. Engels and S. Marks (eds), *Contesting Colonial Hegemony* (1994), pp. 19–54, here p. 19.

2   For the quote, see G. F. Hegel, *The Philosophy of History* (New York, NY, 1956 [1830]), p. 99.

3   For a discussion of the role of colonial discourse theory in African studies, see M. Vaughan, 'Colonial Discourse Theory and African History, or Has Postmodernism Passed us By?', *Social Dynamics*, 20 (1994), pp. 1–23; D. Kennedy, 'Imperial History and Post-Colonial Theory', *Journal of Imperial and Commonwealth History*, 24, 3 (1996), pp. 345–63 and R. Abrahamsen, 'African Studies and the Postcolonial Challenge', *African Affairs*, 102 (2003), pp. 189–210. For a wider discussion, see D. A. Washbrook, 'Orients and Occidents: Colonial Discourse Theory and the Historiography of the British Empire', in R. W. Winks (ed.), *Oxford History of the British Empire*, vol. V (Oxford, 1999), pp. 596–611; F. Cooper, *Colonialism in Question: Theory, Knowledge, History* (Berkeley, CA, 2005), pp. 3–55 and J. Rüsen, 'The Horror of Ethnocentrism: Westernization, Cultural Difference, and Strife in Understanding Non-Western Pasts in Historical Studies', *History and Theory*, 47 (2008), pp. 261–9.

4   See for instance B. Wainaina, 'How to Write about Africa', *Granta*, 92 (2006), pp. 92–5.

5   The literature on the subject is vast. For an introduction, see the entry 'Modernity', in J. H. Bentley (ed.), *Oxford Handbook of World History* (Oxford, 2011), pp. 72–88 and T. Schwinn, 'Multiple Modernities: Konkurrierende Thesen und offene Fragen', *Zeitschrift für Soziologie*, 38, (2009), pp. 454–76. For one of the most influential statements on the subject, see S. N. Eisenstadt, 'Multiple Modernities', *Daedalus*, 129 (2000), pp. 1–30.

6   F. Cooper and A. L. Stoler, 'Introduction – Tensions of Empire: Colonial Control and Visions of Rule', *American Ethnologist*, 16 (1989), pp. 609–21.

7   For the difficulties defining the terms 'the Global North' and 'the Global South', see J. and J. L. Comaroff, 'Theory from the South: Or, How Euro-America is Evolving towards Africa', *Anthropological Forum*, 22 (2012), pp. 113–31.

8   See for instance P. Geschiere, *The Modernity of Witchcraft* (Charlottesville, VA, 1997) and F. Bernault, 'The Shadow of Rule: Colonial Power and Modern Punishment in Africa', in F. Dikötter and I. Brown (eds), *Cultures of Confinement* (Ithaca, NY, 2007), pp. 55–94.

9   J. G. Deutsch, P. Probst and H. Schmidt, *African Modernities: Entangled Meanings in Current Debate* (Oxford, 2002), pp. 1–17 and P. Geschiere, B. Meyer and P. Pels (eds), *Readings in Modernity in Africa* (Oxford, 2008). See also R. Price, 'One Big Thing: Britain, its Empire, and their Imperial Culture', *Journal of British Studies*, 45 (2006), pp. 602–27. For a reflection on the present-day implications of the prevalence of the concept of 'barbarians', see Kalypso Nicolaïdis' chapter in the present book.

10 This chapter was greatly inspired by F. Cooper, 'Reconstructing Empire in British and French Africa', *Past & Present*, supplement 6 (2011), pp. 196–210; J. Iliffe, *Africans: The History of a Continent* (Cambridge, 2007), pp. 187–242 and J. Darwin, *Unfinished Empire: The Global Expansion of Britain* (2012).

11 See R. Burton, *The Lake Regions of Central Africa, a Picture of Exploration*, 2 vols (1860); D. Livingstone, *The Last Journals of David Livingstone in Central Africa, from 1865 to his Death*, ed. H. Waller (1874) and V. L. Cameron, *Across Africa*, 2 vols (1877). On Burton and the context of his writings, see D. Kennedy, *The Highly Civilized Man: Richard Burton and the Victorian World* (Cambridge, MA, 2005).

12 For more detail, see P. E. Lovejoy and J. S. Hogendorn, *Slow Death for Slavery: The Course of Abolition in Northern Nigeria, 1897–1936* (Cambridge, 1993). For the broader picture, see P. E. Lovejoy, *Transformations in Slavery: A History of Slavery in Africa* (Cambridge, 1983).

13 See S. Howe, *Anticolonialism in British Politics: The Left and the End of Empire, 1918–1964* (Oxford, 1993). See also N. Owen, 'Critics of Empire in Britain', in J. Brown and W. R. Louis (eds), *Oxford History of the British Empire*, vol. IV (Oxford, 1999), pp. 188–211.

14 The phrase is taken from Article 22 of the League of Nations Covenant, cited in M. D. Callahan, '"Mandated Territories are not Colonies": Britain, France, and Africa in the 1930s', in R. M. Douglas, M. C. Calahan and E. Bishop (eds), *Imperialism on Trial* (Oxford, 2006), pp. 1–19, here p. 2.

15 F. D. Lugard, *The Dual Mandate in Tropical Africa*, 2nd edition (Edinburgh and London, 1923), p. 211. For the argument that 'indirect rule' policies undermined African aspiration to democratic rule, see J. Comaroff, 'Governmentality, Materiality, Legality, Modernity: On the Colonial State in Africa', in J. G. Deutsch, P. Probst and H. Schmidt (eds), *African Modernities* (Oxford, 2002), pp. 107–34. See also M. Mamdani, *Citizen and Subject: Contemporary Africa and the Legacy of Late Colonialism* (Princeton, NJ, 1996). For a more recent treatment of the problem, see O. Taiwo, *How Colonialism Preempted Modernity in Africa* (Bloomington, IN, 2010).

16 J. W. Cell, 'Colonial Rule', in J. M. Brown and W. R. Louis (eds), *Oxford History of the British Empire*, vol. IV (Oxford, 1999), pp. 232–54.

17 For a detailed account, see J. Iliffe, 'The Creation of Tribes', in idem, *Modern History of Tanganyika* (Cambridge, 1979), pp. 318–41. For the wider argument, see M. Mamdani, 'Historicizing Power and Responses to Power: Indirect Rule and its Reform', *Social Research*, 66 (1999), pp. 859–86 and idem, 'Beyond Settler and Native as Political Identities: Overcoming the Political Legacy of Colonialism', *Comparative Studies of Society and History*, 43 (2001), pp. 651–64.

18 *Ibid.*

19 That indirect rule was 'going nowhere' is a quote from Lord Hailey, the author of the monumental *African Survey* (1938). See D. Killingray and M. Plaut, *Fighting for Britain: African Soldiers in the Second World War* (Oxford, 2012), p. 33.

20 The literature on the history of 'development' is vast, but for a succinct position, see M. Havinden and D. Meredith, *Colonialism and Development: Britain and its Tropical Colonies* (1993) and H. Tilley, *Africa as a Living Laboratory* (Chicago, IL, 2011).

21 The term 'Second Colonial Occupation' was coined by J. Lonsdale. See D. A. Low and J. Lonsdale (eds), *Oxford History of East Africa*, vol. III (Oxford, 1976), pp. 1–63.

22 For more detail, see D. Brinkley and D. R. Facey-Crowther (eds), *The Atlantic Charter* (New York, NY, 1994) and E. Manela, *The Wilsonian Moment: Self-Determination and the International Origins of Anticolonial Nationalism* (Oxford, 2007). See also F. Cooper, *Africa since 1940: The Past of the Present* (Cambridge, 2002).

23 For this argument, see L. Schneider, 'High on Modernity? Explaining the Failings of Tanzanian Villagisation', *African Studies*, 66 (2007) pp. 9–38. For the wider discussion, see C. Ake, *Development and Democracy in Africa* (Washington, DC, 1996).

24 This is very much R. Rathbone's conclusion in idem, 'West Africa: Modernity and Modernization', in Deutsch *et al.*, *African Modernities*, pp. 18–30.

Fading Echoes:
Legacy of Empire and Democracy in India

Sarmila Bose

In a strange irony, democracy in South Asia is usually perceived to be a gift of colonialism. It is seen as a legacy of the British Empire, even though colonial rule was anti-democratic by its very nature.[1] This would seem a counter-intuitive outcome. It appears to rest on the fact that the British had allowed limited electoral participation in the last years of the Raj and presided over a 'transfer of power' in which the successor states adopted Westminster-style parliamentary democracy at the end of the British Empire.

Of the newly created post-colonial nation states, India is seen to have run most successfully with this paradoxical imperial bequest, while others have faltered, with civilian dictatorships or military rule disrupting their experience of electoral politics. The Indian experience demonstrated that widespread poverty and illiteracy was no bar to the establishment and consolidation of democratic political systems. With the exception of a two-year period of 'Emergency' from 1975 to 1977, India conducted regular elections and power changed hands through the ballot box.

However, of late the problems of India's democracy have started to trouble even its admirers. Elections are held regularly, but do not seem to deliver results in terms of addressing the needs of most of the electorate. Corruption and criminalization of politics is rife. Elected assemblies are boisterous, but not necessarily focused on legislative responsibilities, and policy-making too often seems reduced to periods of paralysis punctuated by bursts of pre-election populism. The optimistic view remains that while India's democratic practice is flawed, there were similar problems in Western democracies in the past and it is still early days for a country that is just over 60 years old. Others wonder whether the excuse of 'teething problems' is wearing thin after six decades, and if India is losing ground on its way to realizing the full potential of democracy.

This chapter reflects upon two key aspects of the legacy of British colonialism and democracy in India: first, the inheritance of a powerful centre in a large, diverse and nominally federal state; and second, rule by elected representatives. It considers to what extent these were truly a legacy of colonialism, and in what ways they have changed over 60 years of independence. Do political trends over the decades of freedom indicate continuity and consolidation of the colonial bequests or has the legacy waned or ruptured? If India is diverging from expected paths, what is the shape of its experience, and how does that relate to the legacy left at the end of empire?

It argues that the trajectory for both elements – the political primacy of the centre and the democratic content of India's politics – indicate a waning of the colonial bequest. Regarding the first, the driving forces of representative politics have devolved to regional levels over time, despite the continuing concentration of resources and constitutional powers at the federal level in India. The devolution of real political power to provincial or even village levels need not pose a threat to India as a polity; indeed it may strengthen Indian democracy and be a more effective way to govern a vast and diverse nation. It would move India in the direction of a genuinely federal union rather than being federal in name and unitary in practice. However, the regionalization of Indian politics is a significant structural shift of the key arena of competitive politics from a single powerful centre to multiple locations around the country.

Secondly, even observers celebrating India's democracy cannot but comment on the 'dynastic' nature of India's politics. Actually, India's politics is not always 'dynastic', but frequently seems to be *autocratic* regardless of whether it is 'dynastic' or not. Party leaders of most major parties are not democratically elected, they remain in office indefinitely and run their parties and governments dictatorially. Autocracy would normally be assumed to be entirely incompatible with democracy. However, so far India's autocrats continue to seek political power and legitimacy through the mechanism of the ballot box within the structure of parliamentary democracy – a political practice I termed elsewhere a 'competitive autocracy'.[2] But if key political players are autocratic, what is the future of parliamentary democracy in India in the hands of those who do not believe in its fundamental principles and to what extent is this 'democratic deficit' a failure of the legacy of empire?

The Regionalization of India's Politics

When the British departed they left the illusion of a single state (or rather two nation states – India and Pakistan). They themselves had governed through a patchwork of direct rule over some of the territory that comprises India and indirect suzerainty over a large number of princely states and tribal areas. There was no standard form, but a variety of deals done over time with different parties or authority imposed by various means. What was in common was the ultimate supremacy of British authority, channelled through the imperial capital. It is this aspect that suggests that the state of India would not exist but for the British Empire. Indian nationalists liked to imagine a civilizational unity encompassing the whole of the subcontinent, but in political terms, while the Mughals at their zenith had controlled a large proportion of what is India today, it is the British-controlled area that forms the territorial basis of present-day India. The 'transfer of power' in Delhi in 1947 bequeathed these imperial possessions (minus the territories carved out to form Pakistan) to Indians.

The hegemony of the Indian National Congress Party in India for nearly 50 years after independence, and its dominance at both federal and regional levels, helped prolong this monolithic image. Initial breaks in one-party rule proved short-lived. A non-Congress coalition ruled in Delhi from 1977 to 1980, following Indira Gandhi's 'Emergency', but collapsed within a short period, with Mrs Gandhi returning as prime minister in 1980. Her assassination in 1984 brought her son and successor Rajiv Gandhi to power with a massive majority. Rajiv Gandhi was defeated in 1989 by another coalition, which again collapsed by 1991. Following Rajiv Gandhi's assassination that year, the Congress became the largest party in the parliament and formed a minority government under Narasimha Rao. This government lasted a full term of five years and acquired majority status during the term due to breakaway factions of opposition parties joining the government side.

It was 1996 before India arrived at the age of coalition politics at the federal level. After this no single party held a majority in the central parliament until the BJP led by Narendra Modi won a surprise majority in 2014. However, in reality a long process of regionalization had been in motion over decades, in parallel with a gradual decline of the Congress Party from the dominant position it occupied in the early years after independence. Tamil nationalism in southern India was one of the early challenges, but it seemed to have been contained by the 1960s with a linguistically defined state and the success of regional parties which have held power at the provincial level in Tamil Nadu ever since. By the 1980s, regionally defined parties were well established across India: for instance, Telugu Desam in Andhra Pradesh, Akali Dal in Punjab or Asom Gana Parishad in Assam. The first non-Congress coalition in West Bengal was formed in 1967, though it was short-lived. From 1977, a Left Front led by the Communist Party of India (Marxist) ruled West Bengal until 2011.

Even parties with universal or national ideologies, such as the communists or Hindu nationalists, have found their political base restricted to particular regions.

The influence of the communist parties was limited to the eastern state of West Bengal, the small former princely state of Tripura in India's north-east, and Kerala in the south. The Hindu nationalist Bharatiya Janata Party's appeal seems limited primarily to north-central India, with a recent success in Karnataka a first foray into the south. Since the 1980s the northern plains have been the site of the rise of caste-based parties: Samajwadi Party (Uttar Pradesh), Rashtriya Janata Dal (Bihar), Bahujan Samaj Party (Uttar Pradesh and parts of Bihar and Madhya Pradesh). Several smaller players are also identity-based political formations – for instance, Jharkhand Mukti Morcha (based on a tribal identity) or Telengana Rashtriya Samiti, which sought separate status for the Telengana region which was formerly in the princely state of Hyderabad.

India's choice of a socialist path for economic development until the 1990s also buttressed Delhi's supremacy as the ultimate seat of political competition for several decades. The liberalization of India's economic policy since 1991 has transformed its political – economic relationships. With a loosening of a 'command and control' regime, the centre has been losing relevance in many activities in which it formerly monopolized patronage. India has followed a gradualist path of reform, but the post-liberalization period appears to have accentuated uneven regional development even if some of the inequalities have longer roots. This in turn has turned the spotlight more on state-level performance and interstate comparisons.

Two features of the regionalization of India's politics stand out as we consider its meaning for the legacy of empire. The first is the gradual nature of the regionalization. Despite many centrifugal pulls, India appears to have held together, in some areas by the use of coercive power and in others due to the success of accommodative politics, and the federal centre remains a significant political location. However, regional politics as a concept has been transformed from being seen as in inevitable conflict with the nation state project (as in the Tamil case, the taming of which is frequently described as an example of the accommodative characteristic of the Indian state), to a reality presented as a celebration of the pluralism of the Indian political space.

The second feature is that even though many of the regional governments are led by powerful regional leaders whose principal interest is their own locality, they all continue to seek representation in Delhi. They send members of parliament to Delhi, jockey for places in the federal government coalitions and compete for resource distribution through the centre. Regional politics and being part of an 'emerging' India at the federal level are not seen as incompatible. Delhi does not appear to perceive an existential threat due to the regionalization of India's politics, as the regional powers largely work within the Union of India, retaining a stake in the federal government, which continues to be the repository of enormous financial resources and coercive power. The first signs of a different tune were heard at the turn of the twenty-first century, when some state chief ministers voiced concern that the resource allocation formulas of the central finance commission appeared to penalize well-governed states while rewarding the non-performers. Interestingly, the protest cut across party lines. However, the tone was one of reform, not a radical break from the federal fiscal framework.

'Surreptitious Withdrawal': Regional Politics at the End of Empire

The gradual and accommodative regionalization of Indian politics, and the continued engagement by regional political players with the centre, would appear to indicate that the imperial legacy of a centralized territorial nation state has survived for the long-term. However, both the gradual process of regionalization and the continuing interest of powerful regional players in a stake at the federal centre are in keeping with what happened in India *before* European colonialism, when another imperial hegemony declined and regional power bases emerged as prominent political actors in their own right. Writing about the disintegration of the Mughal Empire in the eighteenth century, Muzaffar Alam observed, 'while there was chaos and anarchy in some regions, an emerging political order tended to be constituted in the form of virtually independent principalities, which nevertheless continued broadly with the Mughal institutional framework'.[3]

According to Barnett, 'the central development of the eighteenth century, as indeed during most of South Asia's history, was the growth and autonomy of distinct cultural and historical traditions possessing unique forms of economic and political organization.'[4] Bayly analysed the 'receding tide' of Mughal rule as itself a result of the creation of new wealth and social power in the provinces where it could not easily be controlled by a distant Delhi. The 'decentralization' of politics was anticipated by the very successes of Mughal expansion. Similarly, the devolution of power to the provinces in twentieth-century India may be viewed as a success of the widening and deepening of its democratic politics. The accommodation of regional identities, for instance, resulted in political parties with local, rather than national, aspirations and limited reach; the successful entry of previously marginalized groups such as 'untouchable' castes into electoral politics has also fragmented the political field. In post-colonial India regional political leaders continue to gather in coalitions at the centre and remain part of the centralized system of resource-sharing – so far. In the fading days of the Mughal Empire the areas that were most successful eventually either revolted openly or 'surreptitiously withdrew' from central control in the eighteenth century.[5]

The process of breaking free took a long time in the post-Mughal period: there was no sudden snapping of ties to the centre. Several autonomous states rose from the ruins of imperial power in the eighteenth century: Awadh, Bengal, Hyderabad, Mysore, various Rajput principalities, and the Maratha confederacy – many of them roughly equivalent to the regional political spheres of influence today. Alam described how these virtually autonomous principalities voluntarily retained their links to the imperial centre for a long time. He surmised that the reasons for this could be because the centre played the role of an arbiter or legitimizer, or because of perceived material benefits or security through symbolic links to a super-structure. There was a 'slow pull to provincial independence', with an 'emerging sense of regional identity which buttressed both political, and to a degree, economic decentralization'. In a parallel to powerful contemporary regional parties retaining positions of influence in weak coalition governments at the centre, such was the 'myth and influence of Delhi' in the eighteenth century that 'even after the total collapse of the central government, the governors of the virtually independent provinces continued to make serious efforts to obtain offices at the Mughal court'.[6]

Mughal rule, which was a complex hierarchy of authority, was not a 'centralized' state in the post-colonial sense. During the Mughal period as in the period of European colonialism, a powerful minority ruled vast territories in complicated arrangements with sections of the local populace. Just as in the late twentieth century 'lower' castes and 'untouchables' in India began to form their own political parties and gain power, 'The eighteenth century saw not so much the decline of the Mughal ruling elite, but its transformation and the ascent of inferior social groups to overt political power.' During the 'long metamorphosis' from provincial government to autonomous kingdoms, the ultimate, if nominal, authority of the emperor in Delhi continued to be respected by almost all the autonomous rulers, for instance in Bengal, Awadh, Hyderabad, or Carnatic. Even the Marathas and Sikhs paid ceremonial homage. Only Tipu Sultan of Mysore called himself 'emperor', but he too was respectful towards the Mughal ruler.[7] However, that nominal respect could not ultimately conceal the altered power relations between Delhi and the regions. Some of the autonomous provinces later formed the basis for the next external imperial power, the British.

The political forms may be different today, but the nature of the relationship between the centre and the regions, in terms of the diffusion of real political power seems strikingly similar in the eighteenth century and in contemporary India. The gradual nature of the realignment process does not mean that the centre is secure. While regional satraps appear to remain interested in a stake in the central government, this may mask a modern round of 'surreptitious withdrawal'. In the eighteenth century, the virtually autonomous rulers of Bengal started making their own appointments, and became irregular in sending tributes to Delhi or stopped altogether.[8] Autonomy was short-lived, however, with one fading empire replaced by a new external colonizer, the British. No equivalent external replacement is evident in the twenty-first century; nor have ideologies with pan-Indian potential, such as communism or Hindu nationalism, succeeded in breaking out of a regional mould. As the arena of politics has nevertheless effectively moved to the regions, it is unclear what the future of Delhi might be, shorn of its imperial purpose.[9]

India's Undemocratic Democracy

The idea of 'democracy' as the best possible political system is virtually unquestioned today in political discussions. Writing about democracy as a 'universal value', Amartya Sen identified the rise of democracy as the pre-eminently acceptable form of governance as the most important development of the twentieth century.[10] There is wide consensus across scholars, policy makers and public opinion about the desirability of democracy as a political system.[11] India's success in sustaining democracy – regular elections and changes of government through the means of elections – is seen as key to its political maturity, stability and progress towards broad-based economic prosperity and inclusive social development. In contrast, the failure to sustain democracy in other post-colonial states in South Asia or other former colonies is perceived as damaging to the prospect of political stability and socio-economic development, and in some sense the transformation of these societies to 'modernity'.

A recent survey of South Asian states found a high level of support for democracy as a political system among Indians. Seventy per cent of Indians surveyed agreed with the statement that democracy was preferable to any other form of government, bettered only by Sri Lankans, whose preference for democracy stood at seventy-one per cent. Only nine per cent of those polled thought that sometimes dictatorship might be preferable. In reality however, Indians are faced with a pervasive lack of internal democracy in their political parties. In this context it is noteworthy that twenty-one per cent of respondents in India – more than a fifth of the 'world's largest democracy' – agreed with the following statement: 'It doesn't matter to people like me whether we have democratic or non-democratic governance.' A more probing examination of the depth of support for democratic rule found a significant level of yearning for 'strong leaders' in South Asia, including India, who would rule unconstrained by democratic checks.[12]

India is a particularly interesting case in this regard due to its long and largely uninterrupted record of electoral politics. The periods of democracy in Pakistan and Bangladesh disappointed their citizens and political analysts alike in terms of the quality of political discourse and governance. However, this is usually explained precisely as a result of not having *enough* democracy – the stunting of democratic political development due to the repeated interruptions. In the case of democracy, the argument seems to be as in so many other activities: practice makes perfect.

India has had plenty of practice, but the quality of its democracy still disappoints. For a country supposedly following the Westminster model of parliamentary democracy, India is noted for its political 'dynasties'. Despite the regular ritual of elections and changes of government via the ballot box, it has produced poor governance. India's performance in key socio-economic indicators in health, education or sanitation has been disappointing, indicating that electoral politics is not adequately responsive to the needs of large sections of the electorate who are poor. It appears to have generated a diverse range of identity groups based on religion, ethnicity or caste, rather than political or socio-economic interests (though in some cases, such as the Bahujan Samaj Party, these may largely coincide).[13] Yogendra Yadav demonstrated the 'deepening' of India's democracy through his empirical studies of Indian elections, but also spoke of India's 'democratic deficit', asserting that 'the existence of this democracy does not deliver what democracies are supposed to' and that the key failures were 'the growing distortion in the mechanism of political representation, the growing distance between the electors and the elected, the inability of the mechanism of competitive politics to serve as a means of exercising effective policy options'.[14] Jayaprakash Narayan, head of Loksatta, the Hyderabad-based civil society organization for democratic reforms probing electoral malpractice and poor governance, assessed India as a 'dysfunctional democracy'.[15]

India's admittedly flawed democracy still retains the confidence of 'democracy optimists'. Most feel they need only compare its relative achievements to the conspicuous failures in the region, notably in Pakistan and Bangladesh, or the wider experience of post-colonial nation states in Asia and Africa. Many point out that all of these are young states, and many of the flaws in their exercise of democracy could be found in earlier eras of European democracies, and may similarly diminish with time and experience. For some, India's democracy is taken to have succeeded merely by its very survival in the inhospitable climate of poverty and conflict. It is celebrated for its institutionalization, despite the many shortcomings of its substantive achievements.[16] For others, democracy's success in India is that it has proved to be more than a superfluous structure. As Oldenburg argued, despite many problems, 'Democracy in India is not a façade behind which one finds dominant classes or other societal institutions that exercise power.'[17]

The more disillusioned, however, wonder about the future of democracy in India, and a few even about the idea of democracy itself.[18] The potential problems of trying to make parliamentary democracy work in post-colonial India were articulated by the chairman of India's constitution-writing committee, B. R. Ambedkar. Himself from the 'untouchable' castes, Ambedkar pointed out that a completely egalitarian idea – one person, one vote – was being suddenly superimposed upon a profoundly unequal society. He worried about how the former was supposed to succeed without addressing the latter.[19]

Continuity and Change at the End of Empire

To what extent was electoral democracy in India truly a legacy of British colonialism? Indians were permitted limited electoral participation at local and provincial levels in the last years of British rule. There were several phases of constitutional reform in British India that preceded the adoption of Westminster-style parliamentary systems in both the successor states of India and Pakistan. Unlike Britain, upon achieving independence its former colonies opted for written constitutions. Bangladesh, when it came into being in 1971, also initially adopted the same system. Sumit Sarkar noted that the theme of continuity between the colonial and post-colonial periods is accepted both by those who view this progression as a positive development and those who are critical of the post-colonial state as a structural continuation of colonial rule.[20]

One interpretation of the limited political participation granted to Indians is that the colonial masters saw it as a means by which 'the natives could discuss their own "schools and drains" without subverting the British Empire'.[21] In this view such political reforms in colonized India were conceded so that 'Indians could be given a safe play-pen in which, if they could harm anyone at all, they could only harm each other.'[22] An alternative, more optimistic view finds some benefit – even if inadvertent – in the practical experience it gave Indian politicians in party-building, electioneering and local government.[23]

Empirical studies of the effect of colonial rule on the establishment of democracy in post-colonial states seem to have produced mixed results. The contribution of the 'British colonial model of tutelary democracy' emerged as a significant factor in Myron Weiner's study of the handful of low-income countries that had managed to retain democratic political systems even with occasional setbacks. Weiner identified two aspects of British colonial rule as crucial factors in successful 'tutelage': the establishment of institutions of governance such as a bureaucracy, judiciary, police and army, and the creation of representative institutions and periodic elections.[24] However, other large statistical studies on the survival of democracy in states have found no significant impact of past colonial history.[25]

Indeed, the adoption of universal democracy by India upon becoming independent may be viewed as a calculated break from British imperial legacy, as it 'went far beyond anything evolved under the late colonial state and indeed represented policies deliberately conceived in opposition to its highly constraining influences. In many ways, the stroke of midnight on 15 August 1947 shattered the links between the colonial past and the national future.'[26] India became independent in 1947 through a 'transfer of power': Indians did not really experience full democracy until 1952, when the first general elections were held under the constitution of independent India with universal adult franchise. If democracy was a legacy of empire, it seemed to have been more of a parting gift, chosen by the recipient and bestowed hastily at the moment of departure.

However, while universal adult franchise may have been a break with the colonial legacy, other aspects of the limited political participation in colonial India endured and contributed to some of the problems of democratic practice in India today. A key measure introduced by the British was separate electorates on the basis of religion and caste. This was introduced through the Morley–Minto reforms in 1909 and consolidated and extended in the 1919 Montagu–Chelmsford package and the 1935 Government of India Act. There is consensus that this 'legitimized the language of communal (i.e. religious) and interest group politics' and 'made it much harder, perhaps impossible, for even professedly secular Indian politicians not, at least tacitly, to do the same'.[27] Washbrook points out that while this has been viewed as 'a peculiarly colonial device constructed by the British for the purposes of "divide and rule"', it may also reflect 'British ruling elite ideas about the nature of representation itself'.[28]

The actual powers of the 'playpen' elected bodies were very limited. It delegated 'petty functions' and even then, 'That the extension of these responsibilities should not involve any meaningful shift in power, however, was guaranteed by a complex system of controls'.[29] As Zachariah put it, 'This caricature of parliamentarianism was the highest form of institutional politics in colonial India: even in the last stages of so-called "training for self-government", at the end of the 1930s, a legislature's decisions could be overridden by the governor of a province or the viceroy of India.'[30]

While British colonial rule – perhaps unsurprisingly – did not provide meaningful democracy, it is noteworthy that the principal opposition to British rule was also anti-democratic.[31] The unquestioned leader of the Indian nationalist movement, Gandhi, neither sought nor held any political office. But those who did hold office did so at his pleasure. In the final years of India's independence movement, the President of the Indian National Congress used to be effectively a nominee of Gandhi. In his choice of candidates Gandhi did not exclude those who held different political views from him on how to dislodge the British from India or what kind of society to build in independent India. On the contrary, he opted for co-option. Most of the time it worked smoothly: the Congress went through the motions of election of the chosen candidate, blessings were sought and received. In 1939, though, it went spectacularly wrong.

In 1937 Gandhi had entrusted the Presidency to Jawaharlal Nehru, who held very different political ideas from him but accepted the status of disciple. The following year he chose the younger, more radical Subhas Chandra Bose. When Bose decided to stand again for the presidency in 1939 it caused consternation. As the members of the Congress Working Committee led by Vallavbhai Patel put it, without even a hint of irony: 'The election, as befits the dignity of this high office, has always been unanimous.'[32] Gandhi did not want Bose to be president again. Bose's refusal to back down forced a real election on the Congress. When Bose was re-elected, defeating Gandhi's anointed candidate Pattabhi Sitaramayya, Gandhi declared it a personal defeat. As it turned out, Bose won the election but lost the war. Gandhi refused to cooperate and as it was impossible to lead the Indian nationalist movement without his cooperation, the democratically elected President of the Congress was eventually forced to resign.

The lack of democracy in the Congress movement, however, did not necessarily affect the legitimacy of Gandhi's leadership. While Gandhi's power was extra-constitutional, nobody could doubt his mass appeal. He did not seek formal office, but he did have immense popular support. Many have viewed this form of leadership as 'saintly', but it would be erroneous to elevate it so.[33] Others who have followed the same strategy do not enjoy the moral status of the 'Mahatma'. In contemporary India Bal Thackeray, leader of the Marathi chauvinistic-cum-Hindu nationalist party Shiv Sena, wielded political authority for decades without holding official positions. From 2004 to 2014, though Manmohan Singh was formally prime minister, everyone knew that the real head of the Indian government was Sonia Gandhi. Sonia Gandhi is a legitimate representative of the people of India: she is an elected Member of Parliament and leader of her party. Her role in government appeared to be accepted by the general public even though she eschewed the official form of exercising her power. Power without office appears to have become routinized; nor is it entirely unaccountable. When elections came around, it was on her shoulders that the verdict for the performance of her party fell.

India's Experiment with Democracy

Even if India received no meaningful 'tutelage' in the practice of democracy before independence, it adopted parliamentary democracy and Nehru, India's first prime minister, is usually described as a politician in the Westminster mould. His daughter, Indira Gandhi, was the only prime minister who attempted to rule directly as a dictator, during the 'Emergency' she declared from 1975 to 1977. However, the Nehru period was also not conducive to the development of democracy in many ways. The Congress enjoyed political dominance in the early decades of India's independence at both federal and state levels. Within the Congress Nehru faced no real challenge to his leadership: he was the only front-ranking nationalist leader to survive to rule in independent India. Though nominally the leader of a democratic state, his was the status of a 'raja' among his people.

Many observers struggle to explain India's actual experience with democracy, which seems at first glance to suggest that parliamentary democracy as a political system has simultaneously succeeded and failed in post-colonial India. The rise of caste-based politics in India, for instance, is seen as a success in terms of empowering marginalized groups in Indian politics, but also as a failure in that it has entrenched caste identities, which many in India had hoped to abolish. An interesting recent argument predicts that the heightened sense of caste identity is actually less permanent than imagined, and that the cross-caste alliances that political leaders have been forced to adopt in a fragmented arena actually weaken the logic of caste politics in the long run.[34]

Discussions about 'dynastic' politics in South Asia sometimes assert that Western democracies also have 'political dynasties', such as the Kennedys or the Bushes in the United States. There is really no comparison between Western 'political dynasties' and family rule in South Asian politics. In Western democracies children do not become prime minister by hereditary succession upon the death of a parent, as Rajiv Gandhi did for example upon Indira Gandhi's assassination. Nor do political parties get handed down to a chosen child in personal wills like family heirlooms, as Benazir Bhutto appears to have done in Pakistan. This development is not a legacy of European colonialism, but a curious product of the interaction between that legacy and the development of India's own peculiar political culture, in which undemocratic political groups compete for power through democracy.

Another feature often overlooked is that India's political leaders are autocratic even when no family dynasty is involved. For instance, the new chief minister of the state of West Bengal, Mamata Banerjee, comes from a humble background and did not have any family connections in politics. She won her place in Indian politics on merit, by sheer perseverance and effort, after a long struggle to oust the communists from power in her state. In the process she left the Congress Party, which she felt was not truly committed to defeating the communists, and formed a new party, Trinamool Congress, which she eventually led to electoral victory. Banerjee is unmarried and has no children, so it is unlikely that there would be a family succession. However, just like the dynastic leaders, she runs her party, and now her state government, in authoritarian style.

Some other notable leaders of political parties in India have secured their political position after defeating traditional family claimants. Jayalalitha, leader of the AIADMK Party in the southern state of Tamil Nadu, saw off a claim from the wife of her political mentor, the film star turned chief minister M. G. Ramachandran. Like Banerjee, she is unmarried and has no children. In Andhra Pradesh, the son-in-law of another movie star turned political leader, N. T. Rama Rao, won the contest to lead his party after Rao's death, extinguishing the hopes of his widow. Mayawati, who became the chief minister of India's most populous state Uttar Pradesh, is a woman from an 'untouchable' caste. She gained the leadership of the Bahujan Samaj Party from her mentor, Kanshi Ram, the founder of the party. She too is unmarried and has no children. Like Sonia Gandhi and all the other leaders who treat political parties as family fiefdoms, the leaders without spouses or children also run political parties as personal autocracies. All swear by India's democracy, but none practises democracy.

If parliamentary democracy was a legacy of British colonialism, rampant autocracy in Indian politics would surely be the sign of a failed gift. Did it fail because limited local elections were merely disingenuous diversions by the colonial authorities? Was it because democracy was imposed suddenly on an unprepared society as the colonizers scrambled to depart before the empire collapsed around them? The supposed 'tutelage' of Britain may also be seen in a different light: perhaps what Indians really learned from the British Empire was not democracy but political hypocrisy, in which one could practise democracy at home while denying it to subjects around the world. Perhaps the art of indulging in the rhetoric of democracy while practising something quite different is the true legacy of British colonialism in India.

However, trying to assess India's democracy in terms of 'success' or 'failure' is an unproductive exercise. Such an assessment always implies a standard, often left unspoken and in any case hard to specify. After all, 'success' need not be achieved by becoming an exact replica of the British model, nor might the open suspension of democracy such as the declaration of Emergency in 1975 be the only possible way to 'fail'. Instead of thinking about India's experiment with democracy in terms of the Western model or the 'British tutelary' legacy, it may be more useful to ask what form of democratic politics has developed in India in the six decades of its practice and in which direction it seems to be headed. How is its trajectory related to its colonial legacy, if at all?

What appears to have developed in India is the retention of the form of parliamentary democracy with the substance of personal autocracy and dynastic rule. The autocratic nature of India's political parties is now widely established and does not appear to be a vote-loser. There have been mass protests in India against endemic corruption, but no organized movement against undemocratic political parties, which have become routine. Educated and westernized politicians accept subordinate positions in 'feudal' family retainerships masquerading as political parties. However, while political parties are undemocratic, they continue to compete for power and legitimacy through the ballot box. Leaders who brook no dissent within their parties accept election losses as the verdict of the people. I have termed this form of political practice, which has developed over the last several decades in post-colonial India, 'competitive autocracy'.[35]

The practice of democracy in India therefore appears to be developing its own particular form, which includes some profoundly undemocratic characteristics. Political parties may be undemocratic, but accept elections as the means to compete for political power and legitimacy. Most political leaders are autocrats, whether representing a family dynasty or not, but may still enjoy genuine popular support and political legitimacy. In this respect India appears to be developing a political system that may be termed *representative*, if not wholly 'democratic' in terms of Western norms. It may be that this hybrid stage is merely a stepping stone to full-blown autocracy. Perhaps it is only a matter of time before India's authoritarian politicians decide to dispense with elections as the means to power. However, it is also possible that India's partially democratic 'competitive autocracy' is a sustainable political practice for the longer term. It appears to marry the notion of 'strong leadership' seemingly valued by a significant section of the electorate with the choice and accountability offered by a democratic system of electing who governs.

Fading Echoes of the Legacy of Empire in India

The shift of the principal location of Indian politics to the regions, its striking parallels with the aftermath of the Mughal Empire, and the widespread phenomenon of autocracy in Indian politics do not mean that India is simply reverting to its pre-colonial past. Rather, it shows how the echoes of European colonialism in the development of democracy in India interact with other societal forces to evolve a new politics which needs to be understood in its own terms.

In 1947 India inherited a centralized nation state and adopted parliamentary democracy. But these were last-minute bequests, rather than a cultivated legacy or the culmination of organic developments in Indian society. The leaders of independent India did not tear down the colonial administrative structures. Nor did the mainstream nationalist movements cultivate democratic values. With the waning of the power of imperial Delhi under the Indian successors to the departed British, the principal arena of politics in India has moved, as in previous post-imperial periods, to the regions. This is similar to the political formations of the eighteenth century, at the end of a non-European imperial period. As at that time, the regionalization of politics in post-colonial India has been a gradual process, and resurgent regions have retained a link to the weakened centre. How long this relationship endures in the face of a faltering centre before covert or overt 'withdrawal' of autonomous regions, or supersession by a new imperial project, remains to be seen.

Democratic governance in the Western mould was arguably never a true colonial bequest. The British did not practise it in India, and most of the Indian leadership in the nationalist movement did not embrace it either. The adoption of democracy can in fact be viewed as a break with British colonial legacy, while the problems of religion- and caste-based politics can be traced to colonial interventions. Over the decades of electoral politics India has developed its own political practice, which includes a host of autocratic political players who – at least until now – seek state power through the ballot box. While not 'democratic', most of these autocratic leaders are 'representative' of their people in a way the colonial masters never were. They gain or lose power through elections. As the memory of European colonialism fades, the inclination to make polite nods towards the formal democratic structures of the former imperialist masters grows ever weaker, leaving India free to develop its own system of competitive autocrats where real power may be unconnected to formal office. This may be 'undemocratic' in the European sense, but nevertheless a 'representative' form of politics which may endure for the foreseeable future.

Notes

1 By 'anti-democratic' I mean hostile to the concept of democracy as a universal value. I use the term deliberately, on the basis that those who had democracy in their own country, but colonized territories around the world and denied the indigenous peoples of those territories the right to govern themselves, did not believe in democracy as a universal value.

2 S. Bose, 'Indians will Vote, but will they get Democracy?', *The Times*, 10 April 2009.

3 M. Alam, *Crisis of Empire in Mughal North India* (Oxford, 1992), pp. 1–2.

4 R. B. Barnett, *North India Between Empires: Awadh, the Mughals and the British, 1720–1801* (Berkeley, CA, 1980), p. 1.

5 C. A. Bayly, *Indian Society and the Making of the British Empire* (Cambridge, 2006), pp. 11–18.

6 Alam, *Crisis of Empire*, pp. 14–17.

7 Bayly, *Indian Society*, pp. 9–18.

8 See P. J. Marshall, *Bengal: the British Bridgehead*, New Cambridge History of India, vol. II (Cambridge, 1987), Chapter 2, resulting in a 'No' vote.

9 Post-colonial Britain has also devolved power in recent times, creating Welsh and Scottish assemblies and fuelling debate about whether there should be an English assembly as well, and whether devolution strengthens or threatens the Union. A referendum on Scottish independence was held on 18 September 2014, resulting in a 'No' vote.

10 A. Sen, 'Democracy as a Universal Value', *Journal of Democracy*, 10, 3 (1999).

11 In the first ever simultaneous survey of attitudes to democracy in Bangladesh, India, Nepal, Pakistan and Sri Lanka in 2004–5, respondents expressed overwhelming support for democracy in spite of significant proportions stating that whether there was democratic or non-democratic governance did not matter to people like them. See Centre for the Study of Developing Societies, *The State of Democracy in South Asia: A Report* (Oxford, 2008).

12 *Ibid.*

13 I addressed some of these issues in 'Is India a Failing Democracy?', Illinois Wesleyan University, March 2005 and 'South Asia's Politics: Can Undemocratic Democracies Work?', Royal Commonwealth Society, Oxford, April 2008.

14 Y. Yadav, 'A Radical Agenda for Political Reforms', *Seminar*, 506 (October) these arguments are reproduced in his essay 'Representation', in N. G. Jayal and P. B. Mehta (eds), *The Oxford Companion to Politics in India* (Oxford, 2001).

15 J. Narayan, 'Electoral Reforms', Loksatta, Foundation for Democratic Reforms, Hyderabad (2002). Loksatta has since launched a political party and Mr Narayan, a former civil servant, was an elected state legislator in Andhra Pradesh.

16 See for instance A. Kohli, 'Introduction', in A. Kholi (ed.), *The Success of India's Democracy* (Cambridge, 2001).

17 P. Oldenburg, 'India's Democracy: Illusion or Reality?', Asian Governments and Legal Systems, *Education about Asia*, 12, 3 (Winter 2007).

18 Notable among those who were originally optimistic but now are concerned about democracy as an idea and as a political system in India is Rajni Kothari, *Rethinking Democracy* (2007).

19 Ambedkar's angst about the contradiction between Indian society and its new political system is famously expressed in his valedictory address in the Indian Constituent Assembly. See for instance *Constituent Assembly Debate*, vol. X: *Official Report* (New Delhi, 1989), p. 979, quoted in Z. Hasan, 'Representation and Redistribution: the New Lower Caste Politics of North India', in Frankel et al. (eds), *Transforming India* (Oxford, 2000).

20 S. Sarkar, 'Indian Democracy: the Historical Inheritance', in A. Kholi (ed.), *The Success of India's Democracy* (Cambridge, 2001).

21 B. Zachariah, *Nehru* (2004), p. 53, citing S. Sarkar, *Modern India* (1983).

22 Zachariah, *Nehru*, p. 35.

23 M. Weiner, 'Empirical Democratic Theory', in M. Weiner and E. Ozbudun (eds), *Competitive Elections in Developing Countries* (Durham, NC, 1987), Chapter 1.

24 *Ibid.*

25 A. Baechtiger, D. Hangartner, P. Hess and C. Fraefel, 'Democracy Survival in Africa and Asia', General Conference of the ECPR, 2007; P. Schleiter and R. Elgie, 'Variation in the Durability of Semi-Presidential Democracies', in R. Elgie, S. Moestrup and Y.-S. Wu (eds), *Semi-Presidentialism and Democracy* (2011).

26 D. Washbrook, 'The Rhetoric of Democracy and Development in Late Colonial India', in S. Bose and A. Jalal (eds), *Nationalism, Development and Democracy* (Delhi, 1998), p. 37.

27 J. Chiriankandath, '"Democracy" under the Raj: Elections and Separate Representation in British India', in N. G. Jayal (ed.), *Democracy in India* (Oxford, 2001), p. 78.

28 Washbrook, 'The Rhetoric of Democracy', p. 40.

29 *Ibid.*, p. 41.

30 Zachariah, *Nehru*, p. 5.

31 Again, I use the term 'anti-democratic' in the sense of being hostile to the idea of universal democracy: see note 1.

32 Statement of Vallavbhai Patel and other members of the Congress Working Committee, 24 January 1939, in *Netaji Collected Works*, Netaji Research Bureau (Oxford, 1995), vol. IX, pp. 69–70.

33 Morris-Jones' classifications of Indian political leadership, discussed by R. Guha, 'Political Leadership', in Jayal and Mehta, *Politics in India*.

34 S. Jodhka, 'Caste and Politics', in Jayal and Mehta, *Politics in India*.

35 S. Bose, 'No Serious Issues in Indian Elections', interview with *Asian Affairs* (May 2009). Online at http://asianaffairs.in/may2009/interview.html (accessed 20 June 2011).

The Imperial Question in the History of Ibero-America: The Importance of the Long View[1]

Jean-Frédéric Schaub

Why the Long View?

In understanding Latin America as a theatre for the deployment of imperial structures, we have the opportunity to listen for the European–Atlantic echoes of a bygone imperial age; and yet doing so today brings us face to face with two still very current political realities. The first is the lasting effect of the two-centuries-old doctrine of United States president James Monroe (coined in 1823) concerning the former Spanish and Portuguese territories in South and Central America. The United States' play for the old Iberian colonial empires remains a permanent source of tension in the relationships between Latin American societies and their powerful neighbour to the north, with the Monroe Doctrine seen as little more than a veil for United States expansionism – a view which finds support in the United States' territorial gains at the expense of Mexico and the entry of Louisiana, Florida and Texas into the Union. These memories and suspicions are present in inter-American relations to this day, with the support given to the Castro brothers' regime by the majority of Latin American heads of state – even the more conservative among them – being one of the more spectacular consequences of this historical mistrust. Against this background, even today, the 'imperial' question in Latin America can be too readily understood as an unequal struggle against United States imperialism, rather than as an investigation into the historical, endogenetic roots of the considerable inequalities in income and social status which lie at the heart of these societies.

The second political reality is that once the questions asked by historians of colonial empires start to attract a certain degree of interest, the result is often simply to reinforce the idea that the colonial structure of Latin American societies disappeared along with the empires which imposed it for three centuries. In this interpretation, nation states are considered incapable of engendering colonial structures, meaning that the extreme nature of some societal inequalities can then be ascribed to a hateful European heritage – a view which is not necessarily easy to defend almost two centuries after the collapse of the Iberian monarchies in America. Nevertheless, these societies remained essentially structured around slavery for several decades after they gained independence, with racial stratification becoming if anything more clearly defined within the framework of post-independence constitutions as, for the first time, the issue of whether to integrate or exclude the indigenous and African populations from civic society was decided on national scales. Indeed, put succinctly, the clear racism rooted in slavery which characterized these societies and persisted into the twentieth century did so under full national sovereignty without much connection at all to the former metropolises which had been, in reality, quite incapable of imposing any kind of measures at all on their former colonies since the early nineteenth century. The dominant social classes in Latin American countries and their political masters can hardly attribute the fundamental inequalities in their societies to the persistence of European colonialism – and even if they may in some small measure, imperial historiography must not be allowed to provide them with comfortable alibis.

Navigating between these two approaches relies on a real understanding of how Latin America has been shaped by the imperial structures imposed on it in the sixteenth and seventeenth centuries: what is at stake is neither the question of 'imperialism' as defined by anti-imperialist rhetoric or the theory of dependency, nor the question of whether the old metropolises can be held permanently guilty for whatever becomes of Latin American societies. Rather, it is about seeing how 300 years of colonial society developed under imperial institutions profoundly structured the societies which became independent in the 1820s on the continent and in 1898 on the islands of Cuba and Puerto Rico. In view of this fact, this chapter will aim to draw on a holistic analysis of the Iberian imperial institutions in the Americas over the whole period of their existence, opening up several perspectives from which to understand this part of imperial history in the context of several centuries of historical development proceeding from the European Middle Ages; in this way, this chapter stretches to its utmost limits the timeframe within which the 'echoes of empire' of the volume at hand may be heard.

Within the overall history of European empires, the colonial activity of the states of the Iberian Peninsula is a special case, first of all due to its chronology: the Iberian imperial story predates the colonial endeavours of other European societies, beginning with the conquest of the Canaries, the establishment of the first trading posts in Africa and the voyage of Christopher Columbus.[2] As conquerors, the Iberian states were as precocious as they proved to be tenacious, being very much the last

European countries to accept, and very reluctantly, decolonization: while Portugal fought in Angola and Mozambique in 1974, its administration in Macao only ending in 1999, Spain maintains its presence in Ceuta and Melilla to this day. Secondly, the territorial aspect of Iberian colonialism sets it apart: up until the golden age of the British Empire, the Iberian territorial conquests in both America and Asia (Sri Lanka, Philippines), as well as their networks of outposts and ports, were the most influential in the world: any reflection on the imperial question in Spanish and Portuguese America can only take place within an awareness of this wider context.

Thus, the history of these empires is part of a very long history; yet intercontinental processes made the history of Latin American societies a dynamic, changing one. Not only is the development of the Iberian monarchies indissociable from the colonial structure of Latin America, but a range of other phenomena with broad repercussions shaped the course which Ibero-America was to follow, the most important of which was the immense transfer of African populations as a result of the Atlantic slave trade. It can be shown that Africans were present from the very start of Iberian conquest in the Caribbean and the Americas, and the scale of this phenomenon is hard to understate, with estimates that more than eight in ten of the 13 million African slaves transported to the Americas were set to work in plantations, towns and mines in Iberian dominions. Within this imperial framework, the uncertainty of frontiers should not be forgotten, with relations between Spain and Portugal being complicated by territorial disputes despite the Treaty of Tordesillas in 1494 and the presence of other colonial actors such as the Dutch, the English, the French and the Danes, especially in the Caribbean.

This chapter takes into account the territorial imperative of expansion and the full length of the timescale on which this occurred, and while this requires a very general account of events, it sheds light on phenomena that the monographic approach has difficulty illuminating. It will begin by charting the imperial models formed in the Latin American sphere in the fifteenth, sixteenth and seventeenth centuries, and will then go on to focus on the exercise of empire in the territories colonized.

Competing Imperial Models

With the Treaty of Tordesillas (1494), the Spanish and Portuguese negotiating parties initiated nothing short of a real intellectual revolution.[3] Under the aegis of the Holy See, the two monarchies divided up between them conquests which had yet to be identified for an undetermined period of time using mathematical coordinates, breaking with the empirical character of territorial negotiations up until that point in a fundamental way. The partition drew on two sources for its legitimacy: the Pope and the rules of geometry. An inviting interpretation is that these empires-under-construction were at once born of the medieval papal tradition and yet also midwives of a modern scientific one.

The problematics of imperial history lead to the initial question of whether the developing imperial character of the Spanish and Portuguese monarchies was the result of colonial expansion, or rather the cause behind it. At the time when the first parts of the imperial construct were being set up in America, Spanish royalty was organizing itself within an already imperial structure: the crowns and principalities inherited by Charles of Ghent (born 1500, Charles I of Castile and Aragon from 1516 onwards, Holy Roman Emperor Charles V as of 1519) were part of a 'composite monarchy' as John H. Elliott calls it.[4] Indeed, the term has become a classic, and can also be applied to the English monarchy during its expansion within the British Isles following Cuthbert Tunstall's famous remark to Henry VIII that 'the Crown of England is an Empire of itself'.[5] The comparison between these two developments, unnoticed for so long, has become a field of comparative studies with a very large historiographical range,[6] and across Europe there has been more general reflection on the links between the composite character of the Hispanic monarchy and the power it attained going into the modern period.[7]

The composite monarchy model rests on several specific characteristics: the territories under it are assembled around a central power either by dynastic line (inheritance, marriage), by negotiation, or by conquest,[8] and the way in which territories enter into the monarchical structure determines the nature of their relationship to the capital. Blood lines and negotiations allow the possibility of the territories in question remaining autonomous inasmuch as they may retain authority over their judiciary, as did Aragon in its relations with Castile or, later on, Scotland with England. Conquest, however, abolishes the right of the new dominion to rule over its own legal systems and maintain its customs, as happened to Ireland and very much to the territories conquered in America.

The processes which lead to composite monarchy are tantamount to territorial growth, and the argumentations used to justify it usually make reference to divine providence.[9] A royal house may be termed 'the eldest child of the church', as was the French, while in the case of the Iberian monarchies, religious justification came through the series of wars known as the Reconquista, which drew on the language used to legitimize crusades to impose a spiritual aura around the chivalrous enterprises of the Castilian, Aragonese and Portuguese kings. The affiliation of the two kingdoms of Aragon and Castile following the marriage between Isabella and Ferdinand (1469) augured the unification of Iberia as Muslim presence on the Peninsula had dwindled to the small rump kingdom of Granada. To give just one example of the use of religious justification, the mythical foundations of the Portuguese dynasty are built on the victory of Prince Afonso Henriques over the Almoravid Moors at the Battle of Ourique; this confrontation between a Christian prince of Portugal and Muslim troops in 1139 would, much later on, become an inexhaustible source with which to celebrate the legitimacy of Portugal as a nation founded during the crusades.[10]

The crusade is not the only element used. The notion of suzerainty gave the holder of the principal crowns of Europe the status of *superiorem non recognoscens* – that is recognizing no superior and being therefore emperors in their own lands. The King of France had himself designated as *Imperator in Imperio suo* accordingly from the twelfth century onwards[11] while Alfonso VII of Castile and Léon (1126–57) carried the title of *Imperator totius Hispaniae*.[12] Meanwhile, the Kings of Aragon, with their naval exploits across the two Mediterranean basins, styled themselves as expansionist maritime monarchs battling against Islam and thereby also blessed with the grace of God[13] the manifest success of the prophetic verses attributed to the shoemaker Bandarra in the mid sixteenth century shows the efficacy of such messianic presentations of political institutions within Iberian society.[14] Put simply, the institutional and spiritual registers within a notion of empire born of Roman and Christian heritage fed the discourse of many a European monarch looking to legitimize his or her reign – well before any kind of colonial expansion had begun.

While the idea of a composite monarchy always seems applicable to the Hispanic monarchy, many historians underline that it is largely unsuited to Portugal, and indeed the metropolis of the Portuguese empire-under-construction was composed of one sole entity. This is why Portuguese and Brazilian historians today prefer to speak of the 'multi-continental monarchy' (Nuno Monteiro).[15] As Portuguese navigators landed in Brazil in 1500 under the leadership of Pedro Álvares Cabral, the royal declaration they carried with them was already worded to express the imperial character of their king, who was titled 'King of Portugal and of the Algarve, of each side of the sea in Africa, Duke of Guinea, and of the conquest, navigation, and commerce of Ethiopia, Arabia, Persia, and India by the Grace of God' – a title worthy of a king of kings, that is an emperor.[16]

In this way, the Spanish and Portuguese political authorities which conquered such immense territories in the Caribbean and the Americas from the end of the fifteenth century onwards were already empires of a sort; then again, there can be no doubt that the sheer size of their conquests in the western hemisphere confirmed and broadened the ideology of divine providence on which their monarchs had based their claims to be emperors. Indeed, while Philip II of Spain did not inherit the crown of the Holy Roman Emperor from his father Charles V, the imperial and divine aspects of his authority remained unquestioned.[17] In the meantime, the success in America and then the union with the Portuguese monarchy in 1581 allowed the power of the Spanish Empire 'on which the sun never set' to take root,[18] and the Holy Roman Empire lost its importance in the face of this king who was suspected across Europe of aspiring to head a Universal Monarchy.[19]

Throughout the long history of Iberian societies, the processes of conquest acquired all of the complexity of imperial structures, with the territorial gains at the expense of the Islamic societies on the Iberian Peninsula taking on a whole range of forms as alliances between princes and emirs periodically punctuated the clash between the two worlds. All of the drama in the emblematic epic of Spanish Christianity, the *Cantar de mio Cid*, is drawn from this two-tiered reality, and this is an important point in understanding that the alliances concluded between the conquistadors and several Amerindian societies against others were nothing new in the sixteenth century. In medieval Spain and Portugal, juxtaposed societies would have coexisted (without any mixing) in often peaceful environments periodically blown apart by explosions of violence.[20] Just as Muslim rulers had allowed communities of Christians and Jews to exist at their very centre, the territories conquered by the Castilian and Aragonese princes kept their Jewish and Muslim communities, albeit in separate quarters of towns and cities, until the collective expulsions at much later dates. It is quite admissible to see this coexistence as a kind of medieval blueprint for the later juxtaposition of European societies and *repúblicas de indios* so typical of colonial America. Furthermore, the conquests by the Christians from the Muslim societies on the Iberian Peninsula were followed by the expropriation of fertile lands in the favour of the new rulers and by strategies for repopulation. This was how the region around Valencia was transformed, as were the Balearics, once Muslim authority had been erased, and certain historians are quite willing to categorize these processes in the conquered territories as colonial situations.[21]

In this manner, even before the great expeditions of the fifteenth and sixteenth centuries allowed them to build colonial empires, the Spanish and Portuguese monarchies had formed their political and territorial structures as empires, and the social and institutional processes this entailed came out of the 'imperial repertoires' as defined by Jane Burbank and Frederick Cooper:[22] internal pluralism; the use of intermediaries; an ambivalent approach to frontiers somewhere between closed and permeable; the complexity of ideological formulae hovering between pragmatism and dreams of world domination – all of these are present in the Iberian experience on the eve of the conquest of America.

Chronologically, the first steps towards the colonization of the Americas were preceded by the first Atlantic expansion of the Iberian monarchies, and indeed David Abulafia has referred to the expeditions to capture the Canary Islands as the 'Discovery of Mankind';[23] and if the 'discoveries' in the 'New World' are characterized as European contact with – and subsequent eradication of – peoples of whom they had previously known nothing, then they do indeed begin in the Canaries. The first expeditions in the fourteenth, the systematic conquest of the fifteenth, and the establishment of colonial society in the sixteenth century were all the first steps in the cycle of the great European Atlantic expansion.[24] With the exploitation of the Atlantic islands – the Azores, Madeira, Cape Verde – the slave traffic started to take on new dimensions and shows that the slave trading network did not need America to function between the Sahara, the Mediterranean, Europe's Atlantic coast and the ocean island groups. Merchants from Portugal, Genoa and Aragon established trade routes for purchasing and selling slaves on a grand scale, constituting the basis for the great Atlantic triangle system of the sixteenth to nineteenth centuries.[25]

The last aspect of medieval heritage in the Ibero-American empires was religious intransigence.[26] The conquest of Muslim territory and the navigation of the African coastline during the fifteenth century occurred concurrently with a series of profound transformations in relations between Christians, Jews and Muslims on the Iberian Peninsula. The symbolic year of 1492, marked by the fall of Granada, the expulsion of the Jews and the voyage of Christopher Columbus, concluded a cycle of phenomena which had been interlocking throughout the fifteenth century.[27] The conquistadors who landed in the Caribbean and on the American continent were of a political culture characterized by Christian society's desire to purge other influences. The *limpieza de sangre* statutes regarding the 'purity of blood' and the techniques of the Inquisition shared the same objective, namely to marginalize and eliminate the groups formed by the descendants of those who had converted to Christianity,[28] and it was with this model of social and cultural relations that the first conquerors in America approached indigenous societies. This is a fundamental point for those seeking to understand the whole range of phenomena which characterized the formation of the new societies in the Americas.

Imperial Practices

The two Iberian empires, the Spanish and the Portuguese, are often considered to be tangibly different, with the main opposition purported to come from the Castilian practice of continental conquest and the control of littoral territory on the one hand and the Portuguese thalassocracy on the other. This is, however, far too general a framework within which to analyse the way in which these empires were deployed, and at the very most it could be said that the territorial ambition of the Castilian conquistadors picks up where the Aztec and Inca empires left off and continues in their tradition. By the same token, the Portuguese model of a non-contiguous empire can be seen to imitate the commercial, political and religious networks which organized the great exchanges between East Africa and China.[29]

When it comes to the American possessions of the two monarchies, however, the grip of this classic theory loosens further. On the one hand, after a century of hesitation, Portuguese colonization takes on the aspect of territorial expansion, whether in Bahia or Pernambuco during the sixteenth century, before the Paulists penetrated into the southern hinterland and Maranhão in the Amazon was conquered in the seventeenth or the Minas Gerais region administered in the eighteenth centuries.[30] Conversely, it is important to recall that, for a long period, the Hispanic institutions remained incapable of exercising their rule over all of the territories to which they had nevertheless laid claim.[31] This was the case not only regarding all of the territories to the north of the Valley of Mexico, but also of the Amazon and the Upper Paraná, meaning that the Spanish institutions too learned how to manage non-contiguous territorial belongings on the American continent.

With an unparalleled demographic disaster caused by genocidal violence and epidemics of disease, local societies were built on the custom of forced labour (*la mita*) and on extremely widespread slavery. Any historical approach to American societies which tries to ignore or detract from the extent and extremity of the phenomenon is doomed to misunderstand the nature of society, politics and culture in the region.[32] The Atlantic slave triangle and the enslavement of the native populations are the most important structural social phenomena on which to grasp the colonial and imperial process in Latin America. In demographic terms alone, the number of African people arriving in the colonies would have been larger by several orders than that of Europeans, and indeed Africans were present throughout the colonial period across the board – whether in towns, on plantations, on the estates of the Europeans, or on their farms and in their mines. Their presence was viewed both as the indispensable fuel of the colonial motor and as a permanent threat to the established order, and the dread of runaway slaves, for instance, was a colonial experience shared by the European subjects of both empires.

At the intersection of Inquisition jurisprudence, the *limpieza de sangre* rules, and the ideological need of a justification for considering children born to enslaved mothers as slaves, the American colonial societies developed systems of racial classification for the populations they administered.[33] One of the examples most often cited is that of the *pinturas de castas* in Mexico, which find their reflection in the iconographic representations of Brazilian towns at the end of the eighteenth and the beginning of the nineteenth century.[34] The society of colonists, administrators and missionaries was premised on the systematic use of slave labour, and this aspect of the empires is far more concrete than any of the imperial institutions imposed by the Spanish and Portuguese monarchies. Indeed, slavery and the slave trade were not abolished as independence came in the liberal era: quite the opposite, and the great *libertador* Simón Bolívar remained – as did his counterparts George Washington and Thomas Jefferson – an owner of slaves, even if he in principle was an advocate of abolition as a way of preventing the war of the races he lived in fear of.[35] In the Atlantic sphere, Brazil was, along with the Spanish colony of Cuba, the last to abolish slavery and the slave trade in 1888 and 1886 respectively.[36]

Beyond these similarities, the institutional forms of the two empires merit analysis by themselves. In the course of the sixteenth, seventeenth and eighteenth centuries, both Spain and Portugal put in place relatively comparable governmental systems based on a proliferation of specialized top-level councils, referred to as the 'polysynody' of the Iberian monarchies. Right through until the middle of the eighteenth century, the administrative model was based on traditional jurisdictions and, as their name indicates, the councils' role was to aid the monarch in taking decisions, while at the same time operating in the monarch's name using their governing delegations. In terms of form, this mode of government is based on the royal authority's judgement of matters submitted to it, and the members of the chambers are usually experts in law, ecclesiastical representatives or members of the aristocracy. To simplify matters, both polysynods can be described as arches built up of chambers and tribunals, at the peak of which sits one council which guarantees the judicial coherency of all of the entities in each monarchy and functions as the highest chamber and place of last recourse (Consejo de Castilla, Desembargo do Paço). Below this, there is a series of councils specializing in matters such as foreign affairs and the cohesion of the empires (state council), finances (fiscal council), military matters (war council), religious issues (council of orders, the Holy Office of the Inquisition), overseas affairs (council for the Indies, overseas council) and in the case of the Spanish crown, councils charged with the home dominions (Aragon, Navarre, Italy, Flanders and Portugal).

Therefore, from the end of the sixteenth century onwards, matters concerning the Castilian Indies and the Philippines were handled by a specialized council, the Real y Supremo Consejo de Indias,[37] whose activities had two distinct sides. In one sense, as the extension of the jurisdiction of the Castilian crown, the council did not depart from the administrative routines and judicial reasoning of the other councils. The recent splitting of the old royal archives, which has isolated the correspondence of the Consejo de Indias at the Archivo General de Indias in Seville, does not do justice to the depth to which this council was integrated into the Spanish polysynody. The meetings of the Council of the Indies were held on the same premises as those of the other high royal tribunals, such as at the Alcázar in Madrid, and the magistrates who sat on the council had often begun their *cursus honorum* in other jurisdictions, and could continue on to others, too, so any research into the American territories must pass through the administrative circuits of the empire; in doing so, the depth to which domestic and overseas questions were intertwined becomes very clear.

Yet in another sense, the distances, delays in communication, and features of the American terrain make it impossible to confuse the ways in which Spanish domestic and overseas affairs were managed, starting with the long-distance administration of native populations and slaves shipped in from Africa. The differences had enough of an effect to call forth specific jurisprudence, termed Derecho Indiano from the seventeenth century onwards by the first to compile it under legislation, Juan Solórzano Pereira.[38] From the first moments of the conquest, the grand tribunals of the American jurisdictions, or *audiencias* (Santo Domingo – 1516, Mexico – 1527, Panama – 1538, Guatemala – 1543, Lima – 1543, Guadalajara – 1548, Bogotá – 1548, Quito – 1563, Charcas – 1559, Chile – 1565, Caracas – 1786, Cuzco – 1787) began to forge this specific set of laws by the decisions they made.

The case of the Portuguese administration was tangibly different. Before the union of the crowns of Portugal and Spain (1581–1640), there was no high council equivalent to the Consejo de Indias and, in the Americas, no equivalent to the Spanish *audencias*. Under the union, there was a brief period in which an 'Indian council' was established (1604–14),[39] but it was only with the new regime installed by the Duke of Braganza under the authority of John IV of Portugal that a stable Conselho Ultramarino came into being in 1641.[40] Born during the rebellion against Spanish rule and the Dutch occupation of the sugar-producing regions of north-eastern Brazil, this was both a governmental and military administration. Royal jurisdiction in the Portuguese Americas cannot really be compared to that of the Spanish territories, however, due to the length of time it took the Portuguese monarchy to set up high-level structures to impose its jurisprudence over the western hemisphere in the same way as the Spanish *audencias*. Indeed, it was not until 1609 that the Relação at Bahia was created under Philip III.[41] By the same token, while the Inquisition had already set up tribunals in America (Mexico and Lima in 1569, Cartagena de Indias in 1610), cases from Brazil were referred up to the Lisbon tribunal. The same is also true of universities with the purpose of training the theologians and lawmakers necessary to govern empires: while the Spanish monarchy supported the opening of around 30 universities throughout that colonial period, the first of which were at Santo Domingo (1538), Lima and Mexico (1551), and Bogotá (1580), Europeans in Brazil who wanted to study for a degree had to do so at the University of Coimbra. Similarly, the first printing press in Mexico was in operation in 1539, while it took until the transfer of the Portuguese Court to Brazil in 1808 for there to be a functioning printing press in this part of the South American continent. This meant that the accoutrements of a working jurisdiction were only present in Brazil much later and in much lower density than in the Spanish Americas,[42] with the result that the Portuguese monarchy did not produce jurisprudence for the Indies or the Americas that was specific or separate from common law in the metropolis.[43]

Nevertheless, the two Ibero-American empires shared a unique sociopolitical structure which can be categorized as a corporative society.[44] This characteristic inherited from the Iberian medieval societies was not put in question by the formation of colonial societies in the Americas; and even if the *encomienda* and *fazenda* systems certainly developed beyond the old feudal model of fiefdoms in the same measure as the control of the labour force replaced the domination of territory,[45] it remains the case that the corporative and hierarchical structure of the municipality and the diocese – and by extension that of the conventual assemblies under the generic term *cabildo* – was retained as the backbone of the sociopolitical system of the Iberian Americas through until the time of independence. The brotherhoods and friaries which shaped parish life, the hospitals for the ill and for the paupers, the colleges and universities there were: all of these were founded on the basis of hierarchy and the collegiate structure.[46]

The society of the Ibero-American empires was therefore designed as an aggregation or assembly of corporate entities, each one with its specific rights or privileges, even though there was no nobility in America as there was in Europe: the society of the European colonists in America and of their descendants, mixed-race to varying degrees, was organized into municipal and ecclesiastical corporations. The other major difference as against European society was that entire sections of the population, including indigenous Americans, large numbers of mixed-race people not integrated into civic life and African slaves (both first generation and those born in America), had no political role in society at all. Portuguese captains and Spanish viceroys created spaces both physical and social for 'Indian republics', both in towns and in the country, and village-scale structures led by missionaries,[47] yet everyone living in the American colonies was required to recognize the supremacy of their monarchs and the unique, indisputable truth of the dogma of the Catholic Church. There were some European structures which were not entirely foreign to them: mainly the brotherhoods formed by the indigenous population and those composed of freed African slaves.[48]

A system of this nature offered the European colonists under the jurisdiction of the Spanish and Portuguese kings in America a considerable degree of autonomy. Not only was royal justice delegated to the magistrates of the *audiencias* and the town councils, most of who were born in America, but royal decrees and laws promulgated at court could also be negotiated and even indefinitely suspended in the colonies; the American authorities were quick to take shelter behind the old medieval judicial adage of '*obedézcase pero no se cumpla*', or 'let it be obeyed, but not enforced'.[49] For this reason, one of the important discussions amongst specialists in Hispanic American history in recent years has been the notion of 'negotiated absolutism', an oxymoron which captures the tension between the metropolis' desire to rule and the power of the local societies.[50] The contractual, collaborative aspect of most of the mechanisms used to rule and enforce in the *ancien régime* societies has now largely been recognized by historians, but what remains to be seen is whether the physical distance (and corresponding time delay) between the metropolises and the overseas territories accentuated the dependence of the court on local elites in the territories to which royal rule was intended to be applied. At this point in the discussions, and given the academic material available, it would appear that a strict mechanical correlation between the distance from the court and the degree of autonomy accorded is not the most convincing of hypotheses. Overall, the system was predicated on very high degrees of inherent flexibility and of autonomy for the colonial societies vis-à-vis the two metropolises, a degree of autonomy which varied over time; there is broad consensus amongst historians that the reforms introduced by the ministers of Charles III of Spain and by the Marquis of Pombal for the Portuguese king tightened the chains of command from Europe to the Americas.[51]

What is by no means the object of academic consensus is the analysis of the actual political efficacy of the imperial institutions, as shown by the lively nature of the historiographical debate in Brazil surrounding evaluations of the functionality of the *ancien régime*. The difference of opinions was provoked by the general framework for this analysis proposed by Fernando Novais: he termed it the 'old Portuguese colonial system',[52] which accords the metropolis (and its ally, Great Britain) almost exclusive responsibility in running a colonial economy based on the predatory extraction of American natural resources and the use of African slave labour. In so doing, this theory presupposes that a colonial state had been forged during the period prior to independence; yet the subsequent generation of Brazilian historians has shown that the critique of the functionality of *ancien régime* monarchies practised in Europe could not remain without relevance for the interpretation of the processes at work in the American territories. They supported their arguments using, amongst others, the work of the Portuguese historian António Manuel Hespanha, who demonstrated the extent to which, through until the late eighteenth century, the Portuguese crown was deprived of modern means of taking action, both in terms of its will to do so and its administrative capacity: his approach to evaluating the royal institutions can also applied to the imperial dimension of the Portuguese monarchy.[53]

This debate called for a re-examination of the development of the societies in the Portuguese Americas proceeding from the new premise that the metropolis was far less capable of giving impulses and implementing orders than had previously been supposed. This counter-model, which has become known as the '*ancien régime* below the tropics',[54] is built on the foundations of powerful research monographs (including examinations of Rio de Janeiro as a new colonial capital and the creole trading networks) and on critical discussion of most recent Portuguese and Spanish historiography. At present, the question at issue is whether societies marked so considerably by slavery can be analysed as *ancien régime* societies as European historians understand them,[55] and whatever the answer, it is worth emphasizing that the question of how to analyse a colonial society like the Brazilian in its imperial form is, in today's environment, liable to provoke vigorous debate, indicating that neither the gaping abyss of dependence theory nor the expertise in development studies has been able to grasp its problematics in their entirety.

What nevertheless remains is the question of what held these entities together for more than three centuries. As with many other imperial societies, the suppleness of the institutional structures goes quite some way to explaining the longevity of the entities under examination here. Under the *ancien régime*, the political reality was essentially founded on the investments made by stakeholders into the institutional structure: that is, the imperial system ran as long as individuals, families, networks and groups grasped the institutional framework offered and imposed themselves and their interests onto it. This is how the two Iberian empires in the western hemisphere attracted magistrates, clergymen, merchants and soldiers between the sixteenth and eighteenth centuries whose pursuit of their own goals gave life to the imperial enterprise.

As works on the *indipatae* – requests for missions in faraway locations formulated by the fathers of the Society of Jesus – show, the *cursus honorum* of religious missionaries was predicated on lifelong comings and goings between the metropolises and the colonies.[56] By the same token, the careers of Portuguese magistrates and military commanders remained intercontinental right through until the end of the colonial period.[57] The trading networks were also based on webs of commercial and familial links between the American territories and the European ports.[58] While the two empires, as already emphasized, did not have the same administrative profile, the fact that the Hispanic possessions in America had Inquisition tribunals which Brazil did not had no effect whatsoever on the efficacy of the Holy Office in hunting heretics with implacable zeal across the continent.[59] On the eve of independence, the two empires were characterized by two apparently contradictory traits. On the one hand, the role of metropolitan ecclesiastical, judicial, military and administrative personnel was as important as it had ever been, which could lead both to competition and to strategic alliances or intermarriage with leading American-born families; on the other, the local power of these American dynasties was becoming decidedly more and more autonomous. Without this latter development, the seizure of power by the 'creoles' as the series of independence declarations started would make little sense.

Yet the capacity of the American-born Europeans within the two empires to act independently and their political determination to do so was clearly evident well before the beginning of the nineteenth century, and this can be illustrated by two examples: the widespread misuse of the royal commercial monopoly by thousands of Río de la Plata merchants in the seventeenth and eighteenth centuries;[60] and the success of prominent Brazilians in fighting the Dutch occupation of Pernambuco and of Angola in the mid seventeenth century without support from the metropolitan armed forces.[61] Throughout the colonial period, the autonomy of the 'creole' societies was also made clear by the general disregard for the territorial delineations between the Spanish and Portuguese empires. In the period from the separation of Portugal from the Hispanic monarchy in 1640 through to the independences of the nineteenth century, the subjects of both kings were not supposed to dwell on the territory of the other; yet the Portuguese presence across Spanish territory from Buenos Aires via Lima and Quito through to Mexico remained significant,[62] as did the Spanish-speaking community of São Paulo at all times. Even while the territorial disputes between the two monarchies were a topic of major import throughout the eighteenth century, the colonists and their families maintained complex identities and selected their places of residence regardless of their national origin. As enlightened as the reforms of the Bourbons and of Pombal may have been, they were not really effective in engendering an interiorization of the territorial demarcations amongst the subjects of the two crowns.

With reference to the overarching theme of this work, this chapter has looked to describe an inventory of the fundamental political processes at work within the Iberian imperial institutions in their American form. To finish, what cannot be stressed enough is the partly artificial nature of the regional division inherent in the term Latin America. The institutional system of empire rests on close, consistent interaction with the entities, authorities, and societies of the metropolis to such a degree that no study of *ancien régime* Latin America can be convincing unless it is carried out with reference to both America and Europe at the very least. Moreover, in examining the formation of Ibero-American societies, the absence of Africa as a factor – the failure to engage to the same depth with the history of the societies of West and Central Africa – is sure to condemn any study to complete academic failure; and there is no shortage of historians who have shown just to what extent it is indispensable when studying the Iberian empires to connect the American phenomena with the grand colonial and commercial enterprises of the European powers in Asia during the modern era.[63]

Beyond this, the citizens of the Latin American countries today will find in this long, multi-regional history some of the elements necessary to understand the historical heritage which continued to weigh on their countries after they became independent nations. Perhaps this is the right place to advance a highly probable hypothesis: these societies are capable of uniting a framework of liberal state institutions with the systematic domination of parts of their populations in ways as colonial as that of the bygone empires. For all the reservations which may arise from the perspective of political liberalism, the repeated electoral successes of Evo Morales in Bolivia and Hugo Chávez in Venezuela are the result not just of continuing, but of worsening racial discrimination against the native, mixed-race, and African-origin populations, and these developments represent a collision of various political concepts. As the charismatic leader in Caracas places himself in the traditions both of socialism and of 'Bolívarism', there are those who, despite understanding that the appeal to Bolívar symbolizes the anti-colonial struggle against Spain, may be surprised that the memory of the republics born of the independence movement is being so celebrated given the status and needs of those at the lower end of the social scale. Just as the racist Jim Crow Laws in the United States were a consequence of the emancipation of African-origin slaves, so did the constitutional recognition of a unique political body in each post-Bolívarian republic in the early nineteenth century give rise to a racial ideology entirely more radical than that of the *ancien régime*, which resulted in a de facto apartheid in some Hispano-American countries. While Las Casas has certainly documented the horrors committed by the first generations of conquistadors in the sixteenth century, the genocide of indigenous peoples in the Pampas by the armies of the Argentine Republic in the nineteenth and that committed by the elites of European origin in Guatemala in the twentieth century – to name but two examples – would seem to suggest that the Age of Empires was not the most brutal time with regard to native populations. Meanwhile, the Brazil of Presidents Lula da Silva and Rousseff has realized that the country's republican claim to embody a kind of Luso-tropical vision of racially harmonious democracy was, in actual fact, standing in stark contrast to the breathtaking economic and thus social inequalities which had persisted after the belated abolition of slavery in 1888; the result has been a sharp increase in social initiatives based on quotas and the principles of affirmative action.

For this reason, viewed from the stance of the populations dominated, the end of the imperial political structure did not bring with it the end of colonial society. While the two phenomena were intrinsically linked under the *ancien régime*, accurate analysis of the societies in the twentieth century uncouples them in the contemporary era when taken beyond platitudes about the universal extension of political rights under republic regimes. In this context, colonial society is territory with populations marked by inequalities of status between social categories and a distribution structure for economic, political and symbolic resources which invariably recalls the history and memory of conquest for some and subjugation for others. As seen at the beginning of the twenty-first century, these aspects have not disappeared with the institutions of the Iberian empires, and there is certainly something to the argument that the colonial dimension of social domination has actually increased in the post-imperial period. That, however, is another story.

Notes

1 Since a full bibliography covering a question of these dimensions would be simply unmanageable, I have chosen the works cited here in accordance with what I thought most pertinent and with the considered aim of offering a multi-lingual set of references.

2 F. Bethencourt and R. Curto Diogo (eds), *Portuguese Oceanic Expansion, 1400–1800* (Cambridge, 2007).

3 L. Adão da Fonseca, *O Tratado de Tordesilhas e a diplomacia luso-castelhana no século XV* (Lisbon, 1992).

4 J. H. Elliott, 'A Europe of Composite Monarchies', *Past & Present*, 132 (1992), pp. 48–71; J.-L. Villacañas, *¿ Qué Imperio ? Un ensayo polémico sobre Carlos V y la España Imperial* (Córdoba, 2008); F. Crémoux and J.-L. Fournel, *Idées d'Empire en Italie et en Espagne: XIV–XVIIe siècle* (Rouen, 2010).

5 D. Armitage, *The Ideological Origins of the British Empire* (Cambridge, 2000), p. 34.

6 J. Arrieta and J. H. Elliott (eds), *Forms of Union: the British and Spanish Monarchies in the 17th and 18th Centuries* (San Sebastian, 2009).

7 C. Magoni, *Fueros e libertà. Il mito della costituzione aragonese nell'Europa moderna* (Rome, 2007); X. Gil Pujol, 'Spain and Portugal', in H. A. Lloyd, G. Burgess and G. Hodson (eds) *European Political Thought, 1450–1700: Religion, Law and Philosophy* (New Haven, CT, 2006).

8 F. Bouza Álvares, *Portugal no Tempo dos Filipes. Política, Cultura, Representações (1580–1668)* (Lisbon, 2000).

9 J. Muldoon, *Empire and Order: The Concept of Empire, 800–1800* (New York, NY, 1999).

10 A. I. Buescu, 'Vínculos da memória: Ourique e a fundação do reino', in Y. K. Centeno (ed.), *Portugal: Mitos Revisitados. Da Fundação à Modernidade* (Lisbon, 1993), pp. 11–50 ; *ibid.*, *O Milagre de Ourique e a História de Portugal de Alexandre Herculano. Uma polémica oitocentista* (Lisbon, 1987).

11 E. Kantorowicz, 'Kingship under the Impact of Scientific Jurisprudence', in M. Clagett, G. Post and R. Reynolds (eds), *Twelfth-Century Europe and the Foundations of Modern Society* (Madison, WI, 1961), pp. 89–111; J. Krynen, *L'Empire du roi. Idées et croyances politiques en France, XIIIe–XVe siècle* (Paris, 1993).

12 M. Perez Gonzalez, *Crónica del Emperador Alfonso VII* (León, 1997).

13 M. Aurell, 'Messianisme royal de la Couronne d'Aragon (14e–15e siècles)', *Annales HSS*, 52, 1, (1997), pp. 119–55.

14 L. F. S. Lima, 'O percurso das Trovas de Bandarra: circulação letrada de um profeta iletrado', in L. Algranti Mezan and A.-P. Torres Megiani (eds), *O Império por Escrito. Formas de transmissão da cultura letrada no mundo ibérico (séc. XVI–XIX)* (São Paulo, 2009), pp. 441–52; L. F. Lima, *Império dos sonhos: narrativas proféticas, sebastianismo e messianismo brigantine* (São Paulo, 2010).

15 João Fragoso and Maria de Fátima Gouvêa, 'Monarquia pluricontinental e repúblicas: algumas reflexões sobre a América lusa nos séculos XVI–XVIII', *Tempo*, 27 (2009), pp. 49–63; N. Gonçalo Monteiro, 'A tragédia dos Távora: parentesco, redes de poder e facções políticas na monarquia portuguesa em meados do século XVIII', in J. Fragoso and M.-F. Gouvea (eds), *Na trama das redes: política e negócios no império português, séculos XVI–XVIII* (Rio de Janeiro, 2010), pp. 317–42.

16 G. Marcocci, *L'invenzione di un impero. Politica e cultura nel mondo portoghese (1450–1600)* (Rome, 2011).

17 M. J. Rodriguez Salgado, *The Changing Face of Empire: Charles V, Philip II and Habsburg Authority (1551–1559)* (Cambridge, 1988).

18 F. Bouza Álvarez, *Imagen y propaganda. Capítulos de historia cultural del reinado de Felipe II* (Madrid, 1998).

19 F. Bosbach, *Monarchia universalis: ein politischer Leitbegriff der frühen Neuzeit* (Göttingen, 1988).

20 D. Nirenberg, *Communities of Violence: Persecution of Minorities in the Middle Ages* (Princeton, NJ, 1996).

21 R. Soto, 'Conquesta, repartiment i colonització de Mallorca durant el segle XIII. Un estat de la question', *Anuario de estudios medievales*, 26 (1996), pp. 605–46; J. Torro, *El naixement d'una colònia: dominació i resistència a la fontera valenciana (1238–1276)* (València, 1999); J. Torro, 'Jérusalem ou Valence: la première colonie d'Occident', *Annales. Histoires Sciences Sociales*, 5 (2000), pp. 983–1008.

22 Frederick Cooper and Jane Burbank, *Empires in World History* (Princeton, NJ, 2009).

23 D. Abulafia, *The Discovery of Mankind: Atlantic Encounters in the Age of Columbus* (New Haven, CT, 2009).

24 F. Fernandez Armesto, *The Canary Islands After the Conquest: The Making of a Colonial Society in the Early Sixteenth Century* (Oxford, 1982).

25 A. Almeida Mendes, 'Les Réseaux de la traite ibérique dans l'Atlantique nord. Aux origines de la traite atlantique (1440–1640)', *Annales HSS*, 4 (2008), pp. 739–68; *ibid*, 'The Foundations of the System: A Reassessment of the Slave Trade to the Spanish Americas in the Sixteenth and Seventeenth Centuries', in D. Eltis and D. Richardson (eds), *Extending the Frontiers: Essays on the New Transatlantic Slave Trade Database* (New Haven, CT, 2008), pp. 63–94.

26 R. Vainfas, *A heresia dos índios. Catolicismo e rebeldia no Brasil colonial* (São Paulo, 1995).

27 B. Vincent, *1492: l'année admirable* (Paris, 1996).

28 J. Hernández Franco, *Sangre Limpia, sangre española: el debate sobre los estatutos de limpieza, siglos XV–XVII* (Madrid, 2011).

29 J. Aubin, *Le latin et l'astrolabe. Recherches sur le Portugal de la Renaissance, son expansion en Asie et les relations internationales* (Lisbon and Paris, 1996, 2006); S. Subrahmanyam, *Explorations in Connected History: From the Tagus to the Ganges* (Delhi, 2004); ibid., *Explorations in Connected History: Mughals and Franks* (Delhi, 2004).

30 P. Puntoni, *A Guerra dos Bárbaros. Povos indígenas e a colonização do sertão. Nordeste do Brasil, 1650–1720* (São Paulo, 2000); C. Damasceno Fonseca, *Des terres aux villes de l'or. Pouvoirs et territoires urbains au Minas Gerais (Brésil, XVIIIe siècle)* (Paris, 2003).

31 C. Giudicelli, 'Les Sociétés indiennes et les "frontières" américaines de l'empire espagnol (XVIe–XVIIe siècle). Une ébauche historiographique', in F.-J. Ruggiu and C. Vidal (eds), *Société, colonisation et esclavage dans le monde atlantique. Historiographies des sociétés coloniales américaines, 1492–1898* (Rennes, 2010), pp. 143–90; C. Giudicelli (ed.), *Fronteras movedizas. Clasificaciones coloniales y dinámicas socioculturales en las fronteras de las Américas* (Mexico, 2011).

32 F. P. Bowser, *The African Slave in Colonial Peru, 1524–1650* (Stanford, CA, 1974); L. F. de Alencastro, *O Trato dos Viventes. A Formação do Brasil no Atlântico Sul, séculos XVI e XVII* (São Paulo, 2000); H. S. Klein and F. Vidal Luna, *Slavery in Brazil* (Cambridge, 2010).

33 E. María Martínez, 'The Black Blood of New Spain: Limpieza de sangre, Racial Violence, and Gendered Power in Early Colonial Mexico', *The William & Mary Quarterly*, 3rd series, 61, 3 (2004), pp. 479–520; E. María Martínez, 'Interrogating Blood Lines: "Purity of Blood", the Inquisition, and Casta Categories', in S. Schroeder and S. Poole (eds), *Religion in New Spain* (Albuquerque, NM, 2007), pp. 196–217.

34 I. Katzew, *Casta Painting* (New Haven, CT, 2004); S. Hunold Lara, *Fragmentos setecentistas. Escravidão, cultura e poder na América portuguesa* (São Paulo, 2007).

35 W. D. Jordan, *White Over Black: American Attitudes Toward the Negro, 1550–1812* (Baltimore, MD, 1973); A. Helg, 'Simón Bolívar and the Fear of Pardocracia: José Padilla in Post-Independence Cartagena', *Journal of Latin American Studies*, 35, 3 (2003), pp. 447–71.

36 R. J. Scott, *Emancipation in Cuba: The Transition to Free Labor, 1860–1899* (Pittsburgh, PA, 2000).

37 E. Schäfer, *Der Königl. spanische oberste Indienrat*, Ibero-amerikanisches Institut (Hamburg, 1936) [Spanish trans.: *El Consejo Real y Supremo de las Indias* (Salamanca, 2003)].

38 A. Garcia-Gallo, *Los orígenes españoles de las instituciones americanas. Estudio de derecho indiano* (Madrid, 1987); I. Sánchez Bella, Alberto de la Hera and Carlos Diaz Rementeria, *Historia del derecho indiano* (Madrid, 1992); E. Garcia Hernan, *Consejero de ambos mundos. Vida y obra de Juan de Solórzano Pereira (1575–1655)* (Madrid, 2007).

39 J.-F. Schaub, *Le Portugal au temps du comte-duc d'Olivares (1621–1640). Le conflit de juridiction comme exercice de la politique* (Madrid, 2001).

40 E. de Souza Barros, *Negócios de Tanta Importância. O Conselho Ultramarino e a disputa pela condução da guerra no Atlântico e no Índico (1643–1661)* (Lisbon, 2009).

41 S. B. Schwartz, *Sovereignty and Society in Colonial Brazil: the High Court of Bahia and its Judges, 1609–1751* (Berkeley, CA, 1973).

42 R. Bentes Monteiro, *O Rei no Espelho. A Monarquia Portuguesa e a colonização da América, 1640–1720* (São Paulo, 2002).

43 A. Manuel Hespanha and C. Madeira Santos, 'Le forme di potere di un impero oceanico', *in* R. Zorzi (ed.), *L'epopea delle scoperte* (Florence, 1994), pp. 449–78; P. Cardim Pedro, 'La jurisdicción real y su afirmación en la corona portuguesa y sus territorios ultramarinos (siglos XVI–XVIII): reflexiones sobre la historiografía', in F. Aranda Pérez and J. Damião Rodrigues (eds), *De Re Publica Hispaniae. Una vindicación de la cultura política en los reinos ibéricos en la primera modernidad* (Madrid, 2008), pp. 349–88.

44 A. Manuel Hespanha (ed.), *O Antigo Regime (1621–1834)* (Lisbon, 2002); P. Fernandez Albaledejo, *Fragmentos de Monarquía. Trabajos de Historia Política* (Madrid, 1992).

45 J. Baschet, *La Civilisation féodale. De l'an Mil à la colonisation de l'Amérique* (Paris, 2006); J. H. Elliott, *Empires of the Atlantic World: Britain and Spain in America* (New Haven, CT, 2006).

46 I. dos Guimarães Sá, *Quando o rico se faz pobre: Misericordias, caridade e poder no imperio portugués, 1500–1800* (Lisbon, 1997).

47 J. Poloni-Simard, *La Mosaïque indienne. Mobilité, stratification sociale et métissage dans le* corregimiento *de Cuenca (Équateur) du XVIe au XVIIIe siècle* (Paris, 2000).

48 J.-P. Tardieu, *L'Eglise et les noirs au Pérou, XVIe et XVIIe siècles* (Paris, 1993); M. de Melo Souza, *Reis negros no Brasil escravista: história da festa de coroação de rei Congo* (Belo Horizonte, 2002); L Reginaldo, *Os rosários dos angolas: irmandades negras, experiências escravas e identidades africanas na Bahia setecentista* (Campinas, 2005).

49 B. González Alonso, 'La fórmula "Obedézcase pero no se cumpla" en el Derecho castellano de la Baja Edad Media', *Anuario de historia del derecho espagnol*, 50 (1980), pp. 469–88.

50 A. Irigoin and R. Grafe, 'Bargaining for Absolutism: A Spanish Path to Nation State and Empire Building', *Hispanic American Historical Review*, 88, 2 (2008), pp. 173–210.

51 K. Maxwell, *Pombal: Paradox of the Enlightenment* (Cambridge, 1995); A. Guimerá (ed.), *El Reformismo borbónico* (Madrid, 1996).

52 F. Novais, *Portugal e Brasil na crise do antigo sistema colonial (1777–1808)* (São Paulo, 1979).

53 A. Manuel Hespanha, 'Arquitectura politico-administrativa de um império oceanico', *Revista Tempo Brasileiro*, 125 (1996), pp. 57–78.

54 J. Fragoso, M. F. Bicalho and M.-F. Gouvêa (eds), *O Antigo Regime nos Trópicos. A Dinâmica Imperial Portuguesa (séculos XVI–XVIII)* (Rio de Janeiro, 2001); M. F. Bicalho and L. Ferlini Vera, *Modos de governar. Ideias e práticas políticas no império português, séculos XVI a XIX* (São Paulo, 2005).

55 L. de Mello e Souza, *O sol e a sombra: política e administração na América portuguesa do séc. XVIII* (São Paulo, 2006); L. de Mello e Souza, J. Ferreira Furtado and M. F. Bicalho (eds), *O governo dos Povos* (São Paulo, 2009).

56 P. A. Fabre and B. Vincent, *Missions religieuses modernes. 'Notre lieu est le monde'* (Rome, 2007).

57 G. Monteiro Nuno, P. Cardim and M. Soares da Cunha (eds), *Óptima Pars. Elites Ibero-Americanas do Antigo Regime* (Lisbon, 2005); G. Frazão and M. Nogueira, 'Redes de poder e conhecimento na governação do império português, séc. XVI e XVII', *Topoï*, 8 (2004), pp. 96–137.

58 J. Ferreira Furtado, *Homens de Negócio: a interiorização da metrópole e do comércio nas Minas setecentistas* (São Paulo, 2006).

59 S. Alberro, *Inquisición y sociedad en México 1571–1700* (Mexico City, 1988); R. Millar, *Inquisición y sociedad en el Virreinato Peruano* (Santiago de Chile, 1998); B. Feitler, *Inquisition, juifs et nouveaux-chrétiens au Brésil* (Leuven, 2003); N. Wachtel, *La Foi du souvenir. Labyrinthes marranes* (Paris, 2001); ibid., *La Logique des bûchers* (Paris, 2009).

60 Z. Moutoukias, *Contrabando y control colonial en el siglo XVII: Buenos Aires, el Atlántico y el espacio peruano* (Buenos Aires, 1988).

61 C. R. Boxer, *Salvador de Sá and the Struggle for Brazil and Angola, 1602–1686* (1952); Cabral de Mello Evaldo, *Olinda Restaurada. Guerra e açucar no Nordeste, 1630–1654* (Rio de Janeiro, 1998).

62 F. Serrano Mangas, *La encrucijada portuguesa: esplendor y quiebra de la unión ibérica en las Indias de Castilla, 1600–1668* (Badajoz, 1994).

63 S. Gruzinski, 'Les Mondes mêlés de la Monarchie catholique et autres "connected histories"', *Annales HSS*, 56, 2001, pp. 85–117; J. P. Zuniga, 'L'Histoire impériale à l'heure de l' "histoire globale". Une perspective atlantique', *Revue d'histoire moderne et contemporaine*, 5 (2007) (54–4bis), pp. 54–68.

Epilogue:
The History, Identity, Crisis and Endemic Submission of the American Continent

Juan José Rossi

From which perspective should we try to hear the echoes of imperialism in today's world? Which groups of humanity are usually considered the subjects of such an analysis – and who considers them as such? Why should the victims and consequences of imperialism be identified, and what is the agenda in so doing? Might the goal be to blur the picture and then consign it to the archives on a 'global' (and perhaps ingeniously utopian) level? Or might the implicit and unconscious aim be to decipher the failed mechanisms of colonialism in order to maintain some kind of hegemony enabling continued territorial, economic, cultural and religious expansion, and upholding the dominion, the aberrant primacy of some over others and the extraction of resources to the detriment of the populations both directly and indirectly affected?

The classic European form of imperialism has been in existence for over 2,000 years, changing and adapting through the centuries, starting in Africa with the beginning of history, continuing in America from 1492 onwards, and present at several points in other parts of the planet; and if the aim really were to investigate this form of imperialism, then the starting point would have to be an analysis of why 'the West' (which is, of course, the East in America and the South in Africa) has this almost congenital predisposition to invade land and gain influence over people over which it is not incumbent, which are not even within its territorial boundaries, and which – for a whole range of reasons – may appear more fragile from a technological or military viewpoint, but which clearly have both the same rights and obligations as 'the West' and legitimate cultural differences worthy of respect. Is it still necessary to stress that there are no superior or inferior cultures, no 'first' and 'third' worlds – just differences?

Why, despite perceiving itself as 'intelligent', could Europe not simply be satisfied with itself during its development? Why this compulsive colonialism, from the empires of its antiquity through to its actions today, driven by a subtle, deceitful political and economic methodology?

The strategic alibis and philosophical reasoning used to justify this kind of endemic illness – considered 'natural' as they are by Europeans – are objectively false and pretentious. Of course, the answer to why Europe (and now the United States, too) is the way it is in its relationship with the rest of the planet is so obvious as to slip by unnoticed: put bluntly, the small subcontinent that is Europe would quite simply disappear as an entity if it did not permanently try to expand. That is, at least, the way things appear seen from the supposed cultural and sociopolitical superiority of Europe itself, which fears that this unconsciously or subconsciously imagined 'superiority' will dissolve for want of the resources which sustain it, leaving Europe at the mercy of its 'enemies'. These foes are classified as the young, virile, ambitious nations with unlimited resources – currently those of Asia and America – who in actual fact have no intention of invading anybody at all.

It is my considered opinion that, in the specific case of America, a victim of Europe's historical disposition to dominate, the real key will not be analysing the 'echoes of (the form of European) imperialism' which subjugated – and continues subjugating in a more underhand manner – the entire continent, even though it doubtless remains necessary to keep examining these aberrational situations and echoes as the present, collective work is trying to do. No, the real key will be looking at why, during their in many respects admirable historical and cultural development, Europe and the United States have shown – and continue showing – such a calling for and such skill at submitting other peoples to their will.

The echoes, or consequences, of imperialism on the American continent are obvious: they are everywhere for those who open their eyes to them in a range of forms which do not require statistics to prove their existence; these echoes become most audible when their fragility is recalled by the crises, interests, and humour of what calls itself 'the first world', on which these echoes depend for their existence.

The Echoes of Imperialism in that Misnomer, 'America'

The specific proposition of the chapter at hand may appear somewhat theoretical and distant in relation to a retrospective examination of the last five centuries of despicable dependency which America has experienced and the current situation this has led to. Yet looking at 'why' entails a radical criticism both of the sociopolitical and cultural system which has subjugated the continent for 500 years and of the classic historiography, still in force today, which underpins and tries to justify this endemic urge to subjugate. It also aims to reinterpret our historical-cultural heritage over the centuries in such a way as the analysis and critical redefinition implied by asking 'why' have an impact both in the political and educational systems and in the everyday life of the individuals in the societies affected, who have been subtly but comprehensively deceived as to the structure and content of the historical and cultural processes which have led to their present situation.

I ought to clarify that I will not develop my hypothesis in direct, explicit relation to the political and economic subjugation of the continent, subtly sustained by an unscrupulous invader and appearing over the last few decades to be almost the most important issue facing both the continent and the world as a whole. The continent's political problems concerning 'democracy' and personal freedom and the economic issues of uneven income distributions and corruption would appear to be the direct result of its historical subjugation, and yet whenever there is any hint of an attempt to shed light on this, it is immediately silenced by a thousand excuses and the complex strategies of that fictional construct, 'the first world', which has been feeling both superior to and proprietary of America since 1492.

Before we go any further, I shall try to explain the existential and epistemological stance from which my points of view originate, and the concrete circumstances which have allowed me to grasp the profound historical-cultural distortions and delays which have been at work without interruption to put us in the critical situation in which we find ourselves today: that is, dissatisfied with the system in all its manifestations (political, economic, educational, etc.), insecure both in material and symbolic terms, and lacking perspectives either in the short- or medium term – and angry. I would even go so far as to say that we are at war against ourselves, that different sections of society are fighting against each other in the misguided belief that we have no common identity. All of this has led us to what seems to be complete dissolution and dependency which get more severe with every passing day. Why is all of this happening despite the fact that the continent itself has a history going back 40,000 years, despite the fact that it is self-sufficient and full of resources both human and natural? What is the root of this situation and how can we begin to surmount it?

Around 1977, after having passed through the education system, in the course of my work and my research, I came into contact with the people of the enormous Gran Chaco plain, the 'impenetrable' part of Argentina. Until then, not actually having been to the region, I had imagined it to be populated with *criollos*,[1] cotton-picking peasants, and livestock farmers on state-owned land; I expected them to be spread thinly, living in typical adobe huts, clothed in baggy trousers, neckerchiefs and canvas sandals with a broad sombrero perched on their heads; the men would spend their days on horseback, the women would slave away at the hearth, and so forth. What I certainly didn't expect, despite all the facts I had in my head following my education (which is all most Americans have after school), was that I would find on this huge wooded plain a parallel society, clearly distinct from both that of the city dwellers and of the *criollos*. Along the courses of the mighty Pilcomayo and Bermejo rivers, near to the inland lakes of the border region between Bolivia, Paraguay and Argentina, I came across village after village, each with its own character. There were groups of houses in circles around a large patio space, a constant setting for work and meetings, for children's games, or for village celebrations. It was a dynamic place, developing ways of dressing, speaking and gesticulating which were completely new to me. There were people who identified themselves with strange names going back one, two, even three thousand years: Chané, Chiriguano, Wichí, Chorote, Chulupí, Kom'lek, Mok'oit, to name but a few.[2] I came to know a broad, dense panorama, and as I did, it started to pose questions: I asked myself what meaning this reality held for us, for the politics and education; it was a reality that was solid once you knew it from the inside, and if it belonged to the country, to the continent, then what was the role of supposedly sacrosanct classical historiography?

I encountered a social spectrum which I could not decipher at that point and which motivated me even before I understood why; from then on, I was able slowly to start to understand the significance and the historical-cultural dimensions of this reality and, with time, I lowered the highly structured defences that come from the kind of hermetic education I received and began to see beyond the sociologically generated categories of 'primitive' or 'disadvantaged'. Despite the deceptive appearances of poverty, I was able to discern the identity of these communities based on thousands of years of historical process: I grasped their philosophy and their lifestyle, their understanding of the cosmos and their historical background, their art and their self-sufficiency in a symbiotic and respectful relationship with nature (*Pacha* in Quechua languages, *Mapu* in Mapudungún, the language of the Mapuche). I am talking about those whom the education system, classical international historiography, government entities both official and unofficial, dictionaries, books, and documents call 'Indians' as if this were not a disqualifying noun which excludes or, at best, differentiates the people described from categories such as 'men and women' or 'inhabitants' much in the way the 'English' are not considered Europeans and the 'Chinese' not Asians.

During this first encounter (around 1976–7) with these societies, several weighty realities left their impact on me and have continued to do so: the tenacity and coherence of these societies over centuries in hostile surroundings; the languages of these peoples, one of the greatest and most admirable expressions of their culture; their solid life philosophy, completely unknown to the rest of us; their art, found on their garments and objects of everyday use; their simple, functional architecture; their internal social structure and the roles used to moderate it; and, as I have mentioned, I was marked by their works, by their dwellings and their patios, each carrying the seal of their own art and technologies, built entirely naturally and freely expressing their designs. All of this was quite simply inexplicable without a very ancient historical heritage and the support of mature traditions.

The more I advanced into the west in the dry, woodland province of Formosa in northern Argentina, bordered by the Salta province, by Bolivia and by Paraguay, the more I was astonished. As I discovered more and more parts both of my home country and of America, I started to get curious. I asked myself: who are these thousands of people in Argentina, these millions across the continent, who identify themselves as the protagonists in and inheritors of a history and culture stretching back millennia? Who are the Wichís, the Guaranís, the Mapuches, Sirionó, Quechuas, Mayas, Nahuatls, Navajos, Sioux, Inuits and the rest of them? Where did they come from? How can they have this widespread spatial presence and solid internal organization, parallel to that of the *criollos* and republics of the continent, and yet be ignored by both the system and the collective consciousness? Why did we learn and acquire knowledge of English, French or Italian, and yet know nothing of Quechua, Guaraní or Wichí – languages which have been spoken in these lands for thousands of years? Why is this other system of villages, clearly defined societal roles, languages, and spectacular art surrounded by dust and largely unknown? How could all of this exist without me having heard anything more than the occasional derogatory, paternal, or oblique reference to it at school? These questions culminated in one: why does the educational system, as well as philosophy, history and politics – including the American constitutions – dilute or ignore this enormous dimension to the extent that the Argentinian constitution of 1994 explicitly affirms that 'Senate recognises the pre-existence' of the indigenous cultures: does the current European political system recognize the pre-existence of the Celts, the Greeks and the Romans? How, I asked myself then and still ask myself now, can it be that these people have, in an act of unacceptable historical irresponsibility, been for the last five centuries systematically termed the 'enemies of civilization', completely resistant to supposedly universal philosophical, ethical, and moral truths? What is *their* history? Or is it simply that, because they aren't human beings, they lack history and culture, much like animals do? Is this the justification for ignoring thousands of years of human development which is just as legitimate as what was happening on other continents?

Seeing these communities and being in constant contact with the people who populated them, with their philosophical approach and their works, I asked myself the same question many of you might have asked yourselves in the same situation: how can people termed 'savages' by European chronologers and intellectuals and westernized Americans through the centuries produce and sustain a range of lifestyles, create and curate languages, and political, scientific and economic systems of greater or lesser complexity, and keep resisting the world around them? How can these 'savages' create artistic wonders, functional marvels, and persist in using their languages, calendars and monuments without any historical-cultural support? Is not their creativity, symbolism and capacity for abstract thought necessarily the fruit of a long historical process?

On the basis of my knowledge of this complete, but largely hidden world – and not losing sight of the permanent absurdity of the continental crisis I see as endemic since the European invasions beginning in 1492 – I shall try to formulate some opinions and propositions shaped by three objectives which by no means exclude each other: firstly, to search for alternative paths which will allow us to grow, becoming conscious of the continental dependency; secondly, to find ourselves as peoples or nations; thirdly, to grasp and protect our own sovereignty and authentic identity. This identity is something that, it would seem, both the world at large and American society has barely looked at in any kind of detail, meaning that the reality does not emerge and does not enter into the American consciousness, for it has been systematically distorted and hidden from view.

In the last analysis, the most important thing will not be so much to weigh up ideological and historiographical positions, but rather to beat and trample pathways which are neither circumstantial nor opportunistic and which transcend ethnic, social, political, and ideological boundaries and short-term considerations to offer people a permanent route to reality. When they confront this reality with the necessary support, they will see how it is the root cause of what today is termed an 'acute crisis'; a crisis which, following my analysis, is not actually acute, but endemic at the very base both of the social-political and economic structures strategically imposed by the invader and of the mentality of the continental population – that is, in our particular way of thinking, interpreting, and making judgements about the development of human societies on the continent.

Nevertheless, recognizing a crisis as endemic both in its historical form and present gravity, and deciding to try and overcome it in some way in order to grow as a free and sovereign people with a distinct history, does not mean simply waiting for some strange 'magic formula' from foreign or local visionaries.

Indeed, an objective look at the 500 years of our continental history (i.e. since the massive intervention of the system called 'Western') allows us to draw the conclusion that there will be no formula, neither from the 'Western' countries of the northern hemisphere, for whom there is no benefit to offering such a solution, nor from those who – despite actually being Americans – think, feel and act like Europeans and share their historically invasive mentality. There will be no such formulae for America, however much the majority of the continent's inhabitants and their governments continue to abase themselves – either out of naivety or misconception – to beg, to plead poverty, disability or orphanage and to demand their rights from a filicidal 'mother Europe' or from an evil 'father First World'.

Issues to be Borne in Mind

In order to avoid semantic and philosophical confusion, I shall outline a few of the prerequisites on which the analysis is based and some pertinent criticisms, both of the real situation of this continent and of the work at hand. The first such prerequisite is strictly historical. Despite the reluctance of a considerable section of America to recognize it, the continent improperly referred to 'America' or 'the New World' (new only from the viewpoint of the invader) has a history that stretches back 40,000 years[3] at the least; there are some remains which would seem to indicate a figure closer to 80,000 or more. This is a unique, long, and fascinating part of human history, starting with the first entrance of humankind from the Eurasian land mass (the exact location and date of which is irrelevant) in the remote regions of the past before recorded history begins. It is the beginning of a story which, for all the attempts that a strategically powerful system has made to destroy or hide it, remains an underlying, living element of the continent today.

Nevertheless, this historical process, initiated millennia previously in the mists of time and continuing to this very day, was shaken by a traumatic incident just over 500 years ago – an incident which, by contrast, has both a date and a name: 1492, Europe. It was not quite the 'discovery' of the continent as it is termed in essays and texts, taught in schools, and celebrated as a national holiday (as if it were cause for rejoicing). No, it was the arrival by chance of foreign explorers on the continent (not the aim of their mission), followed by the compulsive imposition of sociopolitical-economic and cultural systems from the outside on a population of over 70 million at the time. The 'collision' of three European boats with the islands of the Caribbean – unknown to the Europeans, but of course not to the native inhabitants – marked the beginning of an unimaginably disastrous process of philosophical, political, economic, and religious de-structuring. As the sailors clambered down onto the Caribbean beaches, they had no idea of the thousands of years of human history that was beating strong up and down the continent from Alaska to Cape Horn – a beating that is still generally overheard today. Moreover, they also did not know about the processes by which the continent's inhabitants had developed; and as soon as this became known, it was hidden. Indeed, how could this bunch of lost intruders have any inkling of the sheer variety of nations they had stumbled upon? Of the 200 linguistic families and more than 1,000 languages with their dialects, of the ways people on the continent lived their lives, practised science, agriculture, or art – of the gold metalwork, of the ceramics, the pictures and monumental sculpture, their astronomic observatories, magnificent centres of government and worship intimately interwoven, of pyramids and cities of up to 200,000 inhabitants? Of the full range of lifestyles, from the Guaraní culture to the Aztec, from the Quechua to the Selk'nam?

Strangely enough, those European navigators only grasped what this chance encounter with another world meant for them: they stumbled across heaps of raw materials, species, and manufactured wealth, stepped into fertile lands and found free labour and 'souls' (i.e. people) to be converted to followers of a dogmatic and profoundly distorted religious credo which would have lethal consequences for the continent's cultural and economic ecosystem.

The second prerequisite is a point of historiographical methodology. Objectively, when viewed without the lenses of ideology, factors of political or religious power or of supposed biological ascendency on any given continent are all part of history: that is, all human events or processes, no matter whom they effect and where they take place. It follows that the thoughts, feelings, and actions of the Charrúas (a native people of Argentina) as they defended themselves against the invaders is as much a part of history as what these invaders – Spanish, Portuguese, English, mercenaries, *criollos* – did and felt as they acted to dislodge the Charrúas and take over their lands. The same ought to be true of what occurred in Europe, for instance in reference to the 'barbarian' invasion, or on any other continent. Both realities, both that of the invader and of the vanquished, are part of the process: those suffering invasion should be accorded more rights, even though they succumbed, as those invading are rewarded with more power (which is why they succeeded in the first place); yet both are part of the history of a given place. Now, it is entirely possible that, whatever the vagaries of the actual deeds centuries later – in general unreliably recounted by the victor – many of those born later in the place in question will, for ideological, religious, or emotional reasons identify more with the vanquished, or indeed with the invaders. Whatever the case, all of it is regional or continental history due to the fact that the process both before and after the fifteenth century, in some respects irreversible, was the result of human action – presupposing of course, in relation to the events in America in the fifteenth century, that both the invaders and the vanquished were and are still human beings, a point to which I shall return later.

The third prerequisite is a simple statement: for those of us who were born on this continent, and disregarding the element of time for now (i.e. irrespective of how many years ago: 20, 50, 500, 1,000 or even 10,000), as well as dispensing for a moment with what we have 'learned' within the system imposed only five centuries ago, our authentic history is the story in which the protagonists are those who entered the continent around 40,000 years before the present day. Clearly, we cannot forget the circumstances of the coercive invasion from another continent by another culture, in this case Western culture which, incidentally, was never monolithic except in its religious aspect. I should point out that, in using the term 'invading system', I am not only referring to the political and economic sphere, but to the whole of philosophical, artistic, religious life – indeed to the 'cultural' sphere understood as the summation of human strategies for living.

The fourth, and last, prerequisite is of a philosophical and political order. The substantial element in determining America's fate from the fifteenth century through to the present has been the fact that the invader has always acted from an obsessively Eurocentric position: in elaborating strategies and achieving goals, using an artificial logic to underpin these goals, the European invaders have not deviated from the opinion that on the continent misnamed 'America' by none other than themselves, there are no real humans, and by extension no authentic culture. There can then be no legitimate philosophy, no valid system of beliefs, no ethics, languages, territorial boundaries, nations or social structures worth conserving. The invaders concluded that the continent had no real protagonists, no real subjects of a part of human history worthy of respect: they used facts that suited them and absurd theories to deny the presence of humanity with the rights that fit this definition.

The Roots of the Crisis and the Mechanisms which Perpetuate It

On our continent and, above all, in its Southern Cone and in Argentina – which is where I come from and the area I still know the best, despite having crossed the continent several times – we tend to be skilled at identifying the effects and symptoms of the crisis: we work with hundreds of hair-raising statistics regarding corruption, poverty, hunger, social exclusion, unemployment, illiteracy, and the obsequious dependence of our governments in deference to stronger forces (these used to be Europe and have now broadened to the fiscal 'first world'). Without wishing to underestimate the importance of sociological examinations of the crisis and these shortcomings, there ought to be deeper, more serious investigation of the roots and mechanisms which generate these ills and which hold the societies of the continent back in paradoxical contrast to the extreme wealth of their territories in resources both human and natural.

Regarding the specific nature of the crisis referred to, it is not strictly a crisis of political or economic structures, as our analysts tend to claim; after all, any structure or system can be effective and legitimate if its objectives and strategies serve to protect and foster the community that operates them, producing equality of opportunity and general well-being across the whole population.

The crisis is not cultural either, if by culture we understand the capacity to produce and encourage the usual expressions of it (art, literature, music, celebrations, sports, and so on); it is far more a crisis of attitudes, of mentalities, and of historical perspective which began with the system imposed by the invader in 1492, especially by Catholicism and its manipulations of conscience and of consciousness. All of this might be termed a crisis of identity.

It is an endemic crisis, innate to us and to our development after 1492, which has, to varying degrees but quite unswervingly, led Americans to be completely lacking in autonomy, despite the fact that some groups have always felt 'free' at certain times for the simple and small-minded reason that they are not in material distress or because they have adapted to the expectation of Europe and/or the 'first world'. The tangible result of this crisis is submission which is accepted at every level, leading to humiliation, poverty, and underestimation both individual and collective. This feeling is verbalized in oft-repeated set sentences such as 'we don't have an identity', 'we are young societies', 'we are destitute, corrupt, and we need help!'

There are all sorts of circumstances, both internal and external, which lead the continent's own analysts to limit themselves to describing periodical symptoms of the crisis; these can generally be attributed to international economic conditions and to poor government – and there is certainly at least some truth to these arguments. For that reason, for as long as America has been theoretically free as a collection of sovereign republics, it has always imagined that the crisis and its symptoms could be overcome if only the people in America would lastingly adopt the democratic, Christian, capitalist Western political system; a hypothesis which has gone up a little further in smoke with the installation of each political administration on the continent. This is without wishing to detract from the occasional, sporadic display of acumen, such as the political leadership of Cuba and, currently, Bolivia – Bolivia especially, to my mind.

Given this widespread belief in salvation, several questions come to the fore. Just who is saving the continent? From what, to what end, and for whom? Those who governed during the colonial period, then those who took over after the political emancipation, and now those who claim to be running the continent: none of them were or are the stuff of legend or exotic aliens. Quite to the contrary in fact as, since the move towards conformity brought about by the intertwining of different global societies, all of them have issued from the same educational system built on the rigid structure of Western philosophical parameters. This means that throughout history, whenever, say, Argentinians or Columbians have taken on the responsibility of government, they have always ended up seeing things from the viewpoint of the invader, no matter where they went to school or what they claimed during their electoral campaigns. Eventually, they have always capitulated in favour of foreign interests or those of local elites and forgotten the rights, expectations, and needs of society as it is. Of course there has been the odd (very temporary) worthy exception to this sad rule, but none was able to take apart the mechanisms of dependency, nor to change the philosophical perspective or correct the historical trajectory of the continent. The dependency culture has remained, with a feeling of frustration growing greater every time, while at the same time, the inhabitants of the continent have been skilfully led to consider themselves as part of the Western historical-cultural sphere and, by extension, to believe that they owe a debt of gratitude to the West; this is why there is still talk of 'mother countries' and 'father first world', even after all of the repeated attempts at political, economic, religious, and cultural emancipation.

All of which could lead to the conclusion that there is some very deep conditioning at work, leading to a population which is of the mentality that, whatever may be done, the continent will remain submerged in its dependency, indeed will sink further into decadence in matters such as self-determination, dignity, social equality, and sovereignty. Discovering the reality behind this mental conditioning and its incidence both in individuals and societies at large – both unconscious of it – is the *sine qua non* of identifying and starting to overcome the causes of this crisis whether in the short, medium, or long term.

I have outlined two implicit statements that I would now like to underscore so that they do not slip out of view. One is that our crisis is not a new development, resulting from the recent forms of imperialism (even if it is quite possible that said crisis has not always taken on the same appearance and the same intensity of effect as it has today); the other that it is important to identify what makes this crisis specific and locate its roots if we are to escape it. To bring these two points together, this is a crisis which has remained the same since Europe successfully transplanted its entire sociopolitical and philosophical systems with the intent of securing the continent, its people, and its resources; this process was made worse by the fact that, conscious of it or not, forced or willingly, the inhabitants have always played along with this endemic malady. Why this passivity, especially among those who purport to be politicians and pedagogues?

Although many pretend to be, no one is unaware of the chance circumstance which brought the European irruption to this continent (at least according to the most widespread version of events), or of the objectives it generated and which goals the invading society settled upon when it found itself in front of the gift named 'America'. All of the chronicles and documents of the invasion, starting with that of Columbus,[4] express with frightening clarity the rapacious voracity with which the conquerors appropriated, subjugated, and exploited the continent – a voracity that, in a period of three centuries, they managed patiently, methodically, to write into the mentality of the emerging 'new' Americans as a matter of course, a God-given normality. Even today, the Catholic Church, politicians, and the educational system explain matters in a manner almost verbatim.

It requires no exaggeration to show that Columbus' letter from his first voyage, the eldest known authentic document of the European irruption, shows complete disregard for the local peoples and, what is more, explicitly charts the course of invasion and the future relations between Europe and the continent it found by such serendipity.

'For I know', writes Columbus to the kings, 'that it will please your majesties greatly to know of the great victory that our Lord has given me on this journey, and I am writing this to you so that you shall know how I arrived in the Indies and found many very inhabited islands'. It should be borne in mind that the navigator had agreed with the monarchs that he would sail to India, not explore, make money from, and perhaps even take possession of territories outside of Christendom. 'I took possession of them in the name of your Majesties' (first comes misappropriation)

> sending two men into the interior who walked for three days and found infinite petty populations of helpless, fearful people. Nevertheless, as soon as they feel secure and lose their fear, they show a complete absence of artifice and are liberal with their possessions to an extent which remains unbelievable even to those who have witnessed it. Whatever one asks them for, one receives it if they have it, for they are so generous and so loving that they would give their own hearts[...] This is not due to ignorance, for they have a very subtle ingenuity: they are men who navigate across all of these sees and it is marvellous to see how they recount everything.

This praise from the admiral is put into relief by remembering how little the invaders still knew of the sciences, architecture, art, calendars, technologies, and languages of the people they had encountered. 'These islands are to be desired and never to be left', he continues, echoing a feeling which has remained latent in today's global westernized society and is considered to be quite natural. 'I have taken possession of everything in the name of your Majesties[...] In conclusion and referring to everything which has occurred during this voyage, your majesties will see that I shall give them all of the gold they could ever require' (Colombus' sole obsession) 'spices, cotton, gum, linseed, and idolatrous slaves' (read: slaves due to their idolatry) 'as much of everything as your Majesties shall see fit to request' (second, exploitation). 'Thus did our Saviour accord this victory to our most illustrious king and queen, and all of Christendom should rejoice in great celebrations and give solemn prayers of thanks to our Lord that so many peoples shall now be turned to our sacred faith' (third, conversion) 'and for all of the worldly goods that not just Spain, but all Christian peoples shall obtain from this place. This, in brief, is all...'

This is the summary of what the navigator Christopher Columbus wrote to the kings from the Canary Islands on 15 February 1493. It was a project in its embryonic stages which implied three key concepts and attitudes: misappropriation of territory, exploitation of their resources, and, at the strategic vanguard, the pacification or compulsory conversion of their populations to a foreign political and symbolic system.

Once immersed in this process of securing territories and resources while civilizing and pacifying the population, neither the struggle between European powers themselves nor the reassignment of political power from Europe back to the continent, not even the emancipations of the eighteenth and nineteenth centuries, were enough to modify this initial will to misappropriate and subjugate absolutely. This has been imposed, is still imposed, in a fashion more or less obvious and veiled according to the circumstances, all of it subtly justified through the system of education to the point that not even the generations of civil servants which help it to function are aware of this highly efficient form of subjection.

The continent's search, both for autonomy of a political, economic, or cultural nature – this latter based on the continent's original way of thinking (still extant but hidden) – and for a project that would permit its inhabitants to live in accordance with their ancient rights and their expectations (be they of indigenous, mixed, or immigrant extraction) was always conditioned by the presence, pressures, and parameters of foreign politics, religions, and philosophies – especially philosophies.

Despite the supposedly heroic colonial scenery on which the dramas since 1492 have been played out by a succession of imperial actors (Columbus, the kings, the Consejo de Indias, the Casa de Contratación, the chroniclers, the religious hierarchy, the Inquisition, the missionaries, the auditors, governors and viceroys) and the republican politicians who followed them, two recurrent realities are inescapable. As painful as the realization may be, both the predatory, psychologically abusive actions of the invading power and the confused connivance with and acceptance of the European philosophical status quo and all it entails by the inhabitants of the continent continue to this day as if this were normal, indeed beneficial for America.

What ought to be clear is that, from an objective viewpoint, for 300 to 500 years now, the Americans have been the inaptly named 'Indians' of years previous; the self-proclaimed 'first world' wishes to keep them subordinated as a subject, productive, and pacified population (i.e. one which does not rebel against the interests of the conquerors). It is not that the population is not accepted, but it is accepted as a series of different categories which are cognates to those of European society (rich and poor, those with degrees and those without, large-scale entrepreneurs and a working majority, those who govern and those who are governed) in a way which keeps it humble and marginalized, and by virtue of this manageable and cheap on the international market; Africa is the victim of similar processes.

Viewed historically, there has been no substantial change to this, only formal developments. The philosophical system and way of perceiving the universe, inculcated via public education, state religion, and legislation based on Roman law, as well as the political system, have remained largely constant. In this context, there is nothing surprising about the succession of republican governors who signed up to European philosophical propositions and mental conditioning, nor about the chronologically more recent prevalence of coups d'état perpetrated by messianic military or civilian personalities. These are, at most, symptomatic anecdotes, actions taken by actors reading from a 'first world' script; whatever the exact circumstances, the play is directed by political, economic, and religious interests from abroad with the atavistic conviction that they own the continent and are superior in every regard. Behind these phenomena, some of which are simply scandalous while others are quite extraordinary – and all of which should be borne in mind as they form part of history – there are two underlying realities which, for all their impenetrability, are crucial to understanding what is happening in America and which should not be overlooked.

One of these realities is the continuing invasion which, due to its philosophical and strategic origin, has been at the basis of our historiography and the education system since the fifteenth century – indeed, I would say that it is even a part of our mentality and our way of being. The other underlying reality is the uncritical acceptance of the philosophical, political, religious, and education systems imposed; indeed, given that Americans have supposedly European blood, customs and names and identify with the invader, how could it have been any different?

It would appear that neither yesterday's nor today's Americans are sure of who the invaders are and who is being invaded. Whether consciously or not, they have always assumed that it was only the 'Indians' who were considered to be second-class citizens due to having lost in the first instance; it has not occurred to them that indigenous, mixed (*criollo*), and immigrant populations of all extractions (until the immigrants, that is became natives too) are all in the same predicament by *the very fact of living on this continent* which is considered to have been 'made' by Europe. This means that the majority of the population, both philosophically and in terms of its actions, can only see itself as being one of invaders while it is, in reality, one of the dependent natives in the same manner as the pre-colonial, colonial, and republican populations which preceded them. In the minds and intellects of the Americans, it seems to go entirely unnoticed that the economic and cultural transition initiated in the fifteenth century consisted of the undeniably undue appropriation not just of land, but of resources, goods, riches, and people. For the invaders, it was much like the traditional deals their descendants would later carry out when buying estates from each other with everything into the bargain – including the workers. This transition has, with a few short intervals, been more or less continuous, and the most serious aspect of this sordid process is that the current inhabitants of the continent have not realized that they are the workers on the estate being sold.

In this context, what should not be forgotten is that the operational conquest of America, initiated in 1492, had and continues to have two dimensions which are profoundly intertwined and which remain present across the whole process through to the present day. There is the political and military dimension, shown in almost all documents of the early years and most clearly reflected in the *Requerimiento Real* of 1513, written by the theologian Palacios Rubios to be read out to the populations encountered. Amongst the many barbarities of this document, the following sentence stands out: 'I hereby entreat and require you to recognize the Church as your master and the greatest of the universe, and by extension the Holy Father the Pontiff, the King and the Queen[...] Should you not do so[...] I shall with the help of God employ force against you and shall fight a war on you wherever you may be and subject you to the yoke and the obedience of the Church and its fathers. I shall take your people and your women and your sons and shall make slaves of them and sell them as such. I shall take your possessions and will cause you all the damage which I am able to.'[5] The strategic connection between the two powers to serve their objectives is plain to see. The other dimension is an ideological one, based on the dogmatic philosophical principles of both the Greeks and the Romans and taken far beyond their beginnings in medieval Christendom and in the imperial period. Starting from these principles, and in a way which was as diabolical as it was erroneous, the Europeans neutralized and devalued the local ways of seeing the universe and the philosophies of life they found.

Beyond these dimensions, important pillars of the invasion but by no means the only foundations on which it was predicated, there is a serious and subtle phenomenon which should be highlighted as an underlying driving force behind the endemic illness from which the continent is suffering. The invaders, both those arriving from Europe and then those settled in America, blinded by their impulses and interests – and many without realizing it – discontinued the thousands of years of indigenous history on the basis of a categorically false syllogism derived from a fictitious logic and a supposed providential will on the part of their god. In this way, and despite the few European voices who spoke out against it (including Suárez, Vitoria, Las Casas, Pedro de Aragón and Motolinía), the invaders distorted the historical and cultural axis of the continent, twisting it towards Europe in order to convince themselves that the continent was theirs by right because it was either empty of people or, at the very most, inhabited by 'savages' with no culture. In order to convince European society of this mistaken perspective, it became necessary to methodically destroy the autonomous philosophical, sociopolitical, economic, and cultural systems of the continent and apply European ones at any cost. This was achieved using cruel military strategies, religious power, and the compulsive implantation of European languages and hierarchical educational systems conceived from within the continent's philosophical and methodological parameters. This is the reason why it is not a matter of chance, but one of cause-and-effect that Americans generally (with exceptions which are, however, increasing day by day) vaguely suppose that our continent never had real native languages or philosophies, systems of belief or sciences, technologies, arts, or real politics. All of this was obscured by a veil draped over the continent from Alaska down to Cape Horn, and it should suffice to recall the educational texts which were used to form both professors and pupils alike in which the reality of the historical-cultural processes both before and after the invasion is barely mentioned, at best tangentially or in anecdotal form.

In the final analysis, people (and this includes intellectuals and historians) coming from a philosophical and educational system conceived in the Europe of the invaders take it as given that there were no real protagonists of a history measured in millennia in America, only 'Indians' – savages, brutes, infidels. This is not to denigrate the cultural values generated by and for Europe in and of itself; and of course most of those who work on this hypothesis do so with no disingenuousness due to the simple fact that almost all of the American population is imbued with this weighty Western historiography, classical literature, and theoretical suppositions based on a skilfully structured sophism elaborated by obsessive theologians and philosophers of the Eurocentric medieval and Renaissance schools of thought.

It is important to grasp the structure and internal mechanisms of this underlying sophism which, in practice, has adopted and continues to adopt a range of strategic formulations according to whichever concrete goals are being pursued by the invader: that is, whether it wants to appropriate, enslave, exploit, legislate, or convert. Even though readers will surely be able to detect several of their own accord, let us fix our attention on two key examples of the European approach.

'When we Europeans appeared on this continent, there were no people here, only savages and infidels. As a consequence, they could have neither their own history nor culture, and i.e. we brought humanity with us in 1492 and, for this reason, real history and culture begins in this year.'

Here is another version of this perverted, tenacious, and skilful syllogism, presented here in terms of the religious salvation of the indigenous societies and of those which have emerged since the invasion.

'We Europeans came to an empty continent oblivious of the word of God: i.e. there was no owner, and since these lands belonged to no one, the first to claim them owns them, as does the Pope, the representative of God, the absolute owner of everything. All of which means that this continent is ours by natural and divine right.'

This conviction, which pervaded European society from its head – the Pope and the kings – to its feet – the peasants and the likes of Pizarro – had several lamentable effects, one of which was the *Inter caetera* papal bull signed by the corrupt Alexander VI as a matter of urgency on 4 May 1493 to try (in vain) to pre-emptively sidestep a ferocious internal conflict of interests. It constituted the removal of the continent's authority, and one of the series of barbarous provisions reads as follows:

> We, praising your sacred proposition […] and desiring that the name of our Lord and Saviour be introduced to these parts […] hereby decide to pursue in completeness […] such an expedition […] you must induce the peoples [who live there] to receive the Catholic faith […] By the mere fact of the liberal and full use of our power, all of the dry lands discovered and yet to be discovered shall […] by the authority our omnipotent Lord has granted to us in Saint Peter and vicariously through his son Jesus Christ whom we represent on earth with all of the dominions that are his, with cities, fortresses, estates, buildings and all our other belongings […] forever, in the same manner as we rule over these former, shall we make, assign, and dispatch our deputies to them [note this casual use of the word 'them' to apply to nothing less than the entire territories of America] with full authority and jurisdiction in every respect.

This type of reasoning is known as 'sophism' because at least one of its propositions or premises is entirely specious, meaning that the conclusion can only be false even if it is formally correct. In this case, the specious premise is that during (what the Europeans called) the fifteenth century, there were no humans with history, culture, ethics, and rights on the continent, that is no humanity. This assumed lack of genuine, self-contained historical processes lead to a whole range of arguments lacking in legitimation yet able to support the kind of aberration represented by European actions.

I have touched on the falseness or irresponsible nature of the classic sources (chronicles, political and religious documents, contemporary commentaries and essays) which uphold this sophism in traditional historiography and educational instruction. While I would not wish to claim that these sources do not contain truths or concrete facts of a more or less objective nature (at least, in the way those who produced these documents and chronicles saw things), I have a criticism which goes far beyond this level without disqualifying the information contained in these sources, which can of course be of (I stress the word) relative usefulness. Rather, my critical method aims to discredit the focus of these documents about the invasion, as well as that of most commentators who followed and their objectives and the historiographical method used in these writings; for the information presented and the focus used are always superficial, fallacious, and profoundly distorting. It is not so much a matter of the lies or over-imaginative inventions (of which there are more than enough), but of the fact that these sources are rooted in the sophism outlined above, constructed with the messianic, economic zeal of Western Christian civilization. I grant that it is difficult to perceive all the implications or underlying aspects of the sources if they are read and studied in a manner substantiated with the mentality of those who wrote them; many Americans, too, fail to see them by adhering, voluntarily or involuntarily, to the invaders, accepting these thousands of accounts as the truth without keeping the critical distance the mentality and objectives of those behind them would seem to call for, as would the fact that we are dealing with an overwhelming invasion of a pre-existing culture.

I will repeat that the first false premise is that the continent had neither true humans nor human history (while it, in reality, had both in a manner simply different to that of Europe) and no civilization either (while pre-Colombian civilization was as legitimate as the Western Graeco-Latin-Christian one). Yet, based on this specious premise, contemporaries reached perverse conclusions which in turn led to the homogenous tone of the reports, essays, theories, and strategies dressed up as 'age old' philosophy or a theology of 'redemption' (from what?). Let us look at three examples, beginning with that of Thomas Ortiz, the archbishop of the Darien Peninsula, and the theologian Juan Ginés de Sepúlveda in Europe who, around 1540, held against the few intellectuals who argued for the autonomy of the continent, arguing that 'the Indians are natural servants; given their incapacity, their wickedness, and their ineptitude, it is the kinder way to tame, capture, and enslave them.' More recently, in the nineteenth century, the Italian religious man Juan Bosco sent the following directives from Rome – with the full support of the Vatican and the Argentine government – to the congregation he had established in the south. 'The honour of taming the ferociousness of these savages', he says, referring here to the Ona, Tehuelche, and Mapuche, 'is reserved to the Catholic church alone, and in order to achieve this noble end, I have agreed the following plan with the Pope Pius IX and the Archbishop of Argentina', who was also Italian. He goes on to outline what would become the famous missions, before they disappeared after the Europeans and *criollos* had wiped out the three nations which were to be converted. 'We shall found colleges and hospices in the main cities of these lands and surround the Patagonia with our fortresses into which oases of peace and charity we shall bring the indigenous young. We shall attract primarily the sons of the barbarians or semi-barbarians and instruct them in Christianity so that we may penetrate into these regions and open a fountain of true civilisation and progress.' Around the same time, the Argentine parliament enacted Law 947, which required the republic to 'subjugate as soon as possible, whether by reason or by force, this bunch of savages which is destroying our natural wealth and preventing us from definitively occupying in the name of law and progress [...] the richest and most fertile lands of the Republic'.[6] It goes without saying that these three examples show how things are seen when corroborated by the system of the invader.

There were, however, reactions against this hypothesis, both in Europe at the time and in America, of course, which only go to reveal just how conscious the invading societies were of having stumbled upon an authentic part of humanity and of the overwhelming compulsion which led them to misappropriate foreign territory and commit genocide. The theologian Pedro de Aragón, for example, states that 'no king and no emperor, nor the Roman church may, even under the pretext of preaching the gospel, occupy their lands or fight a war against them [...] This is why those who claimed to be spreading the Christian faith by the force of arms have committed a grave sin, and have not legitimately conquered any of these lands, and are obliged to withdraw from them like the unjust usurpers they are.' This convincing piece of reasoning, however, went unnoticed, and not due to the inability of those at the time to understand it, because of their 'mentality': it went unnoticed for the simple reason that it was not convenient – and is still not convenient today. At the most, the usurpers say sorry, but these apologies are forgotten as soon as they are said or archived away, such as the one made by the Pope in 1992.

It is obvious that, faced with this level of blindness on such a powerful continent, it has never been and is still not easy to secure the level of autonomy and growth that we in America deserve: the spider's web is not merely political, but also cultural, philosophical; and, in my opinion, there is no one cultural command or economic strike from on high in our arsenal which could neutralize the effects of Western pressure. What we as natives need to understand is that we must accept the thousands of years of history and cultural heritage with which our continent is imbued – in just the same way as the Europeans do on theirs. This is the starting point from which the population of America today (regardless of the origins of those which compose it) should formulate its objectives and its way out of the current situation. It means affirming its sovereignty in all areas and its cultural identity as proceeding from its own history; it means taking strong, passionate strides across our homeland and being ready to defend it with all of the risks this entails, understanding that the Western ingress onto the continent has always been and remains to this day a complex, disguised, and entirely self-serving invasion.

Having said that, affirming real sovereignty, our identity, and our authentic historical perspective requires us to first become familiar with the cultural content of the process and take on responsibility for correcting the curve of our historical trajectory on a practical, day-to-day level. This is a commitment which must be made by researchers, professors, students, and society at large; and it will not be easy, because it will shake the foundations of many deeply entrenched points of view. It will mean really feeling that life and history here are built on the base of our own process, a fecund historical-cultural background stretching back over thousands of years which actually comes from here, not from the northern hemisphere. At the same time, this commitment should not lead us to ignore or to denigrate the history of the other continents; quite to the contrary, for affirming one's own identity sharpens the eye for others and otherness.

Proceeding from this change in consciousness and an increased sense of our own worth, I think it is entirely possible to look for and find ways towards self-determination, to internal equality, and to overcoming foreign imperialism, orientating ourselves by way of the values which are emerging from our thousands of years of history and philosophy. Alongside this personal and institutional commitment (as soon as it can usefully be made), we should not lose sight of the fact that the invader, using the sophism described and its unrivalled force, established here in America a balance of power and obsequious mentality which has persisted almost intact into the present day – especially through the education system, including instruction at university level – and that these structures must be broken down, as is our good right, if we really aspire to authentic autonomy.

We must also remember that, for the invader, 'defending itself' means declaring war on weak opponents, and with this in mind, it is useful to recall what Bartolomé de las Casas wrote from the Caribbean, although it remained unheeded, faced with the steely obsession with power, domination, and exploitation: 'All wars which are called conquest have always been and continue to be those of the most unjust sort, the wars of tyrants [...] All the kings and leaders of the Indians have been usurped [...] The natives of all of those lands we have entered into have acquired the right to fight the most just of wars against us and to wipe us from the face of the earth, a right which shall persist until the end of days.' In the view of this priest (taken from *Brevísima Relación*), who bore witness to six decades of massacre and pillage, our right is still in force today.

I should like to draw my reflections to a close with two short texts, one by the Mexican Nobel Prize laureate (1990) Octavio Paz in reference to an emblematic figure of the invasion, but which could also be applied to any other person who has abused America (each reader will know who to apply it to); the other is from the ethical tradition of the Yámana people of the Tierra del Fuego.

In 1986, Octavio Paz wrote: 'As a figure, Hernándo Cortés has always provoked contradictory feelings and opinions[...] No one can escape a fascination with him which ranges from idolizing to loathing[...] The cruelty and treachery of some of his deeds, for instance the Cholula Massacre, the execution of Cuauhtémoc, and the destruction of Tenochtitlán, recall the acts of the unscrupulous princes of the Renaissance, of Cesar Borgia or the Malatestas[...] The figure Cortés both invites and offers grounds for the most divergent judgements and the most daring comparisons[...] Cortés is a Mexican myth, a negative one: firstly, he is almost incomprehensible to non-Mexicans; secondly, he appears to be an angry wound. Cortés' (or, I would stress, any other like him) 'is an emblem of the conquest: not as a historical phenomenon' (and if only we could understand this point) 'who, at the meeting of two worlds, united them; but as the image of a violent penetration and an astute, barbarous usurpation, achieved by conquest, i.e. greed, duplicity, cruelty, and the beginnings of oppression and injustice' (Taken from *La Nación*, 16 March 1986).

For their part, the Yámana, gone today after almost 3,000 years in existence at the foot of the continent, used to teach the following to their adolescents from their work, *Chiexaus*.

> Above everything else, we men and women must be good and useful to each other.
> Each must be able to determine their own fate.
> Get up early every morning and you will always be ready.
> Show respect to your elders.
> Don't listen to what the others are saying; and don't be curious about others either.
> If somebody uses rude words or insults you, withdraw [...] later, speak alone to the person
> who offended you when you are both calm.
> Do not take what is not yours [...] if you need something, ask your neighbour.
> Remember that other people have the same feelings as you.[7]

Notes

1 Generally, the word *criollo* today is applied to those who inhabit rural areas and the Gran Chaco. Their origins are decidedly mixed, the result of a deep biological and cultural interaction between peoples from several parts of the world: native or aboriginal Americans, Europeans, Africans and Asians. Historically, the word *criollo* was applied to those born in America of European parents, who are nowadays usually referred to as *gringos* or indeed often refer to themselves as such when they self-identify as descendants of a European bloodline more or less distant (immigrant parents, grandparents, great-grandparents, etc.).

2 Before the Europeans flooded onto the continent today misnamed 'America', it had more than 70 million inhabitants between Alaska and the Cape Horn speaking around 1,200 dialectal languages from 170 linguistic families, according to a meticulous study carried out by the eminent German ethnographer Walter Krickeberg, among others, in W. Krickeberg, *Ethnology of America* (Mexico City, 1982). There were countless countries with their characteristics and many differences in their beliefs about the cosmos, their philosophy of life, their sociopolitical organization, and their technological, industrial and artistic style. While the majority of these nations was wiped out following the invasions beginning in 1492, many subsisted, maintaining the basics of their culture. In what today is called Argentina, more than one million people today consider themselves

'aboriginal', i.e. rooted in the pre-Colombian biological and cultural stock, and divide into 20 nations – each with its own name.

3 On this point, it would be opportune to mention that, since the nineteenth century, and especially during the twentieth century, there has been a range of hypotheses about when human beings emerged and when they entered the continent. The most widely accepted in academic history, anthropology, archaeology and other disciplines is that, with reference to remains found at multiple sites the length of the continent, human history here starts around 35,000 and almost certainly more than 40,000 years ago, which is when humans arrived from Asia across what today are called the Bering Straits. Both personally and as a university professor, I support this latter hypothesis, based substantially on the arguments elucidated by renowned archaeologists and anthropologists in America: A. Bryan, *Historia General de America Latina* (Madrid, 1999), pp. 42–68 and A. Bryan, *New Evidence for the Pleistocene Peopling of the Americas* (Orono, ME, 1986), pp. 203–13; D. Ibarra Grasso, *Examen crítico sobre la antigüedad del hombre americano* (Rosario, 1989) and D. Ibarra Grasso, *América en la Prehistoria Universal* (Buenos Aires, 1982); F. Kaufmann Doig, *Historia General de los peruanos* (Lima, 1986); L. Lumbreras, *Arqueología de la América Andina* (Lima, 1985); S. Osvaldo, *Prehistoria de América* (Santiago, 1983), and many other authors. This hypothesis rests on finds and analyses of a series of fossils dated at 40,000 years or more, including those of Taber, Alberta, Canada, at 40,000 years; American Falls, USA, 43,000; Lewisville, USA, 41,000; Texas Street, over 35,000; Tule Springs, USA, 28,000; Tlapacoya, Mexico, roughly 24,000, etc. These dates which incontrovertibly show human presence refer to the northern half of the continent, but there are abundant finds in the south, too, including at sites such as Los Toldos in Patagonia, carbon-dated to almost 12,000 years, which is extremely old if we consider that humans moved from the north to the south in a process which by its very nature took thousands of years. Due to space considerations, these references will suffice here, but there are plenty more, perhaps different sources, which readers can consult on their own account – some available online.

4 A letter by Christopher Columbus, written during the return from his first voyage to Luis de Santángel for delivery to the kings, dated 15 February 1493; cf. E. Rodríguez Monegal, *Noticias secretas y públicas de América* (Barcelona, 1984), p. 33, among other works.

5 From the very beginning of the invasion, the Catholic Church played a leading role in the territorial appropriation and expansion as an imperial ideology and justification of the actions of the conquistadors in the name of their god. Indeed, the European view of divine providence (shared by Catholics and Protestants), taken to its greatest extent by the Castilians and their crusade mentality (for them, the Crusade lasted seven centuries), is shown most thoroughly in this, the most famous of the official documents, this perverse *ne plus ultra* of Christianity, the *Requirimiento* of 1513, approved by the Spanish court as a way of rationalizing its claims to sovereignty over the 'New World'. Surely there can be no European who does not know of its existence? And surely no academic, sitting as it does in every library on this continent? Unless they do not want to know of its existence, of course.

6 From the *Memorias* of Juan Bosco, the cleric who founded the Salesians, after visiting Patagonia, quoted from A. Latashen, *Marici Weu* (Buenos Aires, 1994), p. 146.

7 Text taken from M. Gusinde, *Los indios de Tierra del Fuego* (Buenos Aires, 1986).

Note from the editors: The author of this chapter prefers to minimize the use of referencing conventions, which he sees as an expression of European-inspired scientific imperialism. Though we do not share this view, we believe that the chapter is an apt polemical epilogue to throw the themes of the book's first section into relief.

Part II

Return to Sender?
Imperial Visions, Imperial Legacies

The Echoes of Rome
in British and American Hegemonic Ideology

Ali Parchami

Rome has provided posterity with a rich and eclectic legacy: from architecture and engineering to the arts of government and warfare, its grandeur has invoked admiration and has been a source of emulation. For over a millennia the ancient polity has served as the template for European empires: Charlemagne, Napoleon and Mussolini – among a succession of European leaders – all claimed to be Rome's heir. The echoes of Rome are particularly discernible in the hegemonic rhetoric and ideology of two of the greatest powers of the last two centuries: the British Empire and the United States. The British liked to boast that their empire was the sole inheritor to Rome's imperial mantle; but, in contrast, it is often America's critics who pejoratively describe it as the 'new Rome'. This chapter will examine two strands of Rome's influence on Victorian and Edwardian imperial thought and on US hegemonic ideology. First, it will show that Rome's echo transcends etymology and can also be seen in the legitimization process through which British imperialists and American hegemonists have sought to justify their respective *imperiums*.

The Romans may not have been the first imperialists in history, but they were the first hegemonic power in the Western world to adopt a sophisticated language that justified interventionist expansionism under a veneer of altruism and even humanitarianism. Second, the chapter will argue that the echoes of Rome can also be found in British and American hegemonic behaviour. During the first two centuries BC, the Romans frequently exercised informal imperialism: where possible, they refrained from direct rule and territorial annexation – preferring instead to use existing sociopolitical structures to control and exploit. While claiming that their own empire was morally and materially superior to Rome's, Victorian imperialists acknowledged that British rule in the dependencies loosely mirrored the Roman model. Conversely, present-day American political commentators tend to dismiss as 'simplistic' any comparison of Roman and US hegemony. Yet, in their effort to discredit the analogy, the rejectionists too often ignore the nuances of Roman imperialism and its echoes in US foreign policy.

Echoes of Roman Legitimization

The Roman contribution to the modern lexicon of imperialism has been widely acknowledged.[1] Outside classical scholarship, however, little attention has been given to the intricacies of Roman imperialism and its echoes in modern hegemonic rhetoric and ideology. The extant writings of Graeco-Roman authors provide us with an invaluable, albeit fragmented, insight into an increasingly sophisticated legitimization process which sought to justify Roman expansionism in benign terms. Ancient apologists claimed that Rome's rise to 'world power' was not by design but rather forced upon it by circumstances; and that Rome only engaged in warfare under the principle of *iusta causa*.[2] They were especially keen to show that Rome had exhausted every avenue of diplomacy before resorting to arms.[3] Their insistence on the righteousness of the Roman cause, and their contention that Rome acquired its empire 'inadvertently', is all the more remarkable because it represents a departure from the rhetoric of previous empires. The Mesopotamian kingdoms of Babylon and Assyria had, after all, boasted about their conquests in the name of glory and with an eye on plunder. In the Melian Dialogue – one of the most quoted passages in the literature of modern international relations – the Athenians had defended their imperialist tendencies on the grounds that might makes right.[4] Philip of Macedonia had justified his invasion of Greece by presenting himself as the unifier of Hellenic peoples and their avenger against the Persians. His son, Alexander the Great, had expressed a desire to conquer the known world and, for good measure, may have also claimed personal divinity. However, Roman apologists preferred to cite self-defence, the protection of weaker allies, and the liberation of others as the legitimization for Rome's singular drive to control the Mediterranean basin: 'Our people have now gained power over the whole world by defending their allies'; and we have fought wars 'in order to render it possible to live in peace without injustice'.[5]

The representation of imperialism in benign colours, and as primarily an altruistic endeavour, can be traced back to Rome's conquest of the Eastern Mediterranean in the second century BC. While in the West they had faced small communities of rural 'barbarians', in the Greek East the Romans had to adapt their strategy against a formidable cluster of Hellenistic states with relatively structured societies and urbanized populations. The vibrant and cultured civilization of the Hellenistic world had to be seduced before it could be furtively conquered.

Therefore, great energy was invested into depicting Rome in normative terms that the Hellenistic nations would find readily acceptable.[6] Ostentatiously proclaiming themselves as Hellenophiles, the Romans initially projected themselves as arbitrators and the guardians of the lesser Greek states against the 'oppressive' policies of Philip V of Macedonia – the most powerful of the Hellenistic kingdoms. Spearheading a coalition of mid-ranking and smaller Greek states, Rome dealt a heavy blow to Philip in two successive wars (214–205 and 200–197 BC). The historian, Livy, records that the Senate of Rome and Titus Quinctius Flamininus, their general, decreed that the Greeks would henceforth be 'free' and 'released from the payment of tribute', and allowed 'to live under their own laws'.[7] In 196 BC Flamininus made a public appearance at the Ismithian Games in Corinth to formally announce the 'liberty' of the Greek states. Livy relates that when they realized the joyful news was true, the Greeks engaged in spontaneous celebration:

> There is, people said, one nation which at its own cost, through its own exertions, at its own risk has gone to war on behalf of the liberty of others. It renders this service not to those across its frontiers, or to the peoples of neighbouring States or to those who dwell on the same mainland, but it crosses the seas in order that nowhere in the wide world may injustice and tyranny exist, but that right and equity and law may be everywhere supreme. By this single proclamation of the herald all the cities in Greece and Asia recover their liberty.[8]

The Greeks did not at first understand that the Roman use of the term 'liberty' only meant they were free to live under their own laws as client-states of Rome.[9] Even as they celebrated their *libertas*, the Romans were proceeding against the Seleucid Kingdom of Antiochus III of Syria – now the major Greek power in the East. In 191 BC Antiochus was deliberately provoked into a disastrous war after the Romans declared his subjects in Asia Minor to be 'free' of Seleucid rule. Antiochus was defeated and bound by a humiliating treaty. Unwilling at this stage to establish direct rule over the Greek East, the Romans reinforced the illusion of Greek 'liberty' by withdrawing most of their troops from the region. 'The Roman people', Livy declared, 'brought not slavery to free peoples, but on the contrary, freedom for the enslaved.'[10] Already the preponderant power in the Hellenistic sub-system, Rome saw to it that the flow of riches to Italy would continue with minimum expense. Accordingly, it relied on subversion when possible – turning Greek against Greek – and force only when necessary. Greek 'allies' were henceforth required to provide Rome with troops and to financially 'contribute' to maintaining the status quo. It soon became evident that any challenge to Roman power was construed as a threat to peace. Livy writes that some of the Greek leaders 'mildly remonstrated against the change in the feelings of the Romans towards them since their victory; others took a much stronger line and declared that without [their] aid [...] [the Macedonians and the Seleucids] could not have been vanquished, nor could the Romans ever have landed in Greece.'[11]

When in 171 BC Perseus, the young Macedonian king, took advantage of the growing disillusionment with Rome to gather allies, the Romans declared war. Perseus was captured in 168 BC and thousands of his subjects were enslaved. Within two decades any remaining pretence was set aside: between 150 and 148 BC, Macedonia was turned into a province under a Roman governor. As for the other Greek states, those who failed to accept the new order were summarily punished, with little distinction being made between former foes and allies. In 146 BC Corinth – the city wherein Flamininus had famously proclaimed the 'liberty' of the Greeks – was sacked: the Romans put its male inhabitants to the sword, enslaved its women and children, and looted its treasures. The ferocity suffered by the inhabitants of Corinth marked the symbolic shift from informal imperialism to outright conquest as one Mediterranean territory after another succumbed to Rome's legions. As the Greek world was reorganized and brought under Roman provincial administration, resistance was crushed systematically and ruthlessly.[12] Attalus III of Pergamum was perhaps wise to bequeath his kingdom to the 'Roman people' in 133 BC. Conversely, those who dared to show some measure of independence, were hunted down like fugitives.[13] Within a century, Pontus and Syria became the latest Roman provinces; Julius Caesar vanquished Gaul; and his adopted son – known to history as the Emperor Augustus – completed the conquest of the Mediterranean by annexing Egypt and ending the insurgency of the tribes in the Iberian Peninsula.[14]

Once established as the dominant power in the Mediterranean, Rome was hailed as the protector of the weak and the benefactor of humanity: instead of the old emphasis on self-defence and the protection of allies, apologists claimed Rome was ordained by the gods to undertake a civilizing mission; that the Romans were burdened with the responsibility of bringing order to a chaotic world; and that they were chosen by Providence to institute the habits of peace under the majesty of the Pax Romana. Although the Pax Romana was never formalized as a concept, it revolved around a sophisticated tapestry of ideas.[15] Domestically, it referred to the end of civil war and the restoration of Rome's institutions, traditions and mores.[16] Externally, it represented Rome's desire to impose its will upon all others – a desire which was encapsulated by the phrase *imperium sine fine*: 'empire without end'.[17] In his masterpiece, *The Aeneid*, the poet Virgil celebrated the imperialism of the early first century AD by giving it a humanitarian dimension. He had Jupiter decree: 'To rule the world shall be thy art Roman, to impose the habits of peace, and to spare the meek and tame the proud.'[18] From its humble beginnings Rome had been elevated by Providence and tasked with the responsibility of acculturating the world: spreading its political and military authority, its laws and institutions, and its customs and values to the far reaches of the earth. Roman imperialism of the Augustan age was unashamedly supremacist with universal pretensions.[19] Its ideology was built upon two central tenets which have echoed into modern imperialism: bestowing upon the conquered the blessings of *pax* and undertaking *humanitas* (civilizing mission).

Pax, often translated into English as 'peace', should more accurately be defined as pacification. The Pax Romana was predicated upon the belief that lasting peace could only be achieved when others submitted to Rome's *imperium*. In the testament to his deeds Augustus – the architect of the Pax Romana – makes it very clear that peace could only be achieved through military victory.[20] He also declares: 'I extended the boundaries of all the provinces which were bordered by races not yet subject to our empire [...] [and] reduced [them] to a state of peace.'[21] During the first two centuries AD, Roman sources repeatedly depict acts of aggression against neighbouring tribes, or the quelling of rebellions by subject races, as unavoidable measures for the sake of maintaining the Pax Romana. The historian Tacitus provides a memorable representation of the Roman peace when he has the Roman general, Cerialis, address a group of Gallic rebels:

> Gaul always had its petty kingdoms and intestine wars, till you submitted to our authority. We, though so often provoked, have used the right of conquest to burden you only with the cost of maintaining peace. For the tranquillity of nations cannot be preserved without armies; armies cannot exist without pay [...] Should the Romans be driven out (which God forbid) what can result but wars [...] Give therefore your love and respect to the cause of peace.[22]

Rome, in other words, is the agency of the divine and the very incarnation of peace; its rule is justified because it is exercised for the benefit of its subjects. The alternative to Rome is chaos, injustice, war and barbarism. Along with the Pax Romana, Roman poets, writers and historians of the imperial age frequently celebrated what the Elder Pliny proclaimed as Rome's mission to 'give civilisation to mankind'.[23] The Roman Empire was regularly referred to as the *orbis terrarum* (the world); what lay outside it was insignificant – inhabited by 'barbarians'.[24] Ancient writers occasionally distinguished between the reality of Roman imperialism and the rhetoric of legitimization: 'Scythia and India still remained unconquered, and in these cases they [the Romans] could have covered up their greed with the not inglorious title of a civilising mission.'[25] But, for the most part, the legitimization process tended to claim that Rome had been entrusted by the gods with a mission to bestow upon mankind the gifts of peace and civilization. This feat could only be achieved once non-Romans were subdued, conquered and eventually assimilated into the *imperium*

Romanum. Roman wars of the imperial age were thus righteous as they were fought for the preservation of the Pax Romana *and* the propagation of civilization.

The Roman Empire eventually declined and gave way to a succession of European states. But its image persisted down through the ages – galvanizing medieval to late modern European polities.[26] While recognizing that the Roman heritage was common to all Western European nations, many British imperialists came to view their own empire as the one true heir to Rome's imperial mantle. The pre-eminence of classical education in public schools, and at Oxbridge, and the milieu of 'new imperialism' that prevailed in the late Victorian era, encouraged Britain's governing elite to draw direct parallels between the Roman and British empires.[27] Rome, a small city-state, had gained mastery over the Mediterranean world; and now Britain, a small island-nation, had been singled out by Providence to subdue a quarter of the world and to extend its rule to one fifth of the human race. The British imperial idea was saturated with the echoes of Rome – nowhere more so than in the adoption of the concept of Pax Britannica.[28] In unmistakably Virgilian language, British imperialist literature frequently alluded to a civilizing mission; to the special destiny of the Anglo-Saxon race; to the responsibility of the British nation to impose the habits of peace; and to undertake the burden of elevating 'backward' peoples to a higher plain of moral and material blessing.[29] Victorian and Edwardian apologists justified British imperialism as an altruistic endeavour: the institutionalization of British rule was depicted in paternalistic terms and the colonialization of the non-European world was explained as a trusteeship for the benefit of the ruled: 'Let anyone think of the general state of the ancient world before the conquest of Rome [...] [and] what Rome did for her subjects, or what England has done in India.'[30] Echoing the speech Tacitus had given to Cerialis, Victorian and Edwardian commentators repeatedly warned that the end of British rule in Asia and Africa would be disastrous for the indigenous population, and would signal a return to injustice and warfare.[31]

Although the Roman analogy peppered Victorian and Edwardian imperialist literature, the three most important works written on the subject acknowledged that the parallels had many limitations.[32] Sir Charles Lucas and Lords Cromer and Bryce – all influential figures at the epicentre of British political and imperial affairs – argued that there were lessons to be learned from Rome, but ultimately the British Empire was both very different and in almost every way superior to the ancient polity. They insisted that, unlike the Romans, the British did not conquer for the sake of booty and exploitation, but were driven by an exceptional sense of morality which bound them to do what they could for the less fortunate races. With its Christian character, and inculcated with a sense of fair play and tolerance, the *raison d'être* of the British Empire was to afford a better spiritual as well as material standard of life for the natives of territories under its control.[33] The analogy was, therefore, considered largely a useful device in the education of young imperial civil servants who would study, examine, and learn from its example in solving their own day-to-day administrative problems. By scrutinizing Rome's frontier policy, its approach to uprisings and rebellions, and its dealing with provincial matters and the locals, the British could improve on what the ancients did right and avoid making the same mistakes. In addition, because Rome was viewed as the first successful empire of its kind in the world, its example could also be used to help inspire the young – the future leaders of the empire.[34] The Cambridge historian J. R. Seeley explained that Rome had represented 'the empire of civilisation over barbarism' in the same way that Britain's empire outside Europe signified modernity over medievalism: 'The light we bring is not less real, but it is probably less attractive and received with less gratitude.'[35] Paradoxically, imperialists wished to project the British Empire as the 'new Rome'; yet they were so perturbed by aspects of Roman hegemony that they also sought to distance Britain from what they regarded as the worst characteristics of Rome's *imperium*: 'The Roman Empire meant despotism, concentration, the absorption of all the parts in a single mass [...] The British Empire means freedom, decentralisation, and autonomy; it will live forever.'[36] The echoes of Rome thus created a dilemma for proponents of empire: how to draw inspiration from the Roman model without succumbing to its perceived physical brutality and moral depravity.[37]

By insisting that the British had morally transcended the Romans, analogists inadvertently provided a platform for the critics of empire. J. M. Robertson was scathing in his condemnation of British behaviour in the colonies, and the obsession of the British governing elite in emulating the Romans and yet conceiting to be better than them.[38] In what was to become a seminal work, J. A. Hobson also denounced the intrinsic hypocrisy of British imperialism.[39] Noting the contrast between the veneer of altruism – with its lofty ideals and appealing language – and the actuality of British colonial practice, Hobson accused his countrymen of pursuing a 'parasitic' imperialism analogous to that of Rome.[40] As far as the critics were concerned, in spite of the effort that went into stressing Britain's higher morality, imperialists were relying on the same dubious rhetoric of legitimization as had the Romans: the Pax Britannica was an 'empty phrase' when warfare and military operations were a fact of life in many parts of the empire.[41] Robertson, Hobson and other radicals derided the logic of British imperialism, built, as it was, on the argument that the end justified the means: 'You cannot have omelettes without breaking eggs; you cannot destroy the practices of barbarism, of slavery, of superstition [...] without the use of force.'[42] Bloodshed, the loss of life among native populations, and pacification were the inevitable price of peace and civilization if 'backward' peoples were to be brought into 'some kind of disciplined order'.[43] Such pronouncements, according to anti-imperialists, were no more than modern enunciations of Rome's doctrines of *pax* and *humanitas*.[44] Even Seeley's remark – that Britain's conquest of 'half the world' was down to 'a fit of absence of mind'[45] – carried the resonance of Rome's 'accidental empire'. If the parallels with Rome had been a useful device for late Victorian imperialists, in the aftermath of the Boer War, its echoes came back to haunt their Edwardian successors.

In the 1890s, across the Atlantic, the McKinley administration in Washington was also actively pursuing an imperialist agenda. It was no coincidence, then, that during this period the phrase *Pax Americana* was creeping into the language of US foreign policy.[46] Partly a pejorative reference to British imperialism, the phrase was also derived from a long-held view that the US was a great republic in the mould of ancient Rome.[47] It is ironic that, over the course of the next century, the more the US sought to distance itself from British (and European) imperialism, the more its language was to betray the echoes of Rome. Less than two decades after McKinley's death, many Americans were already subscribing to the myth that the United States' 'dalliance' with imperialism at the end of the nineteenth century had been uncharacteristic. Conveniently forgetting Washington's policies towards native Americans and Mexico, they argued that the US had never been an imperialist power and that the 1890s had represented an aberration in what was otherwise an inherently altruistic streak in the American psyche. The US was projected instead as a benevolent republic, a champion of self-determination and liberty.[48] In the words of President Woodrow Wilson, the US had

> no selfish ends to serve. We desire no conquest, no dominion. We seek no indemnities for ourselves, no material compensation for the sacrifices we shall freely make. We are but one of the champions of the rights of mankind. We shall be satisfied when these rights have been made as secure as the faith and the freedom of the nation can make them.[49]

As one of Wilson's contemporaries saw it, in America alone existed 'a broad sense of brotherhood, and a new scale of human values'. The US did not 'care to dominate alien peoples'; it did 'not aspire to be the Romans of tomorrow or the "masters of the world"'. America's 'strain of pacifism' demanded 'abstinence from aggression and desire to be left alone to work out' its own destiny.[50]

Just as the Romans had claimed leadership of the 'free' Hellenistic states in the second century BC, by the late 1940s the US was styling itself the 'leader of the free world'. As with Rome's efforts to check Macedonian power, America's Cold War strategy was shaped largely by security fears and a desire to contain the Soviet Union; and, in the same way that the Greek city-states had initially sought Rome's protective shield within the framework of a coalition, the US was to become *primus inter pares* within a new transatlantic security structure.[51] Washington did not have a premeditated plan for hegemony, but found itself gradually entangled in overseas commitments which, in turn, spurred it on to greater militarization and the deployments of additional troops in its global sphere of influence.[52] Its post-war position, and its relationship with its allies, invoke some similarities with Rome's *imperium* in the decades that followed the Second Punic War. However, the aim here is not to draw a direct parallel between the US and Rome because, beyond what has been said, the analogy would be superficial and unhelpful. Of greater interest to our discussion is the echoes of Rome in the language of post-war Washington. Since 1945 the US has played upon the notion of a 'reluctant' superpower: an inward-looking giant elevated to the status of the world's 'policeman' by international circumstances rather than national desire. Not since Rome has such an influential power on the world stage justified one interventionist policy after another in the name of protecting the weak against oppression and defending its allies against aggression. An examination of Washington's justifications for interventionist wars would reveal that they are framed either as self-defence, protecting America's allies, or riding the world of tyranny in favour of self-determination and liberal-democratic norms.[53] The controversial US involvement in Vietnam, for example, was first depicted as a mission to provide assistance to a client-regime and to prevent conflict escalation; and then, following the incident at the Gulf of Tonkin, as self-defence.

Admittedly, the international system today is very different from that of antiquity; and the use of force is prohibited under international law unless it is for self-defence or falls within the remit of a UN Security Council mandate. Nevertheless, critics of US foreign policy contend that Washington has exploited the principle of self-defence on numerous occasions to legitimize its self-serving interventionist policies.[54] The 2003 invasion of Iraq is singled out as the latest egregious act of aggression veiled under the justification of self-defence.[55] The initial case was built upon the assumption that Iraq possessed weapons of mass destruction and that it posed an imminent threat: it was argued that the Iraqis not only had the capability to launch these weapons within 45 minutes but, that given the nature of Saddam Hussein's regime, the intent was there. When the occupation of Iraq failed to produce the WMD evidence, or to tie Baghdad to the attacks of 9/11, Washington sought to legitimize its actions by essentially falling back on the twin Roman mantras of *pax* and *humanitas*: establishing peace under the auspices of *Pax Americana*, replacing the Iraqi political system with democratic institutions, and educating the natives in liberal-democratic norms.

Echoes of Hegemonic Behaviour

Having briefly discussed the echoes of legitimization in British and US hegemonic foreign policy, it warrants looking at the echoes of Roman imperialism in the behaviour of these two powers. When thinking about the nature of Roman imperialism, a number of factors have to be considered. First, the language of Roman legitimization was so skilful that it misled some of the most distinguished classical scholars of the past two centuries. Second, due to the territorial size of her empire, Rome's imperialism was variable and was adapted in response to different conditions, terrains, and the type of societies and peoples that were encountered. Third, Roman imperialism changed significantly during the later stages of the Republic, as well as in the formative years that saw the transformation of the republican state into an imperial system: the predominantly informal imperialism of the mid-Republic was replaced with formal imperialism during the final decades of the Republic, while the expansionism that had characterized the Republican age was in turn largely abandoned for consolidation under the emperors.

There is considerable scholarly debate about the motivation and nature of Roman imperialism during the mid-Republic (*c.*264–146 BC) – the period which saw Rome's conquest of most of the Mediterranean. One school of thought, which dates back to the Victorian era, largely accepts the justifications put forward by ancient apologists. Sometimes referred to as the Mommsen School,[56] these scholars have essentially subscribed to the notion of 'defensive imperialism': the idea that Roman expansion was a reaction to real or perceived security threats. According to the theory, existential fears and entangling alliances compelled the Roman Senate to become involved in a succession of wars that ultimately resulted in empire.[57] Until the middle of the twentieth century 'defensive imperialism' represented the orthodoxy in Roman scholarship. However, beginning in the 1960s, a younger generation of classicists dismissed the thesis of an 'accidental empire' and drew attention to Rome's uninterrupted military campaigns around the Mediterranean. The revisionists argued that Rome had, in fact, embarked upon its imperialist expansion in a far more ruthless and calculated way than ancient sources would have us believe.[58] By questioning historical accounts that removed culpability from the Romans, the revisionists cast a shadow over the Mommsen school: taking its proponents to task for being 'gulled' by Roman propaganda and, as a result, interpreting even neutral sources in such a way as to obfuscate the insidiousness of Roman imperialism. A third group of historians, while endorsing the revisionist thesis, have postulated that Roman imperialism was far more complex than either the Mommsen school or some of their critics have been willing to recognize.[59] These post-revisionists argue that the causes and characteristics of Roman imperialism varied from place to place; and, in particular, a distinction should be made between Roman imperialism in Western Europe and in the Hellenistic East.[60]

In the Iberian Peninsula, where the inhabitants were designated as 'barbarians', no attempt was made to disguise Rome's imperialist intentions nor to mollify the brutality unleashed by its legions. Roman campaigns, undertaken by glory hunters, were largely motivated by economic greed and characterized by mass killings, large-scale enslavement and plunder.[61] But, as we have seen, in the Hellenistic East Roman imperialism was more nuanced, incremental and subversive. Initially, it relied upon divide and rule, a blend of diplomacy and force, and what we would today describe as 'informal' imperialism. Over a course of two centuries, one by one, the major powers around the Mediterranean were either defeated or subverted. Some, like Carthage, were attacked and ruthlessly destroyed; others, such as Egypt, were allowed to retain a degree of autonomy and nominally remained sovereign. As early as 55 BC a Roman garrison had been dispatched to Alexandria, under the pretext of protecting the Egyptian royal family. But given Rome's reliance on Egyptian grain, and with the Egyptian economy increasingly under the control of Roman financiers, the fate of the country was effectively sealed: the country was too rich and too strategically important for the Romans to allow it to retain perpetual independence. Less prized possessions, however, were accorded the right of autonomy as long as the local elite acknowledged Roman suzerainty and were mindful not to challenge Roman power. So even at the height of Augustan imperialism, client-kings, such as Herod the Great in Judea, flourished because they understood and adhered to their place in the Roman order.[62]

Roman imperialism during the imperial age did not confine itself to the territorial limits of the empire, but demanded the projection of Roman power far and wide. In the name of preserving the Pax Romana, expeditionary operations were routinely launched deep into 'barbarian' lands to kill, pillage and terrorize. In a chilling passage, the historian Tacitus gives us a view of Roman imperialism from the perspective of a Celtic chieftain in Britain in the second half of the first century AD:

> Plunderers of the world they are [...] If the enemy is rich, they are greedy; if the enemy is poor, they are power-hungry. Neither east nor west has been able to sate them. Alone of all men they covet rich nations and poor nations with equal passion. They rob, they slaughter, they plunder and they call it empire. Where they make a wasteland, they call it peace.[63]

Beneath its glossy surface, the Pax Romana was essentially a continuation of the strategy the Romans had employed against the Greek East over two centuries earlier: informal imperialism where possible and direct rule when necessary. Terrorization, bloodshed and conquest were justified in Roman imperialist ideology on the account that the world was distinctly divided into the civilized and the barbarian: the Romans had been destined by the gods to rule while other nations were bound to be subject peoples or slaves. The only way for non-Romans to elevate themselves and escape their natural predicament was to be accorded the gift of *humanitas* and Roman citizenship.[64] *Humanitas*, roughly translated as 'civilization', meant acculturation through the dissemination of Roman customs and values. But in order to spread its *humanitas*, Rome first had to eliminate all resistance and assimilate the more pliant segments of the conquered populous. Of course war was not the only instrument used to promote Rome's *imperium*. The provision of amenities in newly subdued territories formed part of the programme of acculturation: temples were built, entertainment was provided, and the children of the local elite were educated in Latin and the Roman way. One only has to think of the *Monty Python* sketch in which a group of Jewish resistance fighters ask 'what have the Romans ever done for us?' Back comes the answer: the aqueduct, sanitation, roads, irrigation, public baths, and peace.[65] Tacitus outlines this process in his account of the campaigns of his father-in-law, Agricola, in Britain. He notes that Agricola first accustomed the natives to a life of peace and quiet which he made manifest in the built environment. Unknowingly, he adds, the natives were 'enslaved' by Rome's *humanitas*.[66]

The complexity of Roman imperialism was a significant element in its attraction to Victorian and Edwardian analogists. Influential figures, such as Lords Curzon and Cromer, saw direct parallels between the type of problems the Romans and the British faced – particularly when it came to frontier warfare and treatment of subject populations.[67] There was recognition that British imperialism in India had followed a similar path: the East India Company had conquered much of the subcontinent through a policy of local alliances and by turning rival indigenous princes against one another. 'Divide and rule' was, after all, a motto derived from the ancient Romans. As with Roman provincial administration under the Republic, British rule was initially bedevilled in Asia by corruption and mismanagement; but in the same way that Augustus had centralized and reformed Roman provincial rule, in the second half of the nineteenth century London had succeeded in drastically improving governance in the dependencies. Like the Romans, the British were plagued with unrest around their vast frontiers; and like the Romans, delivering a bloody noose to unruly tribes was a fact of life under their empire.

Edwardian analogists were aware that differences between Roman and British imperialism outweighed similarities. Lord Cromer, for instance, noted that the Romans did not have to face the dilemma of assimilating races far removed from their own, because their empire had not extended beyond the Near East and North Africa.[68] Critics of empire, however, saw many disturbing parallels between British and Roman imperialism. Echoing Tacitus, J. M. Robertson condemned what he viewed to be a policy of war, plunder and exploitation under the sobriquet of Pax Britannica:

> Observe that the peace-making imperial life [...] without barbarian territory to steal and militant barbarian to shoot, the fabric of tinfoil glory passes away. Blessed are the powder-and-shot peacemakers [...] for they shall always go on inheriting

more earth [...] . Our sentimentalist, himself a barbarian, proclaims a Jehad against barbarism; but without barbarism to fight he is at a dead stand.[69]

The Victorians and the Edwardians did not universally subscribe to the Roman analogy. Nevertheless, Rome was an integral element of the British imperialist discourse. Proponents as well as critics of empire referred to Rome, and drew upon its positive and negative image, in putting forward their own arguments. To understand, and truly appreciate British imperialism, it is necessary to be aware that influential figures at the heart of empire were at least interested in the idea that Britain was Rome's successor state. We are told that one of Cecil Rhodes' favourite quotations was 'remember always that you are a Roman'.[70] Lords Curzon and Cromer published works on Roman and British imperialism; and leading academics and politicians – from Seeley and James Froude to Arthur Balfour and Alfred Milner – drew upon the echoes of Rome.

The world of academia today is more sympathetic to the school that sees only superficial similarities between Roman and British imperialisms: separated by 2,000 years of history, rustic Rome and industrial Britain operated under entirely different sets of conditions and within incomparable international systems. As with the study of any two 'imperialisms', there are analogous patterns and many particular differences. Nevertheless, classicists and historians of the British Empire have found comparative analyses of the two imperialisms a temptation too hard to resist.[71] This is understandable when one considers that both groups of scholars are essentially dealing with the same type of questions: whether the flag followed trade or whether commercial interests entangled the Roman and British states into wider and deeper imperialist policies; the role of the central government versus that of the money-men in Rome and the City financiers in Britain; and distinctions between informal and formal imperialism and between interventionist policies aimed at enhancing security and premeditated acts of aggression.[72] But ultimately Rome's influence in the history of British imperialism should not be sought in the actuality of events on the ground but rather as a notion within the broader context of the British imperial idea. The fact that the latest academic studies of British imperialism continue to highlight the significance of the Roman conception in Victorian and Edwardian thinking is indicative of the ancient entity's continuing resonance.[73]

While the Victorians and Edwardians were by and large receptive to the analogy with Rome, champions of US foreign policy tend to vociferously reject any such suggestions. The analogy has, in fact, become a device used primarily by Washington's critics.[74] The 'American empire debate' has produced a vast body of literature with frequent allusions to America's Roman-like imperialist tendencies. The characterization of the US as a 'new Rome' reached its peak during the presidency of George W. Bush, whose administration was heavily criticized for 'militarizing' US foreign policy. Negative depictions of America, as a 'new Rome', can be traced back all the way to the early twentieth century: in 1914 the Italian historian Guglielmo Ferrero drew parallels with Roman policy vis-à-vis the Greek East when expressing concern about US cultural imperialism in Europe.[75] The German writer Ulrich Kahrstedt was even more explicit in the 1920s, warning that US intervention in Europe was akin to the Pax Romana and would result in the subjugation of Europe.[76] During much of the twentieth century, parallels between Roman and US 'imperialisms' were an ever present, if peripheral, topic of foreign policy discussion. Yet it was the immediate post-Cold War period which drew greater attention to the subject as the US entered its so-called 'unipolar moment' of global domination – a development which some American commentators believed had not been seen since the heyday of the Roman Empire. The trajectory of US foreign policy after the events of 9/11 reinforced the analogy.[77] Characterizing the 'War on Terror' as a conflict between 'civilization' and 'barbarianism',[78] Washington appeared determined to extend its *Pax Americana* across the far reaches of the globe by promoting its brand of democratization, liberalization and Americanization.[79] As Rome had hunted down Jugurtha, a former client-king, so now America was unleashing its wrath against former collaborators Saddam Hussein and Osama bin Laden – provoking the latter to urge resistance to the 'New Rome'.[80] The popularity of the analogy between the 'old' and 'new' Rome has even inspired Hollywood to produce new films depicting Rome's frontier wars as an allegory for US operations in Iraq and Afghanistan.[81]

Advocates of US foreign policy contend that such comparisons are misguided and irrelevant: to draw parallels between the imperialism of an ancient empire and the foreign policy of a twenty-first-century hyper-power would be analogous to comparing ants with elephants. They argue that the US is not an 'empire' nor does it have a desire to become one.[82] The US does not conquer other nations, nor does it collect taxes, or 'maintain garrisons in every foreign territory where its interests lie'. That US policymakers have a fundamentally different goal from the Roman emperors; and though American culture is pervasive, it is foreigners who adopt it so that they can participate in America's extraordinary success.[83] The Roman analogy is described as old and tired: confusing 'hegemony' with 'imperialism' and drawing misleading parallels between a territorial empire and America's global influence.[84]

Although there is merit in these arguments, frequently the rejectionists are engaged with the wrong analogy: the Rome of the emperors rather than the Republic.[85] They also start with the assumption that Roman imperialism was a static, monolithic phenomena underpinned by conquest, subjugation and the creation of the institutions of direct rule for the purpose of exacting taxation. This approach ignores the fact that the connotation of the word *imperium* (translated today as 'empire') changed significantly over the course of Rome's history. *Imperium* in the Republican period was understood by the Romans in terms of control exercised through power rather than of territorial annexation or territorial expansion: it 'did not refer or even relate to annexation or colonisation of other states or nations, but to control of what others did, brought about by the exercise of Roman power and supported by Roman military might'.[86] Roman imperialism in the Republican period should, in fact, be characterized as a series of power-based relationships, the forms of which varied, depending on the different circumstances of those involved.[87] As such, it was not too different from 'hegemony' – the preferred word of American rejectionists. In addition, the rejectionists appear to confuse the possession of an empire with being an empire. Rome represented both: before 31 BC, the Romans had a territorial empire but were governed by a republican system; whereas in the last decades of the first century BC, the state was transformed into an imperial regime. In both periods the Romans were imperialistic – regardless of the type of government they had. So the claim that the United States is a liberal democracy does not in itself negate the case for American imperialism. Indeed, it is somewhat ironic that, in their effort to dismiss the analogy, most American rejectionists fail to see the echoes of Rome in their national footprints.

Conclusion

Imperialist powers often seek to justify their actions by drawing legitimacy from the principles of exceptionalism, altruism, paternalism and imposing peace in the framework of a civilizing mission. The Romans excelled in the rhetoric of imperialist legitimization, developing a language and ideology that was rich in its undertones of humanity, and one that was remarkably flexible in adjusting to the changing nature of their *imperium*. It is a tribute to Rome's legacy that a succession of great powers, including the British Empire and the United States, have deliberately or unwittingly drawn from its example in the vocabulary they use to justify their foreign policies. Incremental subversion, and informal imperialism, were among other attributes of Rome's exercise of hegemonic power which have echoed down through the ages. The Romans were one of the greatest conquerors in history, but it was their system of client-kings, and satellite states, which set them apart from other ancient and medieval polities and made them so relevant to our understanding of modern hegemonic behaviour. Of course differences between the Roman, British and American *imperiums* far outweigh any similarities between them. Yet despite the asymmetry of power, the echoes of Rome have been an ever present feature in British and American hegemonic thinking. The idea of Rome, as a precedent, has been used both positively and negatively by British imperialists as well as American hegemonists. Among both groups, some have endorsed the analogy while others have categorically rejected its relevance. Yet regardless of how the analogy is received, its persistence as a point of reference in the imperialist/hegemonic discourse is in itself indicative of Rome's resonance.

Notes

1 Words such as 'empire', 'emperor' and 'imperial' have been derived from Latin.

2 The Roman conception of 'just cause' should be understood in the context of a religious ceremony known as *fetiales* which sought to obtain the favour of the gods on behalf of the Roman state and its people. When the ceremonial rites were properly observed, the assumption was that the Romans had divine blessing and that their wars were just. S. Mattern, *Rome and the Enemy: Imperial Strategy in the Principate* (Berkeley, CA, 2002) pp. 211–22.

3 See W. Harris, *War and Imperialism in Republican Rome 327–70 BC* (Oxford, 1979); and V. Warrior, *The Initiation of the Second Macedonian War: An Explication of Livy Book 31* (Stuttgart, 1996).

4 Thucydides, *The Peloponnesian Wars*, V, pp. 85–113.

5 Cicero, *On Duties*, III:34 and *The Republic*, III.23. Also see Livy, *History of Rome*, XXXI–LXV; and Polybius, *The Histories*, XV–XLIX. Polybius' history was conterminous with Rome's hegemonic rise, whereas Cicero and Livy were commenting about events which had taken place decades earlier. It should also be noted that, unlike Livy, Polybius distinguishes between Rome's pretexts for war and its desire for empire.

6 Polybius, *The Histories*, XXXVI:2; also see E. Gruen, *The Hellenistic World and the Coming of Rome* (Berkeley, CA, 1986); and J. Rich, 'Fear, Greed and Glory: The Causes of Roman War-Making in the Middle Republic', in J. Rich and G. Shipley (eds), *War and Society in the Roman World* (1993).

7 Livy, *History of Rome*, XXXIII:32.

8 *Ibid.*, XXXIII:33–34; also see Plutarch's *Life of Flamininus*.

9 See Flamininus' speech (194 BC) in Livy, *History of Rome*, XXXIV:49–50.

10 Livy, *History of Rome*, XLV:18.1.

11 *Ibid.*, XXXIII:35.

12 See R. Morstein Kallet-Marx, *The Development of the Roman Imperium in the East from 148 to 62 BC* (Oxford, 1996).

13 For example, Jugurtha, ruler of the client-kingdom of Numidia, was to die in captivity after defying Rome in a protracted insurgency (112–107 BC).

14 Augustus (27 BC–AD 14) presided over the transformation of Rome's government from a republic to an imperial regime.

15 See A. Parchami, *Hegemonic Peace and Empire: The Pax Romana, Britannica and Americana* (2009), pp. 15–30.

16 Velleius Paterculus, *Compendium of Roman History*, II, p. 89.

17 Virgil, *Aeneid*, I, p. 278.

18 *Ibid.*, VI, pp. 851–5.

19 P. A. Brunt, 'Augustan Imperialism', in P. A. Brunt (ed.), *Roman Imperial Themes* (Oxford, 1990), p. 96; and P. Hardie, *Virgil's Aeneid: Cosmos and Imperium* (Oxford, 1986), p. 365.

20 *parta victoriis pax*. Augustus, *Res Gestae* XIII.

21 *Ibid.*, XXVI.

22 Tacitus, *The Histories*, IV:74.

23 Pliny, *Natural History*, III:5:39; also see Aelius Aristides, *Regarding Rome*.

24 Horace, *Odes*, III:3:53.

25 Plutarch, *Pompey*, p. 70.

26 R. Hingley, *Images of Rome: Perceptions of Ancient Rome in Europe and the United States in the Modern Age* (Portsmouth, 2001).

27 See R. Hingley, *Roman Officers and English Gentlemen: The Imperial Origins of Roman Archaeology* (2000); and N. Vance, *The Victorians and Ancient Rome* (Oxford, 1997).

28 Parchami, *Hegemonic Peace*, pp. 61–115.

29 J. Seeley, 'Roman Imperialism', *Lectures and Essays* (Boston, MA, 1870); Lord Cromer, *Ancient and Modern Imperialism* (1910); and C. Lucas, *Greater Rome and Greater Britain* (Oxford, 1912).

30 J. Bryce, *The Ancient Roman Empire and the British Empire In India: The Diffusion of Roman and English Law Throughout the World. Two Historical Studies* (Oxford, 1914), p. 22.

31 *The Times* (30 December 1898), p. 7.

32 Lucas, *Greater Rome*; Cromer, *Ancient and Modern Imperialism*; and Bryce, *The Ancient Roman Empire*.

33 Sir F. Younghusband, 'Our True Relationship With India', in C. Goldman and R. Kipling (eds), *Empire and the Century: A Series of Essays on Imperial Problems and Possibilities* (1905), pp. 613–14; and C. Lucas, *The British Empire: Six Lectures* (1915), pp. 194–215.

34 See C. R. L. Fletcher and R. Kipling, *A School History of England* (Oxford, 1911).

35 J. R. Seeley, *The Expansion of England: Two Courses of Lectures* (1886), p. 244.

36 Sir W. Laurier, 'The Dominion Government and Political Conditions', *The Canadian Annual Review of Public Affairs* (1906), pp. 540–1. Laurier, prime minister of Canada, was speaking as a proud subject of the empire and expressing a viewpoint widely held by British imperialists.

37 See Vance, *The Victorians and Ancient Rome* and Hingley, *Roman Officers*.

38 J. M. Robertson, *Patriotism and Empire* (1899), pp. 193–5.

39 J. A. Hobson, *Imperialism: A Study* (1902).

40 *Ibid.*, p. 365.

41 Parchami, *Hegemonic Peace*, pp. 59–154.

42 Joseph Chamberlain, 'The True Conception of Empire: Speech at the Royal Colonial Institute Dinner', in J. Chamberlain (ed.), *Foreign and Colonial Speeches* (1897), p. 245.

43 *Ibid.*, p. 244.

44 Indeed, it was the Victorians and Edwardians – much more so than the ancients – who should be credited for exaggerating the unparalleled peace and prosperity of the *Pax Romana* in order to draw parallels with their own Pax Britannica.

45 Seeley, *The Expansion of England*, p. 9.

46 See F. Adler, 'The Parting of Ways in the Foreign Policy of the United States', *International Journal of Ethics*, 9, 1 (October 1898), p. 3.

47 A view that dated back to the Founding Fathers. M. Sellers, *American Republicanism: Roman Ideology in the United States Constitution* (Basingstoke, 1994); and C. Richard, *The Founders and the Classics: Greece, Rome, and the American Enlightenment* (Cambridge, 1994).

48 W. Nugent, *Habits of Empire: A History of American Expansion* (New York, NY, 2008); and P. Griffin, *American Leviathan: Empire, Nation and Revolutionary Frontier* (New York, NY, 2008).

49 President Woodrow Wilson, *Address to the Joint Session of Congress* (3 February 1917).

50 Ronald Huggins quoted in G. W. Kirchwey, 'Pax Americana', *Annals of the American Academy of Political and Social Science*, 72 (July 1917), p. 47.

51 G. Lundestad, 'Empire by Invitation?', *Journal of Peace Research*, 2, 3 (1986), pp. 263–77.

52 R. Lock-Pullan, *US Intervention Policy and Army Innovation* (2006).

53 See, for example, M. Boot, *Savage Wars of Peace: Small Wars and the Rise of American Power* (New York, NY, 2002); J. Quigley, *The Ruses for War: American Interventionism Since World War II* (New York, NY, 2007).

54 For example, the US was found guilty of aggression by the International Court of Justice in the 1986 case, The Republic of Nicaragua v. The United States of America.

55 Pre-emption is permitted under international law only if the threat is considered imminent, overwhelming and leaving no other option but the use of force.

56 After the great German classical scholar, Theodor Mommsen (1817–1903).

57 T. Mommsen, *The History of Rome*, vol. II (1894), pp. 401–522; T. Frank, *Roman Imperialism* (New York, NY, 1914); M. Holleaux, *Rome, la Grèce et les monarchies hellénistiques au IIIe siècle avant J.C.* (Paris, 1921).

58 G. de Sanctis, *Storia dei romani*, 4 vols (Turin, 1964); and Harris, *War and Imperialism in Republican Rome*.

59 It also helps explain why the Roman veneer of 'defensive imperialism' was so readily accepted.

60 K. Hopkins, *Conquerors and Slaves* (Cambridge, 1978); Rich and Shipley, *War and Society in the Roman World*; J. Richardson, *Hispaniae: Spain and the Development of Roman Imperialism 218–82 BC* (Cambridge, 1996).

61 Triumph-seeking generals often used war to establish their reputation and acquire enough political kudos and financial capital to embark upon a political career.

62 See D. C. Braund, *Rome and the Friendly Kings: The Character of Client Kingship* (1984).

63 Tacitus, *Agricola*, XXX.

64 See G. Woolf, 'The Roman Peace', in Rich and Shipley, *War and Society in the Roman World*, pp. 177–9.

65 *Monty Python's The Life of Brian* (1979).

66 Tacitus, *Agricola*, XXI.

67 Lord Curzon, 'Frontiers', *The Romanes Lecture* (Oxford, 1907).

68 Cromer, *Ancient and Modern Imperialism*, pp. 18–19.

69 Robertson, *Patriotism and Empire*, p. 54.

70 J. C. Lockhart and C. M. Woodhouse, *Rhodes* (1963), p. 31.

71 P. A. Brunt, 'Reflections on British and Roman Imperialism', in *Roman Imperial Themes* (Oxford, 1992); J. Majid, 'Comparativism and Reference to Rome in British Imperial Attitudes in India', in C. Edwards (ed.), *Roman Presences: Receptions of Rome in European Culture, 1789–1945* (Cambridge, 1999); and A. Eckstein, 'Rome As A Pattern of Empire', *The International History Review*, 24, 4 (December 2002), pp. 844–55.

72 See R. Robinson and J Gallagher, 'The Imperialism of Free Trade', *Economic History*, 6, 1 (1953); P. J. Cain and A. G. Hopkins, *British Imperialism: Innovation and Expansion 1688–1914* (1993); and P. Freeman, 'British Imperialism and the Roman Empire', in J. Webster and N. Cooper (eds), *Roman Imperialism: Post-Colonial Perspectives* (Leicester, 1996).

73 D. Bell, *The Idea of Greater Britain: Empire and the Future of World Order 1860–1900* (Oxford, 2007); and P. Brendon, *The Decline and Fall of the British Empire 1781–1997* (2007).

74 See, for example, C. Murphy, *We Are Rome: The Fall of an Empire and the Fate of America* (Boston, MA, 2007); J. S. Nye, 'The New Rome Meets the New Barbarians', *The Economist* (23 March 2002); P. Bender, 'The New Rome', in Andrew Bacevich (ed.), *The Imperial Tense: Prospects and Problems of American Empire* (Chicago, IL, 2003); J. Freedland, 'Rome, AC ... Rome, DC', *The Guardian* (18 September 2002).

75 G. Ferrero, *Ancient Rome and Modern America: A Comparative Study of Morals and Manners* (1914).

76 *New York Times* (31 October 1920).

77 D. Harvey, *The New Imperialism* (Oxford, 2003); F. Schurmann, 'Like Ancient Rome, America Shifts from Republic to Empire', *Pacific News Service* (9 May 2003).

78 S. Mennell, *The American Civilizing Process* (Cambridge, 2007).

79 P. Rogers, 'If It's Good for America, It's Good for the World', *The Observer* (27 January 2002); R. Watson, 'Military Supremacy at the Heart of Bush Strategy', *The Times* (21 September 2002).

80 O. bin Laden, 'Resist the New Rome', *The Guardian* (6 January 2004).

81 B. Hoyle, 'Romans Recast as GIs in History Lesson for Iraq and Afghanistan', *The Times* (20 April 2009). The allegory has also been the subject of documentaries, such as BBC Radio 4's *America: An Empire To Rival Rome?* (2004).

82 G. W. Bush, Graduation Speech at West Point (1 June 2002).

83 K. Kagan, 'Hegemony Not Empire: How the Pax Americana Differs from the Pax Romana', *The Weekly Standard*, 7, 33 (5 June 2002).

84 G. Baker, 'A Quick History Lesson: America is No Rome', *The Times* (14 September 2007).

85 Kagan, 'Hegemony Not Empire'.

86 J. Richardson, *The Language of Empire: Rome and the Idea of Empire from the Third Century BC to the Second Century AD* (Cambridge, 2008), p. 62.

87 *Ibid.*, p. 45 and 116. The idea of the Roman Empire was really the product of the Augustan imperial regime.

Towards Cosmopolitan Perspectives on Empires and their Echoes? The Case for a European Framework

Berny Sèbe

In his plea in favour of British overseas expansion, the influential theoretician of empire J. R. Seeley pondered on 'a gulf which seemed as unbridgeable as that moral gulf which separates an Englishman from a Frenchman'.[1] Given the depth and longevity of mutual misgivings, it is hardly surprising that the two largest empires of the late modern era have so often been seen as opposite numbers. The benefits of free trade reaped by London, served by the industrial power and naval might of the pioneer of the Industrial Revolution, make an intellectually stimulating contrast with the protectionism of a continental state anxious to isolate potential markets from the nascent world economy for the convenience of its under-competitive manufacturers. The priorities of a society where trade, finance and geographical mobility were paramount offer a striking contrast with the agricultural preoccupations of a country reliant on land-based supremacy. The benevolence of British 'indirect rule' is, on the surface of things, countered by the story of oppressive Gallic 'direct rule'. British willingness to engage in devolution came in opposition to French stubbornness that led the cockerel into costly and futile wars. The list of commonly accepted contrasts could go on for a long time.

Yet this framework risks oversimplifying a vast array of attitudes, beliefs and practices in two empires that covered every continent in the world at one time or another. The British and French empires were among the most resilient and extensive enterprises in modern history, and evolved in a variety of guises in different times, places and circumstances. This chapter discusses the conditions for and benefits of an *histoire croisée*, or 'entangled history', of European imperialisms, using the British–French parallel as a case study and a springboard towards the definition of 'European colonial history' as a valid object of study.[2] It argues that a finer understanding of the Franco-British dynamics of imperial activity (based on attraction and repulsion at the same time) reveals the complex ways in which these 'echoes of empires' have played out since the signing of the Treaty of Rome. In particular, this 'archaeological' approach (in a Foucauldian sense) has the potential to reveal how these two imperial traditions combined to create the current 'European' echoes of empire which are at the core of the present volume. This transnational approach, I argue, would be a first step towards a 'cosmopolitan' history of European imperialisms and their echoes, which would improve our understanding of 'European' echoes of empire.

Marc Bloch suggested a comparative approach to European societies as early as the 1930s;[3] yet until recently comparatively few have considered the relevance of this research agenda to overseas possessions (an omission not unusual when it comes to colonial issues). For a long time, historiographies of imperialism[4] have tended to be centred on national case studies. Apart from a few early attempts to produce general overviews of European imperialisms,[5] some overtly comparative works,[6] and a few projects driven by the geographical proximity of contiguous imperial territories calling for comparison,[7] it is only in the last decade that we have seen highly convincing global histories of empire, such as the pioneering examples offered by John Darwin and Jane Burbank and Frederick Cooper.[8] Though the end of empire has prompted the most significant comparative effort to date,[9] it has not been extended to the post-colonial period, and to the reordering of the world which resulted from the end of European empires. Yet this chapter argues that understanding European imperialisms in a comparative perspective can be useful not only to make sense of the past, but also to understand present patterns in sociopolitical discourses and international relations. Drawing on recent developments in the fields of global and world history, and inspired by the methodological perspectives opened by the theories of connected and shared history, the present chapter posits that a pan-European approach introduces a much-needed new scale of interpretation. The phenomenon that saw Europe take control of the rest of the world has consequences still far-reaching and potent enough to require such a holistic approach, to understand how European countries negotiate their own identities (and that of the supranational ensemble to which they now belong), their national and collective projects, and their relationship with international partners – in the West and in the Third World.

Comparisons Within and Beyond Europe:
The Historical Perspective

In the first place, what can historians gain from comparing European empires, and particularly the British and French examples, more systematically? The imperial experience of these two countries covers the early- and late-modern periods more evenly than their Portuguese, Spanish or Dutch counterparts. France and Britain were among the first unified nation states of Europe, resulting from the gradual political and economic growth of a centre (England or the Kingdom of France) extending power over its immediate neighbours. This early pattern of nation-building, which gave them a competitive advantage and fuelled ambitions of domination, may be seen as a prelude to the overseas expansion witnessed in later centuries. Partly as a result of this early unification, obtained at the price of sometimes savage internal struggles, these countries developed the most administratively effective states, whilst at the same time a vast array of thinkers reflecting on the most adequate forms of government produced sophisticated political philosophies. In addition, the faith in progress that swept the two countries from the Renaissance onwards led to the development of naval and military superiority based on technical invention. Britain and France also shared a strong belief in the universality of their ideas (though the French were, famously, more vocal about this concept than their British rivals).

However, these imperial edifices were never monolithic. They were criss-crossed by competing ideologies which were compatible at times but clashed repeatedly at others. The complexity inherent in any imperial episode makes a transnational analysis of the practices and ideologies of empire all the more relevant in a pan-European context. What were the competing or complementary ideals, principles and goals that drove overseas expansion? How did they relate to the overall national project when it took its modern shape in the nineteenth century? What were the driving forces of these two empires? Their Achilles' heels? To what extent could they demonstrate agency in adverse conditions? The answers devised to such problems have left their imprint on today's nations, and this is where transnational approaches can illuminate present situations across Europe, at a time when national traditions are increasingly interacting and influencing each other.

Seen as dying disciplines in the aftermath of the waves of decolonization, the various national strands of imperial history in European post-colonial metropoles have regained strength in the last couple of decades and they offer precious insights into the 'past of the present' (to use a concept coined by Frederick Cooper).[10] Whereas the two strands of 'imperial history' and *histoire coloniale* have managed to survive whilst remaining essentially based around their national environments, time has come to consider the horizontal questions that could be asked across European countries, and to explore the 'in-between', the manifold instances of reciprocal or unrequited influence that contributed to shaping these empires as much as internal forces (usually foregrounded because they fit into national frameworks of analysis). Such an approach has the potential to highlight some surprising instances of collaboration between empires: for instance, recent research demonstrates that there was more cooperation east of Suez between the British and the French than has been traditionally acknowledged.[11] Such attitudes in an imperial context are all the more instructive as rivalry and cooperation are constantly at play on the European arena.

Revising the national(ist) undertones of the discipline of imperial history reflects the legitimate questions about the role of these historiographies in today's globalized and post-colonial world. Is the study of 'Greater Britain' or *'la plus grande France'* part of the national history of the two countries, or do they deserve a separate treatment? In terms of new historical territories to be explored, do we need to move towards the study of 'European colonial history'? And what would it reveal in terms of similarities and differences between these two case studies?

Shared Traits: Can We Find European Common Denominators in Imperial Matters?

The first evident similarity between the British and French forms of imperialism lies in their initial contingent development. In neither case do we find a unity of purpose giving systematic direction to the course of imperial expansion. The beginnings (or rebirth) of imperial expansion often appeared accidental. Merchants and privateers engaged in a race for riches brought their flags with them, and not always with the full backing of their rulers (contrary to their Portuguese and Spanish predecessors, the long-term structuring role of which is discussed by Jean-Frédéric Schaub in the present volume). Even when some form of initial official involvement was noted, grand designs were generally not on the agenda. In North America, the permanent settlement of Englishmen was not planned by King James I, and the growth of population of European stock at the time of the Crown also resulted from the initiative of dissenters. Similarly, fur trade, more than royal encouragement to export a community overseas, led to the founding of 'New France'. Later, the conquest of Algiers in 1830 stemmed more from French domestic politics than a genuine interest in expanding the French homeland on the southern shore of the Mediterranean: in the first two decades following the landing of Sidi Fredj, this encumbering legacy of Charles X's end of reign was hotly debated in the French chambers.[12] What then were the intentions behind territorial expansion, and the decision-making processes that presided over the destiny of empires on which, finally (and without any apparent grand design from the outset), the sun never set? The gradual addition of territories as opportunities arose (or were stimulated by influential colonially minded circles) explains why both empires look a bit 'like the booty of an obsessive collector whose passions had come with a rush and then gone with the wind, to be replaced in their turn by still more transient interests'.[13]

The absence of clear grand designs for empire-building is not the only similarity between the British and French experiences. Their phoenix-like resilience over centuries also distinguishes them from other, more ephemeral imperial endeavours. Both originated in countries enjoying considerable maritime exposure (an island and one of the two European mainland countries with direct access to both the Atlantic and the Mediterranean). Their preponderance was based to a large extent on their maritime clout: it is no coincidence that the British and French navies were the largest in Europe until a unified Germany increased its sea power, leading the two old rivals to join forces against the newcomer. London and Paris reacted with equal concern to the rise of Berlin because both capital cities had global ambitions, at least partly translated in empire. Having started in the Caribbean (with the sugar islands) and in America, both empires came to span the five continents, through a process of expansion into South Asia, followed by Oceania, Africa in the second half of the nineteenth century and finally the Middle East. In this last case, once again, they had conflicting ambitions in spite of the political rapprochement engineered in 1904 and put to the test during the Great War. Anglo-French relations between the wars were notoriously strained – a sign that the two countries had competing imperial appetites which put them at odds with each other.

Regardless of any value judgement, the imperial experience has become over the centuries a constitutive part of the DNA of the two countries (and this has remained true in the post-colonial era, with the arrival in significant numbers of populations originating from former colonies). National construction, in both its early- and late-modern forms, took place against the backdrop of imperial activity: as David Armitage has demonstrated in the British case, state formation and empire-building have been closely linked since the sixteenth century.[14] The debate as to whether imperial activity was strengthening or weakening the metropole was as prevalent in Britain as it was in France. If the former saw a protracted conflict between 'Little Englanders' and 'imperialists',[15] the latter had to face the anti-imperial feelings of liberal thinkers and also, between 1870 and the 1900s, of die-hard nationalists. In the early nineteenth century, the concept of 'empire' was unpalatable to many in Britain as it had Russian and Napoleonic undertones.[16] Scorn towards colonial possessions was a recurring trend in France, from Voltaire's famous lambasting of Canada in *Candide*[17] to Gustave Flaubert's ironical statement in his *Dictionnaire des idées reçues*[18] and Paul Déroulède's dismissal of colonies as an unsuitable substitute for Alsace-Lorraine.[19] For both countries, the answer to all this questioning about the usefulness of empire culminated at the time of the two world wars of the twentieth century, when their weight in a changing world was put to the test and they clung to their colonies in an effort to counter-balance the threat of power loss.

On the banks of the Thames and the Seine, the journey to the development of major imperial ensembles was long and winding. Since empire was embedded in the long-term historical structures of the two countries, the meaning of imperialism (theoretically and practically), and its relationship to mercantilism, evolved over the '*longue durée*'. If the British Empire, inspired by the liberal tradition, often seemed to promote free trade (for the benefit of British manufacturers, placed in the best position to sell their products on open foreign markets) in contrast with the French leaning towards protectionism (the most famous example being the *régime de l'exclusif* prevalent in the sixteenth and seventeenth centuries), there were also notable exceptions: 'imperial preference' and obviously the Corn Laws were in clear breach of free-trading principles and, conversely, Napoleon III was a partisan of free trade. These similarly oscillating commercial strategies between empires and metropoles, and between different empires, reveal long-term changes in the structural patterns of economic exchanges between European and non-European worlds.

On the ground, any inspection of the dynamics of imperial interaction reveals clear examples of hybridization and creolization in the British (at least until 1857) and French cases. The development of an Anglo-Indian community under the aegis of the East India Company echoes the birth of *mestizo* societies in the Caribbean (a reality for French, Spanish and British-dominated islands) and, later, elsewhere in the French Empire. Late nineteenth-century British fears of 'miscegenation' anticipated colonial anxieties elsewhere, in particular because the more advanced systems of communication prevailing in the British Empire allowed colonial authorities to bring European women to the colonies, making the *mariage à la mode du pays* less acceptable socially as colonial societies moved from an exclusively male environment to one trying to replicate the customs and atmosphere of the 'mother country'. The ambiguous status of hybrid communities has given rise to studies along national lines,[20] but a comparative approach of the administrative reactions and turning points in changing moral standards is needed to explain and contextualize European responses to alterity.

Far from making a comparative approach redundant, these similarities highlight the shared traits of the imperial experience (in its many hesitations as much as its resilience) as a European phenomenon, which has an undeniable echo on the shape and realities of the EU as a modern entity which has taken over part of the legacy of its member states.

The Teachings of Difference

The extensive similarities between these two empires should not lead us to overlook equally significant differences, which have to be taken into account when considering the echoes they have on today's European project. Having been solidly established as a result of the Seven Years War between 1756 and 1763 (which meant quite the opposite for its defeated French rival), and reinforced by the outcome of the revolutionary wars, the British Empire entered the nineteenth century in much more promising shape than its fledging Gallic counterpart.

Although both countries embarked upon seaborne imperial expansion, the geographical realities of the two metropoles differed significantly: while France was regularly drawn to annexation of contiguous territories, Britain's insularity from 1558 onwards and the Union of 1707 meant that overseas conquest was the only opportunity for territorial gain. The size of the national territory also influenced patterns of emigration and settlement. France had more space than the British Isles to accommodate demographic growth.

These differing geographical realities had major consequences when it came to imperial development. Whilst French governments faced constant shortages of candidates for emigration, sustained migratory flows facilitated the birth of 'British worlds' in Australia, New Zealand and, to a lesser extent, South Africa. Whereas Britain laid the ground for enduring dominions worldwide, modelled on the mother country, France repeatedly failed in her attempts to develop settler colonies (first in North America, then in North Africa). The only territory that could be compared to a 'white dominion', Algeria, ended with the almost complete repatriation of its inhabitants of European descent at independence and the complete loss of any form of political or symbolic allegiance (in fact, independent Algeria became one of France's most fervent challengers on the African continent, at least rhetorically).

Naturally, because the template for imperial control was generally based on exclusive paramountcy (apart from a few exceptions such as Egypt for a time, the Anglo-French condominium of the New Hebrides and a few treaty ports), the maps of imperial possessions complemented each other. Areas of success interlocked like the pieces of a global jigsaw, especially in Africa and Asia. In the interwar years, the British and French empires taken together covered 49,550,000 sq km – approximately one third of the earth's land mass – and ruled over around 550 million inhabitants.[21] Yet the French Empire quite clearly lagged behind its British competitor, especially in size and economic profitability.

The economic balance sheet of empire is one of the areas where the most blatant discrepancies between the two cases appear. The role of London as an imperial hub explains why as of the late nineteenth century, the City of London outdistanced Paris as a major international centre for trade and finance – two driving forces of the British Empire.[22] While liberal thinkers such as Adam Smith in the eighteenth century had contested the economic advantages brought to the metropole by imperial possessions, throughout the nineteenth and twentieth centuries the benefits of the British 'world-system' for the national economy were undeniable.[23] By contrast, the metropolitan benefits of the French Empire appear much more fragmentary and limited to certain constituencies. Jacques Marseille, who posited as his working hypothesis the profitability of the empire, came to the exact opposite conclusion: he found that, far from being an engine for growth, the French Empire actually hindered the development of the metropole.[24] The relative backwardness of French capitalism and industrial apparatus due to a late entry into the Industrial Revolution, the relative lateness of imperial expansion and some delay compared with Britain in finding and managing imperial resources may explain this significant difference.

Relations with the colonized were also an area of marked contrasts. Whereas the British, especially after 1857, were reluctant to embark on any large-scale anglicization of their colonial subjects, the French by contrast boasted of the wish to spread the universalist ideals of the republic, which requested them to 'Frenchify' indigenous populations, fuelled by deeply entrenched prejudices which were only strengthened by colonial practices which stemmed from, and perpetuated, a hierarchical vision of civilization.[25] These practices contributed to shape present-day reactions to the development of cosmopolitan societies, with the French colonial tradition of 'assimilation' making 'multiculturalism', as practised in Britain, much more difficult to envisage.

The Benefits of 'European Colonial History' as an Object of Study

The comparison between the British and French empires is a first step towards a 'European colonial history', which taps into several national historiographies to enrich our understanding of European imperialisms, as a national and as a pan-European phenomenon. For instance, can we usefully adapt some pioneering concepts about the British Empire to other colonial systems, in order to improve our understanding of their impact on the metropoles,[26] their modus operandi, their practices, their effect on the colonized? Can the 'invention of tradition', stemming from a monarchical context, be usefully applied to republican France?[27] Some theories commonly used in British imperial history (some of which brought about Copernican revolutions in the field when they first appeared) could well do the same when applied to (or at least tested against) the French case.

One of the most influential concepts of imperial history in the last half century, the distinction between formal and informal empire (the former implying direct military and administrative control; the latter describing the willingness to exert political, economic or strategic influence without seeking direct rule) is not as Anglocentric as its context of development seemed to limit it. Indeed, it can be applied to many empires which were willing to consider the vast range of options available to them to exert their influence. The famous assertion that 'by informal means if possible, or by formal annexations when necessary, British paramountcy was steadily upheld'[28] can throw light on the reasoning behind the early French conquest of Cochinchina in the late 1850s (Napoleon III wanted primarily to sign a commercial treaty with the rulers of Hue) or in the Niger area, where the French were content with indirect influence in the Niger Bend, until the progress of George Goldie's Royal Niger Company started to threaten their interests in the 1890s. Later, the extent to which French assets dominated foreign investment in Russia make it possible to interpret the Franco-British military support for the 'white Russian' generals Kornilov, Denikin or Alexiev as a shift from informal to formal intervention, in an attempt to preserve assets acquired during the Tsarist period and threatened by the breakdown of the Russian polity in 1917.

Other concepts which we owe to Ronald Robinson and Jack Gallagher could usefully see their range of application expanded. The 'official mind' of *Africa and the Victorians* is indeed a concept which depicts well the perceptions, intentions and ideas of imperial policy-makers, which are inherent in all modern colonial enterprise.[29] The 'collaborative bargains'[30] negotiated in any colonial encounter and the role of the 'man on the spot' (the colonial official in charge of a specific area) are universal factors when looking at imperial situations. Sidney Kanya-Forstner produced an early account of the role of the 'man on the spot' (local French officers presenting ministers in Paris with *faits accomplis*) in the conquest of the French Sudan, and although the role of colonial administrators has been the object of many studies and testimonies,[31] it remains under-theorized at a cross-imperial level. In spite of notable efforts, the history of local collaboration is far behind other areas in research on empire (not least because of the dichotomy between colonizers and colonized that has been prevalent in post-colonial studies for a long time), although the establishment of client–patron relationships was a major feature of imperial systems. Looking at these questions in a comparative perspective allows us to reveal the extent to which the powers of local bureaucrats vis-à-vis the metropole in the two cases affected their means of manoeuvre on indigenous affairs. More broadly, it also shows how macro-models of colonization influenced day-to-day political decisions.

The economic history of imperialism, which has seen major breakthroughs despite the unpopularity of economic history in recent decades,[32] is another field where comparative approaches would enrich our understanding of a global phenomenon. Although Cain and Hopkins' concept of 'gentlemanly capitalism' (which posits that 'New Imperialism' stemmed from the interests of the City of London's financiers and the British landed gentry) was shaped by a peculiarly British context, it ought to be tested on other leading financial centres in the nineteenth century – especially Paris and Berlin. Naturally, this would highlight national differences, but it would throw new light upon cases where France had significant economic interests at stake, for instance in Russia or in Egypt.

The link between financial interests and their imperial translation (either formally or informally) is applicable beyond the British case too. Neither Egypt nor Russia became a zone of formal influence, simply because informal paramountcy was long preferred and once formal control became the preferred option the moment had passed (or, in the case of Russia, the option was never really on the table). While in Britain there was palpable tension between partisans of a mercantilist theory and the 'free-traders', France was not immune to these doubts about the best way to safeguard its economic interests.

Economic questions would gain greatly from a broad-scale, international investigation: financial networks, which very often overcame national boundaries, are a clear instance of 'colonial circulations', where cross-fertilization, emulation, competition and transfers of experience shape imperial theories and practices.[33] They embody the prototype of today's globalized world, as Jacques Frémeaux and Gabrielle Maas argue in the present volume.

Although it is generally assumed that the day-to-day running of the empire was an area of blatant contrast between British and French traditions, greater consideration of the variety of situations prevalent in imperial contexts shows that direct and indirect rule took place in each case: Lyautey's views on the preservation of local administrations echo Lugard's theory of indirect rule, whilst the form of imperial government prevalent in some Crown colonies such as Basutoland or Singapore appears akin to direct rule. Jean-Loup Amselle has demonstrated that the traditional association of the French with direct rule and the British with indirect rule neglects many nuances on the spot: for instance, Governor General Joost van Vollenhoven used 'indirect rule' in Senegal in 1917, when he decided to appoint African intermediaries to exert colonial control and strengthened the powers of indigenous chieftaincies. Similarly, Félix Éboué implemented in 1942 in French Equatorial Africa the views he expressed in his book *La nouvelle politique indigène pour l'Afrique équatoriale française*, in which he argued for a greater use in the colonial administration of traditional chiefs.[34] A transnational framework of interpretation of imperial governance reflects vividly the syncretism and plasticity of imperial practice, often shaped by local prevailing conditions as much as principles of government.

In the cultural realm, the reasons for adopting a European analytical framework are countless, from the intellectual networks between imperial capitals and colonies (think of London and Paris), to the training strategies of indigenous elites and the role of religion in both metropoles and colonies, among missionaries as well as settlers and local populations. Building on the ever growing historiography on the London Missionary Society,[35] the White Fathers of Cardinal Lavigerie and French missionaries in general,[36] our understanding of Christian proselytism would gain from moving to a genuinely pan-European scale. Symbolical conceptions of imperial roles often had historical resonances that take on new meanings when they are put in parallel: from the identification of Pax Britannica to Pax Romana (which Ali Parchami analyses in the present volume) to France's projection of herself as the eldest daughter of the Church (with its associated duty to evangelize), and the Italian use of the Roman precedent to give sense to the conquest of Libya, the beliefs and symbols that sustained European imperial thrusts reveal a continent-wide fever when they are compared and contrasted. But it is mainly in the field of 'Popular Imperialism' that useful parallels can be drawn. The research questions posed by John MacKenzie about the British case[37] have been usefully extended to other European countries that saw the development of print capitalism coincide with imperial activity, allowing for a better understanding of how European populations developed to varying degrees an 'imperial mindset'.[38] Clearly, more work needs to be done on the ways in which empires 'struck back' in Europe (to quote Andrew Thompson) or how they influenced metropolitan imaginations, drawing upon existing works in each European case, and distinguishing the common features of this craze for empire, whilst highlighting national differences.[39] In an epistemological effort, the discipline should also endeavour to analyse across several European nations the construction of academic knowledge as part of the colonial process, and their reciprocal influence.[40] Following in-depth research on exploration and geographical societies at the national level,[41] the parallel between the development of geographical science, missionary zeal and the rise of imperial feelings and annexations across European countries still needs to be undertaken. It would look at the connections between these concomitant processes, and would also reveal the multiple instances of connection, exchange and cross-fertilization which sustained this pan-European movement: it is instructive to analyse how the activities of David Livingstone and Charles Lavigerie, or the reports of Henri Duveyrier, Carl Peters and Henry Morton Stanley influenced the expansion of the French, German and Belgian empires respectively, making the most of the development of print-capitalism across these different countries whilst influencing each other.[42]

Lastly, this multilingual approach opens new avenues in the study of colonial and post-colonial societies beyond Europe, allowing us to perceive better pre-colonial trends which have survived across several empires, and to recontextualize imperial disruption across regions which ended up in different colonial spheres. Studying the role of the colonized also needs to overcome linguistic boundaries inherited from the colonial empires, combining sources in various European languages and, as much as possible, testimonies consigned in indigenous languages (where a standard vernacular exists, or when oral testimonies were collected in due course). Anthony Asiwaju or Paul Nugent have shown through their work on colonial borders the benefits of a holistic approach which goes beyond the political and linguistic borders inherited from the colonial period.[43] Focusing more specifically on areas of contact between empires across borders would bring into relief the dense relations between colonized peoples from different empires, but also between European officers of various nationalities, and mutual administrative influences, cooperation and exchange of views across borders. Some wider phenomena, such as the ecological impact of European empires on indigenous peoples and territories, deserve to be considered globally rather than from the standpoint of individual empires – a perspective which had been opened by Alfred Crosby's concept of 'neo-Europes' in his seminal work on ecological imperialism.[44] The combination of sources in a variety of languages, and the holistic approach it allows, enhances our understanding of European imperialisms as a set of global forces, and our appraisal of their worldwide consequences then and now.

Undermining nationalist narratives of empire, a 'European colonial history' is a powerful means of making the singularity of each European empire much more relative. Whilst usefully reflecting variants, it highlights the shared processes which have conditioned the relationship of Western European countries with the rest of the world, and as such provides a useful analytical grid to make sense of the decolonization period, the post-colonial era and the concomitant development of the EU project, which contains in its genes the shared colonial past of its founding members as well as the early joiners.

Towards a Cosmopolitan Approach of 'Echoes of Empires'?

Because it happened everywhere more or less as the same time, the decolonization period has so far attracted the most significant attempts to compare experiences across national borders.[45] This approach allows us to consider the global context that prevailed after World War II, and to highlight the localized nature of responses to nationalist challenges, rather than the prevalence of any dogmatic and systematic approach. The ideological positioning of nationalist movements and their interaction with metropolitan circumstances at a given moment provide the basis for a supranational analytical framework that will reveal many similarities across empires. Though the British devolution process was marked by negotiation in most cases,[46] and therefore allowed the British Empire to be remembered as more enlightened than its French counterpart, a closer analysis reveals that broad-brushed understandings of decolonization patterns on the basis of the colonial power which had to face the insurgency can be misleading. The French decolonization process in West Africa matches the most successful examples of devolution in the British Empire,[47] whilst British reactions to 'communist threats', such as in the case of the Malaya insurgency, were not so dissimilar in nature from French reactions in Indochina. Bernard Porter argued that new developments in the study of the Mau Mau insurgency have demonstrated that 'Kenya was Britain's Algeria'.[48] At the end of 2012, newly opened secret files relating to the assassination of Mau

Mau prisoners at Hola Camp have revealed the unlawful use of violence (torture and arbitrary executions) in cases which had been covered up: colonial counter-insurgency practices were much more widely adopted across a variety of empires than had been previously acknowledged.[49] As is shown by these few examples, looking at the handling of demands for autonomy or independence from transnational frameworks based on categories of reaction (full integration, autonomy, popular consultation, political negotiation, military repression, or a mix of two or more of these) rather than national stereotypes, advances our understanding of this complex but exceptionally synchronic global chain of events.

But it is especially in the field of the 'echoes of empire' that a 'European approach' offers the most conclusive results. The legacy of European empires deserves to be considered globally rather than along national lines, especially because the post-colonial period has been so influenced by transnational developments and the rise of international relations influenced by the shared legacies of cultural imperialism.

A comparison across periods and nations underlines that early modern imperialisms left deeper cultural and linguistic legacies (e.g. English, French and Spanish in North America and the Caribbean, Spanish and Portuguese in South America) than their late-modern counterparts, which were more prone to spare local idioms, customs and religions. Yet late nineteenth-century 'New Imperialism' also left its imprint on post-colonial societies, giving rise in many cases to situations of bilingualism, which are one of the most vivid legacies of empire in many non-European countries. Certainly, no European power was ever able to produce a successful equivalent to the Dominions, overseas replicas of the mother country which proudly claimed their filiation after independence. Elsewhere, the graft was less effective, and in some cases did not survive the decolonization period: Algeria was perhaps the closest equivalent, but the experiment came to an abrupt halt with independence in 1962. Though the 'Anglo-World' was probably unique in its geographical extent, resilience and size (and it largely explains the triumph of English as the global language), the francophone, lusophone and hispanophone ensembles offer an interesting counterpoint to the British experience, highlighting a peculiarly European tradition of cultural imperialism – rarely equalled elsewhere, with the notable exception of religious languages such as Arabic.[50]

Indeed, the field of contemporary cultural diplomacy lends itself very well to a pan-European approach. A comparison of the dynamics and history of the Commonwealth, Francophonie and Comunidade dos Países de Língua Portuguesa organizations, their relationship to each other and with the imperial past of the former metropoles, reveals hitherto underplayed aspects of post-colonial European global influence akin to what Joseph Nye called 'soft power'. Transfers of experience were also key in these processes: for instance, the British Council was modelled on the Alliance française, and the latecomer Instituto Cervantes was certainly inspired by its two predecessors. Strategies to maintain a form of global power in spite of the loss of empire appears as a common denominator of post-colonial European countries; although there is clear competition between these various contenders, the diplomacy of language and culture appears as a key feature of the European relationship with non-European worlds in the post-colonial period.

At home, I argue that a proper understanding of the twenty-first-century 'echoes of empire' cannot be circumscribed to a national context; they take all their significance when placed in comparative perspective across Europe. Many major former European powers cling to their '*poussières d'empire*' (remnants of empire): when taken together, the British Overseas Territories (among them the Falkland Islands), the Spanish enclaves of Ceuta and Melilla, the French Territoires d'Outre Mer or the Dutch island territories in the Caribbean seem to attest a clear European pattern of long-distance territorial control, which has been rarely matched in terms of resilience and consistency. What do these territorial peculiarities tell us about the way these countries approach the post-colonial period? How do they compare with other EU member states (like Italy or Portugal) which lost all colonial territories between 1945 and 1975, out of choice or necessity? The management of post-colonial memory/ ies of the colonial past offers the most fertile ground for comparative work. Confronted with many unsolved issues resulting from their overseas ventures, almost all European countries have uneasily veered between amnesia, celebration and guilt when it came to acknowledging their colonial past. The ways in which the colonial past and decolonization have been discussed, taught at school and memorialized are best approached from a transnational perspective, as many similar debates over the place of the colonial past, and its bearing on the present, have been tearing the European sociopolitical fabric over the last decades.[51] The place of colonial history in the national school curriculum deserves a pan-European consideration, for instance when we saw debates sparked by the French 23 February 2005 law resurface in Britain as former UK Education Secretary Michael Gove (in post between 2010 and 2014) unveiled his plans for the new history curriculum. The memories of traumatic events linked to the colonial past are also too often seen solely from the angle of a national narrative,[52] which obscures the fact that, in many cases, it was a trans-European situation which reflected the reality that imperial metropoles faced comparable challenges against the common background of the Cold War.[53]

Such an approach has the potential to throw new light on the negotiation of the 'after-Empire' in the former metropoles, reflecting the common experience of international power loss, increased racial diversity and the corresponding renegotiation of national identities which these changes entailed.[54] The European project itself is a direct echo of this 're-ordering' of the world, insofar as it was welcomed as a convenient outlet for renewed global ambitions which were no longer sustainable at a national level.[55]

Exploring essentially the potential for Franco-British dialogues about the two countries' imperial past, the present chapter has argued in favour of a European approach to colonial history which would not only complement but also go beyond traditional frameworks of analysis based on national divides. In a short but insightful review, Tony Hopkins sensed that 'preoccupation with the national interest remain[ed] typical of scholarship [in Britain and France]', before adding that 'overcoming it is one of the great challenges facing historians who live in a transnational as well as a post-colonial world'.[56]

Historiographical breakthroughs made in the last decades have provided the groundwork for useful parallels which can enhance our understanding of a phenomenon which, whilst driven by national and patriotic agendas, took place on a global scale and was made more potent and more resilient by its sheer size and appeal. The desired end result will not be to indulge in an exercise of navel-gazing (looking at the singularity of the European imperial experience from a vantage point unifying its various strands), but to reach a scale making it possible to explore the multiple genealogies of the 'echoes of empire' which have contributed to shape, and still influence, the modern project of a European union.

The chronological developments themselves and the voluminous secondary literature that has been produced in the last 30 years justify the methodological effort required for the implementation of an '*histoire croisée*' (in the meaning that Michael Werner and Bénédicte Zimmermann have outlined) of European imperialisms, which would reflect *croisements* (cross-fertilization) at several levels: not only the many cases of reciprocal influences noted in the objects of study themselves, but also a cross-fertilization of the perspectives and the scale of observation.

Adopting a trans-European framework of analysis enriches analytical frameworks and reveals, among other things, processes of mutual influences, transfers of experience, and many other aspects of imperial 'in-betweens' which have hitherto been neglected. Ultimately, this approach reflects a move towards the 'cosmopolitan history of imperialism'[57] which is becoming inescapable to encompass and make sense of such a global phenomenon. Though significant progress has been made thanks to the agenda set out for global history, cosmopolitanism appears as a missing element in the history of empires. The study of empires, as well as their echoes, requires this notion if it is to reflect the lateral (between empires) and vertical (within empires) fluidity which characterized its object of study.

Notes

1 J. R. Seeley, *The Expansion of England* (1891), p. 297.
2 The concept of *histoire croisée*, translated here as 'entangled history', is taken from M. Werner and B. Zimmermann, *De la comparaison à l'histoire croisée* (Paris, 2004).

3 M. Bloch, 'Pour une histoire comparée des sociétés européennes', *Revue de Synthèse Historique*, 46 (1928), pp. 15–50.

4 Imperialism is defined here as 'the attempt to impose one state's predominance over other societies by assimilating them to its political, cultural and economic system' (J. Darwin, *After Tamerlane: The Global History of Empire since 1405* [2007], p. 416). 'Historiography' refers here to the body of historical writing and research produced about a specific topic.

5 Such as, for instance, J.-L. Miège, *Expansion européenne et décolonisation de 1870 à nos jours* (Paris, 1973); M. Ferro, *Histoire des colonisations* (Paris, 1994); or H. Wesseling, *The European Colonial Empires 1815– 1919* (Harlow, 2004) or, by the same author, *Divide and Rule: The Partition of Africa 1880–1914* (Westport, CT, 1997).

6 Such as, for instance, W. Baumgart, *Imperialism: The Idea and Reality of British and French Expansion, 1880–1914* (Oxford, 1982); W. T. August, *The Selling of the Empire: British and French Imperialist Propaganda, 1890–1940* (Westport, CT, 1985) or, more recently, M. Jasanoff, *Edge of Empire* (2005).

7 P. Gifford and Wm. R. Louis, *France and Britain in Africa: Imperial Rivalry and Colonial Rule* (New Haven, CT, 1971).

8 J. Darwin, *After Tamerlane*; J. Burbank and F. Cooper, *Empires in World History* (Princeton, NJ, 2010).

9 See for instance the pioneering article of T. Smith, 'A Comparative Study of French and British Decolonization', *Comparative Studies in Society and History*, 20, 1 (January 1978), pp. 70–102 or, more recently, R. F. Holland, *European Decolonization 1919–1981* (Basingstoke, 1985), D. Rothermund, *The Routledge Companion to Decolonization* (Abingdon, 2006), M. Shipway, *Decolonization and its Impact* (Oxford, 2008) or B. Droz, *Histoire de la décolonisation au XXe siècle* (Paris, 2006).

10 F. Cooper, *Africa Since 1940: The Past of the Present* (Cambridge, 1996).

11 See forthcoming work of J. R. Fichter, presented at the *Greater France* seminar series in Birmingham: 'Britain's French Empire/France's British Empire: Imperial Infrastructure East of Suez, 1815– 1869', University of Birmingham, 14 December 2010.

12 J.-J. Jordi, 'La Prise d'Alger', in J.-P. Rioux (ed.), *Dictionnaire de la France coloniale* (Paris, 2007), p. 29.

13 J. Darwin, *The Empire Project* (Cambridge, 2009), p. 2.

14 D. Armitage, *The Ideological Origins of the British Empire* (Cambridge, 2000). There is no equivalent study on the French Empire, although some background information can be found in M. Ferro, *Histoire des colonisations*, or J. Meyer, J. Tarrade, A. Rey-Goldzeiguer and J. Thobie, *Histoire de la France coloniale des origines à 1914* (Paris, 1991).

15 See for instance B. Porter, *Critics of Empire* (1968) or M. Matikkala, *Empire and Imperial Ambition: Liberty, Englishness and Anti-Imperialism in Late Victorian Britain* (2010).

16 A. P. Thornton, *The Imperial Idea and its Enemies: A Study in British Power* (1966), p. 1.

17 Referring to Canada as '*quelques arpents de neige*' [a few acres of snow].

18 'Colonies (our) – be sad when talking about them.'

19 'I lost two sisters, and you are offering me twenty servants.'

20 See for instance O. White, *Children of the French Empire* (Oxford, 1999); 'Miscegenation and the Popular Imagination', in T. Chafer and A. Sackur (eds), *Promoting the Colonial Idea: Propaganda and Visions of Empire in France* (Basingstoke, 2002), pp. 133–42; and E. Saada, *Les Enfants de la colonie. Les métis de l'empire français entre sujétion et citoyenneté* (Paris, 2007) on the French case, and D. Ghosh, *Sex and the Family in Colonial India* (Cambridge, 2008) on Britain. See also A. L. Stoler, 'Making Empire Respectable: the Politics of Race and Sexual Morality in 20th-Century Colonial Cultures', *American Ethnologist*, 16 (1989), pp. 634–60, and, by the same author, *Carnal Knowledge and Imperial Power: Race and the Intimate in Colonial Rule* (Berkeley, CA, 2002).

21 M. Thomas, *The French Empire Between the Wars* (Manchester, 2005), p. 1, and the size of the British Empire considered here is 14.3 million square miles (for a total population of about 460 million inhabitants).

22 For a comparison between London and Paris as international financial centres, see Y. Cassis and E. Bussière (eds), *London and Paris as International Financial Centres in the Twentieth Century* (Oxford, 2005).

23 See for instance Darwin, *Empire Project*, pp. 276–7.

24 J. Marseille, *Empire colonial et capitalisme français. Histoire d'un divorce* (Paris, 1984).

25 On assimilationist policies in the British and French empires, see S. Belmessous, *Assimilation and Empire: Uniformity in British and French Colonies, 1541–1954* (Oxford, 2013).

26 This approach has been developed in the field of 'Popular Imperialism' by John MacKenzie. See J. M. MacKenzie (ed.), *European Empires and the People* (Manchester, 2011).

27 E. Hobsbawm and T. Ranger (eds), *The Invention of Tradition* (Cambridge, 1983).

28 R. Robinson and J. Gallagher, 'The Imperialism of Free Trade', *The Economic History Review*, New Series, 6, 1 (1953), pp. 1–15.

29 M. Thomas, *The French Colonial Mind: Violence, Military Encounters, and Colonialism* (Lincoln, NE, 2011).

30 R. Robinson and J. Gallagher, 'Non-European Foundations of European Imperialism: Sketch for a Theory of Collaboration', in R. Owen and B. Sutcliffe (eds), *Studies in the Theory of Imperialism* (1972), pp. 117–42.

31 See for instance P. Boilley, E. Bernus, J. Clauzel and J.-L. Triaud, *Nomades et commandants. Administration et sociétés nomades dans l'ancienne A.O.F.* (Paris, 1993), among others.

32 See for instance P. Cain and A. Hopkins, *British Imperialism 1688–2000* (Harlow, 2001) and H. Bonin (ed.), *L'Esprit économique impérial* (Paris, 2008).

33 I owe the concept of 'colonial circulations' to Robert Bickers and Nicola Cooper, who coined the term for their July 2011 conference at the University of Bristol, where a version of this chapter was presented.

34 J.-L. Amselle, *Logiques métisses* (Paris, 1990), pp. 22–8.

35 See for instance R. Bickers and R. Seton (eds), *Missionary Encounters, Sources and Issues* (Manchester, 2000).

36 See J.-P. Daughton, *An Empire Divided: Religion, Republicanism, and the Making of French Colonialism, 1880–1914* (Oxford, 2006).

37 See for instance J. M. MacKenzie, *Propaganda and Empire* (Manchester, 1984), J. M. MacKenzie (ed.), *Imperialism and Popular Culture* (Manchester, 1986), *Popular Imperialism and the Military* (1991) and the 'Studies in Imperialism' series at Manchester University Press.

38 For a comparison of the British, French, German, Dutch, Belgian and Italian cases, see MacKenzie (ed.), *European Empires and the People*.

39 Operating a synthesis of work such as C. Hall (ed.), *Civilising Subjects: Colony and Metropole in the English Imagination 1830–1967* (Chicago, IL, 2002); M. Evans, *Empire and Culture: The French Experience 1830–1940* (Basingstoke, 2004) or the work undertaken in France by Nicolas Bancel, Pascal Blanchard and Sandrine Lemaire.

40 See for instance E. Sibeud, *Une science impériale pour l'Afrique? La construction des savoirs africanistes en France, 1878–1930* (Paris, 2002), or A. Southall, 'The Illusion of Tribe', *Journal of Asian and African Studies*, 1–2 (January 1970), pp. 28–50.

41 See D. Kennedy, 'British Exploration in the Nineteenth Century: A Historiographical Survey', *History Compass*, 5, 6 (October 2007), pp. 1879–900; F. Driver, *Geography Militant: Cultures of Exploration and Empire* (Malden, 2001) or D. Lejeune, *Les Sociétés de géographie en France et l'expansion coloniale au XIXe siècle* (Paris, 1993).

42 On Duveyrier, see for instance D. Casajus, *Henri Duveyrier, un Saint-Simonien au désert* (Paris, 2007). On Peters, see A. Perras, *Carl Peters and German Imperialism, 1856–1918* (Oxford, 2004). On Stanley, see T. Jeal, *Stanley: The Impossible Life of Africa's Greatest Explorer* (2008).

43 See A. Asiwaju (ed.), *West African Transformations: Comparative Impacts of French and British Colonialism* (Lagos, 1991), *Partitioned Africans* (1985) and Paul Nugent, 'Borderland Identities in Comparative Perspective: Chieftaincy, Religion and Belonging Along the Ghana-Togo and Senegal-Gambia Borders', in P. Hernaes (ed.), *The Role of Tradition and Modernity in African Political Cultures and Urban Conflicts: The Case of Ghana in Comparative Perspective* (Trondheim, 2005); 'Cyclical History in the Gambia/Casamance Borderland: Refuge, Settlement and Islam from c.1880 to the Present', *Journal of African History*, 48, 2 (2007), pp. 221–43; 'Border Anomalies: the Role of Local Actors in Shaping

Spaces Along the Gambia-Senegal and Ghana-Togo Borders', in A. Bellagamaba and G. Klute (eds), *Beside the State: Emergent Powers in Contemporary Africa* (Cologne, 2008).

44 A. W. Crosby, *Ecological Imperialism: The Biological Expansion of Europe 900–1900* (Cambridge, 1986). On the subject of the environmental history of empires, see also the forthcoming work of Corey Ross.

45 See for instance D. Rothermund, *Routledge Companion to Decolonization*; Droz, *Histoire de la décolonisation au XXe siècle*; Shipway, *Decolonization and its Impact*.

46 For instance: 'Britain's ultimate commitment was to responsible self-government [...] a goal towards which His Majesty's Government will assist them with all means in their power', D. Low, *Eclipse of Empire* (Cambridge, 1991), p. 227.

47 See T. Chafer, *The End of Empire in French West Africa: France's Successful Decolonization?* (Oxford, 2002).

48 B. Porter, 'How Did They Get Away With It?', *London Review of Books*, 27, 5 (3 March 2005), review article of D. Anderson, *Histories of the Hanged: Britain's Dirty War in Kenya and the End of Empire* (2005) and C. Elkins, *Britain's Gulag: The Brutal End of Empire in Kenya* (2005).

49 http://www.bbc.co.uk/news/uk-20543140 (accessed 5 March 2013).

50 On the concept of 'Anglo-Worlds', see J. Belich, *Replenishing the Earth: The Settler Revolution and the Rise of the Angloworld* (Oxford, 2009).

51 About the French situation see for instance R. Bertrand, *Mémoires d'Empire. La Controverse autour du 'fait colonial'* (Paris, 2006); P. Blanchard, N. Bancel and S. Lemaire, *La Fracture coloniale. La société française au prisme de l'héritage colonial* (Paris, 2005); R. Branche, *La Guerre d'Algérie. Une mémoire apaisée?* (Paris, 2005). About the British case, see A. Thompson, *The Empire Strikes Back?* (2005); K. Tyler, *Whiteness, Class and the Legacies of Empire: On Home Ground* (Basingstoke, 2012).

52 Such as, for instance, B. Stora, *La Gangrène et l'oubli* (Paris, 1996), or C. Elkins, *Britain's Gulag* (2005) and D. Anderson, *Histories of the Hanged* (2005), which are excellent books in themselves, but could be useful stepping stones towards more comparative work.

53 One rare example being S. Howe, 'Colonising and Exterminating? Memories of Imperial Violence in Britain and France', *Histoire@Politique*, 2, 11 (2010), p. 12.

54 Unfortunately, reflections on this topic have remained mostly national so far. See for instance P. Gilroy, *After Empire: Melancholia or Convivial Culture?* (Abingdon, 2004); R. J. Blyth and K. Jeffery (eds), *The British Empire and its Contested Pasts* (Dublin, 2009) or P. Ndiaye, *La Condition noire* (Paris, 2008), among many others.

55 See for instance K. Ross, *Fast Cars, Clean Bodies: Decolonization and the Reordering of French Culture* (Cambridge, MA, 1996) or T. Shepard, *The Invention of Decolonization: The Algerian War and the Remaking of France* (Ithaca, NY, 2006).

56 A. G. Hopkins, review of D. A. Low, *Eclipse of Empire*, in *Cahiers d'études africaines*, 33, 131 (1993), pp. 510–11.

57 A. G. Hopkins, 'Towards a Cosmopolitan History of Imperialism', in O. Pétré-Grenouilleau (ed.), *From Slave Trade to Empire* (Abingdon, 2004), pp. 231–42.

Between Memory, History and Historiography: Contesting Ottoman Legacies in Turkey, 1923–2012

Nora Fisher Onar

The Ottoman Empire is increasingly salient in Turkey, from the use of Ottoman referents in domestic and foreign policy discourses, to the wildfire popularity of cultural commodities inspired by Ottoman motifs. This has not always been the case. The first decades of the Turkish Republic, founded in 1923, were marked by a will to collective amnesia towards the empire on the part of nation-building elites who enacted a nationalist-secularist revolution that disdained the Ottoman–Islamic past. Only gradually have the Ottomans been rehabilitated in the public imagination. Yet today, 'Ottomanism', which I define as 'invocation of Ottoman precedents or legacies, real or imagined, to shape current-day trajectories', figures prominently in debates over Turkey's identity and place in the world.

In this chapter, I explore how rival visions of the Ottoman Empire and its legacies have shaped battles over national identity and the country's trajectory since the inception of the Turkish Republic. I begin by reflecting on the relevance of several challenges identified by the editors of this volume in the study of imperial legacies. These include the habit of naturalizing the experiences of the colonial, nation states of Western Europe as typical of all empire, and other, more diffuse Eurocentric reflexes. Such impulses obscure our readings of the Ottomans, not only because they distort Ottoman 'realities', but because they were internalized, challenged, and reproduced in complex ways by the founders of the Turkish Republic. The same is true for later challengers to republican historiography. On one hand, this presents an analytical challenge, because there is little consensus as to the nature of empire and its legacies. On the other, polysemy furnishes a site for analysis, where contested readings of the Ottomans, and their significance for Turkey, can be mapped over and across time.

To this end, I turn to a leitmotif across Ottomanist debates, namely, whether there was greater continuity or rupture in the transition from empire to republic. I show that the question constitutes a *lieu de mémoire*, a site where memory, history and historiography overlap in charged ways. This is because the transitional moment from empire to republic epitomizes the capture of collective memory by (republican) history and the rejection of an Ottoman role in the Turkish project.

This entailed denial of constitutive aspects of the Ottoman experience, above all, pluralism, public religiosity, and the will to rule far-flung peoples and territories. In its stead, the early republicans instantiated a secularist, nationalist project. The enterprise was based on European models, even as it affirmed Turkish independence vis-à-vis European powers – an ambivalent relationship with the West that amounts to an echo of empire in its own right. This rendering of history, in turn, piqued resistance from diverse quarters which sought to reinstate continuity with, and rehabilitate one or more features of the Ottoman period.

Understanding Empire and its Legacies: The Case of 'Ottomanism'

As Nicolaïdis, Sèbe and Maas observe, the literature on empire and its legacies has long privileged the experiences of the nation state colonial empires of the Atlantic and north-western Europe, namely Britain, France, Holland, Spain and Portugal. The emphasis on national experiences, they note, comes at the expense of a broader vision acknowledging the shared features of a phenomenon that swept through Europe at approximately the same time and against the same world historical backdrop.

One such phenomenon is the emergence of the nation state itself. For each of these entities underwent slow processes of state consolidation along national lines both prior to and in tandem with their colonial undertakings. This means that core national projects were relatively well established at the time of disintegration of empire. Thus, the rise of anti-imperial nationalisms in the periphery – though disruptive – did not shatter core identity and institutions. One consequence was that echoes of empire – when irksome – could be brushed under the carpet. In the case of Britain, for example, 'loss of an empire that covered one quarter of the globe' might have been expected to leave more of a 'political scar than it did [; yet, the] [...] country simply did not believe for a very long time – probably not until the 1970s – that the end of empire had fundamentally undermined its international position as a world power.'[1]

By way of contrast, the Ottoman Empire was a 'traditional', geographically contiguous, multi-ethnic, multi-confessional entity predicated on dynastic authority. Though it collapsed mere decades prior to its 'modern' counterparts, a drop in the sea of imperial time, it did so in the throes of a protracted struggle with nationalism in the core as well as periphery. This culminated in the categorical rejection of Ottoman pluralism, religious/dynastic sources of authority, and will to empire on the part of the founders of the unitary, secular, non-irredentist, Turkish nation state. The break – at once cumulative given the previous century of Ottoman reform, and sudden in light of the dramatic changes wrought in a few short years[2] – made a powerful imprint on the national project. This means that 'echoes' of empire have reverberated in rather more tumultuous ways in Turkey than in the former imperial nation states of Western Europe, where loss of empire was not as obviously constitutive of national identity and purpose. As such, it not possible to disaggregate the legacies of imperial collapse per se, from those associated with other aspects of Ottoman social and political life (e.g. its pluralism and religiosity).

A second and related limitation of extant prisms is their persistent Eurocentrism. After all, the Ottomans, like the Russians, Persians and Chinese, long served as the Other of the European collective imagination. This shapes how they are viewed, from the trope of the 'marauding horde from the East' that still inflects populist perspectives in Europe, to the prevalence of concepts and theories in the social sciences that emanate from 'the narrow experience of European states [...] in fictive opposition to the East'.[3] Ever since the publication of Said's seminal *Orientalism* in 1978, a growing body of scholarship has challenged constructions of Eastern empires as despotic, barbaric, and stagnant in contrast to the enlightened, civilized and dynamic states of the West. Yet Eurocentric frames of reference have proved resilient.

One reason for this, in Turkey at least, is because founding elites in 'non-European' imperial successor states often turned to European – and Eurocentric – templates to impose revolutions from above. Paradoxically intended to enable the states in question to preserve their independence from European powers, the hope was that westernism despite the West would enable the recalibrated state to thrive under Europe-dominated international conditions.

In Turkey, at least, this entailed a will to capitalism and secularism in a manifestly underdeveloped economy and religious society. This spurred critics, in turn, to respond in Marxist and Islamist idiom. Yet, constituted as they were in dialectic response to the foundational republican framework, such platforms displayed their own Eurocentric reflexes vis-à-vis the empire and its legacies. As with post-modernist and post-Islamist narratives today, this speaks to the imperative of teasing out the ways Eurocentrism inhibits, but is also constitutive of, the strands of debate, a challenge to which this chapter will seek to rise.

In short, commentary in and beyond contemporary Turkey on the echoes of empire must grapple with the challenge of what I call 'epistemological nationalism' and 'epistemological Eurocentrism'.[4] These frames circumscribe the interventions of professional historians, politicians and journalists, as well as engaged citizens on wide-ranging substantive questions. Topics include but are not limited to definitions of empire and legacy, and assessments – often emotional – of the roles played by Ottoman-era personalities. They grapple with the evolution of Ottoman institutions and governance, the vicissitudes of centre–periphery relations, shifting balances of power vis-à-vis European actors, the rise of nationalism in the periphery and the core, and the transformations engendered by these phenomena. A leitmotif that emerges across these discussions is the question of continuity versus rupture. It is to this theme that I turn as a site for mapping the volatile relationship between memory, history and historiography in Turkey today.

Lieux de Mémoire: Between Memory, History and Historiography

Pierre Nora famously coined the term 'sites of memory' (*lieux de mémoire*) to describe places where history seeks to colonize memory. Nora understood memory to be the cyclical, communal consciousness, a 'perpetually actual phenomenon, a bond tying us to the eternal present'. History, by way of contrast, is a 'representation[s] of the past' in which memory is captured, disciplined, and objectified by the archivist.[5] In effect, Nora equated memory, both individual and collective, with consciousness/identity, and history with attempts to monopolize consciousness/identity.[6] Thus, the historian – specifically the national historian of the nineteenth and twentieth centuries – sought to claim the consciousness/identity of the population for the national cause. This was achieved through the consecration of *lieux de mémoire* like official holidays, school curricula, museums, and monuments to symbolize national identity. This engendered resistance – the Bastille and Quatorze Juillet, for instance, were canonized only after protracted struggle with monarchist factions. Nevertheless, such readings came to constitute official History.[7]

In revolutionary contexts like France and the United States, but also Turkey, Russia, China (and to a lesser extent the Shah's Iran), attempts to capture collective consciousness by rescripting history necessitated the identification of new sites of memory. For, to paraphrase Renan, a successful nation is one that remembers and forgets the same things to forge a common past as the basis for a common future. That past could not be the recently defunct *anciens régimes*, the memorialization of which would undermine the status of the nation as the only game in town (and the nation-builders as the only game-makers). The impulse to reject the recent past was also steeped in the forward-thinking *telos* of revolutionary programmes predicated on Enlightenment or late Enlightenment logics. Nationalist historians accordingly sought out ancient golden ages, 'inventing tradition',[8] to give the present generation a sense of shared identity and purpose that circumvented, say, Bourbon/Catholic, Romanov/Orthodox or Ottoman/Islamic sources of solidarity.

To be sure, the process of enshrining specific stories and the selection criteria for inclusion and exclusion were eminently political. But the national historian's claim to possess the 'truth' was bolstered by the positivist belief – prevalent at the heyday of the nation state – in the objectivity of recovered knowledge. Especially in contexts, like France and Turkey, where history played a 'strong formative and didactic' role, and/or where the apparatus for political repression was well-instituted, revisionism was considered iconoclastic. For, as Nora[9] notes, the moment one seeks to unpack a site where national consciousness was canonized, then one no longer identifies unquestioningly with that heritage.

The second half of the twentieth century, however, bore witness to the emergence of a historiographical impulse that has yielded a 'history in multiple voices[...] [whose proponents are] less interested in causes than effects; less interested in 'what actually happened' than its perpetual reuse and misuses, its influence on successive presents'.[10] This rise of 'history in the second degree' can be attributed to a confluence of factors: democratization, the rise of new social movements, and identity politics, of globalization, the proliferation of information technologies; it is also a function of the post-modern anti-project of challenging meta-narratives. As a result, the nation's privileged position as the main mnemonic community has been challenged. Increasingly, actors that have been marginalized in national narratives are demanding a place therein, or constructing alternative histories.

As such, the capture of memory/consciousness by History has become a contest over memory/consciousness by rival historiographies. In this context, 'sites of memory' become contested 'turning point[s] where consciousness of a break with the past is bound up with the sense that memory has been torn'.[11] This compels commentators to search at the interstices of continuity and rupture for that which has been lost. The rise of Ottomanism in Turkey may be read through this prism, wherein memory of the empire was colonized by national history with a capital 'H' only to be challenged by alternative historiographies.

Continuity versus Rupture as Historiographical Battleground

The Single-Party Period

Like other late Enlightenment, revolutionary projects,[12] the early republicans sought to make a clean break with the *ancien régime*. They rejected the heterogeneity of Ottoman society, and the religious, dynastic and imperial dimensions of Ottoman governance. Yet, even as they adopted the nation state model of social-political organization emanating from Europe, they sought to affirm the fledgling republic's sovereignty vis-à-vis European powers. This imprinted 'epistemic nationalism' and 'epistemic Eurocentrism' onto the Turkish project (albeit with a nativist twist wherein nationalism was deployed to subvert Eurocentrism). The upshot was that the Ottomans and their legacies were either ignored or demonized. A story of rupture was enshrined, and 'echoes of empire' were denied any relevance in the new polity.

In search of alternative sources of collective memory, nationalist scholars like Ziya Gökalp, the founder of Turkish sociology, flagged the Central Asian Turkic/ish heritage as a source of egalitarian and 'democratic' principles.[13] Others, like Atatürk's adopted daughter Afet İnan, sought at the founding father's behest to recover traditions that would mitigate persistent racism towards Turks on the part of Europeans. The results were the 'sun-language' and 'Turkish history' theses, which rewrote history with Turks at the centre as the progenitors of the world's languages and peoples. Enshrined in textbooks and school curricula, a handful of historians like the Eurasianist Zeki Velidi Togan and Fuat Köprülü denounced the project – primarily on methodological grounds – piquing censure which would later inform oppositional politics.

A second if intertwined strand of republican historiography situated collective identity in pre-Islamic Anatolia. This was epitomized by the moving of the capital from Istanbul, the cosmopolitan seat of the Ottomans, to Ankara, the heart of the Anatolian plateau.[14] Here, the Anatolian Civilizations Museum[15] was founded. Exhibits sought to forge a direct link with the Hittites and other Anatolian civilizations, first in racialist terms, and later, through invocation of a 'homogenized and territorially defined culture'; as Gür[16] notes, this was part of the bid to construct a national identity that could claim historical connections with Europe (e.g. by labelling Neolithic sites as 'Turkish'). At the same time, and like the aforementioned 'sun-language' and 'Turkish history' theses, forays into ancient history sought to affirm authenticity and sovereignty in defiance of European prejudice. This attests to the complex ways Eurocentrism, its negation, and its reproduction were woven into the fabric of the Turkish national project and its denial of empire.

By the late 1930s and 1940s, republican rejectionism of the Ottomans had become less strident (or less stridently enforced). This may have been a function of the life cycle of revolutions, which tend to lapse after an initial militant phase into a Thermidor period concerned with law and order. At this juncture, historians like Ömer Lütfi Barkan suggested that if the search was for a glorious past, the Ottoman Empire at its peak was more attractive and accessible than ancient Central Asian tribes and Anatolian empires.[17] If this resonated with aspirations on the right to reinstate the Ottomans into the collective memory/consciousness, it spoke too to the growing sense on the left that something was missing from the official history. As iconic – and iconoclastic – communist poet Nâzim Hikmet wrote from prison: 'I want – from where, at where, towards where?'

The Multi-Party Period

With the transition to multi-party politics such voices proliferated. A heated debate in leftist circles spoke to Hikmet's question in ways that both negated and affirmed republican rejectionism. At one level, earlier, glowing assessments of the republican equation of modernism with westernism were unpacked. This amounted to a rereading of the ambivalence towards the West that is a legacy of the collapse of empire and foundation of the republic. At another level, left-leaning commentary of this period defended the sovereigntist principles upon which the republican project was founded (thereby affirming epistemic nationalism). As İnalcık[18] observes, this also tended to reduce Turkey's underdevelopment to the legacy of a 'backwards' and 'repressive' Ottoman land tenure system (thereby affirming epistemic Eurocentrism). This reflected, nevertheless, a burgeoning sense of continuity with the past that was inflected with the conviction that continuity was assessed through the prism of a progressive *telos*.

On the right, resistance to republican amnesia was more pronounced, though it too reproduced aspects of the republican story. For instance, intellectuals affiliated with the Hearth of the Enlightened (Aydınlar Ocağı) endorsed nationalism, but sought to redeem religiosity and the public expression thereof that had been a feature of Ottoman life. This view was echoed in the words of the spiritual leader of the Islamist National View Movement (Milli Görüş Hareketi, MGH), Mehmet Zahid Kotku:

> The core identity [...] and character of this wounded nation is Islam. Your main heritage is Islam and as Muslims you can heal this wound by listening to what our Turkish Muslim people want [...] an Islamic sense of justice and the restoration of their Ottoman-Islamic identity.[19]

Here, as in many other permutations of rightist revisionist historiography, the nationalist component of the republican narrative was affirmed. However, Islamic religiosity – considered a core component of the Ottoman heritage – was flagged as constitutive of the nation (thereby affirming epistemic nationalism whilst resisting epistemic Eurocentrism). To be sure, this entailed a claim to continuity over rupture.

Attempts to rehabilitate religiosity and a concomitant nostalgia for the Ottomans began to filter into the official narrative via the centre-right parties that dominated the political scene during the 1950–80 period.[20] They justified such policies by mixing liberal and religious rationales to dismantle aspects of the republican revolution considered repressive in a Muslim majority context.[21] Religion was introduced to the curriculum alongside a religious school (*imam hatip*) track in secondary education. Definitively dropping the Turkish History thesis, they reintroduced into textbooks accounts of the Ottomans that cast the empire in a positive light.

In the wake of the 1980 coup, however, it was not this liberal–religious synthesis but the nationalist–religious synthesis of the Hearth that rose to prominence. For, if the generals' purpose was to crush clashes between the extreme right and left that destabilized the country during this period, they were particularly hostile towards the latter. The upshot was that the 'Turkish-Islamic synthesis' (TIS) was enshrined as a bulwark against the perceived communist threat. As such, a corporatist, ethno-religious vision of collective identity was imprinted onto the post-coup constitution, harkening back to strands of Turkist/ish nationalism which predated the secularist revolution and establised a certain continuity with the Ottoman era.

Reactions to the TIS crystallized at a time when identity politics were displacing right/left cleavages as the idiom in which the battle over memory, history, and historiography was waged. At this juncture, an echo of empire that had long been muted became salient, namely a hankering for pluralism. Advocates included former leftists who had felt the heavy hand of the state and embraced political liberalism. Many allied with the liberal-religious, centre-right to cite Ottoman heterogeneity as a source of tolerance in social and political life. This fuelled, furthermore, a sense of commonality and purpose vis-à-vis the post-Cold War, but also post-Ottoman, Balkans, Caucasus and Middle East. Epitomized in the collaboration between pious politician Turgut Özal and lapsed leftist Cengiz Çandar – who coined the term 'neo-Ottomanism' – the fledging framework challenged the pillars of official history by claiming continuity with Ottoman heterogeneity, Ottoman religiosity and Ottoman involvement in the broader region. It drew sustenance from the economic and political liberalization Turkey underwent in the ensuing decades.

Republican cadres responded with a concerted campaign to affirm the narrative of rupture by returning to the horrific/heroic moment of transition: World War I and the 'War of Independence'. In such accounts, the last Ottoman sultan and his cabinet were vilified along with the occupying Allies. The 1920s and 1930s, on the other hand, were romanticized as an era when Turks became 'civilized'.[22] This went hand-in-hand with a renewal of the cult of personality surrounding Atatürk,[23] and the codification by 'republican nationalists' (*ulusalcı*) of their reading of the legacies of early republicanism into 'Atatürkism', a coherent ideological programme.[24]

A third camp to enter the fray was the MGH with its emphasis on continuities with the Ottoman Islamic heritage and vision of the Turkish Muslim nation as the natural heir to Ottoman leadership in the broader region. In the 1990s, the MGH-inspired Welfare Party (Refah Partisi, RP) swept to power in municipal election across the county. Attesting to the attraction to the Ottomans, they promptly instated celebrations of Mehmet the Conqueror's 1453 capture of Istanbul.

Later, upon coming to the helm of a national coalition government, the RP sought – or was perceived to seek – the reorientation of domestic and foreign policy from the republican pillars of secularism and westernism (despite the West), towards the Muslim Middle East. This precipitated manoeuvres via which the RP was harassed from office by republican cadres. Dubbed the 28 February 'post-modern' coup, this in turn piqued an appreciation, within the Islamist movement, for political pluralism which pundits were quick to rationalize through reference to Ottoman precedents.

In 2001, the moderate wing broke away to found the Justice and Development Party (Adalet ve Kalkınma Partisi, AKP). Self-consciously seeking to situate the party within the liberal-religious, centre-right tradition, the AKP has governed Turkey since 2002. During its tenure, it has displaced the republican establishment, an endeavour for which it initially drew support from liberal-leftists. Today, however, these former allies worry that pro-religious forces are seeking to install their own hegemonic reading of the past and its relevance for Turkey's present and future.

Historiographical Battlefields since the 2000s

In AKP-led Turkey, the 'echoes of empire' reverberate loudly. There are at least three approaches, heirs to historiographical narratives that emerged over the course of the twentieth century. I label these 'republican', 'liberal-leftist', and 'pro-religious', though boundaries between camps are permeable.[25] Each appropriates and/or challenges the early republican rendition of history to make its own claims to collective memory/consciousness.

Republicans continue to reject the relevance for Turkey today of the Ottoman era, including its heterogeneity, religious/dynastic sources of authority, will to empire, and perceived capitulation to European machinations. Echoing obfuscation of imperial legacies in the successor states of Western Europe, if concessions are made to claims of continuity, they tend to be in the form of acknowledgement that the cadres who built the republic came of age in the late Ottoman period. This entails some recognition of the Young Turk era (1908–22) as relevant to the nation's history. Otherwise, the empire is refuted as a site of 'darkness' as opposed to the 'enlightenment' brought about by the republic revolution. Pro-religious cohorts' nostalgia for all things Ottoman is lambasted in a similarly Manichean fashion. Such frames are infused with epistemic Eurocentrism, albeit also with a paradoxical will to align with Europe so as to repel Europe.

Likewise affirming epistemic nationalism, republicans castigate liberal-leftists as cronies of Western neo-imperialism for their endorsement of pluralism as an Ottoman legacy. Many within the republican camp worry that such demands threaten the unitary state, and its territorial integrity. These fears have been dubbed the 'Sèvres syndrome', itself a charged *lieu de mémoire* in the battle over continuity and rupture. Viewed through the prism of Sèvres, demands from within or beyond Turkey for, say, enhancement of minority rights, are equated with Great

Power support for Ottoman minority secessionism, and the 1920 treaty (of Sèvres) which authorized the redistribution of Ottoman territories to Allied forces, Armenians and Kurds.

A number of republican commentators are associated with Inkılap institutes at universities around the country which are devoted to the study of the republican revolution or 'transformation'.[26] A prominent spokesperson is historian, Sına Akşın, chair of the Atatürk Thought Foundation (Atatürk Düşünce Derneği, ADD) and author of *Turkey: From Empire to Revolutionary Republic* (2007). Another looming figure is journalist, novelist and popular historian Turgut Özakman whose bestselling tracts on Gallipoli and the Turkish–Greek war include *Those Wild Turks, Resurrection: The Dardanelles 1915*, and *Republic: The Turkish Miracle*. Özakman is perhaps the gatekeeper par excellence of republican historiography. This was evident in his serialized critique of the biopic *Mustafa* directed by a younger republican journalist who sought to portray the nation's founder in a more intimate and vulnerable light. For Özakman[27] this attempt from within the republican fold to narrate an alternative history was inadmissible, for there is no such thing as 'your or my Mustafa', just the 'one and only Atatürk.'

Liberal-leftists, by way of contrast, are critical of republican rejection of the Ottomans. They are drawn, above all, to Ottoman pluralism. Such a stance entails a challenge to the epistemic nationalism that has long framed the Turkish project. Liberal-leftist engagement of Ottoman legacies emanates too from a broader intuition that both continuity and rupture must be acknowledged. Thus, liberal-leftists also subvert the pro-religious tendency to eulogize the empire, and value features of the republican transition like the investment of sovereignty – at least, in principle – in the people. A case in point is historian Hakan Erdem's work on Ottoman slavery which corroborated neither a 'black' nor a 'white' vision of the past, earning him approbation from both republican and pro-religious quarters. For it destabilizes both orientalism and occidentalism. Erdem responded by lambasting studies of the Ottomans produced in Turkey for – inter alia – their ideological nature, in his book *History the Lame* (Tarih-Lenk 2008).[28]

Erdem, like many liberal-leftist historians, received at last part of his/her training abroad and subscribes to methods and a normative agenda that reflect post-modernist trends in Western historiography. A similar deconstructionist project has been embraced by liberal-leftist public intellectuals like Ahmet Altan, Etyen Mahçupyan and Ece Temelkuran. Such figures became household names when, in 2005, they organized a taboo-shattering conference on the Armenian question. This is one of the most dramatic issues at stake in the current debates over historical legacies, and a site of memory where official rejectionism has proved resilient.

The conference was part of an ongoing attempt to foster domestic debate on the aftermath of the painful process of 'unmixing of peoples',[29] that is of Ottoman Christians and Muslims during the last century of the empire, as well as the impact of the early republican will to homogeneity on Muslim elements like the Kurds. This has yielded intensive civil society activism, and cultural and intellectual production, as well as several official initiatives. However, the assassination of Hrant Dink, an outspoken Turkish-Armenian journalist, and the recent acquittal of most of the defendants in his murder trial, speaks to the entrenchment of resistance to 'confronting the past' when it comes to pluralism in general and the Armenian tragedy in particular.

Finally, pro-religious invocation of echoes of empire comes in at least two intertwined strands.[30] The first, heir to the liberal impulse in pro-religious historiography, emphasizes Ottoman tolerance, itself said to emanate from Ottoman Islam. In the hands of sophisticated commentators, this entails a concerted attempt to deconstruct the epistemic Eurocentrism that infused the republican project, rendering the Ottomans either invisible or barbaric. It is also a challenge to epistemic nationalism, or at least to understandings of the national project that are intolerant towards Other(s). In less able hands, however, it can yield readings which invert but reproduce binary representations of East/West. For example, Ottoman tolerance is often favourably compared in an ahistorical fashion to twentieth-century Western multiculturalism. In such renditions, the empire can be characterized, hyperbolically, as 'the last island of humanity', whilst Western instrumental reason is held accountable for all that is wrong with the world.[31]

A second strand of pro-religious Ottomanism draws on the nationalist-religious impulse of the Hearth and the TIS to extol the glories of empire, often fusing Turkist and Islamist themes. A number of its proponents have roots in the ultra-right Nationalist Action Party (Milliyetçi Hareket Partisi, MHP) from which they migrated to the centre-right and eventually the AKP. A case in point is Minister of State Cemil Çiçek who has called for Turkey to create a commonwealth composed of former Ottoman dominions. Such perspectives reflect a conviction that Turkish activism is welcome in the former Ottoman space, exemplified in the words of a commentator cited in the book *Searching for the Ottomans in Modern Times*:

> Who is making a Greek military attaché say: 'The fault is yours because you abandoned us'? Why do the Anatolian Rum (Greeks) who went to Greece in the population exchange complain that they were 'abandoned to the infidels'? The Hungarian historian cries at his nation's fate in front of the tomb of Gül Baba [an Ottoman saint]. The Lebanese historian who says 'There was Arab unity only at the time of the Turks'. The Yemeni says 'Together with the Turks went peace and plenty'. The Baghdadi who elevates the Ottoman governors to the status of saints [...] What yearning is causing the Syrian to hang a Turkish flag on his home, declaring 'The Turks are coming'?[32]

For all its aspirations to an heightened international role for Turkey, this sort of bombastic Ottomanism is mostly aimed at domestic audiences to bolster a sense of pride and continuity with the Ottomans at their peak. It is evident too in the penchant of the mass media for characterizing initiatives of Turkish prime minister Recep Tayyip Erdoğan in effusive terms as befitting a sultan, an image he appears to enjoy and cultivate.

A number of public intellectuals in both veins have backgrounds in fields like theology or journalism. Particularly amongst the younger generation, however, many have been trained at leading universities in North America and Europe, and/or benefit from the considerable resources being channelled into newly founded institutions like Istanbul's Şehir University whose rector was recently appointed head of the Board of Higher Education. In tandem with the economic and political rise of the pro-religious constituency, this group is well placed to shape the parameters of evolving debate. IT-savvy, they have generated intense discussion on manifold aspects of the Ottoman past in print and online fora.

A favourite topic, to be sure, is the vision of former professor, Foreign Minister Ahmet Davutoğlu. In a nutshell, Davutoğlu's *œuvre* is an attempt to dismantle the epistemic Eurocentrism that, he argues, has blinded Turkish policy-makers to the country's multi-regional potential. His approach also represents a challenge to epistemic nationalism in that he tends to think in civilizational terms. In this reading, Turkey is heir to Ottoman Islamic civilization in both cultural and geopolitical terms. This is said to give it a unique ability to engage other actors in the former Ottoman space, as well as serve as bridge between the West and the Islamic world. The pathway to achieving this is through soft rather than hard power, which may be realized through tools like bi- and multi-lateral diplomacy, intensification of trade, and cultural exchanges. This amounts to an aspiration to reconstitute the *Pax Ottomana* in the Balkans, Caucasus, and, above all, the Muslim Middle East.

Yet, the project is infused with the tension between the two strands of pro-religious Ottomanism. For, on one hand, invocation of Ottoman Islamic sources of pluralism and tolerance is inclusive, in a paternalistic fashion, of non-Muslim and non-practising Muslims in and beyond Turkey. On the other, the presumption of Ottoman Islamic moral superiority is exclusionary vis-à-vis such groups. This tension has yet to be resolved in theory or practice. Davutoğlu, however, is also a pragmatist. To date, he has sought to assuage anxiety piqued by his grand vision of continuity with the Ottoman Empire in quarters within and beyond Turkey by disavowing the term 'neo-Ottomanism'; he is also careful to avoid Ottoman referents when interlocutors are likely to be alienated (e.g. Serbs, Armenians).

Conclusion

In this chapter, I have shown that debates over continuity versus rupture vis-à-vis the Ottoman past constitute *lieux de mémoire*, sites where memory, history, and historiography intersect in charged ways. This is because the transitional moment epitomizes the capture, from above, of collective memory/consciousness by republican history, which rejected any role for the Ottomans in today's Turkey. In so doing, it imprinted what I have called 'epistemic nationalism' and 'epistemic Eurocentrism' onto the Turkish project.

This spurred dissidents to develop alternative historiographies, evident today in the lively debates between 'republican', 'liberal-leftist' and 'pro-religious' constituencies. If republican historiography remains more or less true to the early nation-builders' rejection of the Ottoman past, liberal-leftists tend to recognize elements of continuity from empire to republic whilst criticizing aspects of the imperial period. Finally, pro-religious actors emphasize continuity over rupture, and enthusiastically engage with echoes of empire via pursuit of pluralism, religiosity, and a role for Turkey in the geopolitical space once controlled by the Ottomans. This has gone hand-in-hand with a rereading of Turkey's ambivalent relationship with the West, itself an echo of Ottoman empire.

Notes

1 Hobsbawm identifies three areas in which the loss of territories in the periphery impacted the metropole: first, when the role and structure of core armed forces were affected by anti-colonial uprisings; second, when there was massive repatriation of expatriate core subjects back to the metropole; and third, when there was immigration from the former colonies. All of these are important phenomena to be sure, but only in the case of Portugal did they cause long-term disruption to core institutions and identity.

2 In the 1920s alone, the caliphate and sultanate were dismantled, the Arabic alphabet replaced with the Latin, and the Islamic calendar with the Gregorian. Shari'a was abolished (though it had never been the sole source of law in an Ottoman system predicated on legal pluralism; indeed, by the early twentieth century it had been displaced from most fields except for family law). Civil and penal codes were implemented on the bases of the Swiss and Italian models, respectively. The Islamic clergy and religious schools were disestablished and administration of religious affairs placed under a directorate answerable to the prime minister. Ottoman and Islamic attire (like the fez) was banned or (like the veil) was discouraged. Women were enfranchised. A population exchange with Greece marked the culmination of the 'unmixing' of the Christian and Muslim peoples of the Ottoman Empire which had been underway for at least a century.

3 K. Barkey, *Empire of Difference: The Ottomans in Comparative Perspective* (Cambridge, 2008), p. 5.

4 The two frames exist, moreover, in a state of tension, as nationalism, a European template, was adopted to assure Turkey's autonomy from European powers and thus to empower Turkey vis-à-vis Eurocentrism. Yet, due to the European provenance of nationalism, the project affirmed Eurocentrism by negating the Ottoman Empire. My use of the term 'epistemological Eurocentrism' is inspired by Beck and Sznaider's challenge to the 'methodological nationalism' which characterizes our social science apparatus, arguably blinding us to wide-ranging phenomena. See Ulrich Beck and Natan Sznaider, 'Unpacking Cosmopolitanism for the Social Sciences: A Research Agenda', *The British Journal of Sociology*, 57, 1 (2006), pp. 1–23.

5 P. Nora, 'Between Memory and History: Les Lieux de Mémoire', *Representations*, 26 (Spring 1989).

6 Nora's association of memory with pre-modernity and history with modernity may raise eyebrows today; its Eurocentrism can be eschewed by reading memory as consciousness rather than some

'ethnological slumber' from which newly independent nations are purported to have 'only been recently roused [...] by the rape of colonization' (cited in Heu-Tam Ho Tai, 'Remembered Realms: Pierre Nora and French National Memory', *American Historical Review*, 106, 3 [2001], p. 915).

7 J. Gillis (ed.), *Commemorations: The Politics of National Identity* (Princeton, NJ, 1994).

8 E. Hobsbawm and T. Ranger (eds), *The Invention of Tradition* (Cambridge, 1983).

9 Nora, 'Between Memory and History'.

10 Tai, 'Remembered Realms', p. 906.

11 Nora, 'Between Memory and History', p. 7.

12 Bobby Sayyid uses the term 'Kemalism' generically to refer to westernist, nationalist projects of self-orientalization undertaken by military-bureaucratic elites in the Muslim world. Since the person of Mustafa Kemal, later Atatürk, appears to have been invested in some but by no means all of the projects to which his name has been attached, I have sought here to avoid the label 'Kemalism' altogether, using instead the term 'republican'. See Bobby S. Sayyid, *A Fundamental Fear: Eurocentrism and the Rise of Islamism* (2003).

13 Z. Toprak, 'The Family, Feminism, and the State during the Young Turk period', in *Varia Turcica*, vol. XIII (Istanbul and Paris, 1991).

14 A. Çınar, 'National History as a Contested Site: The Conquest of Istanbul and Islamist Negotiations of the Nation', *Comparative Studies in Society and History*, 43, 1 (2001).

15 Originally called the Ankara Archaeological Museum, it was given its current name in 1968.

16 A. Gür, 'Stories in Three Dimensions: Narratives of Nation and the Anatolian Civilizations Museum', in E. Özyürek (ed.), *The Politics of Public Memory in Turkey* (Syracuse, NY, 2007), p. 49.

17 H. Berktay and S. Faroqhi (eds), *New Approaches to State and Peasant in Ottoman History* (1992).

18 H. İnalcik, 'The Meaning of Legacy: The Ottoman Case', in C. Brown (ed.), *Imperial Legacy: The Ottoman Imprint on the Balkans and the Middle East* (New York, NY, 1996).

19 Cited by L. Doğan in H. Yavuz, *Islamic Political Identity in Turkey* (Oxford, 2003).

20 The Democrat Party (DP), of which Köprülü was a founder, and its successor the Justice Party (Adalet Partisi, AP).

21 These included the rendering of the call to prayer in Turkish rather than Arabic, and the ban on Islamic brotherhoods.

22 Y. Çolak, 'Ottomanism vs. Kemalism: Collective Memory and Cultural Pluralism in 1990s Turkey', *Middle Eastern Studies*, 42, 4 (2006).

23 Y Yashin-Navarro, *Faces of the State: Secularism and Public Life in Turkey* (Princeton, NJ, 2002); E. Özyürek, 'Public Memory as Political Battleground: Islamist Subversions of Republican Nostalgia', in E. Özyürek (ed.), *The Politics of Public Memory in Turkey* (Syracuse, NY), 2007, pp. 114–37.

24 S. Akşın, *Yakin Tarihimizi Sorgulamak* (Ankara, 2006).

25 For more on the difficulty of labelling positions in Turkey see N. Fisher Onar and A. Evin, 'Convergence and Resistance: The European Dilemma of Turkish Intellectuals', in K. Nicolaïdis and J. Lacroix (eds), *European Stories: Intellectual Debates on Europe in National Contexts* (Oxford, 2010), pp. 294–314.

26 Of course, many associated with the Inkılap institutes, like all of the other strands described in this chapter, may embrace only a few, selective aspects of the ideal-typical discourse described here.

27 T. Özakman, 'MUSTAFA' – 1–8, *Cumhuriyet*, serialized December/January 2008.

28 The title was a play on the Turkish for 'Tamerlane', i.e. 'Timur the Lame' (*Timur Lenk*).

29 R. Brubaker, 'Aftermaths of Empire and the Unmixing of Peoples', in K. Barkey and M. von Hagen (eds), *After Empire: Multiethnic Societies and Nation-Building* (Boulder, CO, 1997).

30 For a systematic breakdown of the two strands see N. Fisher Onar, 'Transcending the "West"/"Islam" Binary: Turkey and the Post-Ottoman Mediterranean', in D. Bechev and K. Nicolaïdis (eds), *Mediterranean Frontiers: Borders, Conflict, and Memory* (2009), pp. 57–68.

31 M. Armağan, *Osmanlı: İnsanlığın Son Adası* (Istanbul, 2004).

32 Erol Güngör cited in Çolak, 2005.

The Russian Empire and the Soviet Union: Too Soon to Talk of Echoes?

Alexander Morrison

Russia is often considered to be an anomaly amongst the European empires, and its ambivalent status is further clouded by the 70 years of aggressively modernizing Soviet rule that preceded its collapse. Across all its former territories, elements of the Soviet and even the Tsarist legacy are still live political issues: tangled borders, new nationalities, patterns of migration, strategic imperatives and open warfare all function within the ghostly framework of the Russian Empire. This is so even though the destinies of its constituent parts over the last 20 years have been so divergent, ranging from EU membership for the Baltic States to a return to the personality cult in post-communist Turkmenistan. In part this is simply a function of the empire's vastness, and accordingly any assessment, however brief and superficial (as this chapter inevitably will be), must take into account the long process of Russian expansion, the different circumstances under which territories were incorporated into the empire, and their varied experiences of imperial or Soviet rule. As political circumstances within and outside the former USSR have changed, so, inevitably, have interpretations of Russian imperial history. Immediacy is what makes the Russian case truly distinctive: Russia's relations with the former republics are far from post-colonial, and the Russian Federation remains an imperial polity rather than a nation state. Accordingly, we are not dealing with 'echoes' of imperialism here at all, but with a cacophony of urgent and immediate legacies.

The Expansion of Russia

The course of Russian imperial expansion spanned almost 500 years, and the process of conquest and incorporation exercises a decisive influence over the imperial legacy today. It is useful, if a little over-simplified, to think of the Russian Empire in terms of a series of concentric circles of territory, each of which represents a different phase of expansion, and a process of more or less successful assimilation to the old Muscovite 'core'. Russia itself had been under the suzerainty of the Turco-Mongol Golden Horde until the mid fifteenth century, and the administrative and psychological legacy of the 'Tatar yoke' to the Russian state remains a matter of considerable debate amongst historians.[1] The beginnings of Russian imperialism are usually dated from the fall of Kazan to Ivan the Terrible in 1552, which saw large numbers of Muslim Tatars, together with pagan Turkic and Finno-Ugric groups of the Volga Region, incorporated into what had been a largely Orthodox, Slavic polity.[2] This was followed by the conquest of two other successor khanates of the Golden Horde, Astrakhan (in the Volga Delta) and Siberia. In the seventeenth century Russia would face a threat from the West, in the form of the Polish–Lithuanian Commonwealth, whilst the Crimean Khanate (under Ottoman suzerainty) on the state's southern flank remained a powerful and largely hostile force. Meanwhile Cossack mercenaries and fur-trappers swiftly spread through Siberia, reaching the Pacific coast at Okhotsk by 1641. The indigenous peoples of Siberia soon found themselves swamped even by the limited number of Russian settlers who flowed into the region in this period, and were often decimated by the diseases and alcoholism which they brought in their wake. Russian expansion in the Far East received a check with the Treaty of Nerchinsk (1657) which conceded China's control of the Amur valley; nevertheless the empire had acquired a vast tract of territory which gradually attracted peasant settlers, many from the persecuted Old Believer minority.[3] Stretching from Moscow to the Pacific, all these regions remain part of the Russian Federation today, with Russians in an overall majority in all but a few parts of northern Siberia. However, this apparent political and ethnic unity disguises enormous cultural diversity, some of which is formally recognized through the existence of 'autonomous regions' such as Tatarstan, Bashkortostan and Yakutia, whilst some other minorities such as the Muslim Nogais of the Astrakhan region do not appear on maps of Russia at all.

The emergence of the militarized, bureaucratic Petrine state from the late 1600s saw Russia consolidate and expand her position in the west, whilst also penetrating ever more deeply into Asia. Beginning with victory over the Swedes at the Battle of Poltava in 1709, over the course of the eighteenth century Russia acquired a vast swathe of European territory stretching from Karelia almost to the Danube, taking in the lands of ancient Rus' in Ukraine, the Baltic and most of Poland along the way. These regions were to present the empire with some of its most intractable problems in the nineteenth century. This was partly because their populations tended to be more prosperous and better-educated than those in Russia proper, whilst their political traditions were at odds with the principle of autocracy: it was in this region that the Tsarist state first had to confront the challenge of romantic nationalism.[4] With the annexation of what came to be known as the 'western borderlands' (*Zapadnye Okrainy*) Russia also acquired its vast, and in official eyes contaminating, Jewish population, and struggled to keep it confined to this 'Pale of Settlement'.[5] On the other hand, the empire found some of its most loyal servants in the Baltic German aristocracy, who played a crucial role within the empire's ruling elite until the Revolution.[6] The Crimean khanate finally fell in the 1770s, opening up the European steppe north of the Black Sea to peasant colonization as the Ottoman Empire was rolled back, making this one of Russia's earliest 'oriental' conquests.[7] This region was renamed 'New Russia' or 'Tauride', the first name reflecting its status as a new colony of settlement, the second its classical heritage as the home of Pontic Greek colonies, and both part of a process which saw a conscious elimination of earlier names which were reminders of the region's Turkic and nomadic past.[8]

Russian expansion in the Caucasus followed a slower and bloodier path. The black-earth and steppe areas between the lower Volga and the Caucasus mountains had begun to attract Russian peasant settlers from the early sixteenth century onwards, but until the late eighteenth century Tsarist power in the region was represented largely by semi-independent communities of Cossacks along the Terek River, whose relationship with the Chechen, Daghestani and Circassian mountaineers of the frontier was far from wholly hostile.[9] Peter the Great's capture of the Daghestani city of Derbent in 1722 proved short-lived, but in the early 1800s Georgia and Armenia were annexed, whilst Persia lost the northern part of the province of Azerbaijan at the treaty of Gulistan in 1813. The Caucasus Mountains lay athwart Russia's communications with these newly acquired territories to their south, but the subjugation of the mountaineers would occupy thousands of Russian troops for over 50 years. General Yermolov, in a series of brutal campaigns from 1817–27, espoused a scorched-earth policy which drove an ever-deeper wedge between the Russians and the inhabitants of the Northern Caucasus, 'contracting' the middle ground of cultural and economic exchange which had existed before.[10] His cruelty provoked a general uprising in Chechnya in 1825, which produced the greatest hero of the anti-Russian struggle, Imam Shamil, who was not captured until 1859. The war finally came to an end in 1864, when 300,000 Circassians chose exile in the Ottoman Empire rather than Russian rule. The legacy of the long conflict amongst the Russians was mixed: on the one hand it created a deep and long-lasting distrust of Islam, and brought about a loss of faith in the tactic of absorbing local aristocracies which had served Russia so well in the past, whilst the Muslims of the Caucasus were characterized as 'savages' and 'brigands', an attitude that persists to this day.[11] On the other hand the Caucasus became a vital component of the Russian romantic imagination, inspiring Pushkin, Lermontov and Tolstoy, for whom the mountaineers symbolized a freedom which did not exist in Russian society.[12] Overall, the European and Caucasian territories Russia acquired in the eighteenth and early nineteenth centuries constitute a more liminal zone, where states that are now independent blur into regions that remain part of the Russian 'metropole'. Whilst those who identify as ethnic Russians are usually a minority in these regions, many Russians would still consider the Caucasus, Ukraine and in particular Crimea to be 'ours' (*nash*).[13]

Finally we come to the most 'colonial' of Russia's territories in Central Asia, which were generally excluded from the civic structures of imperial Russia and seen as particularly 'backward' in the Soviet period. With the possible exception of parts of northern Kazakhstan, few Russians today would consider this region to be truly 'Russian'. The Kazakhs of the Inner Horde came under Russian sovereignty with the submission of Abu'l-Khayr Khan to the Empress Anna in 1731,[14] and after 1734 the newly created fortress-town of Orenburg became the centre of Russian influence on the Asian steppe. Despite resistance from part of the Kazakh Great Horde led by Kenesary Kasymov,[15] by the late 1850s a series of campaigns on the Steppe, and the construction of a line of fortresses through Kazakh lands had brought most of this region under Russian control. After a brief check during the Crimean War, the process of conquest continued apace, with the fall of Tashkent in 1865 marking the beginning of Russian incursions into the settled oasis region of Central Asia. Subsequently the Emirate of Bukhara submitted to Russian suzerainty and became a protectorate, whilst Khiva also fell in 1873. 1878 saw the beginning of the exceptionally bloody conquest of Transcaspia, marked by the massacre of thousands of Turkmen by General Mikhail Skobelev at the fortress of Geok-Tepe in 1881.[16] The empire's southern boundary assumed the form it would retain until 1991 with the annexation of the Kushka oasis in 1885, and of the Pamir region in the 1890s. From the mid 1890s the state encouraged peasant migration from the land-hungry regions of European Russia across the Urals to Siberia and south to the Asiatic steppes, and the numbers of Russian and Ukrainian settlers increased exponentially with the construction of the Trans-Siberian and Orenburg–Tashkent railways.[17] By the last years of Tsarist rule there were ambitious plans to swamp the indigenous population of the Steppe and Turkestan with millions more settlers, accompanied by a vast extension of irrigated agriculture.[18] While the demographic balance in the northern steppe was profoundly altered, there was no question that these territories remained alien – *chuzhoi*, and populated by *inorodtsy* – those of a 'different birth'.[19]

Simultaneously the Russian presence in the Far East was consolidated with the annexation of the Amur region and the founding of Vladivostok in the 1850s and 1860s, continuing into the early twentieth century with the acquisition of a warm-water naval base on the Pacific, Port Arthur, in 1897, the construction of the Chinese Eastern Railway to link Vladivostok and Port Arthur with European Russia via the Trans-Siberian railway, and the de facto annexation of Manchuria.[20] Humiliating defeat in the Russo-Japanese War of 1904–5 curbed Russian ambitions in the region, and in the long-term would prove of enormous significance to the other European powers, whose colonial subjects elsewhere in Asia were widely encouraged by this defeat of Europeans by Asians.[21] In this region, then, Russia had been forced to draw in her horns somewhat even before 1917, and today the *Primorskii Krai* or 'maritime region' around Vladivostok remains, for demographic reasons, one of her more fragile possessions.

Understanding Russian Imperialism

The question of how to describe and categorize this enormous polity, spanning two continents, at least fifty languages and three major religions, has exercised historians at least since Nikolai Karamzin wrote his *Memoir on Ancient and Modern Russia* in the 1820s.[22] Russia was a great, land-based empire, with its roots in the early-modern period, whose titular nationality was ill-defined and enjoyed no particular privileges, whose ruling elite was cosmopolitan, with a disproportionate role played by non-Russians, in particular Poles, Baltic Germans and Georgians. It was difficult, if not impossible, to identify a particular territory at the heart of the empire with the Russian 'nation', and at least until the late nineteenth century the core of Russian imperial ideologies was the ruling Romanov dynasty.[23] With leading noble families such as the Stroganovs and Yusupovs descended from Muslim Tatars, with colonists in Siberia 'going native' rather than the natives becoming Russified, racial boundaries seem blurred.[24] Class or *soslovie* (estate), not race, was what determined hierarchies in Russia. Above all, where was that vital distinction between metropole and colony, that barrier between the political, cultural and territorial 'nation' at the heart of empire, and the colonies at the periphery, so characteristic of 'Western' colonialism? Russia's identity is said to be inseparable from empire, her nationalism warped and weakened by it, her people even described as the chief victims of 'their' empire by some historians.[25] Even today one cannot really isolate 'Russia' on a map: the rump of the Russian Federation which was left behind after the break-up of the USSR, with its Far Eastern and Siberian territories and its patchwork of 'autonomous' provinces for different nationalities, is very far from being a nation state. All of this would suggest that if Russia belongs in any 'category', it is that of the early-modern dynastic empires which survived into the modern period, those of the Habsburgs and the Ottomans. Some influential cultural historians have argued that to equate Russian imperialism with that of the British or French is problematic and inaccurate, but there are also some striking parallels.[26]

In the nineteenth century, views of the nature of Russian imperialism varied widely both within and outside the empire. While G. N. Curzon could remark that the Russian conquest of Central Asia was 'a conquest of Orientals by Orientals', other observers such as Eugene Schuyler or Francis Skrine viewed Russian imperialism as simply another (perhaps more backward) manifestation of the wider phenomenon of European expansion.[27] Within Russia there was an 'Asianist' sub-strand of Slavophile thought among some intellectuals and publicists in Moscow and St Petersburg which presented the Russians as occupying a unique position between Europe and Asia, giving them a greater affinity with Asiatic peoples and thus (or so it was argued) a greater right to rule over them. Slavophile philosophers such as Nikolai Danilevsky and Konstantin Leontiev argued that Russia had an imperial *Sonderweg*, qualitatively different from that of the other European powers and characterized by greater tolerance and assimilation to Russian culture among conquered peoples,[28] whilst Fyodor Dostoyevsky famously saw Asiatic conquests as a means of escaping Russia's 'backwardness': 'In Europe we were hangers-on and slaves, whereas to Asia we shall go as masters.'[29]

However, the officials and army officers who actually administered Russia's (largely Muslim) borderlands in the Caucasus and Central Asia generally saw themselves as Europeans on a civilizing mission, frequently finding parallels with the British experience in India or that of the French in Algeria, whilst peasant settlement in the Steppe and Siberia drew forth comparisons with the opening-up of the American West.[30] Accordingly, by and large, although the diversity and peculiarities of Russian imperialism were widely acknowledged by Russians and outsiders alike before 1917, it was not considered entirely *sui generis*, and most Russian commentators were perfectly happy to see Russian expansion across Asia as part of the wider European colonizing and civilizing mission.[31]

It is probable that biological racism was less widespread and influential in the Russian Empire than in the West, but it was by no means unknown, and in any case this was only one of many markers of the difference and inferiority of subject peoples, racial, religious and cultural, which the Russians and other Europeans employed.[32] In the western borderlands, beginning in the early 1860s with draconian restrictions on publications in the 'Little Russian' (Ukrainian) language, the Tsarist state pursued a policy of what is usually known as 'Russification' in an attempt to create a larger 'national' core for the empire, although this policy of repression was never matched by any positive measures to encourage assimilation through schooling, of the kind that took place in France in the same period.[33] Russia may not have had as clear a distinction between metropole and colony as a 'classic'

European maritime empire, but there was an idea of what constituted the 'core' or 'European' areas of the empire, and this was reflected administratively in the distinction between areas under civilian and under military rule, those in which the liberal reforms of the 1860s were applied, and those where they were withheld.[34] There was no single concept of Russian imperial 'citizenship', any more than there was in the British Empire, and all the evidence of the last years of Tsarism suggests that in Russia's fledgling democratic culture the enjoyment of political rights and 'Europeanness' (if not Russianness) were becoming increasingly closely aligned.[35]

Nation-Building in the Soviet Period

The Russian Revolution of 1917 saw an avowedly anti-imperial regime inherit (and in many cases reconquer) almost all the non-Russian territories that had been part of the late-Tsarist Empire. To many it seemed as if the old empire had simply continued in another guise, and indeed that is how the Soviet Union was presented by many Western commentators until its collapse in 1991, with the Soviet 'Nationalities Policy' seen as nothing more than window-dressing, a cunning disguise for the continuation of colonialism.[36] However, the reality was more complex than this, both in practice and in representation. With the demise of the Baltic German aristocracy which had made up such an important part of the old empire's ruling elite, ethnic Russians certainly occupied if anything a more dominant place in the structures of Soviet power than they had in the Tsarist state: but this was true mainly at the centre. In the peripheries, where new 'national' republics were formed, non-Russians in the form of locally recruited party cadres wielded far more power than had usually been the case under the Tsarist regime. The early Soviet policy of *korenizatsiya*, 'striking roots' or nation-building, together with policies promoting mass literacy, industrialization and anti-religious campaigns were qualitatively different from anything undertaken in the Tsarist period, and are better compared with what was taking place simultaneously in Reza Shah's Iran and Atatürk's Turkey.[37] In its Asian borderlands the Tsarist state had been content simply to maintain military security and collect taxes, whilst in Poland and Ukraine it had pursued aggressive policies of Russification. In its early years the Soviet state instead strove to overcome the legacy of 'Great Russian Chauvinism' and shepherd its more 'backward' peoples through the national stage which both Lenin and Stalin thought crucial to the development of socialism.[38] This was reflected in the historiography of the time, which presented Tsarist imperialism as cruel, exploitative and negative, and sought to dissociate Soviet rule from it entirely.[39] To begin with, this was undoubtedly more than just rhetorical window-dressing: even in the traditionally rebellious North Caucasus many Chechens and Daghestanis were active participants in the early Soviet project.[40] Modern

Ukrainian nationalism is arguably in large part a legacy of the *korenizatsiya* policies of the 1920s and 1930s, which for the first time saw 97 per cent of Ukrainian schoolchildren making acquaintance with the literary form of their national language.[41] After World War II, the Ukrainian-speaking regions of Poland were incorporated in the Union republic, whose borders also included large numbers of Russian-speakers in the Don region, the formerly nomadic steppes north of the Black Sea with their diverse settler population and cosmopolitan cities (most notably Odessa) and eventually, in 1954, the Crimean Peninsula, purged of its Tatar population during World War II and now almost entirely Russian-speaking. However, the vagaries of Soviet boundary-drawing ensured that, whilst Ukraine now had a larger 'national' territory than any Ukrainian nationalist of the nineteenth century would have dreamed of, much of its population had never fully identified as Ukrainian in the first place, a legacy which continues to cause severe problems today.

Elsewhere in the USSR, the late 1930s and the outbreak of World War II also saw some significant changes: many elements of *korenizatsiya* were phased out, at least in the Western regions, although in most cases its nationalist legacy was far too potent to be entirely suppressed. The Russians were officially anointed as the 'elder brothers' of the Soviet family of nations, whilst among historians Tsarist imperialism was rehabilitated as having had a 'progressive significance'.[42] The post-war years saw increasingly large numbers of Russians being dispatched to other republics, though normally as urban workers or technical experts rather than as agricultural settlers, with the notable exception of Kazakhstan. In the post-Stalin era the autonomy enjoyed by local party structures was not entirely fictional (the 'great cotton scandal' in Uzbekistan in the 1970s was a clear enough instance of local independence, albeit in the form of corruption),[43] and officially sanctioned versions of 'national culture' continued to be promoted. The history of interethnic relations in the USSR in large part remains to be written. Whilst there were occasional outbreaks of tension, such as the Pakhtakor football riots in Tashkent in 1969, and the Zheltoqsan protests against the appointment of a Russian general-secretary of the Kazakh Communist Party in Alma-Ata in 1986, in general there seem to have been fewer racial tensions than before 1917. Intermarriage between Russians and Muslim peoples (with the exception of the Tatars and Kazakhs) remained relatively rare,[44] but close social relations were not uncommon: to give just one example, the otherwise ill-fated 'Virgin Lands' scheme in northern Kazakhstan gave birth to a strikingly mixed society where Kazakhs, Russian peasant settlers, Caucasian deportees and enthusiastic young Soviet volunteers rubbed shoulders relatively harmoniously.[45] That this coexisted with widespread racial prejudice among European Slavs towards Jews and Caucasian Muslims in particular is one of the many puzzles of Soviet history, although it seems that racist attitudes towards the minority peoples of the USSR were (and remain) more common among those who lived in European Russia than amongst the Slavs who lived in the cosmopolitan cities of Baku, Tashkent or Almaty, where they mixed with 'Asiatics' on a daily basis.[46]

The Fall of Communism and After

The collapse of the USSR in 1991 saw a scramble by historians and political scientists to explain the demise of the beast they had studied for so long, which in many cases led them to come to new conclusions about the nature of Soviet rule. Some espoused the 'deep-freeze' theory – namely that the 'prison of peoples' which was late-Tsarist Russia had remained in suspended animation throughout the 70 years of Soviet rule, before latent nationalist passions were finally unleashed by the crumbling of central authority.[47] The conflicts which immediately emerged in Tajikistan and the Caucasus were certainly a result of the slackening of central control, although in most cases their roots lay in Soviet-era disputes over borders and access to state patronage rather than in events before 1917. In the absence of mediation from Moscow, war broke out between Azerbaijan and Armenia over the Nagorno-Karabagh enclave, whilst Georgia sought to establish full and direct control over the autonomous provinces of Abkhazia and South Ossetia which fell within its borders, with disastrous results. However, it soon became clear that whilst for the Warsaw Pact countries and the Baltic States independence and freedom from Moscow's control could not come soon enough,[48] the other constituent republics of the USSR were much more ambivalent about leaving it, and thus losing the patronage and arbitration of Moscow. The Central Asian republics voted in referenda to maintain the USSR, whilst their leaders almost without exception supported the hardline coup of 1991. Furthermore, many of the 'nationalities' in these regions had not even existed before 1917, and could hardly have 're-emerged' in 1991: the 'Uzbeks' were clearly at least in part a creation of the Soviet era.[49] If anything it was Russian nationalism which destroyed the USSR, as many Russians (not entirely wrongly) saw their republic as subsidizing all the others. The Soviet Union collapsed when Boris Yeltsin succeeded in investing the hollow structures of the Russian Soviet Socialist Republic with real power.[50]

Since then, Russian nationalism has been exploited heavily by the Putin and Medvedev regimes, whilst racism towards migrants from the former Soviet republics of the Caucasus and Central Asia and paranoia regarding Russia's neighbours are increasingly common.[51] This is reflected in much contemporary Russian historiography, where Russia's imperial past is regarded with a mixture of nostalgia, self-righteousness and outright jingoism. A figure such as General Mikhail Skobelev, who was excoriated in Soviet historiography, can now be rehabilitated as a 'Hero of Empire'.[52] Thinly disguised as 'Sobolev', the general has also figured prominently in two of the bestselling Boris Akunin novels, one of which has been turned into a film whose portrayal of the Ottomans is ripe with old-fashioned 'orientalism'.[53] A new statue of Skobelev has apparently been planned for Il'in square in Moscow, to replace the original equestrian statue erected on nearby Tverskaya Street in 1912 and destroyed by the Bolsheviks, although it is not clear if it will ever be built.[54] New statues of General Yermolov, the 'hammer of the Caucasus', have appeared in the North Caucasian towns of Stavropol, Mineralnye Vody and Pyatigorsk, whilst Orenburg also has a new monument to General V. A. Perovsky, who played a leading role in the conquest of Central Asia.[55]

Since 1991, the former constituent republics of the USSR have become nation states, but in most cases their 'new' identities rest firmly on Soviet foundations. This is particularly true in Central Asia, whose republics were carved out of the territories of Bukhara, Khiva and Russian Turkestan in the 1920s, in a complex process of negotiation between the communist leadership in Moscow and local party cadres. This was not, as many Western commentators believed, the product of a deliberate Soviet policy of 'divide and rule' and creation of minorities. Instead it was partly the inevitable product of an attempt to apply ideas of the nation derived from nineteenth-century Europe to a region where this category made little sense, partly a consequence of relying on the categories used by late-Tsarist ethnographers and census-takers, and partly the result of local horse-trading.[56] Whilst the new republics had a territorial form (which continued to shift until the 1980s as boundaries were repeatedly tinkered with) their borders were fairly notional: it was the Soviet State which restricted (and ordered) the movement of labour and the patterns of growth and settlement, not the existence of borders. Since independence the hardening of the borders between the five republics has caused numerous problems, particularly in areas where they are closely intermeshed and pay scant attention to geographical features, most notably the Ferghana Valley.[57] For instance, the region around the city of Khujand (Leninabad in the Soviet era), the northern 'bump' of Tajikistan, is cut off from the rest of the country by a range of mountains, and in the Soviet era was closely integrated both economically and socially with the surrounding regions of Uzbekistan and Kyrgyzstan. After independence Khujand found itself hemmed in on all sides by newly impermeable borders, with the only outlet a dangerous mountain road to the south. Whilst communications with Dushanbe have now improved, continued bad relations with Uzbekistan ensure that the region remains cut off from its economic hinterland, whilst modern Tajik nationalist ideology, which emphasizes both the Persian language and 'Aryan' ethnicity, is particularly alien to this mixed, bilingual semi-enclave.[58] Meanwhile, at the eastern end of the Ferghana valley, many Uzbek families are now divided by the frontier between Uzbekistan and Kyrgyzstan, something revealed clearly when many of those who fled the 2010 pogroms in Osh found shelter with relatives on the Uzbek side of the frontier.[59] In each case, these borders were of little or no importance in the Soviet era, and it was only accidentally that they came to define the limits of sovereignty after 1991. Over the coming years they promise to be one of empire's more intractable 'echoes', as there are few signs that they will become more open or relaxed.

With the exception of Kyrgyzstan, and despite the civil war in Tajikistan, the forms of government of the Central Asian republics show considerable (though not complete) continuity with the Soviet period. The personnel are in some cases the same: Islam Karimov in Uzbekistan, Nursultan Nazarbayev in Kazakhstan and, until his death, Saparmurat Niyazov in Turkmenistan were all the first secretaries of their republics' respective communist parties before 1991. However, all of these countries, except Turkmenistan, are much more open to outside influences than they were in the Soviet period, and the work of nation and state-building continues much more actively than before, often with brutally repressive results.[60] This mixture of change and continuity is reflected in historiography. Despite ritualistic denunciations of Russian colonialism in some new historical work, and Karimov's oft-quoted opinion that 'I do not consider the history written in the Soviet era to be history',[61] the national narratives of the new republics are based largely on those created in the official histories of the Soviet period, complete with spurious theories of ethnogenesis, government-sanctioned 'national heroes', and certain canonical texts in which the culture of the nation is said to reside. The additions normally consist of more monarchical and militaristic characters who were frowned on in the Soviet period (such as Amir Timur in Uzbekistan), and a rehabilitation of the Muslim reformist movements which appeared in the region in the late nineteenth century (denounced as 'bourgeois' in the Soviet period). Nowhere is this truer than in Uzbekistan, where such few historical publications as do emerge follow Karimov's injunction, invariably invoked in the introduction to modern Uzbek historical publications, that 'Historical memory, the restoration of an objective and truthful history of the nation and its territory is given an extremely important place in the revival and growth of national self-consciousness and national pride'.[62] In Uzbekistan history is relentlessly instrumentalized for the purpose of constructing a stronger 'Uzbek' identity: school textbooks portray the Khwarazmshahs, Tamerlane, Babur, Emir Sayyid Muzaffar of Bukhara, the Jadid Reformers and the post-1917 Basmachi as an unbroken line of heroic 'Uzbek' nationalists, engaged in a struggle for 'self-determination'.[63] Access to the national archives has become steadily more restricted to those whose output the regime feels it can control, whilst archival documents are selectively employed to create a narrative of national martyrdom in the Tsarist and Soviet periods.[64] Even academic writing normally echoes older Soviet scholarship on the ethnogenesis of the Uzbek nation, glossing over the complexity of Central Asian society before the national demarcations of 1924, and the degree to which modern Central Asian national identities (particularly 'Uzbek'), far from having been 'suppressed' in the Soviet period, are at least in part a product of early Soviet nation-building policies.[65] The dangers of taking a constructivist approach to the complex history of Uzbek identity were revealed clearly in the furore surrounding the publication of Alisher Ilkhamov's *Ethnic Atlas of Uzbekistan* in 2002, which was heavily criticized by historians close to the Uzbek Government and subsequently banned.[66]

Russian scholars working in Central Asia have responded with anger and bewilderment to suggestions in recent historiography from the region that the Tsarist or Soviet regimes could be considered 'colonial'.[67] In the Soviet period, 'colonialism' and 'imperialism' were things only bourgeois powers were capable of: ergo the Soviet Union – and from the 1940s, by a curious process of extension, its Tsarist predecessor – could not be a 'colonial' power. This strand of thinking became entangled with older Slavophile ideas about the 'natural' and 'organic' nature of Russian expansion until for many historians there emerged a firm belief that the Russian people themselves are not capable of being 'colonial' or racist: a belief which coexists with irrefutable evidence of racism and hate crimes against Caucasians and Central Asians in Russian cities.[68]

In Ukraine, Azerbaijan and Georgia there is now a celebration of the brief periods of 'national independence' enjoyed by these regions between 1917 and *c.*1920–1; the Baltic republics meanwhile romanticize the authoritarian regimes which ruled them throughout most of the interwar period, and have fierce ongoing disputes with Russia over the interpretation and memorialization of World War II, in which Soviet victory over the Nazis saw the re-annexation of Latvia, Lithuania and Estonia to the USSR after 1945.[69] Resurgent Russian nationalism is perceived as a serious threat in this region, whilst Georgia has already discovered to its cost that despite post-Soviet military decline Russia remains a regional if not a global superpower, and that her leaders claim a special sphere of influence in the territories of the 'near abroad' – the former USSR.[70]

Imperial Legacies

The Baltic States aside, there are still numerous ties which bind the republics of the former USSR together, and these are more profound, and geographically closer, than those which link the countries of the British Commonwealth, which has its counterpart in the 'Commonwealth of Independent States' (of which, significantly, the Baltic republics and Georgia are not members). After the collapse of the Soviet Union many Russians left the Central Asian republics (up to a third of the Russian population in Uzbekistan emigrated, mostly to Russia, between 1994 and 2004).[71]

Despite this, many post-Soviet countries still have large Russian minorities (in Kazakhstan they make up over 20 per cent of the population, in Estonia almost a half), and Russian remains a *lingua franca* and a path to professional success in all the Central Asian republics as well as Azerbaijan and Armenia. In Ukraine almost half the population is Russian-speaking. Only in Georgia and the Baltic republics has there been a concerted effort to shed much of this historic and cultural baggage, and that has caused much conflict. Russia itself still contains numerous 'autonomous republics' such as Tatarstan, half of whose population is Muslim, and where there are occasional rumblings which reveal post-colonial tensions.[72] Most obviously there is Chechnya, where Russia has fought several vicious wars of repression since the mid 1990s. The Far-Eastern territories and much of Siberia remain a sparsely populated settler colony, where Chinese commercial and demographic influence is likely to play a crucial role in years to come. Russia herself is suffering from a rapid decline in population, which combined with steady immigration from the Central Asian republics in particular is likely to alter profoundly the nature of Russian society by the end of this century: some Russian commentators make alarmist predictions that by 2050 ethnic Russians will be in a minority within the Russian Federation.[73] This is, perhaps, one of the central paradoxes of the former USSR – that migration between its former constituent parts is far greater now than it was in Soviet times, when movement was strictly controlled by permits (something which is paralleled in the post-colonial migrations within the former French and British empires). One of the most profound Soviet legacies is a vast Russophone cultural and institutional sphere which even Central Asian labourers from remote rural backgrounds can navigate with relative ease, at least compared to migration to Western Europe, or even neighbouring regions with which they may have cultural ties such as Iran, Afghanistan and China. Although some Tajiks fled to Afghanistan during the civil war, the migration flows are overwhelmingly from Uzbekistan, Tajikistan and Kyrgyzstan, all of which suffer from high unemployment, into Russia and Kazakhstan, which throughout most of the 2000s enjoyed an oil-driven construction boom that slowed only temporarily during the financial crisis.[74] Even though much of the immigration is illegal, the Russian state largely winks at this as it needs cheap labour for its construction sites and to sweep its streets – whilst for the Central Asian republics remittances from labour migrants represent up to 30 per cent of GDP, although local governments do little either to facilitate or encourage transfers and investment, and most of the money is spent on traditional forms of immediate consumption, in particular elaborate feasts (*tuys*) and the building of houses.[75] As in Germany in the 1960s, the fiction is that these are all *Gastarbeiter* who will return to their homes once their work is done, but many stay.[76] Xenophobia and hate crimes are a problem, especially in Moscow, and far-right groups and Russian skinheads often appear to target not just migrants, but all those obviously of non-Russian ethnicity.[77] Whilst the Putin–Medvedev regime continues at least to pay lip service to the Soviet ideal of the 'friendship of peoples', it is doing too little to aid integration and acceptance. In some respects this resembles the intolerant reception which migrants from South Asia and the West Indies to Britain and from North Africa to France encountered in the 1950s and 1960s – as one journalist puts it: 'Moscow today is France yesterday'.[78] Conversely, across Uzbekistan, Tajikistan and Kyrgyzstan anything up to 50 per cent of all families (the real proportion is uncertain) have a member working in Russia, and as these are overwhelmingly young men, who are usually married before they leave for work, this leaves hundreds of thousands of husbandless and fatherless families.[79] Usually they return home for one or two months a year, in winter, but in some cases they start new families in Russia, and do not return.[80] Thus the post-Soviet period has seen the creation of new social networks of knowledge, labour and kinship that span the territory of the former USSR, and which are denser and more intimate than the formal political ties and economic control which they have replaced.

Conclusion

The Russian Empire before 1917 had many points of resemblance and divergence with the other European empires. In Central Asia and the Caucasus it looked rather like British India or French Algeria, and these were consciously identified as 'backward', colonial territories that were never fully assimilated to the Russian 'core', even if the loss of the Caucasus remains highly contested. In Siberia it looked more like Canada or the American West – a successful settler colony which largely obliterated earlier peoples and cultures. In its western borderlands it looked more like the Habsburg or Ottoman empires, and here Russia, like its multi-ethnic neighbours, was undone by a gradually rising tide of romantic nationalism. Despite the territorial continuity between the Tsarist and Soviet empires, and the dominant role that continued to be played by Russians, 1917 saw a genuine shift in the nature of Russian imperialism, as the Soviet state sought to transform the lives and identities of its subjects in ways never contemplated under Tsarist rule. Conversely the break-up of the Soviet Union seemed sudden, swift and decisive at the time, and in the case of the Warsaw Pact countries and the Baltic republics this was perhaps true – although even here the imperial legacy continues to do more than merely echo. Economically, Russia and Kazakhstan in particular have seen staggering changes, though Uzbekistan and Turkmenistan still seem to be stuck in the Brezhnev era.[81] In the political and cultural sphere, however, the continuities with the USSR are more striking than the changes. This is not simply because even the rump of the USSR which is Russia remains in many ways an imperial formation, or because Russia has recently shown that it is still willing and able to be aggressive beyond these borders. It is because the demographic and cultural legacy of the Soviet period is extremely profound: the USSR was much more than a 'prison of peoples', and many of its non-Russian inhabitants did not want to leave it and still regret its demise.

Notes

1 See W. Sunderland, *Taming the Wild Field: Colonization and Empire on The Russian Steppe* (Ithaca, NY, 2004), pp. 106–7; S. Panarin and D. Raevskii, 'Predislovie', *Evraziya. Liudi i Mify* (Moscow, 2003), pp. 9–20.

2 J. Pelenski, *Russia and Kazan: Conquest and Imperial Ideology (1438–1560s)* (Paris, 1974).

3 J. Forsyth, *A History of the Peoples of Siberia* (Cambridge, 1992), pp. 28–108; Y. Slezkine, *Arctic Mirrors: Russia and the Small Peoples of the North* (Ithaca, NY, 1994), pp. 11–92.

4 T. Snyder, *The Reconstruction of Nations: Poland, Ukraine, Lithuania, Belarus 1569–1999* (New Haven, CT, 2003), pp. 31–50, 117–32.

5 John D. Klier, *Russia Gathers Her Jews: The Origins of the 'Jewish Question' in Russia, 1772–1825* (DeKalb, IL, 1986); A. Miller and M. Dolbilov (eds), *Zapadnye Okrainy Rossiiskoi Imperii* (Moscow, 2006).

6 D. Lieven, *Russia's Rulers Under the Old Regime* (New Haven, CT, 1989), pp. 32–5.

7 A. W. Fisher, *The Russian Annexation of the Crimea 1772–83* (Cambridge, 1970); B. J. Boeck, 'Containment vs. Colonization: Muscovite Approaches to Settling the Steppe', in N. Breyfogle, A. Schrader and W. Sunderland (eds), *Peopling the Russian Periphery: Borderland Colonization in Eurasia History* (2007), pp. 41–60; S. Dickinson, 'Russia's first "Orient": Characterising the Crimea in 1787', *Kritika: Explorations in Russian and Eurasian History*, 3, 1 (2002), pp. 3–25.

8 Sunderland, *Taming the Wild Field*, pp. 69–70.

9 T. M. Barrett, *At The Edge Of Empire: The Terek Cossacks and The North Caucasus Frontier, 1700–1860* (Boulder, CO, 1999).

10 J. Baddeley, *The Russian Conquest of the Caucasus* (1908), p. 130; T. Barrett, 'Lines of Uncertainty: The Frontiers of the Northern Caucasus', in J. Burbank and D. Ransel (eds), *Imperial Russia: New Histories for the Empire* (Bloomington, IN, 1998), pp. 157–8, 166; M. Gammer, *Muslim Resistance to the Tsar* (1994).

11 V. Bobrovnikov, *Musul'mane Severnogo Kavkaza. Obuchai, Pravo, Nasilie* (Moscow, 2002), p. 169.

12 S. Layton, *Russian Literature and Empire: The Conquest of the Caucasus from Pushkin to Tolstoy* (Cambridge, 1994); S. Layton, 'Nineteenth-Century Russian Mythologies of Caucasian Savagery', in D. Brower and E. Lazzerini (eds), *Russia's Orient: Imperial Borderlands and Peoples 1700–1917* (Bloomington, IN, 1997), pp. 80–99; A. Jersild, *Orientalism and Empire* (Montreal, 2002).

13 This modern sense of possessiveness over the Caucasus is explored rather unsatisfactorily in B. Grant, *The Captive and the Gift: Cultural Histories of Sovereignty in Russia and the Caucasus* (Ithaca, NY, 2009).

14 M. Khodarkovsky, *Russia's Steppe Frontier: The Making of a Colonial Empire 1500–1800* (Bloomington, IN, 2002), pp. 152–60; I. V. Erofeeva, *Istoriya Kazakhstana v Russkikh Istochnikakh XVI–XX vekov*, vol. III: *Zhurnaly i Sluzhebnye Zapiski Diplomata A. I. Tevkeleva po Istorii i Etnografii Kazakhstana* (Almaty, 2005), pp. 51–64.

15 E. Bekmakhanov, *Kazakhstan v 20–40 gody XIX veka* (Alma-Ata, 1947); S. Sabol, 'Kazak Resistance to Russian Colonization: Interpreting the Kenesary Kasymov Revolt 1837–1847', *Central Asian Survey*, 22, 2–3 (2003), pp. 231–52.

16 Lt-Gen. M. A. Terentiev, *Istoriya Zavoevaniya Srednei Azii* (St Petersburg, 1906); D. Mackenzie, *The Lion of Tashkent: The Career of General M. G. Cherniaev* (Athens, GA, 1974); A. Morrison, *Russian Rule in Samarkand 1868–1910: A Comparison with British India* (Oxford, 2008), pp. 11–24.

17 Gulnar Kendirbai, *Land and People: The Russian Colonization of the Kazakh Steppe* (Berlin, 2002).

18 A. P. Krivoshein, *Zapiska Glavnoupravlyaushago Zemleustroistvom i Zemledeliem o poezdke v Turkestanskii krai v 1912 godu* (St Petersburg, 1912).

19 A. Morrison, '"Sowing the Seed of National Strife in this Alien Region": The Pahlen Report and *Pereselenie* in Turkestan', *Acta Slavica Iaponica*, 31 (2012), pp. 1–29.

20 D. Wolff, *To the Harbin Station: The Liberal Alternative in Russian Manchuria 1898–1914* (Stanford, CA, 1999); D. Schimmelpenninck van der Oye, *Towards the Rising Sun: Russian Ideologies of Empire and the Path to War with Japan* (DeKalb, IL, 2001).

21 Something grimly predicted by General Alexei Kuropatkin, the war minister and commander who was widely blamed in Russia for the misconduct of the war. A. N. Kuropatkin, *The Russian Army and the Japanese War* (1908), vol. II, pp. 195–6.

22 R. Pipes (ed. and trans.), *Karamzin's Memoir on Ancient & Modern Russia* (Ann Arbor, MI, 2005).

23 On the symbolic performance of power associated with court rituals and imperial journeys, see R. Wortman, *Scenarios of Power: Myth and Ceremony in the Russian Monarchy* (Princeton, NJ, 1995, 2000), 2 vols.

24 W. Sunderland, 'Russians into Iakuts? "Going Native" and Problems of Russian National Identity in the Siberian North, 1870s–1914', *Slavic Review*, 55, 4 (1996), pp. 806–25.

25 A. Jersild, '"Russia", from the Vistula to the Terek to the Amur', *Kritika*, 1 (2000), pp. 531–46;

26 G. Hosking, *Russia, People and Empire* (1996), pp. 39–40; O. Figes, *Natasha's Dance: A Cultural History of Russia* (Harmondsworth, 2002), pp. 381–2.

27 G. N. Curzon, *Russia in Central Asia* (1889), p. 392; E. Schuyler, *Turkistan: Notes of a Journey in Russian Turkistan, Khokand, Bukhara, and Kuldja* (1876), 2 vols; F. Skrine and E. Denison Ross, *The Heart of Asia* (1899), pp. 408–16.

28 See N. Danilevsky, *Rossiya i Evropa* (Moscow, 2003 [1871]); K. Leont'ev, 'Kakoe sochetanie obstoyatel'stv nam vygodnee vsego?', *Grazhdanin*, 91 (1882), reprinted in *Vostok, Rossiya i Slavyanstvo* (Moscow, 1996), p. 70.

29 F. Dostoevsky, 'Dnevnik Pisatelya III Geok-Tepe – Chto takoe dlya nas Aziya?', in *Polnoe Sobranie Sochinenii* (St Petersburg, 1896), vol. XXI, pp. 513–23.

30 A. Morrison, 'Russian Rule in Turkestan and the example of British India', *Slavonic & East European Review*, 84, 4 (2006), pp. 666–707; W. Bruce Lincoln, *The Conquest of a Continent: Siberia and the Russians* (1993), pp. 263–9.

31 P. P. Semenov, 'Znachenie Rossii v kolonizatsionnom dvizhenii evropeiskikh narodov', in *Izvestiya Imperatorskogo Russkago Geograficheskago Obshchestva*, vol. XXVIII (1892), pp. 358–9.

32 N. A. Riasanovsky, 'Asia through Russian Eyes', in W. S. Vucinich (ed.), *Russia and Asia* (Stanford, CA, 1972), pp. 3–29; E. M. Avrutin, 'Racial Categories and the Politics of (Jewish) Difference in Late Imperial Russia', *Kritika*, 8, 1 (2007), pp. 13–40; M. Mogil'ner, *Homo Imperii. Istoriya fizicheskoi antropologii v Rossii* (Moscow, 2008).

33 A. Miller, *The Ukrainian Question* (Budapest, 2003), pp. 247–60; E. Weber, *Peasants into Frenchmen: The Modernization of Rural France, 1870–1914* (Stanford, CA, 1976). 'Russification' is used to translate two separate terms from Russian: 'rusifikatsiya' and 'obrusenie'. The latter is generally held to have a less politicized meaning, implying voluntary and gradual cultural assimilation.

34 K. Matsuzato, 'General-Gubernatorstva v Rossiiskoi Imperii', in *Novaya Imperskaya Istoriya Postsovetskogo Prostranstva* (Kazan, 2004), pp. 456–8; Olga Maiorova, *From the Shadow of Empire Defining the Russian Nation through Cultural Mythology, 1855–1870* (Madison, WI, 2010), pp. 5–15.

35 A. Morrison, 'Metropole, Colony, and Imperial Citizenship in the Russian Empire', *Kritika*, 13, 2 (2012), pp. 327–64.

36 H. Seton-Watson, 'Soviet Nationality Policy', *Russian Review*, 15, 1 (1956), pp. 3–13; R. Pipes, *The Formation of the Soviet Union: Communism and Nationalism 1917–1923* (Cambridge, MA, 1970).

37 A. Khalid, 'Backwardness and the Quest for Civilization: Early Soviet Central Asia in Comparative Perspective', *Slavic Review*, 65, 2 (2006), pp. 231–51; A. Khalid, 'The Soviet Union as an Imperial Formation: A View from Central Asia', in A. L. Stoler, C. McGranahan and P. Perdue (eds), *Imperial Formations* (Santa Fe, NM, 2007), pp. 123–51.

38 The literature on this period is now enormous. See in particular I. Baldauf, 'Some Thoughts on the Making of the Uzbek Nation', *Cahiers du Monde Russe et Soviétique*, 32, 1 (1991), pp. 79–96; Y. Slezkine, 'The USSR as a Communal Apartment, or How a Socialist State Promoted Ethnic Particularism', *Slavic Review*, 53, 2 (Summer 1994), pp. 414–52; T. Martin, *The Affirmative Action Empire* (Ithaca, NY, 2000); A. Edgar, *Tribal Nation: The Making of Soviet Turkmenistan* (Princeton, NJ, 2004); A. Khalid, 'The Soviet Assault on Islam', in *Islam after Communism: Religion and Politics in Central Asia* (Berkeley, CA, 2007), pp. 50–83.

39 M. N. Pokrovskii, *Diplomatiya i Voiny Tsarskoi Rossii v XIX Stoletii* (Moscow, 1923); G. Safarov, *Kolonial'naya Revolyutsiya* (Moscow, 1921); P. G. Galuzo, *Turkestan-Koloniya* (Moscow, 1929).

40 A. Marshall, *The Caucasus under Soviet Rule* (2010), pp. 161–207.

41 O. Subtelny, *Ukraine: A History* (Toronto, 1990), pp. 324, 524–36.

42 For an as yet unsurpassed account of the contortions of Soviet historiography see L. Tillett, *The Great Friendship: Soviet Historians on the Non-Russian Nationalities* (Chapel Hill, NC, 1969); see also E. Weinermann, 'The Polemics between Moscow and Central Asians on the Decline of Central Asia and Tsarist Russia's Role in the History of the Region', *Slavonic & East European Review*, 71, 3 (1993), pp. 428–81.

43 O. Roy, *The New Central Asia: Geopolitics and the Birth of Nations* (2000), pp. 109–12, 125.

44 Racial intermarriage is the subject of an ongoing study by Adrienne Edgar, some preliminary results of which can be found in A. Edgar, '*Rulers and Victims* Reconsidered: Geoffrey Hosking and the Russians of the Soviet Union', *Kritika*, 13, 2 (2012), pp. 429–40.

45 M. Pohl, 'The "Planet of One Hundred Languages": Ethnic Relations and Soviet Identity in the Virgin Lands', in N. Bregfoyle, A. Schrader and W. Sunderland (eds), *Peopling the Russian Periphery: Borderland Colonization in Eurasian History* (2007), pp. 238–61.

46 There is as yet little work on Soviet cosmopolitanism, but for a thought-provoking, if rather diffuse, anthropological study, see B. Grant, 'Cosmopolitan Baku', *Ethnos*, 75, 2 (2010), pp. 123–47.

47 See for instance G. Hosking, 'The Flawed Melting-Pot', in *The Awakening of the Soviet Union* (Cambridge, MA, 1991), pp. 92–116.

48 Snyder, *Reconstruction of Nations*, pp. 232–55.

49 The first Western historian to fully recognize and explore this was R. Suny in *The Revenge of the Past: Nationalism, Revolution, and the Collapse of the Soviet Union* (Stanford, CA, 1993).

50 J. Morrison, *Boris Yeltsin: From Bolshevik to Democrat* (New York, NY, 1991), pp. 161–2, 259–69, 288–92; Roy, *The New Central Asia*, pp. 125–9.

51 For a fine satire on this tendency see S. Idiatullin and E. Belov, 'Rossiya v kol'tse zla', *Kommersant-Vlast'*, 23 October 2006 (http://www.kommersant.ru/articles/2006/neighbors.html, accessed 5 September 2011).

52 B. Kostin, *Zhizn zamechatel'nykh lyudei – Skobelev* (Moscow, 2000); Evgenii Glushchenko, *Geroi Imperii* (Moscow, 2001) (this jingoistic volume also contains uncritical biographies of K. P. von Kaufman and M. G. Cherniaev); V. I. Gusarov, *General M. D. Skobelev. Legendarnaya slava i neshyvshiesya nadezhdy* (Moscow, 2003).

53 B. Akunin, *Turetskii Gambit & Smert' Akhillesa* (Moscow, 1998), translated as *Turkish Gambit* and *The Death of Achilles* (San Diego, CA, 2005–6).

54 'Pamyatnik generalu Skobelevu poyavit'sya v Il'inskom skvere v Moskve', *regnum.ru*, 19 December 2005 (www.regnum.ru/news/562302.html, accessed 5 September 2011).

55 Sergei Rudkovskii, 'Pamyatnik Generalu Ermolovu otkryli v Pyatigorske', *Rianovosti*, 11 September 2010 (http://ria.ru/society/20100911/274705127.html); I saw the monument to Perovsky when in Orenburg in July 2011.

56 There is now an extensive literature on this – see A. Haugen, *The Establishment of National Republics in Soviet Central Asia* (Basingstoke, 2003); P. Bergne, *The Birth of Tajikistan: National Identity and the Origins of the Republic* (2007).

57 See M. Reeves, 'Locating Danger: Konfliktologiia and the Search for Fixity in the Ferghana Valley Borderlands', *Central Asian Survey*, 24, 1 (2005), pp. 67–81; idem., 'Travels in the Margins of the State: Everyday Geography in the Ferghana Valley Borderlands', in J. Sahadeo

and R. Zanca (eds), *Everyday Life in Central Asia Past and Present* (Bloomington, IN, 2007), pp. 281–300.

58 O. Ferrando, 'Soviet Population Transfers and Interethnic Relations in Tajikistan: Assessing the Concept of Ethnicity', *Central Asian Survey*, 30, 1 (2011), pp. 39–52.

59 M. Reeves, 'A Weekend in Osh', *London Review of Books*, 32, 13 (8 July 2010), pp. 17–18 (http://www.lrb.co.uk/v32/n13/madeleine-reeves/a-weekend-in-osh, accessed 4 September 2011).

60 See Khalid, *Islam after Communism*, pp. 168–203.

61 See for instance D. A. Alimova (ed.), *Tragediya Sredneaziatskogo Kishlaka*, vol. I (Tashkent, 2006), p. 4.

62 I. Karimov, *Uzbekistan on the Threshold of the Twenty-First Century* (1997), p. 86.

63 J. Rahimov, *Istoriya Uzbekistana Vtoraya polovina XIX veka – nachalo XX veka*, Klass 9 (Tashkent, 2001), p. 5; this book was withdrawn from circulation in 2003 at the request of the Russian ambassador, but its replacement by G. A. Khidoyatov, whilst containing fewer anti-Russian sentiments, is otherwise not much of an improvement.

64 J. Sahadeo, '"Without the Past there is No Future": Archives, History, and Authority in Uzbekistan', in A. Burton (ed.), *Archive Stories: Facts, Fictions, and the Writing of History* (Durham, NC, 2005), pp. 45–67.

65 M. Laruelle, 'The Concept of Ethnogenesis in Central Asia: Political Context and Institutional Mediators (1940–50)', *Kritika*, 9, 1 (2008), pp. 169–88.

66 A. Il'khamov, *Etnicheskii Atlas Uzbekistana* (Tashkent, 2002); see D. A. Alimova, 'Neoproverzhimo dokazana antinauchnost' gipotezy o tom, chto uzbekskaya natsiya poyavilas' v XVI veke', Interview with UzA, 15 August 2005 (http://www.centrasia.ru/newsA.php4?st=1124137320, accessed 5 September 2011) in which the then head of the Historical Institute of the Uzbek Academy of Sciences condemns the 'unscientific' nature of Il'khamov's argument that the Uzbeks first appear in recorded history in the sixteenth century (which they did). See further the forum on 'Constructing a National History in the Language of Soviet Science after the Collapse of the USSR: The Case of Uzbekistan', *Ab Imperio*, 4 (2005) pp. 279–360; A. Ilkhamov, 'Archaeology of Uzbek Identity' and A. Khalid, 'The Modernity of Identity: On A. Ilkhamov's "Archaeology of Uzbek Identity"', *Anthropology and Archaeology of Eurasia*, 44, 4 (2006), pp. 10–36, 86–91.

67 On this see in particular the essays by S. V. Timchenko and V. Germanova on, respectively, modern Kazakh and modern Uzbek historiography, which make up appendices 1 and 2 of S. Abashin, D. Arapov and N. Bekmakhanova (eds), *Tsentral'naya Aziya v sostave Rossiiskoi Imperii* (Moscow, 2007), pp. 338–81.

68 Andreas Umland, 'Das Problem der "Unterforschung" des postsowjetischen russischen Ultranationalismus', *Russland-Analysen*, 218 (2011), pp. 16–17.

69 This came to a head in spring 2007 when the Estonian Government dismantled a Soviet-era war memorial; see L. Harding, 'Protest by Kremlin as Police quell riots in Estonia', *The Observer*, 29 April 2007.

70 S. Tisdall, 'The Bear is Back', *The Guardian*, 31 July 2008; 'Russia. A New Confrontation?' *House of Commons Defence Committee Report, Together with Formal Minutes, Oral and Written Evidence* (2009) (http://www.publications.parliament.uk/pa/cm200809/cmselect/cmdfence/276/276.pdf, accessed 7 October 2009).

71 'Grustnaya statistika: za poslednee desyatiletie iz Uzbekistana uekhal kazhdyi tretii Russkii', *fergana.ru*, 6 September 2004 (http://www.fergananews.com/article.php?id=3145, accessed 5 September 2011).

72 Most recently a scandal surrounding the Tatar newscaster and head of the Tatarstan state television company El'mira Israfilova, who openly referred to the Russian population of the region as 'occupiers': 'V Tatarstane otkazalis' vozbuzhdat' delo v otnoshenii tatarskoi zhurnalistki, nazvavshei russkikh 'okkupantami', *regnum.ru*, 10 August 2011 (http://www.regnum.ru/news/polit/1434156.html, accessed 5 September 2011).

73 A. Vaganov, 'Migranty berut revansh. Bogateiiushchaya Rossiya ne mozhet ostanovit sokrashchenie chislennosti sobstvennogo naseleniya', *Nezavisimaya Gazeta*, 25 October 2006 (http://www.ng.ru/politics/2006-10-25/1_migranty.html, accessed 5 September 2011).

74 Guzal' Mirzarakhimova, 'Kazakhstan: gastarbeiterov men'she ne stanet', *fergana.ru*, 9 October 2009 (http://www.fergananews.com/article.php?id=6327&print=1, accessed 5 September 2011).

75 M. Reeves, 'Black Work, Green Money: Remittances, Ritual, and Domestic Economies in Southern Kyrgyzstan', *Slavic Review*, 71, 1 (2012), pp. 108–34; see further E. Marat, 'Labour Migration in Central Asia: Implications of the Global Economic Crisis', *Silk Road Paper*, May 2009 (http://www.silkroadstudies.org/new/docs/silkroadpapers/0905migration.pdf, accessed 5 September 2011) for a useful overview of the migration phenomenon in English. More detailed statistics and descriptions of migrant motivations for Uzbekistan can be found in E. V. Abdullaev, *Trudovaya Migratisya v Respublike Uzbekistan. Sotsial'nye, pravovye i gendernye aspekty* (Tashkent, 2008).

76 V. I. Mukomel and I. M. Kuznetsov (eds), *Adaptatsionnye vozmozhnosti i setevye svyazi migratsionnykh etnicheskikh men'shinstv* (Moscow, 2005).

77 G. Sapozhnikova, 'Hate Crimes in Russia: Citizens of Former Soviet Republics Fear Russia's Streets', *Komsomolskaya Pravda*, 28 April 2008 (http://www.kp.ru/daily/24088.5/320878/, accessed 18 May 2012).

78 M. Kalishevskii, 'Rossiya: Kak byt i zhit' s "ponaekhavshimi"?', *fergana.ru*, 1 October 2010 (http://www.fergananews.com/article.php?id=6747, accessed 5 September 2011). This article includes some remarkable photographs of the prayers for the feast of Qurban Bairam in Moscow.

79 A 2006 Tajik documentary film – G. Dzalaev and A. Abdulloev's 'Novaya Penelopa' ('The New Penelope') – chronicles the lives of wives and children left behind in Tajikistan.

80 See M. Mirovaliev, 'Odissieya uzbekskikh gastarbeiterov v avtobuse – prizrake', *fergana.ru*, 30 August 2009 (http://www.fergananews.com/article.php?id=6282, accessed 5 September 2011) for an account of the lengthy bus journey made by migrants from Uzbekistan to Moscow each year.

81 On the divergent economic trajectories of Kazakhstan and the other Central Asian republics since 1991 see R. Pomfret, *The Central Asian Economies since Independence* (Princeton, NJ, 2006), pp. 1–22.

State of Insecurity:
Self-Defence and Self-Cultivation
in the Genesis of Japanese Imperialism

Christopher Harding

Yamagata Aritomo was one of the leaders of Japan's 'Meiji Restoration' in 1868, which saw the overthrow of the Tokugawa shogunate and the establishment in its place of a self-consciously modernizing regime. In 1890 Yamagata made a speech to the Japanese Diet warning that the current weakness of China and the rather menacing interest taken in the country by Western imperial powers represented a fundamental danger to Japan's security. The focal point of this danger was the Korean Peninsula, for centuries a protectorate of China and now, according to Yamagata, a 'dagger aimed at the heart of Japan'.

The audience in the Diet chamber would have needed little persuading. The previous 20 years lay heavy upon even the most optimistic of Japan's newly elected political class: having watched its centuries-old cultural mentor, China, succumb with terrifying speed to the force of Western imperialism, Japan itself was subjected to the virtual occupation of major ports around its coastline and the imposition of highly unequal treaties. Taken together with a long and largely inglorious history of skirmishing on the Korean Peninsula with various Korean and Chinese dynasties and the attempted invasion of Japan by the Mongols via the same route, it is not hard to see why the issue of the peninsula focused minds and divided opinion in Japan.

Yet the Japanese debate on how to deal with Korea, brought to a brutal temporary settlement with the country's annexation in 1910, was just a symptom of a broader unsettledness in Japan over how to cope with the fundamental insecurity into which the Meiji state had been born. Western military expansionism gave the situation its immediacy, but the depth of Japan's insecurity derived from a dawning realization of the material and cultural achievements of countries like the US and Britain more generally (seen at first hand by a handful of Japanese in the 1860s and 1870s), the manifest failure of Japan's old leaders to develop the country to anything like a similar degree, and finally from a sense that Japan's current inadequacy might stem from something deeper than poor leadership. The result was that the West represented a 'provocation' to Japan in the broadest possible sense, catalysing often contradictory change in strategic, political, literary, religious and other spheres. This is apparent in the trial-and-error nature of early Meiji governance, fluctuating media opinion (including shifting representations of Western and Japanese culture), famous U-turns by major public intellectuals, and the coming together of seemingly diverse areas of life under the almost universally pursued theme of *kuni no tame* – 'for the sake of the nation'.

With this background in mind, three initial claims can be made with regard to what we might call the 'genesis' of Japanese imperialism between 1868 and 1895, all of which will be pursued in this chapter and all of which tie in with themes of insecurity and provocation. Firstly, as Marius Jansen has pointed out, Japanese imperialism was situational as opposed to being planned or calculated. To this we might add that early Meiji Japanese imperialism was, at the strategic level, generally limited to defensive protection as understood in the late nineteenth-century international context. By the 1930s the 'self-defence' claim was odiously inaccurate and propagandist, but this was less because it had been dishonest at the outset than because a clear line never emerged in Japanese policy-making between ever-changing concepts of self-defence and outright imperialistic expansion.[1] Secondly, the relationship of Japanese imperialism to its Western counterparts and to the West in general operated at a number of levels, with a directly mimetic element in colonial rhetoric, administration and ceremony ultimately secondary in importance to the far-reaching consequences of Western infiltration of Japanese life and culture.

Thirdly, as early Meiji newspapers, journals, political tracts, social groups, autobiographies and novels make clear, an educated Japanese minority experienced this period in terms of insecurities that ranged from the geopolitical right through to the deeply personal. A remarkably diverse cross section of quarrelling public intellectuals – from the writers Fukuzawa Yukichi and Natsume Sōseki to the Christian leader Uchimura Kanzō, the Buddhist revivalist Inoue Enryō, and the psychotherapist Morita Masatake – explicitly related the situation and fate of the Japanese individual to that of the nation and its place in the world, in intensely practical and far-reaching ways.[2] Fukuzawa's work, for example, helped to promote the idea that China and Korea represented not just the strategic threat noted by Yamagata but also one of personal and cultural atrophy. Where Yamagata perceived a strategic dagger at Japan's heart, Fukuzawa saw a continent and peninsula that were deeply sick and that threatened to infect Japan if it did not 'escape' in time.[3]

The argument pursued here will be that the early Meiji period was characterized by the connectedness of the personal and political and the ongoing revision of both.

In time, the result was a form of imperialism that appeared to be new, expansionist and predicated upon Western assumptions about a modern world order, but which in large part was an exercise in looking inward, drawing on the domestic past as well as the international present, and grounded in a quest to resolve a range of questions and insecurities rather broader than the purely military or political.

Security and Self-Defence

Most of the core ingredients of Japanese imperialism were in place from the very birth of the new state in 1868. Where the Tokugawa shogunate had failed to appreciate in time the harsh realities of international relations, the leaders of the Restoration moved directly from overthrowing the old regime to demonstrating their familiarity with the current global order's most fundamental dictate: claim and secure your borders.

The first priority was the northern island of Ezochi (Ainu-land), since the remnants of the Tokugawa armies had fled in this direction and it was uncomfortably close to Russian North East Asia. Trade had existed between mainland Japan and Ezochi for centuries, with relations growing steadily more uneven from the seventeenth century onwards as the Tokugawa and their allies sought to exert greater control. Now, after the birth of the new state, the island was to be definitively claimed for Japan, renamed 'Hokkaidō'. The question of whether or not this in itself was 'imperialism' places the concept under considerable pressure. To suggest that Hokkaidō had always been part of Japan is arguably to accept imperialistic rhetoric, and it is certainly a claim that inhabitants of the island, the Ainu, contested across much of the twentieth century. In various ways over the previous centuries, the leaders and traders of mainland Japan had gone out of their way to mark the Ainu out as separate and different from themselves. A combination of Confucian ideas, folk mythology and rhetorically exaggerated distaste at the physical appearance of the Ainu and at their way of life had contributed to an image of 'barbaric' and even demonic people (not unlike the characterization of the Dutch as 'dogs', who were said to wear heeled shoes because the heels of their dog-like feet did not touch the ground).[4] After 1869, social Darwinist notions of 'race' imported from Europe served to invigorate and provide fresh conceptual backing for these ideas. A Western element was also in evidence in the administration of the island by a 'Hokkaidō Colonization Office'. Japanese leaders spoke openly (and approvingly) of *takushoku* (colonization)[5] and encouraged former samurai families from the mainland to move to the island, both as cultivators and as potential defenders. They were given plots of land that had been confiscated on the basis that Ainu had hunted and fished there rather than settled the land for cultivation – colonial logic operating within colonial logic.

When it came to dealing with the Ainu, it could be argued that official oscillation between policies of differentiation and assimilation – a hangover from similar doubts under the Tokugawa – suggested not so much Japanese uncertainty about whether this was imperialism or not as a simple need to reinforce a political securing of borders with an equivalent cultural policy. To this end, Ainu were ordered to alter their hairstyles, stop tattooing themselves, take Japanese surnames, worship at Shintō shrines and allow their children to read Japanese textbooks at school. And yet Hokkaidō was not incorporated into the prefectural system of Japan (set up in 1871) until 1882, and even then it occurred only as a result of a financial scandal over the island's government, with the sense of a 'special status' remaining strong ever after. By 1899 the situation was compounded by the social plight of many Ainu, which forced the government to provide aid under the auspices of a 'Protection Act'.[6]

Whether or not the case of Ezochi/Hokkaidō comes under the heading of imperialism, it demonstrates what we might call the principle of 'simultaneity' in the genesis of Japanese imperialism. The emergence of imperial rhetoric, ceremony and mass public support from the time of the Sino-Japanese War of 1894–5 might tempt us to periodize Japanese imperialism as following on from a formative stage at the feet of the West (Japan's victory over China occurred around the same time as the successful revision of her unequal treaties with the West); in fact, however, the genesis of Japanese imperialism was part and parcel of Japan's attempts to cope politically and culturally with its insecure state right from the Restoration in 1868.[7] In ideological terms, this meant that Japanese concepts – for example, old Tokugawa stereotypes about Ainu – initially dominated and were only joined along the way, as it were, by Western ones. Where a concept of 'race' that eventually entered mainstream Japanese thought as 'common sense'[8] was concerned, the European biological and evolutionary element overlaid rather than displaced a Japanese–Confucian binary of civilized–barbarian, the *kokugaku* (school of Japanese nativist thought) contradistinction between moral purity and impurity, clear class divisions created and embedded in law by successive Tokugawa shoguns, and the concept of ancestry encapsulated in Shintō mythology. (The latter was influential in shifting 'race' in Japan from a purported biological phenomenon [*jinshu*] to one of cultural and ancestral community [*minzoku*].)[9]

Understanding early Japanese imperialism in these terms has the further advantage of allowing us to recognize the influence exerted upon its development by internal public order as well as external security concerns. Early Hokkaidō policy evolved at a time when numerous uprisings were occurring across Japan against the new leadership, including a large-scale rebellion of ex-samurai in 1877, countless smaller disturbances over taxes and other matters,[10] and simmering disagreement as to precisely where sovereignty ought to lie in the new Japanese state. The resulting preoccupation of leaders such as Yamagata and Itō Hirobumi with welding together into a nation groups of Japanese with distinct and frequently conflicting regional and class interests rendered the notion of a racial or quasi-religious community all the more appealing. For all their wariness of Christian infiltration of Japan, many of these leaders envied Christianity its ability to facilitate social cohesion and control in the West. The desire to achieve something similar in Japan was evident in leaders' deployment of the Emperor at the centre of a mythical family-state (*kokutai*) and the promulgation of an 1889 constitution (a 'gift' from the Emperor) that was geared towards united participation in building the new state and hedged any 'rights' for Japanese accordingly.[11] Yamagata in particular was notable for his desire to insulate the military and the bureaucracy from politics and his extreme distaste of oppositional party politics as 'morally wrong'.[12]

The securing of borders to the south as well as to the north was crucial to Japanese leaders' stabilization of their new state and their own positions. Japan initially asserted its control of the Tsushima islands near Korea and then in 1876 it emulated Western gunboat diplomacy to impose upon Korea a treaty of a similarly unequal nature to those under which Japan itself was still labouring – complete with treaty ports enjoying full extraterritoriality. Further south, in the Ryukyu Islands, lack of legal clarity over territory once again equalled lack of effective security: the hitherto complex and shifting relationship between Japan and the Ryukyu Kingdom (traditionally claimed as a Chinese protectorate of sorts) was cleared up in 1879 with the forced abdication of the king and the assimilation of the area into Japan as 'Okinawa' prefecture.

As with Hokkaidō, part of the reason why this is rarely considered 'imperialism' is that mainland Japan was at the time undergoing an administrative shift from domains to prefectures, intended to dilute regional loyalties and encourage people to see themselves first and foremost as 'Japanese'. The addition into this system of Hokkaidō in the north and Okinawa in the south could easily therefore be presented as centralization, clarification, or modernization.

Simultaneity in early Japanese imperialism – of defence and expansion, of internal and external security concerns, and of Asian and Western cultural content – is apparent also in a Japanese expedition to Taiwan in 1874. The expedition was justified in public as the punishment of a group of Taiwanese for the murder of some Ryukyuans, but was privately intended to facilitate at the same time the establishment of colonies on the eastern part of the island. The latter part of the plan, formulated on the advice of a former American diplomat, Charles LeGendre, was abandoned under pressure from the US and Britain (fearing disruption to regional trade). But public reaction to the expedition – in commercial sources such as newspapers, woodblock prints, and books – showed something rather interesting: the slogan of *bunmei kaika* (civilization and enlightenment), which had originally expressed a desire for Japan's renewal through learning from the outside world, had come to be associated with imperialistic assertiveness.[13] While the Japanese government had drawn a relatively bland and non-committal distinction between 'civilization' and 'savagery' in justifying its Taiwan policy, the media went much further, accusing the Taiwanese of cannibalism and implying that the use of force against them was thereby justified. In one visual representation of the expedition, the depiction of the victorious Japanese soldiers is a clear hybrid of samurai valour (complete with swords rather than rifles) and a modern European style of dress, while the message of the piece is that the victory is one for samurai *and* for the Japanese Empire.

One consequence of Japan's early forays into imperialism – political, racial, cultural – was its forfeiture of any credible claim to constructive leadership in Asia, since it ended up displaying a preference for a dichotomized civilized–savage understanding of the world over one where Japan could be an in-between nation, a mediator of sorts.[14] The sense of happiness and pride expressed by India's future prime minister Jawaharlal Nehru on the occasion of Japan's victory over Russia (an Asian finally vanquishing a Western nation) suggested that as late as 1905 Japan was still looked upon in some quarters as a potential hero of colonized Asia. Yet Japanese imperialism was too inward-looking in nature, too bound up with Japan's own process of civilization, to have anything more than rhetoric to offer where a *mission civilisatrice* to other nations was concerned. Of course, as the Saidian turn in the study of European imperialism has shown, Europe's *mission* too was deeply self-referential. But in the Japanese case the balance seems to have been different, with early Japanese imperialism never straying far enough from its basic security dynamic to allow any claim about 'civilizing' to be much more than secondary or cosmetic. Nowhere was this more apparent than in Japan's short-lived, asset-stripping South East Asian empire of the early 1940s.

If Japan's prospects as an 'honest broker' in Asia were damaged by the aftermath of the Taiwan Expedition (bearing in mind that Japanese print media had an international as well as a domestic readership), they were pretty much killed off by the conflict with China in 1894–5. Here again defence and expansion went hand-in-hand, both before and after the conflict. At the very point when victory in war seemed to have brought security as well as a welcome swell of national pride thanks to the cession to Japan of Taiwan and the Liaotung Peninsula, the success of Russian, French and German pressure in forcing Japan to return the Liaotung Peninsula reminded Japan's leaders that it remained under threat in East Asia and that the search for security was not yet at an end.[15]

Japanese Imperialism and Self-Cultivation

Beyond strategic security and the accompanying efforts at racial and cultural 'self-defence' evident in Japanese political and media treatment of Ainu, Taiwanese, and others, a long-standing but newly invigorated Japanese interest in self-cultivation made subtle early contributions to Japanese imperialism. In the late Tokugawa period the concept of self-cultivation had been so broadly conceived that it comfortably covered English-language concepts as diverse as religion, morality, health, and education.[16] Now in the Meiji period it expanded further with an influx of Western influences, the development of Western–Japanese hybrid ideas, and the addition of a new political dimension thanks to the realization amongst Meiji thinkers and leaders that national regeneration needed to encompass a step-change in the attitudes and lifestyles of the Japanese themselves. Some hoped that, as with other areas of the Restoration, a top-down governmental approach could be relied upon to work the necessary magic – through the reorganization of Japan's local communities, education, and the issuing of hortatory messages from the emperor in the form of 'Imperial Rescripts'.[17] Others looked instead to individual self-cultivation fed by a blend of Western and Asian cultural resources, and the relation of the cultivated individual to the nation. Those who focused on the cultivation of the individual formed a broad continuum as opposed to sharing a single view of self-cultivation, and it is to two distinctive thinkers within this continuum – the Confucian scholar-turned-Christian Nakamura Keiu, and one of the founders of 'New Buddhism', Inoue Enryō – that we now turn.

'Self-cultivation', in the sense used here, can take one of two forms: a preparedness to relinquish self altogether to allow something entirely new to emerge, or the retention of an essential core – perhaps conscience or memory – that gives context and direction to the process of cultivation. Influential voices in 1870s Japan could be heard advocating something akin to the former model, with some going so far as to suggest that English should be the national language, Christianity the national religion, and intermarriage with Westerners the familial norm. From the mid to late 1880s onwards this approach lost ground, partly because of anger at its excesses – evident in Japanese journalistic ridicule heaped upon their leaders' absurd affectation of Western dress and manners at ballroom dances inside Tokyo's purpose-built 'Rokumeikan'. Instead, the slogan *wakon-yosai* (Japanese spirit, Western know-how) grew in popularity and came to be understood in terms of the need for any reorganization of Japanese life along Western lines – government, banking, military, education, and so on – to proceed in accordance with a 'Japanese spirit' (*yamato-damashii*).

By the 1920s and 1930s this 'spirit' had become a feature of much right-wing government and media propaganda, but in this earlier period it was a fluid and even elusive concept. The novelist Natsume Sōseki famously lampooned the idea: 'Admiral Togo possesses the Japanese spirit, and the local fishmonger has it as well. Swindlers and murderers also have the Japanese spirit. Since it is a spirit it is always blurry and fuzzy; there is no-one in Japan who hasn't had it on the tip of his tongue, but there's no-one who has actually seen it'.[18] And yet the fuzzier the concept, the more dangerous it was: as media reaction to the Taiwan Expedition showed, the attempt to locate or demonstrate something as amorphous as 'Japanese civilization' tended to proceed along dialectical lines of comparison or competition with other cultures and nations. Academic discussions of Japan's natural surroundings, language structure, history, and shared popular characteristics could easily – and often did – spill over into aggressive newspaper rhetoric, including the forecasting of war and conquest involving Russia, Britain and the United States.

In keeping with the focus of this chapter on the genesis of Japanese imperialism, rather than chart the rise of Japanese imperialist rhetoric in the twentieth century the argument pursued here will be that in this earlier period a flexible, discursive concept of self-cultivation and 'Japanese spirit' started to emerge that was linked in various ways with the broad Western 'provocation' discussed above. Adapting Harumi Befu's concept of 'passive nationalism', we might term the result 'passive imperialism': ideas and sentiments not always immediately emotive, competitive, expansionist, or domineering, but representing nonetheless a mounting stockpile of fuel waiting for the crucial moment – an attack, a crisis, a euphemistic call to 'defend the nation' – to ignite it.[19]

For both Nakamura Keiu (1832–91) and Inoue Enryō (1858–1919), the formation of programmes for self-cultivation involved weighing both the likely effectiveness and the original sources of particular ideas, the latter becoming a particularly pressing concern in the 1880s and 1890s. Here the two men were heirs to a long tradition: ever since the import of philosophical, religious, literary and technical ideas from China and Korea had begun on a large scale in the sixth century, Japan had experienced flashpoints when the desire to distinguish 'Japanese' from 'foreign' ideas had arisen. These ranged from sixth-century arguments about the proper status of Buddhism in Japan (vis-à-vis what we now know as Shintō) to a reference in the eleventh-century Japanese text *The Tale of Genji* to *yamato damashii* and, a few centuries later, the appearance of the slogan *wakon-kansai* (Japanese spirit, Chinese know-how).[20] By the late eighteenth and early nineteenth centuries, *kokugakusha* (scholars of 'national learning') were increasingly strident in their advocacy of self-cultivation along the lines of the distinctly Japanese morality, aesthetic, and closeness to nature that they believed they had found in ancient Japanese texts such as the eighth-century *Kojiki* [Record of Ancient Matters]:

> The Kojiki [contains] the most reliable information on how the Japanese behaved before being infected with Chinese ideas [...] I suggest that one first cleanse oneself of any defiled notions one may have acquired from reading Chinese texts and then, holding fast to one's pristine Japanese heart, study our ancient texts well. If one does this, one will automatically learn about the Way that should be adopted and practiced. To know these things is to adopt and practice the Way of the Gods.[21]

In the advocacy of Japanese self-cultivation for which he became well known in the 1870s, Nakamura Keiu treated the origins of ideas pragmatically rather than ideologically. He defended the unpopular cause of China and Chinese learning on the basis of its practical utility in Japanese self-cultivation: Chinese ethics could be an important source for individual transformation,[22] while the relative conceptual closeness of Chinese and English – particularly where ideas such as 'God', 'heaven', 'spirit' and 'conscience' were concerned[23] – provided a counter-weight to the popular Meiji juxtaposition of a scientific West with a superstitious China that threatened to turn young Japanese away from religion, despite its importance in the building of character. Nakamura was influenced profoundly by his first-hand observation of English society, on the basis of which he decided to publish a Japanese version of Samuel Smiles' *Self-Help*. A copy was soon in many a Meiji pocket (an estimated one million were initially sold), encouraging a generation of young urban men to believe that with earnest individual application all things were possible.[24] Less popular was the further stage to which Nakamura thought self-cultivation should proceed: Japanese conversion to Christianity, with an example to be set by the Emperor himself.[25]

Inoue Enryō's blending of Japanese and Asian ideas in the 1880s and 1890s reflected a shifting mood amongst intellectuals in Japan and a rather more pressurized set of personal circumstances bound up with the precarious state of Inoue's beloved Japanese Buddhism. The religion had been derided by the influential *kokugakusha* Hirata Atsutane (1776–1843) as a product of the 'inferior Indian mind', and elsewhere in late Tokugawa and early Meiji Japan it was viewed as a degraded establishment, hoovering up the meagre earnings of ordinary, decent Japanese and representing a passive and other-worldly stumbling block on Japan's path to modern scientific and political progress.[26] Having witnessed the extent of this anger in the descent of a government initiative to separate out Buddhism from Shintō into physical attacks on temples, monks and nuns, Inoue set out to launder the reputation of Japanese Buddhism by agreeing with much of the criticism and declaring the situation a chance for a much-needed purification.[27] This was to include the replacement of an elite priesthood with a modern *sangha* (religious community) comprising truth-seeking Japanese laypeople. Inoue led the way, giving up his own Buddhist priestly robes, reinventing himself as a philosopher on the basis of his university study of Western philosophy, and jettisoning ritual and monasticism to portray Buddhism as a 'religion based on philosophy' and even congruent with the emerging psy disciplines.[28] Crucially, Inoue was working in a period in which the precise meanings of the neologisms *shūkyō* (religion) and *tetsugaku* (philosophy) had yet to establish themselves in Japanese minds,[29] and in which Western rationalism retained sufficient kudos for Inoue to be able to claim it as the 'impartial' means by which the truths of various religious and philosophical systems could be assessed. Indeed, Inoue claimed to have had his first glimpse of truth while reading Western philosophy, only then seeing that it was there in Buddhism too.[30]

Both men come across as rather hard-headed pragmatists, not overly concerned with the Japanese past: Nakamura was relatively untroubled by the cultural loss of self implied in his advocacy of China and particularly the West, while Inoue was prepared to turn intellectual somersaults and butcher Japan's Buddhist heritage in the interests of salvaging what he regarded as the still-serviceable basics. And yet both were deeply concerned about Japan's future, and were at pains to demonstrate the role that self-cultivation could play in building the nation[31] – a nation that Nakamura envisaged becoming the 'Europe of Asia' in relatively short order. Writing in the preface to his version of *Self-Help* Nakamura noted Smiles' comment that 'national progress is the sum of individual industry, energy, and uprightness, as national decay is of individual idleness, selfishness, and vice'.[32] Smiles' actual meaning here was a warning against state intrusion into the market, but whether Nakamura mistook or deliberately altered Smiles' meaning (both were common features of Meiji translations of Western writing)[33] Nakamura's repeated invocation of 'the country' or 'our country' where the original discussed 'the world' or 'civilization' is perfectly clear in its intent. Similarly, in a Japanese version that Nakamura published of Mill's 'On Liberty', the 'nation' received a great deal more attention than the 'individual', relative to Mill's original.

Specifically, although Nakamura envisaged a proactive, patrician role for government in his translation of 'On Liberty' – often choosing words for 'society' that rendered it more or less synonymous with a ruling elite[34] – in common with the likes of M. K. Gandhi in India a generation later he was dubious about the prospects of any nation whose raw material, its people, remained untransformed. In particular, Nakamura thought, the Japanese tended towards subservience, ignorance, and general lack of virtue,[35] and this was where Christian conversion and Chinese ethics could come in. Crucially, both systems placed limits on the notion of 'freedom', which Nakamura presented in his translation of 'On Liberty' as bounded by the needs of others, to whom each individual is linked by duty and love. 'Individualism' itself was rendered, *pace* Smiles and in accordance with samurai and Confucian emphases on personal effort and achievement,[36] in terms primarily of initiative and self-reliance rather than differentiation, independence, or eccentricity. And an explicit connection was made between freedom of individual conscience and religious liberty, with the suggestion that the latter was valuable in the cultivation of the former. This was a significant departure from Mill's own concerns about the potential power of religion to compromise individual freedom.[37] Nakamura's deployment of Western concepts associated with liberalism had little to do with that brand of political and social thought, and everything to do with purpose, construction, and the sort of communitarian values that were later to become meshed with the *kokugaku*-inspired Emperor ideology and the related theory of *kokutai* (literally 'the body' of the nation).

Inoue's treatment of self and nation was rather more rhetorical, and extended more explicitly to the development and dissemination of Japanese influence in the world. His favourite slogan, *gokoku airi* ('defend the nation and love the truth'), encapsulated both his personal quest and his vision for the transformation of his fellow Japanese. Inoue set out to elucidate – 'for the glory of the whole nation'[38] – an 'Asian' philosophy based on Japanese Buddhism that could deal with intangible truth where its Western counterpart was limited to 'concrete objects'. He hoped that the Japanese would study and live according to this philosophy, forming in the process a revitalized *sangha*[39] (a religious rendering of Nakamura's community ideal) that would be capable of defending Japan against Christian encroachment. Inoue viewed Japanese converts to Christianity as running away from an as yet imperfect community rather than fulfilling their duty to participate in its improvement, and in 1904–5 he went as far as to support the Russo-Japanese War as a crusade against Christianity.[40] Despite conceding that Christianity and Buddhism were alike in their pursuit of the truth, Inoue insisted that 'the West has a nature peculiar to the West',[41] and that the failure to appreciate this – a reference to the dominant pro-Western thinking of the 1870s – placed Japan's cultural and international political status in doubt:

> If we have the slightest desire to maintain our civilization and promote our independence, we must concentrate on a revival of Buddhism. This fine product of ours [Japanese Buddhism] excels those of other countries; the fact that its good strain died out in India and China may be considered an unexpected blessing for our country. If we continue to nurture it in Japan and disseminate it some day in foreign countries we will not only add to the honour of our nation but will also infuse the spirit of our land into the hearts and minds of foreigners. I am convinced that the consequences will be considerable.[42]

Conclusion

Inoue and Nakamura were essentially universalists. For Nakamura, this meant that what might look to some like the abandonment of Japanese culture or kowtowing to China or to the West was in fact nothing of the sort: it was simply a better, more productive way to live, and was essential both for Japanese and for Japan – *kuni no tame*. For Inoue, the 'truth' implied in *gokoku airi* was absolute. Though his protestations about Japanese Buddhism representing the apex of human insight across the world and across time were surely composed with an eye to his peers' preoccupation with *kokusuishugi* (Japanese-ness),[43] Inoue's genuine interest in 'the truth' – a glimpse of which he claimed had brought him safely through a nervous breakdown – and his belief in the fitness of Japanese Buddhism for helping people towards it is beyond doubt.

In this, Inoue and Nakamura exemplified a common trope in Asian cultural nationalism in their time: the claim that there is a shared truth or goal to which human beings have always aspired, and that the West's current vanguard role is compromised by moral hypocrisy, excessive materialism, and ignorance of the remarkable insights contributed to this quest by Asia – including Indian and Japanese religion, philosophy, and psychology. The Indian religious leader Swami Vivekananda owed his fame partly to his ability to present this argument to Western audiences, while in a slightly later period pioneering psychoanalysts in both Japan and India regularly cross-checked and modified Freudian ideas according to the insights of Japanese Buddhism or Hinduism.[44]

How directly the relatively soft, often latent cultural nationalism of Inoue and Nakamura contributed to Japanese ultra-nationalism in later years, or that of Vivekananda to *Hindutva* and inter-communal bloodshed in the 1920s and 1930s, is the subject of ongoing debate.[45] What is clear is that by the mid 1890s in Japan a combination of Western provocation perceived in military, political, and cultural terms and a sense of fundamental insecurity at the loss of the old order and the challenges of the new had given rise to early imperialistic forays of a defensive nature and had begun to generate a passive imperialism centred around the cultivation of an increasingly competitive Japanese sense of duty, community, and the good of the nation. The state of play at the close of this period of 'genesis' for Japanese imperialism was apparent in the language of the Imperial Rescript on Education of 1890, a document often seen by historians of Japan as a crucial marker on the way to Japan's twentieth-century 'dark valley' of authoritarianism, expansionism, and disaster.[46] Addressing the Japanese people, the Rescript stressed continuity with the Japanese past (the 'best traditions of your forefathers') and forms of self-cultivation that would promote 'intellectual faculties', 'perfect moral powers', and finally a 'common good' which, it was foreseen, might one day have to extend to a willingness to 'offer yourselves courageously to the State'.[47]

Notes

1   It was precisely the security of the nation that prompted one faction of Japan's leadership to reject the calls of another group to attack Korea in the 1870s. Such a move, its opponents claimed, would put at risk Japan's people, its finances and its prestige. H. Conroy, 'Lessons from Japanese Imperialism', *Monumenta Nipponica*, 21, 3/4 (1966), pp. 334–45.

2   For religious and 'psy' dimensions here, see Christopher Harding, Iwata Fumiaki and Yoshinaga Shin'ichi (eds), *Religion and Psychotherapy in Modern Japan* (2014).

3   Y. Fukuzawa, 'Datsu-A ron' ('Escaping Asia'), *Jiji Shinpō*, 16 March 1885. See D. J. Lu (ed.), *Japan: A Documentary History*, vol. II (1997).

4   This claim about the Dutch was made by Hirata Atsutane (1776–1843), of whom more below. On the Ainu, see R. Siddle, *Race, Resistance, and the Ainu of Japan* (1996), pp. 8–9 and 26–50. After the Ainu came the turn of the Chinese to suffer harsh physical critiques and wild speculation, fuelled by nationalist sentiment in the 1890s and particularly around the time of the Sino-Japanese War in

1894–5. Stereotyping of the Ainu has not gone away in Japan, and has if anything been made worse by their reinvention as a tourist attraction. The Japan Travel Bureau was censured in 1981 for publishing in the English-language newspaper *The Japan Times* an advert for tourists to see a 'real Ainu village and the famed hairy Ainu'.

5 Richard Siddle has criticized historians of Japanese colonialism for failing to recognize this, and for instead viewing Hokkaidō as a case of a government making an *internal* land settlement. He points out that this common view of Hokkaidō's treatment as *kaitaku* (development, or the opening up of new land), has the effect of obscuring the violent truth of events. Siddle, *Race, Resistance, and the Ainu*, p. 51.

6 For further reading on the Ainu, see T. Morris-Suzuki, 'The Frontiers of Japanese Identity', in S. Tonneson and H. Antlov (eds), *Asian Forms of the Nation* (1996); J. Lie, *Multiethnic Japan* (Cambridge, MA, 2000); G. DeVos, *Japan's Minorities: Burakumin, Koreans and Ainu* (1974).

7 For a critique of existing historiography on Japanese imperialism for understating the simultaneity of Japan's modernization of her colonies and Japan's own modernization, see A. Schmid, 'Colonialism and the "Korea Problem" in the Historiography of Modern Japan: A Review Article', *Journal of Asian Studies*, 59, 4 (2000), pp. 951–76.

8 See Siddle, *Race, Resistance, and the Ainu*, pp. 9–13. As Takashi Fujitani has pointed out in the case of the modern myth-making surrounding Japan's emperor, the past can be supplanted with invented alternatives in remarkably short order. See T. Fujitani, 'Inventing, Forgetting, Remembering: Toward a Historical Ethnography of the Nation State', in Harumi Befu (ed.), *Cultural Nationalism in East Asia: Representation and Identity* (Berkeley, CA, 1993).

9 Over time, the two terms came to be understood at the popular level as having essentially the same meaning. Siddle, *Race, Resistance, and the Ainu*, p. 13. On racialized notions of 'Self' and 'Other' as they made their way into propaganda during the Pacific War, see J. Dower, *War Without Mercy: Race and Power in the Pacific War* (New York, NY, 1997).

10 See S. Vlastos, 'Opposition Movements in Early Meiji Japan', in *Cambridge History of Japan*, vol. V: *The Nineteenth Century* (Cambridge, 1989).

11 On the refashioning of the image and role of the Emperor, see T. Fujitani, *Splendid Monarchy: Power and Pageantry in Modern Japan* (Berkeley, CA, 1996).

12 On the military and on early Meiji leaders' 'negative definition of [party] politics' as essentially disloyal and focused upon private interests , see C. Gluck, *Japan's Modern Myths: Ideology in the Late Meiji Period* (Princeton, NJ, 1985), pp. 53–60.

13 R. Eskildsen, 'Of Civilization and Savages: the Mimetic Imperialism of Japan's 1874 Expedition to Taiwan', *American Historical Review*, 107, 2 (2002), pp. 388–98.

14 *Ibid.*, 399.

15 For a general overview see M. R. Peattie, 'Introduction', in *The Japanese Colonial Empire, 1895–1945* (Princeton, NJ, 1984). On later implications for Korea see P. Duus, *The Abacus and the Sword: the Japanese Penetration of Korea* (Berkeley, CA, 1995).

16 J. Tasca Sawada, *Practical Pursuits: Religion, Politics, and Personal Cultivation in Nineteenth-Century Japan* (Honolulu, 2004), p. 7.

17 These included a Rescript issued to Japan's military in 1882 on the advice of Yamagata Aritomo, stressing loyalty to the Emperor and the avoidance of politics, and another on education issued in 1890.

18 S. Natsume, *Wagahai wa neko de aru* [I am a Cat] (1905–6). Quoted in P. N. Dale, *The Myth of Japanese Uniqueness* (1986).

19 See H. Befu, 'Nationalism and Nihonjinron', in H. Befu (ed.), *Cultural Nationalism in East Asia: Representation and Identity* (Berkeley, CA, 1993), pp. 107–35.

20 M. Carr, 'Yamato Damashii: "Japanese Spirit" Definitions', *International Journal of Lexicography*, 7, 4 (1994), pp. 279–306.

21 Motoori Norinaga (1730–1801), quoted in K. Pyle, *The Making of Modern Japan*, 2nd edition (Lexington, 1996), p. 50.

22 D. R. Howland, *Translating the West: Language and Political Reason in Nineteenth-Century Japan* (Honolulu, 2002), p. 58.

23　*Ibid.*, pp. 50–3.

24　H. Sukehiro, 'Japan's Turn to the West', in B. T. Wakabayashi (ed.), *Modern Japanese Thought* (Cambridge, 1998), pp. 81–3. Natsume Sōseki's classic novel *Kokoro* [The Heart of Things], published in 1914, offered a dark corrective to the optimism of Meiji youth.

25　Howland, *Translating the West*, p. 113. See also A. Hamish Ion, 'Edward Warren Clark and Early Meiji Japan: A Case Study of Cultural Contact', *Modern Asian Studies*, 11, 4 (1977), pp. 557–72.

26　See W. Davis, 'Buddhism and the Modernization of Japan', *History of Religions*, 28, 4 (1989), pp. 310–11.

27　R. Sharf, 'The Zen of Japanese Nationalism', *History of Religions*, 33, 1 (1993), p. 4. See also J. E. Ketelaar, *Of Heretics and Martyrs in Meiji Japan: Buddhism and its Persecution* (Princeton, NJ, 1990).

28　See Christopher Harding, 'Japanese Psychoanalysis and Buddhism: the Making of a Relationship', *History of Psychiatry*, 25, 2 (2014), pp. 154–70.

29　For a debate on the contested emergence of the categories of 'religion' and 'philosophy' in Meiji Japan see G. C. Godart, '"Philosophy" or "Religion"? The Confrontation with Foreign Categories in Late Nineteenth Century Japan', *Journal of the History of Ideas*, 69, 1 (2008), pp. 71–91.

30　One wonders whether this was a little too convenient. Kathleen Staggs concludes that Inoue was sincere at least in terms of his motivation in pursuing truth. K. M. Staggs, '"Defend the Nation and Love the Truth": Inoue Enryō and the Revival of Meiji Buddhism', *Monumenta Nipponica*, 38, 3 (1983), pp. 251–81.

31　See Earl H. Kinmonth, 'Nakamura Keiu and Samuel Smiles: A Victorian Confucian and a Confucian Victorian', *American Historical Review*, 85, 3 (1980), p. 541. See also R. Dore, 'The Legacy of Tokugawa Education', in M. Jansen (ed.), *Changing Japanese Attitudes Toward Modernization* (Princeton, NJ, 1965).

32　K. Nakamura, *Saikoku Risshi Hen*, quoted in Earl H. Kinmonth, *The Self-Made Man in Meiji Japanese Thought* (Berkeley, CA, 1981), p. 20.

33　For a discussion of this theme in the Japanese discovery of Western literature see D. Keene, *Dawn to the West: Japanese Literature of the Modern Era* (New York, NY, 1984).

34　Howland, *Translating the West*, pp. 62–4.

35　*Ibid.*, p. 111 and pp. 57–8.

36　Kinmonth, 'Nakamura Keiu and Samuel Smiles', p. 546.

37　Howland, *Translating the West*, pp. 106–7.

38　E. Inoue, 'Tetsugaku no Hitsuyō o Ronjite Honkai no Enkaku ni oyobu' ('This Society Discusses the Need for Philosophy'), quoted in Staggs, 'Defend the Nation', p. 259.

39　E. Inoue, quoted in J. Snodgrass, *Presenting Japanese Buddhism to the West: Orientalism, Occidentalism, and the Columbian Exposition* (Chapel Hill, NC, 2003), p. 144.

40　Davis, 'Buddhism', p. 327. Uchimura Kanzō, a prominent Meiji-era Christian convert, was obliged constantly to insist on the compatibility of Christianity and Japanese identity by emphasizing the importance in his life of 'the two J's': Jesus and Japan.

41　Quoted in Snodgrass, *Presenting Japanese Buddhism*, p. 148. For Inoue's comment on Christianity and Buddhism's shared basic dynamic, see Staggs, 'Defend the Nation', pp. 266–7.

42　Quoted in *ibid.*, pp. 268, 271.

43　Alongside fellow Buddhists Oouchi Seiran, Shimaji Mokurai, and Ashitsu Jitsuzen, Inoue was a member of the influential *Seikyōsha* group of scholars, whose concerns centred in large part around the subject of Japanese-ness.

44　See C. Hartnack, *Psychoanalysis in Colonial India* (Oxford, 2001); C. Harding, 'The Freud Franchise: Independence of Mind in India and Japan', in R. Clarke (ed.), *Celebrity Colonialism: Fame, Power and Representation in (Post) Colonial Cultures* (Cambridge, 2009). On the 'Ajase Complex', the attempt by the Japanese psychoanalyst Kosawa Heisaku to modify Freud's Oedipus Complex to fit the Japanese context, see: C. Ozawa-de Silva, 'Demystifying Japanese Therapy: An Analysis of Naikan and the Ajase Complex Through Buddhist Thought', *Ethos*, 35, 4 (December 2007).

45　See, for example: B. D. Victoria, *Zen at War* (Lanham, MD, 1998); W. Radice (ed.), *Swami Vivekananda and the Modernization of Hinduism* (Delhi, 1998).

46　See E. K. Tipton, *Modern Japan: A Social and Political History* (Abingdon, 2002), p. 125.

47　Imperial Rescript on Education, 1890.

Epilogue:
Analysing 'Echoes of Empire' in Contemporary Context: The Personal Odyssey of an Imperial Historian (1970s–Present)

John M. MacKenzie

This chapter constitutes a reflection on 40 years of writing aspects of African and British imperial history through the twists and turns of the historiography of the period, at a time when the 'echoes of empire' which are the subject of this book not only took shape, but also proved loci of ideological confrontation.[1] Looking back, historians often realize that in the writing of history, we sometimes stumble over new concepts that seem to represent some of the things they have been trying to do all along. Two examples that are going to be highlighted in this chapter are glocalization, sometimes known as glocalism, and micro-history. These represent the kind of history that I have always found agreeable, and they are profoundly contemporary in their application. Glocalization or glocalism is a concept that has emerged in the past 20 years or so out of business studies and sociology.[2] It concerns the manner in which local markets are integrated into a world economy, the ways that transnational forms operate at the local level and, one hopes, are in turn influenced by the process. Micro-history emerged from Italian writings of the 1970s, particularly promoted by Giovanni Levi and Carlo Ginzburg.[3] It is related to forms of historical anthropology, to notions such as Clifford Geertz's 'thick description', even to history from below. It seeks to analyse a single event, the history of a community or village, of a family or an individual or perhaps of a single institution in one particular place. It has been suggested that it seeks answers to large questions in small places, but that is not quite right, for the places can also be very large, as I shall seek to demonstrate: it is just that we concentrate on individuals and their specific contexts, avoiding mega impersonal quantitative studies or the histories of great men – and as we all know ever since Carlyle it has too often been men – or of big political processes viewed from above. By contrast, empires of all sorts, despite being global phenomena (particularly in modern times) can surely be best understood from the specific experiences 'on the ground' of both dominant and subordinate peoples. Their 'echoes' can best be picked up in the caves, as it were, of local contexts.

But when I started studying imperial history in the 1960s, it always seemed to be about exactly those major political processes, about meta-narratives, great figures, and global quantitative analyses. I remember never feeling entirely comfortable with all of that, even though I had to go through the mill of Hobson, Lenin, Schumpeter, Harlow, Coupland, the greatly innovative Robinson and Gallagher, Fieldhouse and all the rest of them. Official minds were always more important than private passions or personal agonies, individual psychologies or popular responses. Looking back now, I am convinced that individual historians are formed out of their genes, out of their personal experiences, or put at its most basic, out of their gut reactions – even if we do seek to introduce professional modes of distance or supposed objectivity or dispassionate appraisal. How we balance the heart and the mind, the hot and the cool, the gut and the intellect will always remain a prime concern of all of us. In the 1960s, after undergraduate work in Scotland and postgraduate in Canada, my historical apprenticeship was spent in what is now Zimbabwe, then Rhodesia, conducting research, on and off, between 1967 and 1976. There I encountered the work of a historian who led me to new forms of history. I did not encounter him personally at that time because he was already a prohibited immigrant in that country and had moved on to Tanzania.

This was T. O. or Terry Ranger. Ranger is a perfect example of writing history in contemporary context, of pursuing forms of glocalization and micro-history even though – of course – he had no idea at the time that he was doing so. Let me explain why he had a considerable influence on me. When he first went to Southern Rhodesia/Zimbabwe in the late 1950s, the writings about the indigenous response to imperial rule had been minimal to non-existent. His first book *Revolt in Southern Rhodesia 1896–7* came out in 1967 and was a revelation.[4] It revealed what could be written about African resistance from European sources and it also demonstrated that such history could be both exciting and inspirational. Its contention was that African history should be written from below, not from above despite the nature of the sources. It should be about Africans, not about Europeans in Africa. And history could indeed act as a great rallying cry for modern resistance. It unquestionably reflected Ranger's own political commitments as well as his historian's professionalism and was none the worse for that.

It did however also reveal the dangers of writing from a contemporary focus for a modern audience. It tended to the romantic. It replaced the heroic imperial narrative with the equally heroic narrative of resistance. It stressed the importance of major ethnic groups and it suggested that, if they found a single mighty cause and a uniting factor (for Ranger it was indigenous religious forms), they could work together against a common enemy. But the book emphasized resisters to the detriment of collaborators whose objectives were also interesting and worthy of study. It focused on apparently meritocratic leadership – priests and spirit mediums – over that of traditional rulers. And it concentrated upon the big ethnicities rather than marginal peoples. Ranger did not use oral evidence which was about to be one of the basic tools in the Africanist's trade, although he did do so in some significant subsequent works. As soon as some colleagues, sometimes accompanied by myself, established the primacy of fieldwork, we began to see the flaws in *Revolt*. It became a good book to bounce off and there's nothing wrong with that. Moreover, his work created a powerful myth of nationalism which was naturally and inevitably seized upon by nationalist leaders but, sadly, it did not presage either the united leadership or the moral, people-centred politics that Ranger had hoped for. None of that is to detract from the importance of the book or of the many that followed from him. It merely illustrates the manner in which contemporary events and a present-day focus can inspire the writing of truly innovative historical scholarship which can in turn influence current events. It may be suggested that this was a precursor of later modes of doing this, particularly in multi-disciplinary forms, all helping to illuminate the ways in which twenty-first-century Europe relates to the rest of the world (or indeed the other way round).

As it happens, I first arrived in Central Africa in the very year of the publication of that book, 1967. My interest was in African labour migration, in the manner in which Africans from Zambia, Malawi and what was to become Zimbabwe were sucked into migrating to the diamond and gold mines of South Africa as well as to the gold mines and urban employment of white-run Rhodesia. Why did they do it? Was it a purely coercive process, the essentially determinist result of the breaking-up of African societies through warfare, taxation and, above all, through the dispossession of their land? Europeans were determined upon the destruction of what they saw as the 'backward-looking' communal and, from their viewpoint, ultimately unproductive African traditional economies. Africans had to be forced out into modern industrial society and play their role in allegedly developmental processes which marked the supposed 'gift' of imperial rulers in their globalizing imperial thrust. But Europeans were of course obsessed with the age-old dichotomy between opulence and security, between wealth and safety. If Africans were to offer their essential labour to mining, infrastructural developments and urbanization, it had to be on European terms. And those terms had an ineluctable logic about them. A huge urban black population would be highly dangerous, in all sorts of ways, in respect of unionization, the politics of resistance, the supposed protection of white health, and above all wage levels. Seasonal migratory male labour was the answer:

males would be moved into the modernist white economy on a temporary basis, say for a period of nine or ten months. They could be kept there under tight controls. Women, children and the old would remain in the traditional economy, supposedly fed upon the land and not by younger men's wages. Only whites would be involved in the political process. The income gap between the races would of course be enormous. Now all of this is familiar to us from the full development of the whole scheme under apartheid, but the fundamental outlines were framed in the British imperial period and formed in the late nineteenth and early twentieth centuries, starting from the era of the 'mineral revolution' in the Cape and the Transvaal from the 1870s to the 1890s. Moreover, it was highly significant because it was in some respects a system that was replicated in other parts of the imperial world.

But while my focus was on Central rather than South Africa and while I was interested in all the conventional concerns of migratory patterns, that is numbers, recruitment systems, controls and so forth, I was also interested in indigenous motivations. Were the coercive forces always in white hands? Could migration ever be elective? It was well known that African rulers in Southern Africa had sent their young men out to work for whites in order 'to earn a gun', often in the period preceding the imposition of direct imperial controls. In other words labour migration was also seen as potentially a means of enhancing the security of indigenous societies. But what about during a later period? Could we establish anything about motivations from living people? With this in mind, I went out into the field and asked large numbers of elderly informants about when they had first migrated into the white economy, why they had done so, and what effects this migration might have had. Of course the results of such a project were inevitably limited, limited to highly specific regions, limited to a particular generation, and limited to such conditions as proximity to employment opportunities, land availability, marketing opportunities, and much else. Such conditions were inevitably going to change over time, not least as the grip of white rule tightened and as political processes controlled by Europeans repeatedly biased the terms of trade of entry into a market economy in favour of European farmers and white employers generally. But still the results I secured in my interviews were interesting. A high proportion of my informants talked about their opportunities to buy ploughs, industrially produced tools, or means of conveyance like the so-called scotch cart (a small two-wheeled cart, often pulled by a donkey) or the bicycle. Another significant cohort alluded to more personal matters. Through most of the societies of the region, the principle of bride price had been significant in pre-colonial times. The existence of this custom ensured that the marriage practices of young men were securely in the hands of a senior generation. Many of the men I interviewed (women came into my evidence-collecting later) indicated that migrating for pay enabled them to build up the cash required to take control of their own marriage arrangements. Migration – and I stress in some places and at some times – had enabled them to diminish the power of a gerontocracy. Of course I faced two problems: one was the extent to which my 'informants' were telling me what I wanted to hear. The other was the extent to which the economic screws tightened, as it were, more considerably later on. Circumstantial detail was such that the first seemed unlikely, but progressive land and labour legislation, securely in the hands of white settlers after 1923 in the then Southern Rhodesia, made the second a possibility.[5] Even with such caveats, such a mixed approach got me into deep trouble with the dominant Marxist historiography of the time, a historiography that was much more interested in meta-narratives.[6] Being out of step became a familiar condition for me.

Intoxicated by the possibilities of oral evidence-collecting, I later turned to a wholly new, but related, interest. In my visits to so many African villages in the so-called tribal trust lands of what was then still white-ruled Rhodesia, I had been shown ploughs, carts, implements of one sort or another. Sometimes an African informant would show me an item such as a pre-colonial iron hoe and contrast it with an industrially produced one. It must be remembered that at this point I was fortunate enough to be collecting oral evidence in the late 1960s and early 1970s. I was talking to elderly people in their eighties and nineties, and occasionally those 100. I was therefore immensely privileged to be speaking to a generation born in the 1870s, 1880s and 1890s. Their lifetimes had crossed the watershed from pre-colonial to colonial times (the region having been pulled into the imperial orbit in the years after 1890). They had seen the world transformed economically, socially and politically. Most of them were all too aware of this and were alert to the significance of the historical changes through which they had lived. They were also intrigued by my unusual questions, for most previous oral researchers had been interested in genealogies, in politics and traditional leadership, in social structures and forms. To be asked about economic and technological change was something new. In the course of this research I became aware of fascinating paradoxes. Why was it that archaeologists had demonstrated that pre-colonial ironworking seemed to be found in almost all villages in the area while geologists had suggested that really useful deposits of iron ore were only to be found in restricted locations? How were these two to be reconciled? And what would pre-colonial ironworking tell us about trading patterns and that all-important cusp between the traditional and the industrial economy? I embarked on an oral research project to try to find out.

The first step was to consult geologists about iron deposits. The second was to talk to archaeologists and anthropologists about peoples notable for pre-colonial iron working. And the third, of course, was to look at the written sources, particularly those produced by pre-colonial white travellers in Africa. I selected three or four areas of Zimbabwe where oral research might be conducted and duly embarked upon the project. To summarize, I soon discovered that the pre-colonial iron industry could only be understood once it had been divided into sectors. Mining and smelting did indeed take place in restricted areas where good sources of workable iron could be found. But once iron bars had been produced and turned into hoes, knives, axes and other implements, trade was then conducted over extraordinarily long distances. Iron implements were distributed throughout the region. But the story did not end there. Iron was expensive. Hoes became worn out. Every village needed its blacksmith to effect repairs or to cut a larger but damaged implement down to a smaller one. The paradox could be resolved. Smelting was restricted in its incidence; the reworking of iron was universal. And it was of course the very effort and labour intensity of all these sectors that ensured that the modern industrially produced item, like the ubiquitous hoe, would sweep all before it. The price differential was massive. All of the people who had worked in these sectors, with the possible exception of a few local blacksmiths, were denied their pre-colonial occupations and became available for the white labour market.

In all of this, I was enormously helped by the fact that these questions were genuinely new. The sources were not contaminated – that is, damaged by the stories provided by schoolchildren from what they learned at school, fed back to their elders as another form of 'reverse' oral evidence. They had also not been contaminated by earlier oral researchers, who always destroy both the contexts and contents of memory by the very process of asking questions. Moreover, the people I interviewed, proud of their pasts and the dignity of their previous labours with the mystical iron, were genuinely fascinated by my research. It was at this stage that I interviewed some very elderly women who, though generally excluded by the gender restrictions traditionally placed on ironworking processes, were still knowledgeable about aspects of the iron trade and the use and frailties of iron. One such lady presented me with a pre-colonial hoe (no sign of rust) and an industrially produced one (heavily rusted). On another occasion, I well remember a wonderful moment, in an interview with a very old man, probably over 100, when he turned to the people listening in and said, 'How does this *murungu* [white man] know so much?'

This research was published in some obscure journals and has only been noticed by specialists.[7] But of course it was important to me, not just in providing some of the best times of my life, albeit in highly fraught political and occasionally violent circumstances, but also in convincing me of the importance of taking on new and unfashionable projects. And as you can now see I was of course dealing in glocalization and micro-history, the history of individuals caught up in global processes in local contexts. For me, both of these studies constituted some of the essence of imperialism, operating where it matters, on the ground. What I discovered in the wonderful Wedza district of Mashonaland, to use just one example, had all sorts of resonances for people in other parts of the world.

From that day to this, I have never been so excited by what has traditionally been the very meat and drink of imperial history – the high politics, the strategy, and the military activities that constituted imperial processes when viewed from above, from the standpoint of the imperial metropolis. Perhaps that is why I turned to the research for which I am better known. Despite my immersion in the big figures of imperial history, I knew I wanted to branch out on something completely new. I no longer wished to do research in Southern Africa, partly because of apartheid, partly because of the continuing intransigence of Ian Smith, partly because the logistics were becoming increasingly unfavourable. Then I was struck by another paradox. Readings in British history, by such historians as Henry Pelling and A. J. P. Taylor, had told me that the British public had no interest in the empire, that concerns about it were the preserve of an elite, that imperialism in a sense was a characteristic of what came to be known, after Jürgen Habermas, as the bourgeois public sphere. Following Schumpeter, it seemed that empire was a matter for the upper social classes, a system of distant outdoor relief for aristocratic and bourgeois younger sons, for the officials who made it their administrative preserve and consequently their fortune. Although ordinary people migrated in large numbers, they supposedly went principally to the United States, not the British Empire – not strictly true and certainly not in the twentieth century – and the context of a British ideology of empire was in many respects irrelevant. The history of the British Empire and the history of Britain were taught in two separate compartments. The British were the absent-minded imperialists well before Bernard Porter had thought of his Seeley-inspired title.[8] Yet none of this seemed to ring true in terms of the contemporary world in which I lived. Largely brought up in Glasgow, that quintessentially imperial city, as I was later to write, empire had seemed all about me.[9] In the 1940s and 1950s, the Church of Scotland, and the other Scottish churches, though by then often radical in terms of decolonization, seemed to have empire deeply embedded in their history – the history of missions, of missionary publications, of heroes, of lectures and lantern slides by missionaries on furlough.[10] Such matters seemed to form a major source of moral exemplification in sermons, Sunday-school teaching and the like. Empire still floated about in school textbooks and literally floated in the ships of the great imperial shipping lines to be seen on the Clyde. My favourite boyhood walk was to Yorkhill Quay to see the Anchor liners – no locked gates or health and safety regulations then – that plied between Glasgow and Bombay. Glasgow architecture and statuary, the contents of its museums, and the notable, if rapacious, personalities of its industrial, commercial and shipbuilding past were all essentially imperial. People still vividly remembered the Glasgow Empire exhibition of 1938. As a child I had gone to the Saturday morning cinema club and had watched endless exciting serials of imperial 'derring do'. My reading matter, borrowed from the local library, also invariably had empire as the context for the adventures and heroics of its protagonists. Then there was that map, certainly on *my* school walls, with all the red that was supposed to make all true patriots swell with pride.

It is true (and my sparring partner Bernard Porter would find this significant)[11] that my family, notably on my father's side, had migrated to Canada and Australia, that my father had worked in Kenya and in Central Africa in the interwar years and the years after World War II, but that seemed to be the experience of many ordinary working-class Scots. We were certainly not connected with those upper social classes who apparently benefitted from, and were interested in, empire. We lived in a tenement and were firmly in the category of the respectable aristocracy of labour. It is also true that some of my impressionable years in the mid 1950s were spent in Northern Rhodesia, Zambia, where my father was then working in the Public Works Department. But even as I mulled over these connections, I noted the renewed popularity of films and television series about empire in the 1970s and 1980s. At any rate, when I read the transcript of a radio talk by the distinguished sociologist A. H. Halsey, published in *The Listener*, about the manner in which his village classroom of the 1920s had been steeped in nationalism and empire, and the culture of empire that had been all around him at that time, it all seemed to make sense even for my later generation.[12] Once I started researching the incidence of propaganda about the British Empire and of the imperial content of popular culture, it seemed to me to be everywhere in the late nineteenth and twentieth centuries. My boyhood had not been anomalous. My world of the 1950s represented an essential continuity from late nineteenth-century concerns despite the onset of decolonization. I was already well into researching and writing my book *Propaganda and Empire* when a remarkable event occurred. That was the Falklands War in 1982. Suddenly I found myself hearing powerful echoes of the nineteenth century. Jingoism was everywhere, not only in the headlines of *The Sun*, but also on radio and television, in the speeches of Thatcher, in the content of politics – after all even Michael Foot was sucked into the general excitement and the national anxiety not to appease the aggressor. I was reliving the world of J. A. Hobson and the *Psychology of Jingoism*.[13] All this was represented by crowds on the quaysides watching the return of naval vessels and of troop-carrying cruise liners, in victory marches, and in many publications. A modern British public was so swept into this new imperial war that the economic and employment disasters wrought by the Geoffrey Howe budget of 1981 could be forgotten. Thus was Thatcher rescued from the nadir of her popularity and put back into power with an increased majority in the election of 1983. These highly visible events constituted an extraordinary echo of similar moments in the nineteenth century. Moreover, they were followed, as then, by a wave of memoirs and other publications relating to that distant war, even if modern media had made it much more immediate for British peoples in their living rooms. They also seemed to prove that it was possible for historically influenced patterns of thinking to be given renewed lease of life in contemporary times (and in different ways that may also have been true of the Iraq and Afghanistan wars). They also illustrated the ways in which these things really mattered and had important political consequences. I finished the book that year and it was published in 1984, to some howls of disapproval by conventional imperial and British historians.

The point about that book was that I was suggesting that we should get away from the official mind of imperialism and examine the popular psychology. And to do this, we had to get out of the archive. The popular psychology was not to be found in documents in Kew; it was to be found in many other sources, in ephemera, in cultural forms like the theatre, exhibitions, film, the press, visual evidence, school text-books, the everyday material that people read and looked at, in the displays they saw in their streets. Historical phenomena could be reconstructed from many other sources than the purely official. I have to confess that I gave inadequate attention to two important areas: one surprisingly was the church and the other was the press. These have since been repaired and in each case seem to me to demonstrate the importance of the view from outside the official documents.[14] Non-official documents of all sorts seemed to open up fresh vistas that are often more about the lives of ordinary people than the administrators and politicians who were the framers of the policy. And maybe those policy-makers did have an eye over their shoulders at what sort of views and ideas were being promulgated or ought to be promoted among the electors. As John Darwin has recently suggested, those electors seemed to accept that the empire was an important source of foodstuffs, as well as of migratory opportunities. Thus, empire and social reform did not seem to be necessarily incompatible, however different it may seem to us in retrospect. Early in his magnificent book *The Empire Project*, Darwin seems to be convinced by Bernard Porter's contentious work, which he had clearly recently read. Yet towards its end he poses the question: why was it that the British accepted the existence of empire?[15] I would stick by my now 30-year-old conviction that this phenomenon cannot be divorced from the fact that, for many members of the populace as well as Halsey, it was built into the very fabric of their lives. As I have written recently, I stand by that interpretation framed in the late 1970s and early 1980s. Now new work has appeared, or will shortly appear, which has supported my 30-year conviction, particularly in respect of the theatre and of education.[16]

The publication of *Propaganda and Empire* in 1984 led to three consequences. The first was that it did me no favours at all with the historical establishment, for whom it became almost a heretical work.[17] But second, it brought me into contact with large numbers of scholars working in similar fields, often on a cross-disciplinary basis. It was this discovery which led to the foundation of the 'Studies in Imperialism' series of Manchester University Press later in 1984, with the first publications appearing in 1986. It is a source of some pride that it has now (at the end of 2012) passed the hundred-volume mark, a magnificent tribute to the fine work being pursued by younger – and occasionally not so young – scholars across the globe.[18] The third consequence was the appearance of the two edited books *Imperialism and Popular Culture* and *Popular Imperialism and the Military* respectively in 1986 and 1992.[19] Many colleagues emerged who were already working in these fields and they enthusiastically endorsed the whole idea of a series on the social and cultural dimensions of imperialism, a development which, it should be said, well predated the emergence of the post-colonial school and Edward Said's book *Culture and Imperialism*.[20]

Casting around for a new field in the mid 1980s, I sought a return to forms of African history, perhaps in the new field of environmental history. The catalyst was a request from a colleague that I should contribute to a book called *Sport in Africa*. At that point I did not have much interest in the history of sport, a word I interpreted in its modern meaning. I briefly toyed with the thought of writing something about missionaries' dissemination of football and other sports, but I was not enthused. Then I remembered the older meaning of sport – the shooting of animals. I also remembered that whenever I had read books of exploration in Africa I had always tripped over long passages about the killing of elephants and other African fauna. I had invariably skipped these, partly because I found them repetitive and boring and partly because they offended my modern susceptibilities. Should I return to those missed passages, resurrect them, and write something about that form of sport? I duly did so and soon became enthralled.[21] Here was the subject for a book. Notions of shooting for 'sport' soon opened up into much grander concerns. It became apparent to me that it was possible to construct a thesis that Europeans had conquered Africa partly on the strength of the phenomenal richness of its faunal resource. All travellers in Africa, without exception, hunted. They hunted elephants for ivory to finance their exploits. They hunted game, particularly antelope, to feed themselves. The presence of the tsetse fly ensured that the horse could not be used in much of the area embraced by the tropics. Hence travellers had to employ large numbers of porters to carry their possessions, trade goods and ivory. Porters required to be fed and the obvious means was through the shooting of large animals. Missionaries used the great protein resources of Africa for similar purposes. In the next phase, the arrival of settlers, administrators, railway engineers and the like, animals continued to be important. Administrators shot for sport, to protect their African neighbours from depredations to their crops or livestock, and to feed employees. Engineers shot to feed their workers. So did settlers, who invariably started off the process of taking over land by asset-stripping the animals from it. As well as ivory, animals also produced horns, skins and other saleable products. The conquest of Africa would surely have been much more difficult without its animals. It is now apparent that this subject was also glocal.

But the thesis soon spread out in other directions. Most Africans had been great hunters, to protect crops and livestock and provide meat, skins, horns, and ivory. All sorts of techniques, hierarchical customs and sumptuary laws had arisen to surround these activities, much as in medieval Europe. Animals had been important in forming international trade links at one end of the economic process while at the other, they had been significant in staving off famine in time of dearth. I recollected that when I had asked my Zimbabwean informants about changes in their environment, they had invariably mentioned the disappearance of animals.

The study had spread out to such an extent that my ambition knew no bounds. I also wanted to contrast Africa with the practice of indigenous and imperial hunting in India. There it had been one of the most conspicuous ways in which the British took over the symbolic dominance of the environment from the Mughals and other indigenous rulers. Next I noticed the developing concerns of a white elite with the massive reduction in African animals in the late nineteenth century, concerns that led to the framing of game laws and the drafting of international conventions on animal conservation, conventions that led directly to the formation of game reserves and national parks. These were developments that had a tremendous modern resonance, but they were also double-edged swords in the African context. It soon became apparent that European imperial elite hunters and the lawmakers who stood behind them were concerned to protect animals for restricted forms of white hunting while banning African access to game. The self-same criteria about permissible hunting and the creation of such categories as poachers and vermin that had exercised the medieval and early modern mind could be found working themselves out in Africa, India and other parts of Asia. Moreover, anxiety to create game reserves often seemed to render the interests of animals – or at least the interests of elite hunters and tourist game viewers – more important than those of Africans who were excluded from lands they had previously occupied. And it should be noted that I was back in the realm of the interplay of pre-colonial and industrial forms, the contrasting technologies of spears, arrows, and guns (both old-fashioned and modern in the latter case), including the dissemination of the latter throughout the African continent through the agency of Africans as well as Europeans. The whole business of hunting and its aftermath also demonstrated the ways in which Europeans have always sought to impose upon Africa perceptions derived from Europe. Few things change. We still see this in aspects of aid-giving, in the negotiation of rights to oil and other resources, and in such areas as the diplomatic activity relating to fishing rights off the African coast.

This was a vast and sprawling subject that tempted me too far precisely because it had hardly received any attention in the past. The resulting book, *The Empire of Nature*, was published in 1988 and somewhat to my surprise suddenly transformed me into a pioneer of the environmental history movement – at least that was how I found myself being introduced at conferences.[22] Once more I had avoided the high points of imperial history, while interacting with them through the actions of governors, imperial administrators and international conventions. I had set out into unfashionable and at that time little explored territory, albeit territory which chimed with a contemporary set of conservationist ideas which were interpolated within many of the racial and cultural norms of imperialism. A new network of interdisciplinary scholars opened itself up and I was fortunate enough to edit *Imperialism and the Natural World* in 1990.[23] It is of course not without significance that the whole environmental history movement took off at precisely the moment when issues of the environment, which had been circulating at least since Rachel Carson published her *Silent Spring* in 1962, had come centre-stage in modern politics. As anxieties about the environment became increasingly fraught, so did historians, geographers, anthropologists, archaeologists and others become progressively more interested in environmental pasts. Work on hunting and game reserves soon became highly sophisticated.[24]

The next part of my twisting Odyssey got me into really serious trouble. When Edward Said's *Orientalism* was published in 1978, I read it and, like most of the academy, was greatly impressed.[25] The notable exception was Ernest Gellner who described it in his fiercely negative article in the *Times Literary Supplement* as an amusing, but insignificant work.[26] There the matter might have rested had I not attended a conference at which Said gave a keynote. In this he turned to one of his great loves, Western classical music. Using both images and musical examples, he set out to analyse Verdi's opera *Aida* in terms of the new Opera House in Cairo for which it was written, the opening of the Suez Canal which it was supposed to celebrate, and the reorientation of Egypt into Western modernism from its former role as an Ottoman province. For Said, *Aida* represented a classic orientalist construct, a Western re-invocation of the ancient East, in this case Pharaonic Egypt, for Western ends.[27] Here was a typical instance of representation by misrepresentation, of the fabrication of the East in order to be manipulated and dominated by the West. I listened to this with mounting anxiety. It became clear to me that Said did not really know or understand *Aida*, an opera which, as it happened, I knew well. In the question time, I rose and offered my critique, though it was turned aside by the chairman, who gave Said no chance to reply. *Aida*, it has always seemed to me, is about resistance, not dominance.[28] The Ethiopians, not the Egyptians, get the best tunes. Said made no mention of the libretto of the opera, the high point of which is Aida's moving invocation of the environment of her homeland in 'O patria mia'. The second-act triumph scene is consciously rebarbative, even if productions normally treat it merely as spectacle. Aida and her father, the Ethiopian king Amonasro, are the real heroes of the piece and the immolation of the Egyptian general Radames, together with Aida, rather than the dead end that Said saw it as, represents a common nineteenth-century trope in which the virtuous ones find their triumph and union in death. Verdi himself hated imperialism. He was opposed to the Italian involvement in the Scramble for Africa and rejoiced when the Italian army was defeated by the Ethiopians in the Battle of Adua in 1896. He was also highly critical of the British in India. We should never forget that almost all his works are sympathetic to underdogs. However, I should be clear that I base my interpretation on the opera itself rather than on productions of it, which have indeed often been orientalist. At any rate, I was so surprised by Said's complete misreading of the opera that I went back to *Orientalism* and reread it. This time I spotted all the flaws – including the total absence of social class or economic forces like the market. I was impelled to write a critique in which I would use a variety of arts to demonstrate that the alleged Manichean binaries between West and East do not always work, to show the manner in which many creative individuals in the West, like artists, composers, architects, writers and others turned to the East in order to find new inspiration, to find ways of escaping from the dead ends in which so many aspects of the Western arts had found themselves in the nineteenth century.[29] I was convinced that we should be finding instances of rapprochement rather than a never-ending catalogue of an exploitative failure of understanding. This book fitted with many of my own cultural enthusiasms, including my own fascination with Eastern forms, and it seemed to me to be about ways in which we should see imperialism as being about exchanges as well as dominance. But I discovered that he who criticizes a modern saint runs grave risks. Abuse was duly heaped and I found myself 'Othered' as some kind of right-wing reactionary, although I felt that I came to this problem from the left. Moreover, I had always made it clear that I had the most profound respect for Said the Palestinian, Said the man and committed scholar, that I was only critical of some of what I saw as the problematic aspects of his orientalism thesis. The debate became extensive and now, years after Said's untimely death, I feel more at ease with the works of scholarship in this field by writers such as Avril Powell and Robert Irwin.[30] Said's macro approach can indeed be critiqued from glocal and micro perspectives.

It is with some relief that I return to the more normal highways of the historical process and its interaction with contemporary events. This leads me back to what may be considered the oldest truism of historical writing. Freeman suggested that 'history is past politics and politics present history'. It has often seemed to me that this formulation can actually be reversed. History seems so often to be about present politics. Geoffrey of Monmouth wrote propaganda for the Normans in appropriating the story of King Arthur. Shakespeare's history plays famously constituted propaganda for the Tudors. The Tudors and their Stuart successors were of course much concerned with the power relationships among the various constituent parts of what I prefer to call the British and Hibernian Isles. The extension of English power through this Atlantic archipelago was one of the principal features of what we can now see as imperial history between the sixteenth and twentieth centuries.[31] It constituted crucial background to Seeley's vision of the expansion of England in the nineteenth century and the work of Reginald Coupland in the twentieth.[32] Ireland was always an imperial problem; Scotland and

Wales were in many ways imperial opportunities. Yet the British Empire never, in a sense, succeeded in becoming British, despite all the propaganda. In many respects, it remained four empires, those of the English, Irish, Scots and Welsh and modern migration studies, notably in their cultural and ethnic dimensions, now recognize that fact.[33] The British Empire, far from submerging those different ethnic identities, actually succeeded in facilitating their survival. English, Irish, Scots and Welsh all took on global significance and came to frame aspects of their ethnic integrity in terms of their worldwide connections.[34]

Thus, a true understanding of much of the cultural, intellectual, educational, religious, and other characteristics of the British Empire lay in that fundamental need to reflect on the composition of the British and Hibernian Isles themselves. When we examine, for example, the political, legal, religious, intellectual and educational institutions of Canada, South Africa, Australia, and New Zealand, even of India and parts of what were formerly known as the territories of the 'dependent empire', we find that they have to be understood in terms of their Irish, Scots, Welsh or English rather than supposedly synthetic British roots. We are only now arriving at a full appreciation of these essential facts. Even relationships with the environment and with indigenous peoples seem to draw upon the diversity of the so-called British and their variety of experiences at home as well as overseas. Niall Ferguson's coinage of 'Anglobalization' actually only refers to language.

Thus, knowledge of the constituent ethnicities of the British Isles constitutes a set of essential insights for a modern imperial historiography. The history of the empire must be seen as a complex of interactive influences between centre and periphery, periphery and centre. This is even more true now that Britain has itself become a location for settlement for so many Commonwealth migrants. This is why there is an increasing need to understand the complexities of what I call the four empires, the power of their reciprocal effects upon the very construction of the British state, and the ways in which they influenced Irish independence, Northern Irish adherence to Union, and the modern devolutionary processes. We now have an extraordinarily complex and asymmetrical state, in terms of its distribution of powers and legislative authority, and modern imperial history has to embrace these complexities. We are indeed back with the glocal and micro, yet always connected with the macro. This was what seemed to be the important balance in my recent studies of the Scots in South Africa or of the dispersal of the museum idea right across the British Empire into many local contexts.[35]

This personal odyssey through these twisting paths of imperial history indicates that we must always understand what we research and write both in terms of our obvious contemporary perspectives and also in the context of our personal relationships with the never-ending debate in which all historians are involved. Some schools of historians have imagined that it is possible to buck this trend. We need only think of the alleged scientific history of the nineteenth century, writing supposedly about how it really was, or the modern post-colonialists who sometimes imply that their highly moralizing approach to the British Empire represents some new kind of end to history writing. (This is not to deny the undoubted insights of this school which has taken issue with some of the very orthodoxies that I have attacked.) We must also guard against some of the right-wing revisionism that seems to be all around us. Television history reflects this trend. David Starkey junks social and economic history, history from below, to return to kings and queens. Niall Ferguson has sought to reinstate imperialism as a necessary force on the way to globalization. In an interview with *The Guardian* in July 2010, Ferguson suggested that school pupils have to be galvanized into an interest in history through war, war games, and the conflicts of big states.[36] Recently the classicist Richard Miles has talked (in a television series) of civilization as though it were the preserve of the Mediterranean and Middle Eastern worlds, and essentially urban, not rural, a matter of state construction rooted in class formation, war and conflict. Thus we must be alert to the fact that echoes of empire are still prevalent and still influence the thinking of both scholars and politicians in the twenty-first century. Many other examples reflect the ways in which television producers imagine that only this type of history can grip the public, although occasionally we do get something else, as in Michael Wood's series about the history of people in a Leicestershire village, Kibworth, which was a hugely refreshing representation of the glocal and the micro.

Despite the influence of television, books do indeed matter and can sometimes be revelatory. For example, I remember the occasion when I read the anthropologist Marshall Sahlins' highly revisionist book about hunting and gathering peoples, with its defiant opening essay 'The Original Affluent Society'.[37] It refreshingly threw out the stadial evolutionary progressivism of the Enlightenment. That is the kind of vision of the past that continues to enthral and which can surely be made exciting for a wider audience of schoolchildren and the general public. The developments in imperial history in my lifetime indicate the manner in which the best history is about understanding the big events through the local study, grand narratives and patterns explained by a focus on what happens to real people, men and women of all ethnicities, upon the ground. And it seems to me that all of that needs to be set into environmental and climatic contexts, for neither the environment nor the global climates that condition it are respecters of political boundaries. However grand states or individual rulers or warlords may be, they cannot buck those all-important conditions in which the lives of all people are rooted. Ranger and many other Africanists came to realize all that in concentrating on specific localities. As I have wandered from my African migrant workers, iron smelters and traders, with their rich memories, to human impacts upon animal populations and other aspects of the environment, to the manner in which empires have seduced people through the propaganda of popular culture, to the ways in which peoples interact culturally – not least between East and West – to an interest in the constituent parts of these islands in their global contexts, through all of that, the merging of micro- and macro-narratives has always seemed absolutely vital.[38] Ambitious as it is, it also seems to me that imperial history needs to absorb so many of our key modern developments. We need to integrate women's history and the history of science, environmental history and intellectual history before we can arrive at a fully satisfying approach, while still maintaining a glocal and micro focus in order more fully to understand the macro. We also require more insights derived from comparative and parallel narratives, as I have recently discovered in my interaction with Berny Sèbe and other colleagues in the Netherlands, Belgium, Germany, Italy and beyond.[39] British historians, not least of the imperial variety, have been much too introverted for far too long. They have also too often had their noses firmly stuck in the official records and their eyes on the grand processes and meta-narratives of imperial history. Such history, in missing the local and the apparently micro, has missed the vital insights that can be secured from a greater range of documents and techniques, as well as a focus upon real people facing their own problems, dilemmas and sometimes opportunities in specific locations. This volume, in examining echoes of empire in a number of different empires across the globe, helps to facilitate this. Echoes of empire can also be heard in glocal and micro locations: hearing and interpreting those echoes is surely important for the wider understanding of the grander processes of imperialism itself.

Notes

1 This chapter is a revised version of a public lecture given in the University of Birmingham in 2011. This explains its use of the first person and its slightly colloquial style. This has been left to give the flavour of the original. Others have of course worked in these fields and I owe a debt of gratitude to all of them.

2 Much can be found about glocalism or glocalization on the web. See particularly the article by James L. Koch and Uri Savir at http://www.scu.edu/sts/nexus/summer2003/KochSavirArticle.cfm dealing with a glocal forum that took place in Rome in 2002.

3 E. Rothschild, *The Inner Life of Empires: An Eighteenth-Century History* (Princeton, NJ, 2011) offers a useful assessment of micro-history, pp. 6–8 and also in footnotes 13–17 on pp. 312–13.

4 T. O. Ranger, *Revolt in Southern Rhodesia, 1896–7* (1967). 'Revolt' was carefully chosen by Ranger as a more neutral word than 'rebellion', hitherto always used in imperial history. In a long and distinguished career, Ranger published many more works in East and Central African history, though ironically he is better known in the wider academy for his joint editorship, with Eric Hobsbawm, of the celebrated collection *The Invention of Tradition* (Cambridge, 1983), which is still in print.

5 I was also interested in settler political processes and published 'Southern Rhodesia and Responsible Government', *Rhodesian History*, 9 (1978), pp. 23–40.

6 An attack by Charles van Onselen was published in *The Journal of Southern African Studies*, in which he accused me of creating a 'Sambo' figure. My response, 'Sambo and Economic Determinism', appeared in the *Journal of Southern African Studies*, 2, 1 (1975), pp. 98–101.

7 John M. MacKenzie, 'Trade and Labour, the Interaction of Traditional and Capitalist Economies in Southern Zambezia, 1870–1923', *Collected Papers of the Institute of Commonwealth Studies* (1975), pp. 98–101; 'A Pre-Colonial Industry: the Njanja and the Iron Trade', *NADA*, 11 (1974), pp. 200–20; 'Furnace and Bellows Types in Iron-Age Archaeology', *Rhodesian Prehistory*, 6 (1974), pp. 21–2; 'Red Soils in Mashonaland: A Re-Assessment', *Rhodesian History*, 5 (1974), pp. 81–8; 'Colonial Labour Policy and Rhodesia', *Rhodesian Journal of Economics*, 8 (1974), pp. 1–16; 'Chartered Africans: Colonial Office, Settlers and the British South Africa Company, 1890–1923', *Collected Papers of the Institute of Commonwealth Studies* (1973), pp. 77–86; 'African Labour in the Chartered Company Period', *Rhodesian History*, 1 (1976), pp. 43–58.

8 B. Porter, *The Absent-Minded Imperialists: Empire, Society and Culture in Britain* (Oxford, 2004).

9 J. M. MacKenzie, '"The Second City of the Empire": Glasgow – Imperial Municipality', in F. Driver and D. Gilbert (eds), *Imperial Cities* (Manchester, 1999), pp. 215–37.

10 Some of these effects are well charted in E. Breitenbach, *Empire and Scottish Society: The Impact of Foreign Missions at Home, c.1790 to c.1914* (Edinburgh, 2009) and L. A. Orr Macdonald, *A Unique and Glorious Mission: Women and Presbyterianism in Scotland 1830–1930* (Edinburgh, 2000).

11 See Porter's 'Further Thoughts on Imperial Absent-Mindedness', *Journal of Imperial and Commonwealth History*, 36, 1 (2008), pp. 101–17 and my reply 'Comfort and Conviction: A Response to Bernard Porter', *Journal of Imperial and Commonwealth History*, 36, 4 (2008), pp. 659–68.

12 A. H. Halsey in *The Listener*, 6 January 1983, p. 10.

13 J. A. Hobson, *The Psychology of Jingoism* (1901), reflecting Hobson's reactions to another war, the Anglo-Boer of 1899–1902.

14 For the press, see J. M. MacKenzie, 'The Press and the Dominant Ideology of Empire', in S. Potter (ed.), *Newspapers and Empire in Ireland and Britain: Reporting the British Empire, c.1857–1921* (Dublin, 2004), pp. 23–38 and other contributions to the same volume; I have summed up some of the work on missions and the churches in my chapters in *European Empires and the People* (see footnote 39 below).

15 J. Darwin, *The Empire Project: The Rise and Fall of the British World System 1830–1970* (Cambridge, 2009), pp. 15 and 545.

16 M. Gould, *Nineteenth-Century Theatre and the Imperial Encounter* (New York, NY, 2011) offers resounding confirmation of my Chapter 2 in *Propaganda and Empire*. For education, see P. Yeandle, *Citizenship, Nation and Empire: The Teaching of History, 1850–1914* (Manchester, forthcoming 2015).

17 J. M. MacKenzie, *Propaganda and Empire: The Manipulation of British Public Opinion, 1880–1960* (Manchester, 1984). This book remained in print until recent years and is now available in print on demand.

18 Andrew Thompson's edited book *Writing Imperial Histories* celebrates the publication of over 100 volumes in the series (Manchester, 2013).

19 J. M. MacKenzie (ed.), *Imperialism and Popular Culture* (Manchester, 1986) and *Popular Imperialism and the Military* (Manchester, 1992).

20 E. Said, *Culture and Imperialism* (1993) and my review of this book 'Occidentalism, Counterpoint and Counter-Polemic', *The Journal of Historical Geography*, 19 (1993), pp. 339–44.

21 J. M. MacKenzie, 'Hunting in Eastern and Central Africa in the Late Nineteenth Century, with Special Reference to Zimbabwe', in W. J. Baker and J. A. Mangan (eds), *Sport in Africa: Essays in Social History* (New York, NY, 1987), pp. 172–95. See also 'Chivalry, Social Darwinism and Ritualised Killing: the Hunting Ethos in Central Africa up to 1914', in D. Anderson and R. Grove (eds), *Conservation in Africa: People, Policies and Practice* (Cambridge, 1987), pp. 41–62 and 'Hunting and the Natural World in Juvenile Literature', in Jeffrey Richards (ed.), *Imperialism and Juvenile Literature* (Manchester, 1989), pp. 144–72.

22 J. M. MacKenzie, *The Empire of Nature: Hunting, Conservation and British Imperialism* (Manchester, 1988). I was introduced as a 'pioneer' at the conference of the Society for the History of Natural History in Oxford in 1995 and in a major environmental and forestry history conference in Brighton in 2003. J. Beattie, in *Empire and Environmental Anxiety* (Basingstoke, 2011), p. 7, flatteringly describes

me as a pioneer. See also J. M. MacKenzie, *Empires of Nature and the Nature of Empires: Imperialism, Scotland and the Environment* (East Linton, 1997) and 'Empire and the Ecological Apocalypse: The Historiography of the Imperial Environment, in T. Griffiths and L. Robin, *Ecology and Empire: Environmental History of Settler Societies* (Edinburgh, 1997), pp. 215–28.

23 J. M. MacKenzie (ed.), *Imperialism and the Natural World* (Manchester, 1990).

24 J. Carruthers, *The Kruger National Park: A Social and Political History* (Pietermaritzburg, 1995) is but one example of this extensive literature.

25 E. Said, *Orientalism* (1978). This truly seminal work has of course stimulated an enormous literature.

26 E. Gellner, 'The Mightier Pen: Edward Said and the Double Standards of Inside–Outside Colonialism', *Times Literary Supplement*, 19 February 1993, pp. 3–4. This stimulated an extensive correspondence in the issues of 19 March, 2 April and 9 April.

27 Said's view of *Aida* was subsequently published in *Culture and Imperialism*, pp. 134–57.

28 This interpretation was put forward in my article 'Edward Said and the Historians', *Nineteenth-Century Contexts*, 18, 1 (1994), pp. 9–25. This stimulated what the editors described as 'hate mail'. The more printable responses together with my reply appeared in *Nineteenth-Century Contexts*, 19, 1 (1995), pp. 65–100.

29 J. M. MacKenzie, *Orientalism: History, Theory and the Arts* (Manchester, 1995).

30 A. A. Powell, *Scottish Orientalists and India: The Muir Brothers, Religion, Education and Empire* (Woodbridge, 2010); R. Irwin, *For Lust of Knowing: The Orientalists and their Enemies* (2006).

31 J. G. A. Pocock, 'The Atlantic Archipelago and the War of the Three Kingdoms', in J. G. A. Pocock (ed.), *The Discovery of Islands: Essays in British History* (Cambridge, 2005), pp. 77–95.

32 J. R. Seeley, *The Expansion of England* (1883); R. Coupland, *Welsh and Scottish Nationalism* (1954).

33 For example, Marjory Harper and Stephen Constantine, *Migration and Empire* (Oxford, 2010).

34 I first started considering these issues in an inaugural lecture 'Scotland and the Empire' delivered in 1992 (privately printed, Lancaster 1992). This was revised as 'Essay and Reflection: On Scotland and the Empire', *International History Review*, 15 (1993), pp. 714–39. See also 'Empire and National Identities: The Case of Scotland', *Transactions of the Royal Historical Society*, 6th series, 8 (1998), pp. 215–31; 'The British World and the Complexities of Anglicisation: the Scots in Southern Africa in the Nineteenth Century', in K. Darian-Smith, P. Grimshaw and S. McIntyre (eds), *Britishness Abroad: Transnational Movements and Imperialism* (Melbourne, 2007), pp. 109–30; 'Irish, Scottish, Welsh and English Worlds? A Four-Nation Approach to the History of the British Empire', *History Compass*, 6, 5 (2008), pp. 1244–63; 'Scots and Imperial Frontiers', *Journal of Irish and Scottish Studies*, 3, 1 (2009), pp. 1–17; 'Scotland and Empire: Ethnicity, Environment and Identity', *Northern Scotland*, 1 (2010), pp. 12–29; 'Irish, Scottish, Welsh and English Worlds? The Historiography of a Four-Nations Approach to the History of the British Empire', in C. Hall and K. McClelland (eds), *Race, Nation and Empire: Making Histories, 1750 to the Present* (Manchester, 2010), pp. 133–53.

35 J. M. MacKenzie with N. R. Dalziel, *The Scots in South Africa: Ethnicity, Identity, Gender and Race* (Manchester, 2007); *Museums and Empire: Natural History, Human Cultures and Colonial Identities* (Manchester, 2009).

36 'TV and War Games: How Tories' History Man Plans to Bring Past to Life', *The Guardian*, 10 July 2010, p. 5. See also 'Empire Strikes Back: Harvard Academic Asked to Rewrite School Syllabus: Western Domination of the World "The Big Story"', *The Guardian*, 31 May 2010, p. 8. These were contributions to a debate on history stimulated by the former Conservative Education Secretary, Michael Gove.

37 M. Sahlins, 'The Original Affluent Society', in *Stone Age Economics* (Chicago, IL, 1972), pp. 9–32. This was based on a symposium in Chicago and has of course been controversial among anthropologists.

38 Two striking studies of family histories in respect of the British Empire have demonstrated 'micro-history' at its best: S. Foster, *A Private Empire* (Millers Point, 2010) and Rothschild, *Inner Life of Empires* (see footnote 3 above).

39 J. M. MacKenzie (ed.), *European Empires and the People: Popular Responses to Imperialism in France, Britain, The Netherlands, Belgium, Germany and Italy* (Manchester, 2011).

Part III

From Imperial to Normative Power: The EU Project in a Post-Colonial World

Building Eurafrica: Reviving Colonialism through European Integration, 1920–60[1]

Peo Hansen and Stefan Jonsson

From the interwar period until the late 1950s practically all of the visions, movements and concrete institutional arrangements working towards European integration made Africa's incorporation into the European enterprise a central objective. As witnessed by several scholarly, political and journalistic accounts of the time, European integration was inextricably bound up with a Eurafrican project. At the Hague Congress of Europe in 1948, for instance, it was proclaimed that 'The European Union must, of course, include in its orbit the extensions, dependencies and associated territories of the European Powers in Africa and elsewhere, and must preserve the existing constitutional ties which unite them.'[2] Nine years later, upon the conclusion of the negotiations for the Treaty of Rome which established the European Economic Community (EEC), French socialist premier Guy Mollet stated as follows at a press conference in Washington DC:

> I would like to insist upon the unity of Europe: it is now a fact. A few days ago we jumped over the last hurdles that were on its way, and now an even broader unity is being born: EURAFRICA, a close association in which we will work together to promote progress, happiness and democracy in Africa.[3]

Subsequently, in an article for *Chicago Daily Tribune* (9 October 1960), drawn[4] from the English translation of his book *Immuable et changeante*, French sociologist Raymond Aron would lend his support to this blueprint, arguing that the 'development' of 'Eurafrica' could not be accomplished by France alone, but was 'a common European responsibility'.[5] In his magnum opus *Europe: A History*, historian

Norman Davies is thus as far off the mark as he is archetypal of today's prevailing attitude when he claims that '[d]ecolonization was a necessary precondition for the emergence of a new European Community of equal, democratic partners'. In fact, it was exactly the other way around, or as Irwin Wall puts it: 'Neither the construction of Europe nor the building of a French nuclear deterrent was conceived of or understood in Paris as a substitute for a moribund colonialism, as several historians have argued.[6] On the contrary, both were meant to provide the means of maintaining France's Eurafrican hegemony.' In this sense, France's motifs for European integration did not constitute a break with its colonial past but should be seen as a phase in the adaptation of its empire, beginning with the Brazzaville Conference in 1944, continuing with the refoundation of the French Union in 1946, the Loi Cadre in 1956 (which provided the colonies with autonomy in select areas) and the establishment of the French Community in 1958, replacing the French Union.

Mainstream EU studies have yet to cast off a Whiggish approach to the history of European integration[7] that imbues it with a benevolent historical purpose, just as nationalist intellectuals in earlier periods had often refused to scrutinize critically the historical origins of national projects. In keeping with this volume's overall theme, our charting of the Eurafrican history of European integration intends to sketch the contours of what we propose as a new framework for the study of European integration history. According to our framework, the history of European integration deserves a new periodization: 1920–60. It also demands to be cast in a narrative in which the hegemonic Cold War paradigm is decentred in favour of the geopolitical context through which its contemporaries saw it unravel. As we will argue, the Eurafrican project attains central importance once this shift of focus is accomplished. We will demonstrate that there is strong evidence to support that Eurafrica and hence the perpetuation of colonialism was instrumental in the actual, diplomatic and political constitution not just of the European Economic Community. It also influenced most other efforts and institutional arrangements that promoted European integration from the 1920s and onwards. For reasons of space we focus below on the periods before and after World War II. This is certainly not to imply that Eurafrica laid dormant during the war itself; on the contrary, and as can be seen in press reports, it was a guiding idea in the geopolitical visions of the Axis powers, as shown during the German–Italian campaigns in North Africa. According to a report in the *New York Times* in October 1941, for instance, the German view of 'the future of Europe' included Africa since 'the two continents themselves [were seen as] inseparable, as indicated by the joint designation now in vogue: "Eurafrica"'. This Eurafrican scheme was to be built in close collaboration with the French Vichy Republic and was thus also a crucial ingredient in the Vichy administration's colonial outlook.

Configurations of Eurafrica in the Interwar Period

In 1923, Richard Coudenhove-Kalergi[8] published his pamphlet *Paneuropa*, which also launched his Pan-European Union Movement that was to gather both sizeable and influential intellectual and political support from the best and the brightest of his generation, including the brothers Heinrich and Thomas Mann, as well as statesmen like Winston Churchill, Konrad Adenauer and Aristide Briand, the latter serving for a long time as chairman of the Pan-European Union. According to Walter Lipgens[9] *Paneuropa* was by far the most important among the many proposals for European collaboration of the 1920s, and largely mirrored the worldview of internationalists and liberal progressives of the era. A united Europe appeared paramount for political reasons, or simply to prevent a repetition of World War I. This was the argument for peace. A united Europe was desirable also for cultural reasons, as history seemed to indicate that Europe displayed a spiritual and intellectual unity with a specific *Weltanschauung*. This was the argument for civilization. In addition, the 1920s added a third, economic argument: as Europeans compared their own states to the rapidly growing economies of the United States and the Soviet Union, they concluded that both of these foreign powers enjoyed the advantage of being able to organize their economies on a continental scale whereas Europe was politically divided and suffered economically from numerous trade barriers. This economic perspective then gradually turned into a geopolitical one, which touched on the sensitive issue of whether Europe would be able to regain its place on a par with other world powers. From this perspective, Africa was seen as a natural or necessary part of Europe's geopolitical sphere, a part that needed to be more strongly connected to Europe, and to be exploited by united European forces in order to turn its resources to full advantage: 'Europe is Eurafrica's head, Africa its body.'[10]

Africa was seen primarily as a reservoir of natural resources and agricultural produce, but also as a source of hydroelectric power. Africa was often also seen as the solution to Europe's demographic problems: it was widely agreed that Europe was overpopulated, an imbalance that could be resolved by the emigration and resettlement of surplus population in the 'empty' territory south of the Mediterranean. Coudenhove-Kalergi[11] certainly spoke for the majority of Europe's political and intellectual elite as he stated: 'Africa could provide Europe with raw materials for its industry, nutrition for its population, land for its overpopulation, labour for its unemployed, and markets for its products.'[12]

What is important is that all of these arguments for assimilating Africa formed yet another strong argument for the unification of Europe. In interwar thinking, the common or synergetic exploitation of Africa was so unquestionably attractive and beneficial that it constituted in itself a reason for European states to make common cause. A geopolitical calculation based on two symbiotic benefits emerged: the new geopolitical sphere of a united Europe would be sustainable and prosperous thanks to its incorporation of Africa; and correspondingly, the bonds between once antagonistic European states would be consolidated by the shared goal of developing Africa. The unification of Europe and a unified European effort to colonize Africa were two processes that presupposed one another. The idea was succinctly expressed by former French premier Joseph Caillaux, a major supporter of Eurafrica throughout the interwar years: 'Europe supported by Africa. Europe reconciliated by Africa.'[13]

This argument won particular support in Germany, which stood to regain access to the colonial territories that it had lost in World War I if the plan materialized. Africa for Europe (*Afrika für Europa*) became a political slogan and formula for the German Colonial Society, coined after a pamphlet written by its president Heinrich Schnee.[14] Interwar politicians and intellectuals also gave a name to the new great power that would put the European star back in the ascendant. The geopolitical bloc was called Eurafrica, a notion so prevalent at the time that it is difficult if not impossible to find out who actually coined it, although it has been suggested that it was first introduced by Italian anthropologist Giuseppe Sergi.[15] In short, and contrary to a common understanding or standard historiography of the roots of today's European Union – in which Coudenhove-Kalergi is sometimes seen as the father figure of the founding fathers – Pan-Europe was a project not limited to Europe alone but included Africa except for its British possessions. A related geopolitical blueprint was drawn up by Munich architect and urban planner Herman Sörgel (1932). All European nations, he suggested, should unify in the common task of actually damming the entire Mediterranean Sea, thus attaching Africa to Europe, providing the depressed European economy with vital resources and the white race with indispensable *Lebensraum*. Sörgel was among the first ones to propose large-scale technological projects that would enable the extraction of Africa's natural wealth while at the same time facilitate communication – railways, roads, telephony and electricity – between the continents. Such infrastructural designs were to remain a vital concern for Eurafrican planning up until the early 1960s. Sörgel's plan was thus echoed in a prestigious engineering venture, under the supervision of French Euratom president Louis Armand, that proposed, in 1958, to build a channel tunnel between Britain and continental Europe, which 'also eventually would link up with a tunnel under the Straits of Gibraltar and form the great Eurafrica route connecting Europe with Africa'.[16]

Another influential exponent of this geopolitical theory was Eugène Guernier,[17] the French author of numerous works on colonialism including *L'Afrique: Champ d'expansion de l'Europe* (1932), published in the wake of the great Colonial Exposition in Vincennes in 1931. All colonial powers were invited to the exposition to display their colonial possessions, including native inhabitants (Britain declined the invitation, and Spain and Japan were also absent). Top-ranking French politicians such as Paul Reynaud, minister of colonies, and Hubert Lyautey, former governor general of Morocco and the exposition's *commissaire général*, argued that European collaboration at the exposition must now be followed by a European collaboration in the world. As Reynaud explained, 'the colonial reality calls for a European collaboration for which France stands prepared'.[18] Lyautey, for his part, argued for a 'union of all the colonizing nations in a policy of association for the greater moral and material profit of all'.[19]

We could continue the list of other works and plans that advanced similar arguments. It is noteworthy that none of these suggests that there should be any symmetry between the two halves, much less any equality. Coudenhove-Kalergi, known as a pacifist, internationalist and anti-Nazi, comes across as a fully fledged biological racist when he speaks about Africa, claiming that there are inherent differences between the black and white races. 'As long as the black race is unable to develop and civilize its part of the earth, the white race must do it.' At the same time, he states that Europe must at all costs avoid the danger 'that great numbers of black workers and soldiers [might] immigrate to Europe'.[20]

This is where we can locate the underlying structure of the interwar discourse on Eurafrica. It is a racist discourse that allows the rejection of African presence in Europe as an absurdity with the same ease as the affirmation of European presence in Africa as a necessity, without the slightest consideration of the possibility that this position might be self-contradictory.

Post-War Institutionalizations of Eurafrica

Although the interwar plan for Eurafrica was either practically unfeasible or politically defeated, it emerged into the post-war era as a concept ready for revival. After World War II, Eurafrica was developed and institutionalized as a primary aim for many European politicians, institutions, intellectuals and organized interests. Immediately after the end of the war, British foreign secretary Ernest Bevin (Labour) launched his bid to establish a 'Third World Power', working to integrate the African colonies and their vast natural resources into a Western European power sphere able to withstand a world order dictated by the US and the Soviet Union. Built on close colonial cooperation between Britain and France,[21] such a scheme, Bevin believed, 'could have the US dependent on us and eating out of our hands in four or five years [...] [the] US is barren of essential material and in Africa we have them all'.[22] As Anne Deighton aptly elucidates, Bevin's Third World Power enterprise was firmly rooted in the Eurafrican current of ideas of the interwar period.[23]

For all the instances of ideational continuity, however, the post-war period distinguishes itself first and foremost through its institutionalization – and thus operationalization – of the Eurafrica conception. Arguably, the first instance of this took place in the framework of the Organisation for European Economic Co-operation (OEEC, subsequently the OECD), formed in 1948 for the purpose of administering the US Marshall Plan – or the European Recovery Programme. While portions of its funds were used to assist individual recipient states in consolidating financial stability in their respective colonial empires,[24] the OEEC immediately decided to form an Overseas Territories Working Group in order to promote European cooperation in colonial – and particularly African – affairs. In its extensive report from 1951 the OEEC stated that the necessary public and private investment in overseas territories should by no means be limited to Europe's colonial powers, but that all members should be encouraged to contribute: 'It is in the interest of the whole free world that the [colonial] territories, which form part of it, should endeavour to speed up and increase the production of scarce materials.'[25] Although formulated in less grandiose and utopian terms, the report echoes the interwar period's plans for Eurafrica in its focus on large-scale infrastructural projects, water control, agriculture and 'constructional work, on a heavier scale'; the report states, for instance, that 'vast stretches of mosquito-infested swamp must be drained'.[26] What is more, the report is totally void of indications that colonialism in Africa might some day come to an end. Eurafrican planning is unreservedly described as 'a long-term task' in an African terrain characterized by 'political security'.[27]

Whereas NATO, founded in 1949, would contain a minor Eurafrican outfit through its incorporation of France's Algerian *départements*, at the ultimatum of Paris and against US aspirations, it was the Council of Europe (CE), also established in 1949, that would take the Eurafrican scheme to the next level. The CE grew out of the European Movement and its Congress of Europe held in The Hague in 1948. As indicated above, most of the Congress' participant groupings adhered to the Eurafrican tenet of the imperative necessity of developing African colonies for the collective benefit of a war-torn Western Europe striving to emerge as a 'third force' in world politics.[28] 'If we wish to rebuild', said Hendrik Brugmans of the European Union of Federalists (EUF), 'we urgently need "living space" – if you will forgive the expression – on a bigger scale than that of the old, so-called autonomous nations'.[29] In its 'Draft of a Federal Pact', the EUF went on to proclaim the demise of the era of national ownership of colonial territories: 'From now onwards a common European policy of development for certain regions of Africa should be taken in hand.'[30]

While the Council of Europe (CE) failed entirely to embody the federal principles advocated by most parties at the Congress of Europe, it immediately succeeded in turning Eurafrica into one of the organization's defining priorities,[31] a fact largely forgotten today. The unanimous adoption of the 'Strasbourg Plan' by the CE's Consultative Assembly in 1952 provides ample testimony to the Eurafrican momentum during the 1950s. Built on an extensive expert report by the Consultative Assembly's secretariat-general as well as the work of the OEEC, the Plan set out to resolve one of Western Europe's most pressing problems at the time: its chronic and paralysing dollar deficit, which the (by now discontinued) Marshall aid had done little to settle. The answer? Africa! As German representative Johannes Semler, heading the CE's Committee on Economic Relations with Overseas Territories, pleaded for the Plan before the Assembly, he quoted from a speech made a week earlier by former French prime minister Paul Reynaud (now chairman of the CE's Committee on Economic Questions):

> We must also, if free Europe is to be made viable, jointly exploit the riches of the African continent, and try to find there those raw materials which we are getting from the dollar area, and for which we are unable to pay.[32]

In short, why spend precious dollars elsewhere when the same materials could be obtained under Europe's own steam in Africa? Such 'exploitation' would facilitate Western Europe's transition into 'a third economic group standing midway between the Communist and the dollar areas'.[33] However, since the large-scale investments required could not be shouldered by the colonial powers alone, the Plan was adamant in stressing that the contribution of all Council members (by now 14 countries) was essential. As pointed out by the UK representative Lord Layton, 'it is clear that we have to think of these overseas territories not as the possessions of any one country [...]; they have to be integrated with all the countries of Europe and all the overseas territories'.[34] This idea found favour with practically all of the representatives. For instance, Denmark's Hermond Lannung asserted that Europe had just lost the 'battle of Asia', and that its nations now needed to unite in order to avoid losing 'the battle of Africa' as well. 'Here we have before us a great concrete and practical task which calls for the utmost collaboration of us all.'[35]

For this project to become viable, West German, but also Scandinavian, capital and industrial potential was greatly sought after.[36] According to the expert report, all parties stood to gain from such a collaborative approach: 'If European countries without colonial responsibilities contribute to the development of overseas territories it will then be possible to open these overseas markets to them.'[37] With limited access to its traditional markets in the East – now within the Soviet orbit of control – the report argued, such a scenario should provide West Germany in particular with an important incentive to look to Africa as an outlet for its 'tractors, cranes, bridges, dredges, machine tools, etc.'[38] As in the interwar Eurafrica debate, the topic of European emigration to Africa also figured prominently in the

Strasbourg Plan since 'over-population' was still seen as 'one of Europe's most critical human and social problems'.[39]

On 9 May 1950, almost exactly a year after the establishment of the Council of Europe, French foreign minister Robert Schuman presented what was to become known as the Schuman Declaration or Schuman Plan, announcing the Franco-German project for the joint regulation of extraction and production of coal and steel. The Schuman Plan gave birth to the European Coal and Steel Community (ECSC) in the Treaty of Paris a year later, to which France, West Germany, Italy and the Benelux countries were the founding signatories. The ECSC not only created a common market for coal and steel between the six members, but most significantly and symbolically also placed control over production in the hands of a supranational High Authority. With coal and steel constituting the basis for arms production, this arrangement was designed primarily to tie France and West Germany together, or as the Schuman Plan stated: 'The solidarity in production thus established will make it plain that any war between France and Germany becomes not merely unthinkable, but materially impossible.'[40]

As for Eurafrican institutionalization, the ECSC offered little on paper in the ratified treaty itself, but the Schuman Declaration itself spoke in more assertive terms: 'With increased resources Europe will be able to pursue the achievement of one of its essential tasks, namely, the development of the African continent.'[41] The masterminds behind this formulation were René Mayer, Minister of Justice, and the 'Father of Europe' himself, Jean Monnet, both of them keen Eurafricanists.[42] Apparently, Schuman had picked up on Monnet's suggestion that France could give Africa as a 'dowry to Europe'.[43] As such, the Eurafrican passage of the Schuman Declaration follows from the historical pattern sketched above. Since the 1920s, the community and collaboration of Europe's states had presupposed their collaboration in Africa as well. Now, as both the Council of Europe and the ECSC were established, their protagonists obviously felt it important to signal that these institutions of European integration enabled the more far-reaching collaboration that had long occupied debates on foreign policy and geopolitics. Initial steps toward this were also taken in June 1950 through the 'Monnet Plan for Africa' ('Plan Monnet pour l'Afrique'). Although not implemented as such at the time, it envisaged an administrative High Authority for colonial management (modelled on the ECSC's institutional structure) and a European investment fund for Africa.[44] The initiative found support among many intellectuals, among them the influential Austrian writer on foreign policy, Anton Zischka. In his view, the Franco-German coal and steel agreement was but the first step in a process leading to a common exploitation of Africa's resources. Africa, argued Zischka[45] in the title of his book, was 'Europas Gemeinschaftsaufgabe Nr. 1' ('Europe's number one common priority'). However, up until 1956, with the commencement of the Rome Treaty negotiations, divisions within the French political leadership disabled any concrete proposals to open up its colonial possessions to other European states. During this period (1950–4) the six members of the ECSC were bogged down in arduous negotiations on the abortive European Defence Community, in which Paris played Washington and used its European clout to achieve its imperial objectives in Indochina.[46]

As we enter the period of the Treaty of Rome negotiations (1955–7) and their culmination in the establishment of the European Economic Community (EEC), Eurafrica emerges as *the* issue upon which the final stages of the negotiations would hinge.[47] Indeed, it seems safe to say that there would not have been an EEC/EU, at least not at this juncture, had it not been for the German and Dutch governments' decision to yield to the French ultimatum (supported by Belgium and, eventually, Italy) that demanded the incorporation into the EEC not only of France's *départements* in Algeria but also of all the member states' colonial possessions: French West and Equatorial Africa, Belgian Congo and Ruanda-Urundi, Italian Somaliland and the Netherlands' New Guinea. As spelled out in the Rome Treaty, the purpose of colonial association was 'to promote the economic and social [and cultural] development of the countries and territories and to establish close economic relations between them and the Community as a whole'.[48] As part of this, a European Development Fund was established (still in place today) to which all members contributed – West Germany and France being the largest providers – but from which, of course, French colonies benefitted by far the most. It deserves mention that, on the whole, the Treaty of Rome's colonial scheme was established without any prior consideration of the opinions in the territories themselves about their subjection to incorporation or association.[49]

This arrangement whereby the other community members, in particular West Germany, collectively helped finance investments in France's African colonies in exchange for access to colonial markets was, from the perspective of Paris, nothing less than a *sine qua non* for the preservation of its imperial enterprise in Africa, the Union française (French Union), which became the French Community in 1958.[50]

If the Dutch government was the most clearly opposed to the EEC's association scheme – fearing high costs and divergent views on trade policy, and wary of getting involved in France and Belgium's colonial projects and problems[51] – sentiments in West Germany were less clear.[52] Some important figures in Adenauer's cabinet (among them the minister of economy, Ludwig Erhard) were vehemently opposed to the scheme, as was the social democratic opposition.[53] Nevertheless, Adenauer's political force and determination not to spoil an unprecedented opportunity for closer European integration won out – and he had the majority of his cabinet firmly on his side. Arguing for 'der Vision von Eurafrika' before his cabinet on 21 February 1957, Adenauer admitted that no grand geopolitical blueprint for the world is without risk. But, he added, 'the free Europe must be prepared to confront this risk, in order not to be crushed, in the foreseeable future, between the peoples of Asia and Africa should these peoples assume a hostile attitude against Europe'.[54] A week prior to this he had defended his firm belief before his cabinet that France was the country in Europe with the best economic prospects thanks to its latent natural resource wealth in Africa, and that this made Eurafrica a more beneficial choice for West Germany than a simple free-trade agreement with Britain.[55] What Adenauer was referring to more specifically was probably France's discovery in 1956 of huge oil and gas reserves in the Algerian Sahara. In an article published the very same month in the German Journal *Die politische Meinung*, Waldemar Lentz analysed the Eurafrican enterprise as basically boiling down to the French colonial resources in general and Algerian oil in particular. Indeed, as Lentz asserted, 'the Sahara stands at the center of the Eurafrican problematic'.[56]

Adenauer's personal outlook was thus much in line with the general perspective from which Paris and other actors derived their plans for Eurafrican integration. Adenauer's motivation for European integration was primarily political and geopolitical; and it was a geopolitics to no little extent inspired by Coudenhove-Kalergi's interwar Pan-European Movement.[57] Adenauer not only believed in the 'superiority of Western civilization'; he was equally convinced of the inherent racial inferiority of black Africa. It was, therefore, inconceivable, as Adenauer phrased it, 'that Africa, as a black continent, could be independent alongside the other continents'.[58] He also firmly believed that '[t]he domination of the Mediterranean basin by the Soviet Russians would simply be the end for Europe'.[59]

During the Suez crisis, Adenauer's European conviction would be further reinforced. As the unfolding world events challenged Europe's influence in global affairs, it had become all the more important for Europe to stake out its common geopolitical interests in a more independent fashion. 'Then, just as Coudenhove-Kalergi had said in his time', Hans-Peter Schwarz[60] notes, 'Adenauer spoke of the "appearance of non-white peoples on the political stage of world events"'. Adenauer found this 'appearance', and its potential effects on the future constitution of the UN, deeply disturbing.[61]

Adenauer's conviction of the need for a strong European power, built on a solid Franco-German partnership and more independent from the US, thus happened to chime with France's decision to make the realization of the EEC hinge on Eurafrica. The utterly humiliating conclusion of the Suez crisis – when the US and the Soviet Union flexed their superior power and forced Britain and France to withdraw from Egypt, thus dealing a heavy blow to French and British interests and international prestige – would only add further impetus to both France's[62] and Adenauer's objectives. The discomfiting end of the Suez campaign coincided with a high-level Franco-German meeting in Paris to resolve some key obstacles to the EEC negotiations. As Mollet ended a phonecall with the British premier Anthony Eden having failed to persuade him to defy US pressure and prolong the Suez operation for a little longer, Adenauer – a wholehearted supporter of the Suez War – decided to comfort Mollet, telling him:

> France and England will never be powers comparable to the United States and the Soviet Union. Nor Germany either. There remains to them only one way of playing a decisive role in the world; that is to unite to make Europe. England is not ripe for it but the affair of Suez will help to prepare her spirits for it. We have no time to waste: Europe will be your revenge.[63]

As *The Economist* wrote in January 1957, two months prior to the signing of the Rome Treaty: 'since the Suez adventure, [European] integration schemes, far from being suspected as "American plots", have a third force halo'.[64] At its meeting in Stresa, Italy, in September 1956, the Liberal International rallied around a 'United Europe', seeing it as the only potent antidote to figures such as President Nasser of Egypt.[65] 'The efforts of Arab-Asian nationalists to oust Europeans', the *New York Times* reported, 'are seen by many liberals as the newest and most challenging reason for accelerating West European unity'.[66] If Europe had been united, the president of the Liberal International Roger Motz rhetorically asked, 'would Colonel Nasser have dared nationalize the Suez Canal, would the Algerian rebels have thought of gaining something by taking up arms?'[67] Given these strong sentiments, it should come as no surprise that Louis Armand – who was also a close aid to Monnet – went as far as to suggest (in jest) during the ceremony following the signing of the Treaty of Rome on 25 March 1957 that 'We ought to erect a statue to Nasser: To the federator of Europe.'[68]

As should be clear from our account so far, Eurafrica cannot be reduced to a simple auxiliary to the Cold War and the efforts to contain the spread of communism in Africa. To a significant extent, of course, it was part of that too. But to apply Matthew Connelly's astute idea of 'taking off the Cold War lens', Eurafrica must also be construed as a strategy of colonial reinforcement in its own right, targeting various anti-colonial and anti-Western movements that were growing in the southern hemisphere and were not by any means reducible to Moscow puppets: pan-Africanism, pan-Arabism and pan-Islamism, as well as the various strands of indigenous nationalisms.

The political actors, intellectuals and institutions who shaped the content and direction of European integration saw it as deeply entrenched in a North–South struggle, and thus as a response to an allegedly deepening conflict between Christian and Muslim civilizations, between universal values and jihad and between the white European race, on one side, and the 'hordes' of brown, black and yellow races on the other.[69]

But European integrationists' approach to Africa was often also marked by strong reformist, progressive and accommodating currents, particularly from the mid 1950s onwards. Economic development and Eurafrican 'interdependence', rather than exploitation and colonialism, were keywords here. As seen above in the discussion of Dutch and German hesitations over the incorporation of colonial possessions in the EEC structure, this reflected a growing concern in Western Europe to be branded not as reactionary colonialists but rather as pioneers of African development and modernization. In the complex, contradictory and undecided terrain of the late 1950s, this was thus yet another strategy of responding to the 'appearance of non-white peoples on the political stage of world events', to the changing mood in the UN, to the spirit of the Afro-Asian Bandung Conference (held in 1955) and the non-aligned movement. In this context, the EEC's Eurafrican system of colonial association becomes – from a European perspective – the solution to the problem of accepting increasing autonomy or self-government in the colonies, while at the same time continuing to gain from them economically and strategically. Thus EEC association is articulated as an offer of a modern and mutually beneficial partnership to African colonies.

It may be argued that the Eurafrican momentum depended on its dual valence and its ambiguous appeal. On the one hand, Eurafrica represented the continuation of European colonial hegemony. On the other, it enabled a rearticulation of colonial hegemony as 'interdependence'. In this context *independence* was framed as outmoded and harmful for the African territories. As Mollet explained, 'Isolated nations can no longer keep pace with the world. What would Algeria amount to by itself? On the other hand, what future might it not have, as one of the foundations of the Eurafrican community now taking shape.' Instead of moribund independence and national sovereignty, Mollet concluded, 'interdependence among nations is becoming the rule'.[70] In the case of Morocco, the same French policy was offered as 'independence within interdependence' (*l'indépendance dans l'interdépendance*).[71]

In this context, too, the Eurafrican offer of EEC association may be interpreted as a divide and rule strategy, whereby the alleged African benefits of EEC association would thwart the Pan-African movement, attracting and rewarding its moderates while isolating its radical and most committed leaders, foremost among them Ghana's Kwame Nkrumah and Guinea's Sékou Touré.[72] As Nkrumah had it, the Treaty of Rome and the EEC marked 'the advent of neo-colonialism in Africa'[73] whereby the EEC's Eurafrican association scheme represented a newfangled arrangement for 'collective colonialism' – 'stronger and more dangerous than the old evils we are striving to liquidate'.[74] More specifically, leaders such as Nkrumah and Touré saw the EEC's Eurafrican design not only as a strategy to foil national independence in Africa per se; more importantly perhaps, they also saw it as a deliberate attempt to frustrate the formation of any types of independently organized African integration and regionalization projects, which, in fact, had been brewing since the interwar period.

Given the high stakes involved in the EEC's and France's Eurafrican bid, combined with the mixed African reception, there was much work to be done on the international scene in order to persuade and reassure the world of the great boons of Eurafrican integration. This is borne out by the rich international media coverage that Eurafrica received during the latter part of the 1950s. Straight after the conclusion of the agreement on the EEC's Eurafrican integration (in February 1957), Guy Mollet went on a state visit to the US which would amount to a veritable Eurafrican promotion tour: the premier seemingly never missed an opportunity to emphasize that integration was as much Eurafrican as European. As Mollet affirmed before the US Senate, Europe's 'economic development will bring a better standard of living to the European as well as to the African peoples freely [*sic!*] associated to her. This is not a hazy dream. I am firmly convinced that EURAFRICA will be the reality of tomorrow.'[75]

Two weeks before the sealing of the EEC's Eurafrican agreement, the French foreign minister Christian Pineau laid out the plans for Eurafrica to the UN General Assembly's Political Committee. 'Europe in its entirety', he argued, 'bringing to Africa its capital and its techniques, should enable the immense African continent to become an essential factor in world politics.' Linking Eurafrica to the Algerian crisis, Pineau cautioned that an estranged Algeria would 'be pledged to fanaticism and by its very poverty, open to communism'. By contrast, he went on, 'its participation in Eurafrica would mean for Algeria comfort, riches – in other words, the true condition of independence'.[76] Pineau's address chimed appositely with the outlook of the *New York Times*, whose subsequent editorial of 6 February did its utmost to convince the world of the merits of Eurafrica:

> 'Eurafrica' [...] can only be a dream today, but it is the sort of dream that other Frenchmen, like Jean Monnet, have envisaged for Europe herself and have done much to foster. It is the sort of dream that can become reality and that, perhaps, must become reality if the world is to avoid another and greater holocaust.[77]

Conclusion

On 2 June 1960, the German daily *Die Welt* carried the headline 'Is Africa running away from the EEC?' The article asserted that at the time when the Treaty of Rome was drafted, 'the fact that Europe would be faced by independent States in Africa within only a few years could scarcely have been anticipated.' Such independence, the author warned, risked upsetting the EEC's entire edifice of African association. Unless a new EEC strategy towards Africa was promptly launched, the article concluded, the situation could soon prove 'dangerous for Europe and hence for the West in its entirety'.[78] When in 1963 eighteen independent African states decided to retain multilateral EEC association under the Yaoundé Convention, any such fears were, of course, put to rest; by the mid 1970s most African states had opted for EEC association through Yaoundé's successor, the Lomé Convention (today replaced by the Cotonou Agreement).

More plausible, though, is *Die Welt*'s judgement that the Rome Treaty was negotiated under the assumption that most African territories would remain European dependencies or colonies for the foreseeable future. If proven to be true – yet more research is needed here – this hypothesis may explain partly why the 1950s' confident Eurafrican project would peter out in the 1960s – although it never disappeared. While neo-colonial dependency and clientelism, which were to characterize post-independence relations between the EEC and many African states,[79] certainly harmonized with some of the Eurafrican objectives, such relations nonetheless fell far short of sustaining the Eurafrican zeal of the 1950s. The reason for this may be precisely that the conception of Eurafrica always presupposed a Europe more or less in full control of the African scene. To put it differently, since Eurafrica depended conceptually on an idea of civilizational hierarchy and politically on barring Africa from being represented by Africans, it proved ill-equipped even for modest forms of African agency and sovereignty offered under neo-colonial relations. With independence facilitating Africa's full conversion into a battleground of the Cold War, this also eclipsed any real prospects of having Western Europe evolve into a relatively independent third force in global geopolitics. Provided that Eurafrica was in so many ways tantamount to 'third force Europe', such Cold War capture might also explain the rather sudden decline of Eurafrica during the 1960s.

In many ways, then, the study of the rise and decline of Eurafrica in the post-war period becomes a study of the rise of Cold War logic and ideology to dominate international geopolitics. However, and in line with Connelly's argument above, the only way to conceive of this transformation is precisely by decentring the Cold War as the dominant analytical framework. Otherwise the rich material pointing to alternative driving forces behind European integration is incomprehensible. Also, the radically different geopolitical designs for the post-war world order that was encoded in the idea of Eurafrica otherwise remain at best a peculiar historical anecdote, unworthy of further consideration. As we have shown, Eurafrica was far more than that: a decisive factor in the constitution of an integrated Europe.

If our thesis is true, the origins of the EU cannot be separated from the perceived necessity of preserving, prolonging and perhaps even renovating the colonial system. But our hypothesis also has additional theoretical implications. Unlike other accounts of EU history, which are written predominantly from a Eurocentric perspective, and also unlike other analyses of the relation between Europe and Africa which are marked by 'continental' thinking, the category of Eurafrica allows us to discover possibilities for new theoretical departures in both these areas. As we have seen, it sheds new light on the process of European integration, African decolonization and the current relationship of Europe and Africa. As such, Eurafrica also reveals that the EU–African relationship cannot be construed as the sum total of Europe's national colonial histories; secondly, it implies that Europe and Africa, at least in this context, cannot be studied as separate continental units. Rather, it compels us to broach a third theoretical option, in which we go beyond 'continental thinking' and seek to use a larger geopolitical and historical unit as our primary frame of analysis and point of departure.[80]

We all know that the inequality that still exists today between Europe and Africa has a history; but few have explored the role that the EU – and European integration more generally – has played in it. And the essentials remain as they were at the time when Eurafrica was being discussed, at least on the political level. Just as it is self-evident that today's EU does as it pleases to prevent African migrants from entering Europe, it is clear that the EU still feels that it has the right to change the course of history in Africa. Let us finish, then, with a more contemporary echo of colonialism. Speaking in Dakar in 2007, French president Nicolas Sarkozy demonstrated that Eurafrica still remains, in the visions of the highest ranking European politicians, the manifest destiny of two continents: 'What France wants with Africa is co-development, shared development [...] What France wants with Africa is to prepare the advent of "Eurafrica", a great common destiny which awaits Europe and Africa.' If Africa re-emerged as a key sphere in the geopolitics of Eurafrica and the Cold War in the 1950s, it is now re-emerging as a key space of interest in the geopolitics of globalization, with the EU, China, the US and others scrambling for control over Africa's vast natural resources and emerging markets. This being the case, one could wonder whether the echoes of Eurafrica give the EU an edge over its rivals or, on the contrary, contribute to emasculating its current power games.

Notes

1 We would like to express our gratitude to the staff at the Historical Archives of the European Union in Florence for their generous assistance. The research for this chapter was made possible by a grant from the Swedish Research Council.

2 Quoted in A. Hick, 'The "European Movement"', in W. Lipgens (ed.), *Documents on the History of European Integration*, vol. IV (Berlin, 1991) pp. 335–6. The Congress of Europe in The Hague gathered some 750 delegates and political leaders (including Konrad Adenauer and Winston Churchill), representing various interests, movements and parties (excluding the communists and the far right). It was organized by the International Committee of the Movements for European Unity and gave birth to the European Movement and subsequently, in 1949, the Council of Europe.

3 The Historical Archives of the European Union (HAEU), European University Institute, Florence, EN-Emile Noël Papers, EN–2737. 'Statement given by French Premier Guy Mollet on his arrival at the Washington Airport', 25 February 1957.

4 N. Davies, *Europe: A History* (1996), p. 1068.

5 R. Aron, 'The Post-War Destinies of Four European Nations', *Chicago Daily Tribune*, 9 October 1960.

6 I. M. Wall, *France, the United States, and the Algerian War* (Berkeley, CA, 2001), p. 77.

7 M. Gilbert, 'Narrating the Process: Questioning the Progressive Story of European Integration', *Journal of Common Market Studies*, 46, 3 (2008), pp. 641–62.

8 R. Coudenhove-Kalergi, *Paneuropa*, 2nd edition (Vienna and Leipzig, 1923, 1926).

9 W. Lipgens, *A History of European Integration*, vol. I (Oxford, 1982), p. 38.

10 R. Coudenhove-Kalergi, 'Afrika', *Paneuropa*, 5, 2 (1929), p. 5.

11 *Ibid.*, p. 3.

12 See further C.-R. Ageron, 'L'Idée d'Eurafrique et le débat colonial franco-allemand de l'entre-deux-guerres', *Revue d'histoire moderne et contemporaine* (July–September 1975), pp. 446–75.

13 Quoted in Ageron, 'L'Idée d'Eurafrique', p. 463.

14 See H. Schnee, *Afrika für Europa: Die koloniale Schuldlüge* (Berlin, 1924); see also R. Coudenhove-Kalergi, 'Reparationen und Kolonien', *Paneuropa*, 8, 1 (1932), pp. 7–11.

15 L. Ellena, 'Political Imagination, Sexuality and Love in the Eurafrican Debate', *European Review of History – Revue européenne d'Histoire*, 11, 2 (2004), p. 248.

16 'English Channel Tunnel Spurred', *Christian Science Monitor*, 31 March 1958.

17 E. Guernier, *L'Afrique: Champ d'expansion de l'Europe* (Paris, 1933).

18 Quoted in Ageron, 'L'Idée d'Eurafrique', p. 457.

19 P. Morton, *Hybrid Modernities: Architecture and Representation at the 1931 Colonial Exposition* (Cambridge, MA, 2000), p. 314.

20 Coudenhove-Kalergi, 'Afrika', p. 5.

21 For a detailed account of the many but mostly frustrated attempts to institute Franco-British colonial cooperation in black Africa in the first post-war decade, see J. Kent, *The Internationalization of Colonialism: Britain, France and Black Africa, 1939–1956* (Oxford, 1992).

22 A. Deighton, 'Entente Neo-Coloniale? Ernest Bevin and the Proposals for Anglo-French Third World Power, 1945–1949', *Diplomacy and Statecraft*, 17 (2006), p. 845.

23 Deighton, 'Entente Neo-Coloniale?', pp. 836–9.

24 F. M. B. Lynch, *France and the International Economy: From Vichy to the Treaty of Rome* (1997), p. 192; see also OEEC (Organisation for European Economic Cooperation), *Investments in Overseas Territories in Africa, South of the Sahara* (Paris, 1951), pp. 51, 75.

25 OEEC, *Investments* p. 20.

26 OEEC, *Investments* p. 21.

27 OEEC, *Investments* p. 72.

28 See further J.-M. Palayret, 'Les Mouvements proeuropéens et la question de l'Eurafrique, du Congrès de La Haye à la Convention de Yaoundé (1948–1963)', in M.-T. Bitsch and G. Bossuat (eds), *L'Europe unie et l'Afrique: de l'idée d'Eurafrique à la convention de Lomé 1* (Brussels, 2005), pp. 185–229.

29 A. Hick, 'The European Union of Federalists', in Lipgens (ed.), *Documents on the History of European Integration*, vol. IV, p. 16.

30 Quoted in *ibid.*, p. 90.

31 See Palayret, 'Les Mouvements proeuropéens', pp. 200–13, and R. Heywood, 'West European Community and the Eurafrica Concept in the 1950s', *Journal of European Integration*, 4, 2 (1981), pp. 199–210.

32 Quoted in CE (Council of Europe), *The Strasbourg Plan* (Strasbourg, 1952), p. 135.

33 *Ibid.*, p. 15.

34 *Ibid.*, p. 140.

35 *Ibid.*, p. 154.

36 *Ibid.*, pp. 54–7, 175, 190.

37 *Ibid.*, p. 64.

38 *Ibid.*, p. 54.

39 *Ibid.*, p. 58.

40 European Union, 'Declaration of 9 May 1950', *Europa* (official website of the European Union), 2009 http://europa.eu/abc/symbols/9-may/decl_en.htm.

41 *Ibid.*

42 V. McKay, *Africa in World Politics* (New York, NY, 1963), p. 139; Y. Montarsolo, *L'Eurafrique – contrepoint de l'idée d'Europe: le cas français de la fin de la deuxième guerre mondiale aux négociations des Traités de Rome* (Aix-en-Provence, 2010), pp. 85–6; V. Hurd, 'Eurafrica Reechoes', *The Christian Science Monitor*, 21 March 1957.

43 Quoted in McKay, *Africa in World Politics*, p. 139.

44 Montarsolo, *L'Eurafrique*, p. 86.

45 A. Zischka, *Afrika: Europas Gemeinschaftsaufgabe Nr. 1* (Oldenburg, 1951).

46 J. Aimaq, *For Europe or Empire? French Colonial Ambitions and the European Army Plan* (Lund, 1996).

47 P. Guillen, 'Europe as a Cure of French Impotence? The Guy Mollet Government and the Negotiation of the Treaties of Rome', in E. Di Nolfo (ed.), *Power in Europe?* vol. II: *Great Britain, France, Germany and Italy and the Origins of the EEC 1952–1957* (Berlin, 1992), pp. 505–16; Lynch, *France and the International Economy*; P.-H. Laurent, 'The Diplomacy of the Rome Treaty, 1956–57', *Journal of Contemporary History*, 7, 3/4 (1971), pp. 209–20.

48 See further treaty establishing the European Economic Community 1957: Arts. 131–6; 227; Annex IV.

49 Heywood, 'West European Community', p. 210; Lynch, *France and the International Economy*, p. 204.

50 G. Bossuat, *L'Europe des français 1943–1959: La IVe république aux sources de l'Europe communautaire* (Paris, 1996), pp. 320–55; Guillen, 'Europe as a Cure?'; Lynch, *France and the International Economy*; Montarsolo, *L'Eurafrique*, pp. 197–215; Kent, *The Internationalization of Colonialism*; G. Migani, *La France et L'Afrique sub-saharienne, 1957–1963. Histoire d'une décolonisation entre idéaux eurafricains et politique de puissance* (Brussels, 2008), pp. 49–62; K. Muller, 'The Birth and Death of Eurafrica', *International Journal of Francophone Studies*, 3, 1 (2000), pp. 4–17.

51 Laurent, 'Diplomacy of the Rome Treaty', p. 214; Lynch, *France and the International Economy*, p. 204.

52 Lynch, *France and the International Economy*, p. 204.

53 E. Haas, *The Uniting of Europe: Political, Social, and Economic Forces 1950–1957* (Notre Dame, IN, 1958), p. 139, n. 48.

54 Kabinettssitzung, Bundesregierung, 21 February 1957, p. 155.

55 Kabinettssitzung, Bundesregierung, 15 February 1957, p. 144.

56 W. Lentz, 'Eurafrika – Fata Morgana oder Ernst?', *Die politische Meinung: Monatshefte für Fragen der Zeit*, 2, 9 (1957), p. 34. On the wider repercussions of France's oil discovery in Algeria, see B. Sèbe, 'In the Shadow of the Algerian War: The United States and the Common Organisation of Saharan Regions (OCRS), 1957–62', *The Journal of Imperial and Commonwealth History*, 38, 2 (2010), pp. 303–22.

57 H.-P. Schwarz, *Konrad Adenauer: A German Politician and Statesman in a Period of War, Revolution and Reconstruction*, vol. II: *The Statesman, 1952–1967* (Oxford, 1997), pp. 237–8.

58 Quoted in *ibid.*, p. 191.

59 Quoted in *ibid.*, p. 190.

60 *Ibid.*, p. 238.

61 *Ibid.*, pp. 254–5.

62 R. Marjolin, *Architect of European Unity: Memoirs 1911–1986* (1989), p. 297.

63 K. Kyle, *Suez: Britain's End of Empire in the Middle East* (2003), p. 467; See also Bossuat, *L'Europe des français*, p. 335.

64 'M. Mollet Pleads for Europe', *The Economist*, 26 January 1957.

65 M. Hoffman, 'World Liberals See a United Europe As the Best Answer to Nasser's Moves', *New York Times*, 14 September 1956.

66 *Ibid.*

67 Quoted in *ibid.*

68 M. Bromberger and S. Bromberger, *Jean Monnet and the United States of Europe* (New York, NY, 1969), p. 176.

69 M. Connelly, 'Taking Off the Cold War Lens: Visions of North–South Conflict during the Algerian War for Independence', *American Historical Review*, 105, 3 (2000); M. Connelly, *A Diplomatic Revolution: Algeria's Fight for Independence and the Origins of the Post-Cold War Era* (Oxford, 2002).

70 HAEU, EN-Emile Noël Papers, EN–2736. 'Text of the French government's statement on Algeria issued by Premier Guy Mollet', 9 January 1957.

71 A. de Laubadère, 'Le Statut international du Maroc depuis 1955', *Annuaire français de droit international*, 2, 2 (1956), pp. 124–5.

72 That this was indeed the case is amply illustrated in Arnold Rivkin's (at the time Development Advisor to the World Bank) enthusiastic account from 1966 of the EEC's 'fruitful' Eurafrican association scheme. A. Rivkin, 'Africa and the European Common Market: A Perspective', *Monograph Series in World Affairs*, 3, 4 (Denver, CO, 1996).

73 G. Martin, 'Africa and the Ideology of Eurafrica: Neo-Colonialism or Pan-Africanism?', *The Journal of Modern African Studies*, 20, 2 (1982), p. 229.

74 S. K. B. Asante, 'Pan-Africanism and Regional Integration', in Ali A. Mazrui (ed.), *General History of Africa*, vol. VIII: *Africa since 1935* (Oxford), 1993, p. 740.

75 HAEU, EN-Emile Noël Papers, EN–2737. 'Address by Mr Guy Mollet, President of the Council of Ministers of the Republic of France before the Senate of the United States Washington', 27 February 1957.

76 Quoted in M. James, 'France Proposes New Plan to Link Africa to Europe', *New York Times*, 5 February 1957.

77 *New York Times*, 6 February 1957.

78 F. Himpele, 'Läuft Afrika der EWG davon?', *Die Welt*, 2 June 1960. (Translated by European Navigator; retrieved 10 December 2009 from http://www.ena.lu/africa-running-away-eec-die-welt-june-1960-020200670.html.)

79 T. Shaw, 'EEC-ACP Interactions and Images as Redefinitions of Eurafrica: Exemplary, Exclusive and/or Exploitative?', *Journal of Common Market Studies*, 18, 2 (1979), pp. 135–58; Martin, 'Africa and the Ideology of Eurafrica'.

80 This is also why we think that the repressed or hidden category of Eurafrica will especially enrich EU studies, European studies in general, colonial and post-colonial studies and African studies.

Echoes of Colonialism in Trade Negotiations between the European Union and African, Caribbean and Pacific Countries

Emily Jones and Clara Weinhardt

Trade relations between the countries that makeup today's European Union (EU) and African, Caribbean and Pacific (ACP) countries have a very long history that dates back hundreds of years. In this chapter we argue that 'echoes' of past relations, particularly those of the colonial era, can be found in the most recent set of trade negotiations between the EU and ACP countries.

The most recent trade negotiations stem from the mid 1990s, when the EU proposed a radical restructuring of its trade relations with ACP countries. The EU sought to replace the unilateral trade preferences that had existed since the 1970s, with a series of regional free-trade agreements called 'Economic Partnership Agreements' (EPAs). Under these EPAs, ACP countries would commit to opening up their economies more extensively to imports from the EU in return for continued access to the EU market. The EU also proposed the liberalization of trade in services, and the negotiation of rules in trade-related areas such as intellectual property, competition and government procurement, issues which have long been controversial among developing countries.

Despite reservations, in 2000, ACP countries committed to negotiating EPAs by the end of 2007, when the EU was scheduled to withdraw the unilateral trade preferences. The negotiations quickly ran into trouble. While the Caribbean region and the European Union concluded an agreement as planned, negotiations with the five African and Pacific regions were acrimonious and consensus could not be reached on fundamental issues including the scope and depth of the accords.[1] A series of 'interim' agreements were hastily constructed from 2007 to early 2008 between the EU and 21 African and Pacific countries. These were designed to act as bridging agreements to maintain access to the European market after the withdrawal of unilateral preferences, while negotiations continued at the regional level. Although talks resumed, deep divergences remained. In late 2010, an African Union study noted 'the divergences between the EU and Africa seem to be intractable and not resolvable'.[2] As at September 2014, the West African and the Southern African regions had initialled an EPA agreement, while there was no agreement with the Central African, the Eastern and Southern African and the Pacific regions.

In this chapter we explore whether, and to what extent, 'echoes of empire' can be found in the recent EPA negotiations. At the rhetorical level, we find that opponents and proponents of the EPA frequently refer to the colonial era in framing their arguments, suggesting the legacies of the past live on in the minds of actors, shaping the way they approach negotiations. We then probe deeper, comparing and contrasting aspects of the recent EPA negotiations with the trade relations that have existed between European and ACP countries since the colonial era, in order to establish the nature and depth of these 'echoes of colonialism'. We focus on three characteristics of trade relations in the two eras: the substantive content of the trade rules; the way in which power asymmetries were manifest; and the more subtle 'echoes' in patterns of paternalistic behaviour on the European side.

We find evidence of 'echoes' of the colonial legacy in all three aspects of the recent EPA negotiations. While it would be absurd to claim that EU–ACP trade relations at the start of the twenty-first century are no different to the shocking levels of brutality and exploitation that characterized trade relations during the colonial era, we argue that it is also equally fallacious to claim, as some have sought to, that EU–ACP trade relations have somehow left history behind.

The Historical Roots of Trade Rules: Back to the Future?

During the EPA negotiations, the EU tabled a series of detailed proposals. Proponents of these proposals argued that the EPAs were an embodiment of modernity that would enable the ACP countries to break definitively with the colonial relations of the past. The European Commission, which led negotiations for the EU, argued that EPAs were 'the way to help create a modern, twenty-first-century business environment, attract foreign direct investment, to grow markets and trade in order to reduce poverty'.[3] Moreover, the Commission argued that, with EPAs, the historical legacy that had overshadowed previous trade relations could finally be left behind: 'The colonial and post-colonial period are behind us and a more politically open international environment enables us to lay down the responsibilities of each partner less ambiguously.'[4] Similarly, in defending his country's decision to enter an EPA, Jamaica's prime minister justified this step on the basis that the system of unilateral preferences under which ACP countries were exporting to the EU was 'a kind of mendicancy that we need to purge ourselves of'.[5]

Core elements of the EU's proposals were strongly opposed by many, although not all, ACP countries. Opponents argued that the EPAs were economically exploitative and would threaten the development of ACP countries, often referring to the colonial era to frame their arguments. As might be expected, many of the strongest allegations came from civil society actors, some of whom argued they were an attempt at the 're-colonisation of Africa'.[6] Senior ACP leaders also issued public statements reflecting their concerns about the substance of the EPAs, with the most strident critics framing their arguments with reference to the colonial era. For instance, in light of divergences caused within the South African Customs Union as a result of EPA negotiations, South Africa's president called on regional leaders to examine 'how to eliminate all vestiges of colonial systems of domination and dependency';[7] while in a hard-hitting opinion piece, Nigeria's former Central Bank Governor and advisor to the World Bank called the EPA negotiations the 'modern day equivalent of the Berlin Conference', arguing that 'from the time of slavery to the Berlin conference, Africa has either been a source of free labour and profit or source of raw materials and market. Only the dynamics change *but the substance has remained* [emphasis added].'[8]

An examination of the EU's EPA proposals in light of the rules that have governed trade relations between Europe and ACP countries since the colonial era reveals that some of the most controversial aspects of the EU's proposals have deep historical roots. Moreover, it reveals that many of the arguments levelled against European trade policies in the colonial and independence era resonate strongly with the arguments voiced by opponents to the EPAs. Four issues are examined here: reciprocity, industrialization, investment, and trade with third parties.

Reciprocal Preferences

The first area where there is a striking continuity between the past and present is in the structure of the trade relations. At its core, the EPA proposal entailed a shift from unilateral to reciprocal trade preferences. Under the Lomé system of preferences, which governed trade relations between the European and ACP countries from 1975 onwards, ACP countries had duty-free access into the European market for 95 per cent of their exports (although complex rules of origin made it hard for ACP countries to fully utilize these preferences). Lomé preferences were unilateral: there was no obligation for ACP countries to reciprocate; so European exporters did not have preferential access to ACP markets.

Under the EPA, the EU proposed a move to reciprocity, albeit with some degree of asymmetry towards ACP countries. The EU proposed that it would expand the preferential access it provided from 95 per cent to 100 per cent of imports from ACP countries. Crucially, in return, and for the first time since 1975, ACP countries would have to provide preferential treatment towards the EU by eliminating tariffs on 80 per cent of imports from the EU within ten to fifteen years.[9]

Although the EPA proposal retains some asymmetry in favour of the ACP countries, due to the vast differences in the relative size of trade flows and the relative importance of tariffs for both revenue and industrial policy, the burden of adjustment under an EPA is much higher for ACP countries than the EU. EU adjustment costs were low because trade with ACP countries represented only 2 per cent of the EU's total trade in the mid 2000s, so increasing access for ACP imports from 95 per cent under Lomé to 100 per cent under the EPA would have no significant impact on the EU. In contrast, many ACP countries faced substantial adjustment costs. When the EPA negotiations started, the EU was a major trading partner for most ACP countries: 30 per cent of total ACP exports were destined for the EU, and the EU was the source of 28 per cent of total ACP imports.[10] At the same time, ACP countries maintained an average tariff rate on imports from the EU of 14 per cent, with significantly higher tariffs on value-added import competing industrial products.[11] For many ACP countries, opening markets up to 80 per cent of imports from the EU entailed substantial tariff cuts and significant losses of government revenue, particularly in the poorest ACP countries.[12]

The EU advocated this shift from unilateral Lomé preferences to reciprocal preferences under the EPA on the grounds that this would be a more modern way to structure trade relations. However, a review of the historical evidence suggests otherwise. A move from unilateral to reciprocal preferences has strong 'echoes of colonialism'.

Reciprocity was a core feature of French colonial trade relations with ACP countries. France incorporated its colonies into an empire-wide free-trade area, under which trade within the empire was fully liberalized and France set a common external tariff. 'Full reciprocity' was a key feature of the French system, and it privileged the interests of French manufacturers, enabling them to maximize their exports to protected colonial markets. The colonies provided an important market for the most dynamic sectors of the French economy, such as oil-refining, cotton and soap manufacturing, and sugar refinery, as the domestic market was too limited to provide economies of scale, and protected European markets were too difficult for France to enter.[13]

When the European Economic Community was formed in 1957, France lobbied to extend the system of reciprocity that it had with its colonies to the other five founding members. Germany and Luxembourg opposed this move, as they had no colonies and significant economic ties with Latin American countries, which would be adversely affected under the French proposal. However, France won the argument and under the final Treaty of Rome (1957) all the colonies of France, Belgium, Italy and the Netherlands were associated to the European Economic Community (EEC) under a system of full reciprocity.[14]

When they won independence in the 1960s, the French, Italian and Belgian colonies formally negotiated their trade relations with the EEC for the first time. However, their extreme dependency on trade and financial ties with the EEC, and France in particular, meant the former colonies had minimal bargaining power. As a result, there was minimal change, and the French system of reciprocity was retained under the Yaoundé I Agreement (1963).[15]

The British colonial system differed markedly from the French. During the early twentieth century, Britain adopted a system of 'imperial preferences' that demanded what we might term 'less than full reciprocity' from the ACP countries it colonized. Colonies were provided with preferential access into Britain, and while they had to provide some preferences for imports of British manufactured goods, they were allowed to retain some tariffs on British imports. There were repeated calls from the British manufacturing sector to move to a system of full reciprocity like the French, but they were successfully opposed, most notably by the financial services sector. The City of London supported a system of 'less than full reciprocity' as it would ensure that colonies would be left with sterling to pay their debts, instead of spending all the sterling they earned from exports to purchase British imports.[16]

When they gained independence, some of the former British colonies sought to negotiate trade agreements with the EEC, in a bid to gain access to the vast EEC market. However, they were highly critical of the 'full reciprocity' that characterized relations with the former French colonies. The most ardent critics argued, inter alia, that reciprocity had hindered industrialization by denying colonies the right to protect infant industries, structurally disadvantaged them by bringing cheap raw materials to Europe in exchange for expensive manufactured items, and hindered intra-African trade.[17] It is striking that the criticism levelled against the EEC system of reciprocal preferences in the 1960s is so similar to that levelled by critics of the EPA today.

In 1972, Britain sought entry into the EEC and this generated a fresh debate in Europe and among ACP countries about whether trade with the former colonies would be based on the French or the British system. An alliance of leading Caribbean and Anglophone African states convinced Francophone African countries to fight against reciprocal preferences. The resulting Lomé I Agreement (1975) was a significant 'win' for ACP countries as it resulted in the creation of an EEC-wide system of unilateral preferences under which all ACP states had significant access to European markets, without having to provide any margin of preference to Europe.[18] This system was retained from 1975 until 2007.[19]

Seen in light of this history, the EU's proposed shift from unilateral preferences to reciprocity under EPAs appears to be a case of 'back to the future' rather than an entirely new way of structuring EU–ACP trade relations. Moreover, the creation of the Lomé system of unilateral preferences in the 1970s was applauded as a new model of solidarity for North–South relations, which reflected the need for proportional treatment between vastly unequal partners. It is rather ironic that the EU and some ACP leaders have chosen to criticize the Lomé system of unilateral preferences for fostering dependency and advocate a return to the system of reciprocity, originally introduced by France into the EEC in the colonial era, on the grounds that this reflects equality between EU and ACP states.

Industrial Development of ACP Countries

A second debate that has echoes from the colonial era to the present day is the concern that the nature of trade relations with Europe hinders the industrial development of ACP countries.

During the colonial era, trade rules were structured to the advantage of European states. Industrialization in most ACP countries was actively discouraged, lest it compete with industries in Europe. In East Africa, for instance, there is evidence that requests by wealthy Asian traders to establish textiles factories were repeatedly turned down. In one instance such punitive export taxes were imposed by Britain on sisal twine exports from a factory in Tanganyika that it went out of business.[20] In Senegal, quotas were imposed on the export of processed groundnuts in order to keep the processing business in France, and Africans who showed interest in establishing manufacturing businesses were denied access to bank credit.[21]

After independence, ACP states sought to use trade relations with Europe to promote economic diversification and industrialization, but with little effect. As noted above, in the immediate aftermath of independence, there was deep disquiet about the adverse affects of reciprocal tariff liberalization on the ability of Francophone ACP countries to foster industrial development. Under the Lomé I Agreement, Francophone ACP countries regained control over tariff policy, but, as a number of studies have shown, for the main, they were unable to use these to stimulate successfully economic development. Complex and onerous rules of origin imposed by Europe impeded the export of manufactured products by ACP countries.[22]

Current negotiations echo some of these concerns. A key objective of ACP states in the EPA negotiations was to establish trade rules that would foster economic diversification. Many ACP governments have argued, just as Anglophone ACP states did in the 1960s and 1970s, that reciprocal liberalization would greatly hinder their capacity to stimulate industrial development.[23] While the EU has offered to make some improvement to its rules of origin, many experts argue that they remain overly stringent, and continue to impede the export of manufactured products from ACP countries.[24] In addition, many ACP states have argued that the EU's proposal to prohibit export taxes on raw materials would remove an important policy mechanism for stimulating value addition.[25]

Where EPAs have been signed, many ACP countries have insisted on safeguard clauses and tariff exemptions that allow them to make limited use of tariffs for revenue and industrialization purposes, like the Treaty of Rome and Yaoundé Agreements before them. In a similar vein to the Lomé I Agreement, the Caribbean EPA includes provisions on innovation and technology transfer that aim to stimulate economic diversification. However, as with the Lomé I Agreement, the EU's commitments are non-binding, raising questions as to whether they will be implemented.[26]

Given the rapid rise of trade with China, are concerns about trade relations with the EU undermining industrialization now a moot point? Indeed, while economic cooperation with China has brought some important achievements, there is growing concern among African leaders and in international policy circles that imports of Chinese manufactured goods are contributing to deindustrialization in some ACP countries.[27] However, our key argument remains valid: since the colonial era, trade relations with European countries could have been structured differently in order to better support the upgrading of exports from ACP countries and to facilitate industrialization. The EPAs are no exception.

Investment by European Companies

Investment by European companies is a third area where echoes of the past resonate. In the EPA negotiations, the EU has sought significant guarantees for the rights of establishment of its companies as well as guarantees for the free flow of capital. While many assume that these are new demands from the EU in the wake of stalled negotiations on investment at the multilateral level, scrutiny of past trade relations shows that investment has long been a contentious issue between European and ACP countries.

During the colonial era, European trading companies played a crucial role and were in many ways the vanguards of colonialism.[28] Britain's colonial expansion into tropical Africa, for instance, was in part the result of lobbying by British firms.[29] By the end of the colonial era, European trading companies had consolidated their hold. In West Africa trade was exceptionally concentrated and a few large European companies wielded a high level of market power. Data from Nigeria shows that in 1949 the six leading European firms imported 70 per cent of goods, while African firms only imported 5 per cent of goods.[30]

Under the Treaty of Rome, which was modelled on the French colonial trading system, members of the EEC states insisted that their companies be given rights of establishment in the colonies, including national treatment. As a result, the treaty had a section on investment that provided all EEC companies and nationals with equal rights to establish subsidiaries in the colonies as those enjoyed by the colonial powers.[31] Similar clauses were retained in the Yaoundé Agreements. However, when ACP states started to reassert control over trade relations during the Lomé I negotiations in the 1970s, they successfully lobbied for the removal of obligations that granted national treatment to European companies guaranteeing the free flow of capital.[32]

Once again, the debate has come full circle with the EPA negotiations, with the EU requesting national treatment for its companies and provisions guaranteeing the free flow of capital. While advocates argue that such guarantees can stimulate foreign direct investment as they provide greater certainty and flexibility to investors, the reaction of ACP governments has been mixed. The Caribbean region concluded services and investment chapters in their EPA with the EU, but African and Pacific countries have, to date, refused to pursue negotiations in these areas. This is largely out of concern that the EU's proposals would restrict their ability to maximize the benefits of foreign investment and impede initiatives to support local enterprises.[33] Indeed, many argue that premature market opening could undermine economic growth in developing countries.[34]

Controlling Trade with Third Parties

The final area where there are obvious 'echoes' of the past is in the recent debates over whether the EPAs are a bid by European states to maintain a privileged relationship with ACP states and to reduce the influence of third-party countries.

During the colonial era, the French, and later the EEC, model of 'full reciprocity' diverted trade away from third parties in favour of the European states, and was heavily criticized by the United States in particular. In addition, European states took explicit measures to maintain colonies as protected markets for their exports by controlling imports from third parties. For instance, in 1932, when British exports were suffering from Japanese competition, imports of Japanese goods were banned in the Gold Coast and Nigeria. Similarly, to boost the export of French manufactured products, the French imposed a quota on British imports into French West Africa in the 1930s.[35]

In the recent EPA debates, concerns have arisen that Europe might be trying to reassert itself as a privileged partner for ACP states. One model of the trade effects of EPAs highlighted significant trade diversion in favour of the EU, prompting concerns of a 'huge market grab' through EPAs.[36] Similar charges have been levelled in response to the EU's insistence on the inclusion of a 'most-favoured-nation' clause between ACP countries and the EU. This clause states that any market access commitments that ACP states give third-party 'major trading nations' in future need to be passed on to the EU if they allow for better treatment than under EPAs. It poses a threat to growing South–South trade because it reduces the incentives for emerging economies to negotiate bilateral free-trade agreements with ACP countries.[37] This demand has unsurprisingly been fiercely criticized by ACP states and major emerging countries. Brazil raised a formal objection to this clause at the World Trade Organization (WTO) General Council and was supported by other emerging countries, including China and India.[38]

Asymmetries of Power: Who Decides?

In addition to the substantive content of the EPA, concerns that the EU was using coercive tactics during the EPA negotiations generated frequent references to the colonial era. For instance, Tanzania's former president accused the EU of 'using quite blatantly and openly a divide and rule strategy'.[39] Namibia's trade minister called on Europe to resolve the outstanding issues in EPA negotiations without using 'bully tactics or old colonial arrogance'.[40] Guyana's president asserted that the EPA is 'another instance of the European Union using its trade might and economic might bullying a developing country into an agreement'.[41]

Such concerns sit in clear opposition to the EU's argument that the principle of 'partnership' was central to the EPA negotiating process. If power is absent, or present in equal measure on both sides, then a relationship might be said to be a 'partnership' characterized by 'free will, equal weight in terms of influence and ability to shape negotiations and outcomes'.[42] Such a situation of partnership can be contrasted to the profound power asymmetry that was a defining feature of colonial relations. This is implicit in the argument of Nicolaïdis and Kleinfeld, who contend that 'perhaps the most fundamental measure of a non-colonial relationship is that of *voluntary* engagement, usually entailing at least some degree of equality or symmetry rather than a hierarchical relationship'.[43]

A brief exploration of power and resistance in the history of trade relations between Europe and ACP countries shows that power asymmetries continue to persist in the EPA negotiations. While power asymmetries take different forms and have far less effect compared with the colonial era they nonetheless 'echo' the past. Attempts by Europeans to exploit their favourable power position have continued to be a defining feature of trade relations, as has resistance on the part of ACP countries.

Power Asymmetries in the Colonial Era

The highly exploitative trade relations between Europe and ACP countries during the colonial era were ultimately made possible by asymmetries in hard power in the form of military capabilities and the 'gunboat diplomacy' it gave rise to. For instance, towards the end of the nineteenth century, a series of 'unequal treaties' were extracted from African leaders under the threat of military invasion. In the Niger Delta, more than 200 treaties were obtained between 1884–6 alone, ostensibly showing that local rulers had not only relinquished sovereignty to the British, but that they had granted a British company the right to exclude foreigners and monopolize trade.[44] Military coercion enabled the appropriation of vast tracts of agricultural land and forestry for European settlers or plantations, and many colonial rulers claimed rights over mineral resources.

Once colonial rule had been established, colonial powers took steps to reorientate trade relations with ACP countries to serve their interests, including through various systems of preferences explored above. In the domestic economy, control over the administrative structures of state enabled the colonial state to levy oppressive levels of taxes and to manage markets heavily through licences and price controls.[45] Millions of people were forced to labour in slave-like conditions in plantations and mines, including in the notoriously oppressive compulsory rubber-production systems in the Belgian Congo.[46]

Resistance to this oppression continued throughout. People in Africa, the Caribbean, and the Pacific fought to reclaim their autonomy and sovereignty, including through the disruption of economic relations. In Nigeria, for instance, female palm oil traders rose up in protest at new taxes and low prices, beating up colonial officials and local chiefs that were allied with the colonial state, destroying the stores of foreign traders and setting fire to native administration offices. Colonial troops responded by shooting and killing 50 women. In the Gold Coast there were waves of 'hold-ups' by cocoa farmers who refused to sell their produce at the extremely low prices demanded by companies and boycotted British imports.[47] Elsewhere, trade was disrupted by waves of labour strikes and protests on the railways and in the ports.

Despite the profound power asymmetries that characterized the colonial era, this resistance from below limited the room for manoeuvre of colonial rulers. Europeans depended on indigenous collaboration – such as in the case of the Buganda Kingdom in Uganda from 1886 to 1900 – to avert or hold down resistance to be able to impose their system of rules on their empires.[48]

Power Asymmetries in the Independence Era

Rising protests and resistance among the people in ACP countries eventually contributed to the end of colonial rule.[49] With independence, ACP leaders regained sovereignty and formal control over trade policy. This shifted the balance of European and ACP power substantially as ACP states were recognized as sovereign entities, which limited the Europeans' recourse to exercise power by military means.

Despite this, the balance of power was still tipped towards Europe as a result of the deep economic dependence of ACP states on the former colonial powers.[50] During the Yaoundé I negotiations, Francophone African countries were able to participate in negotiations as sovereign states for the first time, but their extreme dependency on trade and financial ties with the EEC, and France in particular, meant they had minimal bargaining power. Many Francophone African countries were unhappy with the outcome but the depth of their economic dependence meant that they had no alternatives and when Mali threatened to walk out, this was not taken seriously.[51]

In the 1970s, the balance of power shifted more firmly towards ACP countries. The 1973 oil crisis sparked fears in Europe that developing countries would exert market power in other key commodities, and this led the Europeans to show some degree of flexibility in the Lomé I negotiations.[52] Together with the formation of a strong coalition across the ACP group, and the use of astute negotiating tactics, this enabled the ACP countries to secure significant concessions, including the creation of the Lomé system of unilateral trade preferences discussed above.[53]

During the 1980s, economic crisis and heavy dependence on aid finance from Europe tipped the balance of power back towards Europe. Although ACP countries managed to hang on to the core concessions of the Lomé I agreement, these were gradually watered down. ACP influence over trade relations ebbed further in the 1990s when it became clear that Europe's interest in a close relationship with ACP countries had waned. Europe had refocused external relations on Eastern Europe after the end of the Cold War, and sought deeper trade ties with the expanding markets of Latin America and Asia.

Following challenges raised at the General Agreement on Tariffs and Trade (GATT) and later the WTO on the compatibility of Lomé preferences with multilateral trade rules on non-discrimination, the Commission started to openly advocate a move to reciprocal trade preference agreements, paving the way for the EPA negotiations.[54]

Power Asymmetries in the EPA Negotiations

At the start of the EPA negotiations, the balance of power looked as if it squarely favoured Europe. In the face of significant opposition from the majority of ACP countries, the EU used a series of common negotiating tactics to try to take advantage of its relative power position and compel ACP countries into agreement on its terms. As in previous decades, the EU's tactical moves met with a series of counter-moves from ACP countries, and in the EPA negotiations they severely limited the EU's room for manoeuvre.

As elaborated below, the form and intensity of coercive power tactics employed by the EU during the EPA negotiations was vastly different to the colonial era, not least because they relied on economic rather than military might. Given this, it is reasonable to ask whether power asymmetries and the reliance of the EU on coercive power tactics are really indicative of an 'echo of colonialism'. Indeed, we should *expect* a larger country to seek to exploit its relative power position when negotiating with a smaller country, irrespective of whether these countries have a colonial past, and we should equally expect the smaller country to respond with counter-moves.[55] This is a valid point. Our argument here is that power asymmetries and the strategic interactions they give rise to are not in themselves evidence of an 'echo of colonialism'. However, just as power asymmetry was a necessary condition for colonial rule, it is also a necessary condition for the persistence of its 'echoes'. Without power asymmetries of some form, such 'echoes' would rapidly fade into oblivion.

During the EPA negotiations, the main source of coercive power was the EU's decision not to apply for a renewal of the WTO waiver that would have enabled the Lomé trade regime to continue after December 2007. The threat of losing unilateral trade preferences meant that ACP states had to agree to an EPA if they wished to maintain the same degree of preferential access to the European market as before. While the EU presented this decision as the only option that was available due to a WTO ruling, several studies show that alternatives were available that the EU decided not to pursue.[56]

Public statements emanating from the EPA negotiations show that ACP countries felt that they were on the receiving end of significant coercive pressure. Two incidents are illustrative. In December 2007, just before unilateral preferences were due to be withdrawn, ACP trade ministers issued a joint statement that 'Ministers *deplore the enormous pressure* that has been brought to bear on the ACP States by the European Commission to initial the interim trade arrangement [emphasis added]'.[57] One incident from the Pacific, disputed by the EU, suggests that threats were made to reduce aid if EPAs were not agreed. In 2007, the European Commission sent an email just ahead of a meeting of Pacific trade ministers stating that financial assistance would have to be 'reprogrammed' if agreement was not reached.[58] The European Commission strongly resisted the allegation that this was tantamount to a threat, and in a rather curt response, one Pacific minister argued that he was educated enough to spot a veiled threat when he was on the receiving end of one.[59]

Power asymmetries were present in other ways too. ACP states had vastly lower levels of negotiating capacity.[60] European development agencies recognized that asymmetry in negotiating capacity undermined the prospects for partnership and made significant efforts to address the imbalance. However, this led to the perverse situation where the EU became a major source of information, expertise and training for ACP negotiators. This generated concerns that assistance was biased, serving to sell the EU's interests to ACP states. In the words of a Brussels-based ACP representative, EU support 'is not advice, it is negotiating on both sides.'[61] A trade official from Malawi noted with concern that 'most consultants were not fully availing themselves to the clear implications of EPAs, since most of them had an attachment to the EU.'[62]

As in earlier decades, the EU's attempts to exploit its relative power position met with counter-moves from ACP states. These took different forms. The Caribbean region adopted a broadly cooperative strategy, agreeing to the EU's general approach to the EPA and investing in deploying technical and legal expertise to negotiate concessions in the margins of the EPA text. African and Pacific countries started by tabling counter-proposals, seeking to positively influence the EPA texts, but when the EU proved intransigent, the majority opted for a strategy of resistance. On the whole, African and Pacific countries that derived few benefits from unilateral trade preferences opted to exit from the EPA negotiations. Others, for whom unilateral preferences were of substantial benefit, successfully blocked many of the proposals tabled by the EU, whittling the agreements down to their core 'trade in goods' elements. Resistance continued after negotiations were formally concluded, with many African and Pacific countries evading the signature, ratification and implementation.[63]

Thus, contrary to the EU claims of partnership, the EPA negotiations were infused with power asymmetries. As in the past, the EU deployed a series of coercive pressure tactics and it met with a series of counter-moves from ACP countries. As in the colonial era, resistance limited the room for manoeuvre of the EU, and in this case, the results were substantial. As at September 2014, only the Caribbean region had agreed to an EPA of the scope that the EU sought, and rather than the result of coercive tactics, this appeared to be due to a consensus among its negotiators that the EPA model was appropriate for the region's development, and the region succeeded in securing concessions in the fine-print of the text.[64] While two more regions, the West African and the Southern African regions, initialled a more minimal EPA on trade in goods in 2014, many other countries proceed to evade signature, ratification and implementation. Those regions who eventually accepted the EPA were significantly influenced by the EU's decision to remove its unilateral trade preferences by 1 October 2014 for countries that have not signed or ratified the EPAs.[65]

This shift in the balance of power towards ACP countries appears, in part, to reflect the global shift in the balance of economic power. As the EPA negotiations progressed, ACP countries, particularly those in Africa, saw a rapid intensification of their trade relations with China and other emerging markets. Statements from ACP leaders during the EPA negotiations suggest that they were very aware of the potential leverage this afforded them. During the Africa–Europe Summit in Lisbon in December 2007, for instance, Senegal's president argued that the EPAs risked causing a 'seismic rupture' between the two continents at a time when China was wooing African countries with loans, infrastructure projects and cheap goods:

'Europe has nearly lost the battle of competition in Africa.'[66] While this shift has not been sufficient for African and Pacific states to see their interests realized, it helped provide a substantial counter-weight to the EU's power.

Paternalism vs Autonomy: Who Knows Best?

Patterns of paternalistic behaviour are the final, and maybe most subtle, aspect of 'echoes of colonialism' that this chapter explores. At the rhetorical level, concerns of paternalism were reflected in the statements of those who opposed the EU's EPA proposals. For instance, Senegal's president refused to sign an EPA, advocating instead a 'partnership deprived of paternalism and without prejudice'.[67] Barbados' Minister of Foreign Affairs and chairperson of the ACP Ministerial Trade Committee noted cynically that 'the EC's insistence on trying to determine what is best for the ACP and how we should configure our economic space seems more than a little disingenuous'.[68] Similarly a leading Caribbean academic argued that the EPA negotiations were constrained by 'Europe's seemingly unchallenged conviction [...] that Europe knows best what [the Caribbean region's] development priorities, needs, and capacities are'.[69]

We argue that deep-seated paternalism on the part of many European officials, and determination among ACP government representatives to preserve and strengthen their autonomy and control, have been a feature of trade relations from the colonial era to the present day. Regardless of whether or not the free-trade models propagated by the EU represented the most effective model for development as such a subtler form of 'echoes of colonialism' was found in the implicit negation of ACP voices in the approaches adopted by the EU.

Paternalism and Autonomy in the Colonial Era

Most historians argue that paternalism on the part of Europeans was a core feature of colonial relations, which stemmed from deep-seated racism. Paternalism was reflected in patterns of thought and action among Europeans that differentiated between 'Self' and 'Other' (ACP peoples) along the lines of benefactor/recipient or superior/inferior. Faced with colonial occupation and stripped of the powers of state, the rights of citizenship and in many instances of their assets, people in ACP countries fought to reclaim autonomy and control over their lives, including in the area of trade.

Advocates of colonial expansion, including chartered companies and government officials, continually justified their actions to the European public in light of the purported interests of ACP peoples. Motivated by genuine belief or political pragmatism, government officials rarely admitted European economic and political interests, justifying colonial occupation in moral terms, citing the aims of ending the slave trade and bringing 'civilization'. In the words of the British colonial minister Joseph Chamberlain, 'we develop new territory as Trustees for Civilisation, for the Commerce of the World'.[70] Even leading merchant traders saw themselves as far more than businessmen, driven by a sense of empire and patriotism, as well as a firm belief in the superiority of the white race. As Rhodes famously noted, 'I contend that we are the finest race in the world and that the more of the world we inhabit, the better it is for the human race'.[71]

Underpinning the *mission civilisatrice* was a set of ideas that, in the words of Thandika Mkandawire, aimed to 'dehumanise the enslaved and the colonised by denying their history and denigrating their achievements and their capabilities' while the colonialists made 'claims to universalism for their cultures and values'.[72] Despite the fact that African countries had been integrated into international trading routes for millennia, Africa was portrayed as having 'no history', in the words of Lord Lugard, a leading British adventurer and explorer and later colonial administrator. Europeans were attributed with 'discovering' the continent and tasked with a 'dual mandate' of bringing trade and 'civilization' to a population portrayed as economically isolated and 'backward'.[73] Under a system that was advocated by colonial governments as 'drawing Africans into the money economy' and 'teaching natives the value of work', people were forcibly removed from their land and farms and often a high level of coercion was involved in making them work for European firms.[74]

A popular humanitarian movement emerged in Europe at the end of the nineteenth century to oppose the brutality of colonial occupation, yet it too was deeply infused with paternalism. Far from opposing colonial occupation per se, their mission was to ensure that 'trusteeship be genuine rather than a rationalisation for exploitation and enslavement'.[75] The movement saw ACP countries as areas to be 'civilized' by Europeans and colonial expansion as a means for furthering European ideals of the Enlightenment, including free trade.[76]

On the ACP side, colonial occupation frequently galvanized strong resistance movements. In addition to fighting economic exploitation, these different pro-independence movements sought autonomy and sovereignty. The underlying argument of these movements was that once formal political control was regained, economic and social development could be pursued. As Kwame Nkrumah, Ghana's independence leader, famously said: 'Seek ye first the political kingdom and all things will be added unto you'.[77]

Paternalism and Autonomy in the Independence Era

After independence, ACP states formally regained control over trade policy but in practice their autonomy was severely constrained as a result of their continued economic dependence on European powers. It is striking that, in addition to opposing the reciprocal liberalization under the Yaoundé Agreement on economic grounds, Anglophone African countries opposed it on political grounds. They argued that reciprocity denied African countries any real control over trade policy and was thus a form of 'indirect rule'.[78] Indeed, a major justification for the switch to unilateral preferences in the 1975 Lomé I Agreement was that it would provide ACP countries with a greater degree of autonomy.

Much of the autonomy afforded by the Lomé I Agreement was lost in the wake of economic crisis in the 1980s and high levels of dependence on European aid. With aid dependence came a deep entanglement between aid donors, with donors largely determining ACP economic and trade policies. Once again, paternalism was a core feature of these relations. The adverse international economic context was frequently overlooked by European officials and there was general consensus among them that economic crisis was exclusively the result of domestic mismanagement by ACP governments.[79] Donor agencies stepped in to 'educate' ACP countries as to the optimal trade policies that they thought they should follow and in many cases took advantage of aid dependence to push through trade reforms.

The shift in power and paternalism was reflected in formal trade negotiations between the European and ACP countries. The negotiations towards Lomé II in the early 1980s were 'extended' and 'abrasive' and for a significant period characterized by stalemate. European negotiators were perceived by ACP countries as 'rude and aggressive' and as treating ACP representatives as 'very junior and very troublesome partners'.[80] During negotiations in the mid and late 1980s, the Europeans tabled a series of demands that they perceived as being necessary for ACP development and which the ACP strongly resisted as they were perceived as an erosion of their autonomy and sovereignty. These included commitments to enter into 'policy dialogue' with Europe, adhere to human rights and labour standards, agree to restrictions on the use of financial assistance, and grant protection to European investors. The ACP argued these implied 'too great a measure of involvement by the EEC in their domestic policies' and were 'not consistent with agreements between sovereign states'.[81] On their part, the Europeans failed to understand the concerns of ACP states: 'What passions were aroused, what anxiety and what misunderstandings caused by this idea, which the Community had put forward *for the sole purpose of making aid more effective* [emphasis added]'.[82]

Paternalism and Autonomy in the EPA Negotiations

It was against this backdrop that EPA negotiations started in 2002. The need to give due recognition to the autonomy and voice of ACP countries in the EPA negotiations was agreed by the EU and ACP alike. They formally agreed that the EPA negotiations would 'aim at fostering the smooth and gradual integration of the ACP States into the world economy, with *due regard for their political choices and development priorities* [emphasis added].'[83] During the EPA negotiations, the EU often noted the importance of negotiating as equals, with, for instance, the EU Trade Commissioner asserting that 'the ACP and EU working together can make policy and build partnerships as equals'.[84]

In practice, many EU officials adopted an approach that undermined these aspirations. Instead of negotiating as equals, the European side clearly expected itself to be in a better position to judge what an economically sound EPA would look like.[85] This led to the implicit delegitimization of many ACP negotiating positions, which were understood to 'ignore economics'.[86] As a consequence, EU negotiators were widely perceived by ACP states as condescending and as showing scant regard for the perspectives of their negotiators.[87] One ACP negotiator noted that the way in which the Trade Commissioner participated in negotiations was 'disrespectful' and 'very rigid.[88] In the EU–Pacific EPA negotiations, the Trade Commissioner allegedly refused to continue negotiations until, as he furiously shouted, 'incompetent' technical advisors of the Pacific team left the room.[89] Another ACP negotiator noted that 'they [the EU negotiators] always try to portray us as being unreasonable and behind'.[90]

However, it would be a mistake to imply that all European negotiators were perceived as being paternalistic. Some ACP negotiators object to the EU being labelled as paternalistic, arguing that their approach is a normal part of the cut and thrust of negotiating. It was argued for instance that '[the] negotiating style and strategy were agreed to by both parties so if it's flawed I wouldn't want to put the blame on the EU'.[91]

When the EU switched trade commissioners from Mandelson to Ashton in 2008, this led to a significant change in the tone of interactions and a more positive mood among negotiators.[92] There appears to have been some acknowledgement by the EU that the negotiating style of the previous commissioner had been infused with paternalism, as the new commissioner said she would introduce a 'different character' in the EPA negotiations, 'listen[ing] to the concerns of each region and replac[ing] controversy over interim agreements with a positive debate on full EPAs'.[93] She explicitly stated that the agreements should be 'based on a genuine partnership rather than paternalism'.[94]

Yet, as one ACP negotiator noted, Ashton's much more diplomatic stance did not necessarily mean that there was a substantive shift in the EU's position.[95] After her appointment, the EU still refused to concede ground on the numerous 'contentious clauses' in the interim EPA texts. Thus it is far from clear that the reduction in overtly paternalistic attitudes resulted in ACP countries having greater autonomy and voice. The EU Trade Commissioner was changed again in February 2010, and the EU returned to a less conciliatory and more assertive tone.

In another move reminiscent of colonial times, the EU went to considerable pains to argue that it was negotiating for the interests of ACP states, rather than its own.[96] A constant refrain of the European Commission was that Europe had no interests at stake and that the development of ACP countries was the EU's only objective. In the words of the Commission, 'DG Trade does not approach these negotiations in the usual way, where we seek to gain economic advantage from each other. [...] Our objective with you is to build on our privileged relationship and to secure and improve your market access into the EU, in order to serve a wider development goal.'[97] Similarly, the first Trade Commissioner often reiterated that his driving mission was 'to ensure [that] the needs of the poorest are at all times at the forefront of our European policy'.[98]

It is of course possible that this was merely a cynical tactic by European negotiators to 'window-dress' the EU's materially driven motivations. Indeed one ACP ambassador in Brussels argued that 'they tell you lies[...] The development thing is rhetoric.'[99] Yet in interactions with EU negotiators one cannot avoid the sense that many were driven, at least in part, by a sense of moral duty to reduce poverty in ACP countries. Nonetheless, what might have been a positive force for solidarity and justice was often undermined by deep paternalism on the part of many EU negotiators, reflected in the conviction that *their* understanding about how trade policy could be used to foster development was vastly superior to that of ACP negotiators.

On the ACP side, many government officials, interest groups and civil society actors criticized the EPAs as an initiative that would further remove ACP control over trade policy. They were perceived as a means of locking-in the policy reforms that were imposed during the 1980s and 1990s, committing ACP states to a raft of trade and industrial policies that, many argue, are poorly suited to their development needs.[100]

Crucially, rather than taking the concerns raised by ACP countries on board, and reconsidering their own beliefs, EU negotiators became more convinced than ever that the problem was ignorance among ACP negotiators. As one EC Development Commissioner shouted furiously in 2008, 'if you want to remain poor, just be against the EPAs.'[101] When the EPA negotiations with Africa and the Pacific stalled, EU Commissioners referred to the need 'to develop a shared discourse that trade is a primary lever of economic prosperity'.[102]

Conclusion

It is often said that the past casts a long shadow over the present, and the EPA negotiations are testimony to this: 'echoes of empire' resonate throughout the EPA story.

In this chapter we have shown that far from being entirely 'modern', many aspects of the contemporary EPA negotiations have clear historical roots. Key aspects of the trade rules proposed by the EU during the EPA negotiations as well as the debates over their likely impact on the development of ACP countries resonate strongly with those that took place in the colonial and independence eras. Legacies of paternalism on the part of Europeans, which profoundly shaped colonial trade relations, live on. Equally, in ACP countries, colonial occupation generated a strong determination to defend autonomy and control over economic policies and this continues to shape the way that ACP countries respond to the EU's trade proposals. Colonial trade relations were made possible by highly and profoundly asymmetrical distribution of power and the persistence of power asymmetries helps account for the strong 'echoes of colonialism' we see today.

While resistance by ACP countries to coercion and domination by European countries has been present since the colonial era (and indeed before) the newfound engagement of China in Africa and the growing alternative of South–South trade, coupled with the 'eurozone crisis', represent important cracks in the foundations of Europe's economic dominance over ACP counties. As a parting thought, it is worth pondering whether these changes might enable EU and ACP states to move to a truly 'post-colonial' relationship, completely devoid of the relics of economic exploitation and paternalism that characterized the colonial era. On one level any attempt to leave history behind is a deeply flawed project. As this chapter has shown, economic and political structures are heavily shaped by the past, and actors are influenced by values and patterns of behaviour that are passed from one generation to the next. To deny this history, to wish it away because it raises uncomfortable questions, and to cover it with innocuous-sounding words like 'partnership' are all ways of perpetuating the inequalities of power that are its legacy.

Yet while history exerts an influence, it is not a binding force. The truly post-colonial project entails staring history in the face, seeing where and how it lives on, and being prepared to change our actions accordingly. Exploring and acknowledging these 'echoes of colonialism' is a step towards the EU being able to eventually embark on a truly post-colonial path with ACP countries.[103]

Notes

1 The ACP countries started the EPA negotiations as six separate groupings that loosely correspond to geographic areas: Caribbean, Pacific Island ACP states, West Africa, East Africa, Central Africa and Southern Africa.
2 African Union, 'African Union Commission / Regional Economic Communities' Common Position Paper on EPAs' (Addis Ababa, 2010).
3 CARICOM Secretariat, 'Press Release: CARIFORUM/EU EPA CAN BE A WORLD LEADER' (Georgetown, Guyana, 2007).

4 *Ibid.*

5 J. Myers, 'Golding Slams EPA Critics – Says they Suffer from Mendicancy', *Jamaica Gleaner*, 1 February 2008.

6 See for instance S. Kwenda, 'An Injury To One Market Is an Injury to All', *Inter-Press Service News Agency*, 2008.

7 J. Zuma, 'Address by His Excellency, President J. G. Zuma', in *Commemoration of the Centenary of the Southern African Customs Union (SACU)* (Windhoek, 2010).

8 C. C. Soludo, 'Africa: From Berlin to Brussels: Will Europe Underdevelop Africa again?', *Pambazuka News*, 29 March 2012.

9 See for instance S. Bilal and D. Lui, 'Contentious Issues in the Interim EPAs: Potential Flexibility in the Negotiations', in *Discussion Paper* (Brussels, 2009), p. 6.

10 E. Jones, 'The Weak vs. the Strong: The Africa, Caribbean and Pacific Countries Negotiating Free Trade Agreements with the European Union' (DPhil thesis, University of Oxford, 2013), p. 8.

11 World Bank, 'Africa – Economic Partnership Agreements between Africa and the European Union: What to Do Now?' (2008), p. 14.

12 For a discussion of the adjustment costs faced by the EU and ACP countries see Jones, 'The Weak vs. the Strong', Chapter 7.

13 D. K. Fieldhouse, 'Review: The Economics of French Empire', *The Journal of African History*, 27, 1 (1986), pp. 169–72; J. Marseille, *Empire colonial et capitalisme français* (Paris, 1984), p. 74.

14 I. W. Zartman, *The Politics of Trade Negotiations between Africa and the European Economic Community: The Weak Confront the Strong* (Princeton, NJ, 1971). Note however that liberalization was limited by a safeguard clause that allowed them to make limited use of tariffs for revenue and industrialization purposes.

15 *Ibid.*, p. 329.

16 D. L. Glickman, 'The British Imperial Preference System', *The Quarterly Journal of Economics*, 61, 3 (1947), pp. 439–70, p. 441. P. J. Cain and A. G. Hopkins, 'Gentlemanly Capitalism and British Expansion Overseas. II: New Imperialism, 1850–1945', *The Economic History Review*, New Series, 40, 1 (1987), pp. 1–26. See also P. J. Cain and A. G. Hopkins, *British Imperialism 1688–2000* (2001).

17 Zartman, *Politics of Trade Negotiations*.

18 However, Lomé I was not optimal for ACP countries. See for instance K. O. Hall and B. W. Blake, 'The Emergence of the African, Caribbean, and Pacific Group of States: An Aspect of African and Caribbean International Cooperation', *African Studies Review*, 22, 2 (1979), pp. 111–25; R. H. Green, *The Child of Lomé: Messiah, Monster or Mouse?* (Oxford, 1980).

19 For a detailed analysis of negotiations between the late 1950s and 2000s, see Jones, 'The Weak vs. the Strong', Chapter 3.

20 W. Robert and R. Maxon Ochieng, *An Economic History of Kenya* (Nairobi, 1992), p. 162.

21 C. Boone, *Merchant Capital and the Roots of State Power in Senegal, 1930–1985* (Cambridge, 1992), p. 48. There were some exceptions for European settlers, however. French textiles companies pulling out of Vietnam were given subsidies to relocate to Senegal, whilst in Kenya the British administration provided significant support to European industrialists, including through protective tariffs.

22 J. Ravenhill, 'Asymmetrical Interdependence: Renegotiating the Lomé Convention', in F. Long (ed.), *The Political Economy of EEC Relations with African, Caribbean and Pacific States* (Oxford, 1980), pp. 33–50.

23 See for instance A. Ouedraogo, 'Why are the Economic Partnership Agreements Detrimental for Africa's future?', in E. Jones and D. Marti (eds), *Updating the Economic Partnerships to Today's Global Challenges: Essays on the Future of the Economic Partnership Agreements* (Washington, DC, 2009), pp. 66–70.

24 E. Naumann, 'Rules of Origin in EU–ACP Economic Partnership Agreements', in *Issue Paper* (Geneva, 2009).

25 Bilal and Lui, *Contentious Issues.*

26 S. Musungu, 'Innovation and Intellectual Property in the Cariforum–EU Economic Partnership Agreement: Lessons for Other ACP Regions', in Regine Qualmann (ed.), *How to Ensure Development Friendly Economic Partnership Agreements: Lessons across Regions* (Eschborn, 2009).

27 For details of deindustrialization trends in Africa see UNCTAD, 'Report 2012: Structural Transformation and Sustainable Development in Africa', *Economic Development In Africa* (Geneva, 2012). On the position of African leaders, see for instance a statement by Nigeria's Central Bank Governor in O. Chima, 'Sanusi: China Is Major Contributor to Africa's De-Industrialisation', *This Day Live*, 13 March 2013.

28 For an analysis of the relationship between foreign investment and the expansion of colonialism see Cain and Hopkins, 'Gentlemanly Capitalism'.

29 *Ibid.* See also J. Darwin, *The Empire Project: The Rise and Fall of the British World-System* (Cambridge, 2009); J. Gallagher and R. Robinson, 'The Imperialism of Free Trade', *The Economic History Review*, 6, 1 (1953), pp. 1–15.

30 P. T. Bauer, 'Concentration in Tropical Trade: Some Aspects and Implications of Oligopoly', *Economica*, 20, 80 (1953), pp. 302–21. For an analysis of Francophone Africa, see P. Manning, *Francophone Sub-Saharan Africa, 1880–1995* (Cambridge, 1988).

31 Manning, *Francophone Sub-Saharan Africa.*

32 I. V. Gruhn, 'The Lomé Convention: Inching towards Interdependence', *International Organization*, 30, 2 (1976), pp. 241–62.

33 See for instance African Union, 'Common Position on EPAs'. Note that the CARIFORUM EPA, which already includes commitments on national treatment, explicitly allows for the continuation of domestic subsidies (Article 60/3, CARIFORUM-EC EPA). It does, however, restrict policy space regarding the level of binding of national treatment. P. Sauvé and N. Ward, 'Services and Investment in the EC–Cariforum Economic Partnership Agreement: Innovation in Rules – Design and Implications for Africa', in G. Faber and J. Orbie (eds), *Beyond Market Access for Economic Development: EU–Africa Relations in Transition* (2009).

34 See for instance A. Saad-Filho and D. Johnston, *Neoliberalism: A Critical Reader* (2005).

35 C. Boone, *Merchant Capital.*

36 A. Beattie and A. Bounds, 'The Wilted Relationship', *Financial Times*, 13 December 2007.

37 Cuts, 'The Most Favoured-Nation Provision in the EC–EAC EPA and Its Implications', *Briefing Paper* (2009), p. 3.

38 See discussion in Bilal and Lui, *Contentious Issues*; World Trade Organization, 'ACP–EC Economic Partnership Agreements: Communication from Brazil (Wt/Gc/W/585)' (2008).

39 B. Mkapa, 'Developing in Dignity: Self-Reliance and an Afro-Centric strategy', in *The 2008 Kwame Nkrumah Memorial Lectures By H. E. Benjamin William Mkapa, Third President of the United Republic of Tanzania* (Accra, 2008).

40 D. Cronin, 'Namibia Stands up to "EU Bullying"', *Inter-Press Service News Agency*, 24 May 2010.

41 'EPA: Caribbean Still Divided on Treaty', *BBC Caribbean.com*, 27 June 2008: http://www.bbc.co.uk/caribbean/news/story/2008/06/080627_jagdeoepa.shtml.

42 M. Farrell, 'A Triumph of Realism over Idealism? Cooperation Between the European Union and Africa', *Journal of European Integration*, 27, 3 (2005), pp. 263–83.

43 R. Kleinfeld and K. Nicolaïdis, 'Can a Post-Colonial Power Export the Rule of Law? Elements of a General Framework', in G. Palombella and N. Walker (eds), *Relocating the Rule of Law* (Portland, OR, 2009), pp. 139–69.

44 F. D. Lugard, *The Dual Mandate In British Tropical Africa* (1922).

45 B. Davidson, *Africa in History: Themes and Outlines*, rev. and expanded edition (1992). The British 'empire cotton growing system' in Uganda, for instance, provided raw cotton to British manufacturers through a system of stringent licensing restrictions that stipulated which companies African farmers could sell to and at what price. A similar system in the Portuguese colonies of Angola and Mozambique set prices so low that cotton became known locally as the 'mother of poverty'.

46 See A. Hochschild, *King Leopold's Ghost: A Story of Greed, Terror, and Heroism in Colonial Africa* (Boston, MA and New York, NY, 1999).

47 G. Padmore, *Africa: Britain's Third Empire* (New York, NY, 1969). See also C. Ifeka-Moller, 'Female Militancy and Colonial Revolt: The Women's War of 1929, Eastern Nigeria', in S. Ardener (ed.), *Perceiving Women* (1975), pp. 128–32; N. Mba, 'Heroines of the Women's War', in B. Awe (ed.), *Nigerian Women in Historical Perspective* (Lagos, 1992), pp. 75–88.

48 R. Robinson, 'Non-European Foundations of European Imperialism: Sketch for a Theory of Collaboration', in R. Owen and B. Sutcliffe (eds), *Studies in the Theory of Imperialism* (1972), p. 120.

49 For a comprehensive account of the reasons behind decolonization see for instance M. E. Chamberlain, *Decolonisation: The Fall of the European Empire* (1985); J. Darwin, *Britain and Decolonisation: The Retreat from Empire in the Post-War World* (1988); H. Grimal, *Decolonization: The British, French, Dutch and Belgian Empires, 1919–1963* (1978); P. Gifford and W. R. Louis (eds), *Decolonization and African Independence: The Transfers of Power, 1960–1980* (New Haven, CT, 1988); M. Shipway, *Decolonization and Its Impact* (Oxford, 2008).

50 A. L. Adu, 'Post-Colonial Relationships: Some Factors in the Attitudes of African States', *African Affairs*, 66, 265 (1967), pp. 295–309.

51 Zartman, *Politics of Trade Negotiations*.

52 Green, *Child of Lomé*.

53 Zartman, *Politics of Trade Negotiations*.

54 European Commission. J. Huber, 'The Past, Present and Future ACP–EC Trade Regime and the WTO', *European Journal of International Law*, 11, 2 (1 January 2000), pp. 427–38. L. Bartels, 'The Trade and Development Policy of the European Union', *European Journal of International Law*, 18, 4 (1 September 2007), pp. 715–56.

55 E. Jones, *Negotiating Against the Odds: A Guide for Trade Negotiators from Developing Countries* (2013).

56 S. Bilal and F. Rampa, 'Alternative (to) EPAs: Possible Scenarios for the Future ACP Trade Relations with the EU', in *Policy Management Report* (Maastricht, 2006).

57 ACP Council Of Ministers, 'Declaration at its 86th Session Expressing Serious Concern on the Status of the Negotiations of The Economic Partnership Agreements' (Brussels, 2007).

58 D. Cronin, 'Small Island States Stand Up to EU', *IPS*, 3 August 2007.

59 'Small Squall in the Pacific, Some Feelings Hurt', *Financial Times Brussels Blog*; A. Bounds, 'Islands Threaten to Halt EU Trade Talks', *Financial Times*, 2 August 2007.

60 African Trade Policy Centre, 'EPA Negotiations: African Countries Continental Review' (2007), p. 55.

61 Interview by authors, phone-to-capital, trade official, January 2009.

62 Response to questionnaire issued by authors, January 2009.

63 For a detailed analysis of the counter-moves of ACP countries see Jones, 'The Weak vs. The Strong'.

64 There was opposition to the EPA among civil society organizations, academics and some heads of state, but on the whole, the Caribbean leadership was supportive.

65 For a detailed analysis of the negotiating behaviour that underpinned the persistent stalemate between the EU and the West African region see C. Weinhardt, 'Playing Different Games: West African and European Perspectives on Negotiating Economic Partnership Agreements' (DPhil thesis, University of Oxford, 2013).

66 W. Wallis and A. Bounds, 'Tariffs will Rupture Relations, Africa Warns EU', *Financial Times*, 9 December 2007.

67 D. Cronin, 'Spare This EU Paternalism', *Inter-Press Service News Agency*, 11 January 2008.

68 B. Miller, 'Speech on the 20 June 2006', in *11th Session of the ACP-EU Joint Parliamentary Assembly on the Negotiations of Economic Partnership Agreements* (Vienna, 2006).

69 C. Thomas, 'Reflections on the CARIFORUM-EC, Economic Partnership Agreement: Implications for CARICOM', in K. O. Hall and M. Chuck-A-Sang (eds), *CARICOM: Policy Options for International Engagement* (Kingston, 2010).

70 Cited in Lugard, *The Dual Mandate*.

71 C. Rhodes, *Confession of Faith* (1877).

72 T. Mkandawire, 'African Intellectuals and Nationalism', in T. Mkandawire (ed.), *African Intellectuals: Rethinking Politics, Language, Gender and Development* (2005).

73 Lugard, *The Dual Mandate*.

74 Manning, *Francophone Sub-Saharan Africa*, p. 39. Manning cites Delavignette, a leading French colonial official who argued that 'the colony has proletarianised them in order to free them, educate them, care for them'.

75 J. S. Galbraith, *Crown and Charter: The Early Years of the British South Africa Company, Perspectives on Southern Africa* (Berkeley, CA, 1974). On the 'New Radicals' movement in Britain in the 1980s an early 1900s, justifying empire on grounds of international moral responsibility, see B. Porter, *Critics of Empire* (1968).

76 K. D. Nworah, 'The Aborigines' Protection Society, 1889–1909: A Pressure-Group in Colonial Policy', *Canadian Journal of African Studies / Revue Canadienne des Études Africaines*, 5, 1 (1971).

77 Cited in A. A. Mazrui, 'Seek Ye First the Political Kingdom', in A. A. Mazrui and C. Wondji (eds), *Africa since 1935* (Oxford, 1993), p. 105.

78 Zartman, *Politics of Trade Negotiations*.

79 T. Hill, 'Whither Lomé? A Review of the Lomé III Negotiations', *Third World Quarterly*, 7, 3 (1985). As Thandika Mkandawire notes, the African state became, in the minds of many Western analysts, 'the most demonised social institution in Africa [...] the state, once the cornerstone of development, had became the millstone around otherwise efficient markets.' T. Mkandawire, 'Thinking about Developmental States in Africa', *Cambridge Journal of Economics*, 25, 3 (1998), pp. 289–313.

80 Green, *Child of Lomé*.

81 R. Namaliu, 'In the End, the Dictates of Mutual Self-Interest and Interdependence which Characterize ACP–EEC Economic Relations Prevailed', *The ACP Courier*, January–February 1985.

82 G. Thorn, 'A Sense of Responsibility: Speech by Gaston Thorn, President of the Commission of the European Communities', *The Courier, Special Issue: Africa-Caribbean-Pacific – European Community* (1985).

83 ACP–EU Ministers, 'Partnership Agreement between the Members of the African, Caribbean and Pacific Group of States of the One Part, and the European Community and its Member States, of the Other Part, Signed in Cotonou on 23 June 2000 – Protocols – Final Act – Declarations' (Brussels 2000).

84 P. Mandelson, 'Speech to the European Parliament Development Committee', 28 January 2008 (Brussels).

85 For a detailed analysis of the beliefs that informed the EU's negotiating positions, see Weinhardt, 'Playing Different Games', Chapter 6.

86 *Ibid.*, p. 209.

87 For an overview of the way in which the EU's negotiation style was perceived by the West African negotiation party in the EPA process, see C. Weinhardt, 'The EU as a Friend of the Developing World? Self-Portrayal and Outside Perceptions in the Negotiations of EPAs', in J. Lieb, N. von Ondarza, and D. Schwarzer (eds), *The EU in International Fora: Lessons for the Union's External Representation after Lisbon* (Baden-Baden, 2011), pp. 110–12.

88 Interview by authors, phone-to-capital, government official, January 2008.

89 Informal conversation with an EPA negotiator in 2008; the EU officially denies this exchange.

90 Interview by authors, phone-to-capital, government official, September 2008.

91 Response to questionnaire issued by the authors (CARIFORUM representative), January 2009.

92 R. Grynberg, 'Op-Ed: An Alphabet Soup of Powerlessness. The Pacific Trade Negotiations', *Papua New Guinea Post Courier*, 14 March 2009.

93 Staff Reporter, 'Replace Controversy with Debate, Says Ashton: A TNI Exclusive Interview with Baroness Catherine Ashton', *Trade Negotiations Insights*, 8, 1 (2009).

94 C. Ashton, 'Economic Partnership Agreements – Remarks to European Parliament', Strasbourg, 23 March 2009, p. 2.

95 Grynberg, 'An Alphabet Soup'.

96 On the EU's self-portrayal of its motives in the EPA negotiations, see Weinhardt, 'The EU as a Friend of the Developing World?', pp. 105–7.

97 Speech by David O'Sullivan at the ACP Ministerial Meeting on EPAs, Brussels, 9 November 2007.

98 Statement by Peter Mandelson to the Development Committee of the European Parliament, 17 March 2005.

99 Interview by the authors, embassy official, Brussels, July 2008.

100 See for instance Soludo, 'Africa: From Berlin to Brussels'.

101 Inter Press Service, 'NGOs Confront EU Over Regional Deals', 2 March 2008.

102 European Commission, K. de Gucht and A. Piebalgs, joint letter to EU ministers, 6 September 2010.

103 On the challenges the EU faces towards becoming a 'truly' post-colonial power see Kleinfeld and Nicolaïdis, 'Can a Post-Colonial Power Export the Rule of Law?'.

From the Soviet Bloc to the New Middle Age: East-Central Europe's Three Imperial Moments

Dimitar Bechev

Europe's presence and actions in the wider world are hard to grasp without a reflection on the continent's own diversity. Writing from his perspective as a historian of Europe, Norman Davies draws a sharp distinction between the West and Europe, two notions often viewed as genetically entwined. In a subversive mode, he observes that the European patchwork of dissonant national histories, fragmented memories and regional cultural cleavages is nothing else but the antipode of the monolith West enshrined in the Plato-to-NATO textbooks familiar to US undergraduates taking classes in 'Western Civ'.[1] As a Briton of Welsh heritage and an authority on Poland and Central Europe, Davies knows all too well that it is next to impossible to conjure up a single seamless narrative of European history.[2] The focus on empire exposes deep-running gulfs that parcel continental geography: it is arguably Wales and Poland, rather than England or France, that have been on the receiving end of empire-building over the last two centuries.

If the memory of imperial rule and colonialism is commonly used to distinguish 'Europe' from 'non-Europe', how do we make sense of Europe's inherent polyphony and multiplicity, of variable national experiences and historical trajectories? The EU now includes member states like Malta and Cyprus which were British colonial possessions as recently as the early 1960s, while the Soviet Empire in Eastern Europe was a fact of life not so long ago. We are not even facing an East–West divergence within the EU, insofar as one can think of 'Western' countries such as Ireland which have had their own experience with foreign domination or even colonization, in the most direct meaning of the term. Finally, former empires differ immensely: think of post-colonial Britain, France, Belgium, Netherlands, Italy, Spain and Portugal, on the one hand, and erstwhile cores of land-based empires such as Austria (and Hungary), Turkey and, with all qualifications, Germany.

Diversity and complexity aside, the trope of 'echoes of empire', at the centre of this volume, may be misconstrued as implying a rather uniform picture of European history. This might be to do with outside perceptions marred by residual 'occidentalism'. From China to India to Latin America, EU-rope is seen as little more than the sum of its big member states, incidentally the same Great Powers which controlled sizeable swathes of Asia and nearly the whole of Africa up until the mid twentieth century. Viewed from outside, it is Paris or London that personify the Union, much less Brussels, let alone obscure national capitals in the newly added eastern marches. External observers should not be faulted for failing to appreciate the mosaic-like character of today's EU. On the whole, the new, post-communist member states are small, preoccupied with their internal politics following two decades of complex and painful socio-economic and institutional transformation, and, no doubt, more parochial in their foreign policy outreach compared to many (though not all) within 'Old Europe'.

Yet the theme of empire is crucial for grasping East-Central Europe's history and its imprint on the present. From Szczecin to Edirne and from Tirana to Tallinn, the 'lands between' still carry the seal of the continent's not-too-distant imperial past and host the relics of empires: Soviet, Habsburg, Ottoman, Romanov, Holy Roman, Byzantine, Venetian and so on. The region has also been the graveyard of the imperial idea as the original target of the Wilsonian principle of self-determination – the very principle which is so influential in the emergence of Third World independence movements challenging the dominance of European colonial powers. But how do these multicoloured legacies and memories in the eastern parts play out in the politics of the present? How do they affect the EU itself, seen by some as a *sui generis* imperial polity? Do they bear, in an indirect fashion, on the Union's rapport with a globalizing, but growingly non-European, world?

This chapter zooms in on three particular imperial episodes, moments or flashbacks within the politics of East-Central Europe over the past 30 years or so. Firstly, the Soviet dominance in the decades following World War II, its end and consequences. Second comes the rediscovery of more distant, pre-1918 imperial past towards the end of the twentieth century, and its use by a motley set of agents, ranging from utopian dissident intellectuals to cynical ethnic entrepreneurs. Thirdly, the chapter discusses the impact of the EU, described by some as a post-modern or a neo-medieval empire, its transformative influence on East-Central Europe but also some aspects of continuity.

The West of the East: The Decay and End of the Soviet Empire

There has been a fascinating debate, now somewhat forgotten, amongst Cold War historians and former Sovietologists on Moscow's rule over the East European satellites (known as 'the outer empire') and its evolution.[3] While the Soviet grip was particularly harsh under Stalinism (1944/5–53), by the time Mikhail Gorbachev assumed the leadership of CPSU in 1985, local rulers in the satellites had a considerable margin of action. Romania, to point out an extreme example, pursued an independent foreign course coupled with repressive, neo-Stalinist policies at home that were inconceivable for Moscow's staunchest allies in Prague, Sofia or Berlin. Soviet leaders had refrained from direct intervention during the Polish 'events' in 1980–1, a departure from the brutal suppression of the revolt in Hungary in October 1956 or the Warsaw Pact invasion that ended the Prague Spring in 1968. As shown by Valerie Bunce and others, Eastern European clients were increasingly becoming a liability for the Soviet hegemon, rather than a useful geopolitical buffer as was the case in the immediate aftermath of the war.[4] Subsidizing the inefficient state-owned economies, the product of rapid industrialization in the 1950s and 1960s, placed an unbearable burden on the USSR right at the time when Gorbachev aimed to carry out an ambitious reform programme and revitalize domestic economy. For their part, vassal regimes were heavily dependent on access to Western credit and trade to maintain living standards and whatever legitimacy they had preserved in the eyes of the population.

Mark Kramer observed that the Soviet Empire was gradually transitioning to more relaxed forms of control over the satellites, which could be described as 'hegemony' or even 'primacy'.[5] Reluctance to resort to military force coupled with Gorbachev's naive belief in the soft power of socialism purified from its totalitarian residue encouraged in the late 1980s reform-minded communists in Eastern Europe to open the political arena for competition while treading very carefully in order not to overstep red lines and let a repetition of 1968 happen. By the time the Berlin Wall fell in November 1989, Solidarity had won in a landslide the first semi-free elections in Poland while the round-table talks with the opposition groups in Budapest, ending the Hungarian Socialist Workers' Party (MSZMP) monopoly on power, had been concluded. Soviet imperial control did not collapse but rather decayed over an extended period of time, though the end of communist rule in the *annus mirabilis* of 1989 came to most observers, including in the academic community, as a surprise. The empire faced its final curtain with the independence of the Baltic States in 1990–1 and the ultimate disintegration of the Soviet Union. With the abolition of the Warsaw Pact and COMECON, the military and economic arm of the bloc, East Europeans could turn their backs on Moscow and advance further on their long and winding journey to the west.

The legacies of the communist period and subordination to an outside centre are manifold and cannot all be explored here. It is tempting to conclude that elites in the new democracies kept a satellite mentality, affecting relations with new patrons, be it Washington or Brussels. This was a line popular with the critics of the New Europeans' support of the war in Iraq and, generally, the neo-imperial policies of the Bush administration in the wake of 9/11. This viewpoint underestimates the fact that Americanophilia was driven not by blind ideological allegiance but by the apprehension of assertive Russia under the authoritarian-minded presidency of Vladimir Putin after 1999, which has been interpreted, rightly or wrongly, as an attempt to bring the Soviet times back. In addition, it overlooks the point that local governments, for instance the Polish administration led by Civic Platform that came to power in 2007, drove a hard bargain, linking military cooperation with important US concessions, suggesting that *Realpolitik* rather than imperial habits is at play. Finally, an important segment of public opinion in a number of countries, for instance the Czech Republic and several of the post-Yugoslav republics, shares anti-American attitudes comparable to those in Western Europe.[6]

One interesting, yet often overlooked, legacy of the Cold War and Soviet imperialism is the exposure of Eastern Europe to the global political arena. Ironically, communist rule had a dual effect: it isolated the citizenry from the emergent globalization but also broadened its geographical horizons. With the notable exception of Yugoslavia, which exited the Soviet bloc in 1948, East-Central Europe was sealed off from the West, especially prior to the détente of the 1970s. In addition, World War II had swept away whatever indigenous traditions of (post-) imperial cosmopolitanism and hybridity that remained: the Holocaust and the post-1945 exchanges of population annihilated much of the ethnic diversity in Central Europe (but not in the Balkans). Ideological uniformity was accompanied by homogeneity of communal attachments.

At the same time, the insertion into the Soviet *imperium* coupled with urbanization, mass education and the growth of popular culture and media raised public awareness of a global world. The Cold War period was the first time when political elites in East-Central Europe cultivated relations with more distant regions and countries aligned with the USSR in the planetary ideological competition. The effort to inculcate a worldwide perspective, in tune with the articles of faith of Marxism–Leninism, is attested by the officially promoted socialist solidarity with Third World leftist self-determination movements, from Indochina in the 1950s to Nicaragua in the 1980s, direct involvement in regional crises (e.g. the Czechoslovak shipment of arms to Israel in 1947–8 and then to Egypt in 1955), and foreign students and workers coming to Prague, Warsaw or Belgrade. Tens of thousands of East European professionals found employment across Africa and the Middle East. In the mid 1980s, there were nearly 30,000 Bulgarians employed in Libya alone.[7]

Communism's globalizing role had to do with Soviet imperial tutelage and ideology but also other contingent factors such as Chinese influence, in the case of Albania, and the megalomaniac aspirations of local strongmen such as Josip Broz Tito in Yugoslavia or Romania's Nicolae Ceauşescu who fraternized with the likes of Kim Il-sung of North Korea. It was Tito who became, alongside Jawaharlal Nehru, Gamal Abdel Nasser, Sukarno and Kwame Nkrumah, the emblematic figure in Non-Aligned Movement, launched in 1961 as decolonization was gathering momentum in Africa.

The collapse of communist rule, and especially the dramatic political and economic changes and upheavals that ensued, signalled a turnaround severing many links and networks between the former Eastern bloc and the Third World. There is no better illustration than the fate of 180,000 Vietnamese guest-workers, who came to a number of countries in the Soviet camp in the 1970s and 1980s. Some of those immigrants headed back to South East Asia while those who chose to remain behind were consigned to the status of a marginalized minority in erstwhile East Germany, the Czech Republic and elsewhere. After 1989, acceptance in the privileged clubs of the West, primarily the EU and NATO, became the main focus of foreign policy in East-Central Europe. Socialist solidarity, eroded ever prior to the 1990s by certain regimes' flirtation with nationalism while lip-servicing proletarian internationalism, was replaced by a mix of introspection and Western-centricism.

The Use and Abuse of Imperial Past after Communism

The decay and demise of the Soviet Empire ushered in a full-blown return of the nation, evident in the primacy of domestic democratic choices over foreign dominance but also the growth of nationalist sentiments. The disappearance of external constraints coupled with the opening of the public sphere rekindled memories of the times preceding the installation of communist regimes. The region's pre-1945, and even pre-1918, history became a paramount point of reference in all debates that sprang up in the wake of 1989: the choice of political institutions, the path towards economic development and market-building, relations with neighbours, the treatment of minorities when present. The memory of Austria-Hungary and especially the Ottoman Empire became politicized (on this latter question, see also Nora Fisher Onar's chapter in the present book) as ethnic problems re-emerged in a number of hotspots. Democratization facilitated the political mobilization across ethno-national lines in countries such as Yugoslavia, which had largely avoided the ethnic cleansing of the 1940s.[8] Minorities sought support from their 'kin-states' across contested boundaries demarcated after the collapse of the great land-based empires of Eastern Europe. Multinational socialist federations disintegrated into their ethnic and territorial components: in Yugoslavia the break-up happened through a bloody conflict that killed more than 100,000 in Bosnia-Herzegovina alone.

The renewed salience of identity, religion and culture in international affairs stressed the pervasive power of historical legacies. 'Back to Europe' voiced by the dissidents-turned-politicians threatened to morph into 'Back to the Future', the phrase security experts such as John Mearsheimer used to warn of impending conflicts animated by past grievances, also part of Europe's historical heritage.[9] Similar to the demise of the Ottoman and Austro-Hungarian empires, the end of Soviet hegemony risked unleashing the ghosts of ethno-national strife across former imperial borderlands such as, for instance, the former Habsburg Militärgrenze (Military Frontier) in Slavonia and Krajina where Croats clashed with local Serb rebels supported by the Yugoslav People's Army in 1991.

The end of the Cold War and the conflicts coming in its wake gave credence to Samuel Huntington's notion of civilizational faultlines as zones of age-old hatreds and violence spurred by culture and identity.[10] To Huntington, former imperial attachments and territorial delimitations structured the politics of the present day. In his view, Transylvania (through curiously, not Banat) differed from the rest of Romania, as did western Ukraine, formerly part of the Austro-Hungarian monarchy, from the eastern provinces exposed to Russification (i.e. Byzantinization). According to this civilizational worldview, '[i]n the Balkans, this line, of course, coincides with the historic boundary between the Hapsburg and Ottoman empires'.[11] This mapping, again, excluded from the western sphere former territories of the Dual Crown such as Vojvodina and Bosnia, all lumped as part of the Orthodox civilization. The Huntingtonian vision therefore gave exceptional prominence to the echoes of the pre-World War I Austro-Hungarian and Ottoman empires, in spite of the communist experience that the whole region went through.

The legitimating power of memories and mental maps was well understood by political leaders. Croatia's president Franjo Tudjman, a historian turned father of the nation, supported Huntington's theory from very early on. If this theory was given credit, violence was not a matter of leaders' choice, and therefore responsibility, but resulted from tectonic upheavals and in that sense was historically inevitable. Furthermore, the cultural argument justified the partition of Bosnia across ethno-communal lines. That Bosnia, as a single borderland entity, had been consecutively part of both Ottoman and the Habsburg Empire failed to impress latter-day adherents of cultural pigeonholing who ignored the ambiguity inbuilt in the notion of imperial legacy. While the hallmark of imperial history was the mixing and hybridization of cultures and ethnic groups, civilizations were supposedly monolith, fixed and internally cohesive.

'Civilizational' affinities and memories of imperial belonging underscored the transnational context within which nationalist mobilization was taking place. Slovenia and Croatia discovered connections with Mitteleuropa as an exit route from the Yugoslav Federation. Crowds in Zagreb chanted 'Danke Deutschland' after newly unified Germany granted its recognition of the country's independence on 23 December 1991. In response, Slobodan Milošević's propaganda machine in Belgrade, run in part by Mihalj Kertes (Mihály Kertész), a Vojvodinian Magyar, trumpeted allegations that Serbdom was (once more) attacked by a cabal bringing together Bonn, the Vatican, and other treacherous enemies. Meanwhile, Tudjman and his entourage disseminated their own version of history portraying Croatia as the past victim of injustices and captive of an alien, Oriental–Byzantine domination commencing in 1918 and reaffirmed in 1945. Historical revisionists conveniently downplayed the crucial part played by Croat politicians, from Ante Trumbić to Tito himself, in the various reincarnations of the Yugoslav state.

In the post-communist beauty contest, 'nesting orientalisms', to quote Milica Bakić-Hayden, became the norm across Central Europe where one's claim to Westernness went hand-in-hand with the portrayal of neighbours as 'backward', culturally inferior and therefore less European.[12] Nowhere was this phenomenon as pronounced as in ex-Yugoslavia where it fed into violence. While Slovenes and Croats sought freedom from neo-Byzantine tyrants in Belgrade, Serbian nationalist discourse painted the nation as the protector of Western civilization against Islamic barbarism, both in the glorious time of the 1389 Battle of Kosovo and in the 1990s. The support by Muslim volunteers and *jihadis* from around the globe for the Bosniak-dominated government in Sarajevo was brought up as a prime piece of evidence testifying to the civilizational origins and dynamics of the conflict. This depiction, discredited by the humanitarian tragedy that it tried to mask, was fully dispelled only with the US/NATO intervention in 1994–5 that brought an end to the policy of inaction, procrastination, and indecisiveness in Bosnia and elsewhere in the Balkans.

The wars of Bosnia and later Kosovo catapulted the conversation on imperial legacy to the centre of academic and political debates, and a number of important studies were published on the Ottoman past of south-east Europe. The rediscovery affected other countries in the vicinity, notably Turkey where it amplified the echoes of a past preceding the institution of the Kemalist republic in the 1920s. The transnational solidarities animated by the conflict raised difficult questions about the country's own traumatic experience with nation-building, ethnic cleansing and destruction of imperial legacies throughout the twentieth century.[13]

Apart from a repository of historical traumas for the benefit of political manipulators, the imperial past promised to provide a script for the smooth overhaul of the socialist system and a return to the West. The prospect of joining exclusive clubs such as NATO and the EU led to the vexing question of who was eligible and who was to be excluded. As the territories of the former Habsburg Monarchy straddled the Iron Curtain, its memory emerged as an umbilical chord linking a supposedly 'kidnapped' Central Europe with its Western self, lost but now regained.

The empire, the pet hatred of nationalists and radicals in 1848, re-emerged on the intellectual radar in its *fin de siècle* sophisticated appeal. As ever, memory was selective. Habsburg nostalgia led back to Robert Musil and Sigmund Freud, rather than Prince Metternich or Kálmán Tisza, the pioneer of assimilationist Magyarization. In marked contrast to both Russia/USSR and the Ottoman Empire, the monarchy was a European polity embodying, particularly after the constitutional reform of 1867, the Enlightenment ideal of a *Rechtsstaat*, even if falling short of the liberal standard. Unlike the Balkans or Russia, Central Europe had its own model of toleration, multiculturalism and, with all due provisos, constitutionalism. The nostalgic rediscovery appealed equally to liberals and conservative nationalists. To the former, the *Rechtsstaat* tradition was a convenient precedent as painful institutional reforms were fulfilled for the countries to 'return to Europe'. The economic success and prosperity of Austria, symbolizing in neighbouring Hungary and Slovakia and elsewhere the essence of Western Europeanness, fed into this portrayal. To the latter, Catholic religion was the basis, in a mechanistic, quasi-Weberian way, of civilization, civic virtue and social development embedded in tradition. This analysis predicating success in transition to democracy and market economy, based on a clearly identified imperial legacy and religious creed was so deterministic that it neglected, as noted by Jacques Rupnik, the authoritarian retrenchment in majority Catholic and post-Habsburg Slovakia and Croatia in the 1990s.[14]

In the former Soviet bloc, the new *Mitteleuropa* was purged of its pan-Germanic connotations, a marked contrast with the Yugoslav context. The new image was close to the vision articulated in the interwar period by Tomáš Garrigue Masaryk, the eminent historian who became Czechoslovakia's first president. Going back to the early 1980s, the exchanges between dissident intellectuals in Czechoslovakia, Hungary and Poland, as well as in emigration, conjured up a regional identity that rejected both Soviet dominance of the present and, more significantly, the heavy baggage of the Third Reich's geopolitics. This was a critical node in Milan Kundera's 1984 piece 'The Tragedy of Central Europe', which started off the conversation on the pages of the *New York Review of Books*, four years after the appearance of Solidarity.[15] Humanists were in the business of reinventing history, not unlike nationalist ideologues. Timothy Garton Ash noted at the time that the celebrated Hungarian dissident György Konrád had identified as Central Europe's essence a certain rationalist, sceptical disposition – a bridge, no less, to Anglo-Saxon empiricism and away from the inhuman utopias of fascism and communism holding the area in their mortifying embrace for most of the twentieth century.[16] The new Central Europe bore little resemblance to the gloomy imagery in the books of Franz Kafka, a quintessentially *Mitteleuropean* author, and reflected the aspirations of utopian intellectuals for freedom of expression, life in truth, and return to the European home after the dark valley of twentieth-century totalitarianisms.

Following 1989, the imperial nostalgia of the dissidents proved a robust transnational thread running over the former Iron Curtain as well as within post-communist Central Europe. It was taken aboard by budding regional diplomatic fora such as the Alpe-Adria scheme, later the Central European Initiative. Once in office, former dissidents such as Václav Havel, now president of Czechoslovakia, added political and institutional flesh to the ideas once floated in *samizdat* pamphlets and the Western media. Visegrád Group (1991) and the Central European Free Trade Agreement (CEFTA), established a year later, aimed at deepening regionalism and embedding it into economic exchanges and societal interdependence. The politics of Habsburg nostalgia were clearly at play, not least because they were a symbolic bridge to geographies on the 'right' side of the Iron Curtain: notably Austria but also northern Italy (nostalgia is an established genre in writings about Trieste and its region), Slovenia and Croatia. Central European revivalism, however, proved very difficult because of multiple impediments: the outstanding frictions amongst the four Central European countries (e.g. between Hungary and Slovakia), economic incompatibility, the inability to liberalize sensitive sectors such as agriculture but, first and foremost, owing to the attraction of the EU whose allure made the individual race towards membership the preferred course of action. It was only after accession to the EU that the idea, which never had enormous traction in Poland anyhow, got a new lease of life both diplomatically and in terms of economic links.

Empire by Invitation: The EU's Enlargement to the East

The eastward expansion of the EU marks the most recent, and perhaps most significant, imperial moment in East-Central Europe. This third episode differs from the preceding two. First of all, the 'post-modern' imperialism carried out by Brussels is not rooted in past experience nor does it come along, in most cases, with a repertoire of historical myths but seeks to transcend it by projecting a new political vision based on pooling of sovereignty and delegating power to a supranational tier of institutions. Secondly, unlike the Soviet Union, the EU has been acting, in both 'Central and Eastern Europe' and 'the Western Balkans', as an 'empire by invitation', to paraphrase historian Geir Lundestad.[17] The expansion came in response to repeated appeals by the post-communist countries in the East. Moreover, it relied on the magnetic pulls of trade and investment as well as on the appeal of Western Europe's peace and prosperity (the famed 'soft power'), rather than on coercion and military might. The EU model contrasted sharply with the imperial imagery, nurtured by reminiscences of past glories or injustice, employed by nationalists in the 1990s. It stressed integration, the pooling of sovereignty, transnational linkages in the form of the four freedoms (goods, services, capital and people), in opposition to the notion of clear-cut and 'natural' boundaries dear to the believers in the nation. Secondly, for all grandiose rhetoric legitimated by and anchored in historical flashbacks, the EU was a pragmatic, future-orientated project based on the logic of market efficiency, regulatory convergence and cooperation in bread-and-butter policy areas which at times sat oddly with the philosopher-kings' musings about the spiritual roots of Europe and their nation's destiny.

As noted by Jan Zielonka and others, the decision to enlarge the EU to the east in the 1990s bore some resemblance to classical imperial policies of projecting order. Key steps were decided at the very moment eastern parts of Europe witnessed upheavals such as the failed putsch against Gorbachev in August 1991, the conflict between President Yeltsin and the Russian Parliament in 1993, the deepening of the Bosnian conflict, NATO's war in Kosovo in 1999. Enlargement and the now sacralized Copenhagen Criteria proved the best way to make post-communist Europe more politically stable and peaceful, immune to the ethnic tensions that had led to the turmoil in Yugoslavia and parts of the Soviet Union.[18] To Zielonka, the end effect has been a more diffuse European Union, at variance with the centralizing instincts of the 1980s federalists, where national and supranational jurisdictions intersect and overlap while power is devolved away from both member states' capitals and Brussels.[19] The direct antecedent of the post-enlargement EU therefore is neither federal states such as the US nor the colonial empires of the nineteenth century but fuzzy medieval polities such as the Holy Roman Empire, part and parcel of Central Europe's history.[20]

The inclusion of East-Central Europe into the (quasi-)imperial structure, neo-medieval or not, that is the EU of the 2000s raises a number of questions. First of all, what have been the transformative effects on the implicated countries? The liaison with Brussels did take away sovereignty at the time when it was being regained after decades of Soviet dominance. The shift was particularly sudden in places such as the Baltic States, Slovakia and Slovenia, which all (re)appeared on Europe's map in the early 1990s, while Poland and the Czech Republic have more recently held up high the flag of national sovereignty. At the same time, one could argue that, on the contrary, accession empowered East Europeans as it gave them voice in EU institutions. It would have been inconceivable prior to 2004 that Lithuania should be able to affect the course of EU–Russian relations. Furthermore, membership in the Union has actually bolstered the governance capacity of the states in question in many regulatory fields, thus making them, in practical terms, more sovereign. The fact that most of the East-Central Europeans, with the exception of Estonia, Latvia, Slovakia and Slovenia, are not part of the eurozone has shielded them from the experience of Southern Europe during the crisis. There has been no backlash against austerity imposed by Germany and the rest of Northern Europe leading to growing levels of euroscepticism. That is true even of countries like Hungary where the government of Viktor Orbán (2010–) has run a populist campaign scapegoating foreign investors in the name of reclaiming power for common Hungarians and passing the burden of the economic crisis on to EU capitalists rather than local taxpayers.[21]

More significantly, the EU – in concert with other international bodies such as NATO, the Council of Europe, and OSCE – pressured East Europeans to implement political reforms related to the empowerment of minorities and solve outstanding territorial disputes with neighbours, such as the bilateral treaty concluded by Romania and Hungary in 1996. Can we therefore claim that the entry into the supranational setup is a catalyst for coming to terms with the post-imperial traumas of the twentieth century as well as reconsidering one's foundational myths in the name of 'Europeanization'? This question is particularly critical for the so-called Western Balkans (former Yugoslavia plus Albania minus Slovenia), which is now knocking on the Union's door and is required to confront the experience of ethnic war in the 1990s.

On the one hand, the consolidation of democracy, catalysed by the EU entry prospect, has advanced the accommodation of minority groups in nearly all countries of the region, the Roma being the single most notable exception. Minority parties are now a key player in the politics of Slovakia, Romania, Bulgaria, Macedonia and, to some degree, Croatia (again the contrast between the Balkans and monoethnic Central European countries is visible). In addition, the 2004 enlargement re-established past links once swept away with the collapse of the Habsburg Empire. Now one can easily reach Vienna by hopping on a low-cost flight to Bratislava, the former satellite town Pressburg (known to Hungarians as Pozsony) thriving at the times of Maria Theresa. Slovakia and Hungary have become part of a single space, a development facilitated by the 2008 enlargement of the Schengen Area. The enlarged EU brings back facets of the cosmopolitan life in the empires of older days, with commercial and cultural links criss-crossing the continental land mass and also spilling over to countries that are still outside the Union: former Yugoslav republics, Moldova, Ukraine (whose western regions have been cultivating their very own brand of Habsburg nostalgia). Timothy Snyder has drawn the comparison between the EU and the Polish–Lithuanian Commonwealth (*rzeczpospolita*, literally 'republic'); a comparison which is rather ambiguous on second reading, given the commonwealth's ultimate fate in the late eighteenth century.[22]

On the other hand, the EU's empire-like expansion has done little to shake up the fundamentals of the nation state, even if it goes a long way in managing tensions inherited from the past. Several relatively recent episodes including the Hungarian Status Law according special rights to ethnic kin in surrounding countries or the rift between the Czech Republic and Slovakia, on one side, and Germany, Austria and Hungary, on the other, over the so-called Beneš Decrees of 1945, should bring it home to observers that the shadow of history is still hanging over East-Central Europe. Indeed Europeanization and the nation have long existed in harmony.

Emerging one by one from the rubble of collapsing empires in the nineteenth and twentieth centuries, East European nations strove, each in their own way, to emulate and catch up with the model societies of the West (primarily France and Germany, less so Great Britain) by adopting their institutions and norms. The gap, whether perceived or 'real', varied from one context to the other: society in Prague differed fundamentally from Bucharest or Belgrade. What was invariable, however, was Herder's romantic doctrine marrying state authority to the presumed spiritual and linguistic identity coded in a given *Kulturnation*'s primordial past. The aspiration to modernity has been tightly linked to the nation state and its claim to homogeneity resting upon historical 'authenticity'.

Peaking with the rise of authoritarianism and right-wing radicalism in the 1930s, such ideas still remain significant in the political and social life in East-Central Europe. Andre Liebich observes that, in contrast to the old EU member states, the newcomers 'have displayed extreme reluctance to countenance state-wide multilingualism, federalist arrangements, or, indeed, any form of territorial autonomy for historic minorities'. To Liebich, there still exists a East–West divide related to the East's 'absence of an overseas imperial legacy' and the fact that 'these countries' sense of national identity has not yet been challenged by the need to position themselves *vis-à-vis* non-Europeans'.[23] While one can legitimately ask questions about how far tolerance of cultural difference goes in certain Western European societies, the contrast invites us to think, yet again, about the boundaries that continue to run across Europe and how 'echoes of empire' actually refer to a variety of situations which sometimes have little to do with each other, apart from stemming from the Latin *imperium*.

The divide also illuminates the new member states' peripheral position in the fledgling European empire. Ivan Berend, a US economic historian of Hungarian origin, sums up the region's experience under communism and beyond as a 'detour from the periphery to the periphery'.[24] In a more recent book, Berend quotes Leopold von Ranke's judgement that the peoples of East-Central Europe 'never exercised any independent influence, they only appear either subservient or antagonistic; they receive [...] only the ebb of the tide of the general movements.'[25] He is not alone, as there is a tradition highlighting the long-term divergences between the western and eastern parts of Europe also upheld by local historians and social scientists: for instance, Jenö Szucz.[26] This distinction need not be perennial and unchangeable: Larry Wolff's *Inventing Eastern Europe* has supplied ample evidence that, in the minds of the Western intellectuals, the distinction with the 'Other' East replaced the older South–North cleavage only in the eighteenth century.[27] However, while discursive constructs or political affiliations shift, material structures are resilient. Anyone travelling on land from Vienna to Istanbul or Kyiv would, no doubt, testify how the socio-economic landscape and physical infrastructure gradually deteriorates, though there the pattern is certainly not linear and the East–West or North–South divides are far from absolute. Thus, 'non-European' Turkey, particularly the western provinces, enjoys higher levels of economic development and infrastructure that is superior to that of 'Western' neighbours in the post-communist Balkans.

Transition from communism strengthened the peripheral position of Eastern Europe. Firstly, it revealed its economic underdevelopment, particularly pronounced in the early 1990s when the post-communist countries experienced a period of negative growth. Secondly, there was a political asymmetry as the purpose of the political and economic reforms was to converge with the standards projected by an external centre and enacted through membership conditionality. Across East-Central Europe, political-party competition shifted away from ideological issues concerning redistribution and towards claims of technocratic competence. Over time, this eroded the legitimacy of political elites and gave ammunition to populist parties claiming to speak in the name of the marginalized, little person, and against the corrupt ways of the politicians and the new business class. Occasionally militating against the EU, populism in some cases actually added to Brussels' legitimacy, at the expense of national authorities. In countries where liberalization processes have been particularly difficult and good governance remains a scarce commodity, like Bulgaria and Romania, sociological data indicates, time and again, that the European Commission's tight control over member states' governments, in the form of post-accession monitoring on judicial reform and anti-corruption policy, enjoys high rates of popularity.[28] What could for some be imperial encroachment is for others a welcome supranational safeguard.

The legitimacy of the empire by invitation has not dwindled post-enlargement, even in Poland or the Czech Republic of Václav Klaus. The temporary exclusion from certain policies and institutions such as the eurozone (apart from Slovenia and Slovakia) and the free movement of labour (the transition arrangement for Germany and Austria was in force until 2011 for the 2004 entrants) does not change the equation. Larger and/or richer countries in the area, such as Poland, the Czech Republic or Slovenia, have asserted an independent role in the Union's institutions and are turning from policy-takers to policy-makers. The trend towards economic convergence between 'new' and 'old' Europe, although temporarily halted by the current crisis, may also relativize the inflexible notions of centre and periphery in the long run, as Slovenia, the Czech Republic and even Slovakia are overtaking or closing the gap with the 'old' peripheries in Mediterranean Europe. Estonia's president Toomas Ilves, for one, is fond of saying that his country, owing to its commitment to fiscal rigour, is fundamentally part of Northern Europe – defined, unsurprisingly, by Protestant culture (as opposed to the lax southern Catholics). The Balkans, for their part, have drifted into being a periphery of the periphery – thanks to their dependence on hardship-ridden economies such as Italy, Greece or even Spain and Cyprus.

Membership of the Union has also given a voice in global affairs to East-Central Europe, despite the characteristic provincialism of the region's politics. For one, the far-reaching economic liberalization associated with pre-accession inserted those countries in to the competitive global marketplace. At the same time, it forced them to contribute to, and participate in, the Union's external policies – from trade to development and humanitarian assistance. In the current Barroso II Commission several portfolios with an international profile have gone to 'new Europeans', including Agriculture, Enlargement and Neighbourhood, and Humanitarian Aid. Occasionally, the abandonment of habitual parochialism happened to the chagrin of old member states. For instance, the Czech Republic's tough stance on Cuba has more than once clashed with the pro-engagement attitude of Spain, the erstwhile colonial master. President George W. Bush's war on terror, in turn, drew 'New' Europeans to military operations in distant corners of 'the Greater Middle East', though their involvement has been more consequential in terms of conferring multilateral legitimacy on US foreign policy actions than adding to the actual military strength of the missions in question.

If EU empire had an empowerment effect on incoming members in Central Europe, what is its role in the outer periphery – the countries of ex-Yugoslavia and Albania which are waiting on the accession queue and depend on Brussels as provider of political stability? In Bosnia and Kosovo, the tasks of pacification, economic development and state-building have entrusted international administrators with broad-ranging powers. As of 2013 the EU has taken on most of the responsibilities earning the label 'post-modern empire', originally attached to it by Robert Cooper, a high-profile Eurocrat. The opportunity to directly intervene in the political process has been criticized by commentators such as Gerald Knaus and Felix Martin of the European Stability Initiative, a think-tank. In an article published by the *Journal of Democracy*, they have likened Paddy Ashdown's term in Bosnia (2002–6) to the Raj in British India, arguing that the heavy-handed international presence precludes local elites from engaging in a genuine democratic process.[29] While the EU could be accused of neo-colonialism – in the rare instances member states actually mandate a joint and coherent policy – one wonders what alternatives it has at its disposal. Particularly after 2006, centrifugal forces have gained an upper hand in Bosnia while Kosovo, home to EULEX, the largest EU mission to date, is stymied by inefficiency and bickering among the member states. It goes without saying that colonial attitudes and practices may be grounded in the historical arrogance of West Europeans towards the Eastern periphery, the Balkans *par excellence*. However, they also reflect the failure of indigenous politicians, institutions and societies to make use of the conditional promise of membership extended back in 2003.

Conclusion

The multifaceted imperial memories and more recent experiences in the lands lying east of the River Elbe and the Julian Alps stand as a reminder of the amazing diversity in the continent's history, despite the forces of convergence, represented most recently by European integration. Now that East-Central Europe has become part of the EU the theme of diversity has become more salient than ever for the Union. One can conceive of many Europes: Nordic, Mediterranean, Central, Balkan, Baltic and, why not, 'Russian Europe'. While other Europes have been defined in various ways in political and academic discourse, imperial legacy is an important point of orientation when one tries to pin down the East–West divide. East-Central Europe's fortunes have been shaped for long centuries by imperial rule, and the reminiscences of the Soviet times are still vivid for many. Witness the success of films like Andrzej Wajda's *Katyń* (2007) depicting the brutal massacre of Polish officers by Stalin's secret police in 1940, the clashes on the streets of Budapest during the fiftieth anniversary of the 1956 Soviet invasion, or the recurrent scandals regarding the files of the former communist security services.

Last in a series of empires, the EU has brought tremendous change to East-Central Europe but sceptics are right to question whether democratization, the free market and the 'Brusselization' of public policies have profoundly altered the very fabric of politics and society. One thing is for sure: enlargement has fast-tracked the region into the globalizing, networked world. This is why the economic crisis hit hard to local export-driven economies, with the possible exception of Poland, benefitting from a large domestic market. Universally seen as a success, eastern enlargement has added to the EU's global posture as a 'normative power', the pragmatic motives behind it and the occasional petty bickering notwithstanding. Yet, it is unreasonable to expect that the outside world will take note of the neo-medieval polyphony resulting from the expansion. This would surely be a mistake. Pushing the boundaries of the quasi-imperial cooperative polity far to the east, next to Anatolia and the Eurasian land mass of Russia, enlargement has presented the most serious challenge to the dichotomy between 'Europe' and 'non-Europe' that still moulds many a mental map.

Notes

1 N. Davies, 'Western Civilisation versus European History', *Europe East and West: A Collection of Essays* (2006), p. 46. The essay develops some themes laid out in Davies' grand synthesis *Europe: A History* (1996), p. 19 ff.

2 J. Lacroix and K. Nicolaïdis (eds), *European Stories: Intellectual Debates on Europe in National Contexts* (Oxford, 2011).

3 See for instance M. Kramer, 'The Soviet Union in Eastern Europe: Spheres of Influence', in N. Woods (ed.), *Explaining International Relations since 1945* (Oxford, 1995), pp. 98–126.

4 V. Bunce, 'The Empire Strikes Back: The Evolution of the Eastern Bloc from a Soviet Asset to a Soviet Liability', *International Organization*, 39, 1 (1985), pp. 1–46.

5 Kramer, 'The Soviet Union in Eastern Europe'.

6 Š. Waisová, 'Between Atlanticism, Anti-Americanism and Europeanization: Dilemmas in Czech Foreign Policy and the War on Terrorism', *Politics in Central Europe*, 2, 2 (winter 2006–7), pp. 83–94.

7 K. Tsonev, *Balgaro–arabskite otnosheniya* [Bulgarian–Arab Relations] (Sofia, 1999).

8 Similar to Czechoslovakia and Poland, Yugoslavia had expelled more than 530,000 'Volksdeutsche' (ethnic Germans) after 1944. There was also a mass emigration of Turks and other Muslims to Turkey in the 1950s.

9 J. Mearsheimer, 'Back to the Future: Instability in Europe after the Cold War', *International Security*, 15, 1 (1990), pp. 5–56.

10 S. Huntington, *The Clash of Civilizations and the Remaking of World Order* (New York, NY, 1996). The original article appeared in the Summer 1993 edition of *Foreign Affairs*.

11 S. Huntington, 'The Clash of Civilizations', *Foreign Affairs* (1993), p. 25.

12 M. Bakić-Hayden, 'Nesting Orientalisms: The Case of Former Yugoslavia', *Slavic Review*, 54, 4 (1995), pp. 917–31.

13 See the chapter by Nora Fisher Onar in this volume.

14 Rupnik analyses the divergence in the trajectories of post-communist East-Central Europe, steering clear from essentializing cultural difference, but still highlights institutional legacies, for instance the Habsburg tradition of what is now called 'good governance'. J. Rupnik, 'The Postcommunist Divide', *Journal of Democracy*, 10, 1 (1999), pp. 57–62.

15 *New York Review of Books*, 26 April 1984.

16 T. Garton Ash, 'Does Central Europe Exist?', *New York Review of Books*, 9 October 1986.

17 G. Lundestad, *The United States in Western Europe: From an 'Empire' by Invitation to Transatlantic Drift* (Oxford, 2005).

18 J. Zielonka, *Europe as Empire: The Nature of the Enlarged European Union* (Oxford, 2006), pp. 44–65.

19 *Ibid.*, pp. 4–14.

20 *Ibid.*, Introduction.

21 See the essays on the Czech Republic, Poland and Bulgaria in N. Walton and J. Zielonka, *The New Political Geography of Europe*, European Council on Foreign Relations, (2013), pp. 83–100.

22 Point made by Timothy Snyder at the round table on 'Where on Earth Does Europe End?', European Studies Centre, St Antony's College, Oxford, 13 October 2004.

23 A. Liebich, 'How Different is the "New Europe"? Perspectives on States and Minorities', *CEU Political Science Journal*, 3, 3 (September 2008), p. 269.

24 I. Berend, *Central and Eastern Europe: Detour from the Periphery to the Periphery* (Cambridge, 1999).

25 I. Berend, *History Derailed: Central and Eastern Europe in the Long Nineteenth Century* (Berkeley, CA, 2003), p. 17.

26 J. Szucz, 'The Three Historical Regions of Europe', *Acta Historica Scientiarum Hungaricae*, 24, 2–4. (1983). Szucz also draws a similar historical boundary between Central Europe and the Balkans.

27 L. Wolff, *Inventing Eastern Europe: The Map of Civilization on the Mind of the Enlightenment* (Palo Alto, CA, 1984).

28 On the rise of populism in the new member states, see I. Krastev, 'The Strange Death of the Liberal Consensus', *Journal of Democracy*, 18, 4 (2007), pp. 56–63. See also D. Smilov in Walton and Zielonka, *New Political Geography of Europe*.

29 G. Knaus and F. Martin, 'Travails of the European Raj', *Journal of Democracy*, 14, 3 (July 2003), pp. 60–7.

The EU and its Eastern Neighbours: Why 'Othering' Matters

Elena Korosteleva

Now our main challenge is to act as a *credible force for good* [...] We therefore have two imperatives: to create greater effectiveness in global governance, but also to uphold democratic legitimacy. To do so will be difficult as it requires new ideas and a sense of compromise ...

Javier Solana, 'Countering Globalisation's Dark Side' (2007), emphasis added

If the EU wants to become a credible global player, it should start from its Neighbourhood ...

Štefan Füle, *European Neighbourhood and Policy Review* (2010)

The EU increasingly envisages itself as a 'credible force for good'[1] in international relations. Despite its modest appearance, this is an expressly profound ambition, which intends to embrace the fundamentals of a 'lasting power', an 'understanding of good' and 'credibility' (being worthy of one's belief) under the umbrella of a single but polycentric player. This vision, in its various incarnations – civilian, transformative, normative, ethical and responsible Europe[2] – has been legitimated, writ large, in scholarly and EU policy-making circles. Yet it has done so either *retrospectively*, referring to the EU's exceptionalism in terms of its to-date realizations and its 'particular historical evolution';[3] or more so, *introspectively*, staking on the EU's 'authority, resources, and capacity to govern'.[4] The world order, however, is changing to become more interdependent and even interpolar;[5] and with it, the hegemonic appeal of traditional powers can no longer be taken for granted.[6] It is therefore surprising how little attention hitherto has been paid[7] to understanding or indeed imagining the EU not only through the lens of its self-perception, tainted by its past colonial overtones of a 'superior Self' on a crusading mission to civilize the world. What is evidently still amiss is the EU's perceptive awareness of the *relational importance* of the outside in its construction of a legitimate and credible Self, whereby the authority to govern is no longer a given, but rather earned through mobilization and electioneering, to ensure allegiance from its counterparts, in a competitive and interpolar world.

The case of the EU neighbourhood is particularly instructive about the complexities of handling the dialectics of the 'outside' vis-à-vis the 'inside' in shaping the EU as a credible and enduring international player. It highlights achievements and success stories,[8] but also brings to the surface a plethora of asymmetrical irregularities in the EU's treatment of its external milieu, driven by a curious mix of the EU's good intentions to govern *rightly* and *by example*, thus perpetuating a colonial trope that excludes 'the outside' from the construction of and reflections on good governance. This has led some scholars to conclude, well before the Big Bang enlargement, that 'it is ironic that the application of a [governance] concept which assumes a blurring of boundaries between inside and outside has largely ignored or downplayed the significance of the "outside" in shaping "the inside"'.[9] Paradoxically, EU practice *post-enlargement* vis-à-vis the outside[10] seems to have continued unaltered, remaining Eurocentric and exclusionary in its external representation. The first steps in devising the European Neighbourhood Policy (ENP) were particularly revealing of the EU's superior feeling of its own Self, associated with rather a prescriptive and disciplinary approach towards its neighbours in shaping their agendas for reform, regardless of their particular normative visions, cultural traditions and individual needs. Blinded by its achievements, the EU was failing or not willing to acknowledge diversity and the plurality of democratic visions, subjecting neighbours to the rigid demands of liberal economies and, more so, to the liberal values of the Western world, which were seen as alien to the lifestyles of many post-communist countries, nurtured on the notions of community and the preponderance of the collective.[11] Consequently, the first EU efforts at engineering like-minded partners resulted in the policy's delegitimation and even resistance to what was perceived as intrusion, thus by 2007 forcing the EU to reconsider its approach to the neighbourhood. It is therefore important, with reference to Solana's aforementioned quote,[12] that if the EU is to transcend its 'colonial DNA' and break free from the overbearing past, some innovative thinking as to how to become *truly* reflective in the EU good governance approach, and how to achieve a deep 'sense of compromise' with the outside in the pursuit of sustainable relations, should be high on the agenda.

This chapter discusses the difficulties of the EU becoming a *credible force for good*, with reference to its eastern neighbourhood. It will argue that in the current climate of uncertainty, instability and insecurity (from financial to human), entwined with the memories and imprints of the EU's heterogeneous colonial past, the *interdependence* and the *interface* of the two dimensions – of the EU's 'Self' and the role of 'the Other' in defining the EU's role as a global actor – should not be taken for granted, and more attention should be paid to the interaction of these two dimensions in developing 'shared meanings' and reciprocated behaviour that also work towards the goals of individual member states.

The EU's representation of 'the Self' – of what it is collectively, and not as a composition of individual member states, when portraying itself to the outside – is realized through an understanding of its present identity as a collective historical 'We' of the past.[13] However, in designing its future – the credible and legitimate 'We' – the EU should not only acknowledge but also learn how its external milieu shapes and contributes to its evolving trajectory. The current internal restructuring triggered by the Lisbon Treaty, and the move to a unified voice for the EU as an international actor through the creation of the European External Action Service (EEAS) is a decisive step to ensure legitimation and sustainability of the EU as a 'credible force for good'. However, it is not a complete one.

The consideration of the 'Other' – multiple and diverse, but united under the banners of perception of being 'different' – and the inclusion of 'the Other', 'the outside' into the process of EU self-identification, are of equal if not greater importance for constructing the EU's image as a global actor. If the 'Other' is not acknowledged or defined, the EU will struggle to achieve the equivalence of commitment and reciprocity from its partners, as well as longevity and trust in building sustainable relations of the future. Therefore, a brief examination of the EU's relations with the outside, under the European Neighbourhood Policy (ENP) as a case study, should offer a broader conceptual discussion of possible pathways for forging the EU's positive image as a transformative force, a force that is able to overcome the diplomatic burden of its colonial past, and ensure cultural and geo-political diversity through cooperation and partnership, rather than compliance and control.

The chapter proceeds by firstly deconstructing the notion of the EU 'Self' inclusive of its *prospective* and legitimate 'We'. Through analysis of the EU's neighbourhood discourse, it will be demonstrated how Eurocentric and colonial it has remained in daily exercise of its external governance. The subsequent section will focus on the importance of 'Othering' in the process of realizing the EU's transformative ambitions, challenged and shaped by the outside. In the final section, and by way of conclusion, the EU's changing strategy and future agenda vis-à-vis its neighbourhood will be considered, to estimate the prospects for reciprocity and legitimation of the EU as a 'credible force for good'.

Examining 'the Self' in EU Governance: Historical Trajectories and Aspirations

In this section we will explore the meaning of the EU's collective 'Self' before juxtaposing it with 'the Other', and evaluate its historical practices vis-à-vis the outside with reference to its eastern neighbourhood.

Understanding the EU's collective 'Self' is important for projecting a cohesive and effective image of a transformative power to the outside world. As Nicolaïdis and Howse argue, in order for the EU to find its international identity, 'consistency is crucial', with greater emphasis assigned to the internal capacity to deliver externally, simply because 'ultimately, the EU would [first] need to model itself on the utopia that it seeks to project on to the rest of the world'.[14]

'The Self', especially of the EU, is not a single entity and draws on the collective 'We' of the past, present and the future as referents. Notably, it relates to the images of the present – collective 'We' – which are premised on the recollection of *to-date memories* and pertaining *practices*.[15] To this extent, the EU often finds itself entrapped in the discourses of its colonial past, gilded with the sense of self-achievement and driven by a mission to model the outside on its own example. Even now, being wrecked by the consequences of the economic and financial crises, the EU still feels it can give a lesson to the outside by imposing its normative visions on those who dare to deviate (Cyprus is a case in point) and those who are perceivably underdeveloped and still attracted by the offerings of the EU's single market (the eastern neighbourhood).

The EU 'Self' is also based on the old-fashioned juxtaposition with 'the Other', which in identity studies is often defined in binary terms, or what 'the Self' ought *not* to be; the two are be sharply separated from each other by 'mutually exclusive sets of assigned rights and duties, moral significance and behavioural principles'.[16] The 'Other' in this reading explicitly echoes the colonial DNA of some EU member states and justifies the discourse of EU exclusivity and desirability as a club,[17] membership of which comes at a price of non-negotiable compliance and convergence: 'like us or not with us'.[18]

Finally, the EU 'Self' also strives for the 'utopian We'[19] or a 'significant We' by identifying 'what we would like to become in the future'.[20] Interestingly however, the future 'We' often appears not only to be the object of aspiration, but also the practical demands made by the EU on others – the club's aspirants – to adopt the norms and values of what the EU's future 'We' ought to be, rather than what it currently is. Furthermore, the future 'We', based on various 'we-group' representations entertains competitive and even disparate visions in a complex process of bargaining for individual interests and aspirations.[21]

This internally contested environment, the side-effect of which is a relative lack of coherence, renders EU external practices often obtuse and unreflective, driven by the need to protect EU collective heritage and to-date realizations, and utilizing empire-building strategies and tactics.[22] As recent rounds of enlargement have amply demonstrated, the EU's geopolitical boundaries and their accessibility are firmly fixed – even if the rules of the game may often appear as 'moving targets'[23] and rather fuzzy. They clearly demand non-negotiable compliance and convergence whereby the future would-be members of the EU are subjected to the strict and rigid process of EU-ization by way of adopting a vast body of EU regulations and rules or *acquis communautaire*, a far cry from the so-called 'civilizational choice' of the post-communist accessions.[24] Furthermore, it is not just the narrative of the 'impregnable fortress' which one often associates with the EU.[25] It is the rationality behind it that renders this exclusionary subjectivity alive, and turns the subjects into the objects of empire-building, as the 2004 and 2007 enlargement rounds clearly attested to: 'Whatever accession was, it was not an "equal treaty". There was a whiff of colonialism in the air.'[26] The EU rationality was simple – to attain the territories which had once been subjugated by the Soviet Union and after its collapse 'became available' – and a new subjectivity was naturally constructed by the EU to ensure its control and political influence.

The neighbourhood case should allegedly tell us a different story: after all, the neighbours are not would-be members, and do not qualify even in a distant future for the prospect of EU accession. If anything, they could aspire to having a stake in the EU internal market, subject to costly and lengthy compliance with the EU's expanding regulatory structures. This scenario has been heavily contested by another regional player in the field – Russia, which has proved far more efficacious in offering the neighbours specific reciprocity in terms of financial and political support. Against this backdrop, the EU strategy of modelling its engagement with neighbours therefore should be drastically different, aiming not to coerce, but rather to incentivize the counterparts for voluntary reform and convergence in order to generate trust and commitment – or what is conventionally known as *partnership* in international relations. This is where the EU clearly stumbles in departing from its imperial past, struggling to reconcile the free will and equivalence of partnership with the EU's embedded rationality and urge for coordination and control in shaping the outside.[27] Initially, whilst developing a strategy towards its immediate neighbourhood, the EU conceived of them as a 'ring of friends', trying to wean them off Russia, their historical regional hegemon. This in theory presumed a relationship of parity in which 'the two sides are clear about the mutual advantages and the mutual obligations'.[28] This was a critical step towards developing a new modality of engagement by the EU, not of imposition, compliance and control, but of mutual reciprocity and interest, thus breaking away from its colonial rationality of the past. The EU, perhaps naively, believed that it would be in the best interests of both powers – the EU and Russia – to modernize the neighbourhood to ensure prosperity, stability and security for the region as a whole. What the EU failed to recognize was that Russia and the EU had differing understandings of what the means for and outcomes of reform should be, and what forms of convergence they should entail – a dependent traditional 'Other' as driven by Russia or a Europeanized and compliant 'Other' as led by the EU. This fabled vision therefore was not to last.

By early 2003 the Commission communicated the final draft of the policy titled 'Wider Europe-Neighbourhood',[29] which identified the practices of enlargement as 'unarguably the Union's most successful foreign policy instrument'[30] and suggested operating through traditional top-down rule-transfer and conditionality in the neighbourhood, assuming that EU self-appeal and financial support would be enough of an incentive for the neighbouring states' compliance and reform. The European Security Strategy further verbalized the initially abeyant colonial discourse of the 'well-governed countries'; and 'the ring of friends' consequently became a moot notion before slipping off the agenda entirely.[31] To be fair, the European Parliament had for a while resisted the concept of 'well-governed countries' for its technocratic and frankly 'colonial' nature, fearing that the incentives for compliance were too limited and potentially damaging for generating allegiances from the neighbours:

> We need to ensure that 'the ring of friends' approach does not turn into a crude argument between those who say that 'neighbouring country' means 'a country destined never to join the EU' and those who believe that the prospect of joining the EU is the only way of achieving closer cooperation[...] We would risk taking the wrong turning ...[32]

This motion however had never sufficiently resonated with the Commission or the Council, and by 2006 the notion of 'a good neighbour' was dropped off the agenda for the lack of alternative visions, and replaced with recommendations to distinguish between the 'geographically European' referring to the east (meaning countries which potentially have the right to apply for EU membership) and the 'non-European' Mediterranean neighbours, and to use conditionality only as a positive incentive for further reform.[33]

By 2007, the concept of 'well-governed countries' had come to a halt, as it lacked reciprocity and commitment on the neighbours' side.[34] To reinvigorate a sense of progress, by 2009 two regional strategies were put in place – the Eastern Partnership Initiative and the Union for the Mediterranean – to cover the neighbouring region in a differentiated and more focused manner. Although they contained an expanded toolbox of policy instruments and financial means, these initiatives remained conceptually constrained by the inherited modus operandi of enlargement – of top-down transfer and conditionality – unfit for the purpose of partnership-building, but agreeable with EU governance rationality.[35]

The ENP has subsequently undergone several rounds of further iteration and revision, including in 2011 and 2012,[36] in an attempt to lift reforms off the ground in the eastern neighbourhood. After almost ten years in operation, the EU approach towards the eastern region has been logistically enriched to offer a complex matrix of opportunities and incentives, and now appeals to all levels of society. The latest policy iterations developed more concrete regional pathways of engagement and a more pronounced structure of incentives – a 'more for more' approach.[37]

Nevertheless, much conceptual indecision, reverberant with the EU's colonial mentality, still remains. The EU may have eased on its demands and expectations, but it has remained EU-centred in its relations with the outside. In particular, lacking a coherent EU self-identity, the policy still reveals the whole gamut of horizontal and vertical discrepancies, when it comes to implementation. Not only has there been continued bickering between various actors, units and divisions of power within the EU's institutional setting,[38] there is also a considerable vertical gap between the executive approach of Brussels and a more nuanced understanding by the in-country officials on the ground, bearing witness to partners' struggles and needs. In particular, off-the-record comments of EU officials in partner-states have explicitly noted the irrelevance of the EU's hierarchical approach and the executive injection of compliance to induce cooperation. Many insisted on a 'stronger and more consistent' policy to the neighbours, being inclusive of their geopolitical and cultural boundaries, and offering reciprocal commitment to those who perform well.[39]

Furthermore, the policy continues to suffer from limited vision. Born with no original blueprint, it still struggles to find common ground in relation to incentives or future prospects for the more committed neighbours, such as Moldova and Georgia. The ENP continues to be an instrument in EU hands for internalizing the outside into the EU's way of thinking. With the post-Lisbon restructuring of the EU's external relations, there are some expectations that the launch of the EEAS may offer a more focused engagement with the outsiders.[40] There is anticipation that with the full entrenchment of the EEAS in the future as a diplomatic corps of 4,000 staff, the EU may eventually develop more substantial capabilities and a better vision for its own Self, especially in the light of the continuing upgrading of the ENP for the rapidly changing neighbouring region.[41] This however comes with a caveat that refers back to the necessity to formulate a 'far clearer idea of what the EU's fundamental aims and objectives are on the international scene as well as consensus on what type of actor the Union wishes to be'[42], before any effective undertaking can occur in the utilization of the EEAS. The stumbling block for effective EU action is the EU's colonial mentality, centred on its own Self and unaware or neglectful of the *relational importance* of the outside in developing the EU's external representations as a legitimate and credible player. Therefore, in order to understand why much resistance still remains in the eastern region towards seemingly incentivizing opportunities under the ENP/EaP, one needs to consider 'the Other', and the reasons and conditions of neighbour states for developing sustainable cooperation and allegiances. After all, the EU may find itself to be not only the subject but essentially the object of mutual boundary construction, on the part of the outside, in an inclusive process of redesigning global political geography.

The Decisive Complementarity of the 'Other'

Not only is the success of the EU as a normative power a precondition for other actors to agree to the norms set out by the EU; it also constructs an identity of the EU against an image of others in the 'outside world'. This has important implications for the way EU policies treat those others, and for the degree to which its adherence to its own norms is scrutinized within the EU.[43]

The EU 'We' embodying its understanding of 'Self', its aspirations and capacities, but also its abilities to act consistently and coherently in the international arena, is an important stepping stone for the EU to become a 'credible force for good'. However, it needs to have clarity about its internal structures and external practices to be able to project its image integrally to the outside. This, however, is only a small part of the 'Grand Strategy'.[44]

As Diez contends, in order for the EU to be an effective and legitimate global player, inclusive of its normative aspirations, it needs to ensure that the 'Other' too constitutes an essential and *positive* referent in EU identity-building: 'it is only through the relation to the Other, the relation to what it is not, to precisely what it lacks, to what has been called its *constitutive outside* that the "positive" meaning of [identity] can be constructed'.[45]

The issue of the 'Other' and the process of 'Othering' appear to be somewhat neglected in contemporary scholarship and the policy-making process, with many studies focusing on the centrality of the EU Self. Even where the 'Other' briefly features as a narrative, its reading, as a rule, is negative and binary.[46]

'The Other' is normally conceptualized as part of the EU Self, or as an anti-image for the EU's self-development.[47] More advanced studies[48] conceive of 'the Other' as part of the 'utopian' narrative for the EU's external projection. 'The Other' in this case is imagined within the space between the EU's current Self and its own aspirational 'utopia' ('better Self'): after all 'the EU can best learn about its own flaws and potentials and become a meaningful utopia for its own citizens by "bringing the outside world back in"'.[49] The potential caveat of this visualization of 'the Other' is that it reflects the future narrative which may 'allow EU actors to disregard their own shortcomings unless a degree of self-reflexivity is inserted'.[50] The EU indeed often struggles to reconcile its high-powered rhetoric of vision for 'the Self' as a 'credible force for good' with its daily practices, ridden by power asymmetries and the perception of its self-righteousness in driving the outside to its standards.

Many scholarly accounts,[51] although in theory recognizing the inter-subjective nature of the 'Otherness' in the process of identifying one's 'Self' and its relations with the external environment, are nevertheless more concerned with the relational *centrality* of the EU in the projection of its appeal as a 'greater power'; while 'the Other has the option of either accepting how it is characterized or challenging its constitution with contending representations'.[52]

In other words, 'the Other' still remains an alien and unwelcome outside, which continues to be seen as a potential threat to the achievements of stability and order within the 'We-group' construct, necessitating respective practices of defensive boundary-closure and control on the EU part, to eliminate the destructive influences of 'the Other'.[53]

In the increasingly changing global order, where one's authority is no longer a given, and one's normative appeal should no longer be taken for granted, a new understanding of 'the Other' as of 'a different kind' which requires an effort of contextualization and a degree of acceptance of different ways of living is long overdue. After all, as M. Smith argues, the EU has now moved towards adopting a more encompassing framework – that of a 'politics of inclusion' – which demands 'diversity of method and paths of developments'; 'the internalization of disturbance rather than its containment'; 'focus on access rather than on control', and which offers the discourse of 'negotiated order', which 'focuses less on difference than on variety'.[54]

To ensure that self-reflexivity is firmly embedded in the EU's relations with outsides, and forms an important part of its construction of 'the Self' especially as a 'credible force for good', the inclusion of 'the Other' in the process of EU identity-building *as different*, and not as subordinate, or inferior or representing a threat, is essential, in order to gauge the success of its actions and the extent of its legitimation by the external milieu. Furthermore, the relationship between the inside and the outside is invariably dialectical and fluid, and requires constant scrutiny of *one's* self against the *other's* perceptions, to achieve reciprocity in their relations and the equivalence of goals and gains:

> Identities are seen always to require another against which they are constructed; an other which they thus construct at the same time [...] Foreign policy, from such an angle, is not the representation of the nation to others

as a pre-given object, but a construction of the nation in the very moment of representation.[55]

The analysis of the EU's treatment of neighbourhood[56] has revealed that the EU's biggest problem is less to do with its policy inconsistency or the lack of cohesion in projecting its representation externally. The EU explicitly stumbles over the conception of 'the Other', which is often acknowledged but not defined. In rhetoric the EU pledges joint ownership and partnership:

> The EU does not seek to impose priorities or conditions on its partners[...] There can be no question of asking partners to accept a pre-determined set of priorities. These will be defined by common consent and will thus vary from country to country.[57]

In practice, EU–neighbour relations remain asymmetrical, and EU-driven, with limited understanding of the partners' internal boundaries – especially of a geopolitical and cultural nature – and perceptions of partners as 'needy' and 'inferior':[58] 'The ENP is not a joint ownership of Ukraine and the EU. From the very beginning the ENP remains a unilateral initiative of the EU, and its framework is not [...] in line with the national interests of Ukraine'.[59]

Even if clarity and internal cohesiveness are fostered, owing to the provisions of the Lisbon Treaty, without better understanding and respective contextualization of its external environment the EU is unlikely to bolster its credibility as a 'force for good', and as a future 'Significant We'. It has taken the EU several rounds to realize, at least on a discourse level, through various iterations of the ENP, that neighbours' representation should form an important part of the EU's agenda-setting, to ensure both policy's effectiveness and modelling of the EU as a 'force for good':

> There is a need for greater flexibility and more tailored responses in dealing with rapidly evolving partners and reform needs [...] The EU does not seek to impose a model or a ready-made recipe for political reform, but it will insist that each partner country's reform process reflect a clear commitment to universal values that form the basis of our renewed approach.[60]

Defining 'the Other', however, does not only entail recognition, but more importantly an understanding of differences, especially pertaining to values, traditions, norms of a behaviour and boundaries such as those that historically have determined other ways of life. This new learning should in turn allow for comprehension of cultural/historical patterns of behaviour, with the view not to inculcate 'better' ones, but to adapt and share best practices through a long-term cooperation and exchange. This cooperation should lead to the development of more sustainable patterns of interaction to ensure that only through reciprocity of interests and tangibility of incentives can a joint future of mutually recognizable best practices be built. As Haukkala aptly connotes, 'the Union should consider a neighbourhood policy that is based less on heavy normative convergence and harmonization and more on tangible cooperation with more modest rhetoric and clearer material incentives'.[61] Only by recognizing 'the Other' as a relational and essential part of the EU's normative global appeal, the EU, alongside the US and other major players, may eventually develop a sustainable strategy of external relations, and shift away from its colonial rationality of compliance and convergence. 'To govern less is to govern better'[62] would allow for accommodation of diversities in the struggle for a sustainable and interpolar future.

The Future Agenda

What of the EU's future relations with the outside, and its eastern neighbours in particular? Since their launch, the ENP and especially the EaP have come a long way. While witnessing a rapid change in the South, and the protracted pace of reforms in the East, the EU has responded with a renewed strategy and a complex governance structure (inclusive of new incentives), to keep up the momentum of convergence. Notably, the 2011 *New Response to the Changing Neighbourhood* by the Commission further detailed a dual-core approach to the neighbours, with more emphasis placed on the multilateral track and on regional partnerships which in turn have been broken down by a number of activities and supported by the whole range of policy instruments.[63] The year 2012 witnessed the development of specific road maps for each region and individual countries, whereby the EU's renewed strategy now offers a complex matrix of flagship activities and platforms, especially under the EaP, with increased financial and political support. These are designed to penetrate and mobilize 'all strands of society', thus purposefully entwining the neighbours into an elaborate scheme of multiple opportunities, with partners' own responsibility for reforms and drive for further convergence.[64] In addition, technical, thematic and financial instruments increasingly abound, often co-opting international stakeholders to ensure success, legitimacy and credibility of the EU's engagement with the eastern region. If successful this matrix of 'self-incentivizing' opportunities could serve as a model for EU external relations in the future.

Now, what about practice? There are principally technical and conceptual caveats here. Technical deficiencies are plentiful, but rectifiable. The involvement of multiple stakeholders, at various levels, for example, requires their proper institutionalization into a system of decision-making in the EU – not an easy objective, but potentially achievable. Furthermore, a comprehensive awareness campaign is necessary to increase partners' interest in the opportunities offered. Once full engagement occurs, the mechanism of 'more for more' is activated. In summary, these technicalities do not per se posit insurmountable obstacles on the way to expanding cooperation with outsiders.

The more fundamental difficulty still relates to the EU's modus operandi, which continues to be expressly Eurocentric, and EU-driven. As Laure Delcour observes:

> **Joint ownership** of the policy process is critical for the EaP's multilateral track, which is underpinned by logic of socialisation. However, the extent to which this track is jointly owned is questionable as the whole process appears to be framed principally by the EU. As a general rule, platforms are chaired by the Commission and the EEAS, which places the EU at the centre of what currently resembles a hub-and-spoke rather than a cobweb model of relations.[65]

Furthermore, the effectiveness of the new 'baiting' strategy – of luring the neighbours into EU-structured opportunities to trigger compliance and convergence – still explicitly depends on whether or not the EU can and is willing to learn about 'the Other' – the partner countries themselves – which not only involves 'hearing them', but also 'listening to' their needs and concerns, and attending to their ideas and suggestions:

> If partners are equal, they negotiate to reach common grounds. It looks as though EU officials have their own explanations for not following this rule: they choose partners who are close to their norms, which is fine from their practical point of view. Foreign policy is however conditioned by national interests and should be independent from regime or the specific nature of any government. Interests are not values. As partners we may have different potentials, but as independent polities, we are equal, and should be treated with respect, which is the basis for a normal and progressive dialogue.[66]

And this is clearly a long-term objective, assuming an overhaul of EU modus operandi and the place of 'the Other' in EU 'self-identity'. The process of 'Othering' and understanding the interface of the two dimensions – of the 'We' and the 'Other' – are vitally important to make the EU's external policies effective and legitimate. The overarching aim is much broader than its constitutive parts, and refers to cultivating the EU's image as a credible and legitimate global player. This may only be feasible by *decentring* the focus from the EU onto partner countries,[67] and treating them as equally significant in the process of propagating EU self-identity and its cohesive self-representation abroad. The equal balancing of 'We' and the 'Other' in the EU's projection of 'Self' as a global actor particularly holds value for what increasingly appears to be an interdependent world. If the EU wishes to become a 'credible force for good', without 'the Other' – no matter how finely crafted a new formula may be – EU governance, on its own, will not succeed.

Notes

1 J. Solana, 'Countering Globalisation's Dark Side', *Europe's World*, 2007, policy dossier, available at www.consilium.europa.eu/uedocs/cms_data/docs/pressdata/EN/articles/96791.pdf (accessed 5 June 2011).

2 F. Duchêne, 'Europe's Role in World Peace', in R. Mayne (ed.), *Europe Tomorrow: Sixteen Europeans Look Ahead* (1972); I. Manners, 'Normative Power Europe: A Contradiction in Terms?', *Journal of Common Market Studies*, 40, 2 (2002), pp. 235–58; Z. Laïdi, *EU Foreign Policy in a Globalised World: Normative Power and Social Preferences* (2008); H. Mayer and H. Vogt (eds), *A Responsible Europe? Ethical Foundations of EU External Affairs* (Basingstoke, 2006); L. Aggestam, 'Introduction: Ethical Power Europe?', *International Affairs*, 84, 1 (2008), pp. 1–11; R. Whitman (ed.), *Normative Power Europe: Empirical and Theoretical Perspectives* (Basingstoke, 2011); H. Grabbe, *The EU's Transformative Power* (Basingstoke, 2006).

3 With minor exceptions whereby the EU's development is explained with reference to the outside in the works of E. Ringmar, 'The Recognition Game: Soviet Russia and the West', *Cooperation and Conflict*, 37, 2 (2002), pp. 115–36; T. Diez, 'Constructing the Self and Changing Others: Reconsidering "Normative Power Europe"', *Millennium, Journal of International Studies*, 33, 3 (2005), pp. 614, 613–36; P. Dekker, A. van der Horst and S. Kok, *Europe's Neighbours: European Neighbourhood Policy and Public Opinion* (Amsterdam, 2009); K. Nicolaïdis and R. Howse, '"This is my EUtopia…": Narrative as Power', *Journal of Common Market Studies*, 40, 4 (2002), pp. 788, 767–92.

4 L. Friis and A. Murphy, 'The European Union and Central and Eastern Europe', *Journal of Common Market Studies*, 37, 2 (1999) pp. 214, 211–32.

5 J. Howorth, 'The EU as a Global Actor: Grant Strategy for a Global Grand Bargain?', *Journal of Common Market Studies*, 48, 3 (2010), pp. 455–74. G. Grevi, 'The Interpolar World: a New Scenario', Occasional Paper No. 79, European Union Institute for Security Studies (Paris, 2009).

6 A. Linklater, 'A European Civilising Process?', in C. J. Hill and M. Smith (eds), *International Relations and the European Union*, 2nd edition (Oxford, 2011).

7 With the exceptions listed in note 3 above.

8 R. Whitman and S. Wolff (eds), *The European Neighbourhood Policy in Perspective: Context, Implementation and Impact* (Basingstoke, 2010); S. Lavenex and F. Schimmelfennig (eds), *Democracy Promotion in the EU's Neighbourhood: From Leverage to Governance?* (2012); L. Delcour, 'The Institutional Functioning of the Eastern Partnership: A Early Assessment', *Eastern Partnership* Review, 1 (Tallinn, 2011).

9 Friis and Murphy, 'The EU and Central and Eastern Europe', p. 213.

10 J. Kelley, 'New Wine in Old Wineskins: Promoting Political Reforms through the New European Neighbourhood Policy', *Journal of Common Market Studies*, 44, 1 (2006), pp. 29–55; K. Smith, 'The Outsiders: the European Neighbourhood Policy', *International Affairs*, 81, 4 (2005), pp. 757–73; F. Bicchi, '"Our Size Fits All": Normative Power Europe and the Mediterranean', *Journal of European Public Policy*, 13, 2 (2006), pp. 286–303.

11 E. Korosteleva, *The European Union and its Eastern Neighbours: Towards a More Ambitious Partnership?* (2012).

12 Solana, 'Countering Globalisation's Dark Side'.

13 T. Flockhart, 'Europeanization or EU-ization? The Transfer of European Norms across Time and Space', *Journal of Common Market Studies*, 48, 4 (2010), pp. 787–810.

14 Nicolaïdis and Howse, '"This is my EUtopia…"'.

15 Flockhart, 'Europeanization or EU-ization?', p. 795 and Howorth, 'EU as Global Actor', p. 458.

16 U. Ozkirimli, *Theories of Nationalism: A Critical Introduction* (Basingstoke, 2000), p. 230.

17 M. Smith, 'The European Union and a Changing Europe: Establishing the Boundaries of Order', *Journal of Common Market Studies*, 34, 1 (1996), pp. 5–28.

18 S. Gänzle, 'EU Governance and the European Neighbourhood Policy: A Framework for Analysis', *Europe–Asia Studies*, 61, 10 (2009), pp. 1715–34.

19 Nicolaïdis and Howse, '"This is my EUtopia…"'.

20 Flockhart, 'Europeanization or EU-ization?', p. 797.

21 For more discussion of what constitutes EU norms and values, see C. Leconte, 'The Fragilities of the European Union as a Community of "Values": Lessons from the Haider Affair', *West European Politics*, 28, 3 (2005).

22 J. Zielonka, *Europe as Empire: The Nature of the Enlarged EU* (Oxford, 2007).

23 Grabbe, *Transformative Power*.

24 Grabbe, *Transformative Power*.

25 D. Hutcheson and E. Korosteleva (eds), *The Quality of Democracy in Post-Communist Europe* (2004).

26 C. McManus-Czubinska et al., 'The Misuse of Referendums in Post-Communist Europe', in Hutcheson and Korosteleva (eds), *Quality of Democracy*, pp. 28–56.

27 T. Börzel, 'European Governance: Negotiation and Competition in the Shadow of Hierarchy', *Journal of Common Market Studies*, 48, 2 (2010), pp. 191–219; E. Korosteleva, *The European Union and its Eastern Neighbours: Towards a More Ambitious Partnership?* (2012).

28 Prodi Commission Report (2004), p. 4.

29 Commission Report (2003).

30 *Ibid.*, p. 5.

31 European Security Strategy, 'A Secure Europe in a Better World' (Brussels, 12 December 2003), available at www.consilium.europa.eu/uedocs/cmsUpload/78367.pdf (accessed 12 April 2010).

32 European Parliament, 'Resolution on "Wider Europe" Neighbourhood: A New Framework for Relations with our Eastern and Southern Neighbours', 2003/2018(INI), Strasbourg, P5_TA(2003)0520, point 2.

33 European Parliament, 'Resolution on Strengthening the European Neighbourhood Policy' 2007/2088(INI), P6_TA(2007)0538 (15 November 2007).

34 Commission Report, 774 final (Brussels, 5 December 2007); E. Korosteleva, (ed.), *The Eastern Partnership Initiative: A New Opportunity for the Neighbours?* (2011).

35 Korosteleva, *EU and its Eastern Neighbours*; E. Tulmets, 'Institution-Building Instruments in the Eastern Partnership: Still Drawing on Enlargement?', *Eastern Partnership Review*, 6 (Tallinn, 2011).

36 European Commission and High Representative of the European Union for Foreign Affairs and Security Policy, *A New Response to a Changing Neighbourhood*, COM, 303 (Brussels, 25 May 2011) and European Commission and High Representative of the European Union for Foreign Affairs and Security Policy, *Delivering on a New European Neighbourhood Policy*, JOIN, 14 (Brussels, 15 May 2012).

37 S. Füle, Speech at the EuroNest Parliamentary Assembly, Speech/12/256 (Baku, 3 April 2012).

38 M. E. Smith and M. Webber, 'Political Dialogue and Security in the European Neighbourhood: The Virtues and Limits of "New Partnership Perspective"', *European Foreign Affairs Review*, 13 (2008), pp. 73–95; Korosteleva, *Eastern Partnership Initiative*.

39 Korosteleva, *The EU and its Eastern Neighbours*; K. Wolczuk and J. Langbein, 'Convergence without Membership? The Impact of the European Union in the Neighbourhood: Evidence from Ukraine', *Journal of European Public Policy* (2011), pp. 1–19; K. Raik, 'From Attraction to Europeanisation – Moldova's Slow Movement towards the EU', *Eastern Partnership Review*, 2 (Tallinn, 2011).

40 S. Hemra, T. Raines and R. Whitman, 'A Diplomatic Entrepreneur: Making the Most of the European External Action Service', Chatham House Report (2011).

41 JOIN (2012), 14.

42 S. Duke and A. Courtier, 'The EU's External Public Diplomacy and the EEAS – Cosmetic Exercise or Intended Change?', Loughborough University Paper (2011), p. 6.

43 Diez, 'Constructing the Self'.

44 Howorth, 'EU as Global Actor'.

45 Hall in Ozkirimli, *Theories of Nationalism*, p. 230.

46 Diez, 'Constructing the Self'; Ozkirimli, *Theories of Nationalism*; Ringmar, 'The Recognition Game', pp. 115–36.

47 Flockhart, 'Europeanization or EU-ization'.

48 Nicolaïdis and Howse, '"This is my EUtopia…"'; D. Bechev and K. Nicolaïdis, 'From Policy to Polity: Can the EU's Special Relations with its "Neighbourhood" be Decentred?', *Journal of Common Market Studies*, 48, 3 (2010), pp. 475–500.

49 Nicolaïdis and Howse, '"This is my EUtopia…"', p. 769.

50 Diez, 'Constructing the Self', pp. 626–7.

51 C. Browning and G. Christou, 'The Constitutive Power of Outsiders: The European Neighbourhood Policy and the Eastern Dimension', *Political Geography*, 30 (2010), pp. 1–10; L. Hansen, *Security as Practice: Discourse Analysis and the Bosnian War* (2006); Ringmar, 'The Recognition Game'.

52 Browning and Christou, 'The Constitutive Power of Outsiders', p. 2.

53 Diez, 'Constructing the Self', pp. 628–30.

54 M. Smith, 'The European Union and a Changing Europe', *Journal of Common Market Studies*, 34, 1 (1996), p. 22–3.

55 Diez, 'Constructing the Self', p. 627.

56 M. Pace, 'Paradoxes and Contradictions in EU Democracy Promotion in the Mediterranean: The Limits of EU Normative Power', *Democratization*, 16, 1 (2009), pp. 39–58; Whitman and Wolff, *European Neighbourhood Policy*; Korosteleva, *EU and its Eastern Neighbours*.

57 European Commission Report (2004).

58 Korosteleva, *Eastern Partnership Initiative*.

59 Ukrainian Ministry for Foreign Affairs statement released in 2010, quoted in Korosteleva, *European Union and its Eastern Neighbours*, p. 89. For more information visit: http://www.ukraine-eu.mfa.gov.ua/eu/en/publication/content/47443.htm (accessed 9 December 2010).

60 European Commission and High Representative of the European Union for Foreign Affairs and Security Policy, *A New Response to a Changing Neighbourhood*, European Commission, 303: 1–3 (Brussels, 25 May 2011).

61 H. Haukkala, 'The European Union as a Regional Normative Hegemon: The Case of European Neighbourhood Policy', *Europe–Asia Studies*, 60, 9 (2008), pp. 1601–22.

62 M. Dean, cited in R. Abrahamsen, 'The Power of Partnerships in Global Governance', *Third World Quarterly*, 25, 8 (2004), p. 146.

63 European Commission (2011), 303.

64 European Commission (2011), 2.

65 L. Delcour, 'The Institutional Functioning of the Eastern Partnership: An Early Assessment', *Eastern Partnership Review*, 1 (Tallinn, 2011), emphasis original.

66 Deputy Minister, Ministry of Foreign Affairs, Belarus (21 September 2009).

67 Bechev and Nicolaïdis, 'From Policy to Polity'.

Southern Barbarians?
A Post-Colonial Critique of EUniversalism

Kalypso Nicolaïdis

They eat with their fingers instead of with chopsticks such as we use. They show their feelings without any self-control. They cannot understand the meaning of written characters.

Boxer, *The Christian Century in Japan: 1549–1650*

Pooling Sovereignty, Pooling Colonies

In today's Japan, one can eat a delicious noodle soup exhibiting a circle of meat swimming at its periphery.[1] The dish is called 'Southern Barbarians', as is an elegant sixteenth-century painting attributed to Kano Sanraku depicting a bunch of white men walking ashore from a grand ship presumably sailing from the South Sea. These were the Europeans of the time, *Nanban* or Southern Barbarians. The Japanese abandoned the term *Nanban* during the Meiji Restoration, as it did not seem excessively compatible with radical westernization. By then, even if the latter had come to be embraced as much as a strategy of resistance to as one of emulation of the West, Europeans could no longer be considered as fundamentally uncivilized or 'barbarian', a term coined by Athenians to designate their own Others, those who fell outside the laws of the *polis*. From their perspective, if by the late nineteenth century Europe was clearly seen as the source of superior technology – the material dimension of civilization – the world over, the same could not be said for European or Western spirit. If the word *Nanban* is still used in today's Japan, we are told that it is meant in picturesque and affectionate spirit, used jokingly to refer to Western people or civilization in a cultured manner – a faint echo of yesterday's intense enmity and rivalry, hardly a matter for passion, desire or hatred.

How should we contemplate the bearing of such subtle *mentalities* beyond the European continent on contemporary attempts at political union within it? Above all, by calling for individual and institutional awareness on the part of 'Europe'. To suggest that today's Europeans remember how their forebears were perceived as *Southern Barbarians* is not only to ask them to consider how colonial echoes linger on in continued perceptions from the rest of the world. It is also an invitation to radical decentring: to free themselves from Eurocentrism and consider the globe from other points of view, whatever place Europeans may hold from the vantage point;[2] to remember that Europe itself was constructed through the fashioning of various 'barbarians', 'Others' beyond its own shifting limits, who defined its own claims to a 'civilized' identity; and fascinatingly, to turn the tables around and consider that Europe might be somebody else's inferior 'South' or yet more unsettling, a faraway province of which is known little – and even to consider that such a reduced status can be the object of a smile, a shrug of irreverence, a nod to irrelevance.

It should come as no surprise that such a 'decentring' mindset is rather marginal in today's institutional incarnation of Europe, the European Union. Instead, the dominant discourse and ambition is that of global purpose and power, that of benign hegemony committed to upholding its values around the world through peaceful means, and to selling its new brand of 'civil' relations between states to other relevant arena of governance, be they regional or global. To be sure, there has always been the sense, with talk of a third way between the US and the Soviet Union, that the only power the EU can claim for itself is that of 'superpowerlessness'.[3] But let us face it. However self-deprecatory, such superpowerlessness has come to be framed as civilian, civilizing or normative powerhood, by Europeans unaware of being seen by many in the 'global south' as the descendants of some version of 'southern barbarians'.[4]

Should not the multifaceted crisis which has befallen the EU since 2009 and saw Europeans seeking rescue from (re-)emerging actors from the global south truly constitute a moment of self-reflection in this regard?

As the many contributions in this volume make clear, echoes of European colonialism are present to this day, and not just in radical leftist anti-imperialist speeches around the world. Nor do these echoes belong only to one member state or another – although to be sure, France's imprint looms large in this story when it comes to Africa, as does Britain's when it comes to South Asia and both when it comes to the Middle East. Instead, as I will argue here, such echoes are linked to the very origins of the European project.

This chapter asks how the EC, and later the EU, dealt with its colonial legacy. Or rather, it points to avenues and ways in which we should ask the question. It is grounded in a broader research agenda committed to 'Rethinking Europe in a non-European World': a 'non-European world' both objectively, as continued US dominance and the rise of new powers imply the progressive marginalization of Europe, and a 'non-European world' subjectively, i.e. a world in stark contrast to the past three centuries when 'southern barbarians' were thought to shape the political geography of the entire globe.

By exploring both the echoes of colonialism in today's EU discourse and practice and the signs of its potential post-colonial maturity, I hope to suggest that Europe has spent a half century negotiating this transition to a non-European world and is now at a crossroads. In one outcome it would succumb to its colonial gene; in the other, it would live up to its post-colonial aspiration. The latter term is intentionally borrowed from the post-decolonization literature to ask whether the EU can truly share in the fate and state of mind of the post-colonial world beyond its borders.

In Part I (The Virgin Birth) I sketch out very schematically the strategies employed by the EC at the creation and in later years to reinvent a Europe that could deny the paternity of its founding member states, embedded as it was in the matrix of war itself. In Part II (The Colonial Gene), I ask whether and to what extent we can nevertheless recognize Europe's core nature in the discourse and practice emanating over the years from the European Union. Finally in Part III (The Post-Colonial Aspiration) I turn to a normative appraisal, defining what I would take to be a post-colonial ethos for Europe and pointing to some of the ways in which the EU could yet invent and fine-tune a genuinely post-colonial agenda.

The Virgin Birth or the Reinvention of Europe

Inconvenient pasts are not all born equal. It is often said that the EU is grounded in the memory of the past and that the need to transcend such a past is still the glue that binds Europeans. But there seems to be only one past relevant to this story, a war which tore the continent apart 50 years ago. Europe's other past, that of its relations with the rest of the world from the beginning of the colonial era four centuries ago until the very creation of the EC/EU, somehow does not figure in this narrative. Yet this past has also never been far from the surface, acting as a backdrop for Europe's cautious self-reassertion on the global stage, first in the context of the Cold War, and above all in the post-Cold War era. Thus, the progressive, tentative and even timid resurgence of the idea and practice of 'Europe as a model' can be seen as the product of a mixed strategy of amnesia, redirection and atonement on the part of public figures, intellectuals and the various actors of foreign policy.

Amnesia and Denial

The European Community was born not only of a desire for a radical break with the past, war and nationalism; it was also born out of desire for continuity and collective management of a colonial world – above all the African continent – that was slipping out of the grasp of its member states individually. As Peo Hansen and Stefan Jonsson illustrate vividly in their chapter, European integration was from the post-war era to the 1960s inextricably bound up with the so-called 'Eurafrica' project of what Nkrumah later called collective colonialism.[5] Starting with initial attempts to institute Franco-British colonial cooperation, through to the Hague Congress of Europe in 1948, the Eurafrica project became that of all founding member states. This meant pooling sovereignty *in order* to pool colonies, as pointed out by the UK representative Lord Layton when he called on the Hague assembly to think of these overseas territories 'not as the possessions of any one country' but lands that 'have to be integrated with all the countries of Europe and all the overseas territories'.[6] If the initial idea was joint exploitation of the African continent to resolve Europe's raw material deficit, demographic deficit, or the dollar deficit, the rationale quickly took on a geopolitical dimension, with Eurafrica as the key to Europe as third force. Even if the 'Monnet Plan for Africa' (a grouping with its own High Authority) was never implemented, Schuman picked up on Monnet's suggestion that France could give Africa as a 'dowry to Europe' with the backing of the likes of Adenauer's Germany as well as many Scandinavians for whom sharing colonies meant sharing markets. And so the Treaty of Rome associated with the nascent EC through trade preferences all of the member states' colonial possessions (French West and Equatorial Africa, Belgian Congo and Ruanda-Urundi, Italian Somaliland and Netherlands New Guinea), without consulting those involved.

Indeed, there was no denying the ubiquitous presence of Europe's colonial past at its creation. But the imprint did not look much like what most Europhiles had planned throughout the late 1940s and 1950s. As France in particular was sealing its reconciliation with Germany with the stamp of a common market, it was caught in a decolonization drama and called De Gaulle to the rescue – although the signature of the Rome Treaty preceded his return to power. So if Le Général presided over the launch of the new European project it was only as a by-product of his newfound Algerian mission. Indeed it is now a forgotten fact that Algeria was part of the original EEC, not of course as a 'member' but as a (dependent) 'territory'. Many proponents of 'European unity' had used the argument that it would contribute to stemming revolt from the colonies, and in particular from Algeria, and the best way to retain this close embrace was to make them part of the new integration scheme. Interdependence, it was argued, was a much better fate than independence, even if from a European viewpoint such interdependence could only be asymmetric.

But history did not quite go along with the plan. When France and the newly sovereign Algeria 'de-commonised' their market and their fates after 1962's independence, there was no formal process of withdrawal or exclusion of the territories now constituting Algeria from the jurisdiction of the EC; the fact that a North African country was an original constituent part of the EC and the process by which it came out of it is so clouded in mystery that no map showcasing the origins of the EC ever includes the southern shore of the Mediterranean (ask schoolchildren in EU countries or indeed their parents). Nor indeed did France deal explicitly with the status of the one million 'Muslim French citizens of Algeria' who had often sided with the metropole during the war of independence and been promised full political rights in the last days of the war: their existence, like that of the land from which they came, was simply erased from the annals, while non-French Algerians simply became a source of cheap labour for the metropole in the post-colonial project. As Shepard argues, the French response to the Algerian revolution gave birth to the certainty that decolonization was a stage in the forward march of Hegelian linear History, making the messy episodes disappear in a familiar liberal narrative of progress.[7] According to this new narrative (new that is with the break of 1962), the French, in general, speaking through the voice of their leader De Gaulle, had not merely resigned themselves to, but had actively embraced the extension of self-determination and the forward march of *liberté, égalité, fraternité* that had begun with the French Revolution.

Beyond France, the narrative of decolonization was shaped or 'invented' in the first decade of the EC's existence as the story of a historical culmination of the internationalization of the European society of nations: a world of sovereign states with territorial boundaries based on presumed homogenous nations which had 'earned the right' to sovereignty. In this context, Algerians would never join Icelanders as a people recorded to have defected from the EC. Since there would never be any attempt to mould Algerians into Europeans, their separation from France had nothing to do with the new Europe. They had never been part of Europe, and would not be party to a contract between equal and similar peoples. If we take Renan's idea of nations as defined by what they choose to remember and forget together, the imagined community of Europe exorcized the demons of its member states by helping to purge their past and its own present of signs that empires had mattered for many of its member states, as well as all of them collectively, right up to the foundation of the EC and during its first few years. In this great process of forgetting, the 1960s were a magical decade. Suddenly, a continent that had been obsessed with its symbiotic and exploitative relations with the colonial world simply rewrote the story that it would tell about itself. Kojève and others' 'Latin empire' in the Mediterranean, the plans for Euro-African integration and the like, simply vanished. The European project retreated into its (small) self in a grand exercise of political amnesia.

And with amnesia came denial, denial that this quickly forgotten and recent past mattered, leading to the widely shared assumption by the end of the 1960s that the idea of a unilaterally defined mission ('domesticating' world politics in its own image) could still be acceptable in this new post-colonial world. As a result, the core tension inherited from Europe's past remained in a different guise. That is, the tension between the two faces of European universalism turned to EUniversalism, namely exceptionalism to the point of justifying domination on one hand and solidarism as trans-national responsibility on the other.[8]

Redirection

To countries like France or Belgium, and later Britain, denial of the relevance of their imperial past to the European project would not and could not mean a simple retreat within the borders of a middle-sized or small power – an EC which without its African backyard could hardly have come to matter as a 'third force'. The Westphalian European order might have put an end (or rather tried to) to expansionist or interfering tendencies within the European continent, but this internal deal had always been balanced by extraterritorial allowance for expansionism beyond. And so with the reinvention of decolonization came the reinvention of Europe as the next frontier of national ambitions. European nations learned to redirect their ambition from without to within. If *la Grande France* could no longer be the *hexagone* enlarged to the 'Départements et Territoires d'Outre Mer' (DOM-TOM) it would become the *hexagone* projected onto the continent of Europe itself, eventually (50 years later) to become 'wider Europe': the label put forth by Brussels to describe the borderlands of Europe destined to become part of its new institutionalized sphere of influence. Clearly, in the case of Germany, redirection – to the extent that it meant allowing its neighbours to police, tax and 'civilize' it – was the straightest road to redemption. It may well be the case that these various projects of redirection did not turn out as initially planned – the EU is certainly not *la Grande France* and Germany has been arguably unsuccessful at getting its neighbours to bind it – but the direction of redirection is still with us 60 years later: the EU is an introverted animal, despite its multifaceted presence abroad.[9]

Such a redirection strategy was much harder for Britain, bent on reconciling its three concentric circles of engagement with the world – the US, the Commonwealth and the EC. Indeed, one of the core reasons for the Labour government of the 1950s to forego the EC option had been a hard-core calculation that 'trade diversion', redirection in the immediate material sense of its trade link from a Commonwealth emerging out of the ashes of empire to the European Common Market, would simply be too costly for food prices, and thus workers in the UK, while weakening the ties with the emerging Commonwealth. De Gaulle's first 'No' in 1963 was grounded not only on the accusation that the UK was a US Trojan horse but – much more ironically, given the then recent French 'invention of decolonization' – in the argument that the UK's failure to decolonize fully and radically could be taken as a sign of its lack of commitment to building Europe.[10] The message was clear: Europeanization could not be complete without genuine redirection. The subtext, of course, concerned competitive advantage in trade, France's obsession with the 'level playing field' and the early convergence between redirection and 'protection' if not protectionism *tout court*.

At the same time, decolonization and the transformation of the old colonies into battlegrounds of the Cold War also erased any prospect of the EC evolving into a relatively independent third force in world politics, confining 'redirection' to the economic realm for the time being.

The strategy of redirection culminated in the process of reunification of the European continent itself at the end of the Cold War, when Europe's east (excluding the troublesome south-east) came to be 'decolonized' from its Soviet master and reappropriated by the EU in one fell swoop. The sphere of influence of Western European member states, especially Germany, increased dramatically as a result. And with this new wave of decolonization of Europe itself, the EU acquired yet a new set of credentials, in theory at least: the membership of nations who had lived under the yoke of empire themselves would presumably bring in an added sensitivity to imperial drift. In truth of course, given the EU's internal power imbalances, the new members have not been in any position to contest dominant narratives vis-à-vis the rest of the world, with some arguing that in this sense at least they are still to some extent in danger of intra-EU 'colonization'.

Atonement

There was however a third strategy in the reinvention of Europe, itself at odds with the first two, but nevertheless a strong theme in Europe's actions in the world since the 1960s. That is the use of the EC/EU as an instrument of atonement on behalf of its ex-colonizer member states; as the actor and identity through which European powers could seek *legitimately* to reassert a role in the world – as if their new instrument, the EC, could offer its member states a genuine virgin (re)birth. The thinking behind the EU's relationship with former colonies did not only emanate from Europe. When public intellectuals like Aimé Césaire called for 'a new humanism' that would open 'unimagined possibilities' to the formerly colonized, this was to be a shared project between the previously colonized and colonizers predicated on a reconceptualized mutual engagement.[11] While European 'Third Worldism' of the 1960s and 1970s has come to be castigated as the 'tears of the White Man' by the likes of Pascal Bruckner, who saw it as a screen against more urgent imperatives of fighting communism – and more recently by Sarkozy and his derision of *repentance* – there is no want of zeal in EU institutions themselves for active EU engagement with 'the South'.[12]

Concretely and early on, the EC's system of colonial association quickly became a setting in which to accommodate the colonies' independence formally and honour the ideal of 'co-development' while continuing to gain from them economically and strategically. At least in theory, the EC's early strategy hinged on inversing the exploitative tropes of the colonial era (fair and stable price for primary commodities through Stabex; unilateral market opening in the interest of infant industries, etc.). More generally and in contrast with the US, the EU systematically favoured diplomatic engagement rather than balancing, containment or coercive diplomacy. From its inception, the EU's complex series of external trade preferences either followed pragmatic economic lines or were based on post-colonial ties. This is not the place to assess whether the EU's considerable development aid programme was used to influence post-independence governments of the former colonies, or in a more benign manner as a way of expiating post-colonial guilt. What is clear, however, is that the more hands-off attitude of the 1960s and 1970s changed somewhat after 1992 and the adoption of the Maastricht Treaty, which made the promotion of democracy and the rule of law in the rest of the world one of the primary goals of the European Union's Common Foreign and Security Policy.[13] Following suit, the Lomé IV agreement in 1989 allowed sanctions and political conditionality to be applied to aid recipients in the ACP in breach of good governance and rule of law requirements. But such conditionality has rarely been applied, and when it has it tends to be in the form of positive rather than negative conditionality. At least in theory, coercion is usually eschewed in favour of enmeshment. To be sure, the EU brand of the development agenda may not have abandoned the old profit motive, but it is now dressed up in the new clothes of partnership. But as the chapter by Jones and Weinhardt illustrates, the EU's attempt to negotiate new 'Economic Partnership Agreements' with ACP countries over the last decade has proved far from convincing to its partners. Indeed, whatever the actual ground for their perceptions, most ACP negotiators involved in the process have shown extreme sensitivity to the ubiquity of colonial undertone and behaviour on the part of their EU counterpart, including the insensitivity of the latter to expert studies contradicting their model of development for Africa.

Over time, the three strategies of denial, redirection and atonement combined to shape a vision of the EU's role in the world as a 'civil', 'benign', 'quiet', 'moral', 'transformative' actor who, through the force of such qualifiers, has slowly recovered the descriptor and indeed the attributes of power. By perceiving itself as a 'community of memory' the EU can in good conscience avoid that part of its past whose echoes are today most difficult to overcome. The strategy of redirection allowed the construction of an 'EUtopia' out of purely internal bargains over sovereignty, and thus a 'European model' which would progressively come to serve as the basis for a new narrative of projection.[14] And the goal of atonement fuelled the EU's commitment to another kind of engagement with the rest of the world. To what extent then has this reinvention of Europe succeeded? To what extent is the EU, actually or potentially, capable of transcending the colonial past of at least some of its member states?

The Colonial Gene or the Nature of the European Project

Unilateral Universalism and European Exceptionalism

We can call 'EUniversalism' the belief that norms and rules developed in the context of EU polity-building and policy-making are largely applicable – even if through necessary adaptation – to different contexts of regional and global governance. Today's brand of EUniversalism is grounded on familiar tropes: rights, values, icons. According to the *Oxford English Dictionary*, universalism is 'the doctrine of universal salvation or redemption'. 'Universal' can depict anything that everyone recognizes and accepts as fundamental, indivisible and relevant to all human beings. In its most general acceptation, universalism then is a shared belief regarding the validity of a set of principles for all human beings. In its secular version, it is a 'belief in the brotherhood of all men in a manner not subject to national allegiances'. In the realm of sociology and economics, it refers to a movement in 'opposition to particularism or regionalism'. The Weberian definition meanwhile reintroduces an ethical dimension, describing universalism as 'the insistence on treatment of all men by the same generalized, impersonal standards'.

In contrast with this (impossible? Incredibly demanding?) 'bird's eye view' version of universalism, the term has historically served to name *particular* discursive traditions, as it is in the nature of universalism itself that it is always in the eye of the beholder. There are of course non-European forms of universalism, such as that of Islam or the Chinese beliefs in the universal qualities of its societal values (e.g. 'ultimate perfection'). But the brand of universalism originating in Europe and directed outside Europe managed to find a material translation which none of the others had found before. As such, European universalism has historically been a *project for* the world as much as a vision *of* the world.

As a project of a particular human community then, universalism has remained a discourse on the ability of one's community to define, embody and uphold whatever it is that is deemed to be universal and the legitimacy of promoting it in the rest of the world. It is a claim about oneself as much as about the rest of the world, conditioned by a geopolitical narrative. If, in Ruggie's formulation, hegemony is the fusing of power and purpose, a unilateral universalist discourse extends this logic by rooting the avowed purpose in the power of attraction rather than power *tout court*.

I use the term *unilateral universalism* to convey the tension associated with the emanation of the universal from a single source. The idea that Europe (or the EU) can be and should be the sources of norms, values and standards applicable to the rest of the world has been enduring to say the least. Like the anthropic principle in cosmology, there is a strong and a weak version of European universalism. The strong version consists of the belief that the standards define Europe itself, its 'soul', its 'Enlightenment inheritance', and that Europe should actively be promoting them as an actor in its own right; whereas the weak version simply asserts that universally sourced values can be or happen to be (best?) promoted by Europeans.

Thus universalism as a project has historically been rooted in what may appear as its contradiction: exceptionalism, or the idea held by a given political community (group, nation, or group of nations) that it is uniquely predisposed by 'who we are' (history, values, culture) to spread these values/principles in the world. Exceptionalism then stands as the condition of possibility of unilateral universalism. To be sure, every nation considers itself somewhat exceptional, from the US as a 'City upon a Hill' to the Chinese eternal empire (how these exceptionalisms differ is a whole topic unto itself). 'Invented here', however, is not only a syndrome of the French and British descendants of those who stormed the Bastille and the Dartmouth to appropriate the brioche and Darjeeling tea. There are also those whose forefathers built the Parthenon and Westminster as they 'invented' democracy, while the Dutch 'invented' democratic peace, the Spaniards constitutionalized regionalism, the Italians the republic of cities. And while exceptionalism is the most widely shared European trait among its various nationalities, it has become the hallmark of the EU itself, all too often described as a unique achievement in human history: 'the most advanced experiment in multilateralism ever devised'[15] – not *a* model, but *the* model.

When José Manuel Barroso, President of the Commission, defined the EU as a 'moral power' he added an essentialist tone to the avowedly more neutral academic idea of the EU as a 'normative power'.[16] Indeed, Kant feared the goal of constitutionalizing ethics as dangerously totalizing,[17] a caution that may ultimately apply to the global constitutionalization of 'universalism' as a European moral project. Moralized universalist approaches have all too often been invoked pragmatically to legitimate harder forms of power discussed in this volume. But the point about either terminology is similar – to try to persuade interlocutors that European power is rooted in ideas not capacity, in ideational rather than material resources. In addition to the basic attempt at contrasting ideas and power, another more subtle shift underpins this discourse, from defending cooperation based on shared interests to one based on shared values or norms – from the conviction that what we do together ought to serve our mutual interests to the idea that it must be consistent with, grounded on *who we are*. Is this such a benign turn? Is it not the case that the politics of identity was precisely what the European Enlightenment (unsuccessfully) tried to escape? Thus the perennial question: to the extent that universalism is grounded in a certain moralism, is universalism the ultimate shared value, or on the contrary a rebranding of localized values?

Europe as a Would-Be Standard Setter: From Standards of Civilization to Standards of Accession

So, to what extent then is EUniversalism an echo of the brand of European universalism which drove the imperialism of yesteryear? European universalism certainly goes back a long way and exhibits a striking continuity in the idea of Europe as standard setter, the centre of a world hierarchically divided between the standard bearers of civilization and its un-less civilized periphery, itself assessed and ordered on the basis of these standards.[18]

We can find the germs of European universalism in late medieval, culturalist formulations of *Christian* fraternity, that is, in the notion that all Christians were created equal in the eyes of God (a claim echoed in Islamic thought). Over time, this universalism

> became increasingly inclusionary, grounded in the rediscovery of classical Stoic thought during the Renaissance, and the dawn of secularism. This transition can be conceived of as a shift from a Catholic with a capital 'C' to a catholic with a lower case 'c' understanding of human relationships and rights. Yet, even as universalism became more open, anyone wishing to partake of the enlarging human fraternity was expected to adopt Christian or post-Christian ideals.[19]

Thus until the eighteenth century, the European-as-international society was grounded on the assumption that only European Christian sovereigns could count as part of the international system of states, or more subtly, that a prerequisite for taking part in the 'international' system as a state in full sovereign standing was conformity with a particular religious and civilizational cultural community, namely that of Europe. That this vision clearly ignored much of European and world history of the preceding millennium remained inconsequential to the Eurocentric narrative which accompanied the early explosion of the Industrial Revolution.[20]

By the late eighteenth century however, aspirations to independence in some former colonies (e.g. the United States) combined with the growing interaction between European and non-European (non-white) communities in trade and commerce at the dawn of the New Imperialism made it necessary to rethink this radical dual premise and come up with some kind of modus vivendi with 'uncivilized Others'. Bridges needed to be built between the two orders by reconceptualizing the criteria of membership in international society. At the same time and on a more practical note, some kind of 'standard' was also required for 'protecting European life, liberty and property in sometimes hostile non-European countries.' Within Europe, however, the secularization of politics in the wake of the French Revolution and the decline of absolute monarchism had brought about a complex situation in which rights to statehood could no longer be based on merely religious terms and notions of a 'Public Law of Europe'. But while in Europe a plethora of organizational and political forms could give rise to sovereign statehood, even progressive thinkers could not imagine that European states should, faced with the seemingly 'savage' and 'backward' social and political practices encountered outside Europe, recognize non-European communities as politically equal and entitled to the privilege of non-intervention conferred upon states under the existing rules governing the European society of states.

In this sense, the recourse to the concept of a common 'European Civilization' (despite all existing differences) whose essential characteristics (its 'standard') could function as a guideline of development for non-European societies was a vehicle to bring into harmony the conflicting necessities of accepting internal diversity and justifying external intervention. So by the end of the eighteenth century, Europe had begun to define in non-religious terms what the 'entrance test' into the club of sovereign states should be. The result was a regime of interacting norms, some formal and others informal, which specified what it meant to be sufficiently 'civilized' and thus gain all or some of the privileges afforded to independent states, such as non-intervention, legal sovereignty, tax autonomy and so forth, as well as membership in emerging international organizations. By the late nineteenth century, these came to be referred to as 'standard of civilization' reflecting both a socio-legal as well as a moral attitude to non-European societies. While there is not one dominant conception as to a single and objective 'standard', these gained overwhelming acceptance and achieved an increasingly explicit status 'codified in treaties, articulated by the publicists, and embedded as a rule of customary international law',[21] which reflected domestic norms as to what 'good government' meant at the time. More specifically, Gong argues that at least five specific requirements formed part of the full-blown 'standard of civilization' at the beginning of the twentieth century and that, depending on a territory's ability to conform to those standards, it was classified as 'fit for sovereignty'. Thus, to qualify for membership in the international society, a state had to maintain: i) a guarantee of basic rights to locals and foreigners. Rights ordinarily considered 'basic' were those of property and commerce, and some freedom of life, religion and movement; ii) functioning political and administrative bureaucracy that could govern rationally and effectively maintain a monopoly of force through military capabilities; iii) a commitment to the rules and obligations of European international law – including the modern law of warfare – and a Western tradition of jurisprudence, that is a rational and efficient system of courts adjudicating in accordance with a written legal code that conforms to European conceptions of basic justice; iv) an adequate diplomatic system to ensure communication between sovereign states; v) a subjective notion that social and cultural customs and practices followed European ideas of morality and prudence. This meant for example that sati, polygamy, and slavery were considered 'uncivilized', and therefore unacceptable. Clearly these criteria were eminently subjective and left existing members of the European 'international society' with a wide margin of appreciation for rejecting membership on grounds of 'otherness'.

A universalist project starts from the presumption that it is legitimate to proselytize, actively 'export' one's values beyond one's shores – at least under the weak version discussed above – arrogate to oneself the responsibility to enforce presumed universal values abroad. How similar are the 'standards of civilization' which determined access to statehood in the nineteenth and early twentieth centuries and the EU's 'Copenhagen criteria' for accession and their corollary definition of 'good governance' – from the enumeration of democracy, human rights and the rule of law to the specific standards set against corruption, judicial independence or the freedom of the press? It could be argued that the latter belong to the panoply of conditionality used not only by the EU but most international organizations. But in the context of enlargement, such standards are not only or even mainly about making prudent loans. Rather, they are part of polity-building, something akin that is to the EU's version of 'manifest destiny' as shaped by the US when it was itself exploring its final frontiers a hundred years earlier. Both polities justified expansion in normative terms, the US by reaching its west coast and the EU by enlarging to the east, while at the same time both decreed a *droit de regard* over their southern neighbours (the Monroe Doctrine and the Barcelona Process). In the process, both essentialized their political project, by claiming for themselves a term that did not belong exclusively to them: EU-ization became Europeanization, and US-ization becomes Americanization. If the second part of the twentieth century has been dominated by another unilateral universalism, that emanating from the United States, and by the re-emergence at different times of counter-narratives of resistance from around the world, the two universalist projects echo one another in striking ways.

Contrary to the US, however, the EU does not only set standards in the context of its interaction with individual countries, candidates for membership or otherwise. Its standard-setting ambitions have continued to expand to the standards adopted by other regional groupings like the Mercosur, or much more recently the Economic Partnership Agreements (EPAs) signed with the ACP countries, as preconditions to inter-regional cooperation; European standard-setting has also extended to global level as many of the standards adopted by organizations such as the ISO, the FAO or even the WTO (e.g. the Singapore standards on competition and government procurement) emanate from the EU. Indeed, it is increasingly in the realm of linkage among standards – for instance between trade and environmental issues – that the EU has been able to claim first mover advantage and shape the debate in global norm setting. The resistance of most other countries to such a normative approach (which happens to correlate better with EU interests than with their own) among WTO members has been palpable.

Provincializing Westphalia: From Hierarchy to Negotiated Sovereignty?

But today's 'echoes of empire' do not arise only from European assertions of 'unilateral universalism', or from the setting of standards with universal claim – an aim which may be more or less reminiscent of nineteenth-century standards of civilization depending on one's analytical premise. They are echoes of another familiar trope as the EU and its member states engage in an altogether more radical project of universal scope and nature: the (re)definition and defence of alternative forms of sovereignties in line with what they see as 'the European model'.

In a nutshell, the argument goes as follows:

Mainstream international relations is welded to Waltz's conceptualization of international anarchy as the absence of world government and therefore the absence of hierarchy.[22] But this conceptualization fails to take into account the existence of power hierarchies not simply as differences in various states' capability to exercise sovereignty as Waltz sees it but as institutionalized differences in the very nature of such sovereignty.[23] Arguably, what the English school describes as the progressive expansion of European international society was in fact an evolution from a two-tiered international society into an increasingly 'global' international society after World War II.[24] Before decolonization, hierarchy was the name of the game: on one hand, a diplomatic system of *recognized* sovereignty – e.g. Westphalian toleration *within* Europe – and on the other, an imperial system of *denied or constrained sovereignty* characterized by hierarchy and the extra-territorial enforcement by colonial powers of special rights and privileges for their own nationals either directly or through capitulation treaties. In this context, the world would eventually be carved into sovereign states even if ideally, access to sovereign status was to be policed by Europe's standards of civilization. Europe's own civilizational wars during the first half of the twentieth century shattered this ambition.

Some would argue that the creation of the EU coincided with the abandonment of this dual pattern of order in the global system. After decolonization, the story goes, the two-tiered system disappeared. Indeed, if anything, we have witnessed an inversion of the prior pattern: Westphalian sovereignty has been rapidly globalized through self-determination while Europeans proceeded to construct a 'civilizing community' among themselves, aiming to civilize each other and justify mutual interference (the latter might be predicated on formal equality not colonization of say Southern Europe, but some observers might even recognize within the EU domination patterns that previously defined colonial relations).

And so here is the paradox of inversion: As Europeans finally succeeded in shaping the world according to their own former (Westphalian) image, a new message was starting to emanate from a new Europe, involving the abandonment of that image: integration across borders, the pooling of sovereignty and the legitimacy of mutual intervention in each other's internal matters. In short, *while deferential recognition of sovereignty was globalized from Europe outwards, civilizational intrusion was internalized within Europe.*

But the story does not stop here. Precisely because Europeans believe they have found and experimented among themselves with a superior form of negotiated sovereignty which can both defer to state interests and transcend them in the name of common interests and individual rights, the EU offers itself as a model and candidate for normative 'expansion' yet again: as Europeans move beyond Westphalia, they propose to take the world with them.[25]

And so, to articulate what is often left unsaid: after inversion must come convergence. The EU's very special brand of triangulation has brought us back to the same pattern of Eurocentric definition of the 'right kind of sovereignty' to be exported to the rest of the world – this time around neither unitary nor conditional but negotiated sovereignty. Indeed, the global system has been converging towards an uneasy mix of indivisible and conditional sovereignty, toleration and interference formally applicable to all under international law.

What is wrong with this picture, one may ask? Are we not evolving towards a truly universal system governed by common concerns for the welfare of all humanity mediated by negotiated sovereignty? The answer to this question is of course highly contested. But the gist of the problem is this. The convergence we are talking about here is hardly 'symmetric'. Elements of hierarchy (beyond mere asymmetries of power) continue to exist in the international system as various modes of coercion are discursively justified and then formalized. The US may not have been a colonial power but it has led this new game (as of course did the Soviet Union). Even if formal hierarchical structures and norms were overturned by the right to self-determination, the new legal order bestowed rather minimal conditions of sovereignty on post-colonial states. Not all sovereigns are born equal. Most 'Third World states' were born insecure and treated as such.[26] The very term 'Third World' for decolonized states framed the construction of such a ranking after decolonization and even the end of the Cold War did not fundamentally change the asymmetry of global security or financial regimes.

And so, the brand of sovereignty 'exported' by the EU may have changed but its mode of promotion continues to exhibit similar forms of uni-directionality.

Moreover, when going global, Europeans (or the West) do not always export 'negotiated sovereignty' but an old familiar form of asymmetrically conditional sovereignty.[27] If sovereignty simply means that recognized states are considered the legitimate location for good politics and the pursuit of economic development, the patterns of EU–ACP relations discussed above do not exhibit a symmetrical regard.[28] In the more extreme cases, we may applaud the duty to intervene contained in the 2005 UN convention on the responsibility to protect; but it is not aimed within European or US borders. Within the EU, coercive interference and intervention has remained taboo, whether in the context of internal conflicts as in Ireland, Spain or Cyprus, or in the context of perceived human rights or rule of law violations in specific member states. And of course EU states would never let non-EU 'outsiders' intervene in their internal conflicts. Arguably the very idea of 'weak' or 'failed' states to justify intervention in post-colonial states contributes to perpetuating the weakness of these states in ways that would be unthinkable for, say, Belgium.[29]

The fate of the term 'civilization' itself is enlightening in this regard. The decolonization era led to the reframing of the civilizing mission as 'the modernizing mission' in order to seek to convey the 'objective connotation' lacking in the former (although ideas of clash of civilizations and the war on terror sought to rehabilitate the notion of civilizational divide). And indeed, as far as self-perception goes, the notion of civilizing as a project continues to characterize the source itself – the EU as a *civilian power* is not quite yet a 'civilized power' itself, but an actor restricting itself to 'civilizing' others through non-imperialist, e.g. 'civilian', means of external action.

Surely, however, there are fundamental differences between the two sequential systems of attempted expansion of European society? Consider both *intent* – what European actors seek to do – and *consent* – what those outside the EU do of their own volition in the context of enlargement, for instance. One would argue that the implications for EU candidates of disregarding EU prescriptions have little to do with the implications of disregarding the 'standard of civilization' in the nineteenth century which effectively determined whose sovereignty was to be respected: non-compliant societies were considered unfit for self-government per se so that no sovereign state was supposed to be obliged to respect that society as independent. The EU criteria, in contrast, merely function as incentives that if fulfilled will confer certain benefits upon the complying non-EU state. The EU does not settle questions of recognition on the criteria of international law alone, or on everyone else's behalf. And of course, presumably, countries can choose to become members or not. But is such a choice real given the structural constraints created by the EU in its part of the world? Were there genuine alternatives to enlargement for East and Central European countries? As Dimitar Bechev discusses in his chapter, these questions have a different connotation in the centre or the periphery of the EU.

Conclusion: The Post-Colonial Aspiration or the Redemption of Europe

So the EU has worked hard to make the world believe in the story of its virgin birth. Colonialism, *moi?* But even with genuine redirection towards its own internal project flanked by what I have termed policies of atonement, it cannot escape the echoes of its own colonialism and pretend that it is possible to simply engage in messianic universalism all over again as if nothing had happened in a previous historical era. Those who see intriguing parallels between the old *mission civilisatrice* and EUniversalism do not simply suffer from post-colonial stress disorder, the infamous imperial guilt derided by well-meaning liberal interventionists. *Europe, pas tout à fait la même, pas tout à fait une autre*, as the poet might have said gazing at the EU in light of its colonial shadow.

This does not mean that Europe, and its current incarnation as the EU, is trapped in a never-ending neo-colonial role. Beyond the critique of Eurocentrism – which is certainly not new – what would it take for the EU to act as a genuine 'post-colonial' power, self-reflexive about the echoes of colonialism and legitimate in the eyes of other countries?

In his preface to Fanon's *Les Damnés de la terre*, Sartre writes, 'We too, the people of Europe are being decolonized [...] let us look at ourselves if we dare and see what we become'. To dare and see ought indeed be the starting point of any post-colonial exploration. And in this realm, the journey must start with self-reflexivity, that is, the ability to reflect critically and openly upon both discourse and practice, the systematic questioning of the assumptions behind one's methods, and the capacity to draw lessons from outside one's world – whether from the past or from the perceptions of others. Some would argue that such self-reflexivity is exactly what *l'Europe éternelle* is all about. They will say that it is the Renaissance that made self-doubt synonymous with modernity, as rooted in the scientific tradition of inquiry going back to ancient Greece. Perhaps. But they forget that Buddhists, Confucians and many other unrecorded individuals and groups practised systematic self-doubt well before Europeans, albeit perhaps under different social and epistemic conditions. More importantly, even if there is no dearth of self-doubt in Europe in this crisis era, somehow, the state of mind seems to wither away when it comes to engaging with its ex-colonial domain. Ask our non-European partners engaged in 'partnership' negotiations, the story told by Jones and Weinhardt in this volume.

To be sure, the 'post-colonial ethos' does not belong to Europeans. It would indeed be the ultimate irony of Eurocentrism to 'steal' post-colonialism from those who have so struggled under its banner. While thinkers like Fanon, Foucault and Said provided crucial initial inspiration, those 'at the origin' of the post-colonial movement were usually fiction writers from ex-colonial countries, whose literary narratives carried a great deal of political significance.[30] These authors were joined by migrants to the west with a strong sense of coming from cultural and political peripheries who did not accept a seamless integration into their new society. Instead, 'armed with the aura of the activism and empowerment of the national liberation movements, they began to ask awkward questions about western history and the implicit assumptions of western knowledge.'[31] Thus, the original post-colonial ethos is marked by an imperative of 'decentring', privileging as it does the margin and migrants over the centre and settlers, the ubiquity of resistance to elite domination on the part of the subaltern and the weak, radical thinking about gender and modernity, the deconstruction of identities as contingent, the emphasis on subjectivity, and the sensitivity of the cast-aside and the concern to see through their eyes.

In recent years, as the field of post-colonial studies has progressively evolved from the particular to the abstract, from local narratives to apprehensions of global cultural and political relations, from the assertion of resistance to embracing hybridity, and from Third World to perspectives escaping ascription and localization, the potential for dialogue with more mainstream IR as well as European studies has also progressively widened (inter alia, Loomba,[32] Huggan and Law[33]). In this area of dialogue, Europe emerges as a complex space, 'which is often imagined and oblivious of its politics of inclusion and exclusion towards migrants, asylum seekers and refugees, as well as of its take on internal conflicts, political transitions and cosmopolitan imaginary'.[34] Yes, it is this obliviousness which we must challenge.

The question remains: If the EU is our agenda, do we necessarily need to follow Dipesh Chakrabarty who calls for Third World histories to be written in a way that marginalizes Europe instead of being simply variants of a master narrative in which Europe remains the subject?[35] Or should we side with Darby who argues that 'the project of marginalizing Europe runs the risk of failing to recognize how much of what was once European has found a place outside Europe and in a sense has become non-European'?[36] The fact is that whatever the dark side of European universalism, we have inherited our understanding of globality from Europe, as Postel-Vinay argues in this volume.

In my view, a 'responsible Europe' ought to be a genuinely post-colonial Europe which does not itself define alone the terms of its own responsibilities. A post-colonial agenda for EU action must be inspired by the ethos of decentring and the adoption of signposts, standards or mindsets to transcend colonial patterns.

One such requisite is to relentlessly demand 'mutuality' between nations or groups, as the obvious opposite referent to colonial patterns of domination and unilateralism. Mutuality implies institutionalized symmetry between actors – if not equality per se given structural asymmetries of power. It can be obtained at many levels. At its most structural, it refers to mutual recognition both in diplomatic and ethical terms, or the idea that processes of recognition ought necessarily to be reciprocal.

Secondly, it implies that understandings of 'free trade', 'human rights' or 'the rule of law' are shared and fine-tuned within multilateral institutions; it underpins the belief that the promotion of avowed universal norms by powerful states without the bedrock of true procedural multilateralism in the end undermines the original claim to universalism.[37] Thirdly, and in the absence of multilateral options, mutuality means some degree of systematic acceptance of influence within each other's polities whereby the inclusion of others is mutually conditioned.[38] Finally, it means if nothing else that the EU is expected to be consistent between its internal and external legal credo. This imperative of consistency – the idea that what we do should reflect who we are – is at the core of EU civilian power thinking, requiring that the EU follow its own guiding principles when acting beyond its borders: integration, prevention, mediation, and persuasion. It would be hard to argue that such consistency is in practice the hallmark of European universalism.

At the same time, a post-colonial agenda for Europe must be bound up with 'empowerment', for lack of a more original term. We always need to ask to what extent external action empowers (certain) local actors to create their own version of this universal ideal – as opposed to receiving a specific and unilateral 'transplant' from the metropole, as it were. EUniversalism may look fine and acceptable when we simply contrast it with parochialism and relativism, or worse, the sovereign right of authoritarian regimes to harm their citizens as they please. But it no longer seems so fine if we contrast it with a true pluralism, where the universal is grounded on the stories and experience of all.

We cannot deny the structural realities of today's global system, its fundamentally hierarchical nature and the asymmetries of power that underlie contemporary international relations, including in the EU's external relations. A relationship of 'influence' by definition involves an element of inequality and hierarchy. But the discourse of the EU-as-a-model has often been grounded in a sense of superior normative or cognitive power which Europeans somehow feel and believe continues to be their prerogative. This is where self-reflexivity is in order, and this is where the Eurocrisis may become a game changer. It may be the case that EU actors learn from the other side not just how the EU model may best be adapted to fit their context, but how the EU model itself may be enhanced based on the experience of other states, regions and peoples. The liberal core of the EU and the pluralist nature of its politics are certainly a good ground to build from.

Notes

1 A preliminary version of this chapter was presented at the conference 'Beyond Westphalia', University of Oxford, 2008. For the input, I would like to thank my co-editors, Berny Sèbe and Gabrielle Maas, as well as Tobias Lenz, Nora Fisher Onar, Juri Viehoff and Andrew Hurrell.

2 For a discussion see N. Fisher Onar and K. Nicolaïdis, 'The Decentering Agenda: Rethinking Europe in a Non-European World', in *Conflict and Cooperation*, Special Issue on Normative Power Europe, 48, 2 (June 2013).

3 See K. Nicolaïdis, 'The Power of the Superpowerless', in T. Lindberg (ed.), *Beyond Paradise and Power: Europe, America, and the Future of a Troubled Partnership* (New York, NY, 2004), pp. 93–120.

4 On these themes, see I. Manners, 'Normative Power Europe: A Contradiction in Terms?', *Journal of Common Market Studies*, 40, 2 (2002), pp. 235–58. See also K. Nicolaïdis and R. Howse, '"This is my EUtopia…": Narrative as Power', *Journal Of Common Market Studies*, Special Anniversary Issue, 40, 4 (2002), pp. 767–92; and the contributions in K. Nicolaïdis and R. Whitman, 'Normative Power Europe Revisited', *Conflict and Cooperation*, Special Issue, 48, 2 (2013).

5 J. Kent, *The Internationalization of Colonialism: Britain, France, and Black Africa, 1939–1956* (Oxford, 1992).

6 Council of Europe, *The Strasbourg Plan*, Secretariat-General Council of Europe (Strasbourg, 1952). Quoted in Hansen and Jonsson, this volume.

7 For a discussion in the context of Algeria, see T. Shepard, *The Invention of Decolonization: The Algerian War and the Remaking of France* (Ithaca, NY, 2006).

8 See R. Kleinfeld and K. Nicolaïdis, 'Can a Post-Colonial Power Export the Rule of Law? Elements of a General Framework', in G. Palombella and N. Walker (eds), *Relocating the Rule of Law* (Oxford, 2009), pp. 139–70.

9 See C. Bickerton (ed.), *European Union Foreign Policy: From Effectiveness to Functionality* (Basingstoke, 2011).

10 See, inter alia, A. Forster, 'No Entry: Britain and the EEC in the 1960s', *Contemporary British History*, 12, 2 (1998), pp. 139–46; *A. Moravcsik*, 'De Gaulle Between Grain and Grandeur: The Political Economy of French EC Policy, 1958–1970', *Journal of Cold War Studies*, 2, 3 (2000), pp. 4–68.

11 A. Césaire, *Discours sur le colonialisme* (Paris, 1955).

12 P. Bruckner, *Le Sanglot de l'homme blanc. Tiers monde, culpabilité, haine de soi* (Paris, 1983).

13 This was also reflected in François Mitterrand's *Discours de La Baule* (20 June 1990). For a discussion see R. Youngs, *The European Union and Democracy Promotion: A Critical Global Assessment* (Baltimore, MD, 2010); See also R. Kleinfeld and K. Nicolaïdis, 'Can a Post-Colonial Power Export the Rule of Law?'.

14 Nicolaïdis and Howse, '"This is my EUtopia…"'.

15 The Rt Hon Chris Patten, Commissioner for External Relations, 'How National is the National Interest?' English-Speaking Union: Churchill Lecture. Guildhall, London, 30 April 2002.

16 I. Manners, 'Normative Power Europe', pp. 235–58. For a set of critical appraisals of the concept see Nicolaïdis and Whitman (eds), *Conflict and Cooperation*, Special Issue, 48, 2 (2013).

17 Z. Laidi, *Norms over Force: The Enigma of European Power* (2000), p. 179.

18 E. Keene, *Beyond the Anarchical Society: Grotius, Order, and Colonialism in International Politics* (Cambridge, 2002).

19 N. Fisher Onar, 'Transcending Universalism? Trajectories for Human Rights in a Post-Western World', in Simon Bennett and Éadaoin O'Brien (eds), *What Future for Human Rights in a Non-Western World?* (2012).

20 J. Hobson, 'Is Critical Theory always for the White West and for Western Imperialism? Beyond Westphalian, towards a Post-Racist Critical IR', *Review of International Studies*, 33 (2007), pp. 91–116.

21 G. W. Gong, *The Standard of Civilization in International Society* (Oxford, 1984). To be sure, such standards of civilization may have been the bread and butter of the legal community in France and Britain, but were far from universally accepted – recall the anecdote of Clémenceau's reluctance to use the concept of civilization since he knew that Germans were bound to use it to demonstrate French inferiority.

22 K. Waltz, *Theory of International Politics* (1979).

23 J. Hobson and J. C. Sharman, 'The Enduring Place of Hierarchy in World Politics: Tracing the Social Logics of Hierarchy and Political Change', *European Journal of International Relations*, 11, 1 (2005).

24 Keene, *Beyond the Anarchical Society*; see also H. Spruyt, 'The End of Empire and the Extension of the Westphalian System: The Normative Basis of the Modern State Order', *International Studies Review*, 2, 2 (2000), pp. 65–92.

25 Ironically, the EU is most often guilty of not practising what it preaches, making for instance the relative closure of its external boundaries close to non-negotiable when so many analysts have argued that a system of circular migration would be good for all sides, including as dictated by demographic imperatives (in 30 years the EU will need 50 million more persons given labour needs unfulfilled by migrants).

26 M. Ayoob, *The Third World Security Predicament: State Making, Regional Conflict, and the International System* (Boulder, CO, 1995).

27 S. Krasner, *Sovereignty: Organised Hypocrisy* (Princeton, NJ, 1999).

28 D. Williams, 'Aid and Sovereignty: Quasi-States and International Financial Institutions', *Review of International Studies*, 26, 4 (2000), pp. 557–73.

29 S. N. Grovogui, 'Regimes of Sovereignty: International Morality and the African Condition', *European Journal of International Relations*, 8, 3 (2002), pp. 315–38.

30 P. Darby, 'Pursuing the Political: A Post-Colonial Rethinking of Relations International', *Millennium*, 33, 1 (2004), pp. 1–32; M. Majumdar, *Postcoloniality* (Oxford, 2007).

31 I. Young, *Inclusion and Democracy* (Oxford, 2002).

32 A. Loomba, *Colonialism, Post Colonialism* (New York, NY, 1998).

33 G. Huggan and I. Law, *Racism Postcolonialism Europe* (Liverpool, 2009).

34 See for instance the network of scholars in PEN (Postcolonial Europe Network); also G. Huggan (ed.), 'Post-Colonial Europe', *Moving Worlds*, Special Issue, 11, 2 (2011).

35 D. Chakrabarty, *Provincializing Europe: Postcolonial Thought and Historic Difference* (Princeton, NJ, 2007).

36 Darby, 'Pursuing the Political', p. 24.

37 R. Rao, *Third World Protest: Between Home and the World* (Oxford, 2012).

38 M. Young, *Inclusion and Democracy* (Oxford, 2001).

Epilogue:
Chinese Empire Meets the West:
A Centennial Conundrum for China

Zhu Liqun and Feng Jicheng

There has been an increasing amount of debate among scholars in international relations over the relationship between China and international society,[1] and China's present identity in particular. Some contend that China is a status quo power,[2] while others argue that China is still a revisionist.[3] We attempt to provide some insight into this question by examining the legacies of the Chinese Empire, and Western colonialism and imperialism within China. Focusing on the interactions between China and the West, we pay special attention to the impact of those interactions in the past century and a half on China's definition of its identity in terms of its relationship with international society. We argue that China, with its traditional identity as the centre of the Chinese tribute system, has undergone a miserable and tortuous quest for its new identity following the intrusion of Western imperialism. The chapter will first look at the legacy of the Chinese Empire, then go on to discuss the details of its encounters with the West and its journey in search of a coherent identity. Finally, we examine China's redefinition of its identity as an integral part of the existing international society.

The Legacy of the Chinese Empire

With the unification of seven states in 221 BC, ancient China naturally evolved into a hierarchical feudal empire which was for more than 2,000 years, with the exception of certain periods, highly unified and centralized. Politically, it enjoyed a highly centralized monarchy with a hierarchical order between the imperial ruler and subjects, and strived for great unity within the empire. This hierarchical order was extremely stable and efficient thanks to its organization on a feudal economic model of self-sufficient small-scale farming. Farming was valued while commerce was discouraged. This hierarchy was justified and further stabilized by the dominant ideology of Confucianism to which *li* (rites or proprieties) and *ren* (benevolence) were central. Rituals were the norms governing people's conduct and were observed by the ancient Chinese in regulating relations with others according to their different roles in society – for instance ruler and subject, father and son or husband and wife – with the latter respectively subordinate to the former. The practice of benevolent policies, according to Confucians, had everything to do with the prosperity and stability of the empire.[4] In order to practise benevolence, Chinese people at that time turned to self-cultivation[5] to set a good example for others to follow, and self-restraint to remain faithful to Confucian proprieties. As a result, the social structure of imperial China turned into a concentric one within which self-restraint was the starting point of ethical relations.[6] So ethics was more important than law, and the cultivation of profound individual character was the key to the stability of the social order.

The domestic social order was also reflected in imperial China's international relations with other polities. This was the tribute system, with China as the Middle Kingdom at the centre and various tributary states at the periphery. It was a virtually self-contained system. Because of the political and cultural pre-eminence of the Middle Kingdom, the system operated such that peripheral states gave 'deference and tribute, whilst receiving legitimizing investiture and gifts in return, but also being left pretty much under their own rule'.[7] This system was clearly different from the Westphalian order. It was governed not by the norm of sovereignty but by the idea of *Tianxia* (All under Heaven) and the management of *guanxi* (relationships). The Chinese of the time, due to their long isolation from the rest of the world and their limited knowledge of world geography, believed that China was the only civilized state in the 'world' and that all others were 'barbarians'. China in this system 'encompassed other units while leaving them considerable room for manoeuvre'.[8] Engaging in *guanxi* with 'barbarians' was seen as a means of exposing others to the Chinese level of civilization. The tribute system was not operated under a balance of power or power politics either. Although China was at the time the only big power within the tribute system, it conducted a reciprocal relationship with outlying states by rewarding magnanimously the tributes paid by vassal states.[9] The Chinese Empire even chose to sacrifice profits in this kind of 'tributary trade'[10] for the sake of safety and security along its borders. It required the tributary states to pay periodic homage but exercised self-restraint in its use of power by giving autonomy to those junior states instead of conquering them, and carried out 'self-cultivation' with the aim of acting as a benign power by ordering its own kingdom well. As such, the tribute system, which combined 'formal hierarchy and informal equality', brought peace and stability to East Asia.[11]

However, the type of principal and subordinate relationship between imperial China and tributary states occasionally resulted in resistance, though political and military domination and resistance were not distinctive features of the tribute system[12] compared with the European international system. The tribute system was also a closed one which confined the vision of the Chinese to the 'world' they knew and encouraged them to value their own order at the expense of alternatives. This meant that when imperial China actually did begin to fall from its strength and prosperity of the eighteenth century, it took a long time for it to recognize its decline – not to mention the great changes taking place in the Western world.[13]

The outbreak of the Opium Wars shook the order. The tribute system was gradually dismantled and replaced by the treaty system, which imposed a series of unequal treaties on China.[14] The long-term peace and stability that imperial China had cultivated for centuries was destroyed by the arrival of Western-style imperialism.[15] China's traditional identity as the centre of the tribute system was forced to change. Under the power politics of gunboat diplomacy conducted by Western powers, some open-minded Chinese officials and scholars began to acknowledge the superiority of Western weapons and to advocate fighting imperialist aggression by attempting to emulate this advanced Western technology. Since then, China has undergone a bitter quest for its identity and has made great efforts to learn, adapt and conform to the norms and rules governing an international society dominated by Western powers. In this process, it has experienced a miserable three-phase transformation: the loss of its traditional identity, a tortuous search for its new identity and a reconstruction of its identity as an integral member of the existing international society.

Identity Lost with Western Invasions

The outbreak of the first Opium War in 1840 ushered in the phase during which China gradually lost its traditional identity through its encounter with Western powers. The humiliating unequal treaties forced on China in the wake of the aggressive war began to transform it from a complete and independent feudal empire into a semi-colony. In face of the stunning change and the weakness exposed by China's defeat at the hands of Western powers, some open-minded officials and scholars advocated learning from the West and its advanced technology, and subsequently carried out a programme of modernization known as the Yangwu (foreign matters) Movement in order to build military power and shield the Qing dynasty from further foreign aggression.[16]

This endeavour of building Chinese might was proved a failure by 'China's stinging defeat in the Sino-Japanese War of 1894', which 'fully exposed the impotence of the Qing government and spelt an end to the movement'.[17] The unequal Treaty of Shimonoseki (1895) forced by Japan on the Qing government further worsened China's status as a semi-colony. The insulting reality of China's defeat by its former tributary state impelled enlightened scholars to reform the old feudal regime. They initiated the Reform Movement in 1898, attempting to go beyond merely copying Western military science and technology as advocated by the Modernization Movement in order to transform China's political system into a constitutional monarchy by adopting Western bourgeois thought and culture.[18] As history unfolded, their efforts also proved ineffectual. This failure further exposed the decay of the Qing government and served as a valuable lesson that reform within the old political framework would not work.

With mounting external aggression and internal crises in the late nineteenth and the early twentieth centuries, and especially the encroachment by the eight-power allied forces in 1900, more and more Chinese patriots became disillusioned with the feudal monarchy because of its powerlessness to resist foreign partition of China, as well as the darkness and decay exposed during the suppression of the internal extremist patriotic movement (the Boxer Movement) in 1901. They finally turned to revolution as the only way out for China. Revolutionaries under the leadership of Dr Sun Yat-sen, who drew his own political ideas from the French and American bourgeois revolutions, concluded from the painful failures of the Reform Movement and the harsh realities in China that the nation could be saved only by overthrowing the Qing dynasty and replacing it with a bourgeois democratic republic.[19] They staged the revolution of 1911 and succeeded in overthrowing the feudal monarchy that had ruled China for over 2,000 years. However, the revolution did not touch the presence of foreign domination. China was still a semi-colony partitioned and exploited by foreign imperialist powers.

China's participation in World War I in 1917 on the victorious side did not bring any change to its semi-colonial status either. China's legitimate demands were rejected at the Paris Peace Conference. The treaty settlement had transferred all former German possessions and privileges in China to Japan. This unfair treatment triggered the indignation of Beijing students and sparked the May Fourth Movement, a patriotic mass protest against foreign imperialism and internal traitors. This anti-imperialist uprising simultaneously upheld the slogan of 'Smash the Confucian Shop', and brought an upsurge in the cultural movement against Confucian ideas.[20]

As such, from 1840 to 1919, China's position in the world had collapsed from an empire at the centre of the tribute system to a marginal state of Western-led international society,[21] a semi-colony under the domination of Western and Japanese imperialism. In the process of interacting with these powers, China had strongly felt its inferiority to them in matters ranging from technology to institutions and even to culture. All this had contributed to a sharp psychological decline recognized throughout the Chinese population. Moreover, the harsh critique of Confucianism represented a complete repudiation of China's traditional culture and a loss of identity.

In the process of self-negation, China's perception of Western-led international society mixed admiration with indignation. On the one hand, China was impressed by the military strength demonstrated by Western powers and became gradually aware of advanced Western institutions and industrial civilization. Indeed, this had driven some open-minded officials and scholars to learn and employ advanced Western technology, science and even political systems as exemplified by the Modernization Movement, the Reform Movement of 1898 and the Revolution of 1911.[22] On the other hand, China perceived that Western powers were aggressive and ready to use force and power politics as necessary means, and ruthlessly imposed a series of unequal treaties on China. In China's eyes, Western powers betrayed the norms of equality and sovereignty that they had advertised with the purpose of turning China into a political dependency.[23]

In brief, China, gradually awakened by the superiority of industrialized civilization shown by Western military strength, started to learn from the West in various ways, yet only to find itself once again bullied and humiliated by foreign powers. From its unequal interactions with the West, China learned the lesson that 'lagging behind leaves one vulnerable to attacks', thus setting anti-imperialism, national revitalization and modernization as its objectives.

The Tortuous Quest for a New Identity

The May Fourth Movement of 1919 in China represents a turning point in the hard journey towards the rebuilding or redefinition of a national identity. After the collapse of the restored feudal monarchy, China fell under the rule of reactionary warlords backed up by various foreign powers which ruthlessly robbed Chinese people and fought incessantly among themselves, bringing chaos to the country and untold suffering to the people. Although efforts were made to revise the unequal treaties with foreign powers, few results were achieved.[24] The unchanged semi-colonial status resulted in China's continued suffering from chronic exploitation by foreign powers. Later on, Chiang Kai-shek turned against the revolution launched by the revolutionary nationalist government against the northern warlords, and started to rule China with reactionary despotism.[25] The already harsh political reality was worsened by the invasion of imperialist Japan in the 1930s. The Japanese occupation of a large part of Chinese territory further intensified the mounting social and political crisis in China at this time.

The great danger of national extinction, coupled with internal political darkness, made Chinese people acutely aware of their national identity, giving rise to a discourse on China's relationship with international society as embodied by the cultural debate in the 1930s. It was nominally a debate about the development of Chinese culture but actually reflected ideological uncertainty about China's identity in its relationship with international society, which was the continuation of past discussions about whether China should keep its traditional culture or be westernized. One school argued that China had lost its cultural particularities and that their revival could only be achieved through cultural restoration. This argument immediately attracted criticism from those who alleged that what its advocates regarded as the essence of Chinese culture actually referred to the old feudal ethical principles such as 'three cardinal guides and five constant virtues'.[26] The opposing school contended that culture could not be divided and wholesale westernization was the only way out for China.[27] This idea also drew much criticism, arguing that different national conditions led to different cultures. Therefore the history, customs and habits of a country had to be taken into account in learning from the West.[28]

In essence, the core issues behind this polemic over Chinese cultural restoration or wholesale westernization were: what kind of relationship existed between China and international society and what was the value system behind each kind of relationship? Put differently, what kind of identity should China adopt in its relationship with international society? How should China be positioned within international society? Fung Yu-Lan, a well-known scholar of Chinese philosophy and culture, argued that it was imperative for China to be modernized and to learn from the West, and that modernization was not the same as westernization. He argued: 'We used to talk about westernization, but now we talk about modernization. This is not just a change of term. It suggests that the reason why western culture was considered to be superior is because it is modern not because it is western.'[29] This was the first time that a third way was advocated for China. This idea of modernization profoundly influenced the Chinese Communist Party (CCP) and China's later choice.

In the struggle for the final liberation of China, the CCP, since its founding in 1921, strongly upheld the banner of anti-imperialism and anti-feudalism and finally founded the People's Republic of China (PRC) after 28 years of tremendous struggle. After the founding of new China in 1949, the Chinese people felt great dignity in defining its national identity. However, the first 30 years after its foundation witnessed a tense relationship between China and the West. China was alienated from Western-dominated international society and in most ways remained an outsider in the struggle for its rightful place in the family of nations.

This identity as an outsider can be attributed to four main factors: the configuration of the international system, Sino-Soviet relations, the policy of the CCP towards the legacy of imperialism, and the central leadership's perception of the then international situation. The first two systemic factors to a great extent produced constraints from which it was difficult for China to escape in its interaction with international society as it then was. The other two domestic factors, which interacted with the systemic ones, also greatly affected the formation of China's identity.

The PRC was founded amidst the hostility created by the fierce confrontation of the Cold War between the two blocs led by the capitalist United States and the socialist Soviet Union. 'By 1949, political, ideological and strategic clashes between the two superpowers had been crystallized after two years of intense Cold War and the division of Europe. World politics was highly dichotomized.'[30] The tensions between the two blocs provided little possibility for 'New China as a Communist state to be accommodated into the American-dominated international society'.[31] The United States, unresigned to its policy defeat in supporting the KMT government, pursued an all-encompassing containment policy towards China effected through political non-recognition, economic embargo and military blockade.

Under such a systemic framework, China had no other alternative but to make an assertive foreign policy choice: lean to one side. That is, to stand on the side of the Soviet-led socialist camp so as to win recognition and support from the socialist countries and prevent the American-led Western camp from subverting the newly born government. Of course, ideological homogeneity and historical relations between the CCP and the Communist Party of the Soviet Union made it easier and reasonable for the CCP to make this decision. On 30 June 1949, in commemoration of the 28th anniversary of the CCP, Mao Zedong wrote: 'The lean-to-one-side policy has been taught to us by Sun Yat-sen's 40-year experience and the 28-year experience of the Chinese Communist Party. We know well if we are to win victory and consolidate it, we must lean to one side [...] the side of imperialism or to the side of socialism [...] there is no third way.'[32] Furthermore, China at that time, weak and poor, was in great need of capital, technology and equipment to rehabilitate its economy and enhance the livelihood of its population. In the face of the economic blockade and trade embargo pursued by the American-led alliance, China could only turn to the socialist states for assistance. It was under such circumstances that Mao Zedong went to Moscow in December 1949 and the Treaty of Friendship, Alliance and Mutual Assistance was signed in February 1950 between the two countries.[33] China therefore became an ally of the Soviet Union, which recognized the newly established government and provided it with invaluable assistance, including 'machinery and equipment, advisers, blueprints and other technical information'.[34]

The policy of leaning to the Soviet side had a great influence on China's economic development and political organization. The CCP adopted the Soviet developmental model, resulting from the fact that China's aspirations of conducting economic cooperation with the United States had been dashed by American anti-communism policy. Just as importantly, to build socialism from scratch was an entirely new cause. China badly needed Soviet aid and experience in building a socialist country.[35] As such, the economic structure of the Soviet Union was taken as a model, representing a planned economy and single public ownership, and focusing on the development of heavy industry. This planned and centralized economy in return strengthened the needs of a centralized government. Inevitably, this blind copying of the Soviet model without due regard to China's own conditions resulted in many problems.[36] By the mid 1950s, especially when the ideological polemics between the CCP and the Communist Party of the Soviet Union (CPSU) broke out in 1956, the CCP began to reflect on its development on the basis of specific circumstances in China.[37]

In addition to the lean-to-one-side policy, China pursued rigorous foreign policies with respect to the legacy of imperialism in China, and particularly the unequal treaties that had made it possible for imperialist powers to continue to dominate China and prevent it from gaining national independence and sovereignty. The resulting policies were titled as 'start anew' and 'clean our house thoroughly before inviting guests'.[38] The former policy meant that the newly established PRC 'would not recognize any old diplomatic relations established by the KMT government with other countries. [New China] will negotiate with those countries for the establishment of diplomatic relations on new terms. Diplomatic personnel from those countries could only be treated as foreign residents in China'.[39] The 'clean our house' policy posited that New China should 'eliminate all prerogatives and influences of imperialist powers in China and establish new diplomatic relations with countries across the world on the basis of mutual respect of sovereignty and territorial integrity, equality and mutual benefit'.[40] These policies were perceived by the United States as a 'repudiation of its [China's] international obligations',[41] though the 'obligations' were actually the prerogatives that the United States enjoyed under the unequal treaty system. In any case, these policies were used by the United States to justify its non-recognition of the PRC.[42]

The fourth factor was the central leadership's perception of the world situation at the time. Judging from the international hostility that China was facing, the early CCP Chinese leaders believed that the main themes of the times were revolution and war. Another world war was inevitable. Thus, the CCP consistently held that the Chinese Revolution constituted one part of the world revolution. Top priority was given to the task of anti-imperialism. Following the ideological debate between the CCP and the CPSU and the subsequent Sino-Soviet split which culminated in military conflict in 1969, China was fighting against two imperialist powers, which objectively alienated it further from international society. Partly because of this, China was perceived by the West as a revisionist of international society. This perception of China was further hardened when leftist thinking won out in the CCP during the period of the Cultural Revolution, in which the PRC 'exported revolution' to the developing world. Faced with grave threats from the two superpowers, the PRC called for an international united front against both superpowers and advocated revolutionary changes in the existing international system.[43] Such a radical approach to the international system was later proved to be against China's national interests, and national security in particular.

The interplay of the four factors resulted in the separation of China from international society for at least two decades after its founding. First contained and encircled by the American-led West and later threatened by both the Soviet Union and the United States, China was compelled to develop its relations out of the then international system with the newly independent countries in Asia, Africa and Latin America by giving moral and/or material support to their national liberation movements. Although it aspired to become an equal member of the Western-dominated international society, China was forced to remain largely an outsider.

The 1970s witnessed some changes in the international environment in which China moved. The PRC's acquisition of a seat in the UN General Assembly and Security Council signalled its formal entrance into the international system. And the improvement of China's relationship with the United States starting from the early 1970s also predicted greater acceptance of China as an equal member in the family of nations. The imminent and predominant threat from the Soviet Union impelled China to play down its revolutionary identity in order to align itself with the United States in the interests of national security, since the United States was the only rival to the Soviet Union. But all this did not bring much change to China's international status, since the United States did not formally recognize China until 1979 and the United Nations was in fact a tool manipulated by the two dominant powers. Nevertheless, these changes suggested the advent of a critical transformation in China's approach to the existing international system.

Responsible Stakeholder of International Society

The adoption of a policy of reform and opening up in 1978 marked a turning point in China's approach to its relations with and identity within international society. As it implemented the policy in a gradual progression, China has experienced a transition from 'incomplete participation' to 'full participation' in the existing international system.[44] For China, it has been a gradual learning process of socialization into existing international norms. In this process, China's identity has been reconstructed and consolidated, transformed from an outsider into a responsible stakeholder of international society.

This change in identity has been made possible by the transformation of Chinese perceptions of the main issues of the times, moving from a perception of the world as one of revolution and war to one of peace and development. In the 1980s, Deng Xiaoping helped change the previous worldview by pointing out that peace and development were the main goals of the world. Deng held that another world war could be avoided and would not break out[45] since nuclear deterrence prevented the occurrence of big wars between great powers and the profound social reforms within Western societies had brought stability. His view dramatically changed the earlier judgement of the world situation and helped China to embark on a new road.[46] In spite of the negative events that China has experienced in recent times, such as the Tiananmen incident in 1989 and the Belgrade bombing incident in 1999, its basic understanding of the current world situation has not changed. Rather, its perception of the world has been extended and deepened in recent years. Cooperation, in addition to peace and development, is conceived as the theme and trend of the world.[47]

This change in perception of the world situation constitutes a precondition for the transformation of China's domestic and foreign policies. Domestically, based on this new understanding of the world, China – discarding the ideology of 'taking class struggle as the principle'[48] – has decided to transfer its focus to economic development and started opening up to the outside world. Internationally, China has abandoned its former policy of taking ideology as a criterion for defining friends or foes. Instead, China has begun to deal with different states according to its own interests and the trend of development in the world, on the basis of independence and the five principles of peaceful coexistence,[49] aiming at creating a friendlier international environment for the construction of societal well-being as well as promoting world peace and global common development. All these changes demonstrate that China has begun to regard itself as a part of the world and incorporate itself into international society.

With top priority given to economic development since the late 1970s, China has vigorously involved itself in the world economy and achieved great economic growth through its close interactions with the world market. China's exports grew by a factor of almost 43 from 1979 to 2004, with an annual growth rate of 17.4 per cent.[50] China's total trade in 2008 reached $2561.6 billion, which accounts for nearly 9 per cent of the world total.[51] China's dependency on foreign trade has witnessed a sharp increase, from 9.75 per cent in 1978 to 66.6 per cent in 2007.[52] More importantly, China has integrated itself into the world economic system by joining multilateral economic institutions including the International Monetary Fund and the World Bank in 1980. Its entry into the World Trade Organization in 2001 further symbolizes that China is a member of the world economic system.

China has integrated itself into other dimensions of the international system since 1978. China's participation in international security institutions has been very noteworthy. China joined the Conference of Disarmament of the UN in 1980 and took part in a series of negotiations.[53] From 1982 to 1996, China's membership in international security institutions rose from 3 to 15, while the total number of international security institutions rose from 9 to 18.[54] China's participation has been noticeable even in sensitive political areas. China participated in the conferences of the UN Human Rights Committee in 1979 and became a council member in 1982.[55] In terms of China's membership in international governmental organizations (IGOs), it was – from its beginnings as a newcomer to international organizations – a member of 50 IGOs by 2000, catching up with most major developing and developed states such as India, the United States and Japan.[56] What is more, 'China became increasingly overinvolved in international organizations given its level of development' over the 1990s.[57]

China's participation in various international organizations and institutions has become more robust since the late 1990s. China was a member of 3,090 international organizations (IOs) in 2000, among which 1,415 are treaty IOs.[58] The total number rose to 4,238 in 2004, among which 1,701 are treaty IOs,[59] and to 4,386 in 2007.[60] As Medeiros and Fravel observe, 'China has expanded the number and depth of its bilateral relationships, and joined various trade and security accords, deepened its participation in key multilateral organizations, and helped address global security issues.'[61] China has participated in organizations supporting counter-terrorism, arms control, development, human rights, law-enforcement, the environment and peacekeeping. Taking peacekeeping as an example, in the past 17 years from 1990 to 2007 China has sent a total of over 7,000 non-combatant troops, police force and civil officers on 16 UN peacekeeping missions.[62]

Through the process of participation, China has interacted with international organizations and institutions. As Qin points out, in these interactions, 'China furthers its knowledge and becomes more engaged in international norms via ceaseless understanding, learning and feedbacks.'[63] And by complying with these norms, China has not only profoundly realized that there is coherence between international interests and its own, but has also gradually constructed and consolidated its identity as a responsible member of the international community.

We are now living in a highly globalized world. Many issues such as economic crisis, environmental protection, anti-terrorism and epidemic prevention have transcended national borders and cannot be solved without international cooperation. China, as the biggest developing country, a socialist state and a peacefully rising power, will continue to fulfil its obligations as a responsible member of the international society. At the same time, it will also make its due contribution to the democratization of world politics and the construction of a fair and reasonable international economic order.

Conclusion

The interaction between China and Western powers has exerted a tremendous impact on China's national identity in its relationship with international society. Firstly, through its encounter with the West, China realized that beyond its own 'world system' there existed a Westphalian system of sovereign states under which Western powers were surprisingly strong due to the development of a capitalist economy, and that the Chinese tribute system was gradually collapsing following the expansion of the Western-dominated international system.

Second, after the encounter, China embarked on a painful and long process of learning to adapt to Western systemic norms. It was a process in which China was subjected to successive intrusions and aggressions imposed by Western powers and Japan. It was also a process through which China undertook to learn from the West and underwent great transformations in national identity in terms of its relationship with international society, moving from the loss of its traditional identity to the tortuous quest for identity and to the reconstruction of its identity as a responsible stakeholder of international society.

Third, China's participation in international society, regardless of the various forms that the country has taken, is at the same time a process of learning to adapt and conform to international norms. In other words, it is a process of socialization into international norms. In this process, China has internalized the international norm of sovereignty, thus becoming sensitive to territorial integrity and the sovereign right of independence. Among the norms governing the Western-dominated international system, China's strongest feelings are about the norm of power politics. China has learned, from its bitter experience with Western powers, that lagging behind others leaves itself vulnerable to attacks, and that only by making itself strong can China win others' respect. China has also deeply felt the inequality between developed countries and developing ones through this encounter, which explains its ceaseless efforts to promote a fair and equal international order and to advocate the five principles of peaceful coexistence in dealing with foreign relations. Since the adoption of the policy of reform and opening up, China has embraced an increasing number of norms including those of a market economy, the rule of law, human rights, multilateralism, cooperation for win–win progress and global governance. China has played its role as a responsible member of international society through various foreign policies and actions.

Last but not least, during the past 30 years of its gradual incorporation into international society, China has achieved great economic growth by involving itself in the world economic system, and has played a part in global governance by joining international institutions. What comes next will be China's social and cultural integration into the world, a process which will of course not be without its challenges. China, a large country with a long history of 5,000 years and profound cultural traditions, is now undergoing domestic institutional transformation and reconstruction, which will be a long and gradual process. Together with the other three dimensions of integration, this interaction with the world on the social and cultural fronts will further influence China's identity.

Notes

1 Among them, see B. Buzan, 'China and International Society: An Unfolding Story' (notes for a presentation to a panel session at 'The 30th Anniversary of the Reform and Opening-up', 16–17 December 2008, CASS, Beijing); A. I. Johnston, 'Is China a Status Quo Power?', *International Security*, 27, 4 (2003), pp. 5–56; A. I. Johnston, *Social States: China in International Institutions, 1980–2000* (Princeton, NJ, 2008); Y. Zhang, *China in International Society since 1949: Alienation and Beyond* (Basingstoke, 1998); Y. Zhang, 'System, Empire and State in Chinese International Relations', *Review of International Studies*, 27 (2001), pp. 43–63; D. Scott, *China Stands Up: The PRC and the International System* (2007); H. Men, 'Yali, Renzhi yu Guoji Xingxiang: guan yu Zhongguo Canyu Guoji Zhidu de Lishi Jieshi' ('Pressure, Perception and International Image: A Historical Analysis of China's Strategy for International Institutions'), *Shijie Jingji Yu Zhengzhi* (World Economics and Politics), 4 (2005), pp. 17–22; Y. Qin, 'Guojia Shenfen Zhanlv Wenhua he Anquan Liyi: Guanyu Zhongguo yu Guoji Shehui Guanxi de Sange Jiashe' ('National Identity, Strategic Culture and Security Interest: Three Hypotheses on the Relationship between China and International Community'), *Shijie Jingji yu Zhengzhi*, 1 (2003), pp. 10–15.
2 Johnston, 'Is China a Status Quo Power?'; Qin, 'National Identity'.
3 Buzan, 'China and International Society'.
4 Xiong 2008, p. 405.
5 Y. Fung, *A Short History of Chinese Philosophy* (New York, NY, 1966), pp. 181–2.
6 X. Fei, *Xiangtu Zhongguo, Shengyu Zhidu* (China's Countryside, Birth Control Policy and Practice) (Beijing, 1998), pp. 27–8, 33.
7 Scott, *China Stands Up*, p. 8.
8 P. J. Katzenstein, *A World of Regions: Asia and Europe in the American Imperium* (Ithaca, NY, 2005), p. 91.
9 S. Chen, 'Shilun Yujia Wenming zhong de Shewai Linian' ('Ideas of Handling Foreign Relations in the Context of Confucian Civilization'), in Chen Shangsheng (ed.), *Rujia Wenming yu Zhongguo Chuantong Duiwai Guanxi* (Confucian Civilization and China's Traditional Foreign Relations) (Jinan, 2008), p. 20.
10 T. Chen and Z. Ding, *TianXia, Shijie, Guojia: Jindai Zhongguo Duiwai Guannian Yanbian Shi* ('Tianxia, the World and State: Evolution of Ideas in Foreign Relations in Late Modern China) (Shanghai, 2008), p. 4.
11 Katzenstein, *World of Regions*, p. 91.
12 *Ibid.*, p. 92.
13 Chen and Zhou, *Tianxia, World and State*, p. 8.
14 Zhang, *China in International Society*, pp. 9–10.
15 T. Zhao, 'Rethinking Empire from a Chinese Concept "All-under-Heaven" (Tian-xia)', *Social Identities*, 12, 1 (January 2006), p. 36.
16 K. Su, *Modern China: A Topical History* (Beijing, 1985), pp. 51–2.
17 *Ibid.*, p. 54.
18 *Ibid.*, p. 68.
19 *Ibid.*, pp. 71–2.

20 *Ibid.*, pp. 97–9.

21 Buzan, 'China and International Society'.

22 Z. Li, *Zhongguo Xiandai Sixiangshi Lun* (A Historical Perspective of Modern Thoughts of China) (Beijing, 1987), p. 312.

23 G. Arrighi and B. Silver, *Chaos and Governance in the Modern World System*, trans. W. Yujie (Beijing, 2003), pp. 247–57, 261.

24 J. K. Fairbank, *China: Tradition and Transformation*, trans. Z. Pei (Beijing, 2001), pp. 526–8.

25 Su, *Modern China*, pp. 125–7.

26 S. Zheng, *Shehui de Zhuanxing yu Wenhua de Biandong: Zhongguo Jindaishi Lun* (Social Transition and Cultural Change: A Late Modern Historical Perspective) (Beijing, 2006), pp. 71–2. The three cardinal guides (ruler guides subject, father guides son and husband guides wife) and the five constant virtues (benevolence, righteousness, propriety, wisdom and fidelity).

27 T. Guo and L. Zaichao, '20 Shiji 30 Niandai Zhongguo Wenhua Jianshe Zouxiang Wenti de Lunzhan' ('A Polemic over the Orientation of Cultural Construction of China of the 1930s'), *Guangxi Shehui Kexue* (Guangxi Social Sciences), 3 (2004), p. 119.

28 *Ibid.*

29 Y. Fung, *Complete Works of San Song Tang*, vol. IV (Zhengzhou, 2001), p. 205.

30 Zhang, *China in International Society*, pp. 46–7.

31 *Ibid.*, p. 47.

32 M. Zedong, *Mao Zedong Wenxuan* (Selected Works of Mao Zedong), vol. IV (Beijing, 1991), pp. 1472–3.

33 N. Han et al., *Dangdai Zhongguo Waijiao* (Contemporary China's Diplomacy) (Beijing, 1987), pp. 24–5.

34 Su, *Modern China*, p. 213.

35 S. Yang, 'Shixi Jianguo Chuqi Wodang Xuanze "Sulian Moshi" de Yuanyin ji Beijing' (Reasons and Background Behind the Choice of the Soviet Model by the Chinese Communist Party in the Early Years of the People's Republic of China), *Lilun Tantao* (*Theoretical Investigation*), 2 (2005), pp. 116–17.

36 Su, *Modern China*, pp. 213–14.

37 Yang, 'Choice of the Soviet Model', p. 117.

38 Han, *Contemporary China's Diplomacy*, p. 3.

39 M. Zedong, *Mao Zedong Waijiao Wenxuan* (Selected Works of Mao Zedong on Foreign Relations) (Beijing, 1994), p. 79.

40 Han, *Contemporary China's Diplomacy*, p. 4.

41 Zhang, *China in International Society*, p. 51.

42 *Ibid.*, p. 52.

43 *Ibid.*, pp. 56–7.

44 Men, 'Pressure, Perception and International Image', pp. 20–1.

45 X. Deng, *Selected Works of Deng Xiaoping*, vol. III (Beijing, 1993), pp. 89, 110–11, 132, 231.

46 *Ibid.*, pp. 110–11.

47 J. Hu, 'Hu Jintao's Report at the 17th Representative Conference of the Chinese Communist Party', October 15 2007. (http://news.xinhuanet.com/newscenterh/2007-10/24/content_6938568.htm, accessed 8 February 2009).

48 'Taking class struggle as a guideline' had been a guiding principle for social construction for the period of the Cultural Revolution. It focused on class struggle, not on economic development, which brought China into a national disaster.

49 These principles are as follows: mutual respect for each other's sovereignty and territorial integrity, mutual non-aggression, mutual non-interference in each other's internal affairs, equality and mutual benefit, and peaceful coexistence. They were first put forward by the late Chinese Premier Zhou Enlai when he met with an Indian delegation in December 1953, and were advocated in the joint declarations issued by the Chinese Premier with the prime ministers of India and Myanmar during the Chinese Premier's visit to the two countries in June 1954. At the

first Asian–African conference (the Bandung Conference) held in April 1955, Zhou Enlai reiterated these principles, the spirit of which was incorporated into the declarations of the Conference. In 1982 these Five Principles were written into the Constitution of the People's Republic of China. They are now a fundamental principle for China in fostering and developing relations with other countries.

50 X. Liao, 'Speech on Bo'ao Forum for Asia 2005 Annual Conference', 2005 (http://news3.xinhuanet.com/fortune/2005-04/23/content_2869786.htm, accessed 8 February 2009).

51 Zhongguo Guojia Tongjiju (National Bureau of Statistics of China), 2008.

52 X. Jiang, 'Zhongguo Kaifang Sanshi Nian de Huigu yu Zhanwang' ('Looking Back on and Looking Ahead of China's 30-Year Opening Up to the Outside World', *Zhongguo Shehui Kexue* (China Social Sciences), 6 (2008), pp. 66–85, p. 69.

53 Men, 'Pressure, Perception and International Image', p. 20.

54 Johnston, *Social States*, pp. 34–6.

55 Men, 'Pressure', p. 20.

56 Johnston, *Social States*, pp. 33–4.

57 *Ibid.*

58 Figure 2.1.1. Geographic distribution: membership of international organization by country: 2000, *Yearbook of International Organizations: Guide to Global Civil Society Networks: 2001–2002*, p. 52.

59 Figure 2.1.1. Geographic distribution: membership of international organization by country: 2004, *Yearbook of International Organizations: Guide to Global Civil Society Networks: 2005–2006*, p. 52.

60 Figure 2.1.1. Geographic distribution: membership of international organization by country: 2007, *Yearbook of International Organizations: Guide to Global Civil Society Networks: 2008–2009*, p. 41.

61 E. S. Medeiros and M. Taylor Fravel, 'China's "New" Diplomacy', *Foreign Affairs*, 82, 6 (2003), pp. 22–35. The number of the countries which have diplomatic relations with China grew from 113 in 1978 to 167 in 2005.

62 Y. Jiang, 'Foreign Affairs Ministry: China's Participation in Sixteen UN Peacekeeping Missions', 2007 (http://news.sohu.com/20070508/n249903335.shtml, accessed 8 February 2009).

63 Y. Qin, 'National Identity', pp. 10–15.

Part IV

Globalism:
From the Colonial to the Post-Colonial Worlds

European Power and the Mapping of Global Order

Karoline Postel-Vinay

International order has not always been global. Until fairly recently there were several functioning international orders, none of them valid for the entire planet. The idea of the 'global', or globality, as a foundation for a new international order started to take shape in the mid nineteenth century and was promoted by the European powers of the time. Globality here refers to the globe, i.e. the earth. It is historically different from the notion of universality. The claim to universality is less concerned with factual geography than with a claim to defend a certain vision of humankind and nature. Proselytizing religions did make people, ideas and norms travel, but their worldview was cosmological rather than planetary. The emergence of globality as the conceptual basis for a global international order happened at a specific moment of Western history that witnessed the end of 'empty space', as Stephen Kern[1] put it, and a general movement towards mastering the earth that was both cognitive – for instance the measurement and naming of mountains ('Mount Everest' in 1865), or the various polar expeditions of the late century – and territorial, as illustrated by European colonialism as well as the expansion of the American and Russian frontiers (leading to the foundation of Vladivostok in 1859). I argue that the long-term implications of this nineteenth-century invention of globality constitute one of the most powerful and lasting 'echoes of empire'.

The purpose of this chapter is to look at how the notion of globality has emerged as both a spatial and normative framework for the regulations of relations between sovereign entities. My topic is not the emergence of the idea of the 'global' as such. This discussion, as it appears in the field of international history, is both methodological and epistemological; its continued relevance is witnessed by a diverse and growing literature, ranging from the 'world history' (*Journal of World History*) to the more recent 'new global history' (www. newglobalhistory.org). Here the 'global' is viewed from a political science perspective, and treated as a more instrumental concept: it is used to look at how the physical finitude of the planet became the fundamental principle of regulation of a specific international order – the European one – and how that order aimed to planetary hegemony.[2]

The first part of the chapter analyses the conditions under which the European powers were able to reorganize international relations on an earth scale – in other words, to produce a global stage for the formulation of a new international order. Among those conditions was the actual globalization of international and transnational exchanges, combining the sudden growth of world trade and finance with the rapid expansion of transport and communication technologies. Then there was the response of Western societies and governments to this major evolution, inspired by a collective will to regulate global dynamics and by ever more competitive power politics. Thus the Western world produced a new international grammar whose ambition was global in every sense of the word, and, in that respect, was deeply challenging for the non-Western world. Indeed, the challenge posed by the West was not only about sheer balance of power but also, in more structural terms, about the definition of the framework within which world order was to be established.

The creation of a global international relations stage in the course of the late nineteenth century eventually led to the creation of a global narrative, the legacy of which is still tangible in today's world politics. The second part of this chapter will discuss why and how this narrative took shape. Its emergence coincided with the internationalist turn of the United States during the Great War and the consequential birth of Wilsonianism developing hand in hand with the expansion of American power in world politics. Although the American global narrative has dominated world affairs since the turn of the century, with a direct impact on the international agenda as well as international organizations, it has been constantly contested. This contestation has never been powerful enough to disrupt the very structure of the international system: it has never actually called into question the global dimension of international order. But the very fact of contestation challenges the legitimacy and, in the longer run, the efficiency of a meta-narrative which aims to reconcile the historical plurality of international order with the contemporary singularity of global order.

The Conditions for Setting a Global Stage

Hedley Bull and Adam Watson have analysed the expansion of the European-made Westphalian regime – the 'international society'[3] – along a path that can appear deceptively linear. What Hedley Bull in particular has defined as the 'emergence of a universal international society' during the late nineteenth century – which could also be called (to avoid the confusion between universality and globality) the actual globalization of the Westphalian regime – constituted a major turning point in the historical trajectory of international society. There is indeed a considerable ontological difference between the political context of the Congress of Vienna in 1815 and that of the Peace Conference at The Hague in 1899. Both can of course be described as specific stages of the expansion of international society. But the understanding of what the 'world' was, the definition of the space of international relations, had drastically changed during the course of the century. Europeans had formed a new worldview based on their experience of 'earth-mastering' and the feeling of 'time-space compression' described by David Harvey.[4]

The Mid-Nineteenth-Century European Obsession with Globality

The reason why Europeans became 'obsessed with globality', as Claude Raffestin[5] put it, was first and foremost linked to a particular moment in the history of human exchanges, marked by the rapid growth of international transportation and communication. The economic crisis of the 1840s that followed the earlier Industrial Revolution pushed European countries towards new paths of development which included spectacular investments, public and private, in distance-shrinking tools, such as steamships and trains, or the telegraph and the telephone. The world railroad network grew from 8,000 kilometres in 1840 to 360,000 kilometres 40 years later. A new laissez-faire mood favoured the reduction of trade barriers and world trade doubled between 1870 and 1913. There was also human movement on a grand scale: during those few decades, 60 million people moved out of Europe, mainly to settle in North America.

Historian Robbie Robertson, along with scholars from the 'global history' school, has called this period the 'second wave of globalization' in human history.[6] Looking at the patterns and degrees of intensity of flows between societies, Robertson defines three waves of globalization: that of the sixteenth century, characterized by the expansion of regional trade, and those starting in the nineteenth and late twentieth centuries respectively. Economists such as Kevin O'Rourke and

Jeffrey Williamson have argued that the real globalization big bang took place in the nineteenth century, when not only did world trade expand, as it also had in the sixteenth century, but markets integrated as well, leading to the convergence of commodity prices.[7] The debates that emerged on the eve of the twenty-first century, while they are revealing of the depth and complexity of the questions brought out by our contemporary globalization, tend to take for granted the very notion of globality. This notion, which again is different from universality, was a fundamental parameter in the evolution of the European-made international society that, in turn, transformed the definition of world order. The literal reference to the earth was indeed part and parcel of the reformulation of how sovereign entities were supposed to relate to each other.

The European mid nineteenth century witnessed the emergence of globality as both intellectual and political reality. The re-association of geography and politics through the new term *Geopolitik*[8] constituted one explicit manifestation of that reality. Although quite different in their contents and purposes, the works of Friedrich Ratzel, Karl Haushofer or Halford Mackinder all expressed a positivist will to understand the world-as-planet, and the belief that this planetary unity of the world was the defining condition of power politics. World geography did of course exist before the mid nineteenth century in the West (as well as in non-Western regions), as illustrated by the remarkable development of cartography from the sixteenth century onwards. But the technological advances of the nineteenth century made it possible to bring this onto an entirely new scale. The axiom of the late nineteenth-century discipline of *Geopolitik* served, following a familiar power/knowledge pattern, as conceptual framework for the elaboration of a new Big Powers agenda. Kaiser Wilhelm II called it '*Weltpolitik*', meaning that the German Empire should truly be a world empire, by making a coherent whole – within a planetary frame of reference – of the motherland and its transnational expansion. The British version, Halford Mackinder's 'geopolitics', did not have the pervasive biological dimension – that engendered the infamous *Lebensraum* concept – of German *Geopolitik*. But it too referred to a worldview that was no longer metaphorically but literally global, and from there contributed to the definition of a new, 'geopolitically aware' British imperial policy. Sir Mackinder himself, as a promoter of geographical education and advocate of imperialist expansion, personified the new focus on globality that underlay the marriage of positivist scientific thinking with international political practice.

Globality and International Society

The current usage of the word 'globalization' is confusing because it tends to conflate various notions that are indeed overlapping but nevertheless distinct. As we have just seen, 'globalization', whether it designates the global expansion of trade or globally regulated markets – or in a more contemporary sense, the multiplication of global issues – does not question the idea of the global, or globality.[9] Again, globality, as an explicit reference to the world-as-planet, was not a component of the configuration of international society before the mid nineteenth century: its emergence is a main characteristic of that specific 'wave of globalization'. But this does not necessarily mean that 'global order' equals 'globalization': this is another confusion engendered by the way the term 'globalization' is used nowadays. Globalization is a process of intensifying exchange; globality is the regulatory arena that seeks to manage international relations in the new conditions created by that process. Global orders, however, can subsist even when competing international orders are competing for mastery of globalization-as-process. The nineteenth-century globalization of exchanges had produced a political understanding of what 'being global' meant that was contradictory from the start. On one hand, it urged powerful governments to think in terms of *Weltpolitik*, or to paraphrase Halford Mackinder, to look at the earth as the new stage for the protection and pursuit of imperial (in this case British) interests. On the other hand, the growth of international flows triggered a multitude of initiatives, both private and public, that aimed at organizing in a cooperative way – at least among so-called 'civilized' nations – one aspect or another of the world's global dynamics.

The faith of the enterprise launched in 1891 by German geographer Albrecht Penck to draw an 'international map of the world' based on a multi-national scientific cooperation was symptomatic of the paradoxical dimension of late nineteenth-century globalization. Albrecht Penck, a leading geographer in his country, wanted to demonstrate that cartography did not need to or should no longer be an exclusive imperial or national exercise whose only purpose was to serve individual territorial ambitions.[10] The project did take off, with the participation of a dozen countries, mostly European. But it was progressively abandoned as diplomatic tensions grew among the participants' respective governments and as its initiator himself started to doubt the political feasibility of such a novel cooperative undertaking (the final blow to the project was the United States' decision to withdraw in 1913). Historical institutionalism in the field of international relations shows us how decisive the European mid nineteenth century was for the development of cooperative world politics and the actual creation of intergovernmental organizations.[11] Around 30 global IGOs were established between the 1860s and the outbreak of the Great War, from the International

Telegraph Union (1865) to the International Labour Office (1901); some of them, such as the International Office of Public Hygiene (1907) which then became the World Health Organization, were incorporated into the United Nations system a few decades later. The analysis Andrew Hurrell gives of our contemporary globalization is also applicable to that of the nineteenth century: 'globalization does not lead to an automatic harmony of interests, but it does create increasing demand for cooperation and also decreases the degree of concern with relative gains'.[12] The awareness of, if not obsession with, globality in Europe was accompanied by a Janus-faced contradictory dynamics: the search for international cooperation on an ever larger geographical scale, and the growth and heightening of imperial ambitions, the intensity of which was illustrated by the devastating war of 1914–18. Yet, from a non-Western viewpoint, the 'globality/international society' paradigm was even more complex.

As Louise Fawcett puts it in her reflection on the history of regionalism, 'regions – like Europe in the nineteenth century – were world leaders, since for those who lived in them, their region was the center of the world'.[13] The geophysical boundaries of, for example, the Sino-centred international order were irrelevant to its definition. It was based on a 'tribute system' that was valid for the whole Civilization (*wenming*): it did not really matter whether the people who lived outside the civilization came from the earth, the moon or any other planet.[14] Hence the European assumption that from now on international order would be global – i.e. planetary and therefore single – constituted a formidable challenge for the governing elite of China. The depth of that challenge is well explained by Xiaobing Tang when describing the experience of leading Chinese reformist Liang Qichao (1873–1929). 'The world as a mappable totality, or rather the concept of a whole world, introduced a sudden spatiotemporal re-orientation [...] To have access to the modern world, therefore, one had both to accept a new global, universal time and to claim a stable and coherent self-identity by means of a territorial nation.'[15] The European project to globalize international order was indeed a two-tiered problem for non-Western powers. They first had to accept that *their* world was no longer *the* world – for instance that their civilization was no longer a unitary and all-encompassing framework – and that the new world was considerably larger. Then they had to define in the most profitable (if not simply the most viable) way their own position within the new international entity. That was especially difficult for those, such as the Chinese or the Ottomans, who were situated at the centre of their own world. But it was a complex question too for the peripheral nations, such as Korea, Japan or Egypt, who could theoretically choose their way between an often unsatisfactory but familiar world order and a radically foreign one.[16] This in turn raises the issue of the possibility of defining a 'non-Western' view of the development of international society: post-colonialism is certainly a helpful point of departure for 'provincializing' the Westphalian system, but it does not always bring out the full complexity of the Western challenge as perceived by nations that were in fact in an infinite variety of situations.

The rich literature on empire, from Jack Snyder's post-Cold War IR approach on 'myths of empire' to the post-9/11 socio-historical work of scholars such as Frederick Cooper and Craig Calhoun on 'lessons of empire', reveals one common assumption: that empire is about the expansion of power. This is of course hardly debatable. If one considers the history of the Roman, the Inca, the Chinese or the British empires, one sees political communities defined by their search for power through territorial expansion. What is now called the US 'empire' – for which Geir Lundestad coined the phrase 'empire by invitation'[17] – can also be defined as a country asserting its influence beyond its national borders through a mix of soft and hard power. Although the non-territorial dimension of America's overseas power suggests the use of the term 'hegemony' rather than 'empire', as John Agnew has argued,[18] the focus of the debate is still the same: the dynamics of the expansion of power. Yet, the notion of empire, when reconsidering the development of European-produced international society, bears another fundamental characteristic which is the postulate of *cosmologic totality*. As we have just seen, from a Chinese viewpoint, the Sino-centric world was not a world within the world, but a discrete entity. The Western challenge to redefine international order within the geophysical contours of our planet therefore had radical implications. The European big powers in East Asia at the time, especially Great Britain and France, clearly expressed their will to impose their own international grammar, which in practice meant to erase the Chinese geopolitical repertoire. The Tianjin Treaty (1858), following the second Opium War, requested that Chinese official documents should no longer use the term '*yi*' which had been translated respectively in English and French as 'barbarian' and '*barbare*'. Traditionally, '*yi*' designated those who did not belong to the civilization; it was a matter-of-fact assessment of otherness more than a clear-cut judgemental understanding of who the outsiders were. However, and beyond linguistic arguments, the implication of the Franco-British request at Tianjin, as seen from Beijing, was at best the transformation of the Sino-centred world into a local one, or a local cosmology; at worst it was the denial of the very existence of that world.

The European powers of the late nineteenth century created a new global stage for the conduct of international relations. They imposed, intellectually and practically, the oneness of the framework of world order. The fact that this enterprise was fundamentally Eurocentric and oblivious to other international orders was not as such entirely novel. One could argue that the civilization was fundamentally Sino-centric and equally unwilling, or unable, to take into account other world orders. The real novelty of the European globalization (i.e. globality as world order) project of that time was that it reinvented the notion of totality. As illustrated by the conjunction of *Geopolitik* with *Weltpolitik*, for the first time international order was defined as a physically inescapable whole. Later on, in the early twentieth century, the United States took this principle of the oneness of the international stage one step further by creating a global narrative that would match the latter.

The Rise (and Fall?) of the Global Narrative

Universalism, religious or secular, is historically plural. The European globalization project of the late nineteenth century progressively tended to conflate globality and universality. It never produced, however, a meta-narrative that actually mixed globality and universality into an undifferentiated whole. The universal claim of visions such as the French *mission civilisatrice* or the British 'White Man's Burden' held two implications. The first one was that there was a global stage – defined by the positivist understanding of the world-as-planet – within which those visions would materialize. The second was that the play being performed on that unified global stage was in fact about Europe – the 'civilizing' endeavour of Europe – and was not the story of the whole world (world-as-planet). It therefore presented some caveats. For example, when Korea found a temporary escape from both Western domination (after the failed French attempt to colonize the peninsula in 1866) and Western modernization, it was then called the 'hermit kingdom';[19] it was considered as no longer part of the main story that, from the West's perspective, was defining world politics.

When the United States made its appearance on the global stage in the course of the Great War, it brought along a story that was meant to include every nation on the surface of the earth: it provided, in other words, a truly global narrative, or supposedly so. The American commitment in the 1914–18 international conflict served as the founding plot of a meta-narrative that has been deployed throughout the twentieth century and which in many ways continues to operate today. The historical conditions under which this narrative has been shaped and reshaped have produced inbuilt contradictions that could be described as realist vs idealist or, in turn, rationalist vs constructivist. Its contradictory dimension also lies, maybe more fundamentally, in its ambition to merge globality with universality, and in doing so to produce an ahistorical form of universality in the field of international relations. That was conceivable during most of the twentieth century, because of a general balance of power that was largely favourable to the West, but it is becoming more challenging as the demands for a plurality of expressions of universalism in world affairs become increasingly vocal.

The 'Earth-Scale War' as Normative Repertoire

The emergence of a global narrative, rather than being a strictly defined American 'invention', pointed to the more general issue of the evolution of the manifestation of power in international politics. It illustrated the trend towards the increasing need for a balance between norm-setting and strength-asserting as a prerequisite for the legitimization of world power status. Wilsonianism, understood as a normative project sometimes reduced to 'idealism', only tells half the story. It neglects the historical conditions under which US foreign policy projected itself on a global scale: these conditions defined an enunciation of diplomatic norms that was still very much about power politics.[20] The production of an 'earth-scale war' narrative is a case in point of how the increase of cooperation through the establishment of new norms actually also leads to novel forms of power and ways of asserting national strength. The introduction in the early twentieth century of historiography as global international norm not only created a collective repertoire for cooperation but opened the way to a new definition of geopolitical power.

From this perspective it is significant that little attention has been given to the normative implications of the notion of 'world war' that is commonly conveyed through the historiographies of 'World War I', 'World War II' and, up to a point, that of the 'Cold War'. The simple fact that what is internationally known as 'World War II' was originally called by the Soviet Union the 'Great Patriotic War' (and is still known as such in Russia), and named the 'War of Resistance against Japan' by the People's Republic of China, tends for example to be overlooked. The history of the labelling of those major conflicts[21] shows how, for all the constructivist apparel now available in the analysis of international relations, the normative enterprise of building an 'earth-scale war' narrative seems in some cases to have passed almost unnoticed. The 1914–18 conflict was for a long time known, and is often still known, as the 'Great War' in Great Britain and the *grande guerre* in France. The actual term 'world war' first appeared in America, both in the media and in government discourse, when the United States entered the conflict, whereas until April 1917 it had commonly been known as the 'European War'. The name became official with the publication, in 1924, of 'The Economic and Social History of the World War', the multi-volume compilation of the preparatory documents for the Paris Conference negotiations.[22] In his famous war message to Congress in April 1917, Woodrow Wilson declared that the conflict initiated by Germany three years earlier was 'a war against all nations'. This early semantic choice by the American president was obviously not made for the sake of geographical precision as indeed large parts of the planet, notably in South America, were not involved in the conflict. Nor was it for the sake of political accuracy: quite a number of nations, because they were colonized or semi-colonized, were not actors per se of the war.

The notion of planetary war fitted with a normative agenda – fighting 'to make the world safe for democracy' rather than being dragged into some messy territorial conflict, a connotation that the term 'European war' could all too easily evoke. 'World war' also conveniently tallied with another global project: that of taking the lead in interpreting international affairs, and imposing one's interpretation on other powers.

By the 1930s, the notion of 'world war' was also established in France and Britain. The 'world war' became a global narrative that described a condition of global disorder, which in turn complemented the idea of global order. Franklin Roosevelt referred to the 'world war' as early as the late 1930s, when commenting on European events. After 1945, 'World War II' became not just standard historiography but history as international norm. In the process of producing this norm two dimensions were conflated: the universal significance of that conflict and the actual globality of the conflict. It can certainly be argued that the war had a universal dimension, such as the fight for human rights. But this does not imply that all nations of the planet were participating in the same story. The fact that the Soviet Union and the PRC used terms other than 'World War II' is one indication of this discrepancy between the universality and the supposed globality of the event. Neither the USSR nor China actually called into question the narrative of 'the global fight of freedom against tyranny' (especially as it would allow them to picture themselves on the side of freedom). But their respective preferences for expressions such as the 'Great Patriotic War', in reference to Russia's Patriotic War of 1812 against France, or the 'War of Resistance against Japan' is not only a sign of a distance taken from the global narrative: it also reveals an identity-building process that is grounded in a nationally rather than globally defined history.

The Cold War as a global narrative describing a world-scale conflict has been more openly contested. The expression 'cold war' was invented in America and popularized by Walter Lippmann's famous eponymous essay, published in 1947. Harry Truman's Cold War speech of March 1947, based on a rhetoric directly inspired by Wilson and Roosevelt's respective war speeches, put forward the argument of the American global mission to make the world safe and free. Again, the involvement of the United States in the new conflict was ostensibly not about solving some local problem – in this case the Balkans; instead, it was explained in terms of fighting a 'world war'. The 1955 Bandung Conference and more generally the Non-Aligned Movement challenged that view. The actual agenda of the Non-Aligned Movement varied and was often contradictory. But the fundamental narrative of the movement did call into question what had been presented as an essential division of the international scene – the East/West division – and proposed to replace it by a North/South division. More than half a century later, one could argue that the 'East/West' global narrative was more efficient, having both a clear beginning and a clear end with tangible consequences, whereas the 'North–South' narrative could not make a similar claim. Yet however problematic it may be to measure the global impact of the North–South narrative, it is undeniable that it did contribute to the shaping of the international society agenda in the second part of the twentieth century. In that respect, the Non-Aligned Movement and its peripheral currents did produce an audible global counter-narrative.

The Structural Paradoxes of the Global Narrative

The tension between an increasing need for international cooperation and the heightening of power politics stakes on which the American global narrative project was built gave it a fundamental fragility. That weakness is also linked, in a deeper way, to the fact that the political understanding of 'being global', that is acting within a new 'globality', was contradictory from the start. The European governmental elite created a global stage; but the stories that were played out on it, such as the *mission civilisatrice*, had an exclusively European focus and relegated non-Western nations to the status of absent or semi-invisible actors. The confusion between European civilization and universalism, which was part and parcel of Europe's normative power at the turn of the twentieth century – and which was taking place within the hard and inescapable contours of a planetary space – had already opened the way to the unlikely overlap between globality with universality. The American creation of a new global narrative was, in a sense, the formalization of the notion that the oneness of globality should make universality singular: it formalized the confusion between 'one earth' and 'one world'.

The paradoxical nature of the global narrative showed signs of unsustainability very early on. The story of the 'earth-scale war' was completed by that of 'earth-scale peace and freedom'. The political translation of globally defined freedom found one of its main expression in Woodrow Wilson's Fourteen Points and more specifically the principle of self-determination. As Erez Manela has demonstrated, Wilsonianism as experienced by non-Western nations such as Egypt, India, China and Korea was a fundamentally ambivalent moment.[23] The principle of self-determination that derived from the 'earth-scale peace and freedom' narrative did not, in reality, live up to its universalist claim as for the 1919 Paris Conference negotiators it only applied to the nations of Europe and not to the faraway countries of Africa and Asia. The shortcomings of the Wilsonian vision, or what could be more broadly characterized as the great misunderstanding that brought about the dissemination of the Western notion of sovereignty,[24] eventually provided the tools for self-expression and positioning within the new global peace order, leading to the rise of anti-colonial nationalism. The Wilsonian moment was indeed as much about exclusion and fragmentation, on the one hand, as it was about inclusion and integration on the other. One should also note, however, that the Leninist vision of communism as the end of colonialism provided a provisional counter-narrative that helped the formation of what later on asserted itself as a Marxist brand of nationalism. The ongoing confrontation between two national models in Korea makes sense only in the light of this ideological divide between two models, which can in turn be traced back to the Wilsonian and Leninist paradigm. Despite this lasting legacy, the Leninist counter-narrative proved to be provisional indeed: it was eventually incorporated into the 'earth-scale war' or the 'earth-scale fight for peace' narrative, and most noticeably in that of the Cold War script initially written in America.

Yet again, however dominant the made-in-the-West global narrative has been, it has also left increasingly larger room for contestation. Another structural explanation for the improbability of a global narrative that would fit efficiently with the oneness of globality is, from a non-Western perspective, the radically alien nature of the global order evoked by the principle of this narrative in the first place. If one takes a hypothetical bird's-eye view of the European prescription of globality as a new framework for the organization of international relations, one could define it as a modernization project on the broadest possible scale. But this bird's-eye view is historically hardly realistic. From the viewpoint of the non-Western nations that were confronted with European imperialism, the late nineteenth-century idea of the global, and the global order that it underlay, constituted a challenge not only because of its claim to singularity, and the specific nature of the norms and practices it induced; first and foremost, this European conception was a challenge for the very practical reason that it established an international order that had to be accepted at best through a more or less balanced process of negotiation, at worst without it. In other words, the 'global' was an exogenous notion, the foreignness of which was all the more acutely perceived because it was apprehended through the brutal dynamics of power politics.

The legacy of this process, where most options for adjustment and negotiation were simply erased, is still embedded in the furniture of the present global order and can be characterized not so much by what is there as by what is not. The origin of the general design of international organizations and international discourses, norms, rules and practices can be traced back to a local site of production, usually Europe or America or both. Since many of the basic features of international regulation are in fact accepted as such globally, what is at stake today is the overwhelming absence of the non-West in this heritage rather than the predominance of the West. It is therefore a matter of representativeness, and of the way the identity of the global is being constructed, rather than a question of being part or not of the global. The 'rise of the Rest', from the early stages of decolonization to the so-called BRICS phenomenon (the emergence of Brazil, Russia, India, China and South Africa), has not affected the Western legacy of international regulation as such, but it has increasingly challenged the way in which this legacy is recorded through the construction of an earth-scale, supposedly 'universal' story. The World War II narrative brought about a fundamental collective reflection on the status of war in international relations, leading to the ban on war prescribed by the Charter of the United Nations. The spirit, albeit not the letter, of the corresponding paragraph of the Charter, and the very existence of this paragraph, has never been called into question. But the World War II narrative itself – the recording, that is, of how this global consensus was reached and is maintained – is becoming problematic.

One major challenge that is now facing the production of a sustainable global order is its capacity for pluralism. For most of the history of humanity, there was not just one world order but several, as there were not just one but several worlds organized by the various political communities that have lived and died across time and space. This multiplicity of international scenes allowed for a plurality of expression of universal ambitions. As cultural history shows, it is highly unlikely that people in vastly differing physical and political conditions will agree on the same universal values. This does not, however, prevent each group from arguing that its vision should be the universally applicable one. The radical dimension of the late nineteenth-century European globalization project was that it eventually implied the disappearance of that room for pluralism. With a mix of positivist thinking, new tools for the intellectual and material mastering of the planet, and the paradoxes of cooperation and competition, the European globalization project led to the reinvention of political totality. World orders until this point, including the European one, had been conceived of as cosmologic totalities. The establishment of 'globality' as the framework for the organization of a new, singular, and therefore 'global' international order meant that those cosmologic totalities would be replaced, through an uncertain and partly unrecorded process, by a planetary totality. By projecting the oneness of the earth onto the definition of international order, Western power opened the way to a problematic conflation of globality with universality. If one acknowledges that universalism as political project is sustainable insofar as it is based on pluralism, then what needs to be revisited is not universality – as some 'clash of civilizations' arguments would suggest – but what we mean by 'global'.

Notes

1 S. Kern, *The Culture of Time and Space, 1880–1918* (Cambridge, MA, 1983).

2 The analysis proposed in this chapter relies on the schools both of geo-history (French *géohistoire* includes authors such as Michel Foucher, Jacques Lévy and Christian Grataloup) and of the revisited English school of international relations (whose authors are well represented in this volume).

3 H. Bull and A. Watson (eds), *The Expansion of International Society* (Oxford, 1984).

4 D. Harvey, *The Condition of Post-Modernity* (Cambridge, 1990).

5 C. Raffestin, D. Lopreno and Y. Pasteur, *Géopolitique et histoire* (Paris, 1995).

6 R. Robertson, *The Three Waves of Globalization* (2004). See also 'Global History' scholars such as B. Gills and W. Thompson, *Globalization and Global History* (2006).

7 K. O'Rourke and Jeffrey Williamson (eds), *Globalization and History* (Cambridge, MA, 1999). See also R. Baldwin and P. Martin, *Two Waves of Globalization* (NBER Working Paper no. 6904, 1999).

8 For a discussion on whether 'geopolitics' was novel compared to previous political/geographical thinking, see R. Mayhew, 'Halford Mackinder's "New" Political Geography and the Geographical Tradition', *Political Geography*, 19, 6 (2000). Also see G. O'Tuathail, *Critical Geopolitics* (1996).

9 My definition of 'globality' is therefore quite different from the one that can be found in the mostly English-language literature on globalization which tends to refer to 'globality' as a stage in a given process, and by doing so pays little attention to the geo-historicity of this notion. For example Ulrich Beck has defined 'globality' as a concept aiming at 'a stronger reality claim' than globalization, i.e. 'world society as an irrevocable fact'. Cf. U. Beck, *What Is Globalization?* (1999), pp. 87–8. This definition is also quoted in T. Luke, 'Ideology and Globalization: From Globalism and Environmentalism to Ecoglobalism', in M. Steger (ed.), *Rethinking Globalism* (Lanham, MD, 2004), p. 67.

10 M. Heffernan, 'The Politics of the Map in the Early Twentieth Century', *Cartography and Geographic Information Science*, 29, 1 (2002).

11 D. Armstrong, L. Lloyd and J. Redmond, *International Organisation in World Politics* (2004); Clive Archer, *International Organizations* (2001); C. Murphy, *International Organization and Industrial Change* (Cambridge, 1994).

12 A. Hurrell, *On Global Order* (Oxford, 2007), p. 15.

13 L. Fawcett, 'Exploring Regional Domains: A Comparative History of Regionalism', *International Affairs*, 80, 3 (2004), p. 436.

14 For an analysis of the Chinese order as 'Tribute System' see Japanese historian H. Takeshi, *Chôkô shisutêmu to kindai ajia* (Tokyo, 1997), and the classic study by J. Fairbank (ed.), *The Chinese World Order* (Cambridge, MA, 1968).

15 X. Tang, *Global Space and the Nationalist Discourse of Modernity* (Stanford, CA, 1996), p. 2.

16 For a longer discussion, see K. Postel-Vinay, *Corée. Au coeur de la nouvelle Asie* (Paris, 2002).

17 G. Lundestad, 'Empire by Invitation? The United States and Western Europe, 1945–1952', *Journal of Peace Research*, 23, 3 (1986).

18 J. Agnew, *Hegemony: The New Shape of Global Power* (Philadelphia, PA, 2005).

19 Cf. William Elliot Griffis, *Korea: The Hermit Kingdom* (New York, NY, 1882).

20 See Neil Smith's analysis of the American projection of power through the political career of Isaiah Bowman: N. Smith, *American Empire* (Berkeley, CA, 2003).

21 D. Reynolds, 'The Origins of the Two "World Wars": Historical Discourse and International Politics', *Journal of Contemporary History*, 38, 1 (2003).

22 J. Shotwell (ed.), *Economic and Social History of the World War* (Washington, DC, 1924).

23 E. Manela, *The Wilsonian Moment* (Oxford, 2007).

24 I have argued that the shortcomings of the Paris Conference did crystallize the gap between the Western promise of self-government and its perception by non-Western nations, but that the elements for the creation of that gap, especially in East Asia, were already present in the late nineteenth century (see Postel-Vinay, *Corée*).

Legal Child vs Step Child?
The Impact of Colonial Legacies
on Brazil's and India's Global Trajectories

Vinícius Rodrigues Vieira

Although this book is about *history* and its legacies, it is worth starting with a short *story*, a tale of globalization. Once upon a time, two countries that had been colonized by European powers adopted for almost 30 years an inward-looking/ import substitution industrialization (ISI) strategy of development. For another 30 years, however, both shifted this strategy incrementally towards economic liberalization, embracing integration with the global economy. At the end of this period, these two federal and multicultural states, long condemned to 'backwardness' by their patrimonialism – the appropriation of the public arena for private purposes – and corruption, came to be considered two of the emerging powers that would influence a post-Western twenty-first century. Nonetheless, while one of these countries rises as a nuclear-, industry- and service-based competitive economy with strong standing in international fora, the other finds its greatest strength in the exports of commodities thanks to Chinese demand for raw materials, and appears to be more flexible in negotiating reform in international treaties, such as the agreements under the umbrella of the World Trade Organization (WTO). What does this divergent trajectory between the latter country, Brazil, and the former one, India, teach us about historical legacies?

I believe that this divergence can be traced back in several ways to the legacies that Brazil and India inherited from their respective colonizers, Portugal and the United Kingdom, which in turn depend on the model of colonization they were each subject to. Whereas Brazil's state and society originated in the transplantation of the mercantilist, rent-seeking Portuguese model to South America, India's post-colonial institutions grew out of the overlap between, on the one hand, the pre-colonial cultural elements existent in its current territory, and, on the other, the bureaucratic organization left by the British Raj. To use a metaphor, Brazil (which, as a distinct entity, is an Iberian creation) can be seen as Portugal's direct 'legal child', whereas India (where there were complex civilizations prior to the European imperialist enterprise) can be seen as Britain's 'step child'. Consequently, the latter drew a clearer distinction between the foreign and the domestic, enhancing a more effective internal cohesion, while the former has been historically more fragmented and less suspicious of international influences.

In short, Brazil and India exemplify two very different colonization models, and as a result two different post-colonial national trajectories towards globalization – understood as a country's economic and political patterns of integration into the international system since the late Cold War (1989). The colonial period in Brazil and India – and in the case of the former the interregnum between independence and the end of World War II (1822–1945) – provide the necessary context. In this chapter, I therefore analyse the ISI period in both countries (1945–1980s), considering the first movements towards economic liberalization. Finally, I discuss the patterns of integration and emergence of the Brazilian and Indian states and economy in the 1980s onwards, identifying the colonial legacies that still pervade political and economic actions in each country.

Let me make four preliminary remarks. First, the step and legal child models do not explain all differences among former colonies in current times. Indeed, more ambitious works in the historical-institutional tradition, such as Mahoney's analysis of Spanish America[1] and Lange's work[2] on British colonial legacies throughout the world, already accomplish this goal through large-N research designs combined with the discussion of specific cases with various socio-economic outcomes. I also do not claim that the step and legal child models provide an exhaustive explanatory framework, although I do argue that they need to be part of the general picture. In sum, these models attempt to frame the discussion about distinct globalization trajectories in non-Western countries which pursued development through industrialization in the context of the post-war Keynesian Consensus Era,[3] with state-intervention in economy and ISI policies.

Second, I need to make clear that the legal child/step child dichotomy does not correspond to the classic opposition between direct versus indirect rule. As Lange[4] argues, direct rule depends on an integrated state apparatus that resembles the state model originating in Western Europe, whereas indirect rule implies collaboration with indigenous intermediaries. What he misses is that rule can be indirect even without the intermediation of native populations: it suffices for the metropolis to rely on third parties that are not part of the state. Furthermore, these classifications (legal/step child and direct/indirect rule) are not mutually exclusive; for instance, Portugal and Britain respectively established the legal and step child models in Brazil and India, but both colonies experienced forms of indirect rule that still pervade their political and social institutions.

Third, this chapter has distinct objectives from earlier works putting newly industrialized economies (NIEs) – and more specifically Brazil and India – in comparative perspective, such as Evans (1995) and Kohli (2004) who explain their developmental trajectories in the twentieth century. While works such as these contribute to my theoretical framework, the data discussed here enrich the existing literature by using case studies to question the Weberian notions of bureaucracy and economic efficiency. For instance, India's political connections with business seem to have played a role in enhancing industrialization, as well as the capacity of civil service, which is a British heritage.[5] Patrimonialism and bureaucratic capacity, then, are not mutually exclusive state characteristics – an observation that applies equally to East Asian developmental states such as Japan[6] and South Korea.[7]

Finally, I employ the word 'child' not to embrace any misleading notion of post-colonial inferiority expressed by the *mission civilisatrice* argument used by European powers to justify colonial rule. Rather, the term 'child' is used ironically in the post-colonial theory reparatory project[8] insofar as colonial offspring/children are taking over their former Western masters/fathers in the 'post-post-colonial', Eastern-centric twenty-first-century form of capitalism.

Pre-WWII: Movements Towards Political and Economic Independence

Brazil started to be formed as a modern political entity in the sixteenth century with the first Portuguese settlements on the eastern coast of the South Atlantic. Since there was not any unified political entity before the Portuguese arrived, colonial rule built the nation state. Decimated by war and disease, most of the native population did not resist colonial rule and was partially enslaved alongside the blacks imported from Africa to work in plantations and mines.[9] Although formal representatives of the metropolis were posted to coastal areas, the landowners who worked on behalf of the Portuguese crown in practice became rulers of the lands where they had settled to cultivate sugar cane in north-eastern Brazil. Indirect rule on the power of plantation owners implied decentralization, and thus the potential for violating state rules.[10] This in turn led to an unclear boundary between the private and the public spheres in Brazil, an adaptation of the Portuguese model arising from the mercantilist state, but with reliance on third parties – i.e. plantation landlords – to govern the colony, as well as to organize its economy. According to Holanda, these are the roots of the patrimonialism that pervades the Brazilian state.[11]

The political independence of Brazil in 1822 did not bring about any major change in economic terms insofar as the country remained a raw-material and commodity exporter until the 1930s. Although recognized as a sovereign nation by the US and the European powers, Brazil remained in the periphery of the international system formed under British auspices in the aftermath of the Congress of Vienna in 1815. In spite of its dominant Western heritage, Brazil – like other states in Latin America – was hardly admitted by the European nations as a full member of international society given the existence of African and Native-American elements in its culture. In practice, the community of 'civilized' nations was formed only by the old world and the emerging US.[12] For instance, the principle of non-intervention that arose after the Congress of Vienna, in 1815, was constantly violated by the US in the region – as happened in Brazil in 1894 – not to mention the notions on inherent Latin American inferiority American diplomacy espoused based on racist ideas.[13]

The process of independence has its origins in 1808, when the Portuguese royal family moved the seat of the empire from Lisbon to Rio de Janeiro, in the wake of the Napoleonic invasion of the Iberian Peninsula. This change led to the alteration of Brazil's status from colony to integral part of the Portuguese Empire in 1815, which gave Brazilian-born elites the right of representation in parliament, and subsequently led to the divergence of indigenous and metropolitan elite interests. When the king of Portugal, John VI, returned to Europe in 1821, metropolitan elites wanted to restrict the autonomy Brazil had been granted in the foregoing years. Among the most important achievements was the end of the trade monopoly with Portugal, which paved the way for the development of direct economic links with Britain.[14] In reaction against their possible loss of political representativeness and autonomy vis-à-vis Lisbon, members of the creole commercial and agrarian elite gathered around the leadership of Prince Peter, who had stayed in Brazil and, being the king's eldest son, was his presumptive heir. Therefore, unlike the Spanish colonies in the Americas which formed elitist republics,[15] Brazil became independent under imperial rule that had its origins in a rupture within the Portuguese royal family.

The Empire of Brazil, founded under the leadership of Peter, kept the former Portuguese colony united under a weak state, although it was strong enough to suffocate separatist movements. These movements lost momentum only after the 1840s when Peter II was considered old enough to ascend to the throne, replacing the regents who had governed the country between 1831 and 1840 following Peter's abdication.[16] The empire maintained the export-orientated agricultural economy based on large plantations, monocropping (with coffee having replaced sugar cane as major export) and black slave labour, while encouraging foreign investment in railroads, banks, and other institutions designed to facilitate exports. The political arena remained highly exclusive but not racially segregated, since free men were enfranchised according to their income regardless of ethnic origin.[17] In 1872, about 10 per cent of the population was composed of slaves, against almost half just before independence.[18] This did not mean an automatic expansion of enfranchisement, since illiterates – most of whom had mixed ancestry – could no longer vote after an electoral reform in 1881. Despite the abolition of slavery in 1888 and the inauguration of the Republic in 1889 following the American institutional model, the Brazilian economy did not change substantially – although the accumulation produced by coffee plantations enabled an incipient industrialization. Combined with immigration from Europe and migration from the countryside,[19] industrialization began to foster an urban class that gained political strength. In 1930, in the aftermath of the collapse of exports provoked by the 1929 crisis, a political–military coup overthrew the national coalition formed by landowners and oligarchs. As a result decision-making on economy and national affairs was centralized in the hands of the federal government, although rural political leaders remained powerful in their regional domains.[20]

Unlike Portugal in Brazil, the British did not create a new society in India, and based their colonial rule mainly on the institutions they found in South Asia in the nineteenth century (Bose, this volume). The territory that is modern India has been occupied by complex civilizations for centuries. Like Portuguese colonization in Brazil, however, the British Raj – which fell under Crown control following the 1857 Indian uprising – was based largely on indirect rule[21] in collaboration with around 500 Princely states and the development of a native, English-speaking bureaucratic elite who worked on behalf of metropolitan authorities.[22] In spite of recurrent resistance to colonial rule, organized mainly around the Indian National Congress (hereby the Congress) founded in 1885, pro-independence movements only gained strength after the Great War.[23] Britain, like Portugal in Brazil, relied extensively on India to balance its national accounts – with the crucial difference of Portuguese decadence in the seventeenth and eighteenth centuries amid the exasperation of the mercantilist model, whilst Britain was in an ascending route with the development of a market economy when it colonized South Asia. According to Kumar[24] by the 1920s Indian exports financed over two-fifths of Britain's balance of payments deficit with Europe and the US. Despite the devolution of powers to the subnational/provincial level in the interwar years[25] and the increasing participation of local elites in the civil service, the 1929 Depression complicated the political situation of the colonizers in India. Indian peasants' income declined rapidly in the 1930s, while the growing urban population faced widespread closures of small-scale business.[26] As Chatterjee[27] argues, the discourse used by local elites in the independence struggle to garner the support of the peasantry and other target groups – such as members of castes considered inferior in the local social system reinforced by the British[28] – combined a Western-based rational theory of power with a non-possessive indigenous spirituality. This combination meant that India did not have to leave behind all the legacies of British colonial enterprise, using the economic and political institutions left by the former European rulers in South Asia[29] to embody, in a modern nation state, local traditions that had been in place for millennia. In a metaphor, the step child (modern India) could reach adulthood being aware of the pitfalls of following both parents: the local past of South Asian civilization and the step-parent – the British.

According to Nobrega and Sinha,[30] Mahatma Gandhi's leadership sought to reject Western-type modernization and Western values, leading the post-independence Westminster-type government headed by Congress leader Jawaharlal Nehru to adopt a strategy of self-sufficiency, with strict restrictions on foreign trade and investment in order to avoid extensive external influences in the country.[31] This, however, could not be done through a Hindu-centric discourse, since the new nation was meant to be a multi-religious and multi-ethnic state, despite the partition that created West and East Pakistan for the Muslim population in the subcontinent. In economic terms, this secularist strategy was twofold: firstly, self-sufficiency of production in general – which implied an almost Soviet-style planning, with long-term plans – and, secondly, state-driven industrialization, aiming to meet the economic needs of 'a fundamental class striving for class hegemony and advance of social production'.[32] Nehru and Congress were able to build the economy of modern India on those two pillars despite collateral effects. The self-sufficient approach required control over consumption and entrepreneurship. As in post-1930s Brazil, decision-making and rule-design for the Indian economy remained centred in the federal government, without removing power from local (and especially rural) elites who still relied on informal institutions such as the outlawed distinctions of caste and patronage networks.[33] Furthermore, states had a relevant degree of autonomy in affairs that concerned traditional elites the most, such as agricultural policy.

Unlike Brazil, however, Indian society remained divided by a variety of identities besides class,[34] with unity provided by a much stronger opposition to Britain than that seen in Brazil vis-à-vis Portugal. In Brazil, there was no strict categorization of race and class or disciplinary power arising from a central source or discourse.[35] The relative ease with which the Lusitanian-Tropical civilization absorbed the 'Other' (non-White, non-Christian) in contrast with Anglo-Saxon racial hierarchies came partly from the non-European (African and indigenous) elements the Portuguese incorporated into the society they created in the Americas (which in turn arguably has its roots partly in Portugal's condition as a colony during most of the Moor domination of Iberia between the eighth and fifteenth centuries).

These are major differences, then, between the early post-colonial experiences of Brazil and India. The divergence arises from the differences between Portuguese and Anglo-Saxon approaches to colonial rule, as well as from distinct pre-colonial legacies. Whereas British rule, with its disciplinary power, eventually laid the foundations for the formation of national identity based on the recovery of what came to be understood as pre-colonial past, Portuguese colonization – being organized around faulty lines of racial categorization which would later constitute Brazilian society – allowed little room for collective action from the people, slaves or peasants against the elites – even during the struggle for independence.

Keynes in the Periphery: Industrialization and Strategic Alliances

Although Brazil did not have to face major divisions beyond class – thanks to the patterns of Portuguese colonization and the early twentieth-century discourse of Racial Democracy in reaction to Scientific Racism, which had predicted a doomed future for mixed-race societies[36] – Brazil remained in practice a fragmented nation, and like India became united under a nationalist-developmental project. This 'Keynesian Consensus' in the periphery raised the status of both countries in the world-system from peripheral to semi-peripheral,[37] with an incipient industrialization mixing public and private capital – although it did not fulfil the Modernization Theory predictions of full westernization through stages of development similar to those in Western Europe and the US.[38] In fact, such national projects did not erase colonial legacies but were rather built on them. Both Brazil and India are archetypes of incomplete developmental states,[39] with semi-cohesive bureaucracies and internal organization between federal and state levels of government, configuring multi-class, fragmented states.[40]

In Brazil, urban labour was incorporated into the political game through state-sponsored labour unions.[41] An ISI strategy was launched and pursued until the 1970s, pervading the economic policy of both dictatorial (1930–45 and 1964–85) and democratic (1945–64) periods. According to Evans, the late ISI process in Brazil focused on the production of capital goods was based on a triple alliance between state, national and international capital, forming the basis for 'dependent development'.[42] As he points out, during the classical dependence phase (agricultural exports in the nineteenth century and the Belle Époque), Brazilian plantations were generally owned by local entrepreneurs. This enabled local capital accumulation and a certain degree of national autonomy – though it was far from the household model adopted in India, where suspicion of foreign partnerships was rife.

The need to advance the ISI process towards the production of capital goods led to the rise of a Bureaucratic-Authoritarian (BA) state in the 1960s, an exclusionary system in which 'central actors in the dominant coalition include high-level technocrats – military and civilian, within and outside the state – working in close association with foreign capital. This new elite eliminates electoral competition and severely controls the political participation of the popular sector'.[43] The BA in

Brazil was implemented after a military coup against a democratically elected centre-left government, with extensive participation of the US behind the scenes in the context of the Cold War and the supposed prevention of communist spread-out in Latin America.[44]

The lack of internal cohesion in the Brazilian state left it vulnerable to the different groups that formed the BA coalition (technocrats/military, local and international capital).[45] Indeed, this coalition depended on concessions from the authoritarian state to its main political base – a middle-class and labour aristocracy formed by technocrats, bureaucrats and employees of state-owned enterprises (SOEs).[46] The 1970s crises jeopardized the ISI strategy because it was based on 'dependent development', which was incompatible with the dictatorship's project of making Brazil a great power. After 1974, this project even led the country to adopt a more independent foreign policy towards the US amid expansion of exports, increased production of capital goods,[47] and the signing of a nuclear agreement with West Germany. The ISI strategy totally collapsed in the aftermath of the 1982 debt crisis as inflows of foreign investment decreased abruptly while external debt exploded, leading to recession and hyperinflation. Although it had promoted economic growth that surpassed 10 per cent per year between 1968 and 1973, the military rule had done so at the expanse of social equality, undermining the expansion of the internal market. As had been the case since the colonial period, the Brazilian state legitimized social hierarchies and remained linked to private interests in spite of the emergence of a modern industrialized society.

By contrast, the household model prevalent in India – created from the combination of pre-colonial cultural traits with institutional legacies from the British Raj – partially explains how the country structured its economy and its foreign relations after independence. The self-sufficient approach preserved, in the rural areas, the village (*panchyats*) as the main sociopolitical unit of organization[48] along with the maintenance of caste hierarchies and an economy organized around agriculture.[49] These elements were now placed in a framework of economic planning inspired by the Soviet model, but within a democratic political system to elect governments at both state and national levels. Private businesses could only operate after obtaining licences in the context of the so-called 'licence *raj*' – the rule that made development of economic activities subject to state authorization. The complex system of state-centred development led to the expansion of the civil service, which according to Kohli was a colonial legacy and 'contributed to effective government and imparted political stability'.[50]

Deeply rooted social cleavages stemming from social identity (e.g. ethnicity and religion) were of less far-reaching importance in East Asian countries, such as Japan and South Korea, which strived to industrialize their economies in the same period with more success than India. In India, however, an initial class compromise between organized labour, the unincorporated rural masses, and private capital under government observance made political consensus converge towards the Congress. However, the struggle for power within the party after Nehru's death in 1964, won by his daughter Indira Gandhi, undermined the basis for cooperation.[51] Also at this time, the first social movements representing underprivileged groups in the social-economic hierarchy, such as untouchables and peasants in general,[52] were taking their first steps out of Congress' umbrella. In 1977, Congress lost the general election following unpopular authoritarian measures imposed under the state of emergency between 1975 and 1977. The fact that Congress lost power, however, did not mean a break with the socialist consensus around self-sufficiency in India. Indeed, the Janata government (1977–80) empowered more labour unions and submitted transnational corporations to strict control, forcing them to establish partnerships with the government,[53] while addressing the nationalist/pro-business agenda of the party.[54] Amid economic instability, Congress recovered power in 1980, when the strategy of self-sufficiency collapsed further, as a result of lack of innovation and consumption, having as its ultimate consequence slow growth in production (see table in the next section with average growth per decade).

If on one hand the world seemed to be converging towards economic liberalism at this time, on the other it remained polarized in political terms. This international situation coupled with its traditional suspicion of the West led India to maintain its non-aligned foreign policy, playing cards with both superpowers – the US and the Soviet Union.[55] This happened in spite of the limits of the non-aligned movement – which India had helped to launch. The movement, however, did not manage to establish international regimes that could support the developmental needs of the de-colonized world.[56] Brazil also insisted on retaining autonomy in its foreign policy, with the 'responsible pragmatism'[57] approach that emerged in the 1970s advocating distance from the main poles of power and particularly the systemic hegemon – the US.[58] However, Washington remained the most important pole for Brazilian diplomacy, as it had been since the beginning of the twentieth century.[59] By that period, the prioritization of relations with the US followed a gradual decline in British influence in Brazil, which, to some extent, had been a legacy of the colonial period, during which Portugal was in practice in a colonial relationship with London:[60] in the early eighteenth century the Portuguese signed a treaty with England agreeing to buy her textiles, constraining any eventual effort towards industrialization. Of course, unlike India, Brazil was clearly in the geopolitical space of just one superpower (the US). Nonetheless, any unconditional alignment with American diplomacy was far from automatic. Such an assumption downplays the role of geographical contingencies or Brazil's latent Western-leaning international identity in defining and explaining its foreign policy. Rather, Brazilian support to the US was a matter of the decision of policy-makers, as different degrees of alignment with the American diplomacy during the Cold War show, ranging from automatic support, as happened in the first three years of the military dictatorship (1964–7), to independent approaches such as 'responsible pragmatism' in the 1970s.

However, Brazil did not show more autonomy than India in foreign affairs in any moment in the twentieth century. In combination with colonial legacies that praised autonomy, non-alignment, and self-sufficiency, the geopolitical situation of India – located in a strategic region for the US, USSR, and China – gave to the country more room for manoeuvre as far as international partnerships were concerned, which, in turn, contributed to a less dependent strategy of development than that found in Brazil. Meanwhile, on the domestic level, India's cleavages beyond class requested a stronger discourse and practice of national cohesion than in Brazil, leading to a more cautious approach regarding the foreign.

Paths Towards Globalization: Back to the Future

As Brazil's trajectory from political independence to economic autonomy shows, it has always been less ambivalent than India in establishing political-economic foreign partnerships. Although one can hardly argue that this is due only to Portugal's legacies, colonial inheritances play an important part in explaining how the Brazilian economy is embedded in society and politics, giving birth to a dependent national trajectory of development under globalization. Likewise, India's colonial experience, first under a 'private' rule and subsequently that of the British Empire, is reflected today in its controlled insertion into global markets and continued suspicion of Western intentions. Furthermore, India – unlike Brazil – built its national foundations on local ancient civilizations, no matter whether the contributions from South Asian societies are original or just contemporary creations derived from an imagined past.

Before embracing integration in the post-Keynesian world of free markets and capital flows, Brazil and India both tried to maintain their strong nationalistic positions. The latter was more successful than the former: unlike Brazil, India managed to partially reform its economic organization in the 1980s before joining the globalized world. The 1980s were disappointing for Brazil: it could neither reform institutions substantially nor achieve good economic performance. The debt crisis and the re-democratization process reduced national expectations for the future, yet Brazil did not entirely abandon the 'responsible pragmatism' approach in foreign policy, keeping its distance from the core of international society made up by the US and Western Europe.[61] In fact, unlike most of its Latin American counterparts, Brazil did not open its economy to international markets in the 1980s despite economic turmoil amid hyperinflation and the rise of the Washington Consensus.[62]

Contrary to dominant interpretations, Kohli argues that the process of liberalization of the Indian economy was launched in the early 1980s.[63] However, many have taken issue with this view. For Srinivasan and Tendulkar, the economic growth achieved in the 1980s was based on increasing fiscal deficit, which eventually led to the balance of payments crisis in 1991, a turning point in India's strategy of development.[64] More fundamentally, Kohli highlights the institutional roots of the 1990s economic reforms. In the 1980s, the government built a strategy based on a pragmatic attitude towards industrial and commercial groups.[65] These incremental reforms, which included the partial removal of the licence *raj*, were interrupted in 1987.[66] Nonetheless, the 1980s reforms heralded a progressive shift from an economy based essentially on state-ownership with socialist traits towards an economic regime favourable to business interests,[67] in which national private economic groups were empowered. This, however, did not mean a pro-market approach, insofar as the country still had several restrictions on foreign investment and national-private capital. As Kohli argues, this strategy emerged after 1991, when the Congress adopted a structural-adjustment programme in order to receive funds from the IMF.[68] The 'licence *raj*' finally came to an end, and the number of sectors reserved for government ownership was reduced from seventeen to four.[69] These measures, however, were not taken to such an extent as to hurt indigenous business, particularly in manufacture. This cautious approach echoes the legacies of colonialism, and particularly the suspicion that too much economic opening could lead the country into excessive dependency analogous to a neo-colonial condition.

Brazil, on the other hand, adopted a more pro-market stance, to use Kohli's classification. This is in line with its historical patterns of development and integration. According to Bresser-Pereira, the focus on economic growth since the 1970s, based on ISI, was replaced by a focus on redistribution of wealth which 'assumes that economic development is assured, be it as a result of the dynamic nature of capitalism or through the inflow of foreign capital'.[70] Such an assumption, Bresser-Pereira concludes, was embraced by the political elite that opposed the military dictatorship of 1964–85. After re-democratization, part of that former opposition to authoritarian rule came into government, and led the market reforms which were part of the successful strategy that defeated hyperinflation, yet reduced the rates of economic growth following the opening of markets through unilateral tariff reduction in the 1990s. Preceded by a foreign debt renegotiation, the successful economic stabilization strategy of 1994 led finance minister Fernando Henrique Cardoso, the head of the team that elaborated the stabilization plan, to victory in the presidential race of the same year running for the Party of Brazilian Social Democracy (PSDB). In contrast to India's cautious approach to globalization, after 1994, many in Brazil advocated relying on foreign investment to revive economic growth.[71] The country, however, was affected by major economic crises between 1995 and 1999.[72]

These general patterns of Brazil and India in the post-Keynesian globalized world remained unchanged even when the parties that led economic reforms were displaced from power. In India, Congress was out of power during most of the time between 1996 and 2004; and between 1998 and 2004 its major opponent, the Hindu Nationalist Bharatiya Janata Party (BJP), led a government formed by coalitions composed mainly of regional parties (a model that defined Indian government between 1989 and 2014, when the BJP became the first party to win a majority of seats within 25 years). The BJP is considered a centre-right party, supporting more private business at the expense of organized labour and unincorporated sectors – an important variable in India, where more than half of the economy is informal. However, BJP also has protectionist stances. India's Congress held power again between 2004 and 2014. In Brazil, the Workers' Party (PT) has occupied the presidency since 2003 and, despite claims of policy shifts in comparison to the PSDB's government because of links with social movements and labour unions, continuity prevailed insofar as there is still a strong reliance on FDI and an increasing importance of non-manufactured goods in exports (Table 1), which reached more than 60 per cent of exports in 2009.[73] The economic policy that aims to keep inflation rates low favours this situation, as long as it is based on high-short-term interest rate and an overvalued exchange rate.[74]

Table 1: Brazil and India – Economic Indicators – Annual Average per Decade (1960s–2000s)[75]

Item	1960s	1970s	1980s	1990s	2000s
Brazil					
GDP growth (per cent)	5.90	8.47	2.99	1.70	3.33
GDP per capita growth (per cent)*	2.98	5.92	0.82	0.13	2.09
Exports of goods and services (per cent GDP)	6.66	7.26	10.14	8.47	13.56
Export of manufactures (per cent exports)**	6.74	23.53	44.29	54.74	50.65
Foreign Direct Investment – FDI (per cent GDP)	NA	NA	0.66	1.47	2.74
Gross Domestic Savings (per cent GDP)	19.83	20.81	23.45	18.51	18.64
India					
GDP growth (per cent)	6.66	2.93	5.69	5.63	7.08
GDP per capita growth (per cent)*	4.23	0.61	3.45	3.72	5.54
Exports of goods and services (per cent GDP)	4.09	5.29	6.00	9.97	17.81
Export of manufactures (per cent exports)**	47.51	53.62	60.11	74.17	70.95
Foreign Direct Investment – FDI (per cent GDP)	NA	NA	0.04	0.39	1.57
Gross Domestic Savings (per cent GDP)	13.61	17.69	19.91	22.63	28.46

*For the 1960s, data for the period 1961–9.

**For the 1960s, data for the period 1962–9.

The differences in economic leverage are projected in both international and national levels. While it is undisputable that India faces more social challenges than Brazil in terms of its lower GDP per capita ($1,100 in India and $8,200 in Brazil in 2009)[76] and Human Development Index (in 2010, high level in Brazil – 0.669, and medium in India – 0.519),[77] India leads in the stakes of power politics. As a legacy of its non-alignment and suspicion of the West, India, on the one hand, is still a harder negotiator in international fora,[78] being known as the country that says 'no', as was the case in the refusal to open its agricultural markets during WTO's Doha Round (in deadlock since 2008), and in the decision to perform a nuclear test in 1998. Such characteristics persist according to most analysts in spite of shifts in India's foreign policy after 1990 to enhance confidence-building through liberalization.[79] Brazil, on the other hand, is regarded as more friendly,[80] and even agreed in 2008 to further reduce manufacturing tariffs in order to have more access to the West's agricultural markets notwithstanding the continuous decreasing competitiveness of Brazilian industry.[81] This puts into question the assumption that former president Lula da Silva, from PT, brought more autonomy to Brazilian foreign policy,[82] and reiterates the role of colonial legacies in shaping global trajectories. Indeed, Brazil seems to be returning to its agro-export-driven past.

Furthermore, while India projected itself as a nuclear power in the mid 1990s amid its continuous rivalry with also nuclear Pakistan, Brazil gave up its nuclear military ambitions as part of its confidence-building strategy with the West. Geopolitical reasons, such as mutual agreements with Argentina since the 1980s regarding the control of nuclear technology, also played a role.[83] This decision can be traced back to Brazil's international identity as a state with strong Western roots. Colonial legacies combined with geopolitical variables – which are to some extent a consequence of the European/Western international society formed through imperialism in the nineteenth and twentieth centuries – make Brazil unlikely to be seen as a 'monster country'. A 'monster country', as Lafer defines it, has a large territory and population, but is located in a strategic geopolitical region for the West, namely locations in the contiguous space of important natural resources, particularly oil reserves in the Middle East, and where fierce disputes among large empires historically took place, as in the case of the Great Game between Britain and Russia in Central Asia during the second half of the nineteenth century.[84] This is the case not only of India but also of China and Russia, the other two major emerging powers. As just after its independence almost 200 years ago, Brazil remains in the periphery of international society: Western concerns are focused on East Asia's rise, as suggested by the US engagement with India to counterbalance Chinese influence.[85]

Conclusion

I have argued that the development trajectories of Brazil and India, and their respective patterns of integration in the international system, bear a strong imprint from colonial legacies. What are emerging powers today were once colonized territories. Just as Portugal's patrimonialist culture and reliance on foreign collaboration shapes Brazil's current reliance on raw material exports, Britain's administrative capabilities and colonial rule have shaped independent India's state configuration and identity, suspicious of the West and reflected in its pro-native-business approach.

While these conclusions do not immediately allow generalizations, they open new avenues of research into causes for post-colonial trajectories to be found in colonial legacies. Firstly, there is the study of characteristics of the state and society of potential great powers. Neither a pure Weberian bureaucracy nor a homogeneous society seems to be a domestic precondition for a country's rise in the international system, as the US and Western European experiences in nineteenth and twentieth centuries suggest. Most of the emerging powers still have to cope with monumental internal challenges, as is clear from increasing levels of inequality in China and India.[86] However, even in the West more internal equality was achieved only after the age of empires, with the class compromise that underpinned the post-War welfare states.

Secondly, it is also worth analysing the role of transnational communities and their impact on nation states' processes of international ascension and domestic cohesion. Like other countries in the Americas, Brazil received large flows of immigrants in the twentieth century, mainly from Europe, which contributed to internalize new technologies as industrialization took off. While these immigrants and their offspring established links with the outside, they did not constitute subnational communities, and were not a cause for concern about national cohesion or unity, at least as of the pre-World War II incorporation phase.[87] In India, the issue of religious diversity requested, in contrast to Brazil, a clearer rhetoric of national unity, rooted in the idea of secularism. This seems to have borne virtuous legacies insofar as, regardless of religious affiliation, migrants of the Indian diaspora contribute to the economic development of the country, be this through remittances, as is the case of transient workers in the Middle East, or based upon technological collaboration, as became evident in the technological services sector, in which Indian-Americans participate significantly.[88]

As potential cases for future comparison, there are countries that are legal children of great colonial powers, such as Argentina in relation to Spain, and step children, such as South Korea in relation to Japan,[89] which have experienced similar trajectories of industrialization under the Keynesian Consensus, although with different results in its aftermath. Whereas South Korea can be considered a winner in the global age, with a buoyant manufacturing sector and high standards of living, Argentina is a legal child that faced far more dependency in globalization than Brazil. There are also mixed cases, where it is not clear which model prevailed; in Mexico, for instance, pre-Colombian cultural traits still pervade social life, such as non-capitalist forms of economic organization based on subsistence agriculture in the countryside, whose population is mainly of indigenous ancestry, alongside Western modes of cultural and economic organization.[90]

It might be too pretentious to claim that these tales of globalization have morals, but it seems that, as children grow up, both legal and step, they 'learn' from their parents' legacies as well as from their indigenous heritage. Based on the contrast between Brazil's and India's respective trajectories, the step children seem to be more successful as they draw a clearer distinction between the domestic and the foreign, building up more effective national cohesion, and drawing strategies that combine pre-colonial and colonial strengths, while legal children lack a basis for cohesiveness, then accepting with more ease international trends in an uncritical manner rather than making them work in their favour, facing a more winding road in the quest for power. In either case, however, they may simply end up imitating the fate of their genitors, reaching glory just to fall again one day.

Notes

1 James Mahoney, *Colonialism and Postcolonial Development: Spanish America in Comparative Perspective* (New York, NY, and Cambridge, 2010).

2 Matthew Lange, *Lineages of Despotism and Development: British Colonialism and State Power* (Chicago, IL, and London, 2009).

3 P. A. Hall, *Governing the Economy: The Politics of State Intervention in Britain and France* (Oxford, 1986).

4 M. Lange, *Lineages of Despotism and Development: British Colonialism and State Power* (Chicago, 2009), p. 4.

5 M. Misra, 'Lessons of Empire: Britain and India', *SAIS Review*, 23, 2 (2003), pp. 133–53.

6 S. Vogel, *Japan Remodeled: How Government and Industry are Reforming Japanese Capitalism* (Ithaca, NY, 2006).

7 A. Kohli, *State-Directed Development: Political Power and Industrialization in the Global Periphery* (Cambridge, 2004).

8 R. J. C. Young, *Postcolonialism: A Very Short Introduction* (Oxford, 2003), p. 133.

9 B. Fausto, *A Concise History of Brazil* (Cambridge, 1999).

10 G. Freyre, *Casa Grande e Senzala: Formação da Família Brasileira sob o Regime de Economia Patriarcal* (Rio de Janeiro, 1983).

11 Sérgio Buarque de Hollanda, *Roots of Brazil* (Notre Dame, 2012).

12 H. Bull, 'The Emergence of a Universal International Society', p. 123, and A. Watson, 'New States in the Americas', pp. 130, 138, in H. Bull and A. Watson (eds), *The Expansion of International Society* (Oxford, 1984).

13 L. Schultz, *Beneath the United States: A History of U.S. Policy toward Latin America* (Cambridge, MA, 1998).

14 Fausto, *History of Brazil*.

15 J. Mahoney, *Colonialism and Postcolonial Development: Spanish America in Comparative Perspective* (Cambridge, 2010).

16 J. M. de Carvalho, *Cidadania no Brasil: o Longo Caminho* (Rio de Janeiro, 2004).

17 J. Nicolau, *História do Voto no Brasil* (Rio de Janeiro, 2002).

18 C. Hasembalg, *Discriminação e Desigualdades Raciais no Brasil*, 2nd edition (Rio de Janeiro, 2005), p. 148.

19 V. Rodrigues Vieira, *Democracia racial, do discurso à realidade: caminhos para a superação das desigualdades sociorraciais brasileiras* (São Paulo, Brasil, 2008), p. 153.

20 Fausto, *History of Brazil*.

21 Lange, *Despotism and Development*, pp. 176–9.

22 Misra, 'Lessons of Empire', p. 139.

23 A. Jalal, 'Exploding Communalism: The Politics of Muslim Identity in South Asia', in S. Bose and A. Jalal (eds), *Nationalism, Democracy and Development: State and Politics in India* (Oxford, 1998), pp. 76–103.

24 A. Kumar, *State and Society in India: A Study of the State's Agenda-Making, 1917–1977* (New Delhi, 1989), p. 33.

25 *Ibid.*, p. 74.

26 *Ibid.*, p. 65.

27 P. Chatterjee, *Nationalist Thought and the Colonial World: A Derivative Discourse?* (Minneapolis, MN, 1993), p. 77.

28 C. A. Bayly, 'Returning the British to South Asian history: The Limits of Colonial Hegemony', *South Asia: Journal of South Asian Studies*, 17, 2 (1994), pp. 21–2.

29 David Washbrook, The Rhetoric of Democracy and Development in Late Colonial India', in S. Bose and A. Jalal (eds), *Nationalism, Development and Democracy* (Delhi, 1998).

30 W. Nobrega and A. Sinha, *Riding the Indian Tiger: Understanding India – The World's Fastest Growing Market* (Hoboken, NJ, 2008), p. xv.

31 S. Bose, '"Hindu Nationalism" and the Crisis of the Indian State: A Theoretical Perspective', in Bose and Jalal, *Nationalism, Democracy and Development*, pp. 111–2.

32 Chatterjee, *Nationalist Thought*.

33 Lange, *Despotism and Development*.

34 Bose, 'Hindu Nationalism'; Jalal, 'Exploding Communalism'.

35 A. L. Stoler, *Race and the Education of Desire: Foucault's History of Sexuality and the Colonial Order of Things* (Durham, NC, 1995), p. 4.

36 Rodrigues Vieira, *Democracia racial*, p. 57.

37 I. Wallerstein, 'The Rise and Future Demise of the World Capitalist System: Concepts for Comparative Analysis', in J. Timmons Roberts and Amy Bellone Hite (eds), *The Globalization and Development Reader: Perspectives and Development and Global Change* (Malden, 2007), pp. 95–113.

38 W. W. Rostow, *The Stages of Economic Growth: A Non-Communist Manifesto*, 3rd edition (Cambridge, 1990).

39 P. Evans, *Embedded Autonomy: States and Industrial Transformation* (Princeton, NJ, 1995).

40 A. Kohli, *State-Directed Development: Political Power and Industrialization in the Global Periphery* (Cambridge, 2004).

41 R. B. Collier and D. Collier, *Shaping the Political Arena: Critical Junctures, the Labor Movement, and Regime Dynamics in Latin America* (Princeton, NJ, 1991).

42 Peter Evans, *Dependent Development: The Alliance of Multinational, State and Local Capital in Brazil* (Princeton, NJ, 1979).

43 D. Collier, 'Overview of the Bureaucratic-Authoritarian Model', in D. Collier (ed.), *The New Authoritarianism in Latin America* (Princeton, NJ, 1979), p. 24.

44 P. H. Smith, *Talons of the Eagle: Latin America, the United States, and the World*, 3rd edition (Oxford, 2008).

45 Kohli, *State-Directed Development*.

46 Rodrigues Vieira, *Democracia racial*, p. 69.

47 V. Bulmer-Thomas, *The Economic History of Latin America Since Independence* (Cambridge, 2003).

48 Chatterjee, *Nationalist Thought*, p.117.

49 Bose, 'Hindu Nationalism', p. 113.

50 Atul Kohli, *Democracy and Development in India: From Socialism to Pro-Business* (New Delhi and Oxford, 2009), p. 5.

51 *Ibid.*, pp. 114–15.

52 C. Jaffrelot, 'Caste and the Rise of Marginalized Groups', in S. Ganguly, L. Diamond and M. Plattner (eds), *The State of India's Democracy* (Baltimore, MD, 2007), pp. 67–88.

53 J. M. Grieco, *Between Dependency and Autonomy: India's Experience with the International Computer Industry* (Berkeley, CA, 1984), p. 10.

54 A. Kohli, 'The Politics of Economic Liberalization in India', in E. N. Suleiman and J. Waterbury (eds), *The Political Economy of Public Sector Reform and Privatization* (Boulder, CO, 1990), p. 370.

55 C.-W. Kim, *Economic Liberalization and India's Foreign Policy* (Delhi, 2006), pp. 63–5.

56 M. Hirst, 'A South–South Perspective', in R. Roett and G. Paz (eds), *China's Expansion Into the Western Hemisphere: Implications for Latin America and the United States* (Washington, DC, 2008) pp. 90–3.

57 P. T. Flecha de Lima, 'Diplomacia e Comércio: Notas sobre a Política Externa Brasileira nos Anos 70', in J. Augusto Guilhon Albuquerque (ed.), *Diplomacia para o Desenvolvimento* (São Paulo, 1996), pp. 219–38.

58 L. A. Moniz-Bandeira, *As relações perigosas: Brasil-Estados Unidos – De Collor a Lula – 1990–2004* (Rio de Janeiro, 2004), p. 55.

59 S. Danese, *Diplomacia Presidencial: História e Crítica* (Rio de Janeiro, 1999), pp. 250–4.

60 Harold Edward Stephen Fisher, *The Portugal Trade: A Study of Anglo-Portuguese Commerce, 1700–1770* (1971).

61 T. Vigevani and G. Cepaluni, 'Lula's Foreign Policy and the Quest for Autonomy through Diversification', *Third World Quarterly*, 28, 7 (2007), pp. 1309–26.

62 The term is a reference to policies recommended and enforced by the International Monetary Fund (IMF) and the World Bank as preconditions for loans, intended to correct balance of payment deficits that originated after the debt crisis. John Williamson (ed.), *Latin American Adjustment: How Much Has Happened?* (Washington, DC, 1990).

63 Atul Kohli, 'The Politics of Economic Liberalization in India', in Ezra N. Suleiman and John Waterbury (eds), *The Political Economy of Public Sector Reform and Privatization* (Boulder, CO, 1990), pp. 364–88.

64 T. N. Srinivasan and Suresh D. Tendulkar, *Reintegrating India with the World Economy* (Washington, DC, 2003).

65 Kohli, 'Politics of Economic Liberalization', p. 371.

66 R. Jenkins, *Democratic Politics and Economic Reform in India* (Cambridge, 1999), p. 42.

67 Kohli, *State-Directed Development*.

68 D. Kumar Das (ed.), *Structural Adjustment in the Indian Economy: Recent Trends and Future Challenges* (New Delhi, 1993), p. 47.

69 A. Karmarkar, 'The Indian Economy: A March Towards Globalization', in *ibid.*, pp. 25–36.

70 L. C. Bresser-Pereira, *Developing Brazil: Overcoming the Failure of the Washington Consensus* (Boulder, CO, 2009).

71 G. H. B. Franco, 'A inserção externa e o desenvolvimento', *Revista de Economia Política*, 3 (1998), 121–47.

72 D. Samuels, 'Fiscal Straitjacket: The Politics of Macroeconomic Reform in Brazil, 1995–2002', *Journal of Latin American Studies*, 35, 3 (2003), pp. 545–69.

73 World Bank, 'World Development Indicators', 2010 (http://esds.mcc.ac.uk/wds_wb/ReportFolders/reportFolders.aspx?sCS_referer=&sCS_ChosenLang=en, accessed 27 April 2011).

74 Bresser-Pereira, *Developing Brazil*, p. 203.

75 World Bank, 'World Development Indicators', 2010 (http://data.worldbank.org/data-catalog/world-development-indicators/wdi-2010, accessed September 2014).

76 World Bank, 'World Development Indicators', 2010 (http://data.worldbank.org/data-catalog/world-development-indicators/wdi-2010, accessed September 2014).

77 United Nations Development Programme, 'International Human Development Indicators', 2010 (http://hdr.undp.org/en/, accessed 27 April 2011).

78 A. Narlikar, *New Powers: How to Become One and How to Manage Them* (2010), p. 30.

79 Kim, *Economic Liberalization*, p. 190.

80 Narlikar, *New Powers*, p. 109.

81 G. Palma, 'Why has Productivity Growth Stagnated in most Latin American Countries since the Neo-Liberal Reforms?', in J. A. Ocampo and J. Ros (eds), *Oxford Handbook of Latin American Economics* (Oxford, 2011), pp. 568–607.

82 Rodrigues Vieira, *Democracia racial*.

83 A. C. Sotomayor Velazquez, 'Civil-Military Affairs and Security Institutions in the Southern Cone: The Sources of Argentine-Brazilian Nuclear Cooperation', *Latin American Politics & Society*, 46, 4 (2004), pp. 29–60.

84 Celso Lafer, 'Brasil: dilemas e desafios da política externa', *Estudos Avançados*, 14, 38, pp. 260–7.

85 M. Sieff, *Shifting Superpowers: The New and Emerging Relationships Between the United States, China and India* (Washington, DC, 2010).

86 P. K. Bardhan, *Awakening Giants, Feet of Clay: Assessing the Economic Rise of China and India* (Princeton, NJ, 2010).

87 Rodrigues Vieira, *Democracia racial*.

88 A. Pandey et al., 'The Indian Diaspora: A Unique Case?', in Y. Kuznetsov, *Networks and the International Migration of Skills: How Countries Can Draw on Their Talent Abroad* (Washington, DC, 2006).

89 For a discussion of Japanese colonial legacies on South Korea in contrast with the impact of Portuguese colonization in Brazil, see Vinícius Rodrigues Vieira, 'Invisible Legacies: Brazil's and South Korea's Shift from ISI towards Export Strategies under Authoritarian Rule', *Journal of International Relations and Development*, 17, 2, pp. 157–90.

90 G. B. Batalla, *Mexico profundo: una civilizacion negada* (Mexico, 1990).

Echoes of Imperialism in LGBT Activism

Rahul Rao

At least one early critical reaction to the emergence of the term 'post-colonial' expressed disquiet about its 'premature celebration of the pastness of colonialism'.[1] Writing in 1992 and citing the then continuing coloniality of Northern Ireland, Palestine, South Africa, East Timor and other places, Anne McClintock worried that this premature celebration ran 'the risk of obscuring the continuities and discontinuities of colonial and imperial power'.[2] While her examples focused on instances of enduring territorial colonialism, it is salutary to bear in mind that imperialism crucially also always had a non-territorial ideational dimension, expressed in projects such as the civilizing mission. It is in the form of this non-territorial dimension that imperialism today is more visible and ubiquitous, enduring long after the reduction of territorial imperialism to a few anachronistic vestiges, and inflecting even those apparently radical and oppositional spaces of politics in which one might least expect it.

In this chapter, I explore the 'echoes of imperialism' in one such space – that of global contention for the recognition of the rights of lesbian, gay, bisexual and transgendered (LGBT) subjects, as well as of other sexual minorities who might not identify in these terms.[3] In doing so, I hear two sorts of echoes. First, my critique of imperial tendencies within contemporary Western LGBT politics parallels and tries to learn from an earlier critique levelled by Third World feminists such as Chandra Talpade Mohanty at white Western feminism. Just as these earlier critiques punctured lazy slogans of 'global sisterhood' that are inattentive to hierarchies of race, class and nationality within women's movements, I question the putative singularity of an assumed global gay subject that seems to underpin some contemporary Western LGBT activism.[4] Second, I attempt to peel away the layers of discourse that encrust such activism in our own time, to reveal the underlying political interests that sustain it. In doing so, I find it helpful to think about the political interests that generated a late nineteenth-century politics of imperial Victorian feminism that saw the rescue of distant global sisters as a means towards improving the condition of women in the imperial metropolis. Both temporal contexts present a bewildering array of tendencies: contemporary Western LGBT activism is a deeply divided space, some of whose constituents are complicit in imperial ventures even as others are deeply antagonistic to them. The past is no less complicated a space, so full of contradictory tendencies that it is difficult to regard our 'post-colonial' age as self-evidently more progressive or reflexive than times gone by.

The construction of a global discourse of LGBT rights and a politics of LGBT solidarity[5] has been empowering for many of its participants. But it has not been an entirely benign development, free from questions of power and hierarchy. Struggles against heteronormativity within Western societies have tended to be marked by a fundamental tension between what might be described as a liberal politics of inclusion or assimilation into the mainstream – marked by such priorities as the right to marry or to serve in the military – and a more radical queer politics that seeks to challenge the very basis of institutions that are seen as oppressive, rather than merely seeking inclusion within them.[6] This fundamental tension has also begun to manifest itself in Western advocacy efforts on behalf of Third World[7] sexual minorities, with the more assimilatory strands of Western advocacy seeking to utilize Western hegemony for the advancement of sexual rights in other parts of the world, antagonizing queer activists and scholars who are deeply invested in contesting such hegemony even as they struggle for sexual freedoms. In the discourse of the former, as LGBT communities have won political and legal battles in the West and have begun to assimilate more deeply into their societies, LGBT rights have become a marker of modernity, resulting in the creation of new hierarchies – or what Jon Binnie calls 'a new racism' – in international politics.[8] States that fail to respect rights around sexual diversity are, in a retrieval of standard orientalist tropes, increasingly characterized as 'backward' and 'uncivilized', with the internationalization of LGBT rights taking on the character of a modern-day civilizing mission.[9]

Scholars have begun to criticize the increasingly apparent orientalism of some contemporary Western LGBT activism.[10] Yet some of these critiques have been overstated. A case in point is Joseph Massad's recent indictment of Western LGBT activism vis-à-vis the Middle East. Massad argues that such activism seeks to replicate the trajectory of gay liberation in the West by attempting to transform practitioners of same-sex conduct in the Arab world into subjects who identify as homosexual.[11] Following Foucault, scholars regard sexuality as having been transformed in the Western world from an aspect of behaviour (what one did) to an aspect of identity (what sort of person one was) sometime in the late nineteenth century, through the operation of discourses of medicine and law.[12] The dislocations produced by industrial capitalism and mass urbanization were simultaneously disrupting traditional family structures and providing the conditions – for some – of individual material self-sufficiency and anonymity that enabled the configuration of new forms of community. These developments in turn provided the demographic basis for the struggle for rights later in the twentieth century, culminating in such epochal moments as the Stonewall Riots that took place in New York City in 1969, widely regarded as marking the birth of the modern LGBT rights movement. In Massad's view, Western LGBT organizations operating in the Arab world seek to replicate this history by pushing those who engage in same-sex practices to 'come out' (i.e. identify) as homosexuals. Yet far from bringing the liberating consequences that this move had in the West, Massad judges that this push from behaviour to identity represents an imperialist imposition that is narrowing the space for same-sex behaviour. Governments that once turned a blind eye to discreet homosexual behaviour are increasingly cracking down on newly visible sexual minorities: it is identity rather than behaviour, in his view, that is considered intolerable and makes individuals vulnerable.[13]

The argument is troubling in a number of respects, not least because it appears to deny the agency and subjectivity of Arabs who are beginning to identify as sexual minorities, appropriating and reworking Western identities in their struggles for sexual self-determination. Massad alternately dismisses these individuals as unrepresentative, regards them as passive victims of a Western-imposed sexual re-education, or more ominously describes them as 'native informants' to Western activists.[14] In the colonial archive, the native informant is a slippery and elusive character, at once powerful and politically suspect from the viewpoint of both the colonial authorities and the natives between whom he intermediates. Comprising, in the words of Thomas Babington Macaulay's infamous Minute on Indian Education (1835), 'a class of persons Indian in blood and colour, but English in tastes, in opinions, in morals and in intellect', he is relied on by the colonial authorities for the knowledge that will inform the power they exercise over the natives.[15] Yet as Homi Bhabha has persuasively argued, his very mimicry of the colonial overlords constantly menaces the racial hierarchies upon which colonial rule is premised.[16] He is the figure through whom the natives formulate their demands in a language intelligible to their colonial masters, yet his very closeness to the latter invites suspicion of traitorous collaboration with the colonizing power. In the context of Western LGBT advocacy in the Arab world, Massad's revival of the trope of the 'native informant' to describe Arabs who identify in terms of a Western sexual ontology stems from his view of them as an unrepresentative metropolitan minority whose motivation for identification in such terms is class-based: 'part of the package of the adoption of everything Western by the classes to which they belong.'[17] Rather than treating the question of motivation as an empirical one, Massad understands it as a function of a self-orientalizing tendency to regard the West as superior in all respects rather than as being the result of reasoned, ethical disagreement with local sexual ontologies.

The insinuations of inauthenticity that attach to his representations of LGBT Arabs deny the possibility and legitimacy of appropriation of ethical categories from outside the moral universes into which they were born. In addition, the fact that Arabs who identify publicly as LGBT often do so at grave personal risk – something that finds no acknowledgement in Massad's argument – makes their comparison to colonial native informants (who profited enormously from their position) particularly inappropriate.

In this chapter, I focus on another problematic dimension of Massad's argument, namely his tendency to flatten out the space of Western LGBT activism vis-à-vis the non-Western word. Massad refers to the institutions of LBGT activism collectively as the 'Gay International' (reminiscent of W. H. Auden's 'homintern') and regards all such activism as being implicated in an imperial politics. This reflects the tendency of some post-colonial work to think of the 'West' in monolithic terms, even as it resists the essentialization of the 'Orient'.[18] In this chapter I disaggregate the 'Gay International' into a number of strands and argue that while some of these have indeed been complicit in contemporary imperial projects, others have not. Critiques of activism that do not make such distinctions have the unfortunate consequence of shutting down activism around sexuality altogether, implicitly denying the seriousness of the homophobia against which it is directed. In contrast, demonstrating that there is no single politics to the so-called Gay International might be a first step towards determining whether there is anything worth salvaging in this politics of putative Western solidarity with Third World sexual minorities. The fractiousness of the 'Gay International' became particularly apparent in the debates that erupted amongst Western activists over how to respond to the execution in Iran in 2005 of two boys alleged to have committed a crime involving homosexual intercourse. Accordingly, much of this chapter focuses on the reaction to these executions, which became the site on which the internal politics of the so-called Gay International played itself out. In keeping with the themes of this book, the chapter attempts to historicize the different strands of the 'Gay International' in light of the record of Western intervention seeking to reshape gender relations in Iran (and other parts of the Third World) since the heyday of colonial times. In doing so, I find that while the contemporary 'Gay International' is a deeply divided space, some of whose constituents are complicit in imperial ventures even as others are antagonistic to them, this is no less true of late nineteenth- and early twentieth-century Western feminist interventions in the colonized world.

Hangings in Iran: Disaggregating the 'Gay International'

On 19 July 2005, two boys – Ayaz Marhoni and Mahmoud Asgari – variously reported to have been between 16 and 18 years of age, were hanged by the government of

Iran in the city of Mashhad for an alleged crime involving homosexual intercourse. Western activists were divided over how to respond.[19] Some regarded the boys as having been hanged on account of their sexuality and denounced the Iranian government, demanding that Western governments take punitive action. British activist Peter Tatchell, whose group OutRage! first brought the story to the attention of Western media, was quoted in a press release as saying that 'this is just the latest barbarity by the Islamo-fascists in Iran [...] the entire country is a gigantic prison, with Islamic rule sustained by detention without trial, torture and state-sanctioned murder', before going on to claim that over 4,000 lesbians and gay men had been executed by the government since the 1979 revolution.[20] Conservative US commentator Andrew Sullivan echoed this language, repeating the claim that the boys had been hanged by the 'Islamo-fascist regime in Iran' for 'being gay'. Expressing disappointment that more gay organizations had not rallied to the war against 'Muslim religious fanatics', Sullivan emphasized that 'this is our war too'.[21] The linkage of Iran with fascism was reinforced by Doug Ireland, a New York-based journalist who described the Ahmadinejad government as being engaged in a 'major anti-homosexual pogrom targeting gays and gay sex'.[22] The Human Rights Campaign, the largest LGBT civil rights organization in the US, called upon the then Secretary of State Condoleezza Rice to issue an 'immediate and strong condemnation' of Iran for its hanging of the teenagers who, it alleged, had been tortured and killed 'simply for being caught having consensual sex'. It urged that 'atrocities committed by foreign governments against all people must be condemned swiftly and forcefully by the world's greatest democracy'.[23] The Log Cabin Republicans, an organization of gay and lesbian members of the US Republican Party, issued a press release in which it noted that 'in the wake of news stories and photographs documenting the hanging of two gay Iranian teenagers, Log Cabin Republicans reaffirm their commitment to the global war on terror'. The group's president, Patrick Guerriero, was quoted as saying that 'this barbarous slaughter clearly demonstrates the stakes in the global war on terror. Freedom must prevail over radical Islamic extremism'.[24]

It was not the first time that Western observers had expressed revulsion at the sexual mores of Iranian society. In an ironic reversal of contemporary attitudes, travelogues of Western visitors to Iran from the seventeenth century onwards frequently record disgust at the observation of same-sex liaisons within aristocratic circles in Tehran. Janet Afary has written about the prevalence of 'status-defined homosexuality' in pre-modern Iran, typically involving partners of different ages, classes or social standings.[25] She chronicles the abundant representation of same-sex love in classical Persian literature, the wealth of allusion to homoerotic relations in the Persian language, and the widespread prevalence of homosexuality and homoerotic expression in public spaces beyond the royal court, including monasteries and seminaries, taverns, military camps, bathhouses and coffeehouses. While not free of moral judgements, she argues that until the late nineteenth century Iranian representations of same-sex love were far less judgemental than the contemporary Western regime of sexuality.[26]

Afsaneh Najmabadi has argued that as Iranian elites came into contact with Europeans and realized that 'polite' European society held such practices to be abominable, their response was one of disavowal and dissimulation.[27] Iranians began to find themselves 'explaining' to European visitors that the latter had mistakenly read homosociality (men holding hands, embracing and kissing in public) as homosexuality. Homoeroticism in Sufi poetry began to be read as purely allegorical and metaphorical for communion between the devout and the divine. Practices of representation underwent dramatic shifts. While notions of beauty were largely undifferentiated by gender in early Qajar (1785–1925) paintings, with beautiful men and women being depicted with similar facial and bodily features, by the end of the nineteenth century the portrayal of beauty had become less androgynous and more gendered. Similarly, while biographical writing well into the nineteenth century contains numerous non-judgemental references to diverse sexual preferences, twentieth-century references to same-sex relationships become more disapproving. Modernist Iranian intellectuals such as the influential nineteenth-century critic Mirza Fath'ali Akhundzadah (1812–78) began to speak of homosexuality as situational, as something that Iranian men indulged in because of gender segregation. By implication, as the sexes were allowed to mingle freely in a modernizing Iran, homosexual relations would disappear. One of the central projects of early Iranian feminism was the transformation of heterosexual marriage from a loveless procreative contract into a romantic one; but the flip side of this was the stigmatization of other forms of desire, leaving – in Najmabadi's words – 'a birthmark of disavowal of male homosexuality on the modernist project of women's emancipation'.[28] The larger point here is that by the late nineteenth century, the heteronormalization of Iranian society had come to be regarded as a marker of modernity. The irony is that the exact opposite has become true in the early twenty-first century.

I would like to anticipate and pre-empt the temptation to extrapolate from Najmabadi's account the claim that European imperialism is to blame for homophobia in contemporary Iran in a straightforward way. This would be a crude, polemical and reductionist conclusion to draw from Najmabadi's complex and nuanced exposition of the transformation of gender relations in Iran. Rather, what emerges from this story is a crucial moment in which even as European imperialism passes judgement on the 'Orient', native elites respond to this challenge, in part, by accepting the European critique and seeking to act upon it. Thus, the heteronormalization of Iranian society (which paves the way for the later institutionalization of homophobia) has to be understood as a transaction involving European and Iranian elites, in which the latter exercise some degree of agency in choosing to reshape their societies in particular ways in the course of the nineteenth-century cultural conflicts between Iran/Islam and Europe/Christianity. Indeed, a growing body of queer scholarship in respect of other parts of the world has begun to locate the institutionalization of homophobia in the colonial encounter in just this way, and to explain it with reference to the desire of anti-colonial elites to construct virile, masculinized nationalisms capable of overthrowing the colonial yoke – a task that entailed the erasure of indigenous traditions of androgeneity and same-sex desire.[29] Massad might suggest that a converse process of 'homo-normalization' of Middle Eastern societies is currently underway as a result of analogous transactions between the 'Gay International' and its 'native informants'. It is certainly too early to conclude, in the case of Iran, whether the process will play out in anything like the same way. Moreover, and crucially to the thrust of my overall argument, one can note the structural similarity of these transactions between Western and Iranian elites in the nineteenth and twenty-first centuries, while taking the view that they have very different political and ethical implications depending on whether they expand or constrict the space for sexual freedom. The more troubling historical continuity is that in both moments, some Western actors have arrogated to themselves (and some Iranian elites have conceded to their Western interlocutors) the power to define the content of modernity, so that being modern continues to mean becoming like the West.

Returning to the events of 2005, Western voices of condemnation of the hangings in Mashhad were divided in terms of the remedial action that they advocated. Some, like Sullivan and the Log Cabin Republicans, regarded incidents such as the Mashhad hangings as vindicating the use of force against 'radical Islam' wherever it manifested itself; others, like Tatchell and OutRage!, sought to clarify that their denunciation of the hangings did not amount to an endorsement of war against Iran.[30] Indeed, Tatchell appears incongruous amongst the many Republican Party-affiliated gay voices in the US who happened to agree with him on this issue, given his history of involvement in left-wing causes and his membership of the Green Party in Britain. Although appearing to share a common position, the different reactions to the Iran hangings were underpinned by distinct sets of political considerations, which I discuss in the following sections.

The more institutionalized activists – those in organizations such as Amnesty International, Human Rights Watch (HRW) and the International Gay and Lesbian Human Rights Commission (IGLHRC) – responded in a very different fashion. Scott Long of HRW was sceptical of the accounts that Tatchell, Ireland and others were providing because they relied mainly on diasporic and exile groups as their sources. These groups, in his view, had long sought to refract situations in Iran that presented human rights concerns through the lens of LGBT rights, in a politically opportunistic attempt to attract the support of yet another international constituency in their struggle against the theocratic regime. In addition, Long believed that conflicting reports claiming that the boys had been executed for raping a 13-year-old boy, while quite conceivably trumped up by the regime to justify the sentence, should not have been dismissed out of hand without careful consideration.[31] HRW, Amnesty and IGLHRC sought to reframe the issue as one about the execution of minors, a violation of the UN Convention on the Rights of the Child and the International Covenant on Civil and Political Rights (both of which Iran has signed).[32] One crucial implication of this reframing was that if Iran was to be censured for its execution of children, the US lacked the moral standing to do so. Of the nine countries that are known to have executed juvenile offenders between 1990 and 2009, Iran topped the list with forty-six executions, while the US followed second with nineteen.[33] (The US Supreme Court declared the use of the death penalty against juvenile offenders unconstitutional in March 2005.)[34] In addition, some activists in these organizations worried that attacking Iran could legitimate the Bush administration's demonization of the Iranian regime at a time when tensions were already running high on account of its nuclear programme and the election of the conservative Ahmadinejad to the office of the presidency only a few weeks before.

Rescue Narratives of the Right

In the wake of the Mashhad hangings, it was possible to discern the emergence of a discourse on right-wing gay websites based in the US and Europe, in which gay rights were pitted against the putative beliefs of 'Islamists'. A central feature of this discourse is that it places LGBT rights at the heart of an enlightened Judaeo-Christian 'West', which confronts a uniformly homophobic 'non-West' 'sunk in ignorance, superstition, barbarism, and moral darkness',[35] evidenced by its failure to respect such rights. Indeed, the very purpose of the comparisons through which this narrative is constructed seems to be the extraction of a hierarchy in which the West is better than the non-West, Israel is superior to Palestine,[36] Christianity is preferable to Islam,[37] and so on. Gayatri Chakravorty Spivak has characterized colonial feminism – exemplified by such acts as the British abolition of sati in India in the nineteenth century – as a case of 'white men, seeking to save brown women from brown men'.[38] Through such gestures, imperialism represents itself as the establisher of the good society by espousing women as objects of protection from their own (racial and national) kind. Something similar appears to be at work in the contemporary eagerness of white queers to save brown queers from brown homophobes. For their part, brown men/homophobes have attempted, just as vigorously, to assert their jurisdiction over brown women/queers and to defend the terrain of brown gender from any perceived encroachment by what are seen to be imperialist modernizing drives. As Partha Chatterjee has demonstrated, the (male) anti-colonial nationalist typically evinced a split mentality, acknowledging his material inferiority but insisting on his spiritual superiority vis-à-vis the colonizer. This meant that anti-imperialist struggle entailed the mimicry of colonial material modernity with a view to catching up with and surpassing the enemy, alongside a rejection of any colonial interference in the social and cultural domains of life. Gender relations were placed squarely in the latter domains, with women-as-mothers functioning as repositories and intergenerational transmitters of cultural capital.[39] The body of the brown woman/queer therefore takes on an overdetermined significance in the Manichean confrontation between white men/queers and brown men/homophobes.

Here I am interested primarily in understanding the impetus for white queer rescue narratives. Jasbir Puar's notion of homonormative nationalism or 'homo-nationalism' is particularly useful in understanding this in the context of contemporary US politics. Borrowing from Lisa Duggan's idea of 'homonormativity', which refers broadly to the phenomenon of gay subjects becoming embroiled in a politics that does not contest dominant heteronormative forms but upholds and sustains them, Puar defines 'homo-nationalism' as a 'collusion between homosexuality and American nationalism i.e. generated both by national rhetorics of patriotic inclusion and by gay, lesbian, and queer subjects themselves'.[40] Contrary to conventional gendered readings of state and nation as being only supportive and productive of heterosexuality and always repressive and disallowing of homosexuality, Puar suggests that 'there is room for the absorption and management of homosexuality [...] when advantageous for US national interests'.[41]

From the perspective of the US state, such absorption might enable the cooption of LGBT rights as an additional legitimation for the 'war on terror' and the project to reshape the Middle East.[42] The harnessing of 'Islamist persecution of LGBT rights' in this fashion is analogous to the use of the Taliban's persecution of Afghan women as justification for the war on Afghanistan in 2001.[43] Yet it might legitimately be asked whether a homophobic Republican US administration – such as the one in power in 2005[44] – had any interest in using alleged LGBT persecution in the Middle East in this fashion. It might be thought that significant constituencies within the party base (evangelical Christians for example) would have been alienated by any advancement of LGBT rights, either domestically or abroad. In what ways might the 'absorption and management of homosexuality' advantage the US state, particularly when it has been captured by the homophobic right?

It is in addressing this question that it becomes clear that the more significant motivations for the gay rescue narrative lie not in the international interests of the US state so much as in the realm of US domestic politics. It is worth recalling that the narrative is produced not by state functionaries, but by mostly right-wing non-governmental gay activists. It could be argued that it is the very incompleteness of their inclusion in the US nation, and the Republican Party more specifically, that furnishes a powerful incentive for collusion between homosexuality and nationalism.

Offering a 'gay' reason for supporting nationalist projects such as the 'war on terror', the gay rescue narrative becomes a means of expressing patriotic sentiment with a view to hastening assimilation into nation and party. Patriotism functions as what Puar calls a 'defensive and normalising' gesture,[45] signalling proximity to a nation and party of which one is not (yet) a full member by emphasizing distance from ultimate Others. Through the gay rescue narrative, the message that right-wing gay activists appear to be sending to a Republican Party whose acceptance they crave seems to be: 'you are against the terrorists; the terrorists are against gays; therefore you ought to be with gays'.

There is a long history of metropolitan subaltern groups participating in a politics of imperialism in the periphery as a means to acquiring full citizenship at home. We can see this in the discourse of many late nineteenth- and early twentieth-century Western feminists and suffragists. The perceived abjectness of their 'sisters' in the colonies, constructed as oppressed by practices such as veiling, sati and foot-binding, provided an Other against whom Western women were able to consolidate themselves as fully formed subjects epitomizing modernity and progress. It also gave them work to do in the colonies, enabling them to escape the stifling confines of Victorian conceptions of femininity which considerably limited opportunities for professional advancement and self-assertion at home. Nima Naghibi has argued that notwithstanding their unequal relationship to men and to the colonial project, Western women were able to argue for their participation in colonial and imperial ventures not despite, but in substantial part *because of*, their gender. Arguing that as women they had unfettered access to female spaces like the harem in which Persian women were oppressed by their men, white Western women were able to define their own unique burden in the context of the civilizing mission.[46]

Travelling to the colonies as missionaries, teachers, reformers, ethnologists and colonial housewives, whether they were feminists or not, Western women were explicitly and implicitly demonstrating that they were the equals of men, playing an integral role in the expansion and consolidation of empire. This was critical in the context of the struggle for female suffrage within the metropolis because it offered a suitable riposte to those opposing votes for women, who had argued during World War I that women should not have the vote because they had not fought in the war or defended the empire.[47] It is no accident that significant sections of the contemporary US LGBT rights movement have invested considerable energy in fighting for a right to serve in the US military: such demonstrations of loyalty to, and participation in, national and imperial ventures have historically been a very effective means of claiming full citizenship.

Of course not all Victorian and Edwardian suffragists were imperialists. As Naghibi reminds us, more militant sections of the women's movement in Britain resisted the dominant tendency to construct white women as active subjects juxtaposed against their victimized Persian counterparts. When the Persian Women's Society addressed an appeal to the suffragists in Britain – 'The Russian government by an ultimatum demands us to surrender to her our independence; the ears of the men of Europe are deaf to our cries; could you women not come to our help?' – the [British] Women's Social and Political Union replies telegraphically: 'we cannot move [the] British government to give political freedom even to us, their own country-women. We are equally powerless to influence their actions towards Persia.'[48] It is a dispiriting response, but one that has the virtue of recognizing a sisterhood founded on shared oppression, rather than being advanced from a position of racial and national superiority.

Rescue Narratives of the Left

If assimilation at home rather than solidarity with distant Others explains the predominant motivation behind the production of rescue narratives by right-wing constituents of the 'Gay International', how do we understand the politics of someone like Peter Tatchell, who would typically be seen as left-wing in both the US and UK? Tatchell was dismissive of the suggestion – which I put to him in an interview in 2007 – that his activism against the Iranian regime might have played into the hands of war-mongering neo-conservatives. Hitting back at his critics (organizations such as HRW and IGLHRC, which distanced themselves from his protests), he offered a straightforwardly anti-consequentialist view insisting on the need to vindicate the rights of persecuted sexual minorities in Iran, regardless of the ways in which this might have strained the West's already fraught relations with that country:

> They seem to take the view that because the United States is against Iran, we mustn't do anything that fuels the argument that Iran is a bad regime. My view is very simple. Human rights are universal and indivisible, whether in Iran, Britain or the United States. There's no ifs, no buts. You defend the persecuted and oppose the oppressor [...] there's no qualifications, there's no exceptions, it's universal, for everyone, everywhere, in all circumstances, at all times.[49]

In analysing Tatchell's position, it is vital to bear in mind that in contrast to conservative activists in the US, he operates from a more gay-friendly jurisdiction in which LGBT citizens have won a number of significant victories, particularly since the election of a Labour government in Britain in 1997. Indeed, for British and Northern European activists, the fulfilment of much of the LGBT rights agenda at home has freed up time and resources and added a moral impetus for the internationalization of activism on behalf of distant Others who are seen as less fortunate. This is not to suggest that sexual minorities in these countries have achieved all their aims, but with the 'great' victories of decriminalization, same-sex partnerships and – in some cases – marriage behind them, the existential crisis experienced by activists as a result of these achievements is alleviated to some extent by human rights abuses in the Third World that can be framed as gay rights violations.[50] Clifford Bob has written about the relationship of mutual dependence between embattled Third World activists and Western patrons, reminding us that while the former depend on the latter for material resources, Western activists derive significant non-material resources from their Third World interlocutors: a *raison d'être*, legitimation for international activism, proof that their agenda remains unfulfilled, symbols for broader campaigns, prestige with their support base, and so on.[51] These are plausible motivations for Tatchell's interest in framing human rights abuses abroad as gay rights violations.

Any criticism of Tatchell's activism is met with the response that his interventions are explicitly requested by sexual minorities suffering oppression in distant parts of the world. Yet closer attention to the requests for help that Tatchell cites to legitimate his activism reveals a deeply ambiguous picture. Arsham Parsi, a gay Iranian activist who obtained asylum in Canada from persecution on account of sexual orientation, is critical of Tatchell's brand of activism, arguing that his commemoration of the 2005 hangings with protests outside Iranian embassies a year later was counterproductive and politically damaging.[52] When I put it to Tatchell that some Iranian activists appeared to be critical of what he was doing he was incredulous at first, arguing that Parsi was initially supportive of the protests and changed his mind only after he had been influenced by HRW's Long. That Parsi was initially supportive appears to be true, given that he had himself incurred criticism from other Iranian activists for standing with Tatchell on the issue.[53] Tatchell is also quick to point out that Parsi does not speak for all Iranian homosexuals. He claims that there were five Iranian LGBT groups at the time of the commemorations, four of which supported his protests. He cites a letter of support issued by MAHA, an e-list which claims a subscription of 1,700 members and a readership of three to five thousand, which strongly endorsed the protests despite the controversy they generated.[54] Tatchell's claims of support are difficult to verify, given his unwillingness to reveal the identity of his interlocutors and the general difficulties of studying the political organization of homosexuals in Iran.

These issues have recurred in Tatchell's relations with African activists, many of whom have publicly dissociated themselves from his campaigns in relation to Nigeria and Uganda in an open letter published in January 2007, citing his failure to consult with local activists and his pursuit of misguided tactics that could endanger local movements.[55] Once again, Tatchell insists that his activism is solicited by many Nigerian and Ugandan activists, citing groups such as Gay and Lesbian Alliance (GALA) and Makerere University Students' Lesbian Association (MUSLA) in Uganda.

He also suggests that his critics – groups like Sexual Minorities Uganda (SMUG) – were animated by petty local turf rivalries. In his view, their denunciation of OutRage! was precipitated by resentment that it worked with other groups in Uganda and fear of a loss of status as these local rivals gained international visibility and prestige as a result of their collaboration with OutRage![56] On a field visit to Uganda in August 2010, I found no evidence of the groups that Tatchell had mentioned. Kasha Jacqueline, founder and director of Freedom and Roam Uganda (a leading lesbian organization in the country), cited a number of instances in which fraudsters posing as NGOs, had solicited human rights funding and support from external donors and activists. She described MUSLA as one such 'briefcase organisation', headed by a group of men and having no lesbians in its membership.[57] Even if we were to give Tatchell the benefit of the doubt, he has at the very least been naive insofar as his interactions with Ugandan and other African LGBT organizations are concerned. At the same time, his interventions in these situations are both powerful and disruptive, as evidenced by the complaints of African activists in the 2007 open letter.

One other possibility that this controversy suggests is that in a field apparently crowded with 'native informants', some Western solidarity activists tend to reach out to those who endorse their project, while ignoring the criticisms of those who do not. Local interlocutors in turn are not abject, apolitical actors suffering oppression, but complex subjects with interests and agendas of their own. The entry of resource-rich solidarity activists into an already fractious terrain can set off a competitive dynamic amongst local actors competing with one another to be privileged informants in anticipation of the potential rewards that might flow from such relationships. Far from assisting in the creation of a united front against homophobia, the external activist can exacerbate local tensions and fracture movements.

Finally, one has to consider the politics of the larger organizations (Amnesty, HRW, IGLHRC, etc.) in the 'Gay International'. Such actors are vulnerable to many of the same criticisms that could be made of Tatchell. They too 'need' human rights violations abroad as a reason for being, and have an interest in framing power struggles in different parts of the world as 'rights violations' with a view to sustaining particular programmes and campaigns. They share a common sexual identity vocabulary with the right- and left-wing gay saviours discussed here. In this sense, Massad is not wrong to speak of the 'Gay International' as a collectivity. In the context of their reactions to the 2005 executions in Iran, however, some crucial distinctions have to be made.

Notwithstanding their common ontological premises, these organizations have generally tended to be wary of foisting a Western sexual ontology on subjects in countries like Iran in the absence of self-identification in these terms. HRW's recent report on the persecution of queers in Iraq, for example, describes the men interviewed for the report as 'gay' only because they themselves used the term in preference to newly coined Arabic equivalents such as *mithli*. Even so, the report cautions against the assumption that being 'gay' in Iraq has the same connotations as it does in the West, noting that the usage of the term in Iraq has as much to do with gender (perceptions of where the subject is located on a butch/fem spectrum, for example) as with the object of one's sexual desire.[58]

In some cases, these organizations have resisted applying an LGBT rights frame to particular instances of abuse. In a virtual reprise of the events of 2005, when Makwan Moloudzadeh, a 21-year-old Iranian man, was sentenced to death in June 2007 on charges of having raped three boys when he was himself only 13, groups like OutRage! and the Italian collective Gruppo EveryOne once again treated the case as one of gay persecution and lobbied the Iranian government in these terms, demanding that the sentence be lifted. In contrast, following investigations which revealed no evidence of any sexual acts whatsoever, Amnesty and HRW flatly denied that Mouloudzadeh was gay and sought to reframe advocacy around the issue as one about the execution of juveniles. Their position was based on evidentiary considerations, but also on the grounds that it was tactically ill-advised to campaign for Mouloudzadeh as a 'gay' person in a country where homosexual conduct, whether consensual or not, could incur the death penalty. Despite a brief window of hope in which the sentence was suspended by the head of Iran's judiciary pending an official investigation into allegations of trial irregularities, Mouloudzadeh was executed in December 2007. Long argues that the framing of advocacy on his behalf in terms of gay rights did real damage to his case, possibly inducing the Iranian authorities to carry out the sentence.[59]

In an interview, Long articulated HRW's preferred approach to such cases in the following terms:

> we were ultimately trying to speak to an Iranian audience. And Iranian audiences, regardless of what they think about *lavat* [sodomy], the main things on their mind are people being arrested for the way they look, the way they dress – particularly women but not just women – and the invasion of privacy, the fact that the Basij – the religious police – can break into anybody's apartment if they think alcohol is being drunk or something bad is going on. So we basically tried to phrase it as an issue of police harassment of people for looking different, and privacy, which I think is something that everybody can understand. And the thing that so pissed me off about this whole Western brouhaha about Mashhad [...] was that there was absolutely no attempt to understand what would resonate in Iran [...] Privacy, yes! Homosexuality, no![60]

The emphasis here is on enlarging the constituency that might be enlisted in the struggle for sexual autonomy by moving beyond identity categories such as 'gay', 'queer' or even 'women', to focus on issues and demands in which multiple groups might have a common interest. Far from seeking to impose Western sexual identities on non-Western populations, key actors within Massad's 'Gay International' seem wary of framing struggles for sexual self-determination in terms of sexuality at all.

It may seem odd to suggest, as I have in this chapter, that the big human rights bureaucracies with their massive budgets and global reach appeared less implicated in an imperialist politics than individual freelance LGBT rights activists, journalists and bloggers. Yet it is certainly the case that insofar as the Western reaction to the 2005 hangings in Iran were concerned, it was the latter group that broke the story, articulated a response that dovetailed neatly with imperial security preoccupations, and set the agenda, capturing the interest and allegiance particularly of a white, Western, gay male public. To many in this public, the professional human rights organizations appeared reactive and weak in their attempt to reframe the debate in ways that avoided a frontal attack on the sexual morality of the Iranian state. But the discussion here has been confined to a single event: in other contexts, the positions of these actors in relation to imperial projects might well be reversed. In other words, there does not seem to be a strong correlation between the levels of material and organizational resources possessed by activists and their distance from imperial projects.

What the reactions to the Mashhad hangings demonstrate is that the 'Gay International' – if it can be seen as a single entity at all – is an extraordinarily fractious space. Its constituents span the entire political spectrum, from right-wing activists concerned about furthering their incomplete assimilation into party, nation and state, to left-wing Greens looking for new causes to replenish spent agendas. It is united by a common Western sexual ontology, but its constituents disagree radically on whether, when and how to export this ontology to the rest of the world. And while some of its constituents seem eager to use gay rights as a means of consolidating Western hegemony in ways that remind us of the heyday of the 'civilizing mission', others seem wary of contributing to such an outcome.

The past, to which I have been comparing the activities of today's 'Gay International', is no less complicated a space. The discourse of suffragist imperialism always coexisted with an anti-imperialist feminism exemplified by figures such as Sylvia Pankhurst, who were able to see the links between patriarchal power in England and colonial practices, and struggled against both.[61] Even as women like Gertrude Bell saw their presence in the colonies explicitly in the terms of Europe's civilizing mission,[62] others such as Annie Besant were staunch anti-imperialists playing leading roles within anti-colonial movements.[63] More pertinently to the subject of this chapter and this book in general, it was precisely his status as a sexual outcast from late Victorian society that gave the homosexual Edward Carpenter an affinity with a range of subaltern groups and movements, including those for decolonization, women's suffrage, workers' welfare and animal rights.[64] Indeed, Carpenter offers an ironic counterpoint to the contemporary orientalist discourse of some Western LGBT activists when he favourably contrasts the valorization of bisexuality and hermaphroditism in Hindu mythology with the homophobia of European culture.[65] It is difficult to think of any Western activists today who draw on the resources of non-Western cultures to argue for greater toleration of sexual minorities within their own societies.

Notes

1 Thanks are due to the editorial collective responsible for the forthcoming *Law like Love: A Queer Perspective of Law in India* (New Delhi, 2011), in which some of the material in this chapter appears under the title 'Queer in the Time of Terror', as well as the editors of this volume. Anne McClintock, 'The Angel of Progress: Pitfalls of the Term "Post-Colonialism"', *Social Text*, 31, 32 (1992), p. 88.

2 *Ibid.*

3 This chapter deploys a distinction between 'LGBT' and 'queer' in two senses. The first is a political distinction between a liberal and a radical politics respectively, explained at greater length in the introduction to the chapter. The second is a distinction based on identity, with 'LGBT' referring to sexual minorities who identify in terms of Western identity categories such as lesbian, gay, bisexual and transgendered (wherever such minorities may actually be located), and 'queer' functioning as an umbrella category encompassing non-Western sexual minorities who cannot easily be accommodated within a Western-style LGBT identity politics.

4 C. Talpade Mohanty, *Feminism Without Borders: Decolonizing Theory, Practicing Solidarity* (Durham, NC and London, 2003).

5 K. Kollman and M. Waites, 'The Global Politics of Lesbian, Gay, Bisexual and Transgender Human Rights: An Introduction', *Contemporary Politics*, 15, 1 (2009), pp. 1–17.

6 M. Warner, 'Introduction', in idem, *Fear of a Queer Planet: Queer Politics and Social Theory* (Minneapolis, MN, 1993), p. xiii.

7 For a critical revival of the term 'Third World', see R. Rao, *Third World Protest: Between Home and the World* (Oxford, 2010), pp. 24–30.

8 J. Binnie, *The Globalization of Sexuality* (2004), pp. 68–76.

9 E. Said, *Orientalism: Western Conceptions of the Orient* (1995 [1978]); N. Hoad, 'Arrested Development or the Queerness of Savages: Resisting Evolutionary Narratives of Difference', *Postcolonial Studies* 3, 2 (2000), pp. 133–58.

10 J. K. Puar, *Terrorist Assemblages: Homonationalism in Queer Times* (Durham, NC and London, 2007); J. Massad, *Desiring Arabs* (Chicago, 2008), Chapter 3.

11 Massad, *Desiring Arabs*, p. 163.

12 M. Foucault, *The Will to Knowledge*, vol. I: *The History of Sexuality* (1998), p. 43.

13 Massad, *Desiring Arabs*, p. 182.

14 *Ibid.*, pp. 172–3.

15 T. Babington Macaulay, 'Minute on Indian Education' (2 February 1835), in *Bureau of Education: Selections from Educational Records, Part I (1781–1839)* (New Delhi, 1965), pp. 107–17.

16 H. Bhabha, *The Location of Culture* (2004 [1994]), Chapter 4.

17 Massad, *Desiring Arabs*, p. 173.

18 Z. Lockman, *Contending Visions of the Middle East: The History and Politics of Orientalism* (Cambridge, 2005), p. 196.

19 R. Kim, 'Witnesses to an Execution', http://www.thenation.com/doc/20050815/kim; P. Schindler, 'The Battle Over Iran', http://gaycitynews.com/site/index.cfm?newsid=17334312 &BRD=2729&PAG=461&dept_id=568864&rfi=8.

20 OutRage!, 'Execution of Gay Teens in Iran', http://www.petertatchell.net/international/iranexecution.htm.

21 Cited from Kim, 'Witnesses to an Execution'.

22 Doug Ireland, 'Iran's Anti-Gay Pogrom', http://www.inthesetimes.com/article/2458/.

23 Human Rights Campaign, 'Secretary Rice Urged to Condemn Execution of Gay Iranian Teens', http://www.hrc.org/1945.htm.

24 Log Cabin Republicans, 'Log Cabin Republicans Denounce Execution of Gay Youth by Iran', http://online.logcabin.org/news_views/log-cabin-republicans-denounce-execution-of-gay-youth-by-iran.html.

25 J. Afary, *Sexual Politics in Modern Iran* (Cambridge, 2009), Chapter 3.

26 *Ibid.*, p. 107.

27 A. Najmabadi, *Women with Mustaches and Men without Beards: Gender and Sexual Anxieties of Iranian Modernity* (Berkeley, CA, 2005), Chapters 1 and 2.

28 *Ibid.*, p. 7.

29 A. Narrain, *Queer: Despised Sexuality, Law and Social Change* (Bangalore, 2004), pp. 41–5; R. Vanita and S. Kidwai, *Same-Sex Love in India: Readings from Literature and History* (Basingstoke, 2001), p. 200.

30 OutRage!, 'Iranian Gay Group Backs 19 July Protests', http://www.petertatchell.net/international/irandemo.htm.

31 Interview with Scott Long, New York, 21 September 2009.

32 Human Rights Watch, 'Iran: End Juvenile Executions', http://www.hrw.org/en/news/2005/07/26/iran-end-juvenile-executions.

33 Amnesty International, 'Executions of juveniles since 1990', http://www.amnesty.org/en/death-penalty/executions-of-child-offenders-since-1990.

34 BBC News, 'US Court Bans Juvenile Executions', http://news.bbc.co.uk/1/hi/world/americas/4308881.stm.

35 P. Varnell, 'Toward a Gay Foreign Policy', http://www.indegayforum.org/news/show/27139.html.

36 See for example, Y. Klein Halevi, 'Tel Aviv Dispatch: Refugee Status', *The New Republic* (19 and 26 August 2002); D. J. Bernstein, 'Gay Palestinians suffer under Arafat', http://www.yaleherald.com/article.php?Article=933; P. Varnell, 'Israel, Palestine, and Gays', http://www.indegayforum.org/news/show/27154.html; W. Goodwin, 'Palestine's Oppression of Gays Should Not Be Ignored', http://www.sodomylaws.org/world/palestine/pseditorials001.htm; J. Kirchik, 'Palestine and Gay Rights', http://www.advocate.com/exclusive_detail_ektid33587.asp. For a critique, see Blair Kuntz, '"Queer" as a Tool of Colonial Oppression: The Case of Israel/Palestine', http://www.zmag.org/content/showarticle.cfm?ItemID=10756.

37 See for example the comparative religious writings of Paul Varnell at www.indegayforum.org. While he acknowledges the universality of homophobia across the monotheistic religions, Christian proscriptions of homosexuality are rationalized and contextualized, even if ultimately criticized, while Islam's lack of pluralism and internal contestation is emphasized.

38 G. C. Spivak, 'Can the Subaltern Speak?', in C. Nelson and L. Grossberg (eds), *Marxism and the Interpretation of Culture* (Basingstoke, 1988), p. 296.

39 P. Chatterjee, *The Nation and Its Fragments: Colonial and Postcolonial Histories* (Princeton, NJ, 1993), pp. 6, 119–20.

40 J. K. Puar, 'Mapping US Homonormativities', *Gender, Place and Culture*, 13, 1 (2006), pp. 67–8.

41 *Ibid.*, p.72.

42 See for example P. Varnell, 'Bombing for Justice', http://www.indegayforum.org/news/show/27137.html.

43 See for example L. Bush, 'Radio Address by Mrs Bush', http://georgewbush-whitehouse.archives.gov/news/releases/2001/11/20011117.html.

44 The administrations of George W. Bush not only failed to extend LGBT rights in any respect, but also sought actively to pre-empt and restrict such rights. Most infamously, the Federal Marriage Amendment, which was a proposed amendment to the US Constitution that would have limited

marriage in the US to unions of one man and one woman and would have prevented judicial extension of marriage rights to same-sex couples, was a centrepiece of the 2004 Republican presidential campaign. The amendment eventually failed to pass in both the House of Representatives and Senate.

45 Puar, 'Mapping US Homonormativities', p. 70.

46 N. Naghibi, *Rethinking Global Sisterhood: Western Feminism and Iran* (Minneapolis, MN, 2007), p. xx.

47 I. Grewal, *Home and Harem: Nation, Gender, Empire, and the Cultures of Travel* (1996), pp. 61–7.

48 Naghibi, *Rethinking Global Sisterhood*, p. 31.

49 Interview with Peter Tatchell, London, 23 October 2007.

50 Here too there are historical parallels. See A. Burton, 'The White Woman's Burden: British Feminists and "The Indian Woman", 1865–1915', in N. Chaudhuri and M. Strobel (eds), *Western Women and Imperialism: Complicity and Resistance* (Bloomington, IN, 1992), who describes Josephine Butler's campaign against the Contagious Diseases Acts, first in England and then in India. Burton argues that Butler turned her attention to India when, in 1886, with the successful conclusion of the campaign in England, she found herself and the considerable campaign infrastructure that she had built in danger of becoming redundant (p. 140).

51 C. Bob, *The Marketing of Rebellion: Insurgents, Media, and International Activism* (New York, NY, 2006), p. 15.

52 Telephone interview with Arsham Parsi (Toronto), 18 October 2007.

53 M. Roshan and K. Shemirani, 'Gays in Iran', http://www.zmag.org/content/showarticle. cfm?ItemID=10772.

54 MAHA, 'The Need for Continued International Solidarity with Iranian LGBTs', http://www.ilga. org/news_results.asp?LanguageID=1&FileCategory=9&ZoneID=3&FileID=879.

55 'African LGBTI Human Rights Defenders Warn Public against Participation in Campaigns Concerning LGBTI Issues in Africa Led by Peter Tatchell and OutRage!', http://mrzine. monthlyreview.org/increse310107.html. The letter accuses Tatchell of exaggerating rights violations committed by African governments, which then left local activists vulnerable to attack by such governments for claims they had never made. As Juliet Victor Mukasa (chairperson of Sexual Minorities Uganda) put it in a letter to Tatchell, excerpts from which were published in background notes to the statement: 'You will sit safely in London while our activists in Uganda pay the price for your deeds.' The letter also addresses a controversy in Nigeria, where differences seem to have arisen over how to respond to a same-sex marriage prohibition bill that had been introduced in the federal legislature. Many activists were opposed to Tatchell's call for a public campaign against the Nigerian government, believing that this would revive governmental interest in a bill that was virtually dead, thanks to behind-the-scenes pressure on Nigerian legislators.

56 Tatchell interview.

57 Interview with Kasha Jacqueline, Kampala, 25 August 2010.

58 Human Rights Watch, *'They Want Us Exterminated': Murder, Torture, Sexual Orientation and Gender in Iraq* (New York, NY, 2009), pp. 9–10.

59 S. Long, 'Unbearable Witness: How Western Activists (Mis)recognize Sexuality in Iran', *Contemporary Politics*, 15, 1 (2009), pp. 120–2.

60 Long interview.

61 Grewal, *Home and Harem*, p. 78.

62 G. Bell, *Persian Pictures* (1928).

63 B. Ramusack, 'Cultural Missionaries, Maternal Imperialists, Feminist Allies: British Women Activists in India, 1865–1945', in Chaudhuri and Strobel, *Western Women and Imperialism*.

64 S. Rowbotham, *Edward Carpenter: A Life of Liberty and Love* (2009).

65 L. Gandhi, *Affective Communities: Anticolonial Thought, Fin-de-Siècle Radicalism, and the Politics of Friendship* (Durham, NC and London, 2006), p. 59.

From the Anti-Colonial Movements to the New Social Movements

Robert J. C. Young

For over three decades now, the fundamental activity of post-colonial studies has been to analyse world history and its cultures from a non-European perspective, to explore, articulate and represent subaltern views and their different marginalized knowledges. Its task with regard to empire and imperialism has been to anatomize empire, imperial practices and their material effects from the viewpoint of the colonized. To that extent it has sought to reconfigure the dominant accounts of the West's imperial history insofar as they appear partial or ideologically driven, even if in certain respects they may be critical of the imperial past. This has meant that post-colonial studies has been less interested in imperialism and colonialism from the viewpoint of the history of particular empires than in the ways in which individual practices, or quite often as in the case for example of Cyprus, Egypt, Mauritius, Somalia, or Sri Lanka, successive imperial practices, affected the historical, political, cultural, social and psychic lives of the local and indigenous peoples who bore the brunt of colonial subjugation. One complaint from historians about post-colonial theory has often focused on the use of common theoretical heuristic paradigms across very different colonial arenas. However, this objection misses the fundamental point – because it still comes from the perspective of the imperial centre. From the viewpoint of the colonized, the structure of domination in fundamental terms was the same, whether it be British, Dutch, French, German, Italian, Japanese or Russian.

There were differences of course. But it is not as if, for example, any of these powers immediately established democracy as the first act of colonial or imperial rule – in fact, the establishment of democracy always marked the end and dissolution of colonial rule. From the viewpoint of a colonized person, the soldier of a foreign power who enforces the rule of the country by force rather than consent represents the same structure of domination whichever national colours he happens to be wearing – for the colonial subject, at one level it makes no difference which particular imperial power the soldier happens to serve. For the same reason, if Britain were occupied tomorrow by the Japanese, and France by the Chinese, British people would be more likely to feel they had something in common with the French than to say that the two occupations were too different in style to compare. post-colonial studies traces the commonality of the colonized.

It was for this reason that I decided to turn the history of imperialism back to front, so to speak, in order to write what amounted to the first history of anti-colonialism and anti-imperialism. My book *Post-Colonialism: An Historical Introduction* (2001), traces a history of the anti-colonial movements over the past 500 years, and seeks to situate the politics of the present in a long history from Las Casas to Burke and Adam Smith, from Toussaint l'Ouverture to Gandhi, from the Communist Internationals and Congresses of Peoples of the East at Baku of 1920 to Bandung in 1955 and the Havana Tricontinental of 1966, from Ho Chi Minh to Nkrumah, Fanon and Guevara, and to the institutionalization of their writings, practices and perspectives as an object of academic study in the discipline of post-colonial studies initiated by Edward Said, Gayatri Chakravorty Spivak, Ranajit Guha and others.[1] One of the things that emerged in the epic narrative of anti-colonial struggle that the book analyses was the importance of events that histories of imperialism typically pass by, such as the Bolshevik Revolution, which established the first ideologically anti-imperialist state, the Chinese defeat of the Kuomintang of 1949, or the Iranian Revolution – which took place in a semi-colony still suffering the effects of the British need for oil – of 1979. Individual histories of particular decolonizations for their part hide the fact that from the late nineteenth century onwards, anti-colonialism was always a globalized phenomenon. The struggle against imperialism involved national campaigns that took international forms and were always conditioned by international contexts. So a post-colonial history of anti-colonialism emphasizes the histories of the formation of transnational networks between anti-colonial activists around the world. Sometimes these were strategic with respect to a common colonial enemy, such as the extensive links that were developed between Boer, Irish and Indian nationalists, for example. In other cases, they were set up in the imperial centres themselves. Affording a political freedom unavailable in the colonies, London, Paris, Berlin, Lisbon, Tokyo and New York were all at various times bristling with anti-colonial activists communicating with each other, establishing international networks of activist cells, and articulating with affiliated comparable struggles. Some organizations themselves operated globally: the Irish Republican Brotherhood, the forerunner of the IRA, was the first international anti-colonial organization: by the late 1860s it was able to effect terrorist acts, including military invasions and naval skirmishes, against the British Empire around the world.

Looking at the long trajectory of anti-colonialism, it is possible to construct general patterns of resistance that formed a common structure across different colonial periods and formations. In fact, from this perspective, colonialism and imperialism themselves become less significant as structures per se than the common history of resistance to foreign rule or domination, by whatever name, ideology or structure it might go under. In many ways, the historical shifts between colonial and imperial rule were less significant in themselves than the late nineteenth-century development of imperialism in its American form as economic – rather than territorial – imperialism (not necessarily just by the Americans; one could instance the British in Latin America). Conversely, one of the lessons of the post-colonial era, starting with Nkrumah's *Neocolonialism* of 1965, was that the achievement of national sovereignty did not necessarily produce full sovereignty.[2] It is for this reason that the concept of resistance has been particularly important for post-colonial studies since what it examines are the forms of resistance to unauthorized or exploitative power structures, particularly those of non-indigenous powers but also those of elites, as in the 'Subaltern Studies' project. From that perspective, the viewpoint of the dominated and exploited nations, the shifts from colonialism to imperialism to post-colonial neo-colonialism to globalization are particular shifts of political and economic formation but not necessarily fundamental structural transformations that require conceptual restructuration. Modern imperialism, the expansion of Europe around the world, was already a form of globalization. So resistance to imperialism and resistance to contemporary globalization may share certain cultural perspectives and political practices. It has become increasingly clear that, contra Hardt and Negri, we do not need a new theory of empire.[3] The forms of oppression and resistance may change, but their fundamental structure remains intact.

Anti-Colonial Strategies

How, though, did the non-Western world resist imperialism? If it was, in a certain sense, a global movement, what strategies were involved? Were they comparable? From the viewpoint of resistance, and more narrowly of anti-colonialism, the choices narrowed down to two alternatives, and these involved an ethical as well as a political decision. Like most anti-colonial strategies, these possibilities were first theorized and formulated by Irish nationalists in the nineteenth century, when, as the great Irish politician known as 'the Liberator', Daniel O'Connell, put it, the choice was deemed to lie between 'physical force' and 'moral force', between violence and non-violence. Throughout anti-colonial history, the two polarities of resistance operated on this axis, between armed resistance against the power of the state and what the Irish called 'moral force', Emerson 'civil disobedience', Tolstoy 'passive resistance', Gandhi *satyagraha* or 'soul-force' and Nkrumah 'non-violent action'. Forms of resistance in our own day can still be mapped according to the polarities of these choices. The ethical basis for armed struggle has typically been justified in terms of the unjustifiable behaviour of the opponent, most famously by Fanon who argued that since the colonizer (for him, the French in Algeria) had established rule by violence, violence was the only effective response.[4] Although in the twentieth century armed struggle has been particularly associated with Leninism and post-World War II radical communism – Mao, Fanon, Che Guevara – the founding document by which it was ethically justified is the American Declaration of Independence, which formally initiated the first successful form of armed struggle against colonial rule in the modern era. It was, ironically, for this reason that Ho Chi Minh's 1945 Declaration of Independence for Vietnam invoked the earlier American example. According to the first paragraph that is often omitted, the American Declaration of Independence of 1776 consists of a justification of the extraordinary steps that the colonists took in taking up arms against the British government. The right to resist that is asserted in the Declaration is essentially based on the claim of tyranny and oppression: in other words, it is argued that there is a level of political oppression, here colonial oppression by an external power, that justifies armed rebellion in the name of freedom. The Declaration of Independence then essentially marshals 'the facts' to make the moral justification for the violence of its own manifestation.[5]

In the twentieth century, the tradition of armed struggle was used by the Irish and the Mau Mau against the British, among many others, but it was after its successful role in the Algerian, and subsequently the Cuban, revolutions that it came to dominate anti-colonial strategy. After the All African People's Conference held in Accra in 1958, armed struggle became the primary mode of anti-colonial resistance in Africa and East Asia.[6] The modern utilizers of that tradition in our own day include organizations such as the LTTE, the United Liberation Front of Assam, Al Qaeda, or any of those contemporary groups designated as terrorist by the EU (there are 47 of them, in a list which includes Hamas but not Al Qaeda). In order to achieve their declared object of sovereignty and autonomy in the Middle East, Al Qaeda has embarked on an international campaign against all those Western powers involved in the various countries of the Islamic domain; bin Laden has traced the origins of this history back to the dismemberment of the Ottoman Empire in 1919 and the Deposition of the Caliphate by the Western powers after World War I. The major Western involvement in the Middle East is the product of a quite specific colonial history that developed after Winston Churchill changed the fuel for British battleships from coal to oil after 1912. Britain had been able to use its own resources for coal, but it lacked any oil.

The Genesis of New Social Movements

In a situation where the axis of armed revolutionary struggle has been appropriated by a political Islam, and where the collapse of the communist bloc has led to an increasing willingness by Western power to tolerate democratic socialist states, such as those of Latin America belonging to Bolivarian Alternative for Latin America and the Caribbean (ALBA), today the secular left draws on the other alternative in the tricontinental anti-imperialist tradition. Many contemporary forms of political activism that operate outside conventional politics, such as new social movements and the anti-capitalist movements, which go by various names including the Global Justice Movement, the Anti-Corporate Globalization Movement, the Movement of Movements (a popular term in Italy), the Alter-Globalization Movement (popular in France), or the Counter-Globalization Movement, as well as the many indigenous movements in the Americas, can be affiliated not with armed struggle, but rather with the alternative forms of non-violent struggle that use moral rather than physical force. Historically this mode of resistance goes back to the early nineteenth century. In the twentieth, many of these strategies were deployed by Gandhi, who during his stay in London took the opportunity to absorb the politics and strategies of late nineteenth-century radicalism in Britain, particularly amongst Irish and suffragette activists, the counter-cultures of modernity which sought to develop anti-hierarchical libertarian ideas particularly with respect to feminism, sexuality, ecology, vegetarianism – and imperialism.[7] Gandhi's original contribution, aside from strategically raising the moral stakes with regard to the methods of anti-colonial struggle, was to deploy such alternative forms of struggle through a highly resourceful use of the international media. It was above all in his inventive use of the media – newspapers, film – as a weapon for wooing international public opinion that Gandhi anticipated contemporary struggles of other kinds in our own day.[8]

In the same way, instead of a direct link to the campaigns of armed struggle of the 1960s and 1970s, the politics of the new social movements can be more directly affiliated with the women's movements, whose relation to the anti-colonial movements varied historically and always to some degree remained in tension with them. It was while I was working on the chapter on 'Women, gender and anti-colonialism' in my *Post-Colonialism: An Historical Introduction* that I began to see most strongly the links between present struggles and the anti-colonial past. One way of putting this would be that while gender struggles always remained problematically comparatively marginal to the anti-colonial movements, the politics of post-coloniality begins from them. Whereas a focus on independence and political sovereignty draws a clear line between the anti-colonial and the post-colonial, from the perspective of women's struggles, the triumph of taking control of the state apparatus in itself did not transform dramatically the social conditions that were being contested. Anti-colonial movements rarely conformed to textbook universal models of political resistance developed by either the Third or the Fourth Internationals. That in many ways is the main lesson to be learned from their extraordinary history, alongside the fact that over the years, these anti-colonial movements developed a whole range of forms of resistance, many of which continue to form the practical basis of struggles today. Post-colonial struggle comprises the rediscovery of how to fight most effectively with the weapons of the weak.

Over the years, the anti-colonial movements developed a whole range of modes of non-violent, so-called passive resistance, many of which continue to form the practical basis of struggles today. Of course some new social movements, such as the demonstrations in Genoa in 2001, become violent at times, if not exactly resorting to armed struggle, just as the Zapatistas today refrain from using violence even though they are armed. In practice, in fact, no liberation movement ever deployed a single tactic alone, despite their specific commitments to one or the other. The liberation movements always negotiated a whole range of strategies of civil and militant resistance, veering between armed struggle and civil disobedience and negotiation. The history of the Irish struggle from 1798 to 1922 involved a constant alternation between these two according to the circumstances, and available technologies, of the day. There was no absolute distinction between them, even for Gandhi. Moreover, there were significant differences even within armed and non-violent struggle. Given that there are different degrees of violence, for example, what kind of violence would be permitted as legitimate? In this connection, we might cite the pamphlet of one of the most famous of Indian women freedom fighters, Aruna Asaf Ali's *ABC of Dislocation* of 1941:

> Dislocation is a common and effective method used by enslaved and oppressed peoples against their rule[...] Thus, if telegraph wires are cut, fishplates on railway lines are removed, bridges are dynamites, industrial plants put out of order, petrol tanks set on fire, police stations burnt down, official records destroyed – they are all acts of dislocation. But a bomb thrown at a market place or a school or a *dharma-shala* [a shelter for pilgrims] is not dislocation. It is either the work of agents provocateurs or misdirected energy.[9]

Ali's account of dislocation, permitting violence against property and communications but not against people, can be compared to the important moral distinction developed by Jean-Paul Sartre in the context of the semi-civil war of early 1970s France, between violence erupting organically from exploited groups, and violence initiated by isolated sectarian groups that have not arisen from the politics of community.[10]

As James Connolly in Ireland, Frantz Fanon in Algeria, Che Guevara in Cuba and the ANC in South Africa always emphasized, armed struggle was the strategy of last resort for any liberation movement. At the same time, as Shahid Amin has shown with respect to Gandhi, a certain possibility of violence always lurks within non-violent movements.[11] That in itself hardly makes them Leninist. Unlike the macho liberation movements of armed struggle intent on capturing the colonial state apparatus, there were also liberation movements whose project was to transform the broader political-social fabric of civil society through new forms of participatory democracy. These mass movements also constitute an important antecedent to post-colonial politics, which an exclusive focus on the wars of national liberation altogether misses. Such popular civil disobedience movements go back to earlier campaigns such as those of the Suffragettes, the Aborigines' Protection Society and even the Anti-Slave Trade Movement. Their techniques were utilized by Gandhi in India and by Nkrumah in Ghana, by the American Civil Rights Movement, and by peace campaigners in Europe (for example, the Campaign for Nuclear Disarmament, the Anti-Apartheid Movement, and even what was originally called the Women's Liberation Movement). It is this tradition of civil resistance, formed through the non-violent anti-colonial movements, that has developed into the new social and indigenous movements across the globe, as well as being institutionalized in international organizations such as Greenpeace or Amnesty International. The World Social Forum now operates as a kind of popular front for a whole range of different interrelated political movements, in the same way as the National Liberation Fronts, or the United Democratic Fronts, brought together a heterogeneous range of different kinds of anti-colonial activism. The new social movements in Europe and the US have predictably received more attention than, say, the Brazilian Sem Terra or the Denotified and Nomadic Tribes Rights Action Group or Dalit activists in India; but they themselves equally employ strategies and forms of civil disobedience – sit-ins, boycotts, occupations, marches and other forms of mass civil disobedience – developed in 'moral force' anti-colonial struggles. Just as a central feature of the anti-colonial movements involved the challenging of the boundaries of the political, so today, grass-roots subaltern new social and indigenous movements operate outside orthodox political spheres and focus on issues that conventional parties have neglected and refused to take on. They have certainly been inspired by the struggles and wars of liberation, but inspired too to define their politics in broader or different terms, and develop their forms of liberation as mass social movements.

Ethics, Economics and Cosmopolitanism

The politics of these movements, and the justice of their material objectives, are largely justified in ethical terms, and in that respect they also embody the practice of 'moral force' over revolutionary physical force. Though Marx himself was scornful of the invocation of ethics, its universal modality can work effectively in the absence of an alternative viable communist economic system or 'science' of historical materialism. Today, in many respects, tricontinental socialism has become an ethics first and an economics second – the Charter of Principles of the World Social Forum, for example, is fundamentally based on ethical arguments. In its 14 principles, as in the UN plan to halve world poverty, the specific demand is for less exploitative relations with respect to both people and natural resources, and for common and general access to wealth, not the complete destruction of the capitalist system as such. The World Social Forum represents an assault on the 'economic fundamentalism' of the World Economic Forum at Davos, against which it pits its ethical and social conviction that 'another world is possible'. The alternative perspective broached by the World Social Forum was prescient: historically it emerged between the times when the communism of the Soviet bloc had collapsed and capitalist neo-liberalism imploded on itself. Unexpectedly, given that economic globalization has always been associated with the rise of neo-liberalism, the unregulated economic forces released by that globalization have now led to a partial return of Keynesian economics, which was itself developed as a way of incorporating some of the concepts and practices of socialism.[12] This perhaps explains why many of the new social movements are not in themselves necessarily antithetical to the liberal wing of capitalism, though that does not, however, stop them from being, as their name states, 'social', and therefore socialist.

Nor, for that matter, should it be assumed that a modern tricontinental politics of difference are antithetical to capitalism. There is, for example, little reason to assume that post-colonial values towards cultural difference are in themselves radically subversive for Western cultures. Consider the following questionnaire in a British newspaper:

DO YOU HAVE A GLOBAL MINDSET?
When you interact with others, do you assign them equal status regardless of national origin?
Do you regard your values to be a hybrid of values acquired from multiple cultures, as opposed to just one culture?
Do you consider yourself as open to ideas from other countries and cultures as you are to ideas from your own country and culture of origin?

If you can answer in the affirmative to all these questions, then the paper assures you that you have 'a global mindset'. In fact the questionnaire formed part of a supplement to the London *Financial Times* called 'Mastering Global Business'.[13]

Just as imperial powers encouraged anti-colonial activists within rival empires, so too today, globalization is not a straightforward process. Even global action against the practices of capitalism turns out not to be so straightforwardly oppositional. Some years ago it was revealed that many anti-capitalist organizations, such as Global Exchange, which seeks to close the World Bank and the World Trade Organization, and the Ruckus Society, which organized the demonstrators who shut down the WTO meeting in Seattle in 1999, had been funded by Unilever – through Ben & Jerry's Ice Cream – the EU, and even the British National Lottery.[14] Why was capitalism funding the anti-capitalist movements that were apparently seeking to destroy it?' One answer would be that the resistance to capitalism has in part taken the form of an ethical movement which rather than trying to destroy it for an alternative that in practice no longer exists, is suggesting essentially that capitalism can afford to provide the alternatives that are being demanded. This is essentially the basis of the struggle between what is still, somewhat anachronistically, called the North and the South. Historically it has been shown that capitalism can adopt and adapt more or less anything for its own benefit and purposes: just as the anti-colonial movements appropriated the forms and ideologies of Western nationalism so now the new social movements seek to appropriate and modify capitalism for the benefit of ethical, socialist principles. In that sense, they once again affiliate to the 'moral force' tradition of anti-colonialism rather than the tradition of revolutionary violence that tended to be more traditionally Marxist in political orientation.

The involvement of liberal capitalism in the anti-globalization movements is no more remarkable than the fact that the Indian National Congress Party was founded by an Englishman. Davos now listens to the World Social Forum. Economists such as Joseph Stiglitz, former Chief Economist of the World Bank, have become far more radical and critical in their views.[15] In fact, and how much more so since the discrediting of neo-liberal economics, a remarkable degree of consensus has developed internationally – as in the transformations of development theory in recent years which has reorientated itself to what are effectively quasi-Gandhian principles, the successful campaigns against drug companies in Africa with regard to HIV drugs, the campaigns over Third World debt and global warming. Indeed, while nation states were denationalizing and dismantling their own economic sovereignty in order to facilitate globalization, paradoxically a leftist social agenda, in effect an updated version of the great Second Declaration of Havana of 1962 was being transformed into a common global social agenda. Ironically and unexpectedly, globalization has produced the situation that we are witnessing now: when a tricontinental politics, the product of the anti-colonial tradition, has finally moved beyond resistance to power to become a power in itself.

Notes

1 R. J. C. Young, *Postcolonialism: An Historical Introduction* (Oxford, 2001).

2 K. Nkrumah, *Neo-Colonialism: The Last Stage of Imperialism* (1965).

3 M. Hardt and A. Negri, *Empire* (Cambridge, MA, 2000).

4 F. Fanon, *Les Damnés de la terre* (Paris, 1961).

5 See R. J. C. Young, 'The Right to Resist', forthcoming.

6 R. J. C. Young, 'Fanon and the Turn to Armed Struggle in Africa', *Wasafiri*, 44 (2005), 33–41.

7 L. Gandhi, *Affective Communities: Anticolonial Thought, Fin-de-Siècle Radicalism, and the Politics of Friendship* (Durham, NC and London, 2006).

8 See Young, *Postcolonialism*, pp. 317–34.

9 Cited in G. Hancock Forbes, *Women in Modern India* (Cambridge, 1996), p. 207.

10 M. Scriven, *Jean-Paul Sartre: Politics and Culture in Postwar France* (Basingstoke, 1999), pp. 73–8.

11 S. Amin, *Event, Metaphor, Memory: Chauri Chaura 1922–1992* (Delhi, 1995).

12 D. Harvey, *A Brief History of Neoliberalism* (Oxford, 2005).

13 'Mastering Global Business', Part 5, 3, *Financial Times* (1998).

14 *Financial Times*, 16 October 2001.

15 J. Stiglitz, *Globalization and its Discontents* (New York, NY, 2002).

Colonization and Globalization

Jacques Frémeaux and Gabrielle Maas

Globalization, like colonization, builds routes and connections. Yet in both cases, these connections are not equally available to all: modern global networks (economic and otherwise), like colonial routes, create power imbalances and rifts even as they connect places. This chapter explores how the unprecedented geographical sweep of European colonial empires, and their criss-crossing web of routes over sea and land, shaped European hopes and fears about a rapidly expanding world of knowledge. The challenge of conquest was also an epistemological challenge: that of introducing order into something incomprehensibly diverse, fitting it into established frameworks for knowledge. As well as a source of material wealth, overseas empires were thus fertile terrain for Europeans to construct a rich fantasy world of endless diversity and sensuousness. The vision of chaos or savagery penned by early colonial ethnographers was another face of what we would now call the orientalist fascination with the sensual possibilities of that 'chaos'. The corpus of attempts to chart the geological, botanical, zoological and anthropological diversity of the overseas territories is thus as much part of the journey of imagination (fantasy, some might say) as the works of the novelists, poets, artists and musicians who painted their own imagined colonial landscapes.

Our aim, then, is not to explore the history of colonial empires, but to give the broadest possible overview of how Europeans have constructed modern overseas empires as a world of the imagination as well as a world of very real profit and power – and to suggest that these two aspects work in symbiosis. Starting from a general observation about the nature of modern colonial empires as projects of metropolitan *rayonnement* on a global scale, we attempt to show here how empires contributed to the formation of networks that were forerunners of contemporary globalization processes. This is clearly a subject that exceeds the scope of the current chapter, but has been dealt with at greater length in a previous work by one of the authors.[1]

Across the Seas

The Roman Empire, a canonical starting point for studies of imperialism, was radically different from the colonial empires of modern European states. Rome's might was founded not on vast maritime expanses but on the command of a territorial bloc, broken only by the few hundred miles of Mediterranean which were themselves crucial to the empire's commanding power. Most of Rome's rival empires, and their European, African or Asian successors from Charlemagne to Tsarist Russia, were based on this model of territorial continuity.

Modern European colonial projects, on the other hand, can without hesitation be described as overseas empires (a notion first evident in the Spanish term *ultramar*). Made up of territories several thousand miles apart from each other, these empires were also separated from the metropole by the vast expanse of the oceans. It was mastery of shipbuilding and navigation techniques that parted the seas for European powers. Colonial empires, indeed, cannot be understood apart from the web of sea routes woven by the competing great powers, with their ports of call and trading posts. In the second half of the nineteenth century, the invention of submarine communications cables coincided with the advent of steam power to crown the technical advances that had made this network of routes ever more dense and reliable. Little surprise, then, that French colonial affairs fell under the exclusive remit of the Ministry of the Navy, or that the special forces posted to the colonies were known respectively as the *artillerie et infanterie de Marine*. Conversely, the substitution of 'overseas' for 'colonial' after decolonization was a natural transition (the Ministère des Colonies becoming the Ministère de l'Outre-Mer, and so on).

Etymologically speaking, 'colony' implies the presence of settlers and the establishment of communities that reproduce the 'mother country' or homeland. From this viewpoint, the modern concept of colonization plays on a double etymological meaning: the Latin etymology of *colonia* posits the appropriation of land and its cultivation by settlers from the conquering country, while the Greek αποικία emphasizes expatriation and long-distance emigration. Successful colonization has always depended on settlers from the colonial power – in addition to military and civil personnel – turning local resources to their advantage and maintaining constant flows of exchange with the metropole. After smaller-scale medieval experiments with this type of colonization, European powers transformed it into a cripplingly powerful modern weapon of settlement, control, and eventually domination.[2]

European colonial powers were initially (and still are, in a looser definition) almost exclusively Western European – and more specifically Atlantic – powers. With a few minor exceptions, neither the Baltic States of Northern Europe nor those of Mediterranean Europe were drawn for any length of time to the open oceans of the Atlantic or Pacific. The fascination with far-off lands grew up along the great estuaries of the Thames, the Rhine, the Meuse and the Scheldt, the Seine, the Loire, the Tagus and the Guadalquivir; and it was from these estuaries that the majority of colonial pioneers launched their expeditions. None of the powers that missed this first wave of colonial expansion was able to catch up later; it was only thanks to continued connections with the Levant that Mediterranean countries were able to secure their share in African and Middle Eastern conquests.

In contrast with non-colonial empires,[3] which could be described as the result of a gradual process of growth around a centre, colonial empires took shape as metropolitan powers endeavoured to spread their influence as far as possible. The symbol of the Roman eagle, often seen in the imperial heraldry of antiquity spreading its wings to cover a vaster and vaster area, is set off by the image of the octopus whose tentacles reach all over. Rome, we might note in passing, had already branded Carthage – a maritime colonial power if there ever was at the time – with this unflattering image; and it was subsequently revived by adversaries of colonial Britain. This model is clearly less suited to the American and Russian colonial empires, which were based above all on territorial expansion (as witnessed by the fact that the American process of 'colonization' referred to the American West and the South before it was extended to Hawaii, Puerto Rico and the Philippines). We should also remember that colonial powers, while prioritizing overseas possessions, sought eventually to constitute these – where possible – in territorial blocs: we need only think of the British 'Cape to Cairo' railway project at the end of the nineteenth century, or the 'African Bloc' advocated in the same period by the French 'Colonial Party'. In any event, the concept of overseas empire is only one part of the story of colonization. To go deeper, we must examine another aspect of colonial empires: their construction of a putative civilizational discontinuity.

The Allure of Exoticism

The notion of difference is at the heart of the 'colonial adventure', which is the story of contacts established between radically different areas of the globe on an unprecedented scale (for European countries at least). The sheer geographical sweep of the empires meant that there was a near infinite variety in the colonies, which spanned the latitudes, climates and flora and fauna of the world, from the poles to the equator, from ice deserts to hot deserts, from the tundra to the rainforest. Tropical and subtropical countries took pride of place, however: with the exception of Canada, part of Australia and the coastal regions of North and South Africa, colonial possessions were places with a tropical, subtropical or equatorial climate and type of vegetation. Images of colonized territories thus became inextricably bound up with heat, dry or humid: talk of the colonies would immediately evoke cyclones, monsoon, the sirocco; it would call up images of deserts, the steppes, the bush; or the jungle, savannah and immense equatorial forests that span the area from twentieth parallel north to south.

This vast diversity – as alluring as it was daunting – gave rise to a popular vision of the colonies as places where the senses reigned supreme. Orientalist painters were largely responsible for this image of a colonial kaleidoscope made up of the ivory, tan or ebony of skin married with the scarlet, emerald or gold fibre of garments. In the orientalist vision, streets 'thronged' with 'heaving crowds' featured the 'bazaars' that invariably offered up 'anything and everything that could be bought or sold' amidst a chaotic carnival of odours (savoury or otherwise) and in the company of all the 'races' of the earth, recognizable by their costumes or physical type. This vision, probably modelled on the trading city-states of the Middle East and the Arabic-speaking world, was subsequently – and erroneously – extended to encompass the 'colonies' as a whole.

This was not a purely aesthetic or impressionistic phase. Commentaries on the diversity of human life and habits go back to the Renaissance, when Montaigne wrote the lines on this subject that are still of the utmost relevance today.[4] European scholars – geologists, zoologists, botanists – had long been working on inventories of their respective fields. In their wake or at the same time, the discipline of human geography set out to enumerate the many and varied methods used by human beings the world over to master their (just as varied) environments; ethnology, meanwhile, started to describe the cultures through which human communities order and make sense of their internal workings and their place in the universe. Yet the great achievement of this endeavour – an unequalled yet inevitably partial body of knowledge about human societies and their future – was also, sadly, the origin of the many simplistic (or, at their worst, caricatured and disfigured) representations of the different groups that made up the imperial construct. 'Comprehension' has a suggestive double meaning; the colonial empires lost sight of comprehensive understanding in their hurry to draw up a cohesive, comprehensive inventory of colonial knowledge.

Geography textbooks remind us of the most simplistic and overdetermined classification system of them all – that of skin colour – in which 'scientific' observations of difference rapidly collapse into a hierarchy giving pride of place to Western civilization and its representative, the white (and preferably blond) man. This construct, if not always openly acknowledged, was always latent in European worldviews of the time. In 1931, the French Minister for the Colonies Albert Sarraut thus compared the 'white race' with the 'coloured races', which he classified as 'yellow', 'brown', 'black' and 'red'. Colonization was further identified as the work of the 'white man'.[5] We should not forget here that the great period of colonial expansion in the nineteenth century coincided with the development of social Darwinist doctrines. Europeans, of course, were guilty of the same error as any other group which sees itself, implicitly or otherwise, as the benchmark of humanity. But it is precisely because Europeans proudly claimed to have attained universal reason and conquered prejudice that their delusion of grandeur – replete as it was with prejudice – seems unforgivable.

Civilizational Faultlines

Many of the territories conquered by European empires since the time of Alexander the Great were, in the eyes of their conquerors, inhabited by 'barbarians' who spoke incomprehensible languages and practised outlandish customs. Conquest undeniably went hand-in-hand with a belief in superiority that often amounted to racism. Yet there is a paradox here: colonial expansion at this time took place on land rather than sea, and the 'barbarians' were thus usually closer to home than the conquerors cared to admit; most had grown out of the Neolithic Revolution that started in the fertile crescent. Jules Harmand, former diplomat and colonial explorer, argued in 1915 that modern colonization had moved from contiguity to diversity: 'modern colonial expansion, in the new conditions and transformations of the present day – that is to say, colonization operating across considerable distances – differs significantly from "natural" or contiguous expansion. It inevitably brings into contact (by subordinating one to the other) elements that had until now evolved independently of one another. It is no surprise, then, to find that they exhibit radical differences of custom, belief, emotion, moral or material demands, ways of conceiving the world – in a word, of everything that shapes human nature and constitutes nations.'[6]

Indeed, colonialism was defined by radical polarization and mutual exclusivity; it compared and contrasted a 'European' civilization – founded on a Christian then humanist and Enlightenment heritage – with a bloc of 'non-European' civilizations that had no knowledge of this privileged heritage. We can see an example of this bipolar outlook in Guizot's 1828 description: compared with others, Western civilization is 'neither narrow, nor exclusive, nor stationary. For the first time in our history, the character of particularity has disappeared from civilization; for the first time, civilization is developing with as much richness and complexity as the theatre of the universe'. To Guizot and his kind, this proclaimed civilizational march forward promoted not only social and political progress but also an improvement in both individual and collective morals.[7] Reading Guizot in retrospect, his subsequent career as prime minister and one of the architects of the July Monarchy conquests – most importantly that of Algeria – makes sense.

Some 50 years later, economist Paul Leroy-Beaulieu asserted that certain peoples, 'with a different civilization but nonetheless compact, coherent and stable' were 'destined by their history and their present character to self-govern and direct their own affairs'. This was the case of the 'Japanese nation' and the 'Chinese nation'. Two categories, on the other hand, seemed to be destined for colonization:

those, firstly, who were judged to be 'fairly advanced in several ways' but who had 'remained stationary', or those who had 'not succeeded in constituting themselves as united, peaceful and progressive nations with a steady course of consistent development', and thus – according to Beaulieu – lived in an 'unstable equilibrium'. If these peoples, 'dormant or powerless' (amongst which Beaulieu cites India and Java), needed their missing energy to be brought to them by others, this was all the more true for the 'barbarous or savage tribes' which were 'incoherent and lacking in any sense of progress', engaged in continuous warfare and incapable of putting the immense territories they occupied to good use.[8] This perceived superiority was used to legitimate conquest. Jules Ferry, in the same speech that evoked the still raw wound of the German annexation of Alsace-Lorraine, emphasized that the 'superior races' had both the right and the 'duty' to civilize the 'lower races'. In Beaulieu's account and others in the same vein, total submission of the world (or as great a part of it as possible) seems a logical and legitimate outcome.

Beaulieu's ideas alert us to the close connection between the colonial project and notions of 'coherence', 'unity', 'stability' or 'regular development' in colonial assessments of the level of 'progress' displayed by their different groups of *indigènes*. The idea that in order to be considered civilized a group must be moving forward with a sense of progress *and* 'coherent, stable' reminds us that colonization worked as a mirror for European insecurities about the continent's own recent past. There is no small irony in the timing of Beaulieu's essay, coming as it did in the immediate aftermath of the Franco-Prussian War and, significantly, of the violent divisions and bloodlet that ended the Paris Commune. The emphasis on unity, pacifism and regular development as criteria for judging progress thus appears as a sort of negative image of what Europeans most feared closer to home and would experience in 1914: the barbarity and violent prejudice that Europe claimed to have banished but that continued, over the course of the nineteenth century and beyond, to resurface with telling regularity.

Cutting the Colonial Cake

The construction of colonial empires, which we paint here only in the broadest of strokes, appears at the height of imperialism in the 1930s as the result of a process already several centuries long. In 1934, for example, Portugal celebrated (a few years late) the 500-year anniversary of the opening of its colonial epic, the Ceuta landing of 1415 on the Mediterranean coast of what is now Morocco. In 1935, France celebrated the tricentenary of the French West Indies. In fact, all of the European colonial powers of the time could have traced their colonial history just as far back, so numerous are the episodes – albeit often brief – in which a European power seized a previously independent African, American or Asian territory and placed it definitively (or so the colonizers liked to think) under European domination.

Yet this expansion was piecemeal and irregular: European domination, far from a steady advance across a steadily expanding area, was something closer to a journey across the globe that liberated certain territories as it occupied others in turn. Though colonial expansion may appear inexorable with hindsight, closer examination reveals that its path was strewn with obstacles and complications – and inevitably so, since the division of the world it implied was under constant renegotiation. Colonial powers won and lost empires one after another; what we see in the 1930s is in fact merely a snapshot of a fleeting moment in a fast-moving historical process. Memory clings on to that moment because it was – as would become clear not long after – the calm before the storm. It is worth remembering that the most common maps of the Roman Empire similarly depict it at its zenith in the second century AD.

The story of the making and the transformations of European empires is in fact a story of constantly renewed struggle. The British Empire, the most prestigious and powerful of them all, did not rise to power in one smooth movement: historians often contrast the 'old Empire', based on the Americas and lost to all intents and purposes when the United States declared independence, with the 'modern Empire' founded in the nineteenth century in Asia, Africa and the Pacific. The same is true of the other great colonial powers. The French Empire built in the nineteenth and early twentieth centuries was a new one; of the *ancien régime* empire, only the 'old colonies' dating back to the sixteenth or seventeenth century – Saint Pierre and Miquelon, the West Indies, French Guiana, Réunion, the French trading posts of India – remained under French domination, with a total area of less than 100,000 km² and a population of just over a million. The 'old colonies', in other words, accounted for less than 1 per cent of the surface area and roughly 1.5 per cent of the total population of the new French Empire. The same is true of Portugal. Portuguese historians regard the essentially African empire consolidated in Angola and Mozambique in the late nineteenth century as the 'third Empire', defining the first wave as the occupation of the East Indies (subsequently taken by the Dutch) and the second that of Brazil, which gained independence in 1880. Only fragments of the vast Asian territories occupied over the past centuries – Goa, East Timor (shared with Dutch control on the western part of the island) and Macao in China – remained under Portuguese control, representing 1 per cent of the surface area and 13 per cent of the empire's population around 1930.

If these colonial powers could soothe their nostalgia for lost lands with the satisfaction of more recent successes, others refused to forget the past and hankered after repossession of territories lost to others. Spain – stripped of the Philippines, Cuba and Puerto Rico by the United States in 1898 – retained only fragmented shards of its vast original possessions, including the Moroccan coast enclaves of Ceuta and Melilla dating back to the Renaissance period. Spain won its remaining colonial possessions – the Rif (Morocco's Mediterranean coast), Ifni and Rio de Oro (present-day Western Sahara) – only at the outset of the twentieth century. Yet

Spanish nationalists did not abandon hope of breathing new life into North African expansion. Other land-hungry countries, however, were waiting in the wings and better equipped to realize their ambitions: Germany, for instance, still smarting from the confiscation of its colonies by the Treaty of Versailles; but also Italy and Japan, countries whose power ambitions far outstripped their territorial possessions.

The following is a table of the surface area and population of colonial empires at the end of the 1930s, at their largest point of expansion:

Table 2: Surface Area and Population of Colonial Empires (end of 1930s)

European states	Area (km²)	Population (no. of inhabitants)
Belgium (1937)	2,385,000	10,000,000
Spain	350,000	1,000,000
France (1935)	11,841,000	66,000,000
Great Britain (1939)	34,363,000	500,000,000
Italy (1939)	3,480,000	13,000,000
Netherlands (1936)	2,079,000	66,000,000
Portugal (1936)	2,098,000	10,000,000
Total	56,596,000	666,000,000
World	134,600,000	2,116,000,000
Percentage of world total	42 per cent	31 per cent
Non-European states		
United States (1940)	1,843,000	18,000,000
Japan (1940)	298,000	32,000,000
Russia	4,000,000	35,000,000
	6,141,000	85,000,000
Total (all colonial empires)		
	63,000,000	750,000,000
Percentage of world total	47 per cent	35 per cent

For Italy: Albania not included, Ethiopia included.

With the exception of states in the Americas, only a handful of groups in colonized areas were still independent in 1939. In Africa, after the Italian occupation of Ethiopia in 1936, only tiny Liberia (100,000 km², with fewer than a million inhabitants) still lay outside European control. Even this exception, moreover, subsisted thanks to American involvement, and the independent Republic of Liberia was proclaimed by freed American slaves rather than an indigenous group. In Western and Central Asia, Turkey, Iran and Afghanistan owed their freedom both to vigorous leadership and to their skill in exploiting the balance of power between Russian ambitions to the north and British claims in the south. In the Arabic-speaking world, Saudi Arabia and Yemen were largely free of foreign domination but remained highly marginal and vulnerable, under pressure from both the British and from growing Italian ambitions, which would ultimately work to their advantage. Egypt's recent independence

(1936), like that of Iraq (1932), meanwhile, placed crippling constraints on these two states, and British paternalism continued to weigh heavily. In the Far East, Siam (which became Thailand in 1939) had the dubious luck of being a buffer state between British-controlled Burma and French Indochina. Although China's leaders succeeded in abolishing the privileges enjoyed by Europeans since the First Opium War and the series of unequal treaties that ensued, they could not prevent the Europeans retaining their power bases in the region, with the port of Hong Kong their most potent symbol. Of the forty-five gunboats that still patrolled the country's major rivers, and became symbolic of an interventionism practised with complete disregard for sovereignty, twenty-six were European (eighteen British and five French) as opposed to ten American and twelve Japanese.[9] European troops were stationed in the concessions until 1937, when the Japanese military invasion of the country began.

However, to informed observers of the time, this situation of near-complete colonial domination was no great arrival or colonial 'end of history'; these are ideas that appeared later, when analysts attempted to read the decadence of colonialism into its final years. Rather, it would at the time have appeared as what it was: just one phase in a continuous open-ended historical development. Georges Hardy thus spoke of a 'stabilization, temporary at least, of the colonial maelstrom'.[10] According to Hardy, Europeans in the colonies 'regarded each other, in general, as men of the same race and representatives of a common cause. In many situations they came to each other's aid. Sporadically, like deer hunters, they forgot their rivalry to form a united bloc against indigenous inhabitants. In short, they more or less consciously established and often observed the duties of a European solidarity.'[11] This is unrealistic; yet it remains true that although hegemonic ambitions were never far away, it was clear from very early on that overseas territories were – of necessity – gains to be shared out rather than controlled exclusively. We can trace this conception back to the 1494 Treaty of Tordesillas, which divided the world between the two Iberian kingdoms along a north–south line running from pole to pole. Colonial politics was the ultimate domain of diplomatic negotiation, of which the Conference of Berlin in 1884–5 that negotiated the division of Africa was perhaps the most representative example. Even after its victories of 1815, Britain did not attempt to strip other powers of their colonial possessions, although it did of course work no less doggedly to ensure more exclusive control of areas judged crucial to its interests. Before 1914, the Franco-German colonial dispute (notably over the Moroccan question) was always solved – or postponed – by compromises. The future Marshal Lyautey, Resident-General of Morocco at the time, announced to his officers on receiving news of the declaration of war in 1914: 'A war between Europeans is a civil war [...] It is the greatest idiocy that the world has ever witnessed.'[12]

And so we are back to the supremacist vision of colonial empires as an appropriation of land by the most powerful and intelligent, justified by the interests – properly understood, their advocates argued – of both conquerors and conquered. The new European empires presented themselves as a marriage of political expediency and the best interests of humanity at large. Expanded to the globe as a whole, they established routes of exchange that opened up a global market. They thus worked as a transition between the old world, understood as a tool of profit for states, and the modern world with its movement towards a unified space criss-crossed with commercial and information flows working in concert with the demands of a global economy but also for the diffusion of an ideal of shared values. The role of ideology and fantasy in all of these representations needs no further demonstration.

Conclusion

Colonial expansion was doubtless an inevitable development given the nature of European culture and above all the evolution of market capitalism followed by industrialism and long-distance finance. In bringing nations and economies closer together, it clearly foreshadowed the world of today. But to recognize the inevitability of the colonial phase is not to endorse its consequences. First of all, even as it created geographical connections between human beings, it erected symbolic and real political walls between them, dividing the dominant from the dominated, consolidating prejudices and establishing grievances whose echoes we still see today. It contributed, furthermore, to the worldwide export of the European nation state model, born in circumstances particular to Europe and often the cause of conflict. We may still ask whether this development might not have been mitigated if, as leaders including Mr Gladstone and Georges Clémenceau advocated at least at one time, the governors of European states had refused to complement the export of Western products and ideas with a politics of imperialism.

Notes

1 J. Frémeaux, *Les Empires coloniaux. Une histoire-monde*, *réédition CNRS* (Paris , 2012).
2 M. Balard and A. Ducellier (eds), *Coloniser au Moyen Age* (Paris, 1995).
3 A term we use to designate imperial projects that do not rely on settlement of metropolitan nationals in conquered territories.
4 M. de Montaigne, 'Des cannibales', *Essais* (Paris, 2009), Chapter XXXI.
5 A. de Sarraut, *Grandeur et servitude coloniale* (Paris, 1931), pp. 68–70.
6 J. Harmand, *Domination et colonisation* (Paris, 1910), p. 53.
7 F. Guizot, *Histoire de la civilisation en Europe* [1828] (Paris, 1985), p. 78.
8 P. Leroy-Beaulieu, *De la Colonisation chez les peuples modernes*, 5th edition (Paris, 1904), pp. 706–7.
9 B. Estival, 'Les Canonnières de Chine', *Revue internationale d'Histoire militaire*, 75 (1995), pp. 97–109.
10 G. Hardy, *La Politique coloniale et le partage de la terre aux XIXème et XXème siècle* (Paris, 1937), p. 447.
11 G. Hardy, *Les Éléments de l'histoire coloniale* (Paris, 1921), p. 186.
12 A. Maurois, *Lyautey* (Paris), p. 165.

Epilogue:
After-Images of Empire[1]

Bernard Porter

The impact of the European imperialisms of the nineteenth and twentieth centuries on their victims (or beneficiaries), on their perpetrators (the European colonial powers themselves), on what one might call their collaborators (European nations that did not have significant empires of their own but were still involved in the movement one way or another, economically, for example, or culturally), and on the rest of the world (extra-European countries that were never formally or even informally colonized but were obviously affected indirectly by the colonization that was going on around them), is a controversial topic, and a complicated one, as my statement of it here suggests. Even more controversial is the question of European imperialism's *after*-effects: its lasting legacy in all the different areas just listed; a question which is muddied still further by the – again contested – issue of whether in fact these should rightly be called 'after'-effects, or whether 'imperialism' is really still going on – in more subtle, indirect ways, perhaps; in the guise of 'globalization'; or in the hands of the Americans. As if this was not enough, we have problems of context: the difficulty that any historian dealing with the 'causes and effects' of things has of extricating one causal factor from another – 'imperialist' from other entirely different but nonetheless compatible motivations, for example – in the bewildering confusion of tendencies, motives and discourses that makes up nearly all human history. This is a veritable minefield. Others in this volume have been brave enough to venture into it. The present chapter, however, will take another path.

As well as after-effects, empires – in common with most other historical events – leave behind them after-*images* (*rémanences*): like the bright shape of an electric light filament we can still see afterwards, for a while, when we close our eyes.[2] It is these that will form the subject of this chapter; mainly in relation to the images left by the *British* Empire, but that empire as seen – or remembered, or imagined, or invented – not only by Britons themselves, but also in the larger or former 'British' community: in Britain's ex-colonies, for example, including the USA. Its argument will be that ever since the (query) demise of the British Empire, the *idea* of it has taken on a life of its own; related of course to the reality that preceded it, but sometimes only very loosely, and occasionally unrecognizably. The chapter will also argue that this new life – or 'after-life', or rather, as we shall see later, 'after-lives' – has become an important historical factor in its own right, entirely separate from any lasting effect we believe the empire itself may have had. Imperialism is not unique in this regard, of course. All great historical events react on later events as myths as well as realities, sometimes hugely influentially. Look at the common United States founding myth, for example (1776 and all that); deeply flawed as history, as most academic historians will tell you, but with an immense potency all of its own. Something similar is happening now in the case of European imperialism in general, and British in particular. The myth has sprouted wings. And also some rather sharp teeth.

Obviously there is no one version of the British imperial myth – unlike the 1776 myth among 95 per cent of Americans. Just as is the case in France, the reputation of the old British Empire is controversial; though probably only for a minority of the British population. (The rest are simply not interested.) Usually the controversy is played out between those on the one side who are critical of the British Empire: perhaps about half the British controversialists, plus a large majority of foreigners; and on the other side its apologists, who are usually British, but with one or two Americans now joining them. The first camp is well represented by the evocative title of John Newsinger's recent history of British imperial atrocities, *The Blood Never Dried*;[3] the second by that of Niall Ferguson's popular and influential *Empire: How Britain Made the Modern World*.[4] These books, and the viewpoints they represent, are of course almost diametrically opposed to each other, in one sense. One thinks the British Empire was a bad thing, the other that it was a good thing – or a good thing on the whole. (Ferguson acknowledges some flaws.) But this is not the main problem with them. Moral judgements are relatively easy to spot – neither Ferguson nor Newsinger is exactly shy about his – and so to discount if we want to. More problematical is an assumption they both share. Each accepts the old British imperialists' view of the *importance* of their empire: of its 'greatness', in their terms; its power, or hegemony; and therefore of its *capacity* for either bad or good. Ferguson's extraordinary subtitle, for example, hangs on this assumption.

It seems to be a general view: though without more research one cannot be sure. When most people today picture the British Empire retrospectively they generally see something – well – *imperial*. That word itself conjures up certain images: usually of great power, domination and pride. In Britain's case this is encouraged by those famous red-daubed world maps that are supposed to have brightened the classrooms of every school in the later nineteenth century; the projection chosen, of course (Mercator's), exaggerating the territorial extent of Britain's colonial dominions, especially in the top left-hand corner; but, even allowing for this (and it could also be argued that Mercator's projection diminishes India's importance), inescapably implying colossal British global hegemony. This is the common image, certainly abroad:[5] of a huge, powerful hegemonic empire, trying to impose British ways on the rest of the world, generally unscrupulously, and in order – basically – to exploit it. But it is deeply flawed; at least as much so as most Americans' view of their 'Revolution'.

Most scholarly work on the history of British imperialism over the past 20 or 30 years has tended to throw doubt on it – to stress on the contrary the essential weakness, ineffectiveness and vulnerability of the British Empire, throughout its history. For example: most of Britain's imperial expansion was 'reluctant', in the sense that Britain would have preferred to get what it wanted in the world in other ways; as a nation it never had any grand imperial *project*, of the kind that is sometimes assumed. It was always relatively weak militarily (not navally), except in the case of India, where its (separate) army was mainly staffed – in the lower ranks – by native Indians. Britain's Colonial and Indian Civil Services together employed just 4,000 men at the very height of the empire (around 1900), which is probably fewer *in toto* than it takes to run just one medium-sized European city. They were incredibly thinly spread. Britain had little money to spend on its colonies: not because it was poor, but because its (mainly middle-class) Parliament had no stomach for spending it in this way. The result of all this was it was forced to run its empire *collaboratively*, with the help of its natives, which meant in very many instances 'appeasing' them. 'Appeasement', in fact, has a long (and often honourable) tradition in the history of British foreign and colonial policy.[6] White settlers in Southern Africa and Australia were appeased by allowing them to tyrannize over their *indigènes*. In the more tropical parts of the empire, especially West Africa, where there were few settlers, this developed into a full-blown philosophy of colonial government in the 1900s, called 'indirect rule', which meant (effectively) leaving the local 'native' inhabitants to rule themselves in their own ways. (In Northern Nigeria it was through Islamic law.) When Britain did not rule 'indirectly', but tried to impose unpopular measures, it had huge difficulty in putting down the revolts that ensued. There are numerous examples of better-armed British armies being embarrassingly defeated by for example African, Afghan and Maori 'savages' (the British name for them), and at least two major imperial wars – the Indian Mutiny and the Boer War of 1899–1902 – where Britain only just squeaked through. Sometimes she resorted to *atrocity*: but that was not necessarily a sign of strength. (It could be the opposite.) Back home – though this is a controversial argument, which not all scholars accept[7] – most Britons cared and even knew very little about their empire; which meant that that empire did not have a very powerful domestic base, either. And it weakened Britain in the rest of the world, preventing it from adequately resisting Russian aggression in the nineteenth century, for example, and German in the twentieth. So the British Empire was emphatically not a particularly powerful – certainly not a *super*-powerful – entity in the nineteenth and early twentieth centuries. The main reason it kept going (and expanding) as long and successfully as it did was that for most of the period from 1800–1950 it had no serious European competitors, except the French Empire; and if France and Britain ever looked like clashing – as they did at Fashoda in 1898 – they were usually able to settle things amicably over a bottle of good French wine. When you look at it closely, therefore, and underneath the display and noise and strutting and silly dressing-up that Britain's political elite employed and encouraged in order to give the *impression* of power and glory, the British Empire was really a very vulnerable thing. What David Cannadine calls its 'ornamentalism'[8] was a big bluff. The British Empire was lucky; not powerful.

Of course this is an over-simple view of it – as simplistic, probably, as some of the 'images' that this chapter will be taking issue with shortly; but every imperial historian would probably agree that it expresses at least a great part of the true picture, and so should be taken into account.[9] It may also be open to the charge of wanting to defend or rehabilitate the British Empire. What it could be interpreted as saying is that that empire was *not as bad as it is made out*. That in fact is a common knee-jerk reaction to any attempt at imperial historical 'revisionism' these days. The very fact of trying to 'revise' some of the accepted versions of British imperial history is enough to damn any historian as a dyed-in-the-wool imperialist blimp.[10] But of course that does not necessarily follow. In the present case in particular, the 'vulnerable' view of the British Empire has unflattering implications as well as exculpatory ones. On a very obvious level: if it was weaker than it sometimes made itself out to be, it also follows that it couldn't have been as positively *beneficial* as its apologists claim; that it could not possibly, as Ferguson's subtitle puts it, have 'Made the Modern World'.

If this was the real situation, therefore, or close to it, why is the common *rémanence* of the British Empire so different? Some of the reasons are fairly obvious. All the superficial signs – starting with that red-bespattered world map (though incidentally that only starts appearing on the walls of elementary schools in the 1900s) – suggest that the British Empire was a 'big thing'. The very word 'empire' – a big, macho one, from the Latin '*imperium*' – corroborates this. It is what contemporary British imperialists themselves wanted to believe. It is what today's Americans also want to believe, for other reasons: firstly because if Britain really was an imperial 'superpower' it makes their own rebellion against it the more heroic (in fact of course the Brits were very half-hearted about defending the Thirteen Colonies, the Americans divided about resisting them, and would not have won without the French); and secondly because they see it through the eyes of their own present 'superpower' status. Peoples generally regard other countries by how they present to *them*. For most of the past 200-plus years Britain has mainly presented to other nations *as* an empire: ruling them, oppressing them, exploiting them, competing colonially with them, or just throwing its weight about generally. It is no wonder, then, that this became a dominant image. Obviously Britain's ex-colonial subjects share this, and are almost bound to regard the British Empire as overwhelmingly oppressive (the key word here is 'overwhelmingly'), which it was if you were being bullied by a red-faced British Army officer in Egypt, as Edward Said was (more of him later),[11] or tortured in a Kenyan detention camp, like (apparently) Barack Obama's grandfather.[12] *Anti*-imperialism is another factor; an ideology which was uniquely fortunate during the Cold War years in being espoused by both sides in that stand-off. (Needless to say, both the Soviet Union's and the United States' professed 'anti-imperialisms' were hugely hypocritical.) Ferguson's *Empire* must also be influential: less, as has been pointed out already, its defence of British imperialism, than the impression it gives of the empire's 'bigness'; and the fact that the book was marketed as such a blockbuster. The British themselves have lost most of the interest they may once have had in their empire, except as a setting for exciting films and TV dramas (*Gandhi*, *The Crown of India*, and so on), which can be critical of imperialism – very few people have much difficulty with that – but which are, again, bound to perpetuate the 'great imperial power' after-image, this time for dramatic effect.

Education may also have had something to do with it. Outside Britain, apart from the United States, where there are some fine imperial historians, albeit vastly outnumbered by post-colonial theorists, very little empirical imperial history seems to be taught.[13] So far as Britain is concerned, my own personal memories may be relevant here. I remember when the lights of the British Empire finally went out, and hardly seeing the shining filament at all then. I do not think I was unusual in this. I am certain that when I was at school and university (in the 1950s and 1960s) I was taught nothing at all about the British Empire; and, in case we think that had something to do with the empire's contemporary demise, my later historical researches have shown me that this state of affairs in fact goes back into the nineteenth century and beyond.[14] There was a certain amount of imperial history being written and taught (a course at Cambridge, for example – but generally reckoned to be for the cerebrally challenged: it was the alternative to the much more prestigious 'History of Political Thought' course), but usually by imperia*lists*, often old 'empire hands', and so widely felt to be tainted. The only alternatives were strident left-wing anti-imperial manifestos. That may be one of the causes of our British problems with the common image of the empire today. When people started getting interested in it again, they had little foundation of reliable knowledge to build on. There were no serious broad academic *un*-imperialist histories of British imperialism before my own *The Lion's Share*, first published in 1976. Even that was considered to be for a small, niche market only, not the mainstream. I remember that when I put on an imperial history course for undergraduates at the first university I taught at (in 1969), it was regarded as a very odd animal indeed, especially by the *social* historians who were in the ascendant then, and who assumed from it that I must be an imperia*list*. (They after all were *social*ists.) It was a decidedly marginal field. I felt very alone.

This of course has changed dramatically in the past 15 or 20 years. It is hard to avoid imperialism now if you are studying history – or many other subjects – at any British school or university. You might think I would be pleased about that. (It must have boosted the sales of *The Lion's Share*.) But the revival took a strange form; and one which – to return to our main theme – is partly responsible for the nature of the 'after-image' that this chapter has been taking issue with. Most of the revivalists were not imperial historians originally: had made no serious study, that is of British imperialism per se before they started writing about aspects of it. Niall Ferguson, the most popular of them, partly because of his very provocative (i.e. relatively pro-imperial) thesis, was a historian of banking before he took up with the British Empire – at the suggestion of the BBC: the book was a spin-off from a TV series. The majority were not even historians at all; for the most remarkable and significant development in this field in recent years has been the entry into it of people from the disciplines of 'literary' and 'cultural studies', many of whom – these of course are the 'post-colonial theorists', or 'po-cos' – have virtually taken over several university departments: 'colonialized' them, if you like; and now probably make up the majority of scholars working on 'imperial' or 'colonial' topics. In a way, one cannot wonder at this. Imperialism was obviously a huge and (to put it mildly) problematical phenomenon in recent world history. Britain was responsible for much of it. Yet most British academic historians were ignoring it, preferring to concentrate on events like the English Civil War (interminably), and themes like the advance of British (domestic) liberty. (Apart from me, of course; but my *Lion's Share* seems to have gone largely unnoticed.) There was a gap here. What came next was almost bound to happen. When people don't have any historical facts, they fall back on 'theory'. In 1993 Edward Said, with a personal background at the sharp end of British imperialism – but very little knowledge at all of its history – revealed that 'imperialism' showed up ubiquitously in European culture too. So the 'cultural theorists' stepped in.

The 'new' imperial history that this fed into has been enormously enlightening and valuable in many ways. It has de-parochialized British history, revealing imperial traces at home that were long ignored by the main British historical establishment. Certain techniques associated with it have furnished some valuable analytical tools: in particular 'discourse analysis' (though I like to think that we older historians used to do a little bit of that, instinctively, before we were told what it was called). Integrated with more conventional historical approaches to the history of imperialism, all this could have enriched our understanding of imperialism enormously; and almost certainly will do, eventually. It is always good to be shown new perspectives on things. (Mainstream history is constantly sucking these in.) Early on, however – and we are still at quite an early stage in this process – any gains to be got from this particular new approach were vitiated by its crudities. One was its semantic laxity: its failure to define its terms, and in particular the meanings of the 'i' and 'e' words ('empire', 'imperialism', and their derivatives); which were often stretched far beyond not what was 'correct', or even plausible: for words like this can mean anything you want them to – but beyond what was *useful*, if you wished to employ them as analytical tools. (All that stuff, for example, about zoos and tea-drinking and Gothic being 'imperial'...) Another was its blindness to *context*, and to the plethora of other 'discourses' that raged in the nineteenth century in a Britain that many post-colonial theorists claimed was dominated by, 'steeped' in, 'imperialism' at that time. Why they *assumed* that imperialism was the dominant (or 'hegemonic') one was never explained. If there is a 'theoretical' argument for this – and the post-colonialists make a great fuss about 'theory' – it is difficult to find it spelled out, clearly. A third 'crudity', arguably, was its often rather simplistic approach to the question of 'power'; which is usually more complex – more *negotiated*, as we have seen already – than the common 'imperial' trope implies. (Other post-modernists are alive to this.) A fourth flaw is post-colonial theory's deafness to *nuance*. As one young historian of South Asia put it recently: the post-colonialist approach 'reduces all imperial experiences to a universally hegemonic colonialism, impervious to the ever-changing geographical, political and temporal realities. [...] Colonialism, in this context, was often viewed as a flat landscape under a uniform imperial power.'[15] Exactly. Indeed, this kind of objection to this school of thought is becoming more and more common now, from historians who have started *testing* it against the empirical evidence; and also, it has to be said, by a new generation of post-colonial theorists themselves. Edward Said's *Orientalism* – a key text in the formation of post-colonialist theory, and for long the Bible (or Qur'an) of his disciples – is a particular casualty of this.[16] (See for example Robert Irwin's recent powerful onslaught on Said's methodology in *For Lust of Knowing*.)[17] It is unlikely that either *Orientalism* or *Culture and Imperialism* will be able to sustain its iconic status much longer. While it does, however, its effect must be distorting. Almost every conclusion of post-colonial theory tends to *exaggerate* the extent, importance and power of what it very vaguely calls 'imperialism' in the world. The reason for this is that the post-colonialists firstly don't know any history; and secondly – and more importantly – do not use the historians' tools. They do not seem to want to *problematize* things. One imagines that most of them would be somewhat impatient of the problems that were posted at the very beginning of this chapter: relating to the *complexities* of these issues. To them it all appears quite simple – and 'imperialist'.

How widespread the effect of this particular influence is, is difficult to say. It certainly stretches a little further than academia, among millions who are unlikely to have read a single post-colonial text. (Some are unreadable anyway, possibly deliberately.)[18] Its findings have found their way into British adaptations of nineteenth-century novels for the big and little screens, for example, which often insert 'imperial' passages that are not found in the originals on the assumption that they were only left out of those because their readers would have taken the empire for granted.[19] (Patrick Brantlinger has a theory that the fewer references to empire there are in a book, the more imperialist they must be.)[20] It could not have been influential at all if it did not appear to fit in with a 'common-sense' view: that the empire *must* have been important, if it was so big. The contrary view appears counter-intuitive. But then (as I have written elsewhere): if all we needed was intuition, there would be no need for scholarship.

So: why does this matter? It is after all 'merely' history now, all done and dusted, water under the bridge. Except that it is not. There are two sorts of harm it can do. The first is purely – 'merely', if you like – academic; but important therefore, or it should be, to academics and intellectuals. The point is this: that when the idea of 'imperialism' is emphasized so much, for example by the 'po-cos', it tends to stifle any more sophisticated analysis of the complexities and varieties of the phenomena that are supposed to be covered by it. 'Imperialism' is often employed as a kind of trump card in discussions of – for example – foreign policy and cultural contact, bringing the game to an end; label the expansion of McDonald's overseas as 'American imperialism', for example, and the tendency is to see that as the last word, the complete answer, rendering any more complicated examination unnecessary. But of course 'imperialism' covers a multitude of evils (and possibly some goods), all of which have characteristics, contexts and significances of their own, and other influences and discourses acting on them besides 'imperial' ones; which it is surely important to examine before we can fully understand them. Reducing them all to 'imperialism' does not get us very far. (It also, incidentally, diminishes the crucial importance to Britain of her clearly non-imperial relationships – with countries in continental Europe, for example. This is greatly misleading.)[21] A few years ago I proposed, at a conference, that we historians agree to a moratorium on the 'e' and 'i' words for five years, denying ourselves the use of them, so that we would be forced to describe the phenomena that are usually placed under that rubric in other terms, which would be bound to be different terms in different situations, thus indicating how complex (again) the phenomenon was (or, more properly, the phenomen*a* were). But there is of course little chance of that.

In addition, however, there are some clear practical dangers. Here are some examples. The first relates to America. We have seen already that the after-image of a great, powerful British Empire appears to be particularly widespread there, for historical reasons. It has had two major (albeit contradictory) repercussions. One is to give the United States something to define itself *against* – its origin was an anti-colonial rebellion – which has made it difficult for it to see itself in 'imperial' terms. 'We don't *do* empire', as Donald Rumsfeld once famously said (just before invading Iraq); which only makes any sense at all if you regard 'empire' in maximalist terms. By defining their national identity against this 'Other' of the British Empire, as they (mis)understood it, Americans blinded themselves to what was undoubtedly imperialistic in their own international conduct.[22] (This self-delusion is in fact quite extraordinary. In 1812 the USA launched one of its many imperial wars, against Canada. In popular American mythology, however, that has become the 'Second War of *Independence*' from the British.)[23] In fact the US pursued policies in the world in the nineteenth and early twentieth centuries which came very close indeed to what in Britain's contemporary case is always *called* 'imperialism'; if Rumsfeld had had a better idea of that latter kind of empire he might have been able to learn some lessons from it. Gladstone's invasion of Egypt in 1882 was the precedent for the Iraq invasion that all of us imperial historians were screaming at him from across the Atlantic – the similarities are quite close – but of course he could not admit that, and the warnings it implied. Instead he took another 'precedent', from one of America's 'good' wars: the liberation of Paris in 1944, with American GIs being welcomed joyously by girls and women waving flowers. That is what he confidently predicted in Baghdad; with of course disastrous results. Without this huge blind spot about the nature of the British Empire, it may not be too fanciful to speculate that the USA might have at least thought twice about repeating Britain's Egyptian mistakes in Iraq.

In another neck of the American Neo-Con woods, however, dwelt those who did recognize the imperial analogy, and actually embraced it; men like Mark Steyn, Charles Krauthammer, David Frum and Max Boot, egged on by Niall Ferguson, whose after-image of the British Empire is the '*beneficent*' red-painted map kind. They wanted America to follow in Britain's tracks.[24] What 'Afghanistan and other troubled lands today cry out for', wrote Boot in 2001, was 'the sort of enlightened foreign administration once provided by self-confident Englishmen in jodhpurs and pith helmets'.[25] Quite apart from the historical howlers involved here – the British did not actually rule in jodhpurs: they were for playing polo in; and of course never in Afghanistan, where they were nearly always soundly beaten (militarily, i.e. not in polo), just like the Americans – the problem with this view is that it gives far too much credit to the *capacity* of the British to do 'good' in this way. In both these cases we can see dangerous practical conclusions being inferred from this over-blown *rémanence* of the old British Empire.

Other examples are easy to find. Here are just a few. President Mugabe of Zimbabwe gained a great deal of the electoral support he certainly once had from his claim that Britain is plotting to 'colonize' his country again; a ludicrous idea, of course, and based on an entirely false view of the power Britain had over 'Rhodesia' even in the past,[26] but potent all the same. In 2004 a journalist writing in the *Guardian* blamed the British Empire for the persistence of homophobia in the

West Indies, though in fact the opposite is just as likely to have been the case.[27] (Even if it were true, 40-odd years after their independence, could not the West Indians think for themselves?) That is not atypical.

My fourth example is a little different. Late in 2007, BBC Four showed a TV documentary series, made by a private production company, called *Clash of Cultures*, about three incidents in British imperial history: the Indian Mutiny, the Sudan Campaign of 1898, and the British Mandate in Palestine.[28] All these events showed the British Empire up in a pretty disreputable light: generally overbearing, greedy and insensitive – perfectly justifiably (in my view). The difficulty was, however, that they were also presented as parts of a deliberate and systematic British Christian crusade to destroy the Muslim religion: which – again any imperial historian will tell you – is a travesty of the truth.[29] The producer of that series was not, of course, a historian, and engaged no general historical advisor; but instead projected modern – and especially modern American Fundamentalist Christian – ideas onto the past. Again, part of the problem was this after-image that *he* clearly had of an all-powerful, proselytizing British Empire. The 'danger' of that, of course, comes from the way it plays to the existing paranoia of Islamic extremists, who always suspected this in any case.[30]

Another example is the sociologist Paul Gilroy's reaction to Linda Colley's suggestion, in a book she published in 2002, that the impact of British imperialism in the eighteenth century was 'uneven [...] shallow and [...] slow'; exactly the point that has been made here for the nineteenth century, and which is incontrovertible, surely, for the eighteenth. Gilroy's complaint against this was that it sought to 'usurp' colonial victims' 'honoured place of suffering'. He also inferred from it that Colley was trying to place the *blame* for empire on its victims; and that she wanted the empire back again: a good example of the kind of 'knee-jerk' reaction to 'revisionism' that has been alluded to already.[31] Quite apart from the monstrous libel implied here, Gilroy's comments are problematical in other ways. They are certainly ahistorical, and in exactly the way all these other misreadings are: i.e. they make out the British Empire to be far more hegemonic than it really was. More than this, however: they seem surprisingly Eurocentric, and even 'imperialist'. If they are meant to imply, for example, that Europe's colonial 'subjects' had no more positive role in the colonial process than to 'suffer' it. That seems disparaging, and surely cannot be helpful to the ex-colonial subjects themselves. A more nuanced historian would at least allow them some *agency*, and consequently dignity, which is better to build on than a constant sense of weak, suffering victimhood.

My final example is the most important. I can best introduce it by referring to the row currently going in the Church of England – the good old, tolerant, 'broad' Church of England, as it used to be – over homosexuality: in particular gay marriage, and the ordination of 'practising' gay priests. The 'traditionalists', as they call themselves, abhor all this; especially homosexuality, which the book of Leviticus tells them is an abomination before God. (Leviticus also tells us that the eating of shellfish is an abomination before God; but we hear less of that.) The details of this controversy are thankfully of no relevance to this chapter; what is relevant, however, is the fact that the wing of the Anglican Church most virulently homophobic is the (mainly tropical) African one, and that it is currently charging that the rest of the C of E's more 'modern' outlook on these matters, and its efforts to persuade other Anglicans to embrace it, are yet another example of 'Western Imperialism'. (Clearly, in view of the West Indian example quoted earlier, 'imperialism' takes radically different forms in different ex-colonies.) Which *it may be*, by some ways of looking at it; but this brings us on to a much more serious aspect of the way the 'e' and 'i' words ('empire', 'imperialism' and their derivatives) are used these days: stemming once again from this fundamentally exaggerated view of the efficacy and significance of the British imperialism of the past.

The problem here is the association of 'imperialism' with 'modernity'. Among the other achievements of imperialism, certainly for its champions but also for many of its critics, is widely supposed to have been the spread of modern ideas and institutions – democracy, the rule of law, secularism, liberalism, toleration, technology, capitalism, rationalism, human rights, shirts and ties, football, and so on: just about every 'modern' trend you can think of – from Europe, where they all originated, throughout the rest of the world. This of course is the 'How Britain Made the Modern World' scenario. It is an extraordinarily widespread set of assumptions, this: firstly, that all 'progress' has stemmed from 'the West'; and secondly, that it was 'imperialism' that facilitated its diffusion into the more benighted – endemically backward, stagnant, reactionary and so on – extra-European world. The latest stage of this, of course, is the recent US mission to forcibly spread 'democracy' (by which it means, of course, its own peculiar capitalist form of it) throughout the Middle East. But it is based, again, on an incredibly simplistic and maximalist reading of European imperialism: its monopoly of 'modernity'; the part played by it in the spread of the latter; its *ability* to enforce 'modernity' on other peoples; and lastly, what 'modernity' really consists of.

These are very big questions, especially the last, which cannot be adequately investigated in this chapter. The point to be made, however, is that they *are*, intrinsically, enormously problematical. First of all there is the question of how 'modern', by many ways of looking at it, the 'West' is by comparison with many non-Western societies and cultures. It is doubtful whether the inmates of Abu Ghraib and Guantanamo prisons, for example, would see it in quite this light. Egyptian Muslims at the time of the French imperial invasion there under Napoleon were impressed by his troops' military efficiency, but shocked by what they regarded as their 'barbarity': 'barbarism', of course, being one *antonym* for 'modernity'.[32] The Austrian sociologist Joseph Schumpeter believed that imperialism generally was a sign of social *regression*.[33]

Everyone can think of non-European customs and institutions which they would like to regard as more 'progressive' than Europe's or America's – Arab hospitality, say. Secondly: it is extremely questionable whether such 'Western' institutions as *have* caught on elsewhere, 'modern' or not, did so on the backs of 'imperialism': unless you want to *define* imperialism as, simply, the spread of Western culture. Most would almost certainly have spread – and are likely to have spread less problematically (with more adaptation to the requirements of the receiving societies, for example) – through what you might call 'normal' intercourse between peoples, including trade. In several instances it has been a case of societies *voluntarily adopting* foreign customs, rather than their being forced on them, and both ways around: West adopting East, as well as East adopting West. David Washbrook has coined a useful new word for this process (in relation to India): *in*culturation (as distinct from *ac*culturation).[34] Lastly, and most importantly: the idea that the 'Western' institutions and values I listed a few moments ago – capitalism, democracy and the rest – only arose in the West is astoundingly Eurocentric, and even incipiently racist. Most of them are found flourishing elsewhere, even before they ever took root in Europe or America. Sometimes it was European imperialism that snuffed out the indigenous versions of them. (Indian cotton manufacture is a good example; African forms of popular rule another.) The Cambridge historian Jack Goody has been indefatigable in recent years in pointing this out: tracing the independent traditions of freedom, capitalism, individualism, the rule of law and so on that are found in China and India in particular. His latest book is called *The Theft of History*: by which he means the way in which Westerners have dishonestly appropriated so many of these 'modern' achievements to themselves.[35] A work that complements this is John Darwin's recent *After Tamerlane: The Global History of Empire since 1405*, which shows firstly how close Europe and Asia were in terms of 'modernity' until around the middle of the nineteenth century – well into 'modern times'; and secondly, how very *un*-modern the majority of European nations and regions remained after then.[36] This should give us pause for thought, at the very least, on the question of imperialism's 'modernizing' function.

But the most serious outcome of this may be the complementary acceptance by many of Europe's ex-colonial subjects of this double-headed myth: firstly, that 'modern' institutions like democracy and capitalism are essentially 'Western'; and secondly, that they were only able to be imposed on them – the non-Europeans – by this all-powerful imperial force. Naturally that leads them to reject modernity (no one likes the idea of being forced to do anything), and strengthens the hands of those with reactionary views – like our West African Anglican bishops, and Muslim fundamentalists – who can now paint it as something alien. (An imperial yoke is alien by definition.) One can see this happening today right across the Middle East: liberal ideas resisted largely because they are associated with Western imperialism. Of course this was (and is) the imperialists' own fault; but it was an unintended one. If there is a prime argument against imperialism, in fact, it must be this: that it is basically counter-productive, even in terms of what you, the imperialist, want to do. That is especially the case when it is presented as having been such a ubiquitous and powerful force in world history; that is when the *rémanence*, that after-image of the glowing filament, is such a vivid one.

Notes

1 This chapter was originally prepared for a Conference entitled 'L'histoire coloniale en débat en France et en Grande-Bretagne', held under the auspices of the Franco-British Council in Paris in January 2009, in a section entitled 'Rémanences de l'empire colonial dans les deux sociétés'. Prior to that, versions of it were aired at the Universities of Chicago and Copenhagen in November–December 2008. I am indebted to my hosts and the participants at all those events for their comments, which have been taken account of here.

2 I am grateful to Robert Tombs for this analogy, which helped me to clarify the meaning of *rémanence*.

3 J. Newsinger, *The Blood Never Dried: A People's History of the British Empire* (2006).

4 N. Ferguson, *Empire: How Britain Made the Modern World* (2003).

5 This is my experience in Sweden, where I mostly live. It may be so in the USA too. When I was there in November 2008 I caught one of their tele-evangelists on my hotel TV. His name is Jimmy Swaggart, and he was talking about Israel, and about how when the Jews reoccupied the Holy Mound (or something) Christ would come down to earth again and convert them. (This is the familiar 'Rapture' line.) In the course of this he happened to mention – though I don't think it was essential to his argument – that Palestine had been part of the British Empire *for a thousand years*. That is quite an exaggeration – by about 970 years, in fact. But all this evidence, of course, is purely anecdotal.

6 In my view it was perfectly honourable, for example, to appease colonial (and Irish) nationalists.

7 On this, see B. Porter, *The Absent-Minded Imperialists: Empire, Society and Culture in Britain* (2004), and the controversy stirred by this, featured (and responded to) in my 'Further Thoughts on Imperial Absent-Mindedness', in *Journal of Imperial and Commonwealth History*, 36, 1 (2008).

8 D. Cannadine, *Ornamentalism: How the British Saw their Empire* (2001).

9 For my more nuanced view, see my *The Lion's Share: A Short History of British Imperialism 1850–2004*, 4th edition (Cambridge, 2006).

10 I am writing here from personal experience of the reception of my *Absent-Minded Imperialists* in some quarters. See my 'Further Thoughts on Imperial Absent-Mindedness'.

11 See E. Said, *Out of Place: A Memoir* (New York, NY, 2000).

12 This was widely revealed in the British press shortly after Obama's election as US President. See for example the *Daily Telegraph*, 3 December 2008.

13 I may be over-generalizing here from an example familiar to me: Stockholm University's history department; which resolutely refuses to teach anything outside Swedish history – with perhaps a little 'Baltic' thrown in, because it can get an EU grant for that. On the other hand, Copenhagen University's 'English, German and Romance Studies Institute' does teach foreign imperial history (I was involved in this). British university history departments may be virtually unique in Europe in typically teaching a *preponderance* of courses centring on countries other than their own. This may be one of the – more acceptable – legacies of empire. (Though it does not appear to have worked this way in France's case.)

14 See Porter, *Absent-Minded Imperialists*, Chapters 4 and 6.

15 From a paper, 'Knowledge Brokers of the Empire', that Manan Ahmed of the University of Chicago delivered in Cambridge (UK) in August 2006.

16 E. Said, *Orientalism* (New York, NY, 1978).

17 R. Irwin, *For Lust of Knowing: The Orientalists and their Enemies* (2006). 'To set my cards out on the table [...] that book seems to me a work of malignant charlatanry in which it is hard to distinguish honest mistakes from wilful misrepresentations' (p. 4).

18 I am still looking for the source of a quotation I once found, but have lost, from a post-colonial theorist who dismissed literary clarity as a 'white, male, colonialist construct'.

19 Two blatant examples are Sarah Curtis' film version of Jane Austen's *Mansfield Park* (1999); and a BBC TV adaptation of Anthony Trollope's *The Way We Live Now* broadcast in 2001.

20 P. Brantlinger, *Rule of Darkness: British Literature and Imperialism, 1830–1914* (Ithaca, NY, 1988), pp. x, 23.

21 The substantial migrations of Britons to continental Europe in the nineteenth century, for example, and *vice-versa*, and the far greater interest that most British people (as well as their governments) evinced in European and American affairs during this period, tend to be marginalized by historians by comparison with relations with Africa and India; simply because it is difficult to convincingly cast English or Irish railway-builders (say) as 'imperialists'. This must distort our picture of British history and even national identity enormously, and possibly even harmfully, with respect to Britain's present-day relations with 'the Continent'.

22 See B. Porter, *Empire and Superempire: Britain, America and the World* (New Haven, CT, 2006).

23 See J. Latimer, *1812: War with America* (Cambridge, MA, 2007).

24 Examples include M. Steyn, 'Imperialism is the Answer', *Chicago Sun-Times*, 14 October 2001; Charles Krauthammer quoted by E. Eakin, '"It Takes an Empire," say Several US Thinkers', in *New York Times*, 2 April 2002; David Frum quoted in J. Heer, 'US Takes on Burden of Empire', *National Post* (Canada), 29 March 2003; M. Boot, 'The Case for American Empire', *Weekly Standard*, 15 October 2001; and N. Ferguson, *Colossus: the Rise and Fall of the American Empire* (New York, NY, 2004).

25 Boot, 'The Case for American Empire'.

26 In fact she devolved that power to the white settlers of Rhodesia very early on. This was a clear derogation of her moral responsibility; whether she could have resumed it later, however, is a moot point. His calculation that she could not, without provoking mutiny in Britain's own military ranks, was one of the reasons for Prime Minister Harold Wilson's refusal to contemplate more forceful action against Ian Smith's government when it declared 'UDI' (Unilateral Declaration of Independence) in 1965.

27 J. Seabrook, 'It's not Natural', *Guardian*, 3 July 2004. If anything the empire was a more tolerant and comfortable environment for homosexuals than was the metropole. See R. Hyam, *Empire and Sexuality: The British Experience* (Manchester, 1990); and R. Aldrich, *Colonialism and Homosexuality* (2003).

28 B. Fagan, *Clash of Culture* (Lanham, MD, 1998).

29 There is no room to elaborate on this here, except to say that the *general* thrust of British colonial policy was to respect and indeed to use Islamic cultures. In Northern Nigeria this was called 'indirect rule'. The only significant exception was the immediately pre-Indian Mutiny years, when Christian evangelicals were given their heads in India to an extent not found anywhere else, especially after the Mutiny taught Britain, very clearly, the dangers of this approach.

30 I took this up with the BBC, first in order to advise them (I saw the pre-airing copy), but got no response the first three times. The fourth time their response was to send my comments to the producer concerned, who wilfully misunderstood them, and whose own defence of his programmes the BBC merely accepted and relayed to me, without query. So I gave up. Perhaps I should not have done; but the BBC's 'complaints procedure', so-called, can really wear one down.

31 I have written about this before, in a review article, 'An Imperial Nation? Recent Works on the British Empire at Home', *The Round Table*, 98 (April 2007). The books are P. Gilroy, *After Empire: Melancholia or Convivial Culture?* (2004), p. 103; L. Colley, *Captives* (2002).

32 J. Darwin, *After Tamerlane: The Global History of Empire since 1405* (2008).

33 J. Schumpeter, *The Sociology of Imperialism* (1919).

34 D. Washbrook, 'Orients and Occidents: Colonial Discourse Theory and the Historiography of the British Empire', in Robin Winks (ed.), *Oxford History of the British Empire*, vol. V (Oxford, 1999).

35 J. Goody, *The Theft of History* (Cambridge, 2006).

36 Darwin, *After Tamerlane, passim*.

Afterword

John Darwin

Perhaps only those with a long memory, or the scars of old struggles, can now remember the time when imperial history was a dying sub-discipline. Forty years ago, however, it was reduced (in Britain at least) to a fugitive band, chased by the heavily armed columns of 'area studies' into its last redoubts: Bloomsbury, Oxford and the Strand. As Bernard Porter recalls, the surviving practitioners risked being accused of 'imperial nostalgia' or of being 'closet imperialists' – so far out of tune with the modern world as to be almost risibly old-fashioned. It was, at least to those for whom the subject remained irresistibly fascinating – as well as (for the moment) their bread and butter – an extraordinary turnabout. Scarcely a decade before, the study of imperialism had been galvanized by those great 'artificers' (to adopt their own phrase), Ronald Robinson and Jack Gallagher. Although their key ideas took some time to catch on, by the early 1960s their reformulation of the history of European imperial expansion, perhaps most vividly set out in their chapter in the eleventh volume of the *New Cambridge Modern History*, seemed to open up not just the historical investigation of European colonial empires, but a huge swathe of world history as well.[1] By showing how European expansion was interwoven with the growth of a world economy, and how Europe's modes of expansion were almost infinitely various, they liberated 'imperialism' from the obsessive preoccupation with 'rule' to which historians were (and remain) so prone. But, above all, by insisting on the importance of studying the ambivalent response of 'local elites' in Africa, Asia and the Americas and their frequent willingness to 'collaborate' (though almost never unconditionally), they showed how the diverse reactions to what would now be called nineteenth-century 'globalization' could be brought into a single field. Here both connection and comparison could be profitably explored. From this viewpoint, imperial history's displacement by 'area studies' or even 'subaltern studies', however sociologically 'necessary', can now be seen as a disastrous regression into an often naive parochialism.

Echoes of Empire sets the seal on what has been an extraordinary revival. It demonstrates the maturing of a field that staggered Lazarus-like to its feet some two decades ago. It seemed for a time as if this reincarnation had been a very mixed blessing. Much of the earlier work of what was carefully called 'new imperial history' (lest the charge of nostalgia be levelled) was curiously Euro- or even Anglocentric. It was mainly concerned with demonstrating that 'empire' had been a decisive influence (for ill) on British society, and too many of those who took up this challenge remained strangely indifferent to the historiography (let alone the archives) of the colonized world. Fortunately, this polemical phase with its literary methodology ('one example makes it true') has now receded, partly because of the 'global' turn among historians. Indeed, we might say that it is the fusion of global history, with its concern for comparison and connection, with an imperial history whose scope has been broadened into social and cultural history (the beneficial legacy of 'subaltern studies' and 'new imperial history'), which gives the field much of its current dynamism. The second very welcome innovation much in evidence here is the exchange of ideas between imperial history on the one hand and the kindred disciplines of politics and international relations on the other. For this is a book that deliberately fuses the approaches and interests of historians and social scientists and has authors drawn from both ranks. It ought to be a flagship for others to follow.

Indeed, the four parts to this book show how subtly and inventively a mature imperial historiography in partnership with politics and international relations, and drawing upon their insights, can be used to illuminate both the recent past and the 'near-present'. Perhaps the leitmotif of the volume is to reject the idea that we can ever be free (at least in the foreseeable future) of the effects of empire. This is not to retreat into post-colonial angst (or rage), but to acknowledge that the world we live in was so largely made by empires (and not just those of Europeans), that to deny their influence is merely futile. Worse still would it be to imagine – as 'nationalist' historiography long encouraged us to – that empires represented a pathological deviation from the high road of progress, towards the 'nation state' world. It does not take a finely tuned ear to catch the echoes of empire all around the modern world. As the chapters in Part I remind us, the 'modernizing' impact of empire needs careful dissection, to take account not only of its local reception among allies and enemies, but also the shifting priorities of those 'modernity-bearers', the colonial regimes. In Part II, we see how the imperialists themselves invoked past visions of empire, or (in the case of Japan) coopted those of their rivals, but often only as top-dressing for their own variation on the 'civilizing mission' or the imperial idea. Berny Sèbe urges us to compare Europe's empires more systematically: two chapters on Russia and the Ottomans show how this could be done. The Russian Federation, says Alexander Morrison bluntly, is 'an imperial polity'. The rehabilitation of Skobelev and Yermolov is a salutary reminder that its imperial ethos is alive and kicking: it is as if new statues of Robert Clive and Lord Roberts (of Kandahar no less), perhaps even one of General Dyer, were to be erected in Parliament Square.

One of the hardiest clichés of the decolonization era was that the European colonial powers after 1945 turned their back on a doomed colonialism and embraced the future – in the form of European unity. When British governments threw in the imperial towel, belatedly and reluctantly, in 1967–8, the Foreign Office in London cast about desperately for a new manifest destiny to replace Britain's 'world role'. The answer of many was Europe! Europe! In the deferential historiography sponsored in Brussels, European union was the summit of European progress, not least because it marked the repudiation of imperialism. This illusion is punctured by the chapters in Part III. They show that imperial ambition was alive and well among the architects of the European Economic Community who arguably expected inter-European cooperation to strengthen, not weaken, their grip on their colonial satellites. The imperial instinct has lingered in parts of Brussels. Towards former colonies and the new member states of East-Central Europe, the European Union often displays a markedly imperial demeanour, not least in its confidence that Europe's institutions and values are unarguably superior. Not for nothing do the EU's more sycophantic admirers invoke the spirit of Charlemagne. But in the last part of the book it is Europe's global claims and ambitions that hold centre-stage. Here Karoline Postel-Vinay offers a subtle investigation of the meanings of globalism and globality, Rahul Rao warns against a global insistence on what have become Europe's sexual norms, and Jacques Frémeaux and Gabrielle Maas neatly reinsert the history of empire into the larger frame of globalization.

The lesson we should draw is that imperial history at its most thoughtful and humane, and allied, as it should be, with scholarship in politics and international relations, is an immensely powerful tool with which to make sense of world history. But the last word should be left to the two grandmasters of the subject whose chapters enliven this book. In his brief intellectual autobiography (let us hope that a full version will follow), John MacKenzie reminds us that the hallmark of a great historian is curiosity, empathy (especially with those who leave no archive behind), an imaginative openness to new ideas and perspectives, and (not least) a certain combativeness. In imperial history's strange trajectory since the 1960s, these qualities have been vital, and anyone who cares for the subject will find his memoir absorbing. At the other end of the book, John's old 'sparring partner' Bernard Porter deploys the imperial historian's other essential, a sceptical intellect that questions the seductive assumptions with which the present rearranges the past to its taste. We do well, he suggests, not to be over-impressed either by the claims of empire-builders, or the lamentations of their victims: the first were less potent, and the second less helpless than they liked to pretend. With that final warning not to pay attention to mere 'noise', we should hear all the more clearly the echoes of empire.

Note

1 F. H. Crawley (ed.), *The New Cambridge Modern History*, vol XI: *Material Progress and Worldwide Problems, 1870–98* (Cambridge, 1962).

Index

abolition (slave trade), 70, 77
Adenauer, Konrad, 211, 217–18, 286
Afghanistan, 167, 196, 363, 390
Africa, 44, 286
  and European integration, 209
  exploitation for slave trade, 29
  as export market, 214
  'modernity' in, 6
  as source of agricultural exports and
    natural resources, 29, 44, 211,
    218
  trading posts in, 64
African history, 10, 190, 196
African, Caribbean and Pacific countries
  (ACP), 227–33, 290
Agricola, 116
agriculture, 37, 44
Aida, 9, 200–1
Ainu people, 177
Akhundzadah, Mirza Fath'ali, 360
Akunin, Boris (Grigory Shalvovich
  Chkhartishvili), 164
Al Qaeda, 376
Alexander the Great, 106, 387
Alfonso VII, king of Castile and Léon
Algeria, 3, 37, 129, 135, 168, 214, 216–17,
  221, 286–7, 376, 387
Ali, Muhammad, 21

aman (Islamic safe passage assurance), 24
Ambedkar, B. R., 54
America, conquest of, 68
American Revolution, 395
anarchy, 12
Anatolia, 146
Anglican Church, 402–3
Angola, 65, 74
Antiochus III of Syria, 107
apartheid, 194, 379
Arab League, 1
Argentina, 83, 88, 97, 350
Aritomo, Yamagata, 175, 179
Armenia, 150, 152, 157
Aron, Raymond, 209
Ashton, Catherine, 243
Atatürk, Mustafa Kemal, 146, 149
Atlantic Charter (1941), 42
Atlantic Ocean, 65, 68–9, 201, 385
Atsutane, Hirata, 183
Augustus, Emperor, 108
Australia, 129, 202
Austria, 258
autocracy, 36, 48
'autonomous regions' (Russia), 156, 163,
  167
Azerbaijan, 166–7
Aztec Empire, 69

Baker, Samuel, 25–6, 30
Balearic Islands, 68
Balfour, Arthur, 117
Baltic States, 155, 163, 166–8, 253, 260
Bandung Conference, 220, 332
Banerjee, Mamata, 58
Bangladesh, 53–4, 55
Barroso, José Manuel, 292
Barth, Heinrich, 23–4
Battle of Ourique, 66
Belgium, 1, 217, 230, 288
Bengal, 52
Berlin Wall, 3
Besant, Annie, 369
Bevin, Ernest, 213
Bhabha, Homi, 10, 357
Bhutto, Benazir, 58
bin Laden, Osama, 118, 376
Black Sea, 156, 162
Bloch, Marc, 124
Boer settlers, 29
Boer War, 112, 395
Bolívar, Simón, 70
Bolivia, 76, 90
Bolshevik Revolution, 161, 374
Bornu (former African kingdom), 22–3
Bose, Subhas Chandra, 56
Bosnia-Herzegovina, 255–6
Bourbon reforms, 76
Brazil, 67, 70, 72–3, 75, 77, 235, 379, 389
Briand, Aristide, 211
BRICS (Brazil, Russia, India, China and
　　South Africa), 7
British Empire, 3, 7, 38, 123–6, 136–7,
　　349, 375, 389
　　identity and 'subempires' of British
　　　Isles, 202
　　and imperial myths, 394–400
　　legacy in India, 47, 55–61, 168
　　local alliances in India, 116
　　'New Imperialism' (late Victorian),
　　　110–11
　　public attitudes to in Britain, 195

rivalry with France, 22, 123, 125–6;
　　see also Raj
Buddhism, 182–5, 299
Buganda (former African kingdom), 22,
　　30, 236
Bull, Hedley, 11, 325
Burckhardt, Jean Louis, 25
Burton, Richard, 26, 27, 37
Bush, George W., 117, 253, 264, 362

Caesar, Julius, 108
Caillaux, Joseph, 212
Cameron, Verney Lovett, 28, 37
Canada, 168, 202, 366, 401
Canary Islands, 64, 68
Çandar, Cengiz, 149
Cannadine, David, 396
Cape Colony, 36, 191
Caribbean Sea, 65, 67, 69, 87, 127–8
Carpenter, Edward, 369
Carson, Rachel, 200
caste system, 50, 52, 54, 58
Castilian monarchy
Castro brothers (Fidel and Raúl), 63
Catholicism, 73, 90, 92, 97, 258, 293
Caucasus, the, 6, 156–8, 161, 168
Ceauşescu, Nicolae, 255
Césaire, Aimé, 289
Ceuta and Melilla, 65, 136, 389
Charlemagne, Holy Roman Emperor,
　　105, 384, 409
Charles III, king of Spain, 73
Charles V, Holy Roman Emperor, 66
Chávez, Hugo, 76
Chechnya, 157
China, 5, 156, 167, 175–6, 183, 291,
　　349, 374
　　Cultural Revolution, 312
　　Communist Party of, 310–13
　　influence in communist Eastern
　　　Europe, 255
　　Sino-centric narrative, 328–30
　　trade with, 232, 235, 238, 242

'traditional' culture in, 10, 310

Christianity, 37, 69, 362, 402
   conflicts with Islam in Iberia, 67, 68
   as germ of European universalism, 293
   in Japan, 179, 185
   in Ottoman Empire, 150; *see also*
     missionary work

Churchill, Winston, 211, 376

'civilizing mission', 5–7, 38–9, 109, 141,
   180, 267, 299, 399

Clapperton, Hugh, 23–4

Clémenceau, Georges, 392

Clyde (River), 195

Cold War, 3, 112, 219, 222, 254, 256, 289,
   310, 331–4, 397

Colley, Linda, 402

'colonial development and welfare', 42–4

Colonial Office (Great Britain), 23

Columbus, Christopher, 64, 69, 92–3

Commonwealth, the, 11, 135, 166, 202,
   288

communism, 49–50, 58, 163, 253–5, 258,
   312, 376

Comunidade dos Países de Língua
   Portuguesa, 135

Confucianism, 177, 184, 299, 306–9

Congo (former Belgian colony), 38, 236

Congo (River), 22

Congress of Vienna, 325, 339

Congress Party (India), 49, 56, 57, 341,
   345, 348, 381

conquistadors, 68–9

Corn Laws, 128

Cortés, Hernándo, 100–1

cosmopolitanism, 137

Cossacks, 157

Coudenhove-Kalergi, Richard, 211–12,
   217

Council of Europe, 214, 261

Council of the Indies, 71

Coupland, Reginald, 201

Crimea, 156, 158, 162

Crimean War, 158

Croatia, 256–7, 261

crusades, 67

Cuba, 64, 70, 90, 376, 389

Curzon, Lord, 116

Cyprus, 251, 270, 298, 373

Czech Republic, 254, 260

dar al-Islam, 24

Davies, Norman, 210, 251

Davutoğlu, Ahmet, 152

decentring, 7, 10, 279, 284, 300

decolonization, 3, 10, 125, 132, 134–6,
   255, 286–9, 296, 298, 374, 409

democracy, 5, 36, 47–8, 55–60, 291

democratic deficit, 49, 53

Denham, Dixon, 23–4

dependence, 4, 12, 64, 74, 343

diaspora, 11

direct rule, 3, 49, 123; *see also* formal
   empire

Dostoyevsky, Fyodor, 160

dynastic politics, 48, 54, 58

East India Company, 116, 128

Eastern Europe, 1, 237, 252, 263

Eboué, Félix, 132

Economic Partnership Agreements
   (EPAs), 227–32, 295

Eden, Anthony, 218–9

Egypt, 21, 131, 200, 373, 391, 401
   as entry point to African interior,
     24–6
   Napoleonic invasion of, 24–5, 403
   in Roman Empire, 108, 115

'end of history', *see* Fukuyama, Francis

Enlightenment, 144, 291–3

Enryō, Inoue, 176, 181–6

Equatoria, 26

Erdem, Hakan, 150

Erdoğan, Recep Tayyip, 152

Ethiopia, 25, 200, 390

ethnic minorities, 159, 162–3, 167, 177,
   255, 261; *see also* racism

'Eurafrica', 7, 209–20
European Coal and Steel Community
    (ECSC), 215–16
European Commission (EC), 228, 238,
    271
European Economic Community (EEC),
    209, 217, 220, 230–1, 409
European integration, 6, 209–20
European Neighbourhood Policy (ENP),
    268–73
European Parliament, 271
European Partnership Agreement (EPA),
    4
European Union (EU), 3, 7, 209, 252,
    267, 284, 409
    enlargement rounds, 259–61, 268,
        271–2
eurozone crisis, 3, 243
expansionism, 63, 67
exploration, 6, 19–22, 198

Falkland Islands, 136, 196
Fanon, Frantz, 290, 376, 379
fascism, 258
Fashoda incident, 396
feminism, 355–6, 364–5, 377
Ferdinand II, king of Spain, 66
Ferguson, Niall, 202–3, 394, 398
Ferry, Jules, 387
Fezzan, 23
'First World', 82, 90, 93–4
forced resettlement, 44, 177, 241
Foreign Direct Investment (FDI), 232, 348
formal empire, 130–1
Foucault, Michel, 299, 356
France, 2, 11, 210, 223, 230, 286–8
Franco-Prussian War, 388
Francophonie, 135
free trade, 128, 227, 301, 325; *see also*
    tariffs; trade
French Community, 210, 217
French Empire, 5, 38, 217, 123–30,
    136–7, 389, 396

French Revolution, 287, 294
Freud, Sigmund, 258
Fukuyama, Francis, 3

Gambia River, 22
Gandhi, Indira, 49, 57, 345
Gandhi, Mohandas Karamchand
    ('Mahatma'), 56, 57, 341, 377
Gandhi, Rajiv, 49
Gandhi, Sonia, 57, 58
Garton Ash, Timothy, 258
Gastarbeiter, 167
Gaulle, Charles de, 286
Geertz, Clifford, 189
Gellner, Ernest, 200
'gentlemanly capitalism', 131
Geok-Tepe, siege of, 158, 163
geometry, 65
Georgia, 157, 163, 166, 273
Germany, 212, 217–18, 230, 288
    atrocities in South-West Africa, 38
    former African colonies, 38
Ginzburg, Carlo, 189
Gladstone, William Ewart, 392, 410
globalism, *see* globalization
globality, 9, 323
globalization, 8, 203, 223, 315, 337, 347,
    351, 375, 382, 383
'glocalization' (glocalism), 189, 202
Gökalp, Ziya, 146
gold mining, 28, 191
Gondokoro, 25
Goody, Jack, 403
Gorbachev, Mikhail, 253, 260
Government of India Act (1935), 56
Gran Chaco plain, 83
Granada, 66
Grant, James, 25, 27
Great Depression, 41, 341
Great Lakes (Africa), 25–7
Greek Empire, 106–8
Grotius, Hugo, 11
Guantanamo Bay detention camp, 403

Guernier, Eugène, 212–13
Guevara, Che, 376, 379
Guizot, François, 387

Habermas, Jürgen, 195
Habsburg Empire, 160, 168, 255–6
Hague Congress, 209, 214, 286, 325
Halsey, A. H., 196
Harmand, Jules, 387
Hausa states, 22, 23
Havel, Václav, 259
Hegel, Friedrich, 35
Henry VIII, 66
Herder, Johann Gottfried, 261
Hikmet, Nazim, 146
Hindu nationalism, 49, 50, 53, 57, 176,
    348
histoire croisée, 124, 137
Hobson, J. A., 111, 196
Hokkaidō (Ezuchi), 176–9
Holocaust, the, 11, 254
Holy Roman Empire, 67, 260
Holy See, 65
Hong Kong, 391
Hornemann, Friedrich, 23
humanitarianism, 105, 108, 241
Hungary, 253
hunting, 198–9; *see also* ivory trade
Huntington, Samuel, 256
Hussein, Saddam, 113

Iberian Peninsula
    Muslim presence on, 66, 68, 341
    Roman Empire on, 114–15
Inca Empire, 69
independence, *see* decolonization
India, 5, 6, 186, 235, 337, 341, 357,
    378–9, 395, 404
Indian Mutiny, 395, 402
indigenous Americans, 68, 73, 83–5, 112,
    340
indigenous elites, 19–22, 132, 236, 338,
    340

indirect rule, 39–42, 49, 123, 395; *see also*
    informal empire
Indochina (former French colony), 3,
    134, 254, 391
Industrial Revolution, 36, 123
industrialization, 232, 339
informal empire, 130–1
International Political Economy, 12
international relations (IR), 8, 11–12,
    106, 327–9, 408–9
Iran, 144, 161, 167, 358–62, 374, 390
Iraq, 113, 196, 253, 391
Ireland, 66, 201–2, 251, 298, 355, 375,
    377
iron mining, 193–4
Isabella I, queen of Spain, 66
Islam, 291, 359
    on Iberian Peninsula, 66, 68
    leaders' tolerance of Christians and
        Jews, 68
    in Russian Empire, 157–8, 162
Islamism
    critiques of secularism, 143
    extremist groups, 30, 359, 362,
        376–7, 402, 404
    party politics, 147–8, 151
Ismail Pasha, 26
iusta causa, 106
Ivan the Terrible, 156
ivory trade, 25, 29, 198

Jamaica, 228–9
James I, king of England, 126
Japan, 5, 307, 343
Jefferson, Thomas, 70
Jim Crow Laws, 77
John IV, king of Portugal, 72
Judaism, 68–9, 156–7

Kafka, Franz, 258
Karamanli, Yusuf Pasha, 21, 23–4
Karamzin, Nikolai, 159
Karimov, Islam, 165

Kazakhstan, 158, 162, 168
Keiu, Nakamura, 181–6
Kenya, 40, 42, 134–5, 196, 397
Keynesian economics, 338, 343, 350, 381
Klaus, Václav, 263
Korean Peninsula, 175–6, 179, 255, 344, 351
Kosovo, 257, 260, 263, 264
Kundera, Milan, 258
Kurdish people, 151
Kyrgyzstan, 164–5, 167

Laing, Alexander, 23–4
Laird, Macgregor, 22
Lander brothers, 22
'Latin America', 63, 76–7, 230
Lavigerie, Cardinal Charles, 132
LeGendre, Charles, 179
Leninism, 376
Leopold II, king of Belgium, 1, 38
Lermontov, Mikhail, 158
Leroy-Beaulieu, Paul, 387–8
LGBT movement, 5
Libya, 30
lieux de mémoire, 2, 142, 144–5
Lippman, Walter, 332
Lisbon Treaty, 269, 276
'Little Englanders', 126
Livingstone, David, 27, 29, 37, 132
Livy, 107
Locke, John, 11
Lomé Conventions, 222, 229–30, 237, 242, 290
longue durée, 128
Lucas, Simon, 23
Lugard, Lord, 40, 132, 241
Lyautey, Hubert, 132, 212–13, 391

Maastricht Treaty, 290
Macao, 65, 389
malaria, 22
Mali, 30
Malta, 251

Manchuria, 159
Marshall Plan, 214
Marxist theory, 12, 254, 334
Masaryk, Tomáš Garrigue, 258
Massad, Joseph, 356, 367
Mau Mau insurgency, 134–5, 376
Mayawati, 58
McKinley, William, 112
Mearsheimer, John, 256
Mecca and Medina, 25
Mediterranean Sea, 21, 67, 106, 108, 114–15, 212, 286, 384
Medvedev, Dmitri, 168
Meiji Restoration, 175, 181, 283
mestizo societies, 128
Mexico, 63, 70, 112, 351
micro-history, 189, 202
migration, 300
    from and to Africa, 41, 214
    within Africa, 191–3
    from Commonwealth to Britain, 202
    from former Soviet satellite states to
        Russia, 6, 166–8
Miles, Richard, 203
Mill, John Stuart, 184
Milošević, Slobodan, 257
mineral resources, 28
mission civilisatrice, *see* 'civilizing mission'
missionary work, 29, 41, 74, 97, 132, 198, 364; *see also* Christianity
Mitteleuropa, 256–7
'modernity', 12, 20–1, 31, 35–7, 44–5, 403, 408
Modi, Narendra, 49
Moldova, 273
Mollet, Guy, 209, 218–21
Monnet, Jean, 215, 286
Monroe Doctrine, 63, 295
Monroe, President James, 63
Montagu–Chelmsford package (1919), 56
Montaigne, Michel de, 386
Monty Python, 116
monuments, 1

Morales, Evo, 76
Morley–Minto reforms (1909), 56
Morocco, 220
Mozambique, 65
Mugabe, Robert, 401
Mughal Empire, 49, 51–3, 199
Muhammad, Hamid ibn, *see* 'Tippu Tip'
multiculturalism, 130, 151
Mussolini, Benito, 150

Napoleon I, 105
Napoleon III, 128, 131
Napoleonic Wars, 23
Nasser, Gamal Abdul, 219, 255
nation states, 142
nationalism, 41, 49, 142, 147, 162, 166, 191, 374
    'epistemic nationalism', 143
    and gender, 363–4
    'romantic nationalism', 156
'Native Authorities', 40–1; *see also* indigenous elites
NATO (North Atlantic Treaty Organization), 214, 255, 260
Nehru, Jawaharlal, 56, 57, 180, 255, 341
neo-imperialism, 4, 220, 223
    economic, 7, 347
    of EU, 259–61, 271
    of Russia, 155, 166
    of USA, 4, 63, 112, 117–18
new social movements (NSM), 377–82
'New World', 68
New Zealand, 129, 202
Nicaragua, 254
Nicholls, Henry, 22
Niger River, 22
Nigeria, 30, 40, 229, 236, 366
Nile (River), 24–5
Nkrumah, Kwame, 220–1, 241, 255, 286, 375, 379
Non-Aligned Movement, 220, 255, 332–3, 345

'Normative Power Europe' (NPE), 7
North Africa, 2
North–South relations, 4, 381
nuclear power, 349

Obama, Barack 397
O'Connell, Daniel, 375
OECD (Organization for Economic Cooperation and Development), 214
oil crises, 44, 237
Opium Wars, 307, 391
oral history, 193–4; *see also* micro-history
Orbán, Viktor, 261
orientalism (concept), 200–1
OSCE (Organization for Security and Cooperation in Europe), 261
Ottoman Empire, 5, 168, 252, 255–6
Özakman, Turgut, 150
Özal, Turgut, 148

Pakistan, 49, 53–4, 55, 349
Palestine, 355, 402
pan-Africanism, 219–20
pan-Arabism, 219
Pankhurst, Sylvia, 369
Papacy, 65
Park, Mungo, 22, 30
Parkyns, Mansfield, 26
parliamentarianism, 55
Patel, Vallavbhai, 56
paternalism, 240–4
patrimonialism, 339
'Pax Britannica', 110, 116
Pax Romana, 109–10, 115
Perovsky, General V. A., 164
Philip II, king of Spain, 67
Philip V of Macedonia, 107
Philippines, 65, 70, 389
piracy, 22–3
Poland, 161–2, 253, 260
polysynody, 71

Portuguese Empire, 5, 38, 67, 339–40, 389

post-colonial theory, 11

Prague Spring, 253

printing press, 72

protectionism, 128, 289, 348

Puerto Rico, 64, 389

Pushkin, Alexander, 158

Putin, Vladimir, 168, 253

racial classification systems, 70

racism, 64, 77, 162–3, 167, 177, 212, 240, 343

Raj, 47, 264, 338, 341, 344

Ram, Kanshi, 58

Rama Rao, N. T., 58

Ramachandram, M. G., 58

Ranger, T. O., 190

Rao, Narasimha, 49

reciprocity, 229, 234–5, 300

Reconquista, 66

regionalization (of national politics), 48, 49–51

Renan, Ernest, 144, 286

resistance, 376

revolutions, 144

Reynaud, Paul, 212, 214

Rhodes, Cecil, 117, 241

Rhodesia, 401
    Northern, 196
    Southern, 42, 191–3

Richardson, James, 23

Roma people, 261

Roman Empire, 4, 106–10, 384

Romania, 253, 261

Romanov dynasty, 159

Roosevelt, Franklin D., 332

Rousseff, Dilma, 77

Royal Geographical Society (Great Britain), 28

Royal Navy (Great Britain), 22

Rubios, Palacios, 95

Rumsfeld, Donald, 401

Russia, 6, 7, 131, 271–2

Russian Empire, 5, 112, 155, 384, 385, 390
    'Russification', 160–1

Russo-Japanese War, 159, 185

Sahara Desert
    as route to African interior, 22–4
    Tripolitanian control over in nineteenth century, 21

Sahlins, Marshall, 203

Said, Edward, 9, 10, 143, 196, 200–1, 299, 374, 398–9

Said, Seyyid, 21, 27, 28

Sarkozy, Nicolas, 223, 289

Sarraut, Albert, 386

Sartre, Jean-Paul, 299, 377

satellite states, 253; see also USSR

Saudi Arabia, 390

Schengen Zone, 261

Schuman, Robert, 215, 286

Schumpeter, Joseph, 195, 403

scramble for Africa, 19, 26, 37, 200, 391

secularism, 142, 350

Seeley, J. R., 111, 123, 201

self-defence (international law), 113

self-defence (racial and cultural), 180

self-determination, 252, 254, 286, 296, 333

Sen, Amartya, 53

Senegal, 36, 240

Seven Years War, 129

Shintō, 182

Silva, Lula da, 77, 349

Singapore, 132

Singh, Manmohan, 57

Sino-Japanese War, 177, 180, 307

Skobelev, General Mikhail, 163–4

slave raiding, 38

slave trade, 25, 65, 69, 71
    British negotiations with African kingdoms over, 24, 26
    end of, 22
    through West African coastal ports, 22

slavery, 36, 70, 339
  and racism, 64
  and social discrimination in Latin
    America, 73–4
Smiles, Samuel, 183–4
Smith, Ian, 195
social Darwinism, 177
'soft power', 135, 253
Solidarity Movement, 253
Sörgel, Herman, 212
Sōseki, Natsume, 181
South Africa, 129, 191, 202, 229, 355
South African War, 38
South-West Africa, 38, 39
Soviet Union, see USSR
Spanish Empire, 5, 67
Spanish Inquisition, 69, 70, 74–5
Speke, John Hanning, 25, 27
Spivak, Gayatri Chakravorty, 10, 362,
  374
sports history, 198–200
Sri Lanka, 53, 65, 373
Stalin, Joseph, 243, 264
Stanley, Henry Morton, 22, 27, 30, 132
Starkey, David, 203
state sovereignty, 2, 6, 12, 64, 241, 294,
  296–8, 333
Stiglitz, Joseph, 381
Stonewall riots, 357
'subaltern' history, 3, 11, 364, 373–5,
  408
Sudan, 24, 30, 131, 402
Suez Canal, 200, 219
Suez crisis, 218–19
Sufism, 360
Suffragette movement, 377
Sukarno, 255
suzerainty, 67

Tacitus, 109, 115
Taiwan, 179
Tajikistan, 163, 164–5
Tamil nationalism, 49

Tanganyika (former African state), 30,
  40, 42
tariffs (import and export), 230–2
Tatar people, 156, 162
Tatchell, Peter, 359, 361, 365–7
Taylor, A. J. P., 195
Thatcher, Margaret, 196
'Third Worldism', 213, 252, 254, 300,
  355, 365
Thomson, Joseph, 28, 30
Timbuktu, 23–4
'Tippu Tip', 28
Tipu Sultan of Mysore, 52
Tito, Josip Broz, 255, 257
Tokugawa shogunate, 177–8
Tolstoy, Leo, 158
Touré, Sekou, 220–1
trade, 3, 41, 44, 198, 214, 286, 290, 339
  expansion of in nineteenth century, 324
  international negotiations over, 227
  trading routes, 21; see also free trade;
    ivory trade; slave trade; tariffs;
    World Trade Organization
Treaty of Rome, 124, 209, 215–17, 219,
  230, 286
Treaty of Sèvres, 149–50
Treaty of Tordesillas (1494), 65, 391
Treaty of Versailles, 390
Trevor-Roper, Hugh, 10
tribute system, 306–7
Tripoli (former African state), 21, 22, 30
Truman, Harry, 332
Tsarist rule, 155, 160–1, 168
Tudjman, Franjo, 257
Tunstall, Cuthbert, 65
Turkey, 2, 161, 257, 263, 390
Turkmenistan, 155, 165
'tutelary democracy', 55, 59

Uganda, 40, 366–7
Ukraine, 158, 160–2, 166–7, 261
Union for the Mediterranean, 1, 271
United Nations, 113, 312, 315, 335

universalism, 9, 330
Urabi revolt, 21
urbanization, 41, 191, 254, 356
USA, 284, 288, 293, 345–6, 362, 394, 396
    Cold War strategy, 112–13
    expansionism, 63, 112, 82, 401
    hegemonic ideology, 105–6
    influence in Africa, 31
    'internationalist turn', 324, 330–3
    relationship with China, 312
    role in Suez crisis, 218–19
    and World Wars, 42, 331–2
USSR, 42, 218, 345–6, 397
    as Cold War superpower, 213, 284
    collapse of, 163
    communism and relationship with
        China, 311–13
    neo-imperialism, 297
    and World War II, 331–2
Uzbekistan, 162, 164–6

Venezuela, 76
Vichy government, 210
Vietnam, 113, 376
Visegrád Group, 259
Vivekananda, Swami, 186
Vladivostok, 159, 323
Volga (River), 157
Voltaire, 126

wage labour, 26
Wahhabi dynasty, 25

'War on Terror', 118, 264, 362
Warsaw Pact, 253
Washington, George, 70
Western Sahara, 389
Wilson, Woodrow, 112, 324, 333–4
witchcraft, 36
world systems theory, 12
World Bank, 381
'world history', 10, 324
World Trade Organization (WTO), 235,
    237, 295, 312, 337, 349, 381
World War I, 6, 127, 148, 324, 331–2
World War II, 1, 11, 41, 162, 210, 254,
    285, 332, 335

Xiaoping, Deng, 312

Yaoundé Agreements, 237, 242
Yeltsin, Boris, 163, 260
Yermolov, General Alexei, 157, 164
Young Turks, 149
Yugoslavia (former state), 254, 255,
    260
Yukichi, Fukuzawa, 176

Zambia, 196; see also Rhodesia:
    Northern
Zanzibar, 21, 26–8, 30
Zedong, Mao, 311, 376
Zimbabwe, 193; see also Rhodesia:
    Southern
Zischka, Anton, 215

CPSIA information can be obtained
at www.ICGtesting.com
Printed in the USA
LVHW080838061221
705401LV00003B/4

9 781784 530518